The Robin Williams Mac OS X Book

Jaguar Edition

Peachpit Press
Berkeley · California

The Robin Williams Mac OS X Book, Jaguar Edition
©2003 by Robin Williams

Cover design and production: John Tollett
Interior divider pages: John Tollett
Interior design and production: Robin Williams
Index: Laura Egley Taylor with Robin Williams
Editor: Nancy Davis
Back cover photo of Robin: John Tollett
The illustrations of Url throughout the book are
from the mouse of the multi-talented John Tollett,
www.UrlsInternetCafe.com
Spine and back cover art illustration: Terry Widener

 Peachpit Press
1249 Eighth Street
Berkeley, California 94710
800.283.9444
510.524.2178
510.524.2221 fax

Find us on the World Wide Web at **www.peachpit.com**
To report errors, please send a note to errata@peachpit.com
Peachpit Press is a division of Pearson Education

ISBN 0-321-16966-2

10 9 8 7 6 5 4 3 2 1

Printed and bound in the United States of America

To my mother, Patricia Williams,

who made it possible,

and to my father, Gerald Williams,

who would have been proud.

Acknowledgments

Many, many thanks to
Nancy Davis *for great editing;*
Laura Egley Taylor *for*
tenacious and great indexing—
I literally could not have
done this without you;
John Tollett *for all of the fabulous*
Url cartoons, the divider page
illustrations, the cover, for writing
a bunch of chapters, and for hanging
in there with me during this long haul.

Contents

Beyond the Basics

The Internet

Back Matter

Introduction

Skip the intro. Read the book. New users, flip through the book and notice the gray "dots" in the upper corners of some pages, like this page. Those are the only pages you need to read. But do check out the tutorial—I guarantee if you actually work through the tutorial you will have more control over your computer than many long-time Mac users.

Experienced Mac users, use the index and look up what you need. But I guarantee that if you actually read entire chapters, you'll be amazed at the tips and tricks you didn't know. I was.

I always write the introduction last, and now I'm really tired. It's been a long and winding book. I do hope you find it useful.

Robin

Mini-Glossary

These three pages contain a list of the terms you are most likely to run into when working on your Mac. If you don't find a word here, check the index because I probably explained the term in the main body of the book. For an incredibly extensive and up-to-date resource of definitions, check **www.webopedia.com** (unfortunately, though, I don't guarantee you will always understand the definition). Also check Sherlock (Chapter 31).

bits

bytes

kilobytes

megabytes

gigabytes

All of the terms listed to the left refer to **size.** It might refer to the size of a file, or how much space that file takes up on a disk. For instance, a small file like an icon might be 3K (kilobytes), and a large file like a high-quality photograph might be 15MB (megabytes). The layered Photoshop file for the cover of this book is 91MB.

Size might also refer to the size of your hard disk. For instance, you might have an 8GB (gigabtye) hard disk, or an 80GB hard disk. The bigger the disk, the more files it can hold.

▾ **bit:** The smallest unit of information on a computer. Each bit is one electronic pulse. These are the ones and ohs you hear about, 1 and 0.

▾ **byte:** 8 bits makes 1 byte. It takes one byte to produce one character, such as the letter A, on the monitor.

▾ **kilobyte:** 1024 bytes makes 1 kilobyte (capital K). A page in a word processor might take about 6 to 12K of disk space, depending on how much formatting was involved.

▾ **kilobit:** 1024 bits makes one kilobit (lowercase k). You'll see this in references to Internet connection speeds. It is not the same as a kilobyte (capital K in abbreviations)!

▾ **megabyte:** 1024 kilobytes makes 1 megabyte (MB). An 8-page newsletter with photographs and nice typography might take about 1.5 to 3MB of disk space, depending on how it was created. A software program like the one I am using to create this book (Adobe InDesign) takes about 90MB of disk space.

▾ **gigabyte:** 1024 megabytes makes 1 gigabyte (GB). Most hard disks are now measured in gigabytes. The Mac I am using at the moment has a 75GB hard disk.

Disk refers to the hardware pieces that hold data. Inside your Mac you have an internal hard disk. You might buy an external hard disk that connects to your Mac through a cable. Removable disks are those that go in and out of a disk drive, which is the mechanism that "reads" the removable disk. Removable disks include floppy disks, Zips, CDs, DVDs, etc.

disk

Download means to copy files from one computer directly to another (as opposed to putting the files on a disk and carrying them to the other computer). Typically, the other computer is "remote," or far away, and you download files from that computer to yours through the Internet. **Upload** means to copy files from your computer to a remote computer.

download, upload

Hardware is hard—you can drop it, break it, and throw it. If you can bump into it, it's hardware. Your computer is a piece of hardware, and so are external hard disks, scanners, modems, and printers. To send a piece of hardware to someone, you need a vehicle. Also see *software*.

hardware

Megahertz (MHZ) refers to speed. In computers, the higher the megahertz, the faster the computer will process information. In 1993, a good computer had a speed of about 20MHz; today, even the cheapest computer is at least 400MHz, and more expensive machines reach a gigahertz. And every day they get faster and faster.

megahertz

Memory is the temporary storage place in your Mac, as opposed to the permanent storage space on a hard disk. There are various kinds of memory, but the one you're most concerned with is random access memory (RAM). The more RAM you have, the better everything on your Mac will work. A minimum amount of RAM is 256MB; a great amount is a gigabyte or two. See page 138 to find out how much RAM you have in your Mac. You can always buy more RAM and install it—it's easy.

memory, RAM

The **operating system** (OS) is what runs the computer. It's kind of like an engine in a car—you can have an entire car sitting in your front yard, but if it doesn't have an engine, it's not going to go anywhere. Operating systems get updated regularly so they can do more and more. You will probably get asked, "What OS are you running?" You'll sound like you know what you're talking about if you say, "Mac OS X version 10.2," which is actually pronounced, "Mac oh ess ten point two." Really.

operating system (OS)
OS X is pronounced
"oh ess ten"

Your monitor is composed of hundreds of thousands of tiny little spots; each one of these spots is a **pixel.** And each pixel is composed of three dots of light: red, green, and blue (RGB). The color in a pixel is a blend of varying amounts of those three colored lights. If all three colors are at 100 percent, the pixel is white. If no colors are sent to the pixel, it appears as black.

pixels

software   **Software** is invisible—it's the programming code written on the disks. You buy software—the applications, utilities, fonts, and games you use—and it comes to you on some sort of disk, or you download the software from another computer to yours (like over the Internet). The disk it came on or the disk you are storing it on contains the software. You can accidentally destroy the software while the disk it's on remains perfectly hard and whole. To send a piece of software to someone, you can use your modem and send it over the Internet.

Vaporware   **Vaporware** refers to software or hardware that has been promised for a while ("real soon now") but hasn't appeared on the market. You might also hear the terms wetware, liveware, or jellyware—that means us, the humans.

third party   Apple is the *first party:* they make the computer and the operating system. You are the *second party;* you use the computer and operating system. Other people who make things for you to use on your computer are the **third party.** This is a third-party book, as opposed to a manual straight from Apple.

volume   A **volume** refers to any sort of disk or part of a disk. A disk can be separated into different **partitions;** each partition is still considered a separate volume. See Chapter 38 on how to divide your large hard disk into separate partitions.

What is .Mac?

.Mac: Formerly known as iTools, .Mac (pronounced *dot mac*) is a suite of services and tools, described below, that have been expanded from the iTools features. Membership is $99 a year. **To sign up for a .Mac account,** go to www.apple.com, click the ".mac" tab at the top of the page, then click "Join Now." Or you can sign up for a **free** 60-day **trial membership.** After you've signed up, log in with your new member name and password.

.Mac email accounts (an IMAP email account with a "mac.com" address) have up to 15MB of storage space on Apple's servers (you can buy more on their web site). You can also add up to ten "email-only" accounts.

Webmail is a browser-based email service that enables you to read or send your email using an Internet browser. From any computer anywhere in the world, go to www.mac.com, log in, and click the Webmail icon.

iDisk is your personal storage space on Apple's servers—now 100 MB of storage, and you can buy more. Store whatever you want on it—backup files on it, place files there for others to retrieve, allow others to put files there for you, serve a web site, publish iCal calendars, and much more. Access your iDisk from any Mac or Windows-based PC. Your iDisk also contains a folder from Apple that contains lots of goodies and extras, such as copyright-free music that you can add to your iMovies or anywhere else, games, software, and more.

iDisk Utility provides levels of control on your iDisk. You can open a Public folder of another .Mac member, set permissions that allow someone else to put files in your iDisk Public folder, add password protection to the Public folder on your iDisk, and open the iDisk of another .Mac member, using their member name and password.

Backup is software that makes it easy to back up your important files. You can back up to multiple CDs or DVDs when file sizes are too large to fit on one disc, back up to your own iDisk, and schedule automatic backups of selected items.

iSync software keeps your calendar and address book information synchronized between multiple Macs or other supported devices, such as a Bluetooth-enabled mobile phone, an iPod, or a PDA (personal digital assistant) device that uses the Palm operating system (such as a Palm or Handspring).

—continued

iCal is a great personal calendar application that helps you manage and organize your time. You can even share your calendars online (useful for families or businesses), or subscribe to other calendars (like from sports teams or bands on tour). Use iSync (above) to synchronize calendars that exist on multiple computers.

.Mac Slides Publisher is a small application that creates a personalized screen saver slide show and publishes it to your iDisk. Jaguar users can subscribe to screen savers that other users have published. See details on pages 333–336 in this book.

Member games and more: With a .Mac account, you can download free games, Apple and Mac OS X software, and other goodies that Apple stores on your iDisk.

Virex anti-virus software protects your Mac from evil, man-made infections. You can regularly download the latest "Virex Definition Updates."

Support gives you access to tips and tricks, discussion boards, FAQs (frequently asked questions), the AppleCare Knowledge Base, feedback, and Help links.

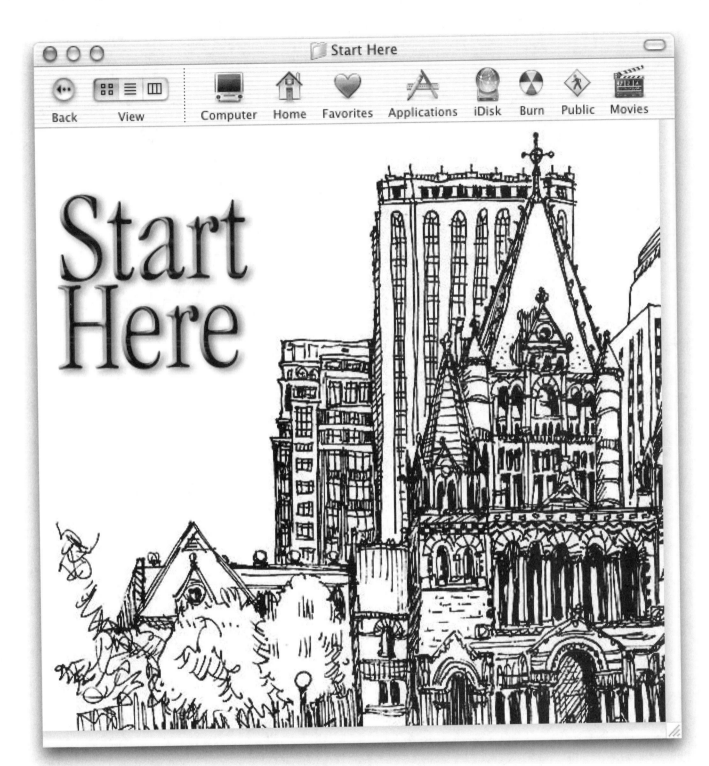

Your attitude is your life.

Robin

Finding Your Way Around

If you just got your first Macintosh or if you just installed Mac OS X and don't know where to begin, start with this chapter. It'll give you a visual overview of what things are and tell you where to go for more details.

- ▼ **If you just plugged in your first Mac** and it's asking how you want to get connected to the Internet, skip to Chapter 30, especially pages 502–505, and fill in the information. Then come back here.

- ▼ **If you're new to the Mac,** after you skim through this chapter, go to the Tutorial in Chapter 2. If you run across any confusing terms in either chapter, check the index to find clarification.

  Remember, as a new user, all you really need to read in this book are the pages with the "dots" at the tops. Come back to the rest later.

- ▼ **If you're an experienced Mac OS 9 user,** skip to Appendix A to find out where all of your favorite features have gone.

Contents of this chapter

The Desktop

The **Desktop** is what you see when you turn on your Mac. It's like home base; you'll get to know it well. ***For details about the Desktop, see Chapter 9.***

*There will always be a **menu bar** across the top of your screen. The options in the menu bar are not always the same! You will see different menu items whenever you open another application or utility.*

- *For an **overview** of this menu bar and the various menus in it, see pages 8 and 9.*
- *For all the **details** about menus, see Chapter 5.*

*This is a window. This particular window is called a **Finder window.***

- *For an **overview** of windows, see pages 4 and 5.*
- *For all the **details** about windows, see Chapter 6.*

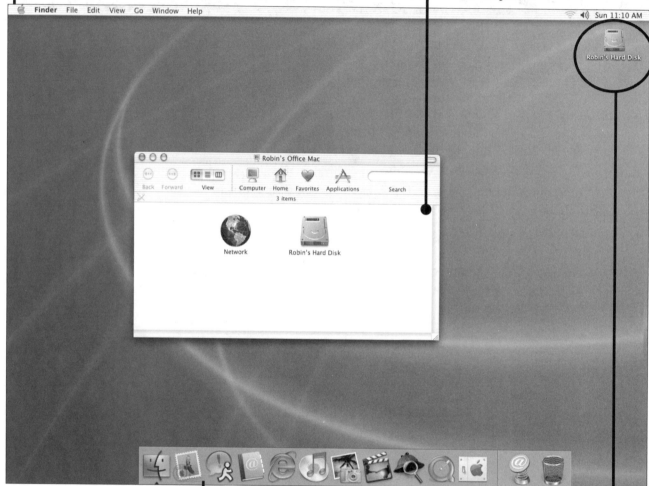

*This is the **Dock**. Each of these icons (pictures) in the Dock will open something when you click on it.*

- *For an **overview** of the Dock, see the opposite page.*
- *For the **details** about the Dock, see Chapter 8.*

*This icon on your **Desktop** represents your hard disk. (It's exactly the same as the icon in the window.)*

- *For an **overview** of the Desktop, see page 126. For all the details, see Chapter 9.*
- *For an **overview** of icons, see page 7. For all the details about icons, see Chapter 7.*
- *For an **explanation** of your hard disk (as opposed to memory), see page 220.*
- *For hard disks and "partitions," see Chapter 38.*

The **Dock** is that strip across the bottom of the screen. It will become your best friend. You might not see all the pictures in yours that you see in the examples below—things come and go from the Dock. You can add items and take items away. Most of the items in the Dock will "open" something when you click once on them: for instance, you might open an application to type in, or a web site on the Internet, or a window in which to find other files. Different things happen when you *click* once or when you *hold* the mouse button down (see Chapter 3 to learn to use the mouse).

The Dock

▼ *For a general idea* of how the Dock works, see below.

▼ *For details* about using and customizing the Dock, including how to resize, hide, or move it, see Chapter 8.

*This is a generic **Dock**. You might see other icons (pictures) in yours, and some of the icons shown above might not be in yours at the moment. Don't worry— it will change constantly as you add and delete items.*

*This is the **Finder icon**. Click **once** on it and the main Finder window will open. **Hold the mouse button down** on this icon and a menu pops up that tells you which other windows are currently open.*

*If something is in the **Trash, press-and-hold** the mouse button on the Trash basket to get this pop-up menu.*

The Finder Windows

The **Finder windows** display all the contents of your hard disk and other removable disks you might put in your computer. Learning how to "navigate" your way around the windows is one of the most important skills you can learn. There are three "views," or different ways you can see the contents of a window, as shown in the examples below. Choose the view you feel the most comfortable with.

▼ ***To learn all about*** finding your way around and controlling and customizing your windows, see Chapter 6.

Click the "Back" or "Forward" button to go back and forth to windows you've been looking at.

Click one of the views in the View button to change the way the window displays the files.

*This is the **Icon View** for my "Home" folder.*

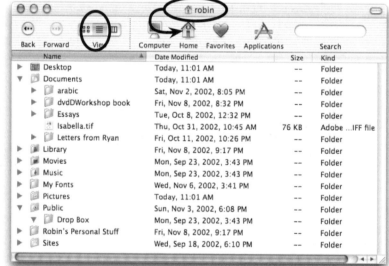

*This is the **List View** of the window above.*

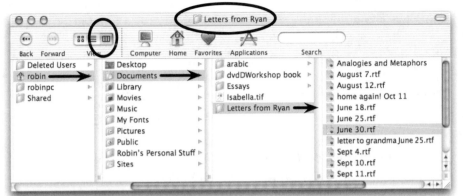

This is the **Column View** *of the same window, my Home folder, but this time you read it horizontally.*

Notice the file "robin" is highlighted, or selected, above. This indicates that the items in the column to its right are contained within "robin."

The folder "Documents" is highlighted in the second column, and its files are shown to its right.

The folder "Letters from Ryan" is inside "Documents." The files in "Letters from Ryan" are show to its right.

The items in the fourth column are contained in the folder called "Letters from Ryan," and one of the letters in the column is selected.

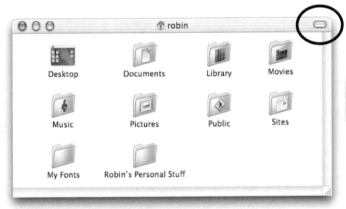

This is the **Hide/Show Toolbar** *button. You might see windows like this one that are missing the Toolbar.*

To show the Toolbar, *click the little, clear button in the upper-right of the window.*

To hide the Toolbar, *click that same little button.*

To show the status bar, *as seen above, go to the View menu and choose "Show Status Bar."*

You won't see the tiny symbols inside the buttons until your mouse is positioned over a button.

Click the **red button** *(x) to put the window* **away.**

Click the **yellow button** *(-) to send the window down to the Dock, called* **minimizing;** *click once on its icon in the Dock to make it visible again.*

Click the **green button** *(+)* **to enlarge or reduce** *the size of the window (each click will do either one or the other, depending on the current size of the window).*

Home

Home

Apple has created features that make it possible for a number of people to use the same computer, yet all users have their own private, protected space which includes a **Home,** your own Desktop, and your own, private Trash basket. Even if you are the only person using your Mac, you have a "Users" folder and a Home button.

▼ Click the "Home" button icon in the Toolbar to go straight to your "home files."

▼ *To learn all about Home* and what it means to you, see Chapter 9.

▼ *To learn how to to add or delete users,* change a user's privileges, and share files between various users, see Chapter 20.

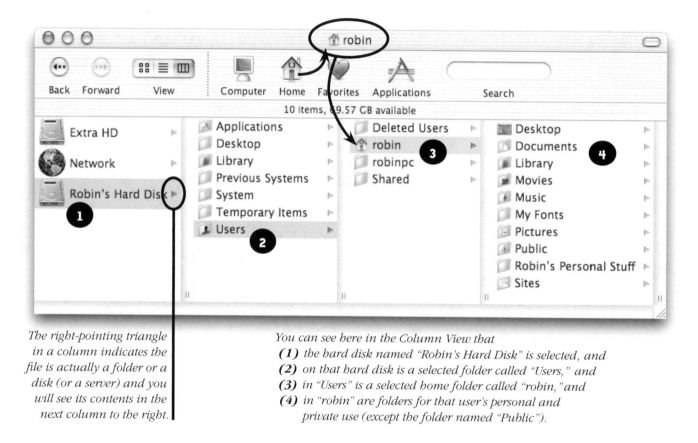

The right-pointing triangle in a column indicates the file is actually a folder or a disk (or a server) and you will see its contents in the next column to the right.

You can see here in the Column View that
(1) the hard disk named "Robin's Hard Disk" is selected, and
(2) on that hard disk is a selected folder called "Users," and
(3) in "Users" is a selected home folder called "robin," and
(4) in "robin" are folders for that user's personal and private use (except the folder named "Public").

Icons are the little pictures you see all over the Mac. Below are some of the ones you'll bump into right away and where you can find more information about them. Sometimes you click once on an icon to activate it, sometimes you double-click on it, sometimes you press on it.

▼ *For all the details* about icons, see Chapter 7.

The Icons

Window Toolbar icons

Computer

Home

Favorites

Applications

Search

Computer: *Click this button to see all the disks in the Mac that your computer recognizes. See Chapter 9.*

Home: *Click this to go straight to your own, personal home folder. See Chapter 20.*

Favorites: *Click this to see all of the folders, documents, web sites, and other files you have designated as favorites. See Chapter 24.*

Applications: *Click this to go directly to the window that stores all of your Mac OS X applications. See Chapter 27.*

Search: *Use this box to find files on your hard disk; type in the name of a file, and matching files that start with that name will appear in the window. See Chapter 25 for all the details.*

Robin's Hard Disk

Network

Finder window icons

Hard disk icons: *This is what a hard disk case inside your computer looks like. Think of this as a filing cabinet— you look inside of it to find your files. See Chapter 9.*

Network: *A "network" is a system of wires and software that allows different people at different computers to share files and information. The Internet is a global network; you might also share files across the office. A click on this icon (in the "Computer" window) opens files that are available over a corporate network. (A click on this same icon in the System Preferences toolbar opens something completely different! See page 344.)*

Dock icons

Finder: *When you click once on this icon, the main Finder window opens. All of the various files on your computer can be found in this window. Think of this as your office—you look inside of it to find your filing cabinets (hard disks) and documents (files). See Chapter 9.*

System Preferences: *This opens up a "pane" with lots of little utilities that let you customize your Mac. See Chapter 22.*

Trash: *This is where you throw away files you don't ever want to see again. Just drag them into this basket. See Chapter 17.*

The Menu Bar

Note: You might have several windows open on your Mac at the same time, but only one can be "active." Whichever one you click on instantly comes to the front and is active. See page 101 for more on active windows and why it's important to know.

As shown on page 2, you will always see a **menu bar** across the top of your computer screen. The items listed horizontally in the menu bar will change depending on what is "active" on your screen. For instance, if you have the general Finder window open because you clicked on the happy face icon in the Dock, you'll see the first menu bar shown below. You can tell the Finder is the active item because you see the word "Finder" in the menu bar.

This is the System Preferences icon you'll see in the Dock. You'll learn all about these preferences in Chapter 22.

If you click on the System Preferences icon (shown to the left) in the Dock to open the System Preferences pane, the menu bar will change. You can tell System Preferences is the active item because you see its name in the menu bar. Notice that some of the other items in this menu bar, as shown below, are different from the Finder's, above.

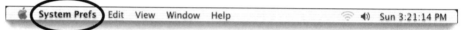

Every application you open will also have its own menu bar, as shown below. The application Preview is open, and you see its name in the menu bar. Notice this menu bar has different items from either of those above. Under the application menu, as shown below, the last item in the list of commands is always "Quit."

Tip: You might someday open a game or watch a DVD movie and discover that you have no menu bar. Even if the menu bar is not visible, you can always press Command Q to quit. See Chapter 5 for details on how to use a keyboard shortcut such as Command Q.

Shown below is every **menu** you'll see while you're at the Desktop and the **Finder** is "active" (see the note on the opposite page). The pages or chapters listed are where you will find information about each menu command.

The Finder Menus

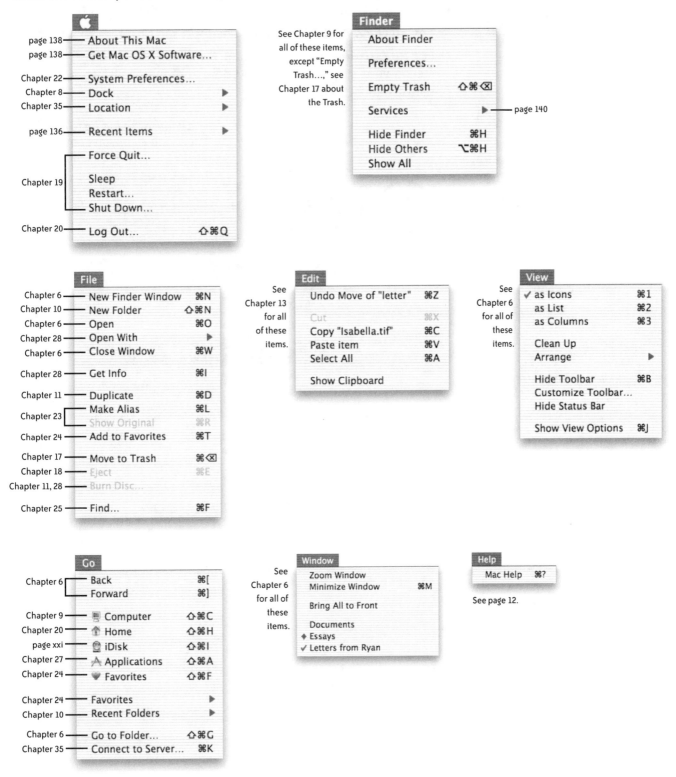

Apple menu

page 138 — About This Mac
page 138 — Get Mac OS X Software...

Chapter 22 — System Preferences...
Chapter 8 — Dock ▶
Chapter 35 — Location ▶

page 136 — Recent Items ▶

Force Quit...

Chapter 19
Sleep
Restart...
Shut Down...

Chapter 20 — Log Out... ⇧⌘Q

Finder

See Chapter 9 for all of these items, except "Empty Trash...," see Chapter 17 about the Trash.

About Finder
Preferences...
Empty Trash ⇧⌘⌫
Services ▶ — page 140
Hide Finder ⌘H
Hide Others ⌥⌘H
Show All

File

Chapter 6 — New Finder Window ⌘N
Chapter 10 — New Folder ⇧⌘N
Chapter 6 — Open ⌘O
Chapter 28 — Open With ▶
Chapter 6 — Close Window ⌘W

Chapter 28 — Get Info ⌘I

Chapter 11 — Duplicate ⌘D
Chapter 23 — Make Alias ⌘L
Show Original ⌘R
Chapter 24 — Add to Favorites ⌘T

Chapter 17 — Move to Trash ⌘⌫
Chapter 18 — Eject ⌘E
Chapter 11, 28 — Burn Disc...

Chapter 25 — Find... ⌘F

Edit

See Chapter 13 for all of these items.

Undo Move of "letter" ⌘Z
Cut ⌘X
Copy "Isabella.tif" ⌘C
Paste item ⌘V
Select All ⌘A

Show Clipboard

View

See Chapter 6 for all of these items.

✓ as Icons ⌘1
as List ⌘2
as Columns ⌘3

Clean Up
Arrange ▶

Hide Toolbar ⌘B
Customize Toolbar...
Hide Status Bar

Show View Options ⌘J

Go

Chapter 6
Back ⌘[
Forward ⌘]

Chapter 9 — 🖥 Computer ⇧⌘C
Chapter 20 — 🏠 Home ⇧⌘H
page xxi — iDisk ⇧⌘I
Chapter 27 — Applications ⇧⌘A
Chapter 24 — Favorites ⇧⌘F

Chapter 24 — Favorites ▶
Chapter 10 — Recent Folders ▶

Chapter 6 — Go to Folder... ⇧⌘G
Chapter 35 — Connect to Server... ⌘K

Window

See Chapter 6 for all of these items.

Zoom Window
Minimize Window ⌘M

Bring All to Front

Documents
♦ Essays
✓ Letters from Ryan

Help

Mac Help ⌘?

See page 12.

Sherlock

If you click the Sherlock Holmes hat you see in the Dock, you'll get the application shown below, called **Sherlock.** Sherlock is a tool you can use to find things on the Internet like old friends, shopping bargains, definitions of strange words, research articles, entertainment, Apple Help, and more.

▼ *For all the details* about using Sherlock, see Chapter 31.

▼ *For an introduction* to the World Wide Web, details on getting your Mac connected, and how to browse web pages, see Chapters 29–31.

Click any of the "channels" **to log on to the Internet** *(providing your connection is set up first) and find various sorts of information.*

This example uses the Internet channel.

1. *Type in the name of something you want to find on the World Wide Web.*

2. *Click the green magnifying glass to tell Sherlock to search the web.*

3. *Single-click any of these results to see information about that web site in the lower pane.*

4. *Double-click any result to make your browser open and go to that web site.*

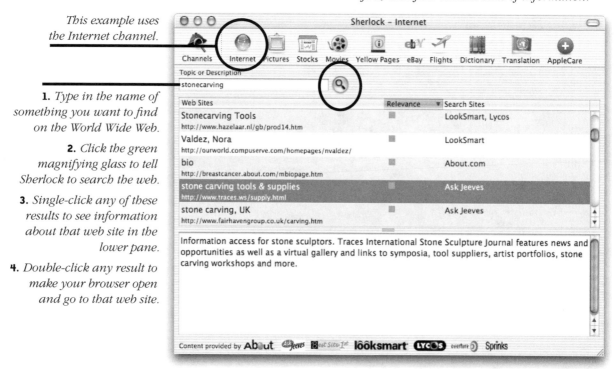

The Mac lets you customize a great number of the features of your computer to accommodate your personal working habits. In the Dock, click the **System Preferences** icon (shown to the right) to get the "pane" shown below (or you can go to the Apple menu and choose "System Preferences…"). You can click on any icon to get a new pane in which you can customize features. You'll be using this a great deal.

▼ *For all the details* about every System Preference shown below, see Chapter 22.

System Preferences

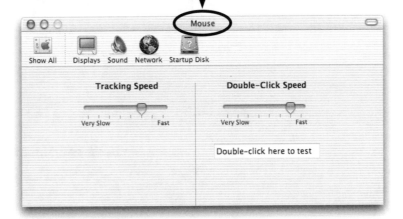

Single-click on one of the icons in the System Preferences and you'll get choices for customizing that particular feature, as shown below. This new "pane," below, will replace the original one, above.

To go back to the entire pane of all System Preferences, single-click the icon in the upper-left corner, "Show All."

Getting Help

Note: Most of Apple's Help files are kept on the web where they can be updated regularly. If you have a permanent Internet connection, such as cable or DSL, you won't even notice. But if your modem has to dial a phone number to get to the Internet, then you must connect first, then go to the Help page you need. Don't worry, you'll know when it happens.

You will always have a **Help menu** in the menu bar, no matter which application you are using. Below are several examples of what the Help menu might display, depending on what is "active" on your screen. When you choose one of these items, you will get Apple's Help files, as shown further below. This is a great place to check for immediate information about almost every feature on your Mac.

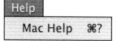

When you're at the Desktop, this is what you'll see in the Help menu.

When you're working in most applications, the Help menu will offer you help for that application.

Non-Apple applications will have different sorts of Help files, not the ones shown below. But you can usually access any application's Help file from this menu.

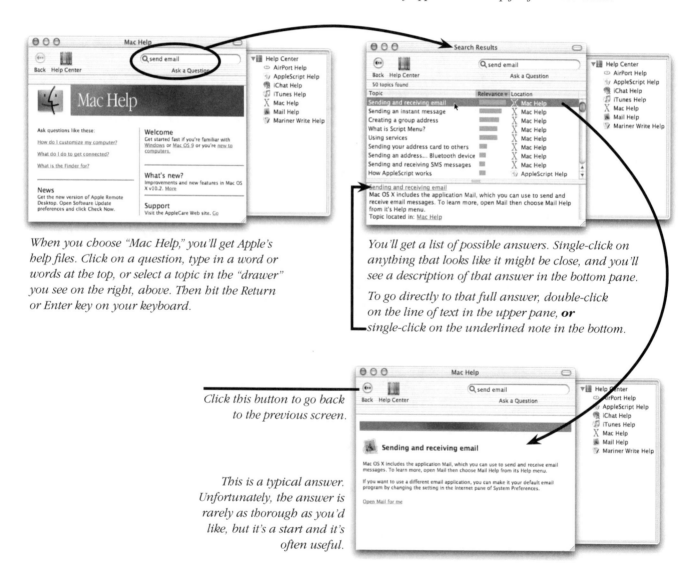

When you choose "Mac Help," you'll get Apple's help files. Click on a question, type in a word or words at the top, or select a topic in the "drawer" you see on the right, above. Then hit the Return or Enter key on your keyboard.

You'll get a list of possible answers. Single-click on anything that looks like it might be close, and you'll see a description of that answer in the bottom pane.

*To go directly to that full answer, double-click on the line of text in the upper pane, **or** single-click on the underlined note in the bottom.*

Click this button to go back to the previous screen.

This is a typical answer. Unfortunately, the answer is rarely as thorough as you'd like, but it's a start and it's often useful.

An Easy Tutorial

If you're new to your Mac, I suggest you start here. This tutorial follows a logical pattern that I have found to be successful in my classes (but it's not meant to be completed in one day!). These steps skip all over the book—I apologize for the hopping around you'll have to do, but you really shouldn't read *everything* about windows or the mouse or whatever at once. You need to know just enough to feel comfortable, then come back later for more. If you get overloaded, turn off the computer and have a cup of tea with me.

After you've finished the brief tutorial, spend a few weeks working on your Mac. Then come back to the book and read other parts that now interest you. Not only will the tips and tricks make more sense, but you'll find you can actually absorb the rest of the information.

Contents of this chapter

Don't Limit Yourself!

You might think, in your eagerness to get right into a program and start creating something or sending email or browsing the web, that you want to skip all these dumb little exercises at the Desktop like making windows smaller and larger or trashing blank folders. But trust me—it's too easy to turn on the computer, find the button for your program, and go right into it. But then you're limited. You won't have complete control over your computer. Some things will always confuse you. You'll never be a Power User (your Goal in Life, right?).

Quick Start

But for the person who wants to instantly create, save, print, and quit, the steps are quite easy, as long as you know what all the terms are, like "icon" and "Dock" and "double-click."

▾ **Open** your word processing program (or other program of your choice):
If the application icon is in a window, double-click it.
If the application icon is in the Dock, single-click it.

▾ **Save** the new document:
From the File menu, choose "Save As…."
Name the file and click "Save."

▾ **Create** something: start typing, drawing, painting, or whatever.
Save regularly as you work (from the File menu, choose "Save").

▾ **Print** the document:
From the File menu, choose "Print…."
Click the "Print" button.

▾ **Quit** the application:
From the File menu, choose "Quit."

This is the same basic process you will go through in any application—it's really that easy. But to be truly powerful—ahh, that takes a little more time.

So here are my recommendations on what you should spend time doing if you are impatient or your time is very limited. Actually, this is a good way to start even if you have lots of time; there is so much information to be absorbed that it works best to absorb a little now, then come back for more later. It also helps to run into a few problems because then when you discover the solution, the solution actually makes sense.

First of all, you don't have to read very many pages of this book to become proficient on your Mac. Flip through the book and you'll see **half-dots** on the edges of the pages—those are the only pages you really need to read. The rest of the book will answer your questions as you bump into things you want to know more about. But to get started, just follow the dots!

On many pages, including some without dots, there are gray boxes that contain short **practice exercises.** This tutorial will direct you to the practice exercises you really need right away, and then you can do the others whenever you feel like it.

Start Using the Tutorial Here

Follow the dots

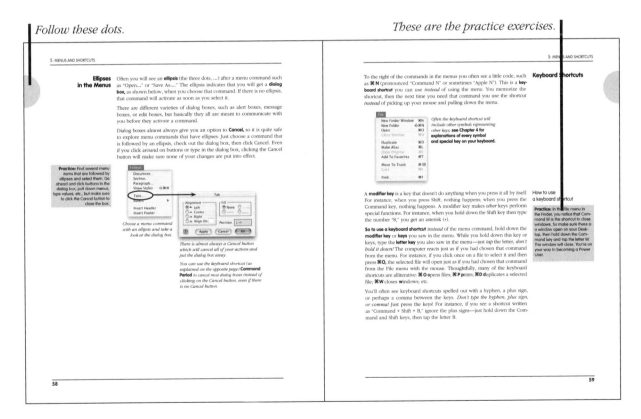

Follow these dots.

These are the practice exercises.

Turning it On

This is the Power symbol.

Some Power symbols look like this.

You've probably already done this, but just in case you haven't, learn how to **turn on** your computer. On most Macs these days you'll find a flat button with the "Power" symbol on it, as shown to the left. The button might be on the keyboard, the monitor (as on iMacs), or the tower (the big box that holds the actual computer parts). (The Power On button is not always the Power Off button—see Chapter 19 when you're ready to shut down your Mac.)

Older Macs have a large button on the keyboard with a triangle on it. This Power On button *does* turn your Mac off, as well as on.

If you work in a large office or a computer lab at school, you might run across other Macs that turn on in different ways, or ones that have been set up to turn on differently—they might have buttons on the back, on a power strip, or somewhere else. But don't let it confuse you—even if you forget half the other stuff in this book, once you figure out how to turn on your computer you probably won't forget it.

The Desktop, Finder, and Home

What you see when you turn on the Macintosh is called the **Desktop.** It is also called the **Finder** because the software program that runs the Desktop is the Finder. You might have seen the map of your Desktop on page 2. Get a general idea of the Desktop features by reading pages 125–127, then learn about your **Home** area on pages 132–133.

Using the Mouse

Read pages 23, 25, and 26. Follow the practice exercises for using your **mouse.** You'll be using the mouse every time you use your Mac, so it's good to practice enough to feel comfortable with it. If you go through the rest of the exercises, you'll quickly become a pro.

Getting Familiar with the Keyboard

Skim through the first part of the **keyboard** chapter, Chapter 4, pages 33 to 41, plus the top half of 42. There are no practice exercises in this section, but try to become familiar with all those odd keys on your keyboard. Don't worry about memorizing what they do—when you need to know, you'll know where to find the information. Just pick out the keys you've been wondering about, or skim through the information and find the keys that you think sound useful for the future.

Using the Dock

You will gradually come to use the Dock more and more as you become familiar with your Mac. At the moment, just read the first three pages of Chapter 8, pages 119–121. This will familiarize you with the Dock enough so you can work effectively. When you want to know more, read the rest of the chapter.

Using Menus and Menu Commands

Read pages 54–58 in Chapter 5 about **menus** and **how to choose commands** (you can read the rest of that chapter some other time). Follow the practice exercises. You will be using the menus and commands constantly every time you use your Mac, so make sure you understand them. By now you're probably pretty good with that mouse, huh?

Controlling the Windows

Chapter 6 about **windows** is pretty long, but windows are *very important*. Almost everything you do at the Desktop/Finder involves a window, and every application you use will display itself in a window, so you need to know how to control them. This is where you should commit to spending a bit of time (won't take more than an hour or two) to go through the chapter carefully, do all of the practice exercises, and make sure you feel comfortable. Believe me, if you don't feel comfortable using the windows, you will never be quite at home on your Mac.

Recognizing Icons

Read pages 105–112 about icons in Chapter 7, and do the practice exercises. Skip the rest for now! Even if you don't see too many icons at the moment, remember that icons tell you a lot; they are rich in visual clues that help you understand your computer.

Don't double-click on anything except folder icons at the moment.

Taking Advantage of Keyboard Commands

Use the **keyboard commands** to do some of the tasks you've already been doing with the mouse and menus. Read page 59, "Keyboard Shortcuts." Using the keyboard shortcuts is a sign of becoming a Power User.

The trick to making a keyboard shortcut work is that you must *first* select the item you want to affect. For instance, if you want to open a folder, *first* click once on the folder to select it, *then* press Command O to open it (as explained on page 59).

Do each of these things using a keyboard shortcut:

❏ Open a window.

❏ Close a window.

❏ Select every item in a window.
(To *de*select the items, click in any white space in the folder.)

Word Processing (typing)

Next to using the windows proficiently, the other main skill you need on a computer is **word processing,** or **typing.** Whether you type a novel or a note, it's important to know how the computer works with text. Learning how to word process will also teach you other important techniques, such as how to open an application, start a new document, cut, copy, and paste. Read and do the practice exercises on pages 195–214. Then recreate the sample shown on page 216. If you spend the time to do this (maybe an hour or two), you'll know more than most people who have been using a Mac for a long time.

Saving your Documents

If you want to keep a document you are working on, you must **save** it and give it a name. Read the first four pages of Chapter 14, pages 219–222, to learn how important it is and why to save your documents, and to learn how to do a quick and easy save. This is very important!

Printing

Now you need **to print your document.** If you are connected to a color inkjet printer like an Epson Stylus or an HP DeskWriter, all you have to do is go to the File menu, choose "Print…," and click the blue Print button. (Of course, first make sure your printer is plugged into your Mac, plugged into a power supply, and is turned on and warmed up.)

If printing doesn't work automatically, you probably need to tell the Mac where your printer is. Read pages 236–240. It's also a good idea to install the software that came with your printer—it's on a CD that arrived in your printer box. Many times you don't have to install the software, but if you do you might discover you have extra printing options.

Quitting

You need to **quit** the application if you are done for the day. Save the document again before you quit: just use the keyboard shortcut Command S. Then from the File menu, choose "Quit." The Quit command is always the very last item, and the keyboard shortcut is always Command Q. You really should read pages 257–261 in Chapter 16 so you understand the difference between closing and quitting.

This is a list of **several other basic Desktop tasks** you need to learn because you will be doing them everyday:

Basic Desktop Tasks

▼ Read pages 145–151 about **folders.** Make a new folder. (What is the keyboard shortcut?!) Name your new folder.

▼ Make a **duplicate** of this new folder: click once on the folder to select it, then find the command for duplicating. Which menu is it in, and what is the keyboard shortcut (see page 171)? Change the name of this duplicate folder.

▼ Use the **Trash** basket (read pages 265–269). Throw away the duplicate folder you just made. Empty the trash.

▼ **Backup** your work! You should do this to every file you want to keep, especially your documents. In case the file on your hard disk gets lost or trashed or your hard disk dies, you will have this extra copy. If you have a built-in CD or DVD burner in your Mac, read pages 176–177. If you have a Zip drive, copy a folder or document onto a Zip disk, as explained on page 173.

Inserting Disks

CDs go in the tray or in the slot with the label-side up. If you have a Zip drive, you'll use **Zip disks** to store extra files or copies of files. The Zip disk goes in the drive with the label-side facing up (or toward the top of the drive, if you have an external drive sitting sideways), the round thing on the bottom. The metal end slides in first. See Chapter 18 about ejecting disks.

Other Very Important Features

There are several **very important features** on your Mac you can learn that will make you the life of any party. Here are suggestions for specific things you need to be in control of:

Search

▼ Learn how to **Search.** Read pages 386–388 and experiment. Later, another day, read the rest of the chapter and learn how to do more complex searches (when you know what you're searching for).

System Preferences

▼ Learn how to use some of your **System Preferences:** skim Chapter 22. Check out only the preference panes that interest you (ignore the others). An easy one to experiment with is the Mouse preferences (see pages 28–29).

Aliases

▼ Learn how to use **aliases.** Read pages 365–369. I guarantee you will find aliases to be one of the greatest features of organization and convenience on the Mac.

p.s.

▼ Read the book called *The Mac is not a typewriter.* It's little.

User Groups!

One of the best things you can do for yourself is join your **local user group!** Macintosh users have a history of joyfully sharing information, and a user group is an incredible source of help and support. To find the user group in your area, check the Apple website: **www.apple.com/usergroups.** You can find the user group nearest where you live or where you will be traveling to, based on the zip code or even by the cross streets.

If you're ever in Santa Fe, New Mexico, on the first Wednesday of the month, visit the Santa Fe Mac User Group! Check our award-winning web site at **www.santafemug.org.**

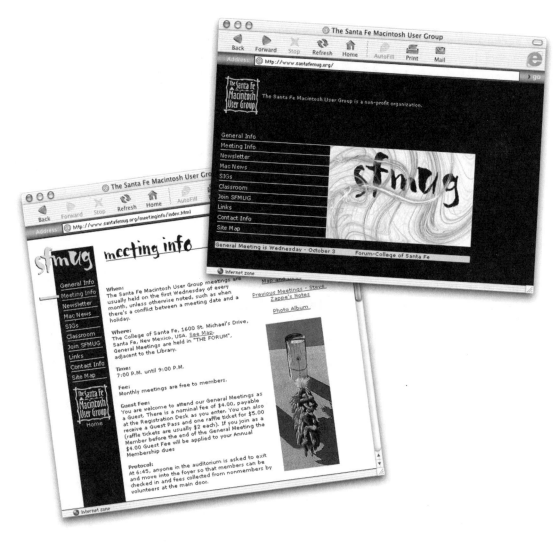

The Mouse

The **mouse,** of course, is that handy little piece of hardware that controls the movement of the pointer on the screen. As you move the mouse across the desk, a pointer, sometimes called a cursor, moves across the screen in the same direction. In most Macintosh applications, you cannot fully utilize the program without the mouse. A few programs give you the option of doing absolutely everything from the keyboard if you choose; but who wants to learn 450 keyboard commands?

This short chapter helps you get familiar with the various ways of using and taking care of your mouse.

Contents of this chapter

Connecting the Mouse

[If your mouse is already connected, skip this page!] The mouse plugs into a port (a socket). Most Macs (including all iMacs, G4s, Cubes, iBooks) have what are called "USB ports" into which you plug "USB devices," including your mouse. You have two USB ports on the top sides of your keyboard; you can plug your mouse into either one. USB ports are rectangular, so of course the mouse cable has a rectangular connector on the other end of the cable. (If your mouse cable has a round connector, see the information below about ADB ports.)

 This is an illustration of two USB ports.

 This is the symbol that indicates a USB port.

Some stand-alone monitors (as opposed to iMac monitors) also have USB ports around their bases, making it even easier to connect keyboards and mice. Check your monitor.

You can plug and unplug your USB mouse while the computer is up and running, although Apple recommends that you first quit any open applications. Plugging and unplugging while the computer is running is called "hot swapping." For more information about USB, see Chapter 37.

Older Macs and ADB ports

Older Macintoshes don't use USB ports; they have something called ADB ports instead. ADB ports are round and have a different symbol identifying them, as shown below. Of course, you must have an ADB mouse to plug into an ADB port. If you have ADB ports, always shut down first before plugging and unplugging anything from your computer, including the mouse or the keyboard. You cannot hot swap from ADB ports!

 This is an illustration of an ADB port.

 This is the symbol that indicates an ADB port.

Left-Handed Mousing

If you are left-handed, all you need to do is plug the mouse into the port on the left side of the keyboard. Unless you have bought a special mouse that curves to fit the right hand, your mouse will fit just as well into the left hand as the right.

Older keyboards with ADB ports often have a port in the middle of the keyboard so you can just move the mouse to the left side.

The Pointer

As you move the mouse, a **pointer** moves around the screen. The only part of the pointer that does the trick is the *very* tip, called the "hot spot." When you need the pointer to activate something, be sure that the extreme point of the arrow is positioned in the area you want to affect. For instance, to click in the little red button in the top-left corner of a window to close it, position the pointer like so:

This is the hot spot . . . .   *The **tip** of the pointer (the hot spot) does the trick.*

Using the Mouse

You'll use the mouse in several different ways. Always, the mouse sits on a flat surface and you roll it around with your hand on top of it, your index finger resting on the front end of the mouse (the part that clicks). We often call the front part of the mouse the "button," even though there's not really a button. Do not hold the mouse in the palm of your hand, and do not pick it up and point it at the screen.

Single-click

A **single click** is a quick, light touch on the front end of the mouse, with the "cursor"—a pointer, an I-beam (page 196) or other shape—located at the spot of your choice on the screen.

> Single-click with the I-beam to set down an insertion point for typing.

> Single-click with the pointer on an icon on your Desktop or in a Finder window to *select* that icon.

> Single-click an application or document icon in the Dock to *open* that application or document.

Practice: Single-click on the icon of your hard disk, in the upper-right corner of your screen. A single click will "select" the hard disk.

Double-click

A **double-click** is a quick click-click on the front end of the mouse, again with the pointer located at the appropriate spot on the screen. A double-click has to be quick and the mouse must be still or the Mac will interpret it as two single clicks.

> Double-click on an application or document icon to *open* that application or document (as long as the icon is not in the Dock—single-click items in the Dock).

> Double-click on a folder icon (not in the Dock) to *open* the window for that folder.

> Double-click on a word to *select* that word for editing.

Practice: Double-click on the icon of your hard disk, in the upper-right corner of your screen. A double-click will "open" the hard disk and show you its window.

Press

To **press** means to point to something and *hold the mouse button down*.

Press on the arrows in a scroll bar of a window to scroll through that window.

Press on items in the Dock to get their menus.

Often directions tell you to "click" on things when they really mean "press." If clicking doesn't work, try pressing.

Press-and-drag

Press-and-drag means to point to the object or the area of your choice, *hold/press the mouse button down, keep it down,* and *drag* somewhere, then *let go* when you reach your goal. (This is sometimes called click-and-drag.)

Press-and-drag to move icons across the screen.

Press-and-drag to select a range of text.

Shift-click
Command-click
Option-click
Control-click

You'll see the terms **Shift-click, Command-click, Option-click,** and **Control-click.** This means to *hold down* that key (Shift, Command, Option, or Control) and then *click* the mouse button once. Different things happen with this action.

Shift-click individual icons (when a window is in Icon view) to *select* more than one icon, or to *deselect* from a group of selected icons (see pages 160–165 for details about selecting).

Shift-click file names (when a window is in Column or List view) to *select* all of the files between the two clicks.

Command-click individual file names (when a window is in Column or List view) to *select* more than one file, or to *deselect* from a group of selected icons.

Control-click on various items on the Desktop to get "contextual menus," which are menus that offer different choices depending on what you Control-click (see page 55).

Option-click on application icons in the Dock to give you a menu choice to force that application to quit.

Option-drag
Command-Option-drag

You'll see terms like **Option-drag** or **Command-Option-drag,** which mean you must *hold down* the Option and/or Command keys and *drag* the mouse.

Option-drag a file from one window to another to make a copy of that file.

Command-Option-drag a file to another folder or to the Desktop to make an alias of it (alias information is in Chapter 23).

You've surely seen or have a **mouse pad,** a small pad to put on your desk to roll the mouse across. The pad has nothing to do with the operation of the mouse, really—the mouse will work just fine without a pad. The purpose of a mouse pad is simply to provide better traction and a clear spot on your desk for the mouse. You can use a book, illustration board, a coaster, paper, or even just the deskop.

Sometimes you may be **moving the mouse** across the mouse pad or the desk and **run out of space** before the pointer or the I-beam gets where you want it to go. Just do this: Keep your finger on the mouse button, pressing it down. Pick up the mouse, keeping the button down, and move the mouse over to where you have more room. Then just continue on your path. Try it.

If you have an **optical** mouse, one with a little red glow on the underside, you can adjust the tension in the click. More tension makes the mouse button feel a little stiffer; less tension makes the clicking easier.

1. Turn the mouse over.
2. There is a plastic ring around the center of the mouse with a small dot at the top. Press on that ring with your thumbs and move it to the right for more tension, to the left for less tension. You can barely see a tiny plus or minus sign in the little round dots as you move it to the right or left.

Mouse Pad

Moving the Mouse
when you've run out of space

Adjust the Tension on an Optical Mouse

Mouse Preferences

This is the System Preferences icon in the Dock. Click it once.

This is the icon that opens the Mouse preferences pane. Click it once.

One of the first sets of preferences you might want to customize are the Mouse preferences (if you have a laptop with a trackpad instead of a mouse, see the following page). You'll read about all the preference panes in Chapter 22, but this one is simple to use and shows you how easy it is to customize many of the features on your Mac, so take a look at it as soon as you feel comfortable using the mouse and pulling down menus. If you are brand-new to your Mac, come back to this page in a couple of days.

1. Click on the "System Preferences" icon in the Dock, as shown to the left, to open the Preferences window. Click the "Mouse" icon, also shown to the left, to open the Mouse preferences panel.

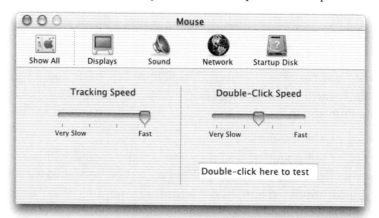

2. When the **Tracking Speed** is set on or near "Very Slow," you have to move the mouse a long way on your desk to move the pointer across the screen. If you choose "Fast," you only need to move the mouse a short distance to move the pointer across the screen. Try it—position the pointer on the colored button and drag it from one end to the other. Let go, then drag your mouse across the screen *without* pressing the button down. You'll notice the effects immediately. Most people find they prefer the faster setting.

When you work in a drawing, painting, or image editing program, you may want to come back to this preference pane and set the speed to "Slow" so you have finer control over tiny details in your drawing.

If you use a tablet with a stylus for drawing, drag the button all the way to "Very Slow."

3. The **Double-Click Speed** adjusts how fast you have to click twice so the computer knows you want a double-click, instead of two single clicks. If you find that you don't double-click quite fast enough to make the computer happy, lower the double-click speed.

   If you set the speed to the fastest setting, you run the risk that the computer will interpret a single click as a double click if you have the slightest bit of shakiness in your click. A good choice is right in the middle.

   To test the double-click speed you chose, position the pointer over one of the words in that sentence you see in the pane, "Double-click here to test." Double-click as you normally would. If the word becomes highlighted (is surrounded by a darker color), that speed is good for you. If the word doesn't become highlighted, set a lower speed and test it again.

4. After you adjust the tracking and double-click speeds, click the close button (the red one in the upper-left corner) to put this preference panel away.

5. To put the entire window of System Preferences away, position the pointer on the bold heading in the menu across the top of your screen, "System Prefs."

   Click once on that heading.

   Click once on the command at the very bottom of that menu, the one that says "Quit System Preferences."

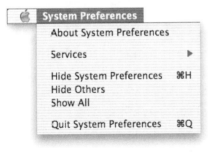

Trackpads and Trackballs

Some people prefer to use a different "pointing device," such as a joystick or a trackball. The Macintosh laptops use trackballs or trackpads.

A **trackball** is like an upside-down version of the roller-ball mouse—instead of moving the little mouse box around to make the ball roll underneath, you use your fingers to roll the little ball on top as it sits in the box. Trackballs have buttons to press that act like the button on the mouse. Depending on what kind of trackball you have, you may click the button with a finger or, as seems to be easier on some laptops, with your thumb.

The **trackpad** is a flat space and you use your finger to drag the pointer around the screen. It takes a little time to get used to it.

Trackballs and trackpads are particularly convenient for those people who have to use the mouse backwards. Yes, I have met several people who have to turn the mouse with the tail facing themselves. When they push the mouse to the right, the pointer on the screen moves to the left. If more than one person uses the same computer, each person has to turn the mouse around. With a trackball or pad, individual idiosyncrasies don't matter.

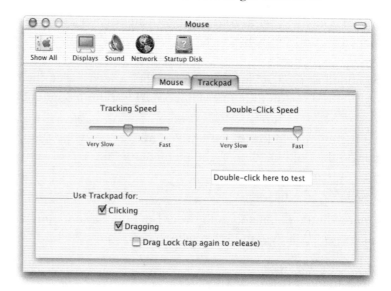

▼ Generally, move your finger around the trackpad. When you want to click on an item, tap the bar under the trackpad.

▼ A checkmark in the "Clicking" checkbox tells the Mac you want to tap your finger on the trackpad (instead of the bar) to click on items. This is a great feature—just roll your finger around and tap to select files (or open Dock icons), tap-tap to open files.

▼ If you check "Clicking," then the checkbox for "Dragging" becomes available. A checkmark in the "Dragging" checkbox lets you click-and-a-half with your finger to drag items: On a regular double-click, you click twice, then let go. In a click-and-a-half, you keep the mouse button down after the second click. Try it. Then you can drag selected files.

▼ Once you check "Dragging," then "Drag Lock" becomes available. This feature will grab the selected item and drag it after the first click. Be careful—this feature can make you crazy if you aren't perfectly aware of what's going on. Experiment.

Cleaning the Mouse

If your mouse has a little **red glow** in the middle, it's an **optical** mouse and uses light to communicate with the monitor. Check the bottom of the mouse regularly—grunge builds up on the white plastic edge and can affect the way the mouse moves around on the pad. You might want to first unplug the mouse from the keyboard to prevent things from happening on your screen as you clean the mouse.

If you have an **older mouse with a ball** on the bottom, it's important to keep the ball and pocket clean—cat hairs and dustballs get inside. Take it apart regularly and clean it, following these steps:

1. Take the mouse in your right hand and turn it upside-down.
2. With your thumbs, slide the round wheel to the left to open the lid.
3. Flip the mouse back over into your left hand so the lid and the ball fall out into your palm.
4. Clean the ball with a soft, dry cloth; clean the rollers inside with a cotton swab dipped in rubbing alcohol.
5. When clean, put the ball in your left hand; with your right hand place the mouse on top of the ball and flop your hands over. This places the ball safely into its little pocket.
6. Put the lid back on and twist it to the right, lining up the marker with the "L" for Lock (if you see one). That's it!

Would you single-click (**S**), double-click (**D**), press (**P**), or press-and-drag (**P&D**) to accomplish each of the following tasks? Circle the appropriate abbreviation in the margin for each task.

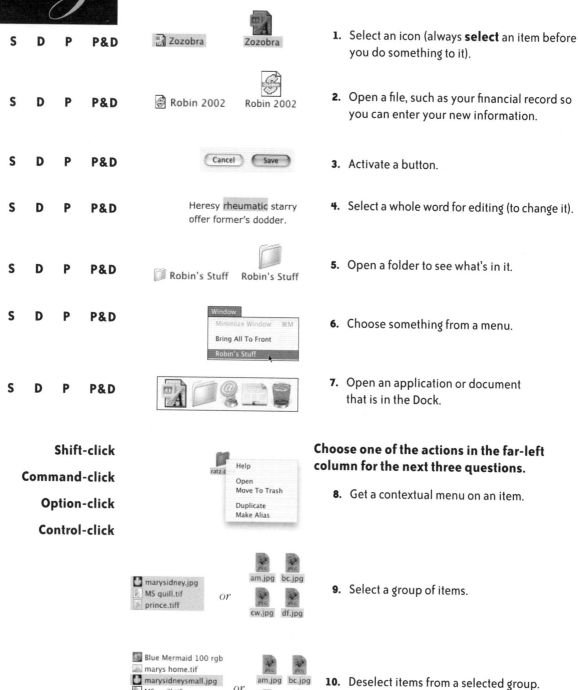

S   D   P   P&D   1. Select an icon (always **select** an item before you do something to it).

S   D   P   P&D   2. Open a file, such as your financial record so you can enter your new information.

S   D   P   P&D   3. Activate a button.

S   D   P   P&D   4. Select a whole word for editing (to change it).

S   D   P   P&D   5. Open a folder to see what's in it.

S   D   P   P&D   6. Choose something from a menu.

S   D   P   P&D   7. Open an application or document that is in the Dock.

Shift-click

Command-click

Option-click

Control-click

Choose one of the actions in the far-left column for the next three questions.

8. Get a contextual menu on an item.

9. Select a group of items.

10. Deselect items from a selected group.

Answers on page 730.

Keys & the Keyboard

There are a number of important **keys** on your keyboard that are particularly useful. They come in handy for shortcuts, manipulating images, accessing alternate characters, and any number of things in specific applications.

All keyboards have certain standard characters, although they may appear in different places on different models. No matter where they are placed, though, all the keys perform the same function (although the function of some keys may vary within different programs).

Don't forget to look at the **underside of your keyboard** and pull out that little lever that puts your keyboard at a slight tilt; the tilt is a better position for your hands.

Contents of this chapter

What are All These Keys?

On these two pages are photographs of the two main sorts of **keyboards** you'll find attached to your Mac, with callouts telling you where to go for more information about particular keys. For a laptop keyboard and its special features, please see pages 45–46.

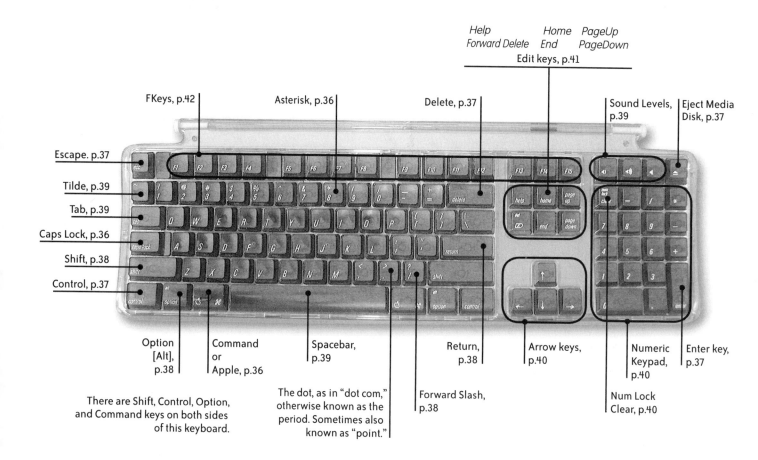

Help
Forward Delete

Home   PageUp
End   PageDown

Edit keys, p.41

FKeys, p.42

Asterisk, p.36

Delete, p.37

Sound Levels, p.39

Eject Media Disk, p.37

Escape. p.37

Tilde, p.39

Tab, p.39

Caps Lock, p.36

Shift, p.38

Control, p.37

Option [Alt], p.38

Command or Apple, p.36

Spacebar, p.39

Return, p.38

Arrow keys, p.40

Numeric Keypad, p.40

Enter key, p.37

There are Shift, Control, Option, and Command keys on both sides of this keyboard.

The dot, as in "dot com," otherwise known as the period. Sometimes also known as "point."

Forward Slash, p.38

Num Lock Clear, p.40

The keyboard shown below is the one that typically comes with **iMacs,** as well as with many other Macs. The Fkeys are smaller, there is no Forward Delete key, and the Edit keys are across the top of the numeric keypad. If you find you don't feel comfortable with this smaller keyboard, you can always buy the larger one (as shown on the opposite page), or any number of other brands of keyboards.

The smaller keyboard

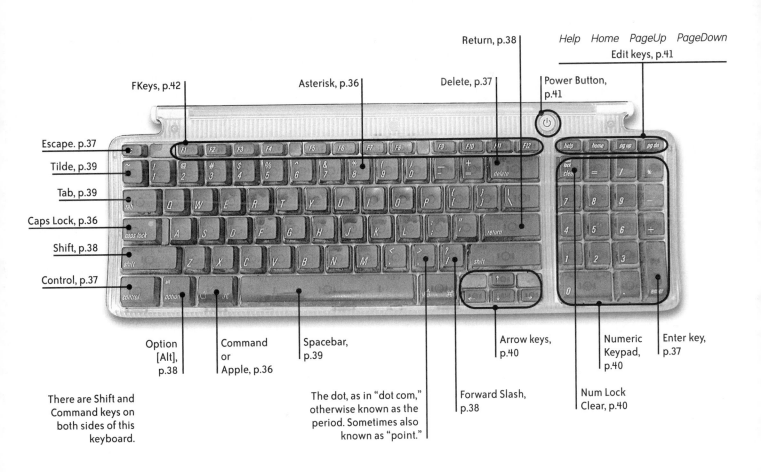

Return, p.38

Help   Home   PageUp   PageDown
Edit keys, p.41

FKeys, p.42

Asterisk, p.36

Delete, p.37

Power Button, p.41

Escape. p.37

Tilde, p.39

Tab, p.39

Caps Lock, p.36

Shift, p.38

Control, p.37

Option [Alt], p.38

Command or Apple, p.36

Spacebar, p.39

Arrow keys, p.40

Numeric Keypad, p.40

Enter key, p.37

There are Shift and Command keys on both sides of this keyboard.

The dot, as in "dot com," otherwise known as the period. Sometimes also known as "point."

Forward Slash, p.38

Num Lock Clear, p.40

Modifier Keys

The symbols shown in the outer column under each of the following headings are the symbols that will appear in menus to indicate those keys.

Some of the keys on the keyboard are called **modifier keys** because they don't do anything by themselves, but are used in combination with regular keys to make something happen, like keyboard shortcuts (see "Keyboard Shortcuts" on page 59). The Shift key, for instance, is a modifier key you are already familiar with: the Shift key doesn't do anything when you press it by itself, but if you hold it down while you type an alphabetic character, you get the capital letter instead of the lowercase letter.

Modifier keys: Shift, Option, Command (also called Apple), Control.

Sometimes a keyboard shortcut uses more than one modifier. Always *hold down all the modifier keys together* (Command, Shift, Option, etc.) while you give *one quick tap on the associated letter key.* For instance, to *paste* an item, the shortcut is ⌘ **V**: hold down the Command key and type a quick V. If you *hold* the character key down (such as the V key) instead of *tapping* it once, you will usually end up repeating the command many times.

Any Key

There is no **Any key.** When a direction tells you to "PRESS ANY KEY," it means to press any key you want on the whole keyboard.

Asterisk Key

*

The **asterisk** (*, Greek for "little star") is used as a multiplication symbol in calculators, spreadsheets, databases, etc. You can use the asterisk on the numeric keypad, or you can press Shift 8 to get the asterisk you see above the number 8 on the keyboard. Thank goodness this key is also known as the Star key because so few people can spell or pronounce "asterisk."

Caps Lock Key

When you press the **Caps Lock key** down, everything you type is in capital letters. If you've ever used a typewriter, you'll find that Caps Lock is different from the Shift Lock on a typewriter: Caps Lock does *not* type the characters above the numbers or above the punctuation, such as the *, $, @, or < >, nor even the ?. If you want to type these Shift-characters you must press the Shift key, even if Caps Lock is down.

Some keyboard shortcuts will not work if the Caps Lock key is down, so check its position if you're having problems.

Command Key
Apple Key

⌘

The **Command key** is on the bottom row, the key with the California freeway cloverleaf symbol on it: ⌘. On most keyboards this key also has an apple symbol on it, and you may hear it improperly referred to as the **Apple key** or **Open Apple** (although in the Mac OS X Help files you may see references to the "Apple" key, even though the symbol in the menus is still the Command symbol.

Most keyboard shortcuts use the Command key. Do not confuse it with the Control key!

The **Control key** is standard on Macintosh keyboards—it's usually on the bottom, far-left, and often on the far-right as well. Contextual menus on the Mac (page 56) usually use the Control key, as do a number of other keyboard shortcuts. Also, this key makes it easier for those who are running DOS or Windows software on the Macintosh. Be sure to read directions carefully and make sure you use the *Control* key when the directions call for *Control* and the Command key when they call for Command.

Control Key
ctrl or control

∧

The **Delete key** is located on the upper-right of the main body of keys. You might hear people refer to it as the Backspace key because it used to be called such. The name was changed to "Delete" long ago because that's really what it does—whatever character is to the *left* of the "insertion point" will be deleted as you "backspace" over it. In applications, whatever item is *selected* will be removed when you hit the Delete key.

Delete Key
(Backspace Key)

There is another delete key located in the little group of Edit keys, called the Forward Delete, that deletes the character to the *right* as you type. I love this key. See page 41.

The **Eject Media Disk key** is not on every keyboard. If you have it, it's on the numeric keypad (the set of number keys on the right side of your keyboard), the very right-uppermost key. Use the Eject Media Disk key to eject CDs and DVDs: *you don't even have to select the disk,* just hit this key. As its name implies, this key only works on CDs and DVDs (media disks, as opposed to data disks); that is, this key will not eject a Zip or Jaz cartridge.

Eject Media Disk Key

⏏

If you don't have an Eject Media Disk key, try the F12 key.

Also use this key in combination with the Control key to shut down your computer: Hold down the Control key, press the Eject Media Disk key, and you'll get a message asking if you want to shut down your computer now, along with options to restart, sleep, and cancel.

Keyboard shutdown

The **Enter key** on the *numeric keypad* (the set of number keys on the right side of your keyboard) will also activate buttons with the double border, just the same as the Return key (following page), and Enter will usually start a new paragraph as well. Different programs use the Enter key in different ways.

Enter Key

⊼ or

The **Escape key** (labeled **esc**) on the upper-left of the keyboard is used in a few applications.

Escape Key
esc

> **Tip:** Press Command Option Esc to bring up the dialog box to force quit an application. (See pages 262–263 about force quitting.)

Forward Slash

/

The **forward slash** (/) is used as a division symbol in calculators, spreadsheets, databases, etc. It's also used in World Wide Web addresses. You can use the slash on the regular keyboard (the same key as the question mark) or the one on the numeric keypad. Don't use the straight slash (|) or the backward slash (\, backslash), which are both situated above the Return key, when you want to divide or when you type a web address.

The forward slash is an "illegal" character in file names in Mac OS X, which means you are not allowed to use it (it means something important to the Mac operating system). You can't use a colon (:) either.

Option Key
(Alt Key)

Next to the Command Key is the **Option key.** The Option key is often used in combination with the Command key and/or the Shift key. With the Option key, you can type the special characters such as ¢ and ®, as well as accent marks, as in résumé and piñata (see page 215).

This key sometimes has the word "alt" on it as well because the Option key is often comparable to the **Alt key** when using Windows programs on the Mac (if the Alt key doesn't work in a Windows program, try the Shift key).

Return Key
¶

The **Return key** is used for many things other than simply beginning a new paragraph. For instance, any button that is "pulsing" can be activated with the Return key instead of the mouse. Different programs use the Return key in different ways. Most things you do with the Return key you can also do with the Enter key, which is found in the numeric keypad.

Whenever you see a button pulsing, like the "Save," "Open," or "Create" buttons shown above, you can always press the Return key (or the Enter key) to activate that button instead of clicking on the button with the mouse.

Shift Key

The **Shift key** is one of the most commonly used modifier keys in keyboard shortcuts, as well as regular typing. Its symbol is an upward arrow, as shown to the left. You have a Shift key on both sides of your keyboard.

Some keyboards have **Sound Level keys** just above the numeric keypad. Use the two keys that have vibration symbols to lower or raise the volume. The key with no vibrations in the symbol is the **Mute** key; press it and your computer will not make any sounds, not even alert sounds. Instead, when it wants to beep at you, your menu bar will flash.

Sound Level Keys

The **Spacebar** is represented in menus by the symbol shown to the right, or sometimes *as a blank space.* That blank space can really throw you. How long does it take to figure out that "⇧⌘ " means to press the Shift key, the Command key, and the Spacebar?

Spacebar

The Tilde (~, pronounced *till´duh*) is located on the upper-left of the main set of keys on most keyboards and next to the Spacebar on older keyboards. This Tilde was never used much in English until the World Wide Web was invented—now we see it all the time in web addresses so you had better know how to type it (hold down the Shift key, then tap the Tilde key).

Tilde

~

The **Tab key** in the upper-left acts like the Tab key on a typewriter (if you've ever used a typewriter) in that after you press the Tab key you'll start typing at the next tab stop that's set. In most **word processing** programs, there is a default tab set every one-half inch; to make others, simply click in the ruler you see across the top of the screen to create a tab stop in the selected paragraph (to remove tabs, press-and-drag the tab markers down off the ruler).

Tab Key

» →

You won't see a symbol for the Tab key in menus, but you might see it on your word processing page; the symbol varies from program to program.

In **spreadsheet** and **database** programs, the Tab key will move the selection to the next cell or field *to the right,* just as it would move your typing to the right (the Return key will move the selection to the next cell or field *down*). Hold the Shift key down as you press Tab to move the selection backwards to the left (or Shift Return to move up).

When you are in **dialog boxes,** press the Tab key to select *edit boxes* (the small spaces where you can type something new, as shown circled to the right). Just try it: Open a dialog box, then press the Tab key to cycle you through the edit boxes. If there is something in an edit box already, the box will highlight; *anything you type will replace what is highlighted*

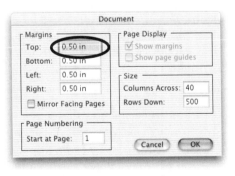

Do you see the seven edit boxes in this small dialog window? The first one, "Top," is highlighted and ready for you to enter a new value. Hit the Tab key to select the next edit box.

(which means you don't have to hit the Delete key first—just type). If the edit box is empty, the insertion point will flash to indicate you can now type in it. Using the Tab key to select the next field also works on most forms on **web pages.**

Arrow Keys

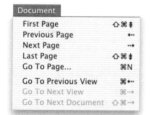

These are examples of menu commands that use the arrow keys for shortcuts.

Depending on your keyboard, you may have **arrow keys** (keys with nothing but an arrow on each of them) tucked in with your letter keys, or you may have a separate little set of four arrow keys, or on laptops your arrow keys are added onto existing character keys. Arrow keys are used for different things in different programs.

In **word processing** programs you can use the arrow keys to move the insertion point (the insertion point is that thin, flashing, vertical bar that moves along with the text as you type).

> **Tip:** In most programs, hold down the Shift key as you press the arrow keys, and the text will be *selected* as the insertion point moves along. Try it.

In some programs, such as **page layout** or **graphics** programs, you can use the arrow keys to nudge objects around on the screen. In **spreadsheets** and **databases,** the arrow keys might be used to move the insertion point or to select other cells or fields. In **dialog boxes,** the arrow keys will move the insertion point within the selected edit box.

RightArrow
LeftArrow
UpArrow
DownArrow

You'll notice when I write about commands that use **arrow keys** I write them out like this: RightArrow, LeftArrow, UpArrow, and DownArrow. For instance, I might tell you to press Shift LeftArrow. I do this because I have seen beginners follow a command such as "Press Command + left arrow" by pressing the Command key and then looking for the key that says "left," plus an arrow key. (And many new users also try to press the + key.) So even though it may seem odd at first, combining the two words that describe the arrow keys makes it clearer that there is just one key.

Numeric Keypad
Clear Key
Num Lock

On the far-right of the keyboard is a **numeric keypad** that looks like calculator keys. If you have a laptop, don't think you are missing a numeric keypad—see pages 45–46. In some applications, these numeric keys will type numbers, and in other applications they will move the insertion point (see page 196 for a description of the insertion point).

In some applications these keys can do both—they can type numbers *or* they can move the insertion point, depending on whether the **Num Lock** key is down; when down, it locks the keypad into typing numbers instead of moving the insertion point.

When you use the Calculator utility (see Chapter 28) or work in a spreadsheet or financial program, use the numeric keypad to enter data into the Calculator and perform functions. The asterisk (*) is the multiplication key, and the forward slash (**/**) is the division key. The **Clear key,** of course, acts like the clear key on a calculator.

The **Power key** might be an actual key on the keyboard, or it might be a round or oblong **Power button** embossed or printed with a left-pointing arrow or the standard power symbol (both shown to the right). It you have one on your keyboard, it's at the top-center of some keyboards and at the upper-right in others. Various models of iMacs also have a Power button on the monitor. Some of the newest keyboards do not have either a Power key or button on the keyboard itself—you have to use the button on the case or the monitor. A Power key on the keyboard makes it very easy for your cat or your small child to turn on your Mac when you least expect it.

The Power button or key will also **shut down** your Mac, or on some models you can set the Power button to put the Mac to **sleep** (check your Energy Saver preferences, Chapter 22). If you have a Mac tower with the Power button on the tower, you might have to hold the button in to the count of five to turn off the machine (or use "Shut Down" from the Apple menu).

If you have cats and kids swarming around your house, you might find your computer turning on or off at odd times. Fortunately, you do get a warning beep asking if you really want to shut down, and even if the cat steps on the Return key (which chooses "Okay" to shut down), the Mac will save any files that were left open before it turns itself off. See Chapter 19 for more details about shutting down your computer.

If you have an extended keyboard, you have an extra little set of keys between the alphabet keyboard and the numeric keypad called the **edit keys.** These keys help make the Macintosh compatible with PC programs, as well as provide you with extra little features. Not all Mac programs use these keys, although if you read your manual you may be surprised. Try them in your word processor. Or open a Desktop window and try the **PageUp** and **PageDown** keys, as well as Home and End. Try them in Save As and Open dialog boxes. At the Desktop, the **Help** key will open the Apple Help file. In some applications, hitting the Help key gives you a question mark—you can then click on any menu item in your application and you will get the Help file about that menu item.

In most browsers on the World Wide Web, you can hit **End** to take you to the bottom of the web page, and **Home** to take you to the top of the web page. PageUp and PageDown might take you up or down a window's length. Experiment.

The **Forward Delete key (del),** one of the edit keys mentioned above, is a particularly handy key: it deletes the character to its *right* (forward) as you type. This is just the opposite of the Delete key we usually use, which deletes the character to its *left* (backward). Unfortunately, some keyboards (like the ones that comes with iMacs) don't have this useful key. On your **laptop,** press the **fn** key (lower-left, see page 45) and tap **F8** to forward delete.

Power Key
Power Button

Edit Keys

⑦? Help

I←Home

→IEnd

⬍PageUp

⬍PageDown

⊠Del

(In AppleWorks, the ⬍ symbol refers to the Enter key, not the PageUp key.)

Forward Delete Key
(del)

Fkeys
F1–F12 or F1–F15

The **Fkeys** run along the top of your keyboard, that row of keys labeled F1, F2, F3, etc. Fkeys are used in many shortcuts, as you can see in the menu to the left.

If you're using an application in Classic (see Chapter 39), you can press F1 to undo your last action; press F2 to cut an item, F3 to copy, and F4 to paste (see pages 210–212 for explanations of undo, cut, copy, and paste). In Classic you can also program the extra keys yourself: use the Keyboard control panel and click the button "Function Keys…." But in Mac OS X, you cannot program the Fkeys.

Keyboard
Repeat Rate

In the Dock, click once on this icon to open System Preferences.

In the System Preferences pane, click once on this icon.

You can control a couple of features on your keyboard through the **Keyboard** system preferences. To get the "pane" shown below, click once on the System Preferences icon (shown to the left) that you'll find in the Dock. Then click once on the Keyboard icon (also shown to the left).

Every key on the Macintosh keyboard will *repeat,* meaning if you hold the key down it will continue typing that character across the page. In the Keyboard pane, shown below, the **Key Repeat Rate** lets you control just how fast that key repeats across the page—drag the marker left or right.

The **Delay Until Repeat** options, either "Off" or between "Long" and "Short," give you control over how long you can hold your finger on a key before it starts to repeat. This is wonderful if you're heavy on the keys—set it for a long delay so even if your fingers plod along on the keys, you won't end up with extra characters all over the page. If you drag over to "Off," the keys will not repeat at all, no matter how long you hold them down.

Use this pane to see how your settings affect your typing— just type and it will replace the text in "Type here to test settings."

Full Keyboard Access lets you do a lot of actions with your keyboard so you don't have to pick up the mouse to click buttons, use menus, open applications and menus in the Dock, jump from tab to tab in dialog boxes, and more. This might be a convenience for you, or you might have trouble using a mouse and so it might be a great and necessary tool.

Full Keyboard Access only works in applications that have been created specifically for Mac OS X—it does not work in Classic, nor does it work in applications that open in both OS 9 and OS X.

Open the Keyboard preferences, as explained to the right, and click the "Full Keyboard Access" tab, as shown below.

Full Keyboard Access

In the Dock, click once on this icon to open System Preferences.

In the System Preferences pane, click once on this icon.

Check the box to **turn on full keyboard access.** As it says, you can press Control F1 at any time, whether this pane is open or not, to turn keyboard access on and off.

Once it is turned on, press the Control key plus one of the function keys noted above to focus on a certain part of your screen. **For instance:**

To use the menu bar with the keyboard instead of the mouse,
press Control F2. The Apple menu will instantly drop down.

Once the menu bar is thus selected, **use the RightArrow and LeftArrow keys to select menus;** each menu will drop down as you get to it.

When a menu is visible, **use the Up and DownArrow keys to highlight items,** and the **RightArrow** to open a submenu.

When the menu command you want is highlighted, press the **Spacebar.**

To choose nothing, press the **Escape key.**

You can also use Tab to move to the right across the menu bar, and Shift Tab to the left, but who cares since the Arrow keys work just fine.

—continued

The Return or Enter key also works to choose highlighted items, but if there is a pulsing blue button, the Return or Enter key will activate the blue button instead of your selected item. So it's a good idea to get in the habit of using the Spacebar.

You can use the same technique to access the **Dock** and use the arrow keys to select each item in the Dock. **To open an application,** press the Spacebar. **To pop up a Dock menu,** press the UpArrow. **To select an item in the Dock menu,** press the Spacebar.

If an application has a Toolbar, as in Mail or Address Book, you can select the Toolbar and its items. You can select palettes that a program might use.

If you choose to highlight "Any control," you can select every button and edit box in the entire dialog box from the keyboard. That is, as you press the Tab key, each button, edit box, checkbox, or radio button is highlighted in turn, and then you can use the keyboard (as listed below) to act on the selected item.

If you use Keyboard Access regularly, you might discover that it is difficult to type some of the key combinations. For instance, Control F6 really takes two hands. So you can choose to use letter keys instead, such as "Control d" to focus on the Dock. Or choose the "Custom keys" option and select your own keys to use as shortcuts.

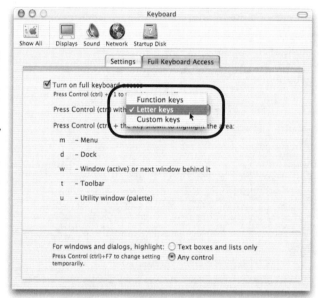

Once you focus on the item of your choice, use these keys listed below to highlight and select.

To highlight items:

Highlight the next item in a list, set of tabs, or in a menu: **Arrow keys**

Highlight the next control: **Tab**

Highlight the next control if an edit box is currently selected: **Control Tab**

Highlight the next window in the active application: **Command ~** (Tilde key, upper-left)

Move sliders and spin buttons*: **Arrow keys**

Highlight a control attached to an edit box**:
Control Arrow keys

Reverse the order of selection: Add the **Shift key** to the Tab or arrow keys you were using

To choose highlighted items:

Select the highlighted item: **Spacebar**

Click the default button (pulsing blue) or perform the default action: **Return** or **Enter**

Cancel a dialog box or close a menu without choosing an item: **Escape**

*Spin buttons are the ones that cycle around, like when moving the hours, minutes, and seconds up and down in the Time pane.

**As in an edit box where you can type in a font size, and next to it is a menu with font size choices.

On most Mac **laptops,** there is a key with the tiny symbol **fn** on the bottom-left, in a different color. You see other keys with tiny symbols or characters also in that color, such as *num lock, clear, home, end, pg up, pg dn* (page up or down), as well as numbers. Also check the Fkeys. If you press the **fn key,** then the keys change their standard function to the symbols or characters in that matching color (the color that matches the **fn**), as described below.

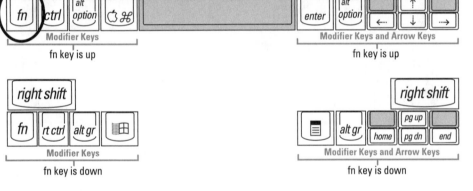

F5	Num Lock
F7	Insert (used in some applications)
F8	Forward Delete

*This shows the regular keys on your keyboard when you **do not** press the fn key.*

*This shows how the regular keys change when you **do** press the fn key.*

Hold down the **fn** key and tap F8 to **forward delete.**

The **arrow keys** on the bottom-right turn into Home, PageUp (pg up), Page-Down (pg dn), and End (see page 41) when you hold down the **fn** key.

The **Control key** becomes the Right Control key (rt ctrl), and the **Shift keys** become Right Shift keys, which are necessary in some games where the right-side keys can have different features from the left-side keys. The **Option keys** become Alt GR keys, and I haven't found anyone who knows what these are.

The **Option, Command,** and **Enter keys** take on the functions of a PC keyboard when you hold down the **fn** key. This is useful if you're running Windows emulation software, such as Insignia SoftWindows or Connectix Virtual PC, that lets your Mac run Windows: The Command key becomes the **Windows key** that brings up the Windows Start menu. The Enter key becomes the **Windows Menu key** that accesses the right-button menus (like the Mac's contextual menus). And the Option key becomes an official **Windows Alt key.**

 This icon represents the Windows key.

 This icon represents the Windows Menu key.

Numeric Keypad on Laptops

If you look carefully at your laptop keyboard, you'll see tiny numbers and mathematical symbols in a different color on the keys under your right hand (u, i, o, p, etc., as shown below).

If you hold down the **fn** key, this embedded **numeric keypad** becomes active. Use these numbers as you would in any application on any Mac, such as a spreadsheet or the calculator. *You have to keep the fn key down to use the numbers.*

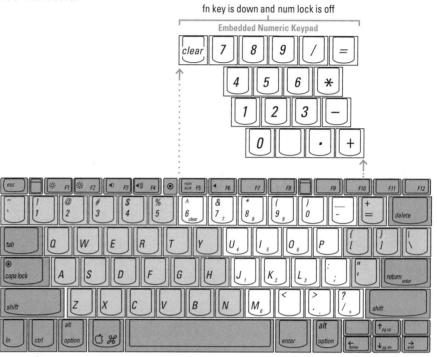

Lock in the numbers

As shown above, you have to hold down the **fn** key as you type numbers. However, you can disable all other keys *except* for the numeric keypad so you won't have to hold down the **fn** key as you type numbers: press **fn** and the **num lock key** (F5), then you can let go of **fn**. To type the alphabetic characters again, press the **fn** key once more to release it.

*Some applications, such as Microsoft Word and Adobe PageMaker, have always utilized the numeric keypad for moving the cursor, and you have to **turn on** num lock if you want to type numbers. On a laptop, these keys can't do both (move the cursor **and** type numbers), so in Word and PageMaker, when the fn key is down and num lock is on, the cursor moves—you don't get the numeric keypad.*

If you need to type with the characters of another language, you can—see the following page. You can also choose a language in which to see the menus, dialog boxes, and even the Apple Help files. Use the International preferences pane, as described below.

To change the language shown in menus and dialog boxes:

1. Click once on the System Preferences icon in the Dock.

2. Click the "International" icon. You'll get the pane shown below.

3. Click the tab "Language," if it's not already visible.

4. In the "Languages" list, drag the language you want to the top of the list—press and drag the name. You'll see a black bar appear as you drag; when that black bar is all the way to the top, let go. The language you want should be the first one in the list.

5. In the lower-left portion of this pane, select the appropriate "script" for your chosen language. On the lower-right, choose the "text behavior" for the chosen language. Quit the System Preferences (press Command Q or use the File menu).

6. If any applications were open, **quit** them (don't just *close* their open windows), then reopen the application to see the new language in that application. To change your entire Mac to the new language, log out (go to the Apple menu, choose "Log Out…"), then log in again.

International Keyboard Layouts

This is the System Preferences icon in the Dock.

This is the International icon in the System Preferences.

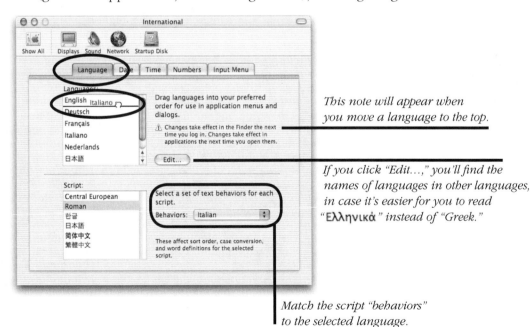

This note will appear when you move a language to the top.

If you click "Edit…," you'll find the names of languages in other languages, in case it's easier for you to read "Ελληνικά" instead of "Greek."

Match the script "behaviors" to the selected language.

—continued

After you log out and log back in again, or after you shut down and/or restart, your Finder menus and dialog boxes will appear in the chosen language. It's amazing.

If you plan to switch your entire computer to another language, also click each of the other tabs in this International preferences pane and choose the same language so your text inputs correctly (see the following two pages).

Notice the new menu item next to "Help," which is called the "Keyboard" menu. For information about this menu and how to input text with the special characters of another language, see the opposite page.

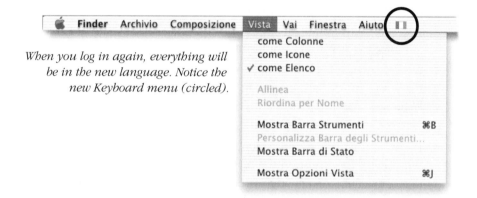

When you log in again, everything will be in the new language. Notice the new Keyboard menu (circled).

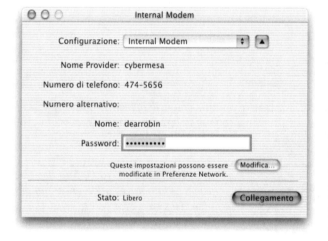

As explained on the previous pages, you can enable your Mac to display menus, dialog boxes, and even Help files in another language. But you might also want to *type* using the special characters of another language, whether or not your menus display English.

To change the keyboard layout and the input language:

1. Click once on the System Preferences icon in the Dock, then click the "International" icon. You'll get the pane shown below.

2. Click the tab "Keyboard Menu."

3. Put a checkmark next to each language that you would like to have accessible in the Keyboard menu in the Finder.

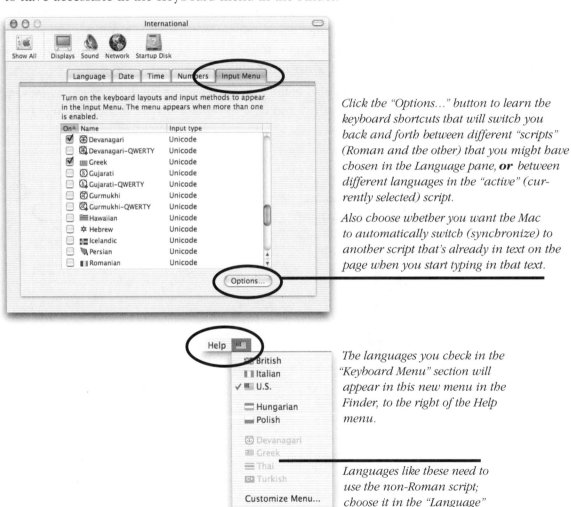

*Click the "Options..." button to learn the keyboard shortcuts that will switch you back and forth between different "scripts" (Roman and the other) that you might have chosen in the Language pane, **or** between different languages in the "active" (currently selected) script.*

Also choose whether you want the Mac to automatically switch (synchronize) to another script that's already in text on the page when you start typing in that text.

The languages you check in the "Keyboard Menu" section will appear in this new menu in the Finder, to the right of the Help menu.

Languages like these need to use the non-Roman script; choose it in the "Language" pane, as shown on page 47.

International Date, Time, and Numbers

There are a number of applications and features on your Mac that automatically format dates, times, and numbers—from the date in your menu bar to your spreadsheet or financial application—according to the language of choice. For instance, in the United States we write the date with the month first, then the day, then the year; but in most other parts of the world, the date is written with the day first, then the month. If you want the date, time, and/or number formatting to use the style of a particular region, use the International preferences pane.

This is the System Preferences icon in the Dock.

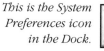

This is the International icon in the System Preferences.

To choose a regional format for dates, times, and/or numbers:

1. Click once on the System Preferences icon in the Dock.

2. Click the "International" icon. You'll get the pane shown below.

3. One at a time, click the tabs "Date," Time," and "Numbers." In each pane, choose the "Region" that creates the formatting you want. An example of the formatting is displayed at the bottom of the pane.

   You can also enter your own formatting: just select any existing text in an edit box and type to replace it with the formatting of your choice.

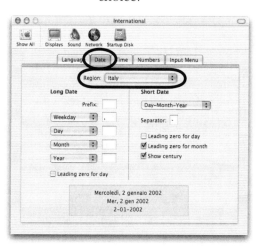

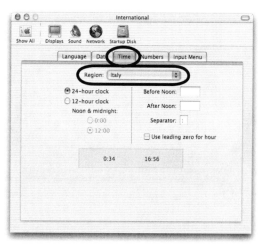

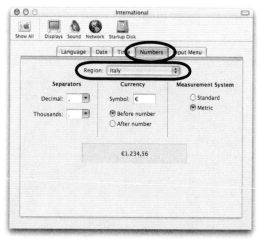

In Mac OS X, the character encoding technology has changed. In all previous versions, the Macintosh operating system used ASCII, an international standard for Roman characters, that allows a maximum of 256 characters. Mac OS X uses something called Unicode, which allows over 65,000 characters, which means the Mac can now set type in alphabets such as Japanese, Arabic, or Chinese. But in Mac OS X applications that use Unicode, such as TextEdit, fonts like **Zapf Dingbats** and **Webdings** do not appear correctly. In fact, they don't appear at all. If you want to use characters from a dingbat font, you'll have to go through the steps described below.

To type with a dingbat font or symbol font:

1. Click once on the System Preferences icon in the Dock.

2. Click the "International" icon, then click the tab "Keyboard Menu." You'll get the pane shown below.

3. Put a checkmark next to "Character Palette." Close the pane.

4. In your menu at the Finder, you now have a new item, a little flag, to the right of the Help menu. This is the Keyboard menu, as shown in the sidebar to the right.

5. When you want to set a character in one of these fonts, click in your document at the place where you want the character; your insertion point should be flashing (as explained in Chapter 13).

6. Go to the Keyboard menu and choose "Character Palette." This brings up the Character Palette, as shown below.

7. Find the character you want to set, double-click it, and it will appear in your document where the insertion point is flashing. Close the Character Palette window (click in the tiny red button).

Using Zapf Dingbats, Webdings, or Symbol

Only read this if you've discovered a problem typing with these fonts!

Zapf Dingbats:

Webdings:

Symbol:

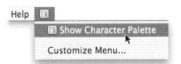

This is the Keyboard menu.

Choose "Character Palette" in this dialog box. Even if you use it rarely, it won't hurt anything to have it available at all times.

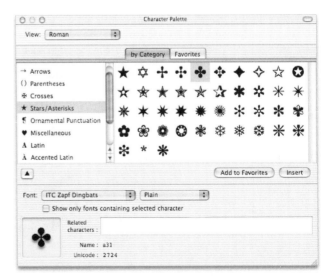

For more details on how to use this Character Palette, see Chapter 26.

1. If you want to select another edit box in this dialog box, ("Find" is currently selected), which key would move the selection from box to box?

_____

2. If you want to activate the "Next" button in the dialog box above, but don't want to pick up the mouse, which key would you press?

_____

3. Which keys would you press to:

Hide the menu bar? _____

View the bookmarks folder? _____

Close all the open windows? _____

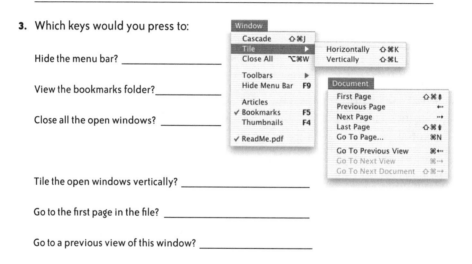

Tile the open windows vertically? _____

Go to the first page in the file? _____

Go to a previous view of this window? _____

4. Write the letter identifying the key with its symbol:

Escape key _____	a)	‡	PageUp key _____	l)	⌥
Option key _____	b)	⇡	PageDown key _____	m)	⇧
Control key _____	c)	esc	LeftArrow key _____	n)	⌦
Command (Apple) key _____	d)	~	RightArrow key _____	o)	↓
Tilde key _____	e)	→	UpArrow key _____	p)	/
Asterisk, or Star _____	f)	⌘	DownArrow key _____	q)	⌃
Shift key _____	g)	⇤	Home key _____	r)	→|
Forward slash _____	h)	⇕	End key _____	s)	⇢
Backslash _____	i)	⌫	Forward Delete key _____	t)	*
Tab key _____	j)	\	Enter key _____	u)	⇠
Delete key _____	k)	⏏	Spacebar key _____	v)	⌣

Answers are on page 730.

Menus & Shortcuts

Whenever you are at the Finder level of your Macintosh or whenever you're in any program on the Mac, you'll see a **menu bar** across the top of the screen, as shown below. Also shown below is a **drop-down menu:** when you click on a word in the menu bar, a list of menu commands drops down. In addition to these drop-down menus, on the Mac you'll also find pop-up menus, contextual menus, and others. This chapter discusses all the various sorts of menus, the commands, and how to use them.

You'll see a lot of typical "dialog boxes" in this chapter from a variety of applications. Don't worry that you haven't seen that same dialog box yet—the Mac is amazingly consistent and if you don't see that exact dialog box, you will run into something similar.

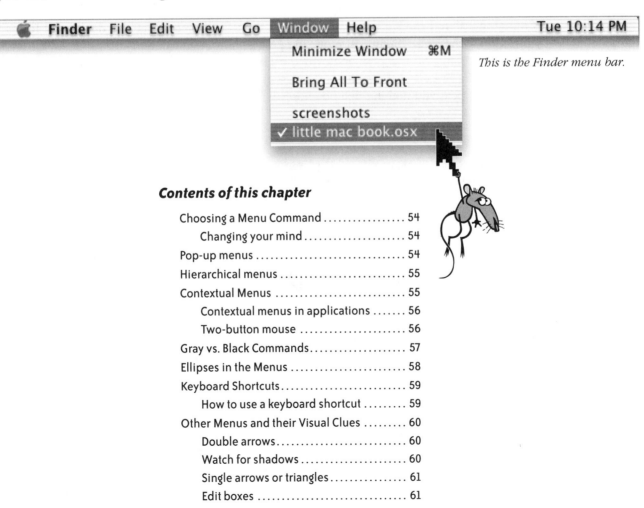

This is the Finder menu bar.

Contents of this chapter

Choosing a Menu Command

To choose a command from a menu, click once on any of the choices along the menu bar. The menu will pop open for you. As you move your mouse down the list of commands, the different choices *highlight,* or become *selected,* as you pass over them. When the one you want is highlighted, click on it.

Practice: Position the pointer over any word in the menu bar, then click on that word. Run the pointer down the list and watch the various commands highlight.

Don't click anything yet unless you know what it will do!

The command "Clean Up" is highlighted—click on it to activate it.

Changing your mind

If you change your mind halfway through the menu list and don't want to choose anything, just move the pointer off of the list, then click. If you were dragging the pointer down the list with the mouse button down, simply move off of the menu and let go of the mouse button. The menu will disappear and nothing will be chosen.

Pop-up Menus

You will also find **pop-up menus** where you press on an item toward the bottom of the screen and the list pops upward.

This is an example of a pop-up menu. The Dock uses pop-up menus.

In some programs the menu itself contains a **pop-out menu** where you not only slide *down,* but also *out to the side,* usually in the direction of the arrow. These are also known as **hierarchical menus,** or **h-menus.**

Hierarchical Menus

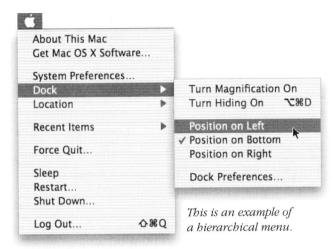

This is an example of a hierarchical menu.

Practice: Go to the Apple menu, as shown to the left, and position the pointer over any menu item that has an arrow to its left. Practice moving your mouse over to the right and sliding down the hierarchical list — it can be tricky!

Don't click on any command yet unless it has an ellipsis in the menu (see page 58), which means you will get a dialog box that you can cancel out of.

The Finder has **contextual menus:** hold down the *Control* key (not the Command/Apple key), click anywhere, and a menu pops up. These are called "contextual" menus because the context of the menu varies depending on what you click upon: an application icon, a folder icon, a document icon, a disk icon, a blank spot inside a window, a blank spot on the Desktop, etc. What you see in these menus might also change as time goes by and more features are added.

Contextual Menus

Practice: Hold down the Control key and click on a folder, a blank spot in a window, a disk icon, a document, or an application.

To put away a contextual menu, just click anywhere outside the menu.

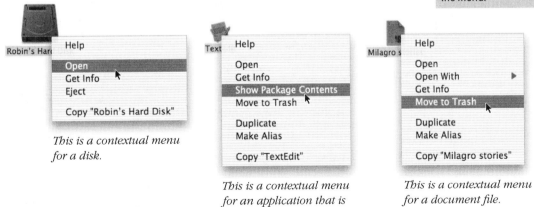

This is a contextual menu for a disk.

This is a contextual menu for an application that is "packaged" into one icon.

This is a contextual menu for a document file.

Also see the following page about contextual menus in applications.

Contextual menus in applications

Many **applications** use contextual menus. Try this in your favorite program: hold down the Control key and click on the window in your program, or on an object, the text, any buttons in the toolbar, etc., and see what happens.

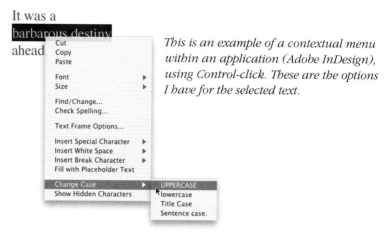

This is an example of a contextual menu within an application (Adobe InDesign), using Control-click. These are the options I have for the selected text.

In some programs, such as most **web browsers,** you don't even need to hold down the Control key—just press. **Try it:** In a blank area on a web page, press and *hold* the mouse button down and you'll get a contextual menu with options for that page. Press on a graphic and you'll get choices to save or copy the graphic. Press (don't click) on a link and you can open that link in a new window, which means you'll still have the current page visible on your Desktop. (In Internet Explorer, you have to hold the mouse button down for too long before contextual menus appear; if you use the Command key, they pop right up.)

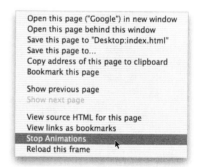

Press on a link and get a contextual menu that lets you save the link, open it in another window, and much more. This is one of my favorite features in OmniWeb—I can open a link in a new window that goes behind my current window so I can continue to peruse my list of search results. I often open six or eight pages this way, then go back and see what came up.

Press on any blank spot on any web page and you'll get a useful contextual menu.

Two-button mouse

If you have a **two-button mouse,** you can use the right-hand button to open contextual menus, without holding down the Control key!

In a list of menu commands, some **commands** are in **black** letters and some commands are in **gray.** When a command is gray, it means *that particular command is not available at that moment.*

The most common reason a command is unavailable is that you did not *select* something before you went to the menu. For instance, you cannot choose "Open" from the File menu until you select a disk or file as the item to be opened. You cannot "Copy" text unless you first select the text you want to copy. (To select *text,* press-and-drag over it; to select an *object,* click *once* on it.)

Gray vs. Black Commands

Some commands are gray; some are black. In this example, "Cut" and "Copy" are gray because there is no text selected to cut or copy. If nothing is selected, the Mac has no idea what you want to cut or copy, and the computer certainly can't make that decision on its own.

One important rule on the Mac is this: Select first, then do it to it.

Practice: Click on a blank area on the Desktop so nothing is selected, not even a folder or window; then click on the View menu and notice how many items are gray. Now click on an open window and take another look at the View menu.

*This is the same menu as shown above, but this time I selected some text on the word processing page before I went to the menu. Now I am able to cut or copy the **selected** text.*

Ellipses in the Menus

Often you will see an **ellipsis** (the three dots, **...**) after a menu command such as "Open**...**" or "Save As**....**" The ellipsis indicates that you will get a **dialog box,** as shown below, when you choose that command. If there is no ellipsis, that command will activate as soon as you select it.

There are different varieties of dialog boxes, such as alert boxes, message boxes, or edit boxes, plus dialog "sheets" that drop down from the title bar, but basically they all are meant to communicate with you before they activate a command.

Dialog boxes almost always give you an option to **Cancel,** so it is quite safe to explore menu commands that have ellipses: Just choose a command that is followed by an ellipsis, check out the dialog box, then click Cancel. Even if you click around on buttons or type in the dialog box, clicking the Cancel button will make sure none of your changes are put into effect.

Practice: Find several menu items that are followed by ellipses and select them. Go ahead and click buttons in the dialog box, pull down menus, type values, etc., but make sure to click the Cancel button to close the box.

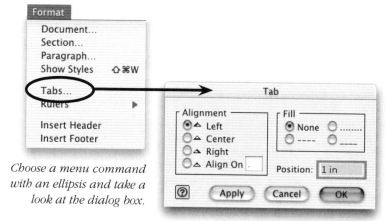

Choose a menu command with an ellipsis and take a look at the dialog box.

There is almost always a Cancel button which will cancel all of your actions and put the dialog box away.

You can use the keyboard shortcut (as explained on the opposite page) **Command Period** *to cancel most dialog boxes instead of clicking on the Cancel button, even if there is no Cancel button.*

To the right of the commands in the menus you often see a little code, such as ⌘ **N** (pronounced "Command N" or sometimes "Apple N"). This is a **keyboard shortcut** you can use *instead* of using the menu. You memorize the shortcut, then the next time you need that command you use the shortcut *instead* of picking up your mouse and pulling down the menu.

Keyboard Shortcuts

File	
New Finder Window	⌘N
New Folder	⇧⌘N
Open	⌘O
Open With	▶
Close Window	⌘W
Get Info	⌘I
Duplicate	⌘D
Make Alias	⌘L
Show Original	⌘R
Add to Favorites	⌘T
Move to Trash	⌘⌫
Eject	⌘E
Burn Disc...	
Find...	⌘F

Often the keyboard shortcut will include other symbols representing other keys; **see Chapter 4 for explanations of every symbol and special key on your keyboard.**

A **modifier key** is a key that doesn't do anything when you press it all by itself. For instance, when you press Shift, nothing happens; when you press the Command key, nothing happens. A modifier key makes *other* keys perform special functions. For instance, when you hold down the Shift key then type the number "8," you get an asterisk (∗).

So to use a keyboard shortcut *instead* of the menu command, hold down the **modifier key** or **keys** you saw in the menu. While you hold down this key or keys, type the **letter key** you also saw in the menu—just *tap* the letter, *don't hold it down!* The computer reacts just as if you had chosen that command from the menu. For instance, if you click once on a file to select it and then press ⌘**O**, the selected file will open just as if you had chosen that command from the File menu with the mouse. Thoughtfully, many of the keyboard shortcuts are alliterative: ⌘ **O** **o**pens files; ⌘ **P** **p**rints; ⌘ **D** **d**uplicates a selected file; ⌘ **W** closes **w**indows; etc.

You'll often see keyboard shortcuts spelled out with a hyphen, a plus sign, or perhaps a comma between the keys. *Don't type the hyphen, plus sign, or comma!* Just press the keys! For instance, if you see a shortcut written as "Command + Shift + B," ignore the plus signs—just hold down the Command and Shift keys, then tap the letter B.

How to use a keyboard shortcut

Practice: In the File menu in the Finder, notice that Command W is the shortcut to close windows. So make sure there is a window open on your Desktop, then hold down the Command key and tap the letter W. The window will close. You're on your way to becoming a Power User.

Other Menus and their Visual Clues

You'll find other menus in all kinds of odd places. Well, they won't seem so odd once you become accustomed to the **visual clues** that indicate a menu is hiding. In the dialog box below, can you see the menus?

Double arrows

Double arrows are one visual clue that a dialog box contains a menu. Whenever you see that double arrow, as shown below, you can click anywhere in that horizontal bar and a menu will pop up or down.

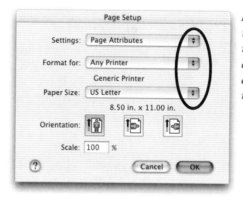

Do you see the three menus in this dialog box? You recognize them by the double arrows. Click on any one of these and a menu will pop up or down.

Watch for shadows

In the example below, the box next to "Field Type" has a little **shadow** behind it, as well as an arrow. Even without the arrow, that little shadow is your **visual clue** that if you press or click on the word, you will get a pop-up menu, as shown in another example further below. Look for that shadow!

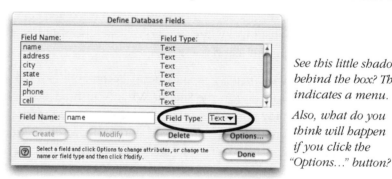

See this little shadow behind the box? That indicates a menu.

Also, what do you think will happen if you click the "Options..." button?

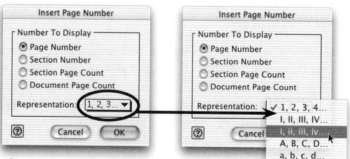

This is an example of what happens when you press on a menu in a dialog box.

A **single** downward-pointing **arrow** or **triangle** does *not* indicate a menu. A triangle typically expands a dialog box to present more information, as shown below. The fact that this information is hidden indicates that it is not necessarily critical at all times—you only pop open that information when you need it. As you are learning to use your Mac, click that arrow or triangle whenever you see it so you become familiar with the options, whether you use them or not.

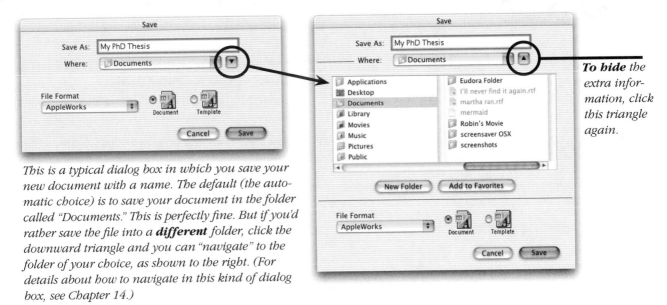

*To **hide** the extra information, click this triangle again.*

*This is a typical dialog box in which you save your new document with a name. The default (the automatic choice) is to save your document in the folder called "Documents." This is perfectly fine. But if you'd rather save the file into a **different** folder, click the downward triangle and you can "navigate" to the folder of your choice, as shown to the right. (For details about how to navigate in this kind of dialog box, see Chapter 14.)*

The boxes that do *not* have shadows behind them (as shown in the dialog box below) are called **edit boxes.** You can type into these edit boxes to change the specifications.

Edit boxes

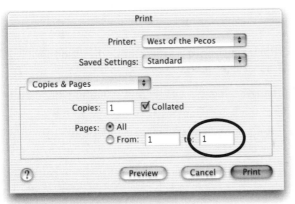

*These are called **edit boxes.** Type in them to change the values. There is no shadow behind them, which means they are not menus. How many edit boxes do you see here? How many menus?*

Watch for those visual clues!

1. Which menu command is selected?

_____

2. How many of these commands have h-menus (hierarchical menus that pop-out to the side)?

_____

3. How many of these commands will give you a dialog box when you choose them?

_____

4. How many of these commands are not available at the moment?

_____

5. How many of these commands have keyboard shortcuts?

_____

6. What is the keyboard shortcut you could use to activate the selected command instead of choosing it from the menu?

_____

7. If you were to press Command P, what would happen?

_____

8. How many menus are there inside the dialog box shown to the left?

_____

9. How many edit boxes are there inside this dialog box?

_____

10. What keyboard shortcut could you press to Cancel this dialog box?

_____

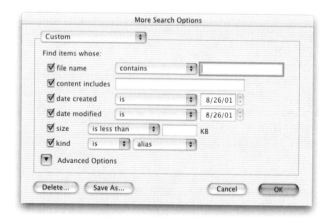

Answers on page 730.

How to Use the Windows

6

A **window** is a basic, fundamental element of the Macintosh.

When you open any **folder** or **disk,** including your hard disk, the Mac displays the contents of the folder in a **Finder** window.

When you open an **application,** such as a word processor, database, or spreadsheet, the Mac gives you a **document** window in which to type a letter, work with a database, or create a spreadsheet.

Although they are very similar, on the following page is a visual explanation of the main differences between these two types of windows. The major part of this chapter is devoted to the features you will find in the windows on the **Desktop,** the **Finder** windows that open to display the contents of **folders** and **disks** (not document windows). Once you know how to maneuver your way through the Finder windows, the document windows will make perfect sense to you. And that's most of what you need to know on the Mac.

Contents of this chapter

Finder Windows vs. Document Windows

Below you see two different windows. On the top is a **Finder** window, sometimes called a Desktop window, the kind you'll see when you open a folder or disk on the Desktop. A **document** window is the kind you'll see when you are using most applications, or programs, in which you create your work. You'll notice both sorts of windows have a number of similar features, but the Finder windows are more complex and confusing. I'll first explain the details of the Finder window, and later in this chapter you'll see how those features are also built into document windows.

*When a Finder window is open and **active** (in **front** of any other windows), this menu item is always "Finder."*

*You can tell this is a **Finder window** because in the menu bar across the top of the monitor, just to the right of the apple, is the word "Finder." The Finder is the software that runs the Desktop, so all of the windows on the Desktop are considered **Finder windows.** Don't let that confuse you—just think of the Desktop and the Finder as the same thing, for all practical purposes.*

The items inside a Finder window might be shown as icons, as a list, or in columns.

*This is the name, or **title,** of the Finder window that is open. This particular window is called "robin" because it is my "Home" folder that contains my personal files.*

Under the title of the window is the Toolbar, which I explain at length on the following pages.

This area at the top of the window is the Toolbar.

This is the name of the application.

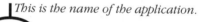

*You can tell this is a **document window** because in the menu bar across the top of the monitor, just to the right of the apple, is the name of the application in which this document is being created. TextEdit is a word processing application on your Mac (see Chapter 13 for tips on how to use it).*

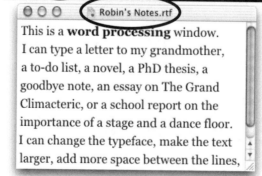

*This is the name, or **title,** of the document I have created in this application. Every document you create will be in its own window.*

You can see that the biggest difference between this window and the one above is that there is no "Toolbar" across the top of this window.

Finder Windows

Finder windows are those windows that open to display the contents of folders or disks, including your hard disk.

The Macintosh allows you a great deal of control over the look and the feel of your computer and the options available so you can arrange your work and your working environment in a way that is most effective for *you*. The **Finder windows** are a good example of the control you have on the Mac—you can choose to display what's in your window in a variety of ways, all appropriate for different purposes or styles; you can organize the windows any way you like; and you can customize the window Toolbar for your convenience. You can even change the color or add a picture to the background of a window, which might help you organize certain projects or recognize important folders.

There are so many options in OS X that it can be very confusing, so you might want to read through this entire section to get an overview of how things work, spend some time with the windows, then go back through it again and decide how to customize your windows so they work best for you.

Close button; *see page 69.*

Minimize button; *see page 69.*

Zoom button; *see page 69.*

Title bar icon; *see page 102.*

Title of window; *see page 68.*

Title bar; *see page 67.*

Search box; *see Chapter 25.*

Hide/Show Toolbar button; *see page 79.*

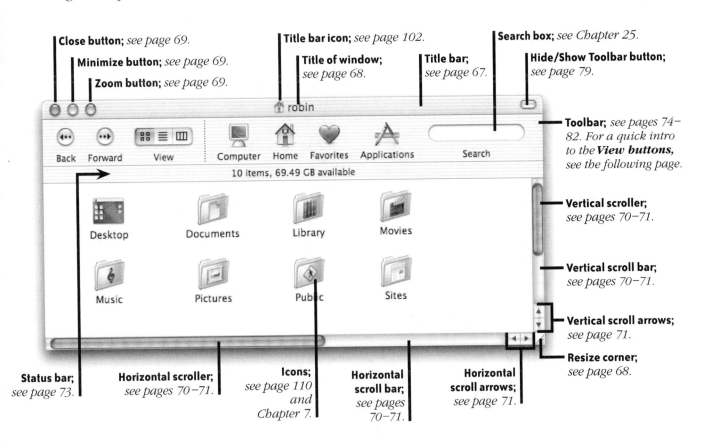

Toolbar; *see pages 74–82. For a quick intro to the **View buttons,** see the following page.*

Vertical scroller; *see pages 70–71.*

Vertical scroll bar; *see pages 70–71.*

Vertical scroll arrows; *see page 71.*

Resize corner; *see page 68.*

Status bar; *see page 73.*

Horizontal scroller; *see pages 70–71.*

Icons; *see page 110 and Chapter 7.*

Horizontal scroll bar; *see pages 70–71.*

Horizontal scroll arrows; *see page 71.*

10 items, 69.49 GB available

Back Forward View Computer Home Favorites Applications Search

Desktop Documents Library Movies

Music Pictures Public Sites

Three Views of the Same Contents

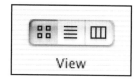

These are the View buttons you see in the Toolbar—click one to change the view of the active window.

You can also change the view of the active window by using the "View" menu at the Desktop.

You can change how you **view the contents** of a Finder window. Some people like to see their window's contents as icons, some prefer to view a list of names, while others prefer columns showing the contents of multiple folders at once. Below you see the same window contents in three different views. We're going to look at each of these views in detail later; for now, I just want you to know what they are and how to change them if you like.

This is the contents of the Applications folder, shown in **Icon View.**

Double-click any folder icon to see the contents of that folder (the new contents will **replace** what you see in this window now).

See pages 83–87 for details of Icon View.

Practice: In the Dock, single-click the "Finder" icon (shown below) to open a Finder window. In that open window, click the View buttons one at a time to see how the contents appear in each of the different views.

Finder icon

Choose the **Icon View** and do the short Practice exercises on the following five pages.

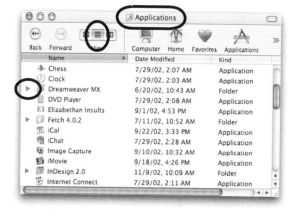

This is the contents of the Applications folder, shown in **List View.**

Single-click on the triangle pointing to a folder to display a sub-list of what is contained in that folder.

Or double-click a folder icon to display its contents in this window.

See pages 88–91 for details of List View.

This is the contents of the Applications folder, shown in **Column View.**

Can you see that "Applications" has the darkest highlight? That's a **visual clue** that the contents in the column to the right belong to the highlighted Applications folder. The title in the title bar tells us the same thing.

See pages 92–94 for details of Column View.

The **title bar** is the striped bar across the top of a window in which, logically, the title appears. This title is the name of the disk, folder, or document you have opened. The title bar also holds the little colored buttons.

Every window has a title bar.

Moving the window

To move any window around the screen, position the pointer in the title bar of the window, then press-and-drag. Just let go of the mouse button when you have the window placed where you want.

The active window

If you have more than one window open, only one will have the little round buttons *in color* in its title bar. The colored buttons are a **visual clue** that this window is the **active window.** If windows are overlapping, the active window is the one that is in front.

The **active window** is the only window that the commands from the keyboard or the menu will affect. For instance, if you go to the File menu and choose "New Folder," the new folder will appear in the *active* window. If you go to the File menu and choose "Close," it will close the *active* window. It's very important to be conscious of which window is active!

To make a window active, simply click on any visible part of it; this will also bring that window to the front of any others. If you know a window is open somewhere but you can't see it, go to the Window menu and choose its name (see page 95).

Practice: Try **moving** any window around the screen—just press in the title bar and drag.
The next time you find more than one window open on the screen, notice which one is **active.** Click on a window that is not active and watch its title bar change.

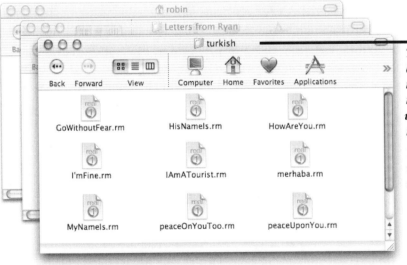

*The title is dark, the buttons are in color, and the window is in front of the others. Each of these **visual clues** indicates that this is the active window.*

You can actually close or minimize windows that are not active—nice feature.

Tip: To move a window that's behind others *without* making it active, hold down the Command key while you press-and-drag the title bar. Try it.

The path in the title bar

The title bar can always tell you where a particular folder is stored. The list that you see dropping down from the title bar below is called the **path** to the document.

To see the "path" to where a folder is stored, hold the Command key down and click on the title bar; a menu will appear. You can slide the mouse down the menu and choose any item to open that item's Finder window. (Don't worry if you don't quite understand what a path is and what it's telling you—you might never need to know this information!)

Practice: This technique works in document windows and Finder windows. So try it on any window that is open: Hold down the Command key (not the Control key), and while the key is down, click on the name in the title bar.

You'll learn more about paths, if you care to, in Chapter 14.

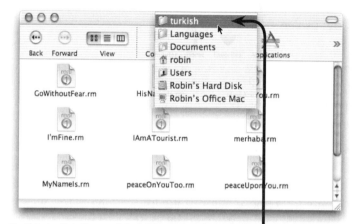

So this path tells me this folder named "turkish" is stored in a folder called "Languages," which is stored in a folder called "Documents," which is in the Home for "robin," which is in the folder called "Users," which is on the hard disk named "Robin's Hard Disk," which is on the computer named "Robin's Office Mac."

Notice the tiny icons to the left of the path names are **visual clues.**

Resize Corner

The bottom-right corner is the **Resize corner.** Press-and-drag in that box to manually make the window larger or smaller (as opposed to clicking the green zoom button, as described on the following page). This is useful when you have several windows open and you want to resize and rearrange them so they all fit on your screen without overlapping. Or you might want to resize a window smaller or larger than the zoom button will automatically make it.

Practice: Open any window. Press in the lower-right corner and drag in any direction.

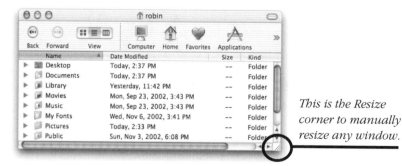

This is the Resize corner to manually resize any window.

In the upper-left corner of each window are **three little buttons: red, yellow, and green.** These are in color in the *active* window and gray in all other windows behind that one (although when your mouse brushes over the buttons in any other window, they burst into color and you can click them without making that window active).

Window Buttons

If your buttons are gray instead of colored, see page 73.

From left to right, the buttons are red, yellow, and green.

When the pointer is positioned near the buttons, tiny symbols appear.

▼ Click in the **red** button to **close** the window. This puts it away, back into the folder or disk it came from.

Or press Command W.

▼ Click the **yellow** button to **minimize** the window, which sends the window down into the Dock, as shown below.

Or double-click in the title bar.

Or press Command M.

This is the minimize button.

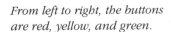

When a window is minimized, it floats down into the Dock as an icon, out of the way until you need it again. When you want it back, simply click once on its icon. See Chapter 8 for details about using the Dock.

If you have several windows in the Dock, position your mouse over one (don't click) and that window's name will appear above the Dock.

▼ Click the **green** button to **zoom** the window large enough to see everything, or to zoom it smaller. How large or small the window becomes depends on what is in the window and how large or small it was before you clicked the button.

Practice: If you don't have a window open, click once on the Finder icon in the Dock to open one. Use the **red** button to **close** the window.

Open a window, then use the **yellow** button to **minimize** it. To open the minimized window again, click once on its icon in the Dock.

Open a window, then use the **green** button to **resize** it.

Useless Tip: To minimize an open window in **slow motion,** hold down the Shift key when you click on the yellow button.

Tips: To **close all** open windows in the active application, hold down the Option key and click the red button. You will be asked to save any unsaved documents.

To **minimize all** open windows in the active application, hold down the Option key and click the yellow button.

Scroll Bars and Scrollers

Along the right and bottom edges of the window are the **scroll bars.** The scroll bars allow you to view everything in the document, even if everything cannot all fit on the screen at once or if the window is sized too small.

Scroll bars are huge **visual clues.** When a **blue scroller** appears **in the scroll bar,** *that's a visual clue that there is more information in the window that you can't see.* In fact, how big the scroller is and how much space is above and below the scroller tells you exact*y* how much you can't see.

You see a scroller in the vertical scroll bar on the right side of the window, which tells you there are more items in this window that you can't see at the moment.

In this example, there is no horizontal scroll bar at all, which tells you there is nothing more in the folder in the horizontal direction than what you can already see.

If there are no "scrollers" or "arrows" in the scroll bar area (as you can see, above, on the bottom edge), that tells you there is nothing more in that direction—you are viewing everything there is.

In the example below, however, you see scroll bars and scrollers on *both* edges, so you know there are items or information that you can't see in both directions. You can also tell, in the example below, by the proportions of the scrollers in the lengths of the bars, that you're not missing much.

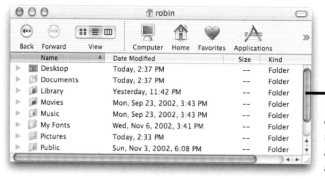

*These scrollers **almost** fill each of the scroll bars, which is your **visual clue** that **almost** everything is visible in the window.*

Use the scrollers to make the other items in the window visible. **Press-and-drag a scroller** to move it to any position on the scroll bar, let go, and the window will immediately *jump* to that particular place rather than slide past everything. This is very handy inside a window with hundreds of items where scrolling with the arrows (described below) would take a while. Instead of holding the mouse button down on an arrow, just drag the scroller all the way to the bottom.

Press-and-drag the scroller

There's yet another way to use the scroll bars: simply **click** the pointer in any *gray* area of the bar, and the window will move up, down, or across. It will jump you right to that position in the window (say, in the middle of the window, vertically) if you click in the middle of the vertical scroll bar.

Click in the scroll bar

If you want to jump from one section of the window to the next, you can use the PageUp or PageDown keys. Depending on your keyboard, these keys might be in the small section of "edit keys" to the left of the numeric keypad, or they might be tiny little keys directly above the numeric keypad (see Chapter 4 if you can't find them). Experiment with these keys. Also try them on web pages or in page layout applications.

Use PageUp and PageDown

("pg up" and "pg dn" on some keyboards)

When a scroll bar has a scroller, it also has two **scroll arrows.** These arrows might be at either end of the scroll bars, or they might both be at one end, depending on what is chosen in the General preferences (shown on the following page). When you see scroll arrows, *press* on one arrrow to make the contents of the window glide past, like the scenery outside a train window. If you've never used scroll arrows before, it might seem like things are gliding past in the opposite direction you expect, but you'll soon get accustomed to it and you'll instinctively learn which arrow to press to slide the contents in the direction you want.

Scroll Arrows

This window has no scrollers or arrows at all. What does that tell you? That you are seeing everything there is to see in this window.

Practice: Open a window. Click once on the Applications icon in the Toolbar. Use the techniques on these two pages to see all of the contents in the window.

If there are no blue scrollers in a window that you want to practice on, use the Resize corner (as explained on page 68) to make the window smaller so the scrollers show up.

Status Bar   If you like, you can add a **status bar** to all your windows that tells you how many items are in an open window. The bar also tells you how much disk space is available, how your icons are arranged, as well as the sharing status (for more information on sharing, see Chapter 34).

*This is the **status bar**. As you can see, it says there are ten items in this window. Since you can see eight of them, you instantly know exactly how many are not visible at the moment.*

This bar also tells you how much empty space you have left on this hard disk.

The status bar will also tell you if your icons are using a special "arrangement" (see pages 85–86) and if there are any limitations on the "privileges" (see Chapter 34). For instance, this status bar tells you the icons are using the "Keep arranged by" option, and no one is allowed to "write to" (add anything to) this window.

To add the status bar to all windows in all views:

1. Open any Finder window.

2. From the "View" menu, choose "Show Status Bar."

   When you want **to get rid of the status bar,** open any Finder window, go to the View menu, then choose "Hide Status Bar."

As mentioned on the previous page, you can choose to have one scroll arrow at either end of the scroll bars, or set them together at one end of the scroll bar (which allows you to scroll through a window in either direction without having to move your mouse to the other end of the scroll bar).

You can also choose what you want to happen when you click in the gray area of a scroll bar, as shown below.

Window Scroll Preferences

System Preferences

General

To change the scroll arrow and scroll click options:

1. In the Dock, click on the "System Preferences" icon (as shown above-left).

2. When the System Preferences window opens, find the icon named "General" (also shown above-left), and single-click on it. You'll get the "preferences pane" shown below.

3. Find the options circled below. Click to make your choices.

4. Quit the System Preferences: press Command Q.

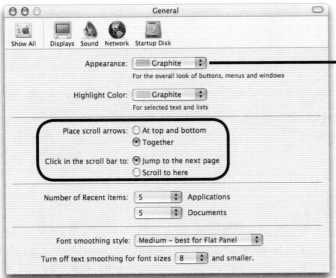

If you change the "Appearance" from "Blue" to "Graphite," then the red, yellow, and green buttons in your windows will all be the same color of gray.

Tip: *Once you become accustomed to what will happen when you click in the scroll bar, you can try this trick. Hold down the Option key and click in the scroll bar—it will do the opposite of what you have selected in these preferences.*

The Toolbar The Toolbar is an important and useful feature of Finder windows. Below and on the following pages you see what each Toolbar icon represents (each icon is a button; click *once*). On pages 80–81, learn how to customize the Toolbar to help you work more efficiently.

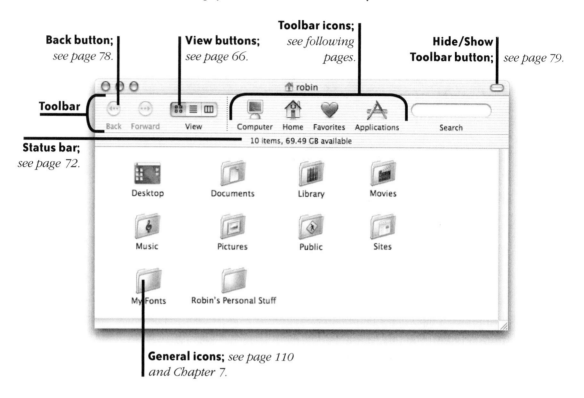

Back button; *see page 78.*

View buttons; *see page 66.*

Toolbar icons; *see following pages.*

Hide/Show Toolbar button; *see page 79.*

Toolbar

Status bar; *see page 72.*

General icons; *see page 110 and Chapter 7.*

*These **Toolbar icon** buttons are discussed individually on the following pages.*

*The **Search** feature is discussed at length in Chapter 25. Often in this book you won't see this box in the Toolbar because I took it out—it takes up too much space for me. I press Command F to bring up the Search dialog box instead.*

*Sometimes you see these **double arrows** on the right end of the Toolbar. This indicates that one or more of the icons can't fit in the Toolbar.*

Press on the double arrows to get a menu from which you can select the icons you can't see.

The Search box becomes the word "Search" in the little menu that pops out.

Computer: This window displays the icons of your hard disk and any other disks that are in your computer, as shown below. Any disk icons in this window will also appear on your Desktop.

Every time you click the Finder icon in the Dock, the window will open or change to display this Computer level. If you would rather it always open to your Home folder, see page 96.

The Computer icon in the Toolbar

This is what you named your computer when you first started it up. To change this name, see page 635.

Your "Computer" window *will always show at least these two icons.*

The "Network" icon *gives you access to any files or applications that are available over a corporate network, if you're on one.*

The hard disk icon *is labeled with whatever you named your hard disk (see page 115 if you want to rename it).*

To see what is stored on your hard disk, *double-click the hard disk icon (**not** the "Computer" icon).*

*This is the same window, but on a different computer. You see **two hard disk icons** here because I installed an extra hard disk inside my Mac.*

The network icon *called "**jtratz**" represents another computer that I am sharing files with over the network in my home office (see Chapter 35).*

*The icon that looks like a **CD** is a music CD I'm listening to.*

*The icon called "LMB OSX v2 represents a removable **Zip disk** that is in the Zip drive (if you have a floppy disk drive, its icon looks just like the Zip drive icon).*

To see the files that each of these disks contains, *double-click each icon. When you double-click, the contents of that disk you double-clicked will **replace** the contents you currently see in the window. If you want to come back to the "Computer" window, either single-click on the Computer icon again, or single-click the "Back" button on the left side of the Toolbar.*

Practice: Click once on the **Computer** icon to see the disks that are "mounted." Notice that every disk icon in this window is also sitting right on your Desktop.

The Home icon in the Toolbar

Home: When you first turned on your Mac with OS X, you had to create a name and a password for yourself; this is your "user" account. If more than one person uses the computer, each person can have his or her own user account. All users can customize the Mac to their own particular likings, and all persons' files are protected from everyone else. You need a password to enter your own Home, and don't ever lose that password! Write it down!!

Each user has their own "Home" space, with their own Home folders, as shown below. When you single-click the "Home" button icon in the Toolbar, your Home files are displayed in the window. To learn all about your Home and how to take advantage of it, see Chapter 9.

Practice: Click once on the **Home** icon to see the folders that Apple has already set up for you.

You can open each folder (double-click the icons) to see what is inside each one, but there is probaby nothing there yet. It's up to you to put files inside.

This is my Home. Noticed I have added a couple of extra folders ("My Fonts" and "Robin's Personal Stuff"). You can add as many folders and documents into this window as you like.

Favorites: On the Mac, "Favorites" are folders, documents, web site addresses, or any other files that you want easy access to. Once you create a Favorite, you can access it a number of ways. If it's a web address, you might want to go to the site; if the Favorite is a folder, you might want to save items into it; if the Favorite is a "server" (another computer that you are connected to), you might want to copy files from the server or store files onto it. All of the Favorites you create will be stored in this Favorites folder. For all the details, see Chapter 24.

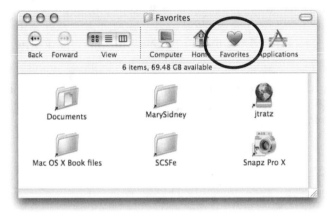

The Favorites icon in the Toolbar

Practice: Click once on the **Favorites** icon to see any Favorites you might have created. Don't worry if this folder is empty at the moment; when you learn why and how to create Favorites (Chapter 24), they will automatically be stored in this folder.

Applications: Apple has supplied a number of applications for your education and entertainment and has stored them in this special Applications folder. You'll notice, as you poke around your Mac, that there is more than one folder called Applications. The one that appears when you click the button in the Toolbar is the "system-wide" folder; that is, anything in this folder is available to all users. If you want to install a new software application just for your own use, you'll install it into the Applications folder that you find in your Home window. For details about how to use some of the applications provided by Apple, see Chapter 27. For details about users and Homes and how to install new applications into this folder, see Chapter 20.

The Applications icon in the Toolbar

Practice: Click once on the **Applications** icon to see the applications Apple has provided. Use the scroll arrows or scrollers to see the applications stored toward the bottom of the window.

The Back and Forward buttons in the Toolbar

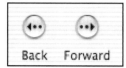

Back   Forward

Practice: Single-click the **Computer** icon in the Toolbar, then the **Home** icon, then the **Favorites** icon, then the **Applications** icon.

Now click the **Back** button once and you'll go back to the contents of the Favorites window. Click the Back button once more and you'll see the Home window, etc. Try it.

Back and Forward buttons: Your Mac is automatically set up so that when you click a new Toolbar icon to view its contents, the new contents *replace* what was already in the window. This prevents having a screen full of individual windows all displaying their contents.

If you want to go back and forth between the contents you're viewing *in this particular window,* click the Back and Forward buttons. If you've used a web browser, you'll find it's much the same.

Sometimes the buttons are gray. This happens when you get all the way to the first or last folder window you looked at. If you open a *new* window, the Back button is gray since the window is new and there is nowhere to go back to.

It's possible to individually open *new* windows instead of *replacing* the contents of the current window, if you prefer. See page 91 for details.

Hide/Show Toolbar button: As its name implies, click this button to hide the Toolbar; when it's hidden, click this button to show the Toolbar. When the Toolbar is hidden, a very important change takes place.

When the Toolbar is visible, double-clicking on a folder icon displays the new folder's contents in the *existing* window, replacing what was there.

When the Toolbar is hidden, double-clicking on a folder icon opens *another* window to display the contents of that folder.

Once you hide the Toolbar, all new windows that open from this one will automatically have a hidden Toolbar.

If you *always* want folders to open to new and separate windows, whether or not Toolbars are hiding, see page 96.

The Hide/Show Toolbar button in the Toolbar

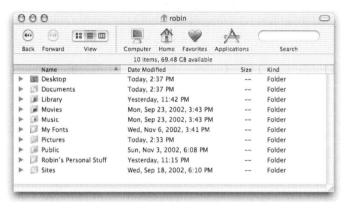

This is the window with the Toolbar showing.

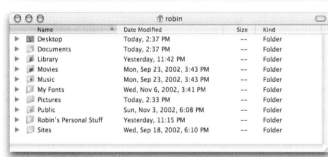

This is the same window as above, with the Toolbar hiding.

Practice: While the Toolbar is visible, double-click any folder. The contents of the new folder **replaces** the previous contents.

Click the **Back** button to go back to the previous folder.

Click the **Toolbar Hide/Show** button to hide the Toolbar.

Double-click a folder icon and you will see it open into a **new window,** and the previous window will still be on your screen. The new window has no Toolbar (click the button to bring the Toolbar back).

Remember, to **close** a window, click in the red button in the upper-left of the window.

Customize the Toolbar   You can **customize the Toolbar** to suit your working habits. You can *rearrange* items, *remove* any of the existing button icons, and *add* icons of folders, applications, files, servers, and more. Once you rearrange or add new items to a Toolbar, they appear in the Toolbar of every Finder window.

To rearrange items in the Toolbar:

Just drag them (for some items you have to hold down the Command key and drag). As you drag sideways, other icons move over to make room. When you have an item positioned where you want it, let go.

To customize the Toolbar using the "Customize Toolbar" pane:

1. Open any Finder window.

2. Hold the Shift key down and click the Hide/Show Toolbar button. **Or** from the View menu, choose "Customize Toolbar...."

3. From the pane that appears, press-and-drag any icon you like into the Toolbar and drop it there (if you change your mind, just drag the icon off the Toolbar and drop it on the Desktop; it will disappear).

This little menu changes how the icons are displayed in the Toolbar. Choose each one to see how it looks. The last one you choose is the one that will apply to the Toolbar when you close this pane.

Click "Done" when you are finished.

4. If you add more icons than will fit, a tiny double-arrow icon will appear at the end of the Toolbar, indicating there are more items in the Toolbar. Click on that double-arrow and a tiny menu will appear with the other items listed; you can select from that menu.

5. Click the "Done" button in the bottom-right corner when you are finished and want to apply the changes you made.

Some of the **icons in the Customize pane** represent items you already have in your Toolbar. They exist because it's possible to remove every single item from the Toolbar, even the Back button or the Views button, and you might one day want something back that you previously removed. Below is a list of the items we haven't already talked about that you can put in the Toolbar and what they do:

Icons in the Customize pane

Path: An open window represents the contents of a disk or a folder. Click on this Path button to see where the current disk or folder is located on the computer; you'll get a menu showing the folders inside of folders, etc., of where the item is stored. You can choose any location from this menu to open *that* window.

Eject: If you *select* a removable disk in the Computer window, you can then click this Eject button to eject the *selected* disk. This button doesn't work if you select the disk icon on the Desktop. See Chapter 18 about ejecting disks.

Burn: If you have a writable CD or DVD drive, you can click this button to begin the burn process. First *select* the CD or DVD icon in the Computer window.

Customize: Click this button to open the Customize pane (the one shown on the opposite page).

Separator: Drag this into position on the Toolbar to create a dividing line between groups of icons.

New Folder: Click this to put a new folder in the *active* window (which would be the one whose Toolbar you're clicking in).

Delete: Click this to delete any *selected* item(s) in the window. This button will be gray until you select something. The item you delete will go into the Trash basket (see Chapter 17).

Connect: Click this to connect to any other computers in your office that are already networked (see Chapter 35 about networking).

Find: Click this to open Search, which you can use to find files on your computer (see Chapter 25).

Get Info: Select a file, then click this to open a Get Info window, which provides lots of information about the file (see Chapter 28).

iDisk: If you bought a membership to Mac.com, this icon will open your storage space on Apple' server. See page xxi.

Documents, Movies, Music, Pictures, Public: Each of these represents one of the folders in your Home. Put its icon in your Toolbar, then you can just click to access that folder. Or you can drop files onto the icon in the Toolbar and the files will actually go into the folder.

Default set: Drag this entire block up to the Toolbar and it will replace everything you have customized and make the Toolbar exactly how it was when you first started.

Add folders or files to the Toolbar

You can **add any folder** to the Toolbar. When you put a folder in the Toolbar, you are actually placing a *copy* of the folder icon in the Toolbar; the real folder stays right where it is. But you can drop files onto the Toolbar folder and the files will go straight into the real folder. You can click the folder icon in the Toolbar and its window will instantly appear, as shown below.

You can **add any document** file to the Toolbar. When you click a document icon in the Toolbar, the application you created that document in will open and your file will appear.

You can **add any application** to the Toolbar. When you click an application icon in the Toolbar, it will open that application.

To add folders, files, or applications to the Toolbar:

Just find the file icon in a window, then drag it to the Toolbar and let go. Remember, you can always rearrange icons by just dragging them left or right. (To rearrange Apple's icons, Command-drag them).

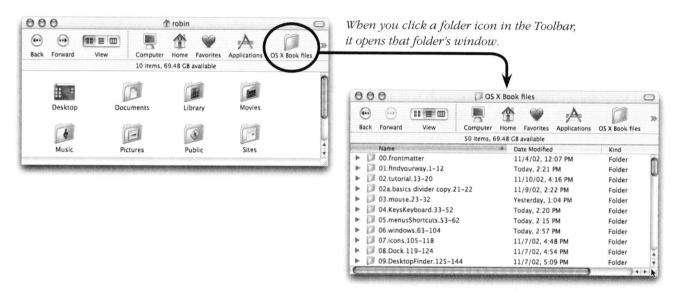

When you click a folder icon in the Toolbar, it opens that folder's window.

Remove items from the Toolbar

To remove items from the Toolbar: When the Customize pane is open, you can just drag any icon off of the Toolbar and drop it on the Desktop.

You can also remove any icon anytime you like, *without* having to open the Customize pane: Some icons you can just drag off and drop on the Desktop. If that doesn't work, hold down the Command key and drag it off.

If you have a lot of items in the Toolbar, the item you want to remove might not be visible. You'll have to open the window wide enough to see the icon (drag the Resize corner, see page 68), then drag it off.

As I mentioned on page 66, you can **view the contents** of a Finder window in three different ways, one of them as **icons.** Icons are the pictures that represent the various types of files on your computer. The biggest advantage to viewing windows in icons is that you can quickly and easily tell what is a folder, an application, a document, e. (see Chapter 7 about icons).

Using Icon View

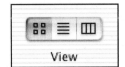

To view a window as icons: Click the Icon View button in the Toolbar (shown circled, below). Or go to the View menu and choose "As Icons."

Icon View obviously shows icons.

To select an item that you know is in this folder but you can't see it: Type the first couple of letters of its name. For instance, in the example above, you can't see the application called Stickies. So type "st" and the window will instantly scroll itself down and Stickies will be selected.

Tricks in Icon View

To "launch" (open) an application: Double-click its icon.

To open a folder and display its contents, double-click a folder icon. This will open the new folder *in this same window;* the contents of the new folder will *replace* the contents of the current window.

To open a folder in a new window: Hold down the Command key and double-click the folder. You will get a new window, plus the previous window will *remain* on the Desktop. The Toolbar is automatically hidden in the new window.

As I mentioned on page 79, whenever the **Toolbar is hidden** (click the little button in the top-right of the window), a folder will open into a *new* window when you double-click on it. The new window automatically has the Toolbar hidden; once the Toolbar is hidden, you can double-click on any folder in that window and it will automatically open into a new window (you don't have to hold the Command key down).

Always open a folder into a new window: If it makes you crazy to have only one window for all your folders, use the Finder preferences (see page 96), to make sure every time you double-click a folder icon (or single-click a folder icon in the Toolbar), you get a new and separate window.

Clean up the arrangement of the icons

There are two items in the View menu that pertain only to windows in Icon View: "Clean Up" and the "Arrange" options. If your window is in any other view, these items are gray, which is a **visual clue** that you can't use them.

There is an invisible underlying grid in every window, and when you choose to **Clean Up** the window, the Mac moves each icon into the nearest little square on that grid, the nearest square that the icon is already next to. This means there might still be gaps between icons.

When you choose **Arrange** plus one of the options from its submenu, the Mac moves each icon into that particular order. The icons are placed in neat rows and fill every invisible square in order.

The arrangement of the icons is also affected by the options you can choose in the "View Options," as discussed below and on the opposite page.

To clean up the icons in a window:

1. Make sure the window you want to clean up is active: click once on it.

2. From the View menu, choose "Clean Up" or an option from the "Arrange" menu.

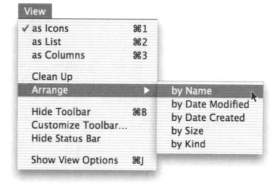

Practice: Open a window and view it by icon. Using the mouse, drag the icons around in the window so they are a mess. (If the icons won't move into new positions, see the information about "Icon Arrangement" on the opposite page.)

From the View menu, choose **Clean Up** and see what happens.

Now from the View menu, choose **Arrange,** and **by Name** and see what happens.

There are several features you can change in the Icon View, using the **View Options** dialog box, as shown below. To get this dialog box, go to the View menu and choose "Show View Options," or press Command J.

Once this dialog box is open (as shown below-right), you'll notice that its title bar changes its name depending on which window is *active*. That is, once you open it, you can open a whole bunch of other windows and whichever window is in *front,* the one that has the three buttons in color, is the one that this View Options box will apply to. Even if you have only one window open, if you switch to another folder in that same window, this View Options box will switch to displaying the options for the new contents.

What you see in the View Options depends on which view the active window is displaying. For instance, if you have a window in Icon View and you click its button to change the window to List View, the View Options box will change.

Here are explanations for each of the Icon View options. First of all, you have two choices that determine where you will see any options you apply.

> **This window only:** This option means just what it says. Any changes you make in View Options will apply only to the *active* window whose name appears in the title bar of the View Options box.
>
> If you make individual changes to a window, then at some point decide you don't like those individual changes, at any time you can open the View Options, click "All windows," and the active window will revert to your global options.
>
> **All windows:** If you click "All windows," any changes you make in this View Options box will apply to every window on your entire computer (when viewed in Icon View).

View Options in Icon View

*The View Options title bar shows the name of the **active** window. The changes you make in this box will apply to the window whose name is in this title bar.*

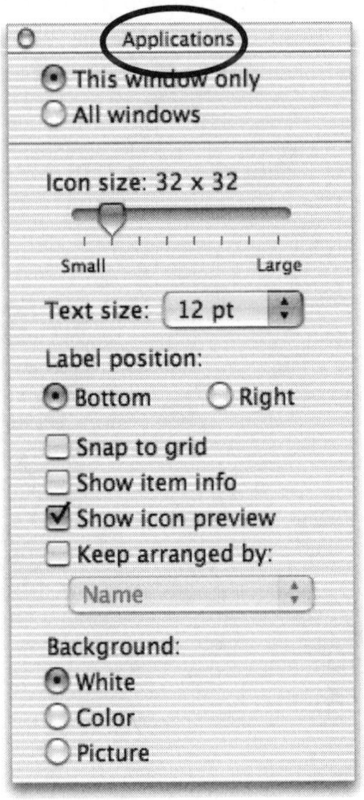

Below the dividing line in **View Options** are your choices.

Icon Size: Simply slide the blue slider back and forth to choose a size for your icons. As you slide, you'll see the changes take place immediately in the active window.

Text Size: This changes the size of the labels under the icons.

Label position: Choose to see the names of your files below their icons, as they typically are ("Bottom"), or to the right side ("Right").

Icon Arrangement

> **None:** With this button checked, you can move the icons around wherever you please.
>
> **Always snap to grid:** With this button checked, when you move icons around in the window, they will always snap into the nearest open

—continued

screamer.jpg → screamer.jpg

"Show icon preview" displays the actual image.

square in the underlying invisible grid that I mentioned on page 84. This keeps the window looking nice and neat. The size of the grid depends on the icon size you chose in the scroller (described above).

Show item info: Check this button and you will see not only the name of the file, but how many items are in a folder, how large some graphic files are, and how long some sound files are.

Show icon preview: This will change generic graphic icons into small representations of what they really look like, as shown to the left.

Keep arranged by: If you check this button, not only will your icons stay in the nice, neat grid, but they will automatically arrange themselves by whatever you choose from the pop-up menu (shown to the left). That is, if you drop a new folder or document or application into a window that is arranged by *name,* then that item will automatically put itself in alphabetical order and all the other icons will shift places to accommodate it. (You won't get the pop-up menu until you click the "Keep arranged by" button.)

Name: In alphabetical order.

Date Modified: The date you last opened and saved changes to this file.

Date Created: The date the document, folder, application, or other file was originally created.

Size: How large the file size is, which means how much space it takes up on your disk in kilobytes or megabytes.

Kind: Whether this file is a document, application, folder, etc.

If you choose to organize your icons by "Always snap to grid" or "Keep arranged by," you will see a little icon in your status bar (if you choose to show your status bar, as described on page 72).

This icon indicates the window is organized in "Always snap to grid."

This icon indicates the window is organized as "Keep arranged by."

Background: You can leave the background of your windows white, or you can apply a color or a photo. As with the other options, you can choose the background for all windows (global) or just the active window. Or both: You might have a global color, but choose to put a photo in one or two windows.

White: Removes any existing color or picture.

Color: Click this button and a little box appears. Click on the box and you'll get Apple's Colors palette, as shown below. Choose a color "model" along the top of the palette (the model called "Crayon" is fun and easy). Then click on a crayon. The color in the box across the top of the palette when you click OK is the color that will appear as the background of the active window.

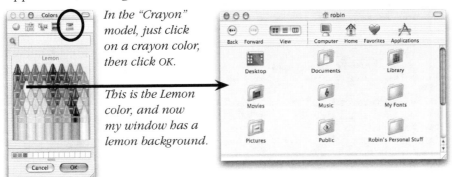

In the "Crayon" model, just click on a crayon color, then click OK.

This is the Lemon color, and now my window has a lemon background.

Picture: Click this button and a "Select…" button appears. Click that button and you'll get the standard "Open" dialog box that will automatically open to "Desktop Pictures," as shown below. If you know how to use this dialog box, you can "navigate" (see Chapter 12) to any folder on your computer and select a photo of your choice instead of the ones that are already in the Desktop Pictures folder.

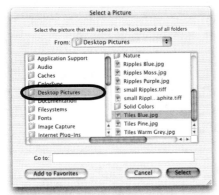

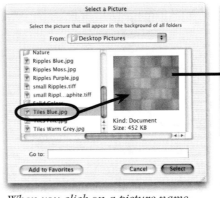

The folder "Desktop Pictures" is probably selected for you. Click once on a picture name in the right column.

When you click on a picture name, you'll see it on the right. Click "Select" and it will appear in the window.

Depending on which photo you choose, it might fill the entire space or just a corner.

Using List View

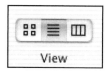

View

The **List View** is another way of looking at the items in a window. Below you see a typical list. Notice there are several columns; you can resize these columns, rearrange them, get rid of them, or choose different ones. You can organize each column in order backwards or forwards. The List View lets you "expand" several folders in the same window (you can see the folder "Documents" expanded in the example below) rather than opening a new window for each one as with Icon View.

This is the List View button.

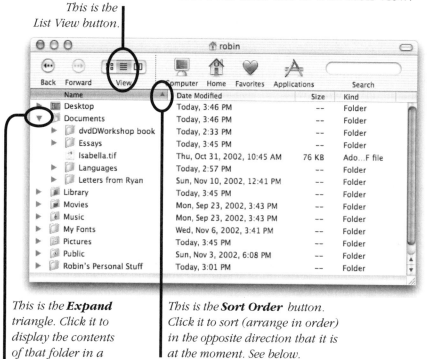

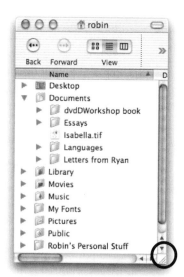

*This is the **Expand** triangle. Click it to display the contents of that folder in a List View. See below.*

*This is the **Sort Order** button. Click it to sort (arrange in order) in the opposite direction that it is at the moment. See below.*

This is the same window as shown to the left, just resized narrower.

Practice: Click the List View button. You'll see the **expand triangles.** Click one to view the contents of that folder in this same window. To close it up, click the triangle again.

Click on another **column heading** to organize the contents by that heading.

Click the **sort order triangle** to reorganize the contents in the opposite order.

Expand triangles: Click on an **expand** triangle to open and display the contents of that folder in this same window. This triangle allows you to see the contents of a number of windows in the same folder. This makes it easier to move files from one folder to another, to compare folders, and even to select items from several different folders at the same time. As you can see in the example above, you can expand folders inside of folders (as with the "Essays" folder inside the "Documents" folder). Click the triangle again to **collapse** the folder. See Chapter 10 for details on this feature.

Sort Order triangle: When a column heading is selected (click on it to select it; it will turn blue), a tiny upward- or downward-pointing triangle appears. This indicates the order in which the contents in that column are **organized,** or **sorted.** For instance, in the example above, the "Name" column is organized alphabetically in order from A to Z (the pointy tip of the triangle indicates the lower end of the sort order). If you want this column organized from Z to A, click that triangle; the triangle will point downward and the items will be sorted alphabetically backwards. Try it.

You can **resize and rearrange the columns** of information that are displayed in your window when you view items in the List View.

> **To rearrange the columns,** press directly on any column heading (except Name) and drag to the left or right. As soon as you start to drag, the pointer tool turns into the grabber hand, which is your **visual clue** that you are about to rearrange the columns. The only column you cannot move out of position is "Name."

> **To resize the columns,** position the pointer on the line between two column headings. The pointer will turn into a two-headed arrow, as shown below, which is a **visual clue** that you can resize the columns—just press that two-headed arrow and drag to the left or right.

Resize and rearrange the list columns

Practice: Just follow the directions to the left.

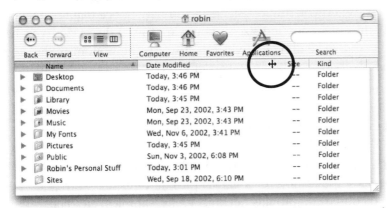

*If you see a one-headed arrow, that's a **visual clue** that you can only resize that particular column in the direction the arrow is pointing.*

*How can you tell by looking at this window that the files are arranged by name? (The obvious **visual clue** is in the column heading.)*

You can **choose which columns** will appear in a List View, as well as how **dates** will appear (if you choose to show dates), and the **size** of icons.

Options for List View

1. Open any window and click the List View button.

2. Go to the View menu and choose "Show View Options," or press Command J to get the dialog box, as shown to the right.

3. As explained on page 85, click **This window only** if you want to make changes just to the active window. Click **All windows** if you want changes to apply to *every* window when shown in List View.

4. Experiment with the **Icon Size** and **Text Size** options.

5. The column headings you check under **Show Columns** will appear in the *active* window as headings. See the following page for explanations of each column.

6. **Use relative dates** will display "Today" and "Yesterday" where appropriate (as shown above), and regular dates for older files.

7. If you check **Calculate all sizes,** your window will display the size of folders and various other files that it doesn't normally show, but it can be kind of slow to do this sometimes.

Choices in "Show Columns"

Below are explanations of the columns that can appear in your List View.

Date Modified lists files in chronological order according to the last time you opened a file or folder and changed something in it. Arranging folders by either Date Modified or Date Created can come in handy when, for instance, you have several budget documents and you want to see the most recent edition.

Date Created lists the files in chronological order according to when they were first made. The Mac looks at the creation date as determined by the date and time you've set in the Date & Time preferences (details for Date & Time are on page 351–352).

Size lists the files in order of how much space they take up on your computer. When you are in List View, you may notice that folders and certain other files show no size. If you want to see their sizes, you have to check "Calculate all sizes" which is towards the bottom of the "View Options" dialog box (shown to the left).

Kind lists the files in groups: applications, various sorts of documents, and folders. This is handy if you want to see a list of all the photographs in your family folder or all the documents you've stored in your budget folder.

> **Tip:** "Arrange by Kind" is particularly useful for a folder that holds an application (or a game) plus all of its accessories—the dictionaries, tutorials, technical files, samples, etc. The view by "Kind" will usually put the application (or game) at the top of the list so it's easy to find.

Version displays the version number of each application. The version number tells you how current the software is; every time it is updated, it gets a new version number. For instance, your Mac is now using the tenth major version of the operating system.

Comments will display the first several characters and the last characters of any text that was typed into the Comments box in the Get Info window (see page 478), as shown below.

This is what the Comments might look like in the window.

If you hold the pointer over the Comments (don't click!), in a couple of seconds the entire message will appear.

To make the entire comment appear instantly, *press the Option key (don't click).*

You can **open folders,** as shown on page 88, by clicking the expand triangle and the contents of the folder will drop down in the list. **Or** you can double-click any folder and the contents of that new folder will replace the contents of the current window, as shown below.

Opening folders in List View

I single-clicked this triangle to display the contents of this folder right in this window, in a list.

*I could **single-click** this **triangle** to display the contents of this folder (which is inside the Documents folder) in this list.*

*Instead, I **double-clicked** the **folder icon** and it replaced the contents of this window with the new folder's contents, as shown to the right.*

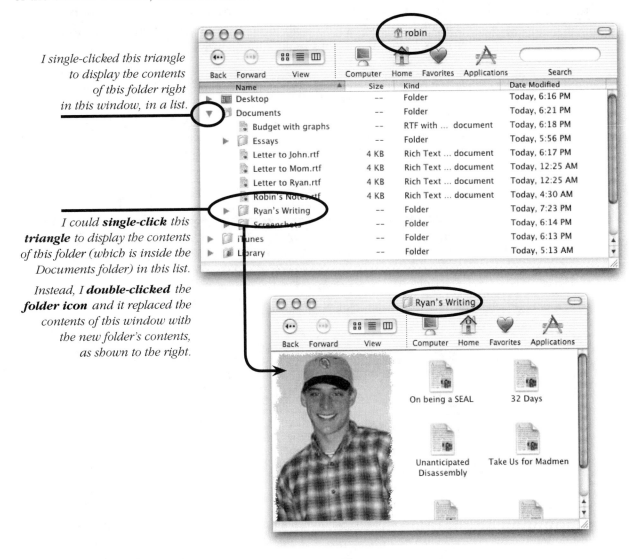

Notice the new window displays the contents **in the same view that I last used in this folder,** *not* in the view of the window I just came from. You might love this feature or hate it. You can use the Finder Preferences to make all new windows open in the same view, and even make all new folders open in a new, separate window; see page 96.

Using Column View

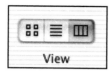

The **Column View** is a new thing on Macintoshes. At first, it can be quite confusing and frustrating to work with, so walk yourself through these two pages to get the gist of how it works, and then you'll simply have to use it enough until it begins to make sense. It's important to understand the Column View concept because every time you save a document or have to "navigate" or "browse" through your computer to open a file, you'll bump into this Column View. It's really quite handy.

*This is the Computer level of your Mac, shown in Column View. Notice each of the icons on the far left, on the Computer level, show a triangle pointing to the right. This is a **visual clue** that you can single-click on that name (the "Hard Disk" or the "Network" icon) and you will see, in the next column, what is stored on that level (shown below).*

*Following the example above, in this window you can see by the highlight (the darker area) that I single-clicked on **Robin's Hard Disk** to see what was stored on the hard disk. Its contents are displayed in the second column.*

*In the second column, I clicked on **Users,** which I can tell is a folder, to see what is stored in that folder. Its contents opened in the third column.*

*In the third column, I clicked on my own Home folder, **robin** (I can tell it's actually a folder because of the tiny triangle pointing to the right), to display what is stored in my Home folder. There I see the folders I know and love.*

(These columns can be handy, but you can already understand that it would be much easier to see your Home folders if you just click on the Home icon button in the Toolbar.)

Continue following the progression on the next page.

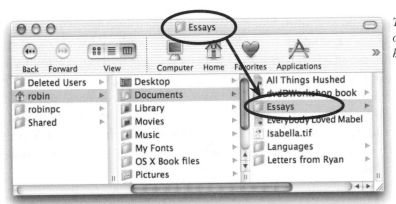

The title bar displays the name of the folder that is selected, or highlighted.

*You can still see the **robin** Home folder on the far left, highlighted, but it is a lighter highlight than in the next column, where **Documents** has a darker shade. This indicates that it is actually "Documents" that is the **active** item here (because I clicked once on it).*

The column on the far right shows the contents of the Documents folder.

*How many **scrollers** do you see? The one across the bottom indicates that you could scroll back to the left, back to the Computer level. The two vertical scroll bars indicate there is more in each of those columns.*

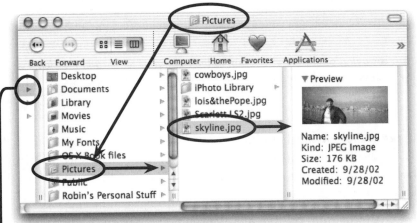

*This final column will display either an icon or the actual image of the **selected** document.*

If you select a movie, you can actually play the movie right here in Column View.

Options for Column View

If the preview makes you nuts, you can turn it off in the Column View Options.

You can also turn off the icons so you see just a text list in each column.

In the example at the top of the page, I clicked on the Pictures folder, then I clicked on one of the pictures inside that folder. This made the Home column (with "robin" and "Shared") scoot to the left, where you can barely see it; you can just see the tiny triangles, and "robin" is still highlighted, although you can only see the triangle.

*The **Pictures** folder is highlighted, which is a clue (along with the name in the title bar) that the files in the next column are stored in the Pictures folder.*

*Now we are finally looking at documents (notice the documents have no tiny triangles pointing to the right). The file **skyline.jpeg** is highlighted, and it's the darkest highlight so we know this is actually what is **active** at the moment, and this is what is shown in the very last column.*

Once you find a file in a column, you can double-click it to open it within its application.

Navigating in Column View

Navigating refers to finding your way around the Desktop on your Mac, or in a dialog box or window. You have to navigate to the document you want so you can open it, or to a disk icon so you can eject it. In the Column View, you can use the arrow keys to select items left and right, as well as up and down. For instance, in the example below, "robin" is currently selected (its highlight is the darkest; the lighter highlights to the left show where it came from). If I press the RightArrow key, I will select the first item in the next column. Once in that column, I can press the UpArrow or DownArrow keys to select a folder.

When you get to the Open and Save As dialog boxes, you'll find the Column View there as well, where you can still use the arrow keys to navigate.

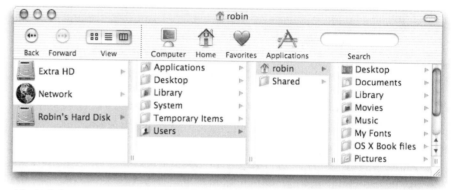

The Tab key will also move the selection to the right, and Shift-Tab to the left, but the arrow keys are easier and more consistent throughout the Mac.

Resizing columns in Column View

You can **resize the columns** in Column View. You've probably noticed the little "thumbs" at the bottoms of the scroll bar column dividers (circled below). **To resize,** just press and drag on any thumb. This actually resizes all of the columns at once.

To resize one individual column at a time, hold down the Option key and drag the thumb.

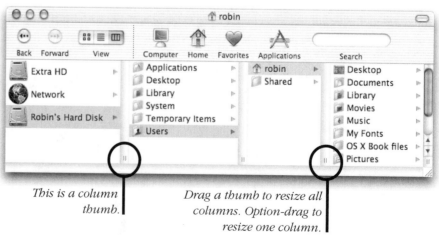

This is a column thumb.

Drag a thumb to resize all columns. Option-drag to resize one column.

At the Desktop, you have a menu called **Window.** In it you will find a list of the titles of every window that is currently open on your Desktop. (When you are in an application, this menu will list the open documents in that application.)

▼ A checkmark next to a window title indicates the active window.

▼ A diamond indicates that window is minimized (in the Dock).

▼ Select any title in the menu to bring that window to the front.

You might have a number of windows open—some from applications, several Finder windows, and a couple from a utility you're using. These windows might all be visible on the screen at once, layered over and under each other. Click on one Finder window, then choose "Bring All to Front" from the Window menu, and all of the windows of that type will come forward (although only one can actually be *active* and on top of the others).

The Window Menu

If you see a round dot in the Window menu, see page 102.

There are a number of ways to close or minimize all windows at once.

▼ To simultaneously **close every window** that is open on your Desktop, hold down the Option key while you click in any window's Close button (the red one); all the windows will go away one after another!

▼ In the File menu there is a command to "Close Window." If you hold down the Option key, that command changes to "Close All."

▼ The keyboard shortcut to close a window is Command W. **To close all the windows at once,** press Command Option W.

▼ **To minimize all the windows at once,** hold down the Option key and click the Minimize button (the yellow one) in the upper-left corner of any window. This also works in applications when you have more than one window open.

▼ You might have the feature turned on that always opens folders in new windows (see the following page), but often the folder you want to open is buried within several folders. To prevent having too many windows open that you don't need, hold the Option key down while you double-click to open those folders to get to your file. **The windows will close up behind you** as you go along.

▼ When you turn off the computer, the Macintosh remembers which windows were open when you left. When you turn the computer back on, those windows will re-open in the same position in which you left them. You can take advantage of this fact and arrange your windows before you Shut Down.

Close or minimize all of the Windows

...and other window tricks

Finder Preferences

There are a couple of items in the **Finder Preferences** that refer to using Finder windows. These options are global, meaning they will apply to all windows on the Desktop until you go back and change them.

To open the Finder Preferences:

1. Make sure you are at the Finder/Desktop. Look at the menu bar: If the menu item next to the apple is not "Finder," then click once on an empty spot on the Desktop, or click on a Finder window.

2. When you see "Finder" in the menu bar, click on it and choose "Preferences…" from the menu. You'll get the box shown below.

    ▼ Whenever you open a new Finder window, it automatically opens to the "Computer" level. You probably don't need to use much on the Computer level; everything you need is in your "Home." In the Finder Preferences you can choose to have **new Finder windows open to your Home level** instead.

    ▼ If you are an experienced Mac user, you're probably accustomed to a new window opening every time you double-click a folder icon, instead of the contents of the new folder *replacing* what was already in the window. In the Finder Preferences you can choose to **have a new window open every time you double-click a folder.**

    ▼ If you prefer one window view over another, it might make you crazy that you never know what view the next folder will appear in. You can choose that all views *in the window you're working in* will stay the same as the view you have currently selected. That is, if you set a window to Icon View, all the folders that open *within that window* will be in Icon View.

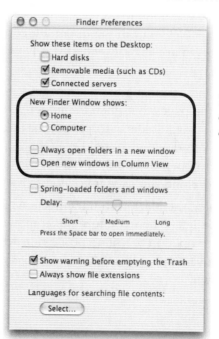

These are the options that apply to Finder windows, as explained above.

All the information in the previous pages has pertained to Finder windows, the ones you will use at the Desktop. But the Mac also uses windows in every application; when you open an application and create something, you create it in a **document window.** A document window has most of the same features as Finder windows, with a few differences. Below is a typical document window (although every application is slightly different). You can see that it has the same features as the Finder windows, without the Toolbar.

Document Windows

Important note: *If you open an application in Classic (Mac OS 9), your windows will not look quite like this. If you don't know how to use Classic windows, please see Chapter 39.*

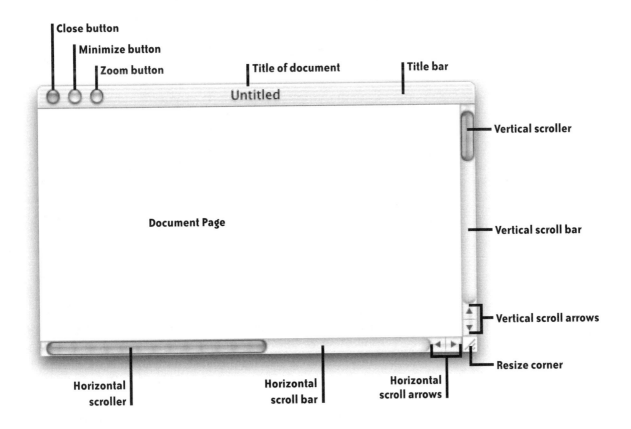

On the following page are examples of document windows.

Examples of document windows

This is an example of a **document window** in a page layout application. Notice there are differences between this window and the one on the previous page; every application applies its own details. But all of the items in the example on the previous page are also present in this window.

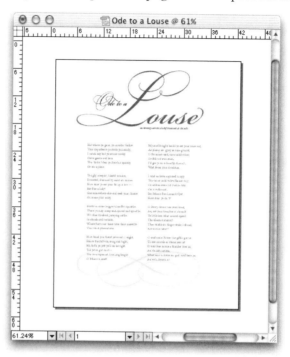

You'll find the buttons and scrollers and title bars and resize corners in just about every application on the Mac, no matter what the "document" looks like. Below is the iTunes application for listening to music on your Mac. Notice this window has the same features as every window we've talked about so far, you should feel comfortable with it as soon as you open it—you already know how to close it, minimize it, move it around the screen, resize it, etc.

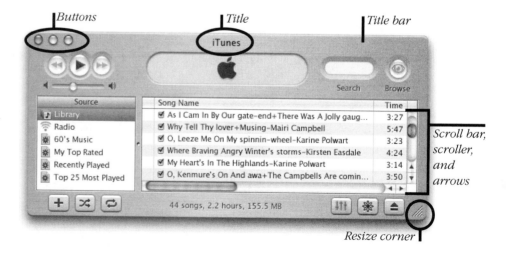

Buttons *Title* *Title bar*

Scroll bar, scroller, and arrows

Resize corner

The **scroll bars and scrollers** are particulary important in document windows because they tell you how much of your document is not visible, or even where it is. Many times I have been called to students' desks who were panic stricken because the papers they were writing "disappeared." I would point out that the scroller was all the way to the bottom of the document window, and that if they dragged it back up, their papers would reappear. In a page layout application, the scrollers might be all the way to the left or right, hiding the page that is in the middle.

Document scroll bar clues

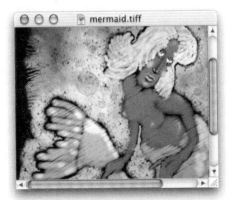

> An Entertaining Creature
>
> Yes, that's what she called him. "An entertaining creature." As if he had been born and raised to provide her amusement. How droll, she had said. She acts like she's some long-lost countess who has just been released from a time warp. Well, he would show her. He would just turn himself into a real creature and

In this example, there is no horizontal scroll bar at all, which tells us there is nothing more in the document in the horizontal direction than what we can already see.

There is no scroller in the vertical scroll bar on the right, which tells us this story ends right where we see it—there is nothing more to see in the vertical direction.

> creature." As if he had been born and raised to provide her amusement. How droll, she had said. She acts like she's some long-lost countess who has just been released from a time warp. Well, he would show her. He would just turn himself into a real creature and . . . and what? He didn't know how to turn himself into a creature. He wasn't some gall-darned warlock or anything. Oh, he could cast simple spells like the kind to make acne go away or to find enough money to take himself to a movie, but not the kind to make babes like Eliza fall in love with him. Or to turn

The size of the scroller in the scroll bar is proportionate to how much of the entire window is visible to you.

The amount of space above and below the scroller is proportionate to how much of the window you cannot see at the moment.

This example has scroll bar scrollers along both the right and bottom edges, indicating there is a lot more of this image than is visible in the window at the moment.

To open the window *enough to see the entire image (if it will fit on your monitor), click the green button.*

Tip: **To go to the very end** of the document (in most applications), hit the "End" key.

To go to the very beginning of the document, hit the "Home" key.

Title bar in a document

Document windows also have **title bars,** the striped bar across the top of a window in which, logically, the title appears. This title is the name of the document you have created. *You* are responsible for the title; when you *save* the file, its name will appear here (see Chapter 14 about saving).

Remember, you can also double-click in the title bar to **minimize** a window.

Every window has a title bar.

The document path in the title bar

The title bar can always tell you *where* a particular document is stored, once you have actually saved the document and given it a name. The list that you see dropping down from the title bar below is called the **path** to the document.

> **Practice:** This technique works in document windows and Finder windows. So try it on any window that is open. You'll learn more about paths, if you want, in Chapter 14.

To see the "path" to where a *saved* document is stored, hold the Command key down and click on the title bar; a menu will appear. You can slide the mouse down the menu and choose any item to open that item's Finder window.

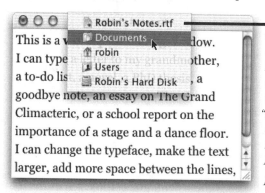

So this menu tells me that this document named "Robin's Notes.rtf" has been saved into a folder called "Documents," which is in the Home for "robin," which is in the folder called "Users," which is on the hard disk named "Robin's Hard Disk."

Notice the tiny icons to the left of the path names are also visual clues.

Moving the document window

To move any document window around the screen, position the pointer in the title bar of the window, then press-and-drag. Just let go of the mouse button when you have the window placed where you want.

If you have more than one document window open, only one will have the little round buttons *in color* in its title bar. The colored buttons are a **visual clue** that this window is the **active window.** If windows are overlapping, the active window is the one that is in front.

The **active window** is the only window that the commands from the keyboard or the menu will affect. For instance, if you go to the File menu and choose "Close," it will close the *active* window. If you choose "Save," it will save the *active* window. It's very important to be conscious of which window is active!

To make a window active, simply click on any visible part of it; this will also bring that window to the front of any others.

The active document window

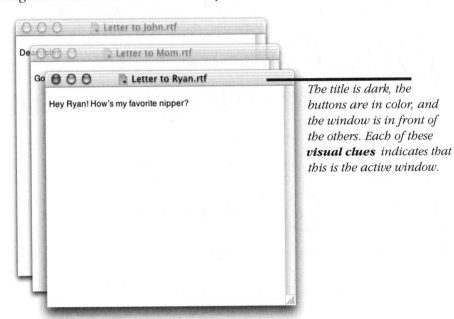

The title is dark, the buttons are in color, and the window is in front of the others. Each of these **visual clues** indicates that this is the active window.

Tip: To move a window that's behind others *without* making it active, hold down the Command key while you press-and-drag the title bar. Try it.

Dot in the red button of a document window

Sometimes you may see a round dot inside the red button, as shown in the example below. This dot is a **visual clue** that you have made changes to the document but haven't "saved" them yet. That is, a new document is "untitled" and unsaved until you go to the File menu, choose "Save As...," and give the document a name. This process puts a new, permanent file in your Documents folder. But whenever you make any changes to that document, such as adding more text, those changes are *not* included in the permanent file until you "Save" once again (either press Command S to save, or go to the File menu and choose "Save"). See Chapter 14 for all the details about saving.

In this example, you can see the red dot that indicates there have been changes made to this file and they are not saved yet. Also notice that the small document icon in the title bar is gray.

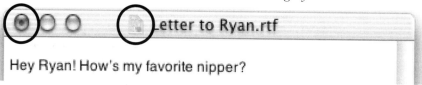

Hey Ryan! How's my favorite nipper?

I saved the changes to the file, and now the red button has no dot, plus the document icon in the title bar is now darker.

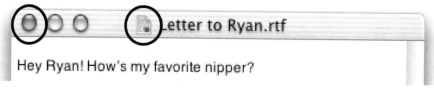

Hey Ryan! How's my favorite nipper?

Dot in the Window menu

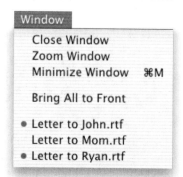

This menu indicates there are three open documents in this application, and two of them have unsaved changes.

Most applications have a "Window" menu that lists all the open documents in that application, as shown to the left. Notice in that list of document windows, two files have dots to the left of their names; these dots are **visual clues** that changes have been made to those documents but haven't been "saved" yet (as explained above). You can select one of the names in the menu to bring that document forward, and then save it. (Remember, to do something to a file, the document must be the *active* window, as explained on the previous page).

Because windows are so incredibly important and because there are so many details about them to know, this quiz is two pages long!

1. Label the window below with the following parts:

   a. **Close button**
   b. **Scroll bar**
   c. **Title bar**
   d. **Minimize button**
   e. **Title**

   f. **Scroll arrows (2)**
   g. **Resize corner**
   h. **Scroller**
   i. **Zoom button**

2. Describe three ways to **minimize** a window.

   _____

3. How can you instantly tell **how much you can't see** in a document?

   _____

4. How can you **move a window** without making it active?

   _____

5. What is the **visual clue** that tells you a document has not been saved recently?

   _____

—*continued on next page!*

continued from previous page!

6. Do you single-click or double-click on anything in the Toolbar?

_____

7. How would you arrange a Finder window to see how large your files are?

_____

8. Name two ways to open a folder into a new, separate window (without changing the Finder Preferences).

_____

9. In List View, what is the quickest way to organize files by another column heading?

_____

10. How would you resize a single column in Column View?

_____

11. How can you alphabetically organize a window in Icon View?

_____

12. How can you close all the Finder windows at once without touching the mouse?

_____

13. How can you see a list (the path) of all the folders in which a folder or document is nested?

_____

14. What would you do if you want to change the positions of your scroll arrows?

_____

15. How can you add a status bar to your windows?

_____

Answers are on page 730.

All About Icons

Icons—the little pictures you see on the screen—are an intrinsic part of the look and feel of the Macintosh. Instead of having to type a code to open an application or document (which you had to do before the Mac was invented), you simply double-click on an icon.

An icon can represent any kind of **file**—a file is any form of information you see on your computer. The term "file" might refer to an application, document, clipart, photograph, folder, email letter, web page, or other items.

The icons offer rich **visual clues.** At first they may look like an odd collection of stuff, but once you really look at them you'll see how much information icons instantly provide. This information is valuable to you, and that's the purpose of this chapter—to help you take advantage of these clues.

Most of the techniques in this chapter, such as moving an icon or changing its name, apply whether your files are represented by icons or shown as names in a list.

Contents of this chapter

Highlighted, or Selected, Icons

Favorites

When an **icon is dark,** like the one shown to the left, it is **highlighted,** or **selected**—it got selected because you clicked once on it, or perhaps you typed the first letter or two of its name. Selecting is important because you must select an icon before you can do anything with it. For instance, menu commands, such as "Open" or "Duplicate," only affect highlighted (selected) icons. Selecting is so important I wrote an entire chapter on it (Chapter 11).

Icons: Single-Click or Double-Click?

Icons represent files on your Mac. You need a basic understanding of what the various icons are telling you about themselves, which is the main point of this chapter. But you also need to know that you must treat icons differently *depending on where they are on your computer.* For instance, to **open** an application from the Dock, you **single-click** on the icon; to **open** an application from the Applications folder, you **double-click** on the icon. This can be confusing, so let's look at it visually right now.

In any Toolbar

Practice: Single-click each item (except iDisk, if you have it). The window contents will change to show you what is contained in each item.

Single-click icons in the Toolbar. The icons on the left side of this Toolbar are buttons; on the right side, they actually represent folders that contain other files.

In the Dock

Practice: Single-click the "Finder" icon (circled, to the right) to open the Finder window.

If you clicked on any other icon and don't know what to do now, do this: hold down the Command key (⌘) and tap the letter Q to quit.

Single-click to activate any icon in the Dock. However, what each one does when you activate it is different—some of the icons represent applications which will open, others represent system tools that provide information, and several connect you to the Internet. See Chapter 8 for details.

On the Desktop

Practice: Select your hard disk icon: Single-click on it.

Open your hard disk window: Double-click the hard disk icon.

To close the window: Single-click on the tiny red button in the top-left of the window.

Robin's Hard Disk

Robin's Hard Disk

To select an icon on the Desktop, ***single-click.***

To open a folder, document, or application icon (as described in the following pages), ***double-click.***

This window is showing the Icon View.

To select *an icon in a window in Icon View,* **single-click.**

To open *a folder, document, or application icon (as described in the following pages),* **double-click.**

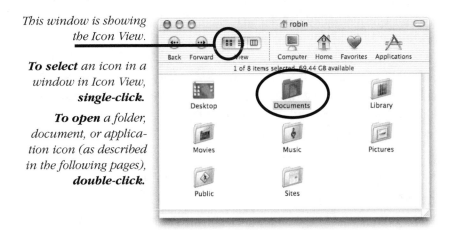

In the Icon View of a window

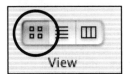

To change any window into the Icon View, click the button circled above. (If you don't see this "toolbar" above your window, click the tiny oval in the upper-right of the window.)

This window is showing the List View.

To select *an icon in a window in List View,* **single-click** *the icon itself,* **not** *the tiny triangle to its left.*

To open *a folder, document, or application icon (as described in the following pages),* **double-click** *the icon itself,* **not** *the tiny triangle to its left.*

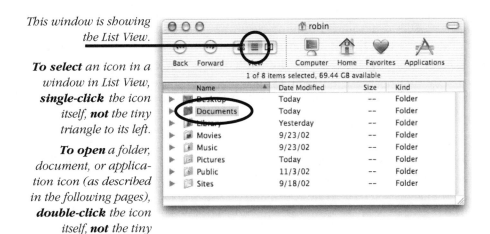

In the List View of a window

See Chapter 6 for details about the List View, and see Chapter 10 to learn how to use folders within the List View.

This window is showing the Column View.

To select *an icon in a window in Column View,* **single-click.**

To open *a folder, document, or application icon (as described in the following pages) in its own window,* **double-click.**

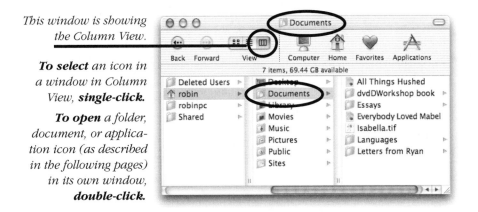

In the Column View of a window

See Chapter 6 for details about how to work in the Column View, and see Chapter 10 to learn how to use folders within the Column View.

Types of Icons

Now let's look at individual **types of icons.** Having a general idea of what the icons represent is helpful while working on your Mac.

Disk Icons

When your Desktop is visible (the Desktop is shown and described on page 2), you'll always see icons of any **disks** that are in your Mac. When a disk icon appears on the Desktop, we say that disk is "mounted."

▼ You will always see the hard disk icon, as shown below, that holds all of the files on your computer.

▼ When you insert a CD or a DVD, an icon of the CD or DVD will appear.

▼ If you have bought something called a "Zip drive" in which you insert a small, removable hard disk called a "Zip disk," you'll see its icon on the Desktop as well.

You might, at some point, "partition" your main hard disk into several separate compartments; the Mac considers each of these partitions a separate hard disk and so you would see individual icons for each one. You might buy another hard disk and install it inside your computer or plug it in to the back of your Mac so the "external" hard disk sits on your desk; its icon will also appear on your Desktop.

▼ Single-click on a disk icon to *select* it.

▼ Double-click on a disk icon to *open* it; you will see a window displaying all the files on that disk.

Practice: To **select** the hard disk, single-click the icon on the Desktop or in the Finder window.

To **open** its window and display its contents, double-click the hard disk icon.

To **close** the hard disk window, click the tiny red button in the upper-left of the window.

Mac OS X

*Hard disk icon
(your icon is
probably named
something else)*

FontDisc

CD icon

CASABLANCA

DVD icon

Little Mac Book

Zip disk icon

Folder Icons

Whenever you have a Finder window open, most likely you'll see **folder icons.** They act just like folders in your filing cabinet in that you store items in them for organization, and you can open them to see what's inside. Be sure to read Chapter 10 on folders since they are an incredibly important tool that you will be using constantly.

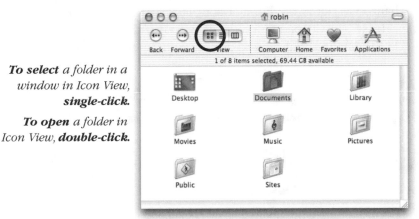

To select a folder in a window in Icon View, ***single-click.***

To open a folder in Icon View, ***double-click.***

To select a folder in List View, ***single-click*** *the icon itself.*

To "expand" a folder so you can see its contents in this window, ***single-click*** *the tiny triangle.*

To open a folder in a new window, ***double-click*** *the folder icon or name.*

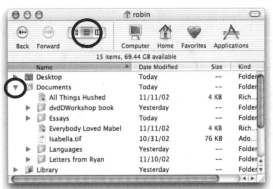

To select a folder in Column View, ***single-click.***

To open a folder into its own window, as shown on the far-right, ***double-click.***

Which view your window displays depends on your Finder preferences as described on page 96 in Chapter 6.

Fancy Folders

Many of the folders you see are identified with special icons. These **fancy folders** are created by the Macintosh operating system and they have special functions. Below you see the folders that are in your Home window. If more than one person uses the computer, each person can have his or her own Home window and their own set of these folders. Anything a user puts in these folders is accessible only to that user, with the exception of the Public folder; whatever is put in the Public folder is accessible to anyone using the machine. Please see Chapter 9 for details about each of these folders, and Chapter 20 for details about how to add more users to your Mac.

The Desktop and Home icons are actually folders, but their icons have been totally changed.

Don't change the names of any of these folders! Many of them have very specific purposes that depend on their names.

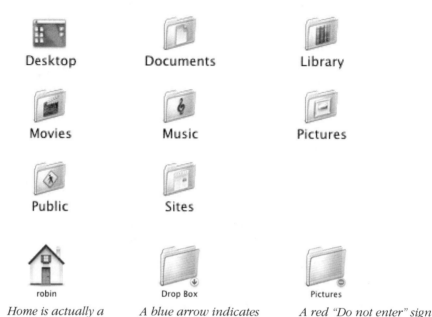

Desktop   Documents   Library

Movies   Music   Pictures

Public   Sites

robin   Drop Box   Pictures

Home is actually a folder with a special icon.

A blue arrow indicates a folder with write-only privileges. See page 135.

A red "Do not enter" sign indicates a folder with no privileges. See page 134.

Trash, or Wastebasket Icon

The **Trash,** or **waste basket,** icon in the Dock is an important icon that you will use regularly. Its icon represents exactly what it does: items that you don't want anymore, you drag down to the Trash and throw them away. Please see Chapter 17 for all the details.

Application (or **program**) **icons** are typically rather fancy ones. These belong to the actual applications (the software programs that you work in). Each application has its own design so they all look different, but what they have in common is that many try to give some sort of **visual clue** as to what they do. For instance, below you can see that the TextEdit icon represents a word processing program; the iMovie icon represents a movie-making program. When you create your own *document* in an application, the document usually has some visual clue that it belongs to that particular application, as you can see below and on the following page.

Application Icons

TextEdit   martha ran.rtf   iMovie   summer.mov

Each of these application icons (TextEdit and iMovie) gives you a visual clue of what it does. Each of their documents also gives you a visual clue that it was created in that particular application.

Practice: Single-click the Application icon in the Toolbar (shown circled, to the left).

Find the **Chess** icon.

To open the Chess application, double-click the Chess icon.

To play, drag a white piece into the square of your choice. The Mac will make the next move. To get a hint of where to move next, go to the Move menu and choose "Show a hint."

To quit the application, go to the "Chess" menu and choose "Quit."

Document Icons

Document icons represent documents, or files, that **you** (or someone like you) have created in any particular application. Whenever you are working in an application and you save your document with a name, a document icon is created for you somewhere on your Mac.

Document icons almost always look like a piece of paper with the top-right corner folded down, as you can see in the examples below. Typically document icons have some resemblance to the application they were created in, as shown below and on the previous page.

Notice most document icons have an "extension," which is a two- to four-letter code at the end of the name. Although you don't always see them, these extensions are very important in Mac OS X; see page 227 for more about extensions.

▼ Single-click a document icon to **select** it.

▼ Double-click a document icon to open the application **in which the document was created,** which will also place that particular document on the screen. This means the application will open first, and then the document will open inside that application. *A document cannot open on the screen without some sort of application opening first.*

Now, just because you have a document icon doesn't guarantee that you also have the application that created it! For instance, your friend might send you a file in a word processing application that you don't have. There are a number of things to do in this situation; see the information on the opposite page, as well as page 478.

summer.mov Travel Stories.rtf xmascard.pdf sonnets.idd

You can see the top-right corner turned down in all of these document icons.

Quicken Robin Acrobat xmascard.pdf

Each document icon matches its application icon.

The document icons below actually represent **graphics** (you can tell by their extensions; see page 227). Graphic documents can be opened in a number of different applications, and they can also be placed on the pages of other documents; for instance, you can *insert* a photo of Jane in your letter to the dog pound, even if you didn't have an application that *opens* Jane.

jane.jpg jane.jpeg family photo.tiff ex.gif BookaCook logo.eps

Occasionally you will see a **blank document icon.** This usually means one of two things:

1. A blank document icon often means that the application in which this document was created is not on your computer. For instance, the blank document shown below, left, is the same file as the InDesign document (Adobe InDesign is a page layout program) on the right. When this file is in a computer that has InDesign installed, it looks like it belongs to InDesign. But if I copy the same file to a computer that does **not** have the application InDesign installed, the icon is blank.

Hondo ad.idd   Hondo ad.idd

Sometimes, just to confuse you, your document does appear with an icon, even if the application is not in your Mac.

2. Many of the files that help operate Mac OS X look like blank document icons. To protect you from messing up your computer, you're generally not allowed to open these. If you try, you get the message shown below. You'll only find these blank system icons if you go poking around where you shouldn't be (anywhere except your own Home folders).

iCal.order   version.plist

Many of the files in the system folders are blank. Just leave them alone.

If you double-click a blank document icon, you will usually see this message:

You can click "Choose Application..." to get an "Open" dialog box where you can choose from your list of applications; select one that you think might open this document.

Or instead, try dragging the **document** icon on top of various **application** icons, as illustrated in Chapter 12. If an application can open a file of this type (AppleWorks, for instance, can open almost any text file), the application icon will become highlighted. This is your clue that this application can open this file; let go of the document and it will try to open in that program (it doesn't always work).

Blank Document Icons

Tip: Sometimes if you rebuild the Classic Desktop, as explained in Chapter 39, blank icons will get their icons back, depending on why it was blank in the first place.

dreamland.hqx

You might also see this "generic" icon, which indicates that Mac OS X recognizes it as a file but is not sure which application it belongs to.

System Icons   If you click the Computer icon in the Toolbar and view it in Column View, as shown below, you'll see several "system" folders, or folders that the system uses to run your Macintosh. Inside most of these folders are **system icons** that represent programming that performs essential operations. You'll see a variety of types of icons, most with some sort of "extension," or additional file abbreviation after a period.

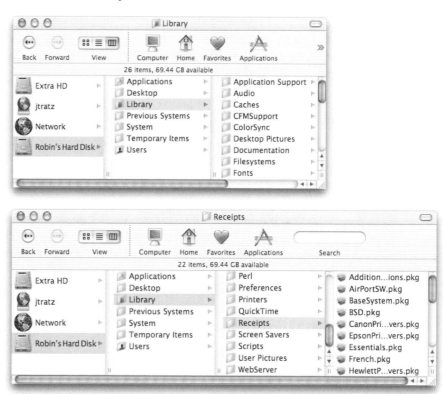

▼ Double-clicking on most system icons (the ones that aren't blank, as discussed on the previous page) will give you the message shown below. This is because most system icons are just visual representations of the data on your disk that makes them work—there's really nothing to look at besides the cute little icon.

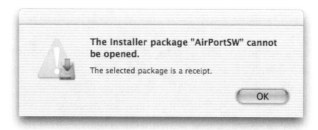

To rename any icon—a folder, a document, a program, a disk—just click once on the icon's *name* (not on the icon's *graphic*); wait a second or two until a box appears around the name so you know you're changing it, then simply type the new name. **Or** instead of clicking directly on the name, click anywhere on the icon to select it, then press Return to get that box around it (this is actually faster than clicking on the name).

Renaming Icons

Don't rename any of the folders in your Home folder!

All Things Hushed

Click once on the name to select it . . .

All Things Hushed

you'll see a box around the name . . .

Sweet Silent Thought

then just type to replace the selected name.

In changing the name, you can use standard word processing techniques, as detailed in Chapter 13, to set an "insertion point" (the flashing vertical bar, your **visual clue** that you are in typing mode). Or double-click a *word* to select the whole word, backspace to delete characters, etc. You can use your arrow keys to move the insertion point. In fact, press the UpArrow or DownArrow to move the insertion point to the very beginning or the very end of the name. As soon as you click somewhere else, or hit the Return or Enter keys, the name is set.

Tip: You can also use the Get Info box to change the names of icons. Open Get Info for a selected icon (press Command I), then retype the name at the top of the box.

If you do **accidentally change the name** of an icon (which is very easy to do—files have been known to mysteriously change their names to \\\\\\ \\\\\\ or ˋˋˋˋˋˋ while you weren't doing anything but leaning on the keyboard), you do have one chance to restore the name to its original form: **Undo.** As soon as you see the mistake has been made, from the Edit menu choose "Undo." *If you haven't done anything* since this minor catastrophe (and things could be worse), Undo will restore the original name, even if you forgot it. In fact, you can undo the name on one file until you change another name—check the Edit menu; if you can still Undo the change, the first thing in the Edit menu will be "Undo Rename"; choose it. If you are too late to catch Undo, you'll just have to rename it yourself (if you know what it was). Remember, the keyboard shortcut for Undo is Command Z.

Undoing a Name Change

You **cannot change the name** of a folder, disk, application, or any other icon that is **locked,** as described on the following page.

If You Can't Change the Name

Locking a File

You can see information about every file icon in a **Get Info** window (details about Get Info are in Chapter 28). One of the things you can do in a Get Info window is **lock** a file so no one can make changes to it.

To get the Get Info window: In the Finder, click once on an icon, then press Command I *or* go the the File menu and choose "Get Info."

There is a "Locked" checkbox in the lower-left corner of the Get Info window. If you check this box (click once on it), this file cannot be renamed or inadvertently thrown away—as soon as it hits the Trash, a dialog box comes up telling you a locked file cannot be thrown away. It also becomes a **read-only** file: anyone can open and read the file, but no one can save any changes to it. You can't even change the Get Info comments. This is handy for sending around copies of a document and ensuring no one accidentally changes anything.

To lock the file, click in the checkbox.

To unlock the file, click in the checkbox again. If there is no ✔, the file is unlocked.

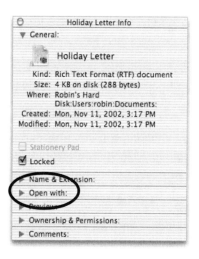

If you look very closely at a locked file, you'll see a tiny padlock in the lower-left corner.

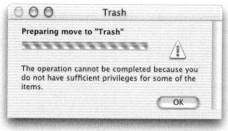

This message can mean a file is locked.

As you can see, this isn't a very secure way to safeguard a file—all anyone has to do is Get Info and unlock it. It's just a way to prevent things from happening to the file accidentally.

You'll find there are a number of files you cannot lock, including all of your Home folders. Apple is trying to protect you from yourself.

Tip: If Mac OS X yells at you because a file is locked, but the "Locked" button is not checked in Get Info, it may have been checked in OS 9 in Get Info. Restart your Mac in OS 9, unlock the file, then go back to OS X.

To move icons, simply press-and-drag them. You can put any icon into or drag any icon out of any *folder* icon.

▼ When you drag an icon (or any file, no matter what it looks like) from one place to another **on the same disk,** the computer **moves** it to the other place.

▼ When you drag a file **from one disk to another disk,** the computer **copies** it to the other disk. For details about copying, see Chapter 11.

You can **create your own icons** and apply them to any existing icons, and you can copy icons from one file and apply them to another.

▼ Open an OS X graphic program like AppleWorks (paint or draw). Or use any clipart or photo image instead.

▼ In the graphic program, create the little picture that you want as your icon. No matter what size you make the art, the Mac will reduce it to an appropriate size as it becomes the new icon. But if you make it too large, it will be unrecognizable when reduced.

▼ Select the image you created or found; copy it (from the Edit menu).

▼ Go back to a Finder window.

▼ Click once on the icon whose picture you want to replace. From the File menu, choose "Get Info" (**or** press Command I).

▼ Click once on the icon that appears in the upper-left of the Get Info window (see below, circled).

▼ From the Edit menu, choose "Paste" (**or** press Command V).

▼ Close the Get Info window (press Command W).

Although this can be a wonderful trick, I don't like to encourage beginners to change all their icons because that original icon tells you so much information. If you start changing icons, how do you know what will happen when you double-click? Is this object a folder that will open to a window, or is it an application, a document, a system icon, or what? Just be sensible.

Click here to select the icon's image, either to paste in a new one or to clear out an existing one.

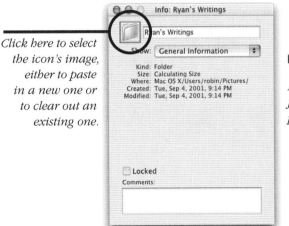

Ryan's Writings

I changed the standard folder icon, above, to a photo of Ryan, below.

Ryan's Writings

To change an icon back to the original, select its tiny icon in the Get Info window; from the Edit menu, choose "Cut." The original icon will appear.

Draw lines to match the description with the icon. Carefully read through the list first—although there are several similar icons, each has a different visual clue.

application

hard disk

CD

folder

document

Zip disk

unknown document

selected icon

locked icon

Trash can

DVD

ready to rename

stationery/template

Little Mac Book

Ryan's Writings

FontDisc

sonnets.idd

CASABLANCA

Favorites

version.plist

All Things Hushed

To Do List

Mac OS X

Holiday Letter

TextEdit

Answers on page 730.

All About the Dock

The **Dock** is that strip across the bottom of your screen that contains a number of icons. Apple has put those icons in the Dock for your use, but you can customize it endlessly, as explained on the following pages. You can add folders, applications, web sites, documents, windows, or just about anything else to the Dock—once an item is in the Dock, you just single-click to open it. You can delete items, rearrange items, move the Dock to the left or right of your screen, enlarge it, reduce it, hide it, and more.

This is the Dock. If you're a Mac user from way back, you'll discover that the Dock takes the place of the traditional Apple menu, the Application menu, and the Application Switcher.

Contents of the chapter

The Basic Dock

Below is a typical Dock with brief explanations of what each item does and where you can find more information about it. Items marked with an asterisk (*) will *automatically* connect you to the Internet (if your connection has been set up and is ready to go; if not, see Chapter 30).

Finder: click to open the main Finder window. Chapter 9.

iChat: chat with other people. Chapter 33.*

Internet Explorer: a browser for viewing web pages. Chapter 31.*

Sherlock: find information on the Internet. Chapter 31.*

***Dividing line:** applications to the left, everything else to the right.*

Trash: throw files away. Chapter 17.

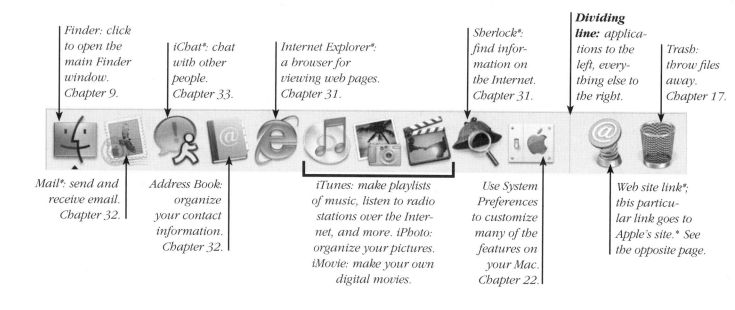

Mail: send and receive email. Chapter 32.*

Address Book: organize your contact information. Chapter 32.

iTunes: make playlists of music, listen to radio stations over the Internet, and more. iPhoto: organize your pictures. iMovie: make your own digital movies.

Use System Preferences to customize many of the features on your Mac. Chapter 22.

Web site link; this particular link goes to Apple's site.* See the opposite page.*

Every now and then one of your Dock icons might turn into a question mark or the generic OS X icon.

Drag the question mark out of the Dock and replace it with the original item, as explained on the opposite page.

The generic icon is okay. It still works just the same, and when you restart your Mac, your real icon will probably come back.

Position your mouse over a Dock item (don't click or press), and a "tool tip" appears above the Dock to tell you what that item is.

To find the window that stores a particular icon, press (don't click!) to get a pop-up menu; choose "Show in Finder" and the window that holds the icon will open.

***Or** Command-click (don't press!) on the icon and the folder that holds the icon will instantly open.*

Add Items to the Dock

You can **add** anything you want to the Dock. Typically, you'll add files and folders that you want easy access to. You'll notice when you add *application icons,* they go on the *left* side of the dividing line. All other icons must stay to the *right* of the dividing line.

To add a file: Find its icon (folder, application icon, document icon, etc.), then simply drag that icon down to the Dock and let go. You are not actually *moving* the file—you are simply adding an "alias" of it to the Dock (an alias goes and gets the real file; see Chapter 23 about aliases).

To add an open application: While the application is open and active, you will see its icon in the Dock. Press on that icon and you'll get a pop-up menu; choose "Keep in Dock" (shown to the right).

To add a web site: Using Internet Explorer, go to the web site you like. In the Address bar, drag the little @ symbol (circled, right) down to the Dock. If you are using Netscape, drag the Bookmark icon (next to the Location box) to the Desktop, then drag that icon into the Dock.

When you add a folder, you can *click* its icon in the Dock to open the folder window, or *press* to pop up a menu listing every item in the folder (shown to the right). Slide up to choose an item in the list and that particular file will open. If you have folders inside this folder, you will get a submenu showing the items in that subfolder. Notice, however, that the folder icon in the Dock gives you no visual clue as to *which* folder it is. You can customize its icon, if you like (see page 117), so you can identify individual folders without having to mouse over each one.

When you press on a folder in the Dock, there is a slight delay before the folder menu pops up. To make it pop up instantly, Control-click the folder icon.

Rearrange Items in the Dock

To move the positions of items in the Dock, simply press-and-drag them. Only application items are allowed to the left of the dividing line, however; everything else must stay to the right.

Remove Items from the Dock

To remove items from the Dock, simply press-and-drag them off the Dock and drop them anywhere on the Desktop. A cute little "poof" will appear. Don't worry—you won't destroy the original files. All you remove is an icon from the Dock—you won't hurt the original application, folder, file, web site, or anything else. (You cannot remove the Trash basket or the Finder icon, though.)

This is the "poof" that appears when you remove something from the Dock.

Dock Preferences

System Preferences icon

Dock icon

You have control over several aspects of the Dock. To get the Dock preferences pane shown below, click the System Preferences icon (as shown to the left) in the Dock, and then click the "Dock" icon (also shown to the left).

Or from the Apple menu, choose "Dock...." From there you can either change several settings using that menu, or choose "Dock Preferences..." to get the preferences pane shown below.

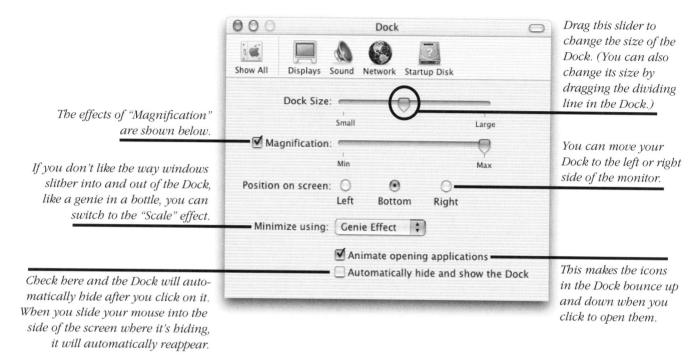

Drag this slider to change the size of the Dock. (You can also change its size by dragging the dividing line in the Dock.)

The effects of "Magnification" are shown below.

If you don't like the way windows slither into and out of the Dock, like a genie in a bottle, you can switch to the "Scale" effect.

You can move your Dock to the left or right side of the monitor.

This makes the icons in the Dock bounce up and down when you click to open them.

Check here and the Dock will automatically hide after you click on it. When you slide your mouse into the side of the screen where it's hiding, it will automatically reappear.

When "Magnification" is checked, the Dock icons grow as you run your mouse over them. How large they grow depends on where you set the Magnification slider.

*There is a **shortcut** to get the Dock preferences: Control-click on the divider line in the Dock and change your preferences from the pop-up menu.*

The **triangles** you see under certain icons in the Dock are very important **visual clues.** A triangle means that particular application is open at the moment. Because you can see the Dock at all times (unless you choose to hide it), you are constantly aware of which and how many applications are open at any given moment.

To **quit an application,** you don't even need to bring the application forward: just *press* on its icon in the Dock, and in the pop-up menu, choose "Quit."

The triangle indicates the application is open. Press on the icon to get the pop-up menu to Quit.

Here are a few extra tips and tricks for using the Dock.

To enlarge or reduce the Dock, simply grab the dividing line (shown at the bottom of the opposite page), press, and drag. The Dock will enlarge or reduce as you drag. Let go and it will stay that size until you change it again.

To hide the window that's currently in the foreground when you open or go to another application: Hold down the Option key when you click an application icon in the Dock, or when you click any visible area of the Desktop.

To hide all the windows of all other open applications, hold down the Command and the Option keys when you click an application icon in the Dock.

To find where a docked item is located on your hard disk: Hold down the Command key and click on its icon in the Dock—the folder in which the item is stored will open on your Desktop. As mentioned and shown on page 120, you can also press on the icon to get a pop-up menu, then choose "Show in Finder."

To switch between open applications: Hold down the Command key and tap the Tab key. Each time you tap the Tab key, the next open application icon in the Dock (moving towards the right) will highlight. Just keep pressing Tab until you select the icon you want—then let go of the Command (and Tab) key and the selected application will come forward. (The Finder is considered an application.) Try it.

To cycle through the open applications in the other direction (going left in the Dock), hold down Command and Shift, then Tab.

To switch instantly to the last application you used: Command Tab just once and let go.

To send windows to the Dock in slow motion: Hold down the Option key when you close a window. Useless trick, but pretty. Try it.

Triangles in the Dock

Quit an Application from the Dock

Dock Tips and Tricks

Practice: Position your mouse over the dividing line in the Dock, press, and drag upward to **enlarge** the Dock. Drag downward to **reduce** it.

Hide and show the Dock:

1. Hold down the Control key and click on the dividing line to get the pop-up menu; choose "Turn Hiding On."

2. Now move your mouse away from the Dock and watch the Dock slide away.

3. Then move your mouse down to the bottom of your screen (don't press the mouse button down) and the Dock will slide up; when you move your mouse away, the Dock disappears.

4. If you want the Dock visible all the time, slide your mouse down so the Dock appears. Hold down the Control key and click on the dividing line to get the pop-up menu; choose "Turn Hiding Off."

1. Describe two ways to move the Dock from the bottom of the screen to either side.

   _____

2. How do you remove an item from the Dock?

   _____

3. How do you rearrange items in the Dock?

   _____

4. Which items in the Dock cannot be moved nor rearranged?

   _____

5. What sort of files can you add to the Dock?

   _____

6. If you add a folder to the Dock, what happens when you **click** on the folder icon?

   _____

7. If you add a folder to the Dock, what happens when you **press** on the folder icon?

   _____

8. How can you resize the Dock itself?

   _____

9. Describe three ways to get the Dock preferences.

   a. _____

   b. _____

   c. _____

10. How can you hide the Dock?

   _____

Answers on page 730.

The Desktop, Finder, and Home

The **Desktop** is what you see on your computer monitor when you start up your Mac. It's the background that the windows and the Dock sit on, and you probably have disk icons also sitting on the Desktop. The Desktop is a *place*. (In your Home area you'll see an icon called "Desktop" which is actually a folder that holds the same things you see on the Desktop itself.)

The **Finder** is actually a *software application* that displays and controls the windows, menus, icons, etc., that you see on the Desktop. **Finder windows** are those windows on the Desktop that show you what is stored inside of your computer.

Home is a collection of folders that are for *your* use, as opposed to the collection of folders that the *Mac* uses to run itself with. You'll keep all of your work and personal files, fonts, and applications in your Home folders. You can create multiple users for one computer, and every user has his or her own Home. When more than one person uses the machine, or on a "network" of connected Macs, as in a school or office, everyone's Home folders are protected from every other user.

Contents of this chapter

The Desktop

Below you see a working **Desktop,** which probably looks very similar to the one on your Mac. You can store items directly on the Desktop, as shown below—you don't have to put everything in the Dock that you want to keep handy. The big difference between storing things in the Dock vs. on the Desktop is that the Dock is always available and accessible, no matter which application you are using, whereas the Desktop might be covered up by the window of an application. Keeping that in mind, feel free to store some of your most-used folders, documents, or applications right on the Desktop. It's best to use **aliases** for most things you want to keep on the Desktop—see Chapter 23 for alias details.

This is my mother's Home window. Click once on the Home icon in any Toolbar, like you see here, to open your Home area.

This is actually a folder. It contains the same things you see sitting directly on the Desktop (except for the hard disks, which are displayed in the Computer window.)

You can see here that she's storing several files right on the Desktop. If you were to double-click the "Desktop" icon in the window you see above, it would display the same document and folder items.

*The folder named **Desktop (Mac OS 9)** is an "alias," or an empty icon that goes to get the real thing. If you were using Mac OS 9 and had stored items on the Desktop, you'll now find those items in this folder.*

You might not see this folder. It is only useful if you have Mac OS 9 installed on the same hard disk or "partition" as Mac OS X. If you have multiple partitions, each volume will have its own "Desktop Folder" with all of the items that you had left on the Desktop.

*If you double-click this folder and you get a message that the **original item could not be found**—don't worry. Just throw this icon in the Trash basket (see Chapter 17).*

You can **change the background of your Desktop.** Apple provides several collections of images for you, from solid colors to nature scenes to wild abstract graphics. Or you can use any graphic you have on your computer as a background. You might want to use your favorite holiday photo, a family portrait, or your daughter's kindergarten handprint.

If you have images outside of your computer and don't know yet how to get them inside, have a friend help you. Once an image is "digitized," or turned into a digital image so the computer can handle it, put the image in your Pictures folder, which is in your Home. Then follow the directions below to use it as a background.

To change the background of the Desktop:

1. From the Apple menu, choose "System Preferences…."

2. In the System Preferences pane, click on the button "Desktop," shown to the right. You'll get the Desktop pane, as shown below.

3. Now you can do one of several things:

    ▼ You see a row of images along the bottom. Click once on any one of those images and it will appear in the "well" above.

    ▼ **Or** click on the "Collection" menu and choose from other collections Apple has provided, as shown below. —*continued*

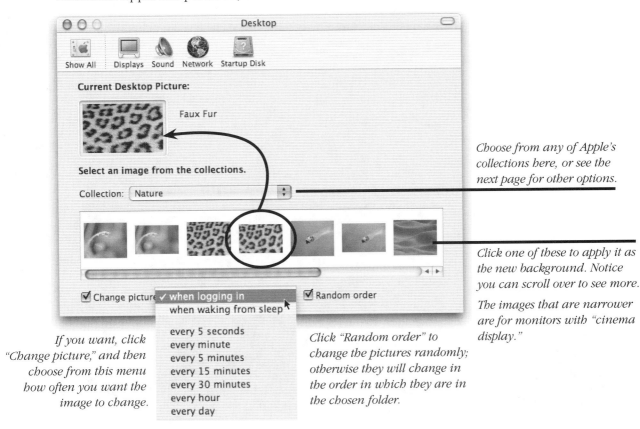

Choose from any of Apple's collections here, or see the next page for other options.

Click one of these to apply it as the new background. Notice you can scroll over to see more.

The images that are narrower are for monitors with "cinema display."

If you want, click "Change picture," and then choose from this menu how often you want the image to change.

Click "Random order" to change the pictures randomly; otherwise they will change in the order in which they are in the chosen folder.

▼ **Or** drag an image from anywhere on your computer and drop it right into the well. You'll have to find the file you want to drop in and position it on your screen so when you open the Desktop pane, you can still see the file. Then just drag it from your Desktop to the well.

▼ **Or** store images you want to use in your Pictures folder in your Home. Then in the Desktop pane, click the "Collection" menu and choose "Pictures Folder." All of the images you have in your folder will appear in the slot along the bottom. Click one of them.

When you choose your own picture as a background, you get options to fill the screen with the image, stretch it, center it, or tile it.

Fill screen: *enlarges the image to fill the entire Desktop, which will cut off the edges of most images.*

Stretch to fill screen: *distorts the image to cover the Desktop.*

Center: *centers the image at actual size, and gives you a color box (click it) where you can choose a color for the rest of the background.*

Tile: *repeats the image across the entire Desktop.*

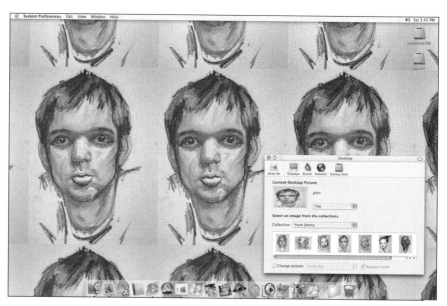

This image is tiled.

These portraits are drawn by my son, Jimmy Thomas. He's studying print-making at the Pacfic Northwest College of Art in Portland, Oregon. He's great.

This image is enlarged to fill the screen.

If you like to keep icons on your Desktop, you have a few **options** for how they are arranged and how large they appear. You can also use the "Clean Up" and "Arrange by Name" choices in the View menu (see Chapter 6). Just make sure you first click on the Desktop so the *Desktop* is active, not a window, before you go to the View menu and make a choice.

To change the size of icons and text labels on the Desktop:

1. Make sure the Desktop is active: click once on it.

2. From the View menu, choose "Show View Options," or press Command J.

3. In the View Options dialog box, as shown to the right, you should see the word "Desktop" in the title bar. If you see anything else, just click right now on an empty spot on the Desktop and the name in this title bar will change to "Desktop."

4. To change the size of icons, just drag the "Icon size" slider bar (circled, left). You'll see the icons currently on your Desktop change shape. Choose a text size. Close the box when items are sized to your liking.

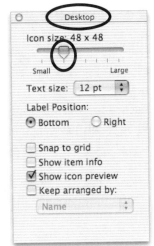

Desktop View Options

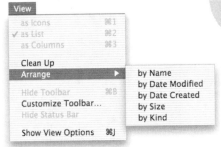

You can tell when the Desktop is properly selected because all other options in this menu will be gray except the ones shown above.

There is an invisible, underlying grid on the Desktop that is sized to fit your icons. You can force all Desktop icons to snap into the cells of this invisible grid: choose **Snap to grid,** as shown below.

Show item info adds information that tells you how many items are in a folder, how large some graphics are, and how long certain sound files are.

Show icon preview will display a small picture of a graphic files instead of a generic icon.

As you add and delete icons from the Desktop, you can force them to stay in a pre-arranged order: check **Keep arranged by,** then click on the menu that appears and choose the order in which you want them arranged.

With the "Keep arranged by" option on, you might think your icons are "stuck" in certain spots because you can't move them out of their arranged positions. **To move icons freely,** open the Desktop View Options and uncheck "Keep arranged by." **Or** hold down the Command key and drag icons.

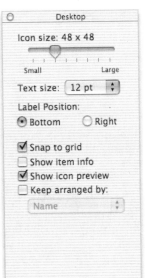

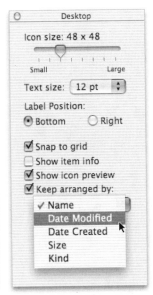

Tip: Whether you choose to "Keep arranged by" or not, you can always ***override*** the current setting: hold down the Command key and drag an icon.

Computer Level

The **Computer level** in a Finder window shows you all the possible "storage devices," or "volumes," you have available. Storage devices include your own hard disk, including any "partitions" you might have separated it into (see Chapter 38 about partitions). If you are in an office or school facility that uses "servers," or big computers that store files and send them out to other computers for others to use, you will see icons for the servers in the Computer level. You will also see any computers that you are connected to over any kind of network, such as in a small home office (the Mac considers all computers that you are connected to in any way to be "servers").

If you have an extra hard disk attached to your Mac, such as a FireWire hard disk, its icon will appear here. Any removable disks you have "mounted" (inserted into your Mac and are now available to use) will show their icons here. So this level basically shows you every possible media that is connected to your computer at the moment, media that you can take files from or store files onto.

Click this icon to see the Computer level of your Mac. Notice the title bar tells you whose computer you are looking at.

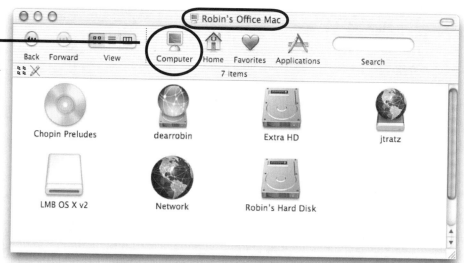

*This **Computer window** shows two hard disks because I installed an extra one in my Mac.*

You see a network icon (jtratz), which is one of the other computers in my home office that I can share files with.

You see a removable disk (LMB OSX v2); this particular one is a Zip disk.

You see one CD (Chopin Preludes), which is a music CD.

The big world icon named "Network" is actually a folder that provides access to your corporate network, if you're on one. If you have a small office on a local area network or if you have no network at all, you will never need to use this icon.

Finder Preferences

In the **Finder Preferences,** you have control over several Desktop features.

To open the Finder Preferences:

At the Desktop, go to the Finder menu and choose "Preferences...."

"Show these items on the Desktop"

You can decide which icons automatically appear on the **Desktop.** As shown below, you can uncheck the "Hard disks" box so hard disk icons do not appear on the Desktop. You can also uncheck "Removable media," which means you won't see any CD, DVD, Jaz, Zip, floppy, or any other kind of icons that represent disks you have inserted into drives. If you are on a network and can connect to other computers, an icon appears on your Desktop that represents the other computer, or server; you can turn off that icon as well. The reason it's not important to have these appear on your Desktop is that every one of these icons appears in your Computer level window, as described on the opposite page. So you can uncheck these boxes and clear off your Desktop.

"New Finder Window shows"

When you first click on the Finder icon (the smiling face) in the Dock, and whenever you press Command N to get a new window, the Mac automatically opens a **Finder window** that displays the **Computer** level, as shown on the opposite page. It might be more useful to you if the window always opened to display your **Home** folders instead; if so, click in the "Home" button. Home is explained on the following pages.

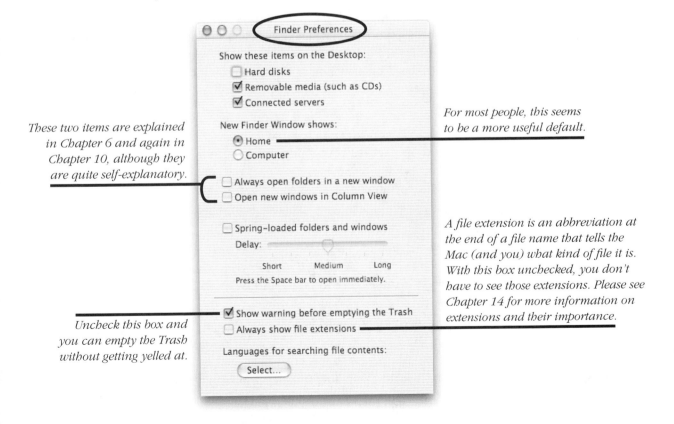

These two items are explained in Chapter 6 and again in Chapter 10, although they are quite self-explanatory.

For most people, this seems to be a more useful default.

A file extension is an abbreviation at the end of a file name that tells the Mac (and you) what kind of file it is. With this box unchecked, you don't have to see those extensions. Please see Chapter 14 for more information on extensions and their importance.

Uncheck this box and you can empty the Trash without getting yelled at.

Your Home **Home** is an area of your Mac that Apple has set up for you to work in. It has a number of folders already created in which you can store your work, and a Public folder in which you can put files you want to share with others who might use the machine. If you are the only person who ever uses the computer, you are still considered one of the "users" and you have a password—remember that password you choose the first time you turned on the machine? You had better remember that password.

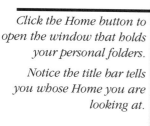

Click the Home button to open the window that holds your personal folders.

Notice the title bar tells you whose Home you are looking at.

Do not move or rename any of the folders in your Home area! They have important jobs to do and Mac OS X depends on being able to find their names and locations. Below are descriptions of how you can use these folders on your own Mac; if you have a .Mac account (see pages xxi–xxii), your Mac will use these folders to post items to the web in a variety of ways.

Desktop: Although its icon is different, this is actually a folder. It contains any folders or documents that are sitting on your Desktop, as described on page 126. Anything you put on the Desktop (except disks and servers) will appear in this folder, and anything you put in this folder will appear on the Desktop. (Disk and server icons appear in the Computer level window, as explained on page 130.)

Documents: When you are creating your own documents, such as letters, brochures, flyers, etc., and choose to "Save" the file, the Mac automatically opens your Documents folder so you can save it in there. This way you always know where to go to find what you created. It's certainly possible to save your documents into any other folder you want, including new folders you make; see Chapter 14.

Library: The Library folder stores a lot of other folders that hold information the Mac needs to run your Home. This is where you might put new fonts (in the Fonts folder inside the Library folder), where your new applications will store their own preferences, and more. Fonts are about the only things you will ever put in your Library folder.

Movie: If you use iMovie to create a movie from your video camera, the Mac will automatically save your movie into this folder. If you have a still digital camera that records short clips, the Mac will automatically offload them from your camera to this folder.

Music: Store music files in this folder. If you've used iTunes already, you'll find a folder inside Music called "iTunes." When you import songs from audio CDs, they are automatically stored in this folder. You can change the location of this folder through the iTunes preferences.

Pictures: When you import photographs from your digital camera, they are automatically saved into this folder. You can put the photos anywhere else you like, but if they are in this folder they are easily accessible when you want to change your Desktop background (see pages 127–128) or make a customized screensaver (Chapter 28).

Public: Files you put in the Public folder are accessible to other users of the computer, while the rest of your Home folders will be locked to anyone else. No one can *remove* the file from your Public folder— it will always be automatically *copied* to another user.

Other users can put files *for you* into your "Drop Box" folder, which is inside your Public folder (see the following page). But no one can take anything *out* of your Drop Box, so if you want to give someone a file, be sure put it in your Public folder.

Sites: If you turn on "Web Sharing" in the Sharing preferences pane, any web pages you store in this folder can be seen on the Internet, once you are connected and tell someone the address. See Chapter 36.

The **Shared folder** is not in your Home area, but one level back, in the "Users" level (as shown on the following page). Anything you put in this folder can be used by all other users, and they won't have to open your Home area to get to it. If you want to share a file with every other user on this computer, like a teacher might in a school lab, you can put the file in this Shared folder and everyone can copy it to their own Home Documents folder. This is an easier way to share among multiple users than to copy the file into every one of their Drop Box folders.

A file from the Shared folder cannot be *removed*—it will be always be *copied* to another user's folder.

Every user uses the same Shared folder. But only the user who put the file inside the Shared folder in the first place will be allowed to move it, rename it, trash it, etc. Everyone else can only copy it.

The Shared folder

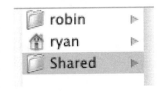

In the Users folder, you will see icons for every user. Only the person who is logged in will have the Home icon next to their name.

The Shared folder is accessible to everyone.

Safe and protected   An important feature about the Home area is that it is automatically **protected** from anyone else who uses the same computer. And there are several extra ways you can protect your personal files, fonts, and applications.

▼ You can make the Mac ask for a login password when the machine is turned on, even if you are the only user.

▼ You can set up the screensaver to turn on when you are away from the computer, and then make it password protected—someone must type in a password before the screensaver turns off.

▼ You can "lock" your computer when you walk away from it instead of waiting for the screensaver to turn on, or instead of having to type in a password every time the screensaver turns on; see page 285.

▼ You can set up two users for yourself: Create one that has administrative privileges so you can add and delete applications, fonts, etc. Set up another user for yourself that does not have administrative privileges, then log on as that user. Even if someone did use your machine, they could not add or delete any files in critical folders (although they would have access to your personal folders).

See Chapter 20 for details on how to make all of these things happen.

Sharing files with another user   When others log in as **different users,** they each get their own Home areas. They can load their own fonts; safely store their own documents; set the Desktop preferences, Finder preferences, and window view preferences to accommodate themselves; add new folders; and organize their files however they like. Even the Trash basket belongs to each alone—every user has their own Trash and can choose to empty it when they feel like it.

This computer has two users, me and Ryan. You can tell I am the user logged in at the moment because the Home icon is next to "robin."

*But I have selected the user folder "ryan" and I can see his Home folders. Notice every folder except "Public" and "Sites" has a "Do not enter" symbol on it. This is a **visual clue** that I cannot open or put anything into his other folders.*

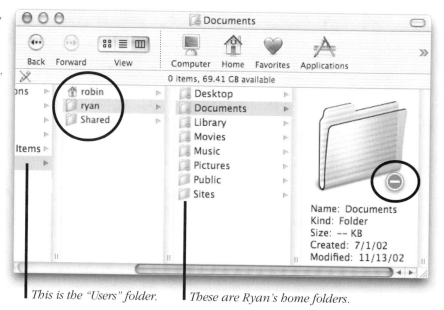

This is the "Users" folder.   *These are Ryan's home folders.*

Although you are locked out of most of the other users' folders, you can **give a copy of a file** to someone else by dropping it in their **Drop Box,** which is located in their Public folder, as shown below. (For more information about moving or copying files from one folder to another, see Chapter 11.)

The Drop Box

This is Ryan's Home folder.

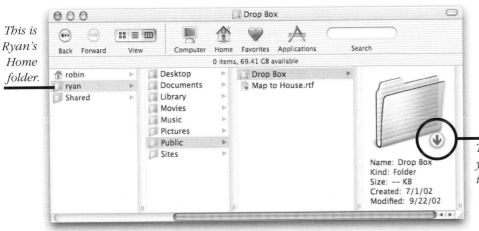

This symbol indicates you can put things inside this folder.

I am logged on as the user "robin." Here, I selected Ryan's Home folder, then his Public folder, then the Drop Box.

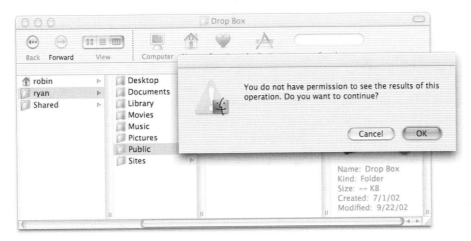

*I dragged a document file from the Desktop and dropped it in Ryan's Drop Box (**not** in the Public folder—you are not allowed to put things in someone else's Public folder). This message appears, which is okay— it just means you can't open the Drop Box and make sure the file really got put inside.*

For details about how to create new users, delete others, share files, add applications and fonts to your Home, and more, see Chapter 20.

General Preferences

The **General** preferences give you several options that apply to different parts of your computer. To open this, go to the Apple menu, choose "System Preferences...," then click on the "General" icon.

If you change this option to "Graphite," the red, yellow, and green buttons in your windows will all be gray.

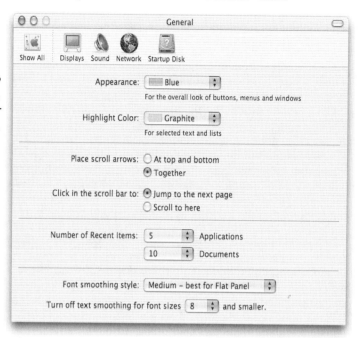

Appearance: Choose between the Blue or the Graphite look for all of your buttons, scroll bar sliders, the selection bar in menus, etc.

Highlight Color: Click this menu to get a list of color choices, or choose "Other..." and build your own color. The one you choose will be the color of the selection when you select text in a word processor, a file in a window, or an entry in an "edit box" in any dialog box.

Place scroll arrows and **Click in the scroll bar to:** I explained these in Chapter 6, page 71 and 73. They're fairly self-explanatory.

Number of Recent Items: Click these menus to choose how many applications and documents the Mac will keep track of and list in the "Recent Items" command in the Apple menu. See page 139 for details.

Font smoothing style: Choose your monitor type here.

Once you know how to do one thing, move on to the next. —*James Baldwin*

Once you know how to do one thing, move on to the next. —*James Baldwin*

These two examples are the same text, same size, same typeface, in the same application. The top example has text smoothing applied; the bottom one doesn't.

Turn off text smoothing: Text smoothing is a feature that blurs the edges of text so it appears smoother on the screen (not in print). Sometimes, however, in very small type (say, 8 or 10 point) the blurring effect makes the type more difficult to read; hence you have this option to turn it off for smaller sizes. You can't turn it off altogether, though. Experiment with the size options and see what you prefer. For Photoshop, make sure you set this to 8 points.

If you've worked with image-editing programs, "text smoothing" is "anti-aliasing."

Each of the items on the *left* side of the **Finder menu bar** are explained either in the following pages or in other chapters, as noted below. The items on the far-*right* of the menu bar appear not just in the Finder, but in every application. That is, you will always have access to whatever is on the right side. They are explained on this page.

You can remove these items, if you like, and there are others you can add. If you *can* add or remove something, you'll find a checkbox in its preferences (found in the System Preferences pane) that says something like, "Show the clock in the menu bar."

The Finder Menu Bar

If you have an AirPort card installed in your Mac, you'll see this icon. See Chapter 28 about AirPort.

See pages 138–139.   *See page 142.*   *See Chapter 6.*   *See page 95.*   *See page 285.*

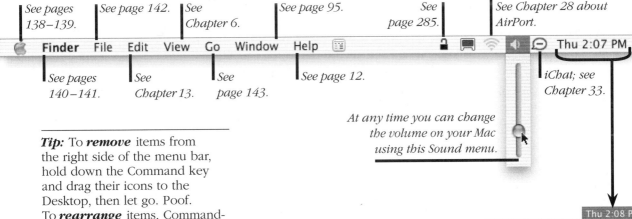

See pages 140–141.   *See Chapter 13.*   *See page 143.*   *See page 12.*   *iChat; see Chapter 33.*

At any time you can change the volume on your Mac using this Sound menu.

Tip: To **remove** items from the right side of the menu bar, hold down the Command key and drag their icons to the Desktop, then let go. Poof. To **rearrange** items, Command-drag an icon left or right.

Click once on the time and you'll get this menu where you can see the full date, choose to view a simple clock icon instead of the time, and open the "Date & Time" preferences pane, as shown below.

*If you change your monitor resolution or number of colors often, you can choose to "Show displays in menu bar," which will give you this icon and menu on the right side of your menu bar. **To add "Displays" to your menu bar,** open the System Preferences pane (click once on its icon in the Dock), then click the "displays" icon, and you'll see the checkbox.*

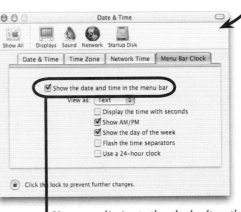

You can eliminate the clock altogether from the menu bar if you uncheck this box.

The Apple Menu

This is the Apple menu, something you will become very familiar with.

Tip: Click on the version number in the "About" box and you will see the "build" number of the version of Mac OS X you're running. Click again and you'll see the serial number of this Macintosh.

Click "More Info…" to get the Apple System Profiler that displays technical information about your Mac.

The **Apple menu** is the only menu on the left side of the menu bar that stays the same no matter which application you are using or where you are in your computer, so everything you see in this menu you can use at any time. Some of these items are discussed elsewhere in this book, but the others are explained below.

About This Mac: Choose this item to check on which version of the operating system you are using, as well as how much RAM (random access memory) you have installed in the machine. It also tells you, in case you didn't know, which "processor," or chip, is running your machine. As you can see by the dialog box to the right, this machine is "running" the operating system Mac OS X, version 10.2.2. It has 1.25 gigabytes of memory installed, and the Mac is using a PowerPC G4 processor.

Get Mac OS X Software: When you select this item, your web browser software will open, your Mac will try to connect to the Internet and if it is successful, you will be taken to Apple's web site where you can download software that you can use in OS X. You'll find free software ("freeware"); free updates for software you might already have ("updates"); software you can download to see if you like it ("demo") and if you do, you can buy it; and more. Also see the "Software Update" preferences in Chapter 22.

If you want to use this command and you have a "dial-up" Internet account (your modem dials a phone number and you're not permanently connected), *first* open your connection, *then* choose this command.

System Preferences: This opens the System Preferences pane, where you can customize a number of the features on your Mac, as well as set up your networking, choose to share files, and more. Choosing this item from the Apple menu is exactly the same as clicking on the System Preferences button in the Dock. Some of these preferences are explained individually in the chapters where they are pertinent, and the rest are in Chapter 22.

Dock: This provides a menu where you can change some of the Dock preferences, as you might have learned in Chapter 8, instead of having to open the Dock preferences pane. Choosing this is the same as Command-clicking on the Dock dividing line.

Location: A "location" is a set of networking preferences for connecting to the Internet or to other computers. Depending on your situation, you might only have one set that connects you to everything and so you never need to worry about this item. Or, like me, you might have one set of networking preferences to dial up through your modem to get connected to the Internet, and a different set that uses an "Ethernet" connection to share files with other computers. Or you might use a laptop and need different locations to get your laptop connected in different places. If so, use the Apple menu to quickly switch to a different location. For details about why and how to make locations, see Chapter 35.

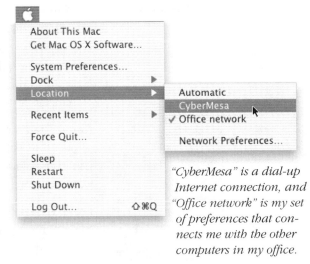

"CyberMesa" is a dial-up Internet connection, and "Office network" is my set of preferences that connects me with the other computers in my office.

Recent Items: Your Mac keeps track of a certain number of applications that you have recently used, as well as a certain number of documents that you have recently opened. Sometimes it is faster to go to the Apple menu and choose an application or document from Recent Items than it is to go digging around in your folders for them. You can determine how many items (if any) the Mac keeps track of in the General preferences, as shown on page 136. If you want to get rid of everything in the list and start over, choose "Clear Menu" from the list.

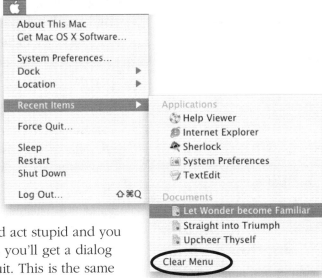

*You have a list of **"Recent Folders"** in the Go menu; see page 143.*

Recent items also appear in "Save As" and "Open" dialog boxes.

Force Quit: Sometimes applications get hung up and act stupid and you have to force them to quit. If you choose this item, you'll get a dialog box asking which program you want to force to quit. This is the same dialog box you get when you press Command Option Escape. Details about force quitting are in Chapter 16.

Sleep: When you put your computer to sleep, the Mac goes into a low-power mode that saves energy. The screen fades to black and your Mac sounds like it turned itself off, but it didn't. Depending on your computer, your power button might "pulse" yellow when it's asleep. Use the Energy Saver preferences (Chapter 22) to make your Mac go to sleep automatically after a certain period of inactivity.

Restart and **Shut Down:** Restart will power down your machine and bring it back up again without actually turning off the power to it. Shut Down will close everything up neatly and turn off the power. See Chapter 19.

Log Out: If there are multiple users on a machine, one logs out so the other can log in and access her own Home files. See Chapter 19.

Finder Menu

Most of the items you see in the **Finder menu** also appear in every program's **application menu,** which is what this actually is—it's the Finder's application menu. For instance, when you open the application Grab, there is a "Grab" menu that has these same menu items. When you open Internet Connect, there is an "Internet Connect" menu that has these same items. So below are explanations of these items that you will see in every program.

About The Finder: This gives you a small commercial about whatever application you're in. It might tell you who created it and when, and usually provides the "version number" of the software (every time software is improved and updated, it gets a new version number).

Preferences: Every application has preferences that you can change to customize the program for yourself. The **Finder Preferences** are explained on page 131.

Empty Trash: This is a feature specific to the Finder (that is, you won't find it in the application menu of other programs). Notice in this example there is an ellipsis (three dots) in the menu command. The ellipsis, remember from Chapter 5, is a **visual clue** that you will get a dialog box when you choose this item. In this case, the dialog box asks if you really want to throw away the stuff in the trash. Now, if you go to the Finder Preferences as shown on page 131 (choose "Preferences..." from this menu) and uncheck the box to warn you about emptying the trash, the ellipsis will disappear from this menu. This indicates, of course, that you *won't* get the warning dialog box.

Services: This is an interesting feature that you'll find in most applications that were created specifically for Mac OS X. It integrates the capabilities of a number of other possible applications into the one

you're using. For instance, let's say you're viewing a web page that has an interesting article. You can select the text in the article (click at the beginning, hold down the Shift key, and click at the end to select everything between the two clicks), then go to Services and choose "Summarize"; the Mac will take the first couple of sentences of each paragraph and put them into a TextEdit document for you. Or you might want to email a quote from the article: select the text you want to quote, from Services choose "Mail," then choose "Mail Text," and the Mac will open your email program, create a new message, and paste this quote into it. Or you might want to save a piece of text as a note to yourself: select the text, choose "Make New Sticky Note," and the Mac will make a sticky note with your text in it. Maybe you want your mail read out loud to you: Open a message, select the text you want read, then choose the Service "Speech" and "Start Speaking Text." (Check the index to learn how to use Mail, Stickies, and Speech.)

Hide Finder: Every application will change this command so it lets you "hide" the current application you are using; that is, if you're using AppleWorks, this item will be "Hide AppleWorks." When you hide something, it just temporarily disappears from the screen. It doesn't close or quit or really go away—it just becomes invisible. You will always know an application, document, folder, or window is still open because its icon will be in the Dock with a triangle under it. You can always go to any application menu (this menu, in any application or at the Desktop) and choose "Show All" to make everything that was hiding reappear (everything in every open application).

In the Finder (at the Desktop), when you choose this item, all of the open windows will disappear without getting sucked into the Dock; just click once on the Desktop and they will all reappear.

Hide Others: This will hide (as explained above) everything else on the screen *except* the windows in the current application. You will still see any icons you have sitting on the Desktop.

Show All: As explained above, this command will make everything reappear that had been previously hidden. "All" really means everything—every application and window that is open on your Mac—not just the windows in the active application.

Tip: To automatically hide the application you are currently working in when you go to the Desktop, hold down the Option key and click on any visible part of the Desktop. Your application will hide so you have a clear view of the Desktop.

File Menu

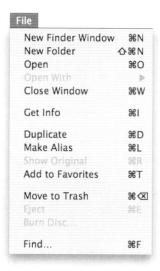

The **File menu** in the Finder has a collection of commands that only apply to certain things that are *active* or *selected* in the Finder. Be sure to make the desired window *active* first (click once in it) or *select* the icon first (click once on it) before you choose one of these commands.

New Finder Window: Opens a new window (you don't need to activate or select anything first). Actually, it opens another window of the *same* window that's on your screen. This is useful when you want to open, say, the Applications window, but you don't want to close the current window on your screen. Just open a new Finder window and click on its Application icon.

New Folder: This creates a new, untitled folder in the *active* window.

Open: This opens the *selected* icon, whether it's a folder, document, application, or anything else.

Open With: Instead of double-clicking on a selected document, come to this menu and choose the application you want to open that document, which might not be the one it was created in at all. Hold down the Option key to change this to **Always Open With** which will force all documents of the type selected to open in a chosen application.

Close Window: This closes the *active* window.

Get Info: The Get Info dialog box tells you information about the *selected* icon; hold down Option and this becomes **Show Inspector.** See pages 477–479 for details about Get Info and Show Inspector.

Duplicate: This makes a copy of the *selected* icon. The copy will appear in the same folder and its name will be the same as the original, with the word "copy" at the end.

Make Alias: This makes an alias, or a pointer, to the *selected* file. See Chapter 23 about how to use aliases.

Show Original: *Select* an alias icon, then choose this command to open the folder that stores the original item, which will be highlighted.

Add to Favorites: This makes an *alias* of (a pointer to) a selected item and puts that alias in the Favorites folder. Once an item is in that folder, you can open it from the Favorites submenu in the Go menu (see the opposite page), or you can open the Favorites folder and double-click the item in there. You can save into or open Favorites right from the Save As or Open dialog boxes. See Chapter 24 about Favorites.

Move to Trash: This moves the *selected* item or items to the Trash basket.

Eject: This ejects the *selected* removable disk. It will also disconnect you from a *selected* server.

Burn Disc: If your Mac can burn (copy or record onto) CDs and/or DVDs, use this menu command to start the process. See Chapter 14 for details.

Find: This command brings up the Search box so you can search for files on your computer. See Chapter 25.

Back and **Forward:** This is the same as clicking the Back or Forward buttons in the Toolbar. Notice there are keyboard shortcuts you can use instead (Command LeftBracket and RightBracket), which are the same shortcuts that will take you back and forward through pages in most web browsers.

The next five commands in the **Go menu** provide you with menu access or keyboard shortcuts to open the various windows of the icons you see in your Finder window Toolbar. For instance, even if there is no window open at all, you can choose "Applications" from this menu, or press Option Command A, and the Applications folder will open. You could close up your Toolbar, if you like, and use these keyboard shortcuts instead.

Favorites: You can open the Favorites folder or directly open any of the individual Favorites you have saved (see Chapter 24).

Recent Folders: Gives you a list of the ten folders you last opened. The list is in alphabetical order, not the order in which you opened the folders.

Go to Folder: In the box that appears when you choose this item, you can type the "path" to a folder name, hit Return, and that folder will open. The trick is you have to *know* the path, or the folders within folders where this particular folder is stored. Heck, if you know the path, it will take longer to type it in than to just open the folders and find the dang thing yourself. It's more useful if you're on a huge network.

The forward slash (/) indicates folders; type a slash between each folder name. The tilde (~) indicates Home folders; type ~ryan to open Ryan's (or whichever user you named) Home folder.

Go Menu

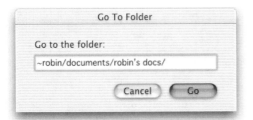

If there are no windows open on the Desktop when you choose "Go to Folder…," you get this dialog box.

You do not have to worry about capital letters when typing the path in this box.

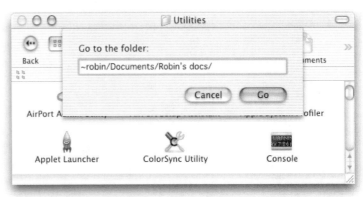

If a window is open, this "sheet" drops down out of the title bar.

If the folder you want is in this window, you don't have to type the path. (But if the folder you want is in this window, all you have to do is type the first couple letters of its name to select it anyway.)

Connect to Server: If you are on a network and want to connect to another computer to share files, use this command. See Chapter 35 for details.

1. Every disk and server icon that you see on the Desktop is also displayed in which window?

_____

2. Every document and application icon you might see on the Desktop is also displayed in which window?

_____

3. How would you make the "New Finder Window" command (Command N) open to the Home level instead of the Computer level?

_____

4. Can you stores files directly on the Desktop, instead of keeping all of them in the Finder?

_____

5. Describe how to arrange the files on your Desktop alphabetically.

_____

6. How do you change the color or picture of the Desktop?

_____

7. How can you change the size of the icons on the Desktop?

_____

8. How can you temporarily get rid of (hide) the windows of all applications you're not using at the moment?

_____

9. What is the Power User tip to go to the Desktop and make the windows of the active application disappear at the same time?

_____

10. If you want to share a file with everyone who uses the computer, where would you put it?

_____

Answers on page 730.

How to Use Folders

Folders are essential to organizing your work on the Mac. Folders are, of course, visual representations of our office and home environments, and they function in much the same way.

You can consider your computer to be a big filing cabinet. When you store items in a filing cabinet, you don't just toss them in the drawer, do you? Can you imagine what a mess your filing cabinet would be without folders? A Macintosh can become just as messy and just as difficult to find work in if you don't have some sort of organizational system. It's very important to learn to take advantage of the folders.

Contents of this chapter

Organizing Your Disk Using Folders

Folders keep your computer **well-organized.** Your Mac is basically arranged like a filing cabinet. You have several "drawers" already set up for you: Computer, Home, Favorites, and Applications. You can set up new storage drawers by placing your own folders in the Toolbar (see page 153). Within each drawer/folder (except Computer) you can add other folders, and folders inside of folders.

If you're a new user, you'll probably end up keeping most of your files in the Documents folder. That's fine until you start amassing a large collection of work—then you'll want to start organizing.

This is what your Documents folder can look like if you don't take advantage of organizing your files with folders.

Make new folders inside the Documents folder (or almost anywhere, actually) to organize all of your files.

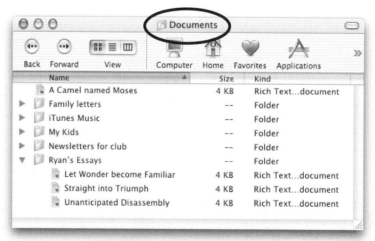

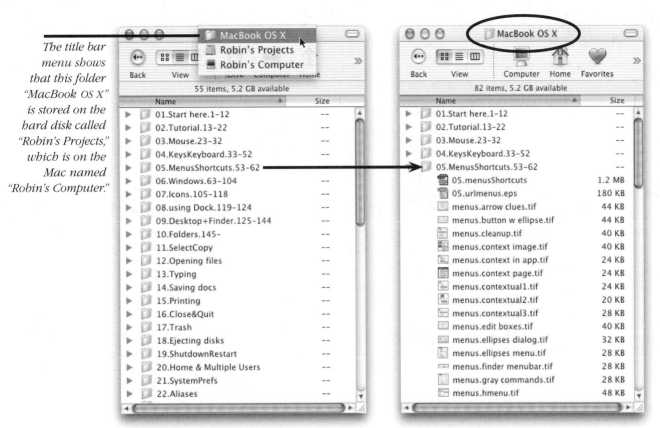

The title bar menu shows that this folder "MacBook OS X" is stored on the hard disk called "Robin's Projects," which is on the Mac named "Robin's Computer."

To store all of the files for this book, I made one folder named "MacBook OS X." Inside of that folder I made a separate folder for each chapter.

Each chapter folder contains the page layout file for the chapter, plus every illustration or screenshot (picture of something on the screen) that belongs in that chapter.

I named the folders according to their chapters. The numbers at the ends of the folder names are the current page numbers for that chapter so I can easily find what I'm looking for either by chapter number, title, or page number.

Understanding Folders

and how they display their contents in the different views

The contents of folders are always displayed in windows. As explained in Chapter 6, you can choose to see the contents of any window in three different views: Icon View, List View, and Column View. How you **open and display the folder** is a little different in each of these views.

Icon View

Icon View: In Icon View, **double-click** a folder to see its contents. Typically, the contents of this newly opened folder will *replace* what was just there. You can, as explained in Chapter 6, arrange to have a *new* window open every time you double-click a folder; see pages 79 and 96.

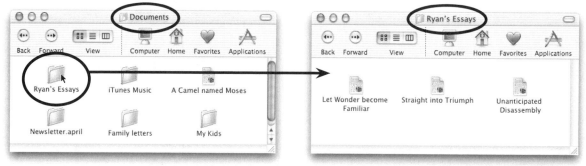

Double-click a folder to display what is stored inside. Notice the title bar will tell you which window is open.

Here you see the contents of the folder "Ryan's Essays," as you can tell by the title bar. Click the Back button to go back to the previous folder window.

Column View

Column View: In Column View, **single-click** a folder to see its contents in the column to its right, as shown below. You can also **double-click** a folder in Column View and its contents will open to *replace* this entire window instead of appearing in the next column. There are two exceptions to this:

▼ *If* you checked the box in the Finder Preferences (page 96) to make sure every window opens in the same view as the one before it, then nothing will happen when you double-click a folder.

▼ *Or if* you checked the box in Finder Preferences to always open folders into new windows, then a double-click opens a new window.

If you checked *both* boxes, the folder will open in a new window *and* it will be in Column View. But that's too much to think about—just work with the Column View and it will slowly start to make sense. As you grow accustomed to columns, experiment with the Finder Preferences; see page 96.

Single-click on a folder icon to display its contents in the column to the right.

The title bar tells you which folder the contents on the far right are contained in.

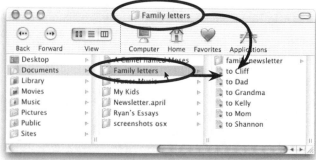

The **List View** is sometimes known as the **outline mode.** There's a tiny triangle next to each folder's name, and if you **single-click on that triangle** you can see what's in that folder without opening another window—as in the folder "Family letters" shown below. The items contained within a folder are indented just a little from the left, which is your **visual clue** that the items are *inside* the folder.

In the outline mode, you can keep opening folders within folders until you are all the way to the bottom level of your filing system, *with everything displayed in the same window.*

One benefit to this view is that you can see at a glance exactly how your files are organized and what's in them. You can move items from one folder to another, even if the folders are several levels apart. You can Command-click (page 163) to select items from any number of different folders, which is impossible to do if the folders are opened as individual windows. (See Chapter 11 about selecting files.)

▼ **To expand,** or *open* a folder, single-click on the little sideways-pointing triangle (or click on the folder icon and press Command RightArrow).

Expanding a folder

▼ **To compress,** or *close* a folder, single-click on the downward-pointing triangle (or click on the folder icon and press Command LeftArrow).

Compressing a folder

▼ To simultaneously **expand all the folders,** press Command A to select everything in the window. Then press Command RightArrow.

Expanding all folders

▼ To simultaneously **compress all the folders** that are expanded, press Command A to select everything in the window. Then press Command LeftArrow.

Compressing all folders

▼ **To open a folder in its own window,** *double-click* the folder icon, not the triangle. The contents of the new window will replace the current contents.

Opening a folder in its own window

Single-click the triangle to see the contents in a list.

Double-click the folder (not the triangle) to open the folder in its own window.

Creating a New Folder

It's easy **to create your own** new, empty folder.

1. If you want the new folder to sit directly on the **Desktop** (not in another window), first click on the Desktop.

   In **Icon View** or **List View,** make sure the window in which you want a new folder is *active* (click on it).

   In **Column View,** it's a little tricky to select the proper column; see the illustrations and captions below.

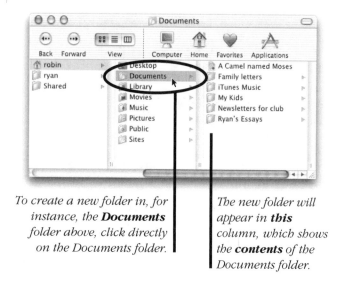

To create a new folder in, for instance, the **Documents** folder above, click directly on the Documents folder.

*The new folder will appear in **this** column, which shows the **contents** of the Documents folder.*

***Or** click an empty spot in the column that shows the **contents** of the Documents folder. The column will get a dark border around it, which is your **visual clue** that this column is selected and the new folder will appear in here.*

2. Once the proper location is selected, from the File menu, choose "New Folder," or use the keyboard shortcut, Command Shift N. A new, "untitled folder" will appear in the active window, as shown below. See the opposite page on how to name it.

This is the new folder in Icon View, ready for you to name it.

This is the new folder in Column View, ready for you to name it.

You can also create a new folder when you save a document, as described in Chapter 14.

Naming the New Folder

When the new folder appears in the active window, it's already *highlighted,* or *selected* (the **visual clue** is that it's dark), it has the name "untitled folder," and there is a border around the name, as shown below, because the Mac assumes you want to **change the name.** So while the folder is highlighted and has a border, **just type the name you want it to have and the new name will appear.** Yes, really, all you do is type. If you type an error, just backspace over the error (use the Delete key in the upper-right of the main keys) and continue typing. (See the following page if you blew it already.)

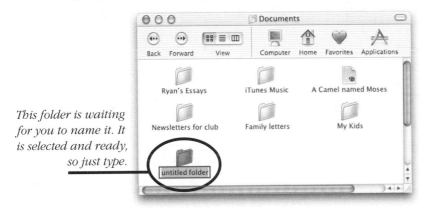

This folder is waiting for you to name it. It is selected and ready, so just type.

Tip: Don't start a folder name with a period (.), and don't use a colon (:) or a slash (/) in the file name. Those characters are reserved for special items within the Mac.

You can type up to 256 characters in a folder name, but you can't type a colon. If you *try* to type a colon, the Mac will substitute a hyphen. And don't ever start a folder name (or any file name) with a period.

After you name the new folder, the border disappears as soon as you click anywhere else, or when you hit the Return or Enter key. When the border disappears, you are no longer in the naming mode.

A **file extension** is a short abbreviation after a file name, always starting with a period, such as "Letter to Mom**.rtf**" or "Family Photo**.jpg**." In Mac OS X, extensions are very important; they often tell the Mac which program to open a document in. Many users add extensions to their files so they will know what kind of file it is themselves; for instance, I always put extensions on different graphic formats so I know what they are, and I add extensions to documents to tell myself which versions I'm working on. But Mac OS X will yell at you if you try to add certain extensions, as shown in the experiment below. Depending on the extension, this can be a problem—the icon can actually turn into something else if you put the wrong extension on it. See page 227 for more information about extensions.

Names with file extensions

chapter8

chapter8.dock

The folder above was just fine until I added the extension ".dock." Then the Mac thought it was an entirely different file! It will no longer open as a folder. (If I take the extension off, it turns back into a folder.)

The Mac assumes that anything after a dot (period) is an extension.

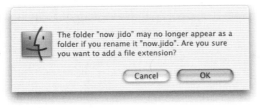

The folder "now jido" may no longer appear as a folder if you rename it "now.jido". Are you sure you want to add a file extension?

Cancel   OK

Changing the Name of a Folder

If you accidentally un-highlight the new folder before you change its name, or if you want to **change the name** of any other folder (or any icon of any sort), it is still very easy to do: simply click once on the *name* and the icon will change color, the name will highlight, and a border will appear around the name. The border and highlight are **visual clues** that whatever you type will *replace* the current title. So go ahead and type the new name while you see the border.

Tip: Once you click on the name, it seems to take a "long time" (like a whole second or two) for the border to appear. If you want faster service, click on the icon or the name, then hit the Return key to get the border.

Use standard word processing procedures (Chapter 13) to type the new name: press-and-drag to select text; click to insert an insertion point; backspace to delete characters, etc. Hit the UpArrow to move the insertion point to the beginning of the name, and hit the DownArrow to move it to the end of the name.

Whether your window is in Icon View, List View, or Column View, when you click once on a folder its name will highlight and you'll see the border around the name so you can change it.

Where Did Your New (or renamed) Folder Go?

How your window is arranged or sorted, such as by name or by size, will affect where your new, *untitled* folder will appear. For instance, if you view your window as a list which you have sorted by "Name," the untitled folder will appear near the bottom of the list, alphabetized as "untitled." If you sort by "Date Modified," the untitled folder will appear first in the list because it is the most recent.

After you name the untitled folder and click anywhere or hit the Enter key, *the new folder gets arranged in the list according to the view you have chosen.* That is, if the list is sorted by "Name," the folder instantly gets alphabetized into the existing list, *which means it may disappear from your sight.* You can use the scrollers to go find it, or just type the first letter or two of its name and it will pop up again right in front of your face.

Putting Something inside a Folder

To put something inside a folder, press-and-drag any file icon (except a disk) over to the folder; when the folder changes color (highlights), let go and the file will drop inside. This **moves** the file from one place to another. Remember, it is the *very tip* of the pointer that selects the folder, *not* the shadow of the icon that goes inside.

You can have folders inside of folders inside of folders, which is technically called the *Hierarchical File System* (HFS). You can drag an item from one window and put it into a folder in another window.

A folder does not have to be closed to place an item inside of it. The folder window can be displaying icons, a list, or columns.

The only trick to putting something inside a folder is that you have to be able to see both the *item* you want to drop in and the *folder* you want to drop it into. Since the contents of new folders replaces the previous contents, this can be kind of tricky; sometimes it requires opening multiple windows and moving your windows around the screen so you can see both items at once. Following are several techniques that make it easier to access folders without having to have lots of open windows: putting folders in the Toolbar, putting folders in the Dock, and storing folders on the Desktop.

Storing a Folder in the Toolbar

You'll find that you use some folders more often than others. And you might use one folder for a while and then you're done with that project and need to use two or three other folders for a while. It can be annoying and sometimes tricky to keep digging up the folder you want, either to put stuff in or take stuff out, but here is a great trick: **Drag the folder into the Toolbar.** This actually creates an "alias" in the Toolbar, a *copy* of the folder's icon, but it acts just like the real thing. You can drag files into it, single-click to open it, and it's always available right in front of your face.

When you no longer need such easy access to your favorite folder, **just drag it off the Toolbar—**the folder alias will disappear in a poof. *Only the alias icon disappears—*the real folder stays safe and secure right where it was.

Of course, you can drag files directly into the Home, Favorites, and Applications windows by dropping the files directly on top of the Toolbar icons.

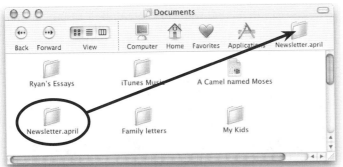

Drag a folder into the Toolbar to make the folder easy to access. To put things in this folder, you can drag them to this Toolbar folder and drop them in—the items will actually move to the real folder.

Storing a Folder in the Dock

You can also store a "copy" of a folder in the Dock: just drag the folder down to the *right* side of the Dock and drop it. The other items will move over to make room. This does not *move* your folder—it automatically places an "alias" in the Dock. Your original folder stays right where it is. But now you can open the folder from the Dock: you can open a full window, or you can pop up a menu that displays all of the items stored inside this folder.

To see the name of the folder in the Dock: Position the pointer over the folder icon in the Dock and just "hover" (don't click). The name of the folder will appear just above the Dock.

To open a folder in the Dock to a new window: Click once on the folder icon in the Dock.

To pop up a menu that displays the contents of the folder: Press (don't click) on the folder icon in the Dock.

To put a file inside a folder in the Dock: Drag it to the folder and drop it in.

To take a file out of a folder in the Dock: Click once on the icon to open its window, then drag the desired file out.

When folders are in the Dock, they all look the same so you have to hover over the icons to see which name pops up. You might want to customize your folder icons (see page 117) so when they're in the Dock you can tell which is which.

images for jaguar

This is actually a folder; I customized the icon so I can tell which folder it is in the Dock.

Tip: Once you've opened a window whose folder is stored in the Dock, try to remember not to **minimize** that window—**close** it instead. If you minimize the window, you'll end up with two icons in the Dock for the same thing: the folder icon *plus* the minimized window icon.

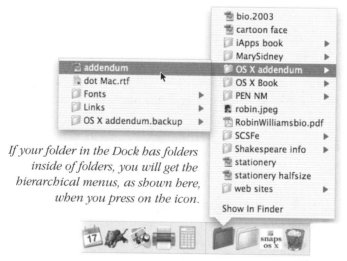

If your folder in the Dock has folders inside of folders, you will get the hierarchical menus, as shown here, when you press on the icon.

Single-click *the folder in the Dock to open its window.*

Press *on the folder icon and in about two seconds a menu will pop up. Slide up the menu and select an item to open it, as shown above.*

You can always make a **new folder** directly on the Desktop: click on the Desktop to select it, then press Command Shift N.

Or you can **drag any folder** from a window to the Desktop. This doesn't make a copy or an "alias" of the folder—it literally *moves* the original folder onto the Desktop (unless you are dragging it from another disk, in which case it does make a copy).

Or make an **alias of a folder** on the Desktop. The alias, as explained in Chapter 23, looks just like the original, but it's actually kind of like a spirit image—it's not *really* the folder. But you can put files into the alias and they will actually go straight into the real folder. **To make an alias,** hold down the Command and Option keys and drag the folder to the Desktop. When you get to the Desktop, let go, and the alias will appear on the Desktop. You'll know it's an alias by the tiny arrow in the lower-left corner.

Storing a Folder on the Desktop

john

An alias has a tiny pointer in the lower-left corner.

Opening a Folder in a New Window

To move items from one folder to another, you can also **open the folders in two different windows.** As explained in Chapter 6, hold down the Command key and double-click a folder icon to open that folder into a new, separate window. Then you can arrange the two windows side by side so you can **move** items from one folder to another.

Or click the Hide/Show Toolbar button in the upper-right of the window, then when you double-click a folder icon it will open in a new, separate window.

Now, this can get sort of frustrating because you have to open one folder into a new window, then go back to the first window and navigate around to find the file you wanted to move into the second folder. So here is yet another option:

New Finder Window

Open the window that contains the file you want to move. Press Command Shift N to get a **new Finder window** (the new window is probably a duplicate of the one that's already open). Position the two windows side by side. In the new window, find the folder icon that you want to move the file into. Then just drag the file from one window and drop it onto the folder icon in the other window.

Drag a File to the Desktop

Sometimes it's easiest to **drag a file to the Desktop,** then find the folder icon you want to move the file into, then drag the file from the Desktop into the folder icon (or its open window).

As I mentioned earlier, if you use certain folders often, just drag them to the Toolbar or the Dock so you can move files in without having to find the folder in a window. Plus you'll always have that folder accessible so you can single-click to open it.

Spring-Loaded Folders

To turn spring-loaded folders on or off, go to the Desktop (click once on it), then from the Finder menu, choose "Preferences...."

With **spring-loaded folders** turned on, you can drag a file to a folder, and *if you don't let go,* that folder will open up. Without letting go of the file, you can then drag the file to another folder and either drop it right on top, or hover for a second and *that* folder will open for you. All folders between the first and last will automatically close when you let go of the mouse. Try it. Disk icons and Toolbar icons also spring open. Unfortunately, you cannot spring open folders that are in the Dock. Dang.

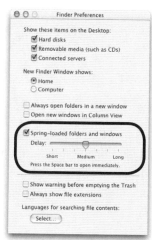

*The **Delay** indicates how long you have to hover your mouse over a folder or icon in the Toolbar before its window opens.*

*Press the **Spacebar** when your mouse is positioned over a folder and it will open instantly, regardless of how long your delay is set, even if you **uncheck** spring-loaded folders.*

To **move or remove** something from a folder, you have to *open* the folder first so you can see the files inside. Open a folder in the various views as explained on pages 148–149. Then simply press-and-drag a file out of the folder; drag it either to the Desktop or to another folder or window, then drop it. The important thing to remember is this:

Moving vs. Copying Files

If you drag the file to someplace else **on the same disk,** the file will just pop out of that first folder/window and **move** into the other folder.

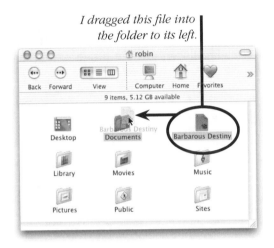

I dragged this file into the folder to its left.

*The file **moved** into the folder and is gone from this window.*

BUT if you drag the file **to a different disk or to a server,** the original file will stay put in the original folder and the Mac will put a **copy** of the file on the other disk.

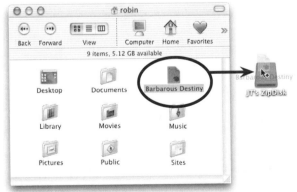

*I dragged the file onto the Zip disk. Notice the tiny plus symbol next to the arrow—a **visual clue** that the file will be copied, not moved.*

*The file was **copied** onto the Zip disk and the original stayed right where it was.*

See Chapter 11 for tips on selecting more than one file at a time, as well as for moving and copying files.

1. What is the purpose of a folder?

   _____

2. At the Desktop, when you go to the File menu and choose "New Folder," how do you know where that new folder will appear?

   _____

3. What is the keyboard shortcut to create a new folder?

   _____

4. How do you rename a folder, and what is the **visual clue** that tells you a folder is ready to be renamed?

   _____

5. How do you open a folder in each of the three views?

   _____

6. What happens when you open a folder, and what do you see?

   _____

7. What are the keyboard shortcuts for expanding and compressing folders in the List View?

   _____

8. How can you close all of the expanded folders at once?

   _____

9. What are two big advantages to the List View?

   _____

10. Name four ways to make it easier to move files from one folder to another.

    _____

    _____

Answers on page 731.

Selecting, Moving, and Copying Files

You'll often need to **move** files around to rearrange them. And **copying** files is an everyday task. You may need to copy a small utility from its original disk onto your hard disk; copy a report to give to a coworker; copy a document and its graphics to take to a service bureau for high-resolution printing; create the ever-necessary backup copy; etc., etc., etc.

Copying files usually involves moving them, and before you can move or copy any file, you must first **select** it.

Apple has made it as easy as possible to copy files on the Mac (which is why *pirating,* or copying software without paying for it, has always been such a problem). Copying files has no effect on the *original file,* nor is there any loss of quality in the new version—there is absolutely no difference from the original to the copy.

Contents of the chapter

Selecting Individual Files

Before you can move or copy files, you have to know how to select them. **Selecting one file** is easy—as long as it's not in the Dock or a window Toolbar, click once on it. (If you click once on an icon in the Dock or Toolbar, it *opens* that item instead of selecting it.)

Type the first letter

To select any single file, even if you can't see it in the window, **type the first letter** of the name of the file and it will be instantly selected. If there are several files with the same first letter, quickly type the first two or three letters. This technique makes it a lot easier to find your folder named "Waldo" in an alphabetized list, for instance, or a file that starts with "Z," or any icon in a crowded folder.

Arrow keys

You can also use the **arrow keys** to select files. *Once you have a file selected,* either by clicking on it or typing its first letter, the arrow keys will select the next icon or file name in the window. In List View and Column View, the UpArrow and the DownArrow select, of course, the next file in the list. In Icon View, the four arrows select the icon to the left, right, up, or down, unless there is nothing else in that direction. Take a minute and try it.

Select the next file alphabetically

No matter how you select a file, you can select the next file alphabetically. For instance, perhaps you typed the letter "S" because you wanted to select the folder named Scarlett, but instead it selected Sally. *Except in Column View,* you can do this:

▼ To select the icon that would be alphabetically *after* the currently selected icon, tap the **Tab key.** You can continue to tap the Tab key to keep selecting files in alphabetical order.

▼ To select the icon that would be alphabetically *before* the currently selected icon, hold down the **Shift key** and tap the **Tab** key. Continue to tap the Tab key to select files in backwards alphabetical order.

Selecting more than one file at a time

You've probably noticed that once a file is selected, it gets *de*selected the instant you click somewhere else. So an important trick is knowing how to **select more than one file** at a time. Once you select multiple files, you can drag them *all together,* either to the Trash, into another folder, onto another disk, or simply to clean up the joint.

How you select multiple files depends on which view you are in. In Icon View and Column View, you can only select items from inside **one folder.** In List View, you can select multiple items from **different folders.** We'll look at how you can select files in each view.

Practice: Open a window, like your Home folder. Select a file by clicking once on it (not on a Dock icon!). Then try each of the techniques listed on the page.

Selecting Multiple Files in Icon View and on the Desktop

You may have noticed in **Icon View** or on the **Desktop** that when you *press in an empty space and drag the pointer,* a colored rectangle comes out of the tip—this is the **selection marquee** found in many Mac programs. Any file that is even partially enclosed in this marquee will be selected. You can tell which files are selected because they are highlighted, as shown below.

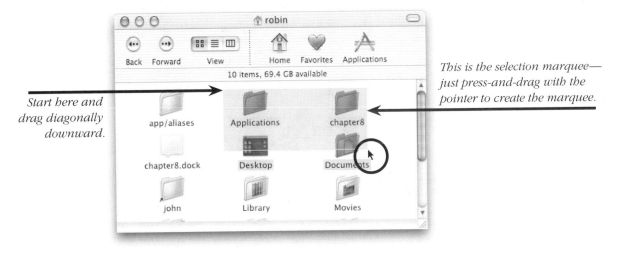

Start here and drag diagonally downward.

This is the selection marquee— just press-and-drag with the pointer to create the marquee.

Selecting icons this way will highlight all of the icons that were touched by the marquee. Now:

▾ When you press-and-drag on the *highlighted* area of one of the selected items, they will all drag together.

▾ Click in any *white* space, on any unselected icon, or on the Desktop to *deselect* all the files.

Add or delete individual icons from the selection

Using the above method, you can only select files that are *next to each other.* But often you might want to **add** another icon to this collection, or you might want to **pick and choose** individual files that are not next to each other. Or you might want to **deselect** just one of the selected files in a group. Here's how to do it:

To SELECT individual files to add to a group of selected icons, hold down the Shift key *or* the Command key (not the Control key), and single-click on individual files.

To DESELECT individual files that are in a collection of selected icons, hold down the Shift key *or* the Command key (not the Control key), and single-click on individual files.

Practice: This is a technique you will use daily, so follow the directions above to select multiple files, then deselect individual files from the group.

Selecting Multiple Files in List View

If you view your window as icons or columns, you can select items *from only one window or column at a time.* But in List View, you can **expand** the folders and **select** *any number of files from any number of expanded folders within that one window,* as shown in the examples below.

Drag the selection marquee

Just as in Icon View, you can **drag to select files that are next to each other:** Press in a white space in the window next to a file name and start to drag. The colored **selection marquee** will appear when you drag, and any item that is even partially enclosed within the marquee will be added to the selection.

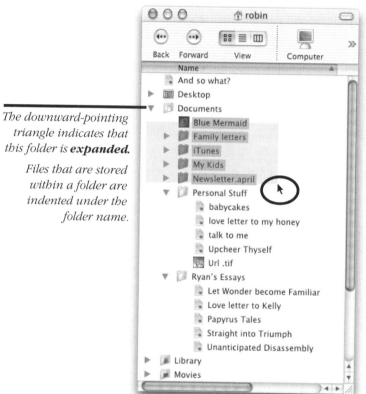

The downward-pointing triangle indicates that this folder is **expanded.**

Files that are stored within a folder are indented under the folder name.

Press-and-drag to select adjacent items in a List View. The five highlighted files you see in this window are **selected.**

Press on any one of them to drag them all together, to open them all at once, to print them all (if appropriate), etc.

Click anywhere else to **deselect all** *of the items in the group.*

To SELECT INDIVIDUAL files to ADD to the collection, hold down the Command key (not the Control key, nor the Shift key) and single-click on individual files that are not already in the collection. Each file you click on will be *added* to the group.

To DESELECT INDIVIDUAL files FROM the collection, hold down the Command key (not the Control key, nor the Shift key) and single-click on individual files that are in the collection. Each file you click on will be *deselected* from the group.

Practice: If you don't learn the difference between the Shift key and Command key while selecting, it can make you crazy! Try these techniques.

To ADD CONTIGUOUS files to the top or bottom of the collection, hold down the Shift key and tap the UpArrow or DownArrow key.

To DESELECT all files, click in any white space.

To select individual files from different folders in List View, first expand the folders whose contents you need to see: click once on the tiny triangles pointing to the folders (see Chapter 6 for tips on expanding and compressing all folders at once). Then **Command-click** on the files you want to select (hold down the Command key while you single-click on icons).

Command-click

Notice the four selected files are each in a different folder.

If I press-and-drag any one of these items, all four of them will move. I can copy, trash, print, open, or move them, all at once.

To DESELECT individual files FROM the collection, hold down the Command key (not the Control key, nor the Shift key) and single-click on individual files.

To DESELECT all files, click in any white space.

Practice: This is the selection technique you will probably use most often. Try it.

Shift-click   Another method of selecting more than one item in List View is to **click–Shift-click.** This method only selects items that are *contiguous,* or next to each other, although you can always use the method on the previous page to add individual files to the collection.

1. **Click once** on the first file in the list you want to select.

2. Hold down the **Shift key and click** on the last file in the list you want to select. Everything between the first click and the Shift-click will be selected.

Click once on the first file, then Shift-click on the last file.

To ADD CONTIGUOUS files to the collection, hold down the Shift key and click a file higher or lower than the selected collection, or tap the UpArrow or DownArrow keys (with the Shift key down).

To DESELECT CONTIGUOUS files from the collection, hold down the Shift key and click a file inside the selected collection; all files between the beginning or the end of the collection (whichever your pointer is closest to) will deselect.

> **Practice:** This technique also works when you select text: Click, then Shift-click and everything in-between (text or files in a list) will be selected. Try it.

To ADD INDIVIDUAL files to the collection, hold down the Command key (not the Control key, nor the Shift key) and single-click individual files.

To DESELECT INDIVIDUAL files from the collection, hold down the Command key (not the Control key, nor the Shift key) and single-click individual files.

To DESELECT all files, click in any white space.

The **Column View** gives you the impression you can select files from different columns, but you can't. Column View is a cross between Icon View and List View, as far as selecting items goes.

To select multiple individual files in one column, hold down the Command key and click on each one.

To select contiguous files in one column, press-and-drag to draw the selection marquee around the files. Any file even partially enclosed by the marquee will be selected.

OR click on the first item in the list, then hold down the Shift key and click on the last item in the list. All files between the first click and the Shift-click will be selected.

All of the tips listed on the bottom part of the opposite page also work in one column of Column View.

Selecting Multiple Files in Column View

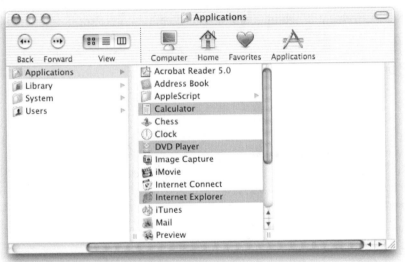

Command-click to select individual files in one column.

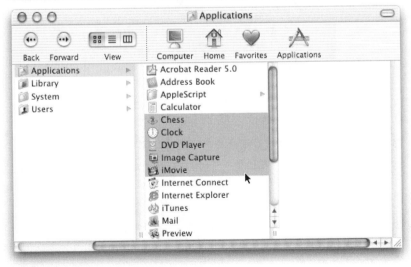

Press-and-drag or click-Shift-click to select a range of contiguous files.

Add individual files to the selection with Command-click.

Using Search to Select Files

You can also **use Search to select files** from all over your Mac (see Chapter 25 for all the intimate details).

All of the found files will be shown in one Results window, and you can select their icons from that Results window and drag them to the Trash, open them, move them, etc. (Remember, press on *one* selected item and *all* selected items will follow.) Make it a point to learn to Search—you'll discover it comes in handy in a number of ways.

I often Search to select a file even when I know where it is because it's so much faster than digging through levels of folders. If I need a document, I hit Command F, type in a few letters, hit the Return key, then lo and behold, there is my file in front of my face. I double-click the file name to open it, and off I go.

I want to find a file with "marysidney" in its title, and in case I have a lot of those, I want to find only the one that is a PDF.

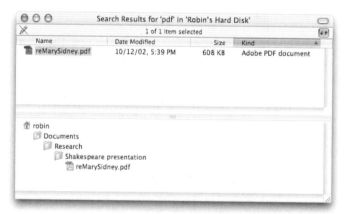

Here is my file—I can see where it is stored, but all I need to do is double-click the title to open it right up.

You can use the **edit keys** on an extended keyboard to **scroll** through a window. This doesn't *select* anything, but it makes it easier for you to find and click on files. The edit keys are that little set between the alphabet keys and the numeric keypad on most keyboards, or above the numeric keypad on smaller keyboards, like the ones that usually come with iMacs.

Although the edit keys don't select anything, they come in handy when you want to get to the top or the bottom of a window instantly or if you want to scroll through the window in a hurry.

> **Home** scrolls the window straight to the top.
>
> **End** scrolls the window straight to the bottom.
>
> **Page Up (pg up)** and **Page Down (pg dn)** scroll the window one window-sized section up or down.

Moving Around in a Window

Moving Files

Once you have selected a file or two or more, you can **move** them to another place on your Mac. When you move a file, it's just like moving something in your kitchen—the thing is no longer in the position you took it from. That is, moving does exactly what it says—it does not leave a copy behind.

To MOVE a file or files from one place to another:

1. First make sure you can see the files you want to move **and** the folder or window you want to move them into.

   There are detailed explanations on pages 153–156 on how to make folders easier to access. Briefly, you can open a folder into a new, separate window (Command–double-click on it); store a folder in the Dock; store a folder in the Toolbar; or keep an alias or the original folder right on the Desktop.

2. **Select** the files as explained on the previous pages.

3. Then, *making sure you have no keys pressed,* grab one of the selected files and **drag** it to its new position. Dragging one selected file will drag *all* of them, as shown below.

4. As usual, the **tip of the pointer** is the critical factor—wherever the tip of the pointer is when you **let go** of the mouse button, that is where the files will move to.

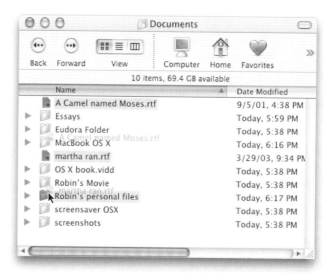

If the folder you want to move files into is in the same window as the files you want to move, then just select the files and drag them.

Above, I Command-clicked on the two document files, "A Camel named Moses.rtf" and "martha ran.rtf."

*Then I let go of the Command key, **pressed** on "martha ran.rtf," and dragged both selected files to the folder.*

*Notice the **tip** of the pointer is directly on the folder "Robin's personal files," selecting it, and the shadows of the selected files are following along.*

If the folder you want to move files into is not visible, first make it visible (as explained on the opposite page) before you select the files.

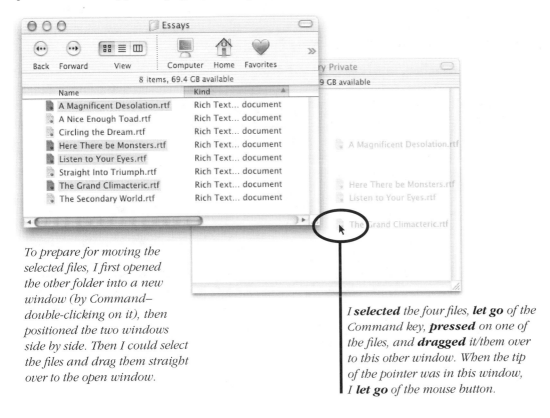

To prepare for moving the selected files, I first opened the other folder into a new window (by Command–double-clicking on it), then positioned the two windows side by side. Then I could select the files and drag them straight over to the open window.

I **selected** the four files, **let go** of the Command key, **pressed** on one of the files, and **dragged** it/them over to this other window. When the tip of the pointer was in this window, I **let go** of the mouse button.

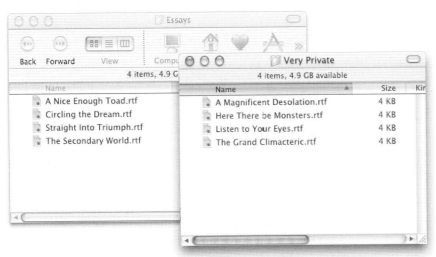

After I let go of the mouse button, the files moved right into the new folder. Notice they are no longer in their original folder.

Copying Files

Copying files is an everyday task. You'll copy files from one folder to another so you can have multiple versions; you'll copy files onto removable disks to give to someone else or as backup for yourself; you'll copy files from removable disks onto your Mac's hard disk so you can use them; and you'll probably find a number of other reasons to copy files. When you duplicate or copy *folders,* every item contained within that folder is also copied.

Go back to work while the computer is copying

If you have a large file to copy, you can **go back to work** on something else while the computer is going through its copying process. You can go back to your application, browse through your windows, empty the Trash, connect to the Internet, or do other Finder tasks. Most machines today are so fast, though, you will rarely have time to get back to work before they're finished copying! Also, you don't have to wait for one file or collection of files to finish copying before you start another.

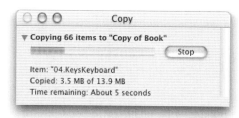

*This message will appear when you copy. The lines in the title bar are a **visual clue** that you can drag this box around on the screen. For instance, you might want to move it out of the way so you can do something else while the item is copying.*

Your visual clue of the copying process

Sometimes you might think you are just *moving* a file, but the Mac actually *copies* it. This is because when you "move" a file from one *disk* to another *disk* (rather than from one *folder* to another *folder*), the Mac automatically makes a copy instead of moving the original. Your **visual clue** that you are actually copying a file is in the arrow—you'll see a small plus sign (+).

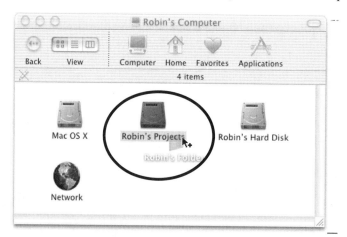

You can see the shadow of the file I dragged to the hard disk icon. Because this file was originally on another one of these partitions (which the computer sees as a separate hard disk), when I drag the file to another partition, the Mac automatically copies it. I realize this when I see the arrow sprout a plus sign.

Sometimes you want to make another **copy of a file on the same disk.** The Mac *automatically* copies a file when you drag it to another *disk,* but to make a copy on the same disk you have to do it yourself. There are three ways to do this.

Duplicating or copying a file on the SAME DISK

1. To make a COPY (DUPLICATE) of the file in the same folder:

1. Duplicate

1. First click *once* on the file icon to select it, or select several files as described on pages 162–165.

2. From the File menu, choose "Duplicate" (*or* press Command D). This creates a second version in the same folder named "_____ copy." If you make more copies of the same file, they will be named "_____ copy 1," "_____ copy 2," etc.

whitel
whitebox copy 3.tif

This looks odd because I held down the Command key and tapped the D key three times. This made three duplicates in the folder, stacked one on top of the other.

whitebox.tif   whitebox copy.tif   whitebox copy 2.tif   whitebox copy 3.tif

I just dragged the duplicates off to the right so I could see their individual icons and names.

When you use the Duplicate command, the new file appears with the word "copy" at the end of its name. If you want to avoid this, just Option-drag a file to make a copy, as detailed below.

2. Option-drag

2. To drag a copy of a file into another folder on the same disk or onto the Desktop:

▼ Hold down the **Option key and drag** the file to the other folder or to the Desktop. This puts a copy of the file into the other folder or on the Desktop, but does not rename the file "_____ copy."

You'll know it's making a copy instead of moving the file because you'll see the plus sign appear next to the arrow as soon as you hold down the Option key.

(Actually, you can also Option-drag a file in the *same* folder to make a copy, but because you cannot have two files in the same folder with the same name, you will still get the word "copy" at the end of the file name.)

3. Contextual menu

There is a great little technique to copy a file into another folder without first having to arrange both folders on the screen, like you do when *moving* a file from one folder to the other. (I wish this technique worked for moving, as well as copying.) This only works in Icon or Column Views.

3. To put a copy of a file (or multiple files) into another folder on the same disk or onto the Desktop (or on any other disk, actually):

Tip: Use this technique or the one on the opposite page to **back up** your files—make a copy on another disk. If you have very important files, makes copies on two different disks, then store one of the disks off-site. This way if your office is plundered or caught in a fire or flood, you still have copies of your important files.

1. First click *once* on the file icon to select it, or select a number of files, as explained on pages 162–165.

2. Hold down the Control key (not the Command key) and click on one of the selected files to get the contextual menu, as shown below. Choose the "Copy items" command. (If *one* item is selected, the copy command will name the item.)

If several files are selected, you only need to Control-click on one of the selected files to get the contextual menu.

3. Open the window or the column where you want to put the file(s).

4. In an empty space in that window or column, hold down the Control key and click; you'll get a contextual menu, shown below.

5. Choose the "Paste items" command and the file(s) you copied will be pasted into this window or column.

You can't select a folder icon to have the items pasted inside that folder—you must open its window first.

You can also use the Paste command from the Edit menu, as shown on page 175.

You can copy from your hard disk onto a removable disk, from a removable disk onto your hard disk, or directly into a specific folder on any other disk. In every case, make sure the icon of the disk or folder you are copying *into* becomes *highlighted* (highlighting is darker or colored), which is your **visual clue** that the disk or folder is *selected* as the place to copy to. When the icon is highlighted, that means it's ready to accept the file(s). If the icon is not highlighted, you'll end up just placing the file *next* to the disk or folder, not *inside* of it. The *tip of the pointer* is what highlights any icon, as you can see in the example below.

Make sure the disk or folder you are copying to is selected!

When you drag a file to another *disk* or partition, the Mac automatically copies the file. This is how to back up your files onto Zip or Jaz disks.

Copying files from the Mac to a REMOVABLE DISK
(not onto a CD; for that, see pages 176–177)

To COPY a file from one disk to another disk (such as from your hard disk to a Zip disk):

1. At the Desktop, click once on the file you want to copy.

2. Press-and-drag that selected file to the icon of the disk that you want to copy it onto. This icon might be right on the Desktop or in the Computer window—you can drag to either one.

   You will see a small plus sign appear next to the arrow, and a little message comes up telling you the file is being copied.

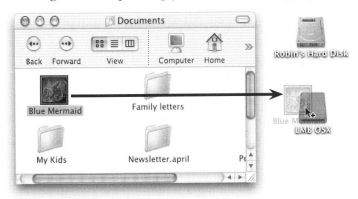

You can see three things here:

1) *The shadow of the icon I am dragging over to the Zip disk.*

2) *The tip of the pointer is positioned directly on the disk icon to select it— that's what highlights the disk.*

3) *The pointer sprouted a small plus sign as soon as it reached the disk, which tells you the file will be copied, not moved.*

You could also drag a file to the disk icon that appears in the Computer window, but that is not as easy as dragging it to the Desktop, generally.

Copying FROM A REMOVABLE DISK to the Mac

There are a couple of ways to copy files from your **removable disk** (such as a Zip disk, a CD, or a floppy) to your hard disk, depending on whether you want to copy selected files or the entire removable disk. Although these methods specifically detail copying from your "removable disk" to your "internal hard disk," you can use these same methods to copy from one disk to any other disk or volume, as long as there is room on the other volume.

To COPY SELECTED FILES from a removable disk to your internal hard disk:

1. Insert the removable disk.

2. Double-click the removable disk icon to open its window.

3. Take a look at the files on the removable disk, *then selectively* choose the ones you need to copy. Press-and-drag the chosen files to the hard disk icon, or drag them directly into a folder on the hard disk. As usual, you need to be able to see the folder, window, or column you want to drag the files into.

To COPY THE ENTIRE DISK to your internal hard disk:

This method copies *every single item* from the removable disk to your internal hard disk. Make sure that's what you really want to do.

1. Insert the removable disk into its drive.

2. If you try to *drag* the removable disk icon onto your hard disk icon, you'll notice a tiny curved arrow will appear next to the pointer, as shown below. This indicates that dragging the item will create an *alias*—it will not *move* the disk, nor will it make a *copy*. (See Chapter 23 about aliases.)

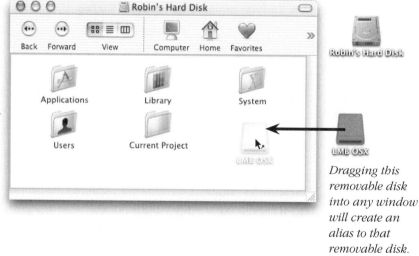

*Notice the border around the inside of the window. This is a **visual clue** that this window is selected as the destination for the file.*

Dragging this removable disk into any window will create an alias to that removable disk.

3. **Instead** of dragging the disk, hold down the Control key and click on the removable disk icon to get the contextual menu, as shown below.

4. From the contextual menu, choose the "Copy item" command.

5. Open the window you want to copy the entire removable disk contents into. The contents will copy into the *active* window.

6. From the Edit menu, choose the "Paste item" command (or use the contextual menu as shown on page 172).

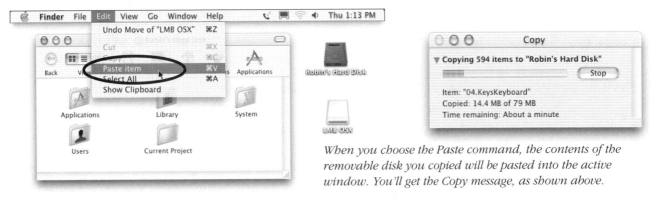

When you choose the Paste command, the contents of the removable disk you copied will be pasted into the active window. You'll get the Copy message, as shown above.

7. After the copy/paste process is finished, you'll have an icon of the removable disk in the window. Don't get confused and think that this represents the actual removable disk! It doesn't—it is a *copy* of the entire contents on that disk. The icon is actually a folder with a customized image.

This is the "folder" that holds a copy of the contents of the Zip disk.

Copying Files onto a CD

When you **copy files onto a CD,** it's called **burning a CD.** A CD burner uses a laser beam to burn digital information into the surface of a CD. You can't just burn any ol' CD, though—you need to understand the differences between CD-ROM, CD-R, and CD-RW.

CD-ROM (Compact Disc–Read Only Memory): You cannot erase information from or copy information to a CD-ROM, such as an old application installation disc that you don't need any more. If you've been saving that stack of AOL CDs to use for backups, forget it. They're CD-ROMs.

CD-R (Compact Disc–Recordable): CD-Rs are the most common type of disc for burning data and music files. Using Apple's CD burning software, you can "write" once (a single burn session) to a CD-R. You can't erase a CD-R. Some other CD burning software, such as Roxio's Toast, enables multiple CD burn sessions of data files, but not if you're burning a music CD. CD-Rs hold between 650 and 700 megabytes of data and are very affordable, usually in the range of one dollar per disc or lower. However, the disc quality and dependability drop along with the price.

CD-RW (Compact Disc–ReWritable): CD-RWs can be rewritten and erased many times, making it a media that's ideal for backing up files that change over time. If you use Apple's CD burning software, you can write to a CD-RW more than once, but only if you erase its current content. Some CD burning software, such as Toast, allows you to selectively erase or rewrite files repeatedly on a single CD-RW, or you can choose to rewrite only files that have been changed since the last backup to the disc. Depending upon the quality of the CD-RW and the quantity you buy, the price per disc may be similar to CD-Rs, or maybe two to three times more.

Do not use CD-RWs for creating music CDs—they only work in computers, not CD audio players.

To burn a CD:

1. Insert a blank CD.

2. From the "Action" pop-up menu, select what you want to happen: choose "Open Finder" for the most common burn procedure, which is copying data files from your computer to the CD.

Tip: To avoid potential problems, before you burn a CD, make sure your Mac will not go to sleep during the process. To do this, go to the System Preferences, and choose Energy Saver. Set the top slider (System Sleep) to "Never," and uncheck the bottom two options (Display Sleep and Hard Disk Sleep).

This is the CD icon before burning. The letters "CDR" indicate this is a CD-Recordable disc that has not been burned.

Generally, media created optically (burned with a laser beam, such as CDs and DVDs) is spelled "disc."

Media created magnetically (internal hard disks, Zip disks, floppies, external FireWire drives) is spelled "disk."

*Use the **CDs & DVDs system preferences** to predetermine what happens when you insert a blank CD.*

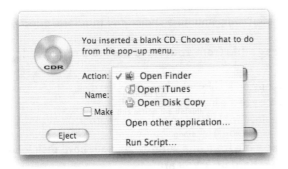

Choose the **Open Finder** option to copy data and multimedia files to a CD that can be read by a Mac or a PC. These data files can be recognized by a computer, but not by a CD player or MP3 player.

Choose **Open iTunes** to create *music* CDs that you can play on standard CD players or on your computer. If you choose this option, iTunes opens so you can select a Playlist (or selections from a Playlist) to burn.

Choose **Open Disk Copy** if you want to burn a "disk image" file (.dmg) that exists on your computer onto a CD.

3. Drag folders and files to the CD icon, according to the choice you made in Step 2:

If you chose the **Open Finder** option, drag the folders and files you want to copy and drop them on top of the CD icon on your Desktop. A "copy" window opens to show the progress.

If you chose the **iTunes** option to create a music CD, select a Playlist (or songs in a Playlist) from the iTunes window that opens, then click the "Burn CD" button in the top-right corner of the iTunes window.

If you chose the **Open Disk Copy** option, a "Burn Image" window opens in which you select an existing disk image file (.dmg), then click "Burn" in the bottom-right corner.

4. Drag the CD icon to the Trash. If the disk has not yet been burned, the Trash icon changes to the "Burn CD" icon, shown to the right. Or Control-click on the CD icon, then choose "Burn Disk."

5. As your files are prepared, burned, and verified, the "Burn Disc" window shows your progress.

6. The letters "CDR" are gone from the icon, indicating that this disc has been burned. Eject the disc—select it and press Command E, or press the Eject Media key on the upper-right of newer keyboards.

Circle the correct choice in the following multiple choice and true/false questions.

1. **When you drag a file from your hard disk to a removable disk, you are:**
   a. Making a copy of the file onto the removable disk.
   b. Making a copy of the file onto the hard disk.
   c. Simply moving the file from one place to another.

2. **When you drag a file from one window on your hard disk to another window on your hard disk, you are:**
   a. Making a copy of the file onto a removable disk.
   b. Making a copy of the file onto the hard disk.
   c. Simply moving the file from one place to another.

3. **When you drag a file from a removable disk to your hard disk, you are:**
   a. Making a copy of the file onto the removable disk.
   b. Making a copy of the file onto the hard disk.
   c. Simply moving the file from one place to another.

4. **If you want to make a copy of a file on the same disk, the fastest and most efficient way is to:**
   a. Make a copy onto a removable disk, then drag that copy back onto the hard disk.
   b. Select the file, then from the File menu, choose "Duplicate." Or select the file and press Command D.
   c. Hold down the Option key as you drag the file into another folder or window.

5. **In the List View, you can select multiple files:**
   a. By dragging around them with the pointer tool.
   b. That are in different folders.
   c. Both a and b.

T F **6.** It's always okay to drag the icon of the removable disk onto the icon of the hard disk when you want to copy something onto your hard disk.

T F **7.** To select more than one file at a time, hold down the Option key as you click each one.

T F **8.** You can press-and-drag the pointer around any number of files to select them all.

T F **9.** The quickest (and coolest) way to select a file is to type the first letter or couple of letters of its name.

T F **10.** Once a file is selected, the Tab key will select the next largest file.

Answers on page 731.

Opening Applications & Documents

12

A **file** is a generic term referring to just about any icon on your computer. A file might be an **application,** which is the program you use to create things, or a **document,** which is the thing you created in your application, or a "font," which is a typeface, or a number of other sorts of digitized pieces of information. The files you will work with the most are applications and documents. This chapter gives you some basic guidelines so you can understand and work with them.

Contents of this chapter

What is an Application?

AppleWorks 6

*This is **not** an application icon—it is the folder that stores the application. Open this folder to find the application icon.*

The terms **applications** and **programs** are often used synonymously (although an *application* is only one form of programming). *Application* refers to the software package you use to create your documents, such as AppleWorks, PageMaker, FreeHand, Quicken, Photoshop, Internet Explorer, Mail, etc. They all do something different; they each have a particular function. For instance, you can keep track of your finances in Quicken, but you can't open photographs in Quicken. You can open and edit photographs in Photoshop, but Photoshop will not help you with your finances. Sometimes it takes a little research to discover which software applications meet your specific needs.

Application versions

Every application has a **version number** that tells you how up-to-date it is. For instance, you might have AppleWorks 6 and your friend has AppleWorks 5. Version 6 is newer and has more features (does more stuff) than version 5.

Sometimes the company adds just a few new features and fixes a few old problems instead of revising the entire program. In that case, they usually don't jump to a whole new number, like from 6 to 7; instead, they might say this is version 7.2 (minor updates) or 7.5 (fairly serious update when it's a half number), or 7.5.2 (*very* minor fixes when it's the third number).

The period in these version numbers is pronounced "point." So version 7.5 is pronounced "seven point five." And 7.5.2 is "seven point five point two." Sometimes, of course, we shorten it to say, "Oh, this is version seven five."

AppleWorks 6   **Chess**   **Internet Connect**

These are application icons. They are stored in various folders on the Mac, but the same application will always have the same icon, although the icon might be larger or smaller, depending on where you see it.

To open an application, or software program, you need to find its icon or file name on your hard disk. Application icons, as noted in Chapter 7, typically look "fancier" than most other kinds of files.

▼ If an application's icon is in the Dock, *single-*click on it.

▼ If an application's name, icon, or alias is in a Finder window or sitting on the Desktop, *double-*click on it.

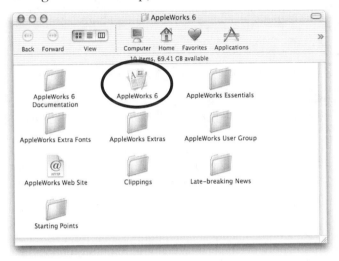

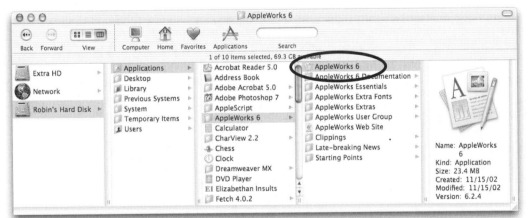

Opening an Application

These examples use AppleWorks, which might or might not be on your Mac. You can follow along with TextEdit, found in the Applications folder.

Find the Application

Some applications have very busy folders and it can be difficult to **find the actual application icon** to double-click. If you use the List View, you can sort your window by "Kind," as shown below, which forces the *applications* towards the top of the list. Simply click on the heading "Kind" to change the organization of the columns.

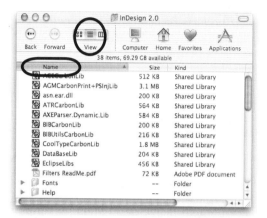

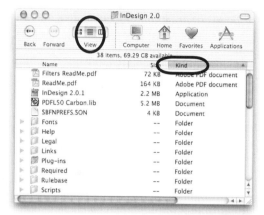

All the files in this folder belong to Adobe InDesign. The window is organized by "Name," as you can see by the colored column header, circled above. You really have to look to find the actual InDesign application. Do you see it? (No.)

This is the same folder, but now the items are organized by "Kind." (Just click in a column header to organize by that column.) Do you see that the application is now listed first towards the top of the window?

Practice: Find and **open the application TextEdit:**

Open any Finder window.

Click the "Applications" icon.

Type the letter "T" to select the TextEdit icon (or scroll to find it).

Double-click the TextEdit application icon to open it.

When your application opens, *one* of the following things will happen:

A. A blank page will open for you, as shown to the right, ready for you to create a new document. Go ahead and start working.

B. You will get a dialog box asking what sort of document you want, as shown below, or how you want your pages set up.

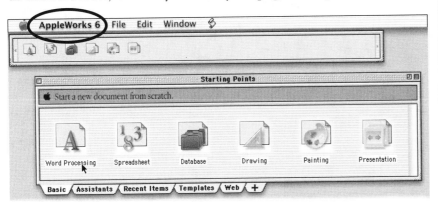

Because AppleWorks has several different modules, when you first open the application it asks you which module you want to create a new document in. Click the icon of your choice.

C. You'll get a commercial that will go away when you click on it. Then see **D,** directly below.

D. It appears that nothing happened. It did—look carefully at your menu bar and you'll see the name of your application on the left, next to the Apple. You need to go to the File menu and choose **"New"** to create a **new,** blank page, or **"Open"** to find a document you previously created that you want to **open** again.

Your application opens

Many applications will automatically open to a blank page, waiting for you to create something. Shown above is a new page in TextEdit.

Practice: TextEdit automatically opens a clean, blank page for you to type on.

Read as much as you can take of the rest of this chapter, **or skip right now to the next chapter** and learn word processing techniques. Just leave this new window open and use it for the practice exercises in the next chapter.

Application icons in the Dock

You'll notice, after you open an application, that **its icon then appears in the Dock** and has a triangle beneath it, which indicates it is open, as shown below. If you are opening an application in Classic (see Chapter 39), it may take a few minutes; be patient. You can tell an application is trying to open because the icon bobbles up and down (depending on how you have set your Dock preferences).

Tip: See Chapter 8 if you want to add icons to the Dock, and see Chapter 23 if you want to know how to use aliases to access your applications without having them clutter up the Dock.

You can see that AppleWorks is open.

Tip on switching applications

Advanced tip: When there are several applications open, you can **switch** between them with this keyboard shortcut: Command Tab. For instance, let's say you're using your word processor to work on a report and you want to pop over to your web browser to check some information on the Internet (assuming you have a full-time connection). The web browser is already open because you used it this morning. Just hold down the Command key and tap the Tab key—you'll see the application icons in the Dock highlight with each Tab tap. When you have selected the application you want to switch to, let go of the Command key and it will appear in front of you.

The Tab order moves from left to right and then back to the beginning again. If you want to go in the reverse order, hold down the Shift key along with the Command key, then tap the Tab key. Try it.

Extra-Great Tip: Press Command Tab just once and let go—you will pop to the last application you used, instead of having to cycle through all of the open applications in the Dock.

Once an application is up and running, in the File menu you see two choices: **New** and **Open.** This confused me at first because I thought, "Well, I want to *open* a *new* one." The difference is this:

▾ **New** creates a clean, blank page on which you can begin a *new* document from scratch.

▾ **Open** takes you to a dialog box (shown and explained on pages 190–193) where you can choose to *open* a document that was previously created and saved.

A **document** is a file that you or someone else created in an application. For instance, if you open an application like AppleWorks and type a letter, that letter is a document. If you open a page-layout application such as PageMaker and create a newsletter, that newsletter is a document. If you open an image-editing applicatin such as Photoshop and edit a photo, that photograph is a document.

You can't create a document without an application, and **you can't open a document unless it has an application to open into.** When you double-click a document icon to open it, it will try to find the application that created it, then *both* the application and the document will open. If the Mac cannot find the application that created the document, it will try to find some other application to open the document in. If the computer can't find anything, it will ask you what to do; see pages 186–188 if you have trouble opening documents.

New vs. Open

What is a Document?

letter to mom

This is a document icon. As explained in Chapter 7, all documents have the upper-right corner turned down.

Opening a Document

Tip: To open a number of documents at once, select all the files (see Chapter 11 about selecting multiple files), then press Command O. Every document (and every necessary application) will open.

To open a document that has already been created and saved in an application, find its icon. Then:

▼ If a document's name, icon, or alias is in a Finder window or sitting on the Desktop, *double*-click on it.

letter to mom

Double-click any icon except when it's in the Dock or in a window Toolbar.

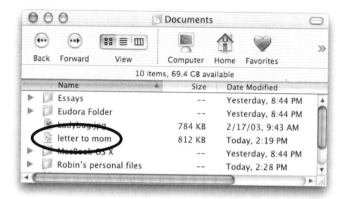

▼ If a document's icon is in the Dock, *single*-click on it.

Important reminder: When you open a document, *you actually open the application also!* That's because a document cannot put itself on the screen—only an application can put a document on the screen. If you get a message complaining that "There is no application available…," all is not necessarily lost. See the next two pages, as well as page 478.

Opening a Document with Drag-and-Drop

You can also open a document by **dragging the document icon** and **dropping it** on top of its application icon. The application icon might be in the Dock, in an Applications folder, anywhere in your Home area, or even an alias on the Desktop.

You'll notice that the application icon will highlight (turn dark), which is the **visual clue** that if you let go your document will open. (Usually.)

*I dragged this AppleWorks **document** icon and dropped it onto the AppleWorks **application** icon. If the application is not open, this will open it.*

Now, the great thing about this trick is that you can often **open a document in an application other than the one it was created in.** For instance, the application AppleWorks is able to open documents created in many other programs. If you have a word processing document someone gave you but you don't have the program they wrote it in, you can drag the foreign document on top of the AppleWorks application icon. If AppleWorks highlights, let go of the document and the program will (probably) open the file. (If not, try the technique on the following page.)

So if you ever get a blank document icon with no clue where it came from or even whether it's a photograph, a letter, or a spreadsheet, drag the icon over every application program you own. Whichever application icon highlights will (usually) open the document.

Drag a file onto application icons to see if an application can open that file. (Sometimes the application attempts to open the file, but then decides it can't.)

In this example, I dragged a graphic I found on the Mac and dropped it on top of the Photoshop application icon. The application icon highlighted, as you can see, and it opened the file.

Aliases for application icons

Check Chapter 23 on **aliases** for directions on creating an alias of each application you own. You can keep these aliases in your Dock or on your Desktop, either individually or in a folder. This makes them easily accessible for opening files with the drag-and-drop method.

Opening a Document in a Different Application

Now, just because you have an icon representing a document you or someone else created in a certain software application doesn't mean you can open up that document on any computer. Clicking on a document icon will only open it **IF** the application itself is also in the computer, either on the hard disk, on another disk that is inserted into one of the drives, or if it's accessible on a network. If the application can't be found, then the document doesn't have anywhere to put itself! Generally, you must have the same version of the application (see page 180) as the one in which it was created.

Sometimes, however, certain applications can open certain documents that were created in other applications. And sometimes you *want* to open a document in a different application; for instance, perhaps you want to open a photograph in Photoshop instead of Preview, but when you double-click the photograph icon, it automatically opens in Preview. And sometimes the document is from an earlier version of the application, and the new version really can open it. In any of these situations, first try the drag-and-drop technique explained on the previous page. If that doesn't work, then try the suggestion below. For a more permanent solution, see page 478.

For details on how to use the Open dialog box, see pages 190–193.

1. First open the application that you are pretty sure will open the document.

2. From the application's File menu, choose "Open." This will display the "Open" dialog box, as shown below.

3. In the Open dialog box, find the name of the file you want to open. If the name is visible and is black (as opposed to gray), the application can probably open it. Double-click the file name.

    If the name doesn't appear at all, the application can't "naturally" open it, **BUT** the Open dialog box in your application might have a little menu or two, like the ones circled below, that give you more options for what sorts of files this application can open. If it does, choose something like "All Types" or try to find the specific "extension" (abbreviation at the end of the name) and see if that makes your document name appear in the list. If the document's name does appear in black, it will probably open when you double-click its name.

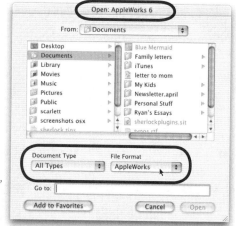

Check the "File Format" menu to see what other sorts of files can be opened.

Some documents don't really need to be *opened* before you can use them. For instance, you don't have to "open" photographs or clipart if you want to put them on a page of a text document such as a letter, newsletter, or email. Instead, you need to "insert" or "place" the image into the document.

Opening Clipart or Photos

To place clipart into a document:

1. Click the insertion point at the position where you want the clipart or photograph to be in the document.

2. Find the command in that application to "Insert," "Place," "Get picture," or something similar.

3. Use the dialog box that comes up to find the photo or clipart you want to place on the page. (This assumes you know how to "navigate" in an Open dialog box; if not, see the following pages.) When you find the name of the graphic you want, double-click it.

4. The image will land in your text right where the insertion point was flashing. In most programs you can resize the image: click once on the image, hold the Shift key down, then drag the bottom-right corner diagonally upward.

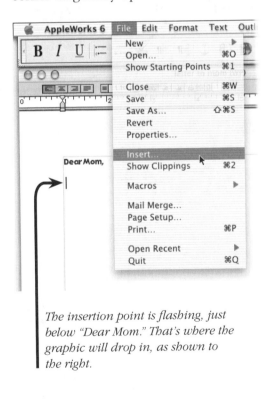

The insertion point is flashing, just below "Dear Mom." That's where the graphic will drop in, as shown to the right.

An "Open" Dialog Box

Finding your way around an **"Open" dialog box** is called "navigating." It's one of the most important skills you can learn, and you'll need this skill in other dialog boxes, like when you save documents or when you import or export text. Try to take the time to understand and absorb what each part of the dialog box is telling you. (Skip the opposite page until you need it.)

*The name in the **From menu** is the specific folder or disk that contains the files you see in the directory (lists) below.*

*In this example, the "From" menu **(A)** says you can open a file from the Documents folder. The Documents folder is selected in the left column **(B)**, and the contents of the Documents folder are listed in the right column **(C)**. At the moment, then, you can open any document stored in that Documents folder— just double-click on the file name in the right column.*

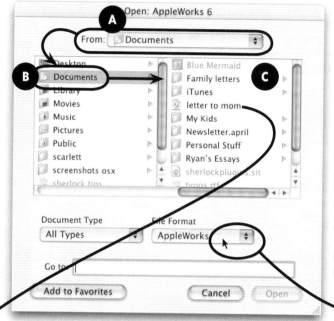

*The **documents** that appear in black (as opposed to gray) in this list are documents that the current application can open. (The **folders** are always black because you can always open them to find more documents.)*

*Single-click any name to **select** that file, as shown below.*

*Double-click the name to **open** the file, which will place that document on your screen.*

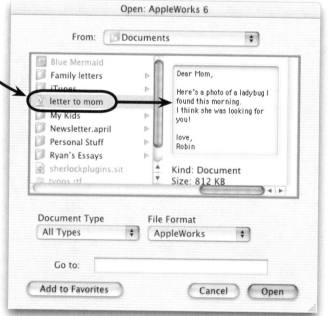

*If you **single-click** on a document name, that column slides over to the left, and in the new column on the far right you'll see a preview of the selected document.*

*Use the horizontal **scroller** to go back to a previous column, just as you would in a window in Column View.*

*Click **Cancel** to take you back to where you were before you chose "Open" from the File menu.*

*Click **Open** to open the **selected** file; or double-click directly on the file name in the list.*

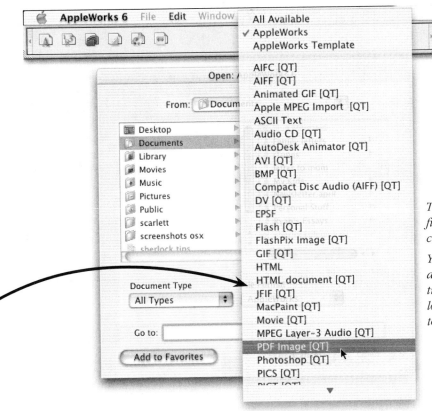

These are some of the different file formats that AppleWorks can "read," or open.

You don't have to know what all these are—I don't. Just try to find one that sounds or looks like the file you're trying to open.

File won't open?

If the name of the file you want to open is shown in the list in gray (instead of black), that doesn't necessarily mean it's impossible for the current application to open it. Most applications have a number of other "file formats" they can "read," or open. Click on the "File Format" menu (circled on the opposite page), if your application has one, to get the list of formats it can open. As you can see above, AppleWorks can open an incredible range of file formats.

If your application has a menu like the one shown above, called something like "Document Type" or anything similar, make sure it is set to try to open "All Types" of documents.

— continued

Open another folder If you've been saving all of your documents in the Documents folder, then you won't have to navigate anywhere else to find your documents. But at some point you will start making new folders in which to store your work, and you need to know how to find these in the Open dialog box.

If you learned how to work with the Finder windows in Column View (Chapter 6), you'll find the Open dialog box very familiar—you can enlarge the dialog box and go find other folders, as shown on the opposite page.

There is also a list of menu options that will take you to **certain folders or disks** on your Mac, as shown below. This menu can be a shortcut to help you find the document you want to open.

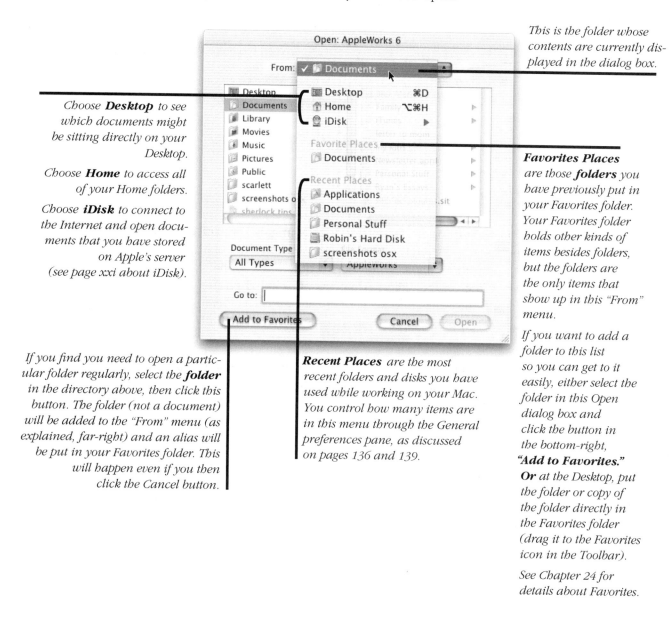

This is the folder whose contents are currently displayed in the dialog box.

*Choose **Desktop** to see which documents might be sitting directly on your Desktop.*

*Choose **Home** to access all of your Home folders.*

*Choose **iDisk** to connect to the Internet and open documents that you have stored on Apple's server (see page xxi about iDisk).*

Favorites Places *are those **folders** you have previously put in your Favorites folder. Your Favorites folder holds other kinds of items besides folders, but the folders are the only items that show up in this "From" menu.*

If you want to add a folder to this list so you can get to it easily, either select the folder in this Open dialog box and click the button in the bottom-right, ***"Add to Favorites." Or*** *at the Desktop, put the folder or copy of the folder directly in the Favorites folder (drag it to the Favorites icon in the Toolbar).*

See Chapter 24 for details about Favorites.

*If you find you need to open a particular folder regularly, select the **folder** in the directory above, then click this button. The folder (not a document) will be added to the "From" menu (as explained, far-right) and an alias will be put in your Favorites folder. This will happen even if you then click the Cancel button.*

Recent Places *are the most recent folders and disks you have used while working on your Mac. You control how many items are in this menu through the General preferences pane, as discussed on pages 136 and 139.*

You can open the dialog box wider and **navigate** through it just like you navigate through the Column View windows on the Desktop. Press the Tab key to select the From menu or the columns below. Use the arrow keys to move left or right from column to column, or up or down in one column.

Drag the bottom-right corner to widen the window.

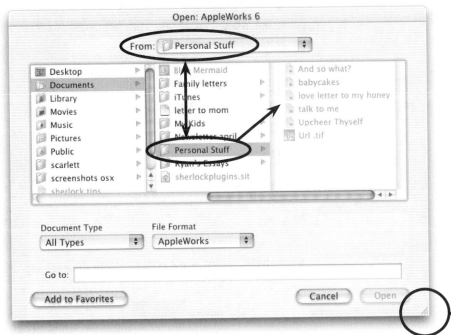

Single-click a folder or a disk *to see a list of the files inside that folder or on that disk, and the title of that new folder or disk will be displayed in the "From" menu above the list.*

Drag here to make the window larger or smaller.

Use the slider bar to scroll to the left and get to the Home level of your Mac, or even to the Computer level, so you can locate the folder and document you want to open.

Splash.mov

1. Is this file an application or a document?

_____

2. What will happen when you double-click on the icon in #1?

_____

Internet Explorer

3. Is this file an application or a document?

_____

4. What will happen when you double-click on the icon in #3?

_____

5. What would be the fastest way to view a window by "Kind" so you can tell which file is the application?

_____

6. In the File menu in an application, what is the difference between "New" and "Open"?

_____

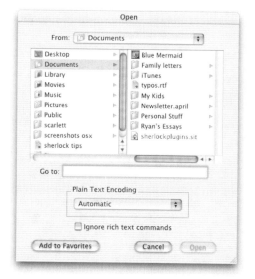

7. Label these parts of the Open dialog box to the left:

   a. the directory, or list of files and folders you can open.

   b. a document that can be opened.

   c. the name of the folder that contains the files you see in the list.

   d. the menu that will display favorite and recent folders.

Answers on page 731.

Word Processing

also known as "typing"

You may have grown up **typing** on a typewriter or you may have grown up **word processing** on a computer of some sort. Typing and word processing are very similar, of course, in that they use a similar keyboard. The difference is that word processing is much more fun. You can delete text with the click of a button; rearrange single words, paragraphs, or entire pages of text; automatically number all the pages; resize the text so it fills out the requirement for your project; use italic, bold, and different typefaces for emphasis; and much more.

You're going to be typing everywhere on your Mac. In some applications typing is the main point, as in word processing, page layout, and email. In others, it is the way to input the data (information) you need to manipulate, as in databases or spreadsheets. In others, typing is a sideline that is occasionally necessary, as in paint programs. And all over your Mac you'll find dialog boxes where you type some answer or other, and even on your Desktop you type the names of files and folders. Fortunately, in the consistent Mac environment, typing follows the same patterns and features everywhere, so you should read this chapter no matter how you plan to use your computer.

Contents of this chapter

I-Beam

You may already be familiar with the Macintosh word processing **I-beam** (pronounced eye-beam). It looks like this (or very similar): ⌶ The tiny cross-bar just below the center of the I-beam indicates the "baseline" of type, that invisible line that type sits upon.

On the Mac, the I-beam is a **visual clue** that you are now in a typing mode, as opposed to seeing an arrow or a cross-hair or any number of other "cursors" that appear in various applications.

> *The I-beam is simply another pointer.* And just like the pointer, it doesn't do anything until you *click it* or *press-and-drag it.*

Insertion Point

When you move the I-beam pointer to a spot within text and *click,* it sets down a flashing **insertion point** that looks like this: │ (but it flashes).

This insertion point is extremely important! After you click the mouse to set the insertion point, then you can move the I-beam out of the way (using the mouse)—**the insertion point is what you need to begin typing,** *not the I-beam!!* The I-beam just positions the insertion point.

Practice: Open TextEdit (it's in your Applications folder), or your favorite word processor.

Just start typing. Type about a paragraph, ignoring typos. Notice how the **insertion point** moves in front of the characters as you type.

At the ends of lines, **do not** hit the Return key—the text, as you type, will bump into the far-right edge and bounce back to the left side automatically. (See page 200 about using the Return key.)

Now move the mouse around, and notice how the cursor is not a pointer, but an **I-beam**. (It might be a pointer when you move off of the word processing page, but when when you move it over the text, it becomes the I-beam.)

Position that I-beam anywhere in your paragraph, click, shove the mouse out of the way, and start typing. Notice the insertion point moved to where you clicked the I-beam, and your new typing starts at that point.

With the insertion point flashing, anything you type will start at that point and move out to the right. This is true whether the insertion point is at the beginning or the end of a paragraph, in the middle of a word, in a field of a dialog box, in the name of an icon at your Desktop, or anywhere else. (The only time the words will not move to the right in a word processor is if the text is centered or flush right, or if you've set a tab other than left-aligned.)

At any time you can use the mouse to move the I-beam pointer somewhere else, click, and start typing from the new insertion point.

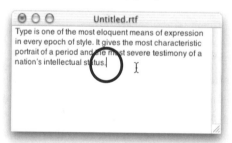

Do you see the insertion point at the end of the paragraph? If I start to type again in this story, it will begin at that insertion point. The I-beam (do you see it?) is just hanging around waiting to be useful.

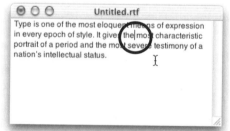

Do you see where I moved the insertion point to? If I start to type again in this story, it will begin at that insertion point.

Also from that insertion point, press the **Delete** key (found in the upper right, called the **Backspace** key on older keyboards or typewriters) to backspace *to the left* of the insertion point and remove any text along the way.

So you can backspace/delete to **correct typos** as you type, *or* you can click to set the insertion point down anywhere else in your text and backspace from that new position.

When you want to continue typing at the end of your story, use the I-beam to position the insertion point at the end of the story.

**Delete
(or Backspace)**

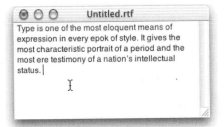

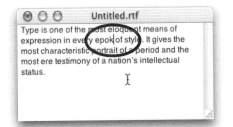

This paragraph has a typo. Do you see it? I need to go back and fix it.

*I used the I-beam to move the insertion point just to the **right** of the typo. Now I can hit the Delete key to erase that wrong letter and type the correct one in its place.*

Practice: In the paragraph you typed earlier, take note of where the insertion point is, then hit the **Delete** key several times. Watch as it deletes the characters **to the left** of the insertion point.

If you have a **Forward Delete** key (del), experiment with that one as well.

If you have a full-sized keyboard with the little pad of edit keys in the middle, as shown on page 34, you have a **Forward Delete** key. It's marked with "del." This is a fabulous key—it deletes characters *to the right* of the insertion point (the regular Delete key deletes to the left, or backwards as you type).

Forward Delete key

What?! One space after a period? If you grew up on a typewriter, this is a difficult habit to change, I know. Or if you were taught keyboarding skills by someone who grew up on a typewriter, they taught you typewriter rules. But characters on a Macintosh are not *monospaced* as they are on a typewriter (except for a few typefaces such as Monaco, Courier, and Andale Mono), so there is no need to use two spaces to separate two sentences. Check any book or magazine on your shelf; you will never find two spaces after periods (except publications produced on a computer typed by someone still using typewriter rules). If you find this hard to accept, read *The Mac is not a typewriter*. If you're interested in creating fine typography, read *The Non-Designer's Type Book*. Yes, I wrote them.

**One Space
After Periods**

For the ultimate authority on the question, check the question-and-answer page on the web site for the *Chicago Manual of Style:* **www.press.uchicago.edu/ Misc/Chicago/cmosfaq.html**

Selecting (Highlighting) Text

When you **select text,** it becomes **highlighted.** Once it is selected, you can do things to it, such as change its size, the typeface, delete it, etc.

If you take the I-beam and double-click on a word anywhere on the Mac, the entire word is selected, indicated by the highlighting.

This word is highlighted. I double-clicked on the word to select it.

To select more than one word, press-and-drag over the entire area you wish to highlight. The entire sentence is highlighted.

To select all of the text in an entire document, use the keyboard shortcut Command A.

To un-highlight (deselect) text, click once anywhere, even in the highlighted space.

Practice: In the paragraph you typed earlier, use the I-beam to **double-click** on a word to select it.

Select a range of text: Position the I-beam somewhere toward the top of the paragraph, press the mouse button down and hold it down, then drag the mouse downward. You can move backward as well, as long as you keep the mouse button down. When you have a range of text selected, let go of the mouse button.

Replacing highlighted text

Once a word is selected (highlighted), anything you type will **entirely replace the selected text.** That is, you don't have to hit the Delete key first to get rid of the text—just type. This is true everywhere on the Mac.

While the text is selected you can now change the font (typeface) or style or size of the text using your menu commands. Or you can copy or cut or delete that text. Or you can paste something in to replace it. In fact, you *cannot* do any of these things *unless* the text is first highlighted. (Each of these procedures is explained in this chapter.)

Practice: In the paragraph you typed earlier, use the I-beam to double-click on a word to select it. Without hitting the Delete key to delete the selected text, just type a new word and watch it replace the selected word.

Try selecting a range of text, as above, and while it is highlighted, type a new sentence.

Try these shortcuts for **selecting text** anywhere on the Mac:

▾ Double-click in the middle of a word to select the whole word.

▾ Triple-click in the middle of a sentence to select either the whole line or the entire paragraph (depending on the application).

▾ The arrow keys move the insertion point backward and forward, up and down. Hold down the Shift key as you use the arrow keys, and the text will be *selected* along the way.

▾ If you have a lot of text to select, try this:

1. **Click** (don't press and drag) at the *beginning* of the text you want to select.

2. Scroll, if necessary, to the *end* of the text you want to select, even if it's on another page.

3. Hold down the **Shift** key and **click.** Everything between **click and Shift-click** will be selected. You gotta try it.

This also works in spreadsheets and database lists. In page layout applications, it only works within one linked story.

▾ In many applications, the numeric keypad will either type numbers (when the Num Lock key is down) or it will move the insertion point (when Num Lock is not down). Experiment with it. For instance, in Microsoft Word or Adobe PageMaker, the number 1 will bounce the insertion point to the beginning of a line, and the number 7 will bounce it to the end. Other keys move the insertion point up or down a paragraph, a page, a word, etc. And if you hold the Shift key down, the text will be selected as the insertion point moves.

Several selection tips

Very few applications* let you select "discontiguous" text— that is, it's generally not possible to select one line from the first paragraph, plus a line from the third paragraph. The selected text must all be contiguous, or connected together.

*One notable exception is the great word processor called Nisus Writer from Nisus Software, www.nisus.com.

Practice: You can skip these techniques if you are new to word processing—come back later when you feel more comfortable.

If you've been word processing for a while, experiment with each of these techniques. They are incredibly handy.

When to Use the Return Key

A word wrap is sometimes called a soft Return (although technically it isn't).

For typewriter users: The Return key is the equivalent of the carriage return on a typewriter.

Word wrap: In a word processor, you should *never* hit the Return key at the end of your line *unless* it is the end of the paragraph or unless you *really do* want the line to end there, as in an address. This is because word processors *word wrap*—when the words get close to the right margin, they just wrap themselves around onto the next line. Why is that? Well...

Hard Return: When you press the Return key you insert what is called a *hard Return* that tells the computer to always stop the line at that point. So if you change your margins, your line *always* breaks at that hard Return, as shown below. Just keep those nimble fingers moving along and only hit the Return key when you really want a new paragraph.

Practice: In Text Edit, type a paragraph, but this time hit a Return at the end of each line as you approach the right margin.

Then take your mouse and position the pointer (notice it's not an I-beam once you are out of the word processing space), and drag the bottom-right corner to resize the window. Notice how your lines always break at those Returns you typed, no matter how you change the margins.

(If your margins don't change in TextEdit, go to the Format menu and choose "Wrap to Window.")

As you make the margins narrower, you will get other line breaks where the text automatically adjusts itself to the new margins, as they should.

Although you can't see it, I typed a hard Return at the end of each of these lines. It looks fine at the moment.

Type is one of the most eloquent means of expression in every epoch of style. It gives the most characteristic portrait of a period and the most severe testimony of a nation's intellectual status.
Peter Behrens

When I widened the margins by enlarging the size of the window in TextEdit, the lines still broke at the hard Returns. This can be okay sometimes.

Type is one of the most eloquent means of expression in every epoch of style. It gives the most characteristic portrait of a period and the most severe testimony of a nation's intellectual status.
Peter Behrens

But when I made the window narrower, which in TextEdit makes the margins narrower,* you can see the problem that results from those hard Returns.

Type is one of the most eloquent means of
expression in every epoch of style.
It gives
the most characteristic portrait of a period
and the most severe testimony of
a nation's
intellectual status.
Peter Behrens

*In TextEdit, if your margins don't change when you make the window narower, go to the Format menu and choose "Wrap to Window."

Tip: To the computer, a **paragraph** is created every time you hit the Return key. So the computer thinks a return address of three lines is really three paragraphs.

Double-Return: Hitting the Return key twice creates a double space between the lines. This is for extra space between individual paragraphs (although in any good word processor you can ask for an automatic increase of space between paragraphs instead of a double-Return).

If you want the entire document, or even just a piece of it, double-spaced—that's different: there is always an instant way to change your spacing to double-spaced, usually just a button to click *after you select all the text.* Check your manual for the method for your particular application.

Removing a Return: The computer sees a Return as just another character, which means to remove a Return you simply *backspace over it* with the Delete key, just as you would to remove an unwanted character. The problem is that in most programs you can't *see* the Return character. So you must set the insertion point just to the left of the first character on the line and backspace/delete, like so:

> Let's say I'm typing away and my dog shoves his big head under my arm
> and suddenly
>
> my text starts typing on the wrong line, like this. What to do?

Tip: Most word processing programs (but not TextEdit) have a command for showing invisible characters such as Returns and spaces, which makes it easier to get rid of unnecessary ones. The command might be something like "Show invisibles," "Show ¶" or "Display ¶." Check your menus.

Set the insertion point directly to the left of the text that's on the wrong line (as shown below).

> Let's say I'm typing away and my dog shoves his big head under my arm
> and suddenly
>
> my text starts typing on the wrong line, like this. What to do?

Hit the Delete key to remove the empty line above that new, unwanted paragraph (**you** don't think it's a paragraph, but the computer does). Now it will look like this:

> Let's say I'm typing away and my dog shoves his big head under my arm
> and suddenly
> my text starts typing on the wrong line, like this. What to do?

Delete again to wrap the sentence back up to the one above.

> Let's say I'm typing away and my dog shoves his big head under my arm
> and suddenly my text starts typing on the wrong line, like this. What to do?
> Oh, it's all fixed!

Changing Fonts (typefaces) and Rule No. 2

Or as my friend Don Nissen, a design instructor at Ivy Tech State College, explains more elegantly: "Select, then affect." "This seems to clarify to students that, if something isn't selected, it ain't gonna be affected."

Throughout the entire Mac environment, to make any changes to anything you must follow this rule, Rule No. 2:

Select First, Then Do It To It.

For instance, **to change to a different font,** or typeface:

1. First *select* the characters you want to change (press-and-drag over the text). If you want to change all of the text, press Command A to select all.

2. Then *choose* the font name you want to change it into.

   The font list is found in your menu under various labels, depending on your application. It might be under Fonts, Type, Format, or something similar.

   In TextEdit, go to the Format menu, choose "Font," then "Font Panel...." Select a font from the list that appears.

Formatting the insertion point

Notice that the insertion point picks up whatever font, style, size, and alignment *is directly to its left*. No matter where you set the insertion point, you will type in the font, etc., of the character to its left, even if that character is an empty space. **But you can format the insertion point.**

Now, let's say you want the next few words you're going to type to be in a different font. Do you need to type the text first and then select those characters and change the font? No!

1. Make sure your insertion point is positioned where you are going to type with the new font.

2. *With no text selected*, choose the font (and style and size, if you like).

   When there is no text selected, all the formatting gets poured into the insertion point—whatever you type next will be in the font you just chose.

   As soon as you place the insertion point elsewhere, though, it will again pick up all the formatting of the character to its left.

Practice: Use the paragraph you typed earlier and **change some text to a different typeface,** like this:

Double-click a word to select it, or drag over a range of text.

Then go to the Font menu in your application and choose a new font.

Or change the typeface before you type:

Position your insertion point at the end of your existing text.

Hit Return.

Now, while the insertion point is flashing, choose a different font.

Start typing.

Style refers to whether the type is plain, **bold,** *italic,* condensed, etc. To change the style of the type, you need to follow Rule #2: *select first, then do it to it.* **Select** the type you want to change (highlight it), then **choose** the style you want from the menu. Depending on the application, you can choose more than one of these; for instance, you can have a face that is ***bold italic condensed.***

Not all typefaces have all of the options, as shown below. Many applications limit you to just the designed faces; that is, in some programs you can force a typeface to fake an italic, but in most you can't do that anymore.

If you're using an application that lets you apply pretend italic or shadow or outline to a typeface, you can remove all of the style choices at once: *select* the text and *choose* Plain or Normal from the font style menu.

Changing Style

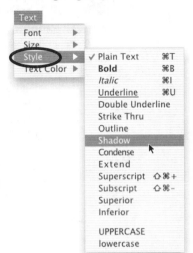

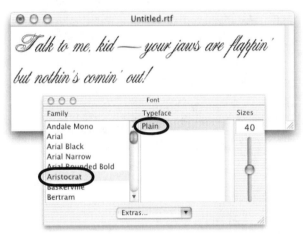

In the Font panel in TextEdit, you see a list of fonts on the left. On the right are the individual style choices that are available for the selected typeface. Notice this typeface, Aristocrat, has only one option, Plain. That's because you can't have an italic version of a script like this, and the designer apparently did not create a bold face for this font (well, she might have, but it's not loaded on this Mac).

In AppleWorks, this is the list of styles you can apply, whether they are designed into the font or not. To remove all applied styles, choose "Plain Text."

(In TextEdit, however, "Plain Text" is something completely different! Don't choose it—see the following page for information about what "Plain Text" is in TextEdit.)

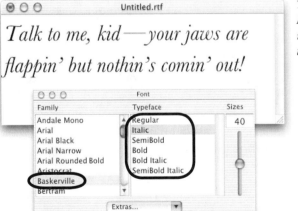

This selected font family, Baskerville, has a broader range of styles from which to choose.

> **Practice:** Follow the practice exercise on the opposite page, but this time choose a different style for the selected text.

Changing Styles Mid-Sentence — without using the menu

As explained on page 202 about changing *fonts*, you can just as easily choose the style you want from the menu *before* you type the text (as long as you don't move the insertion point after choosing). But even that's a pain if you just want to italicize the next word and then return to normal text. This is an easier method:

Notice the keyboard shortcuts in the menu shown below? In most applications they are the same: Command **B** for Bold, Command **I** for Italic, etc. (Some programs may use Command Shift B and Command Shift I, etc.)

Learn these keyboard shortcuts!

▼ As you're typing along, simply press Command **B** and the next word you type will be **bold.**

▼ When you want the next word to be *not* bold, press Command **B** again and it will take *off* the bold (that's called a *toggle switch*— when choosing the same command turns that command off).

▼ Logically, you can press Command **B I** to create a word that is (guess!) ***bold italic.***

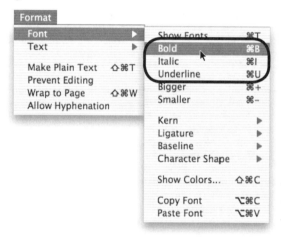

These are the typical keyboard shortcuts to make selected text bold, italic, or underline.

Remember, though, you should only choose italic or bold if you know that typeface has a real italic or bold designed in the family.

If you don't know how to find out (see Chapter 26 if you care), just look carefully at the text on the screen. If it looks like regular text that has been fattened or slanted instead of designed, it's fake.

Practice: In your word processor, go to the Style menu and see exactly which keyboard command it uses to apply the bold or italic style (it's most likely Command B for bold and Command I for italic).

Type a few words.

Press the keyboard command for **bold,** then type a few more words. They should be in bold.

Now type the keyboard command for **bold** again, which will remove it.

Type a few more words and they should be in the regular style, not bold.

Try it again, this time press Command B I to change to both bold and italic at once.

▼ If you want to take all the extra formatting off at once (for instance, you want to remove the shadow, the outline, and the bold), select the text and apply the shortcut for Plain, Normal, or Regular style—whatever your application calls it.

(This trick doesn't work in TextEdit. "Plain Text" in TextEdit actually refers to ASCII text, which is type stripped down to nothing but standard characters—no italic, no bold, no underline, no indents, only one font, etc. Choose "Plain Text" in TextEdit when you want to send this document to someone using a PC so their machine doesn't get confused by the character formatting.)

Size in type is measured in *points*. There are 72 points in one inch, but you don't have to remember that. In your menu you see different numbers (points) referring to the size of type; logically, the bigger the number, the bigger the type.

As usual, **to change the size of characters:** *select first, then do it to it.*

1. Select the text.

2. Go to the Size menu and choose a point size.

   In TextEdit, there is no "Size" menu. Go to the Format menu, choose "Font," then "Font Panel…." You'll see the size slider on the far right, as shown below.

Or set your insertion point and choose the size from the menu *before* you type (see the previous two sections on changing fonts and styles).

Changing Type Size

8 point type

48 pt.

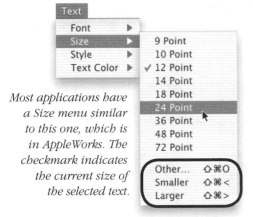

Most applications have a Size menu similar to this one, which is in AppleWorks. The checkmark indicates the current size of the selected text.

Choose "Other…" to type in a number that isn't on the list.

Use the other two keyboard shortcuts to make the selected type smaller or larger right in front of your eyes: Hold down the Shift and Command keys, then tap the LessThan (<) or GreaterThan (>) symbols over and over; each tap reduces or enlarges the selected type by one point.

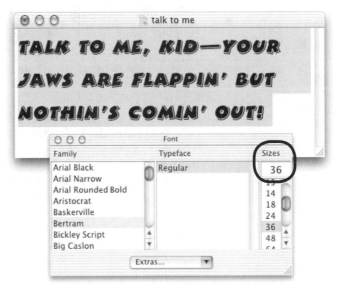

This is TextEdit. Notice the text in the window is selected. Once your text is selected, you can either type in a new number in the box on the right side of the Font panel, or click to select one of the sizes in the scrolling list.

Practice: Follow the two steps above to change the point size of selected type.

If you're using AppleWorks, try the keyboard shortcut.

Alignment

Alignment refers to where the text is lined up.

▾ *Align left:* text is lined up on the left side, and the right is ragged, as shown in these sentences. Also known as *flush left.*

▾ *Align right:* text is lined up on the right, and the left edge is ragged. Also known as *flush right.*

▾ *Align center:* text is centered on a vertical axis *between your margins.* If you change your margins, your centered text will shift.

▾ *Justified:* text is lined up on both the left *and* right margins, as seen in the paragraphs below.

To change your alignment, you know what to do! That's right: *select first, then do it to it*—highlight the text, *then* choose the alignment from the menu or the buttons, as shown below.

Alignment is **paragraph-specific** formatting; that is, whichever alignment you choose will apply to the *entire paragraph*—it's not possible to apply it to only one line in the paragraph. (Remember, to the computer, every time you hit a Return you create a new paragraph.)

The important thing about this concept is that you don't have to select every character in a paragraph to change the alignment—selecting a few characters or even just clicking your insertion point anywhere in the paragraph *selects the entire paragraph.*

This is different from **character-specific** formatting such as font, size, and style, where the commands only apply to the *individual, selected characters.*

Rulers

Every word processor has a **ruler** that appears at the top of a document, as shown below. If you don't see it, you'll find a menu command that says something like "Show Ruler." Generally, all the buttons you see in the ruler are also listed as menu commands, but the ruler makes it so convenient.

If you're practicing in TextEdit right now and you don't see the ruler, go to the Format menu, choose "Text," then choose "Show Ruler." Or just press Command R.

Alignment buttons: left, center, right, and justified.

This changes the spacing between lines.

This typical ruler is the one in AppleWorks.

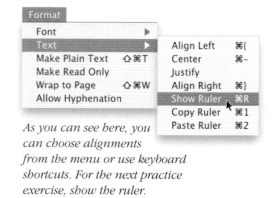

As you can see here, you can choose alignments from the menu or use keyboard shortcuts. For the next practice exercise, show the ruler.

Below are two examples of text that is **selected** to change the alignment. If you want to apply an alignment to more than one paragraph, you must select every one that you want to change. The paragraphs must be contiguous, or next to each other; that is, in most applications you cannot select the first paragraph and the third paragraph at the same time.

Here is an important thing to remember about rulers: ***every paragraph has its own ruler.*** Alignments, margins, tabs, line spacing—everything applies to the *entire* paragraph and *only* to the selected paragraph(s)!

These are the alignment buttons in TextEdit's ruler. Just select the text and click a button.

The circle in the headline is around the insertion point—to select a paragraph, all you need to do is click the insertion point in it (the computer thinks the headline is a paragraph).

This is another way to select a paragraph— just grab a piece of it, as much or as little as you want. The alignment will apply to the entire paragraph no matter how little of it you select.

Practice: The important thing to be aware of when changing alignment is **exactly what gets changed.** For instance, click once in the headline, then change the alignment to centered. Notice the change in the headline did not affect the rest of the page!

Now click once in the body copy, and take a look at the alignment buttons— the flush left button is still selected, **not** the centered button. That 's because **the ruler affects only the selected paragraphs.** If you click once again on the headline, you'll see the centered alignment button selected.

Blank Spaces

The computer thinks a **blank space** is just the same as any other character—it has no idea that you can't see that character. Every Tab, Return, Spacebar space, etc., that appears invisible to us is an actual thing to the Mac. This means you can select blank spaces, blank lines, blank tabbed spaces, or Returns to delete them. Select and delete them just as you would any other character.

The space between these█words is highlighted.

████████This tabbed space is highlighted.

If you hit double Returns, you can also select the blank space between the lines, as shown below, and delete it.

██

The bar above is the blank space indicating an empty line.

Also, since these blank spaces are characters, you can actually change the size of them (font size, that is, as explained on page 205), as well as the *leading* (space between the lines), the paragraph spacing, etc., all of which would affect the size of the empty space.

But the most important thing to understand about blank spaces is that the Mac takes them into consideration when you center lines or paragraphs, when you try to align columns, and during other word processing techniques. So you must be conscious of where those blank spaces are!

Practice: Type a couple of paragraphs. Use several double-Returns and a couple of tabs (just hit the Tab key, then type).

Now using the selection techniques you practiced on page 198, select not the words, but the blank spaces.

Centering Text

As explained on the opposite page, when you center a word or line, the Mac takes all those blank spaces into consideration, so any Spacebar spaces or any indents or any tabs you've inserted will be used to calculate the center of the line, making the line appear to be uncentered!

If you want to center a headline or a paragraph of text, *do not* use a centered tab to do so! Instead, find the button in the toolbar (shown on pages 206 and 207) to center the text. Centered tabs are only for centering columns of text.

This line is centered.

This line is also centered ⟵

but the line includes an invisible tab.

I hit the Tab key before I typed the first word in this centered line. Thus the line appears, to our eyes, to be uncentered. (The Mac, however, believes it to be centered.)

The invisible tab character
that is disrupting the alignment
must be highlighted
and removed, like so:

This line is also centered. ⟵

I selected the tab space and deleted it.

Then it will center just fine:

This line is also centered. ⟵

After I deleted the invisible space, the line centered just fine.

Cut, Copy, and the Clipboard

Almost anywhere you can type, you can cut or copy text. When you **cut** text (or graphics), it is *removed* from your document and placed on the "Clipboard." When you **copy** text (or graphics), the original text *is left in your document* and a *copy* of it is placed on the Clipboard. Well, what the heck is a Clipboard?

The **Clipboard** is an invisible "container" somewhere in the depths of the Mac. It holds whatever you have *cut or copied,* be it text, spreadsheet data, graphics, an entire folder, etc. Once something is on the Clipboard, it waits there until you paste it in somewhere (we'll get to that in a minute).

The most important thing to remember about the is that it holds *only one thing at a time;* that is, as soon as you cut or copy something else, whatever was in the Clipboard to begin with is *replaced* with the new selection.

In some programs, including the Finder, you'll find a menu command called *Show Clipboard,* in which case it appears as a window with its contents displayed, as shown below. In most programs, though, you never see the actual Clipboard—simply trust that it's there.

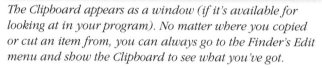

The Clipboard appears as a window (if it's available for looking at in your program). No matter where you copied or cut an item from, you can always go to the Finder's Edit menu and show the Clipboard to see what you've got.

If your application lets you see the Clipboard, it will be a command in the Edit menu.

Items will stay on the Clipboard even when you change applications: you can put a paint image on the Clipboard in a paint program, then open a word processing document and paste the paint image into a letter.

Items will disappear from the Clipboard when the computer is turned off or if there is a power failure—the contents are stored in RAM (memory), so anytime RAM gets wiped out, so do the contents of the Clipboard. (There's an explanation of memory on page 220.)

Practice: The practice exercise for cut, copy, and paste is on page 212.

How to Copy: Simply select, then do it to it. For instance, select the text you wish to copy (press-and-drag over it), then from the Edit menu choose "Copy." The text will *remain* in your document and a *copy* will be placed on the Clipboard.

Copy

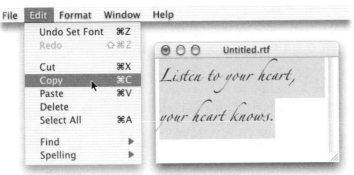

This text is selected and the Copy command is chosen. You can see it on the Clipboard on the opposite page.

OK, it's on the Clipboard. Now what? Well, the Clipboard holds objects for *pasting*. You can take text or a graphic out of one place and paste it into your document somewhere else, just as if you had a little glue pot. We'll get to that in just a moment (next page).

How to Cut: Simply select, then do it to it. For instance, select the text you wish to remove from the document (press-and-drag over it). Then from the Edit menu choose "Cut." The text will be *eliminated* from your document and placed on the Clipboard. (Be sure to read about "Delete" further on in this chapter.) Now you can paste it somewhere; see the following page.

Cut

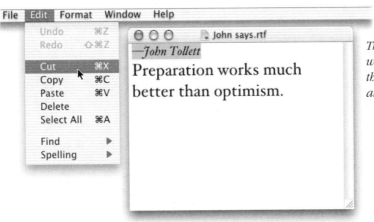

*This text is selected. I don't want this text at the top of the page like this—I want it at the **end** of the quote.*

Paste   **How to Paste:** All you do is go to the Edit menu and choose "Paste," but it's important to know *where* it will paste into.

▼ Whatever was on the Clipboard will be inserted in your document *beginning at the flashing insertion point.* So if you want the pasted item to appear at a certain place in your document, **first** click the I-beam to position the insertion point.

▼ If you have a *range of text selected,* the pasted item will *replace* what was selected.

Say you have a paragraph in Letter A that you want to use to replace a paragraph in Letter B. Copy the paragraph in Letter A, open Letter B, select the paragraph you don't want in Letter B, paste, and the paragraph from Letter A will *replace* the selected paragraph in Letter B.

▼ Spreadsheet data, graphics, etc., can be pasted in as well. In some programs, especially graphic programs, the pasted object will just land in the middle of the page.

As long as something is on the Clipboard, you can paste it in a million times in many different applications.

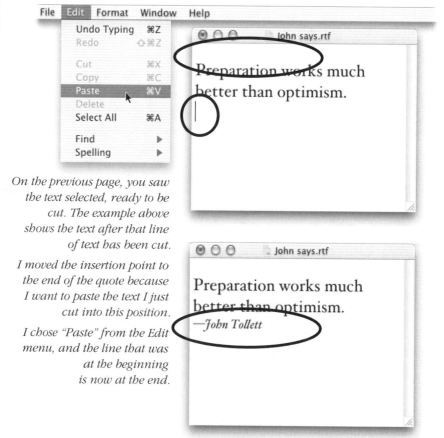

On the previous page, you saw the text selected, ready to be cut. The example above shows the text after that line of text has been cut.

I moved the insertion point to the end of the quote because I want to paste the text I just cut into this position.

I chose "Paste" from the Edit menu, and the line that was at the beginning is now at the end.

Cut, copy, and paste are not limited to text. You will use these features in every program you have, as well as the Desktop. Below is an example of copying a graphic image from a drawing program and pasting it into the text in a word processing document. The application I used is AppleWorks, which includes not only drawing and word processing, but paint, database, spreadsheet, and slideshow modules.

Cut and paste graphics, also

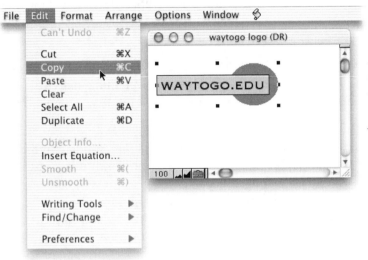

I created this little logo in the drawing module of AppleWorks. I selected it, then opened my word processor, below, and pasted it in.

Delete or Clear and the Clipboard

Now, the **Delete** key (on the upper-right of the main group of keys, called **Backspace** on older keyboards and typewriters) works a little differently from Cut: if you hit this key while something is selected, whatever is selected is *deleted* but is *not* placed on the Clipboard. This means if you are holding something in the Clipboard to paste in again, whatever you *delete* from your document will not replace what is currently being held in the Clipboard. But it also means that you don't have that deleted item anymore—whatever you delete is really gone. **Clear,** in the Edit menu, does the same thing as the Delete key.

Undo

Undo can sometimes save your boompah (no, that's not computer jargon —it's Grandma's euphemism). When you do something that makes you scream, "Aack! Oh no!" then try Undo. It's always the first command in the Edit menu (or press Command Z).

> **Note:** What Undo can undo is *only the last action that occurred.* For instance, if you selected two paragraphs of brilliantly witty text that you spent three hours composing and then the cat walked across your keyboard and obliterated the entire work, Undo could give it back to you **IF** you Undo before you touch *anything.* If you start fiddling around with the keys and the mouse, then what you will undo is that fiddling around. So if something goes wrong, don't scream—**UNDO.** Then scream.
>
> (Some applications, such as illustration programs and page layout applications, can Undo multiple times. Check your manual.)

Commands Z, X, C, V

Thoughtfully, the keyboard shortcuts for the undo/cut/copy/paste commands are very handy. Notice on your keyboard the letters **Z, X, C,** and **V,** all lined up in a row right above the Command key. Remember, select first (*except to Undo*); then hold down the Command key and lightly tap the letter.

Command **Z** will Undo (Z is very close to the Command key).

Command **X** will Cut   (X like eXiting or Xing it out).

Command **C** will Copy (C for Copy).

Command **V** will Paste (V because it is next to C; it's sort of like the caret symbol ^ for inserting).

Special characters are the symbols you have access to on the Macintosh that weren't available on typewriters, such as upside-down question marks for Spanish (¿), the pound symbol for English money (£), the cents sign (¢), the registration or trademark symbols (® ™), etc. You can view all these with your **Key Caps** utility; see pages 464–465.

Below is a short list of special characters you can experiment with. For each character, hold down the modifier key (Option, Shift, etc.) and tap the character key noted. For instance, to type a bullet, hold down the Option key and tap the number 8 on the top of your keyboard (not the number 8 on the keypad). It's no different from typing an asterisk, where you hold down the Shift key and tap the 8. A complete list is in Appendix B.

•	bullet	Option 8
©	copyright	Option G
™	trademark	Option 2
®	registration	Option R
¢	cents	Option $
°	degree	Option Shift 8
…	ellipsis	Option ;
–	en dash	Option Hyphen
—	em dash	Option Shift Hyphen

You can type **accent marks** on the Mac, as in résumé and piñata. There is a complete chart in Appendix B, but it's easy to remember that you use the Option key, and the accents are hiding beneath the keyboard characters that would usually be under them. For example, the acute accent over the **é** is **Option e;** the tilde over the **ñ** is **Option n.**

To type accent marks, follow these steps (using the word Résumé):

1. Type the word until you come to the letter that will be *under* the accent mark; e.g., **R**

2. *Before* you type that next letter (the letter **e** in this case), type the Option combination (**Option e** in this case, which means hold down the Option key and tap the **e** once)—*it will look like nothing happened.* That's okay.

3. Now type the character that is to be *under* the accent mark, and both the mark and the letter will appear together; e.g., **R é s u m é**

Using Real Accent Marks

Here is a list of common accent marks:

´	Option e
`	Option ~
¨	Option u
~	Option n
∧	Option i

Practice: Type the word **résumé** as explained here.

Now type **piñata.**

How about **Voilà!** You'll find that accent mark in the far upper-left of the keyboard, on the same key as the tilde (~).

Practice What You Learned

In TextEdit or your favorite word processor, type the text below, or make up your own. Just type it in as you see it, with double Returns after each paragraph, then format it as you see on the opposite page.

▼ **To type the bullet (•),** hold down the Option key and type the number 8 on the keyboard (not the number 8 in the numeric keypad).

▼ Remember, when formatting on the opposite page, that ***every paragraph has its own ruler settings.*** That is, you can select the first paragraph, click the centered alignment button, and it doesn't affect any other text on the page.

My Summer Vacation

Type two Returns to create this extra space. If you plan to do a lot of word processing, find out how to add extra paragraph spacing automatically (read the manual for your word processor). This will do two things: You won't have to hit two Returns, only one; and you won't have this huge gap between paragraphs because you can choose a smaller amount of space.

Well, my summer vacation was too boring to tell you about because all I did was work every day, all day, sometimes all night. But if I could do whatever I wanted, this is what I would do:

• I'd take a long hike across the desert every morning at sunrise.

• I'd carve massive pieces of stone into vibrant sculptures.

• I'd mosaic landscapes and ravens and dancing people onto my walls, and a mermaid in the bathroom.

• I'd read and study a Shakespeare play every week.

• I'd cook hot and spicy soups and hearty bread.

• I'd go back to school, some big, fancy school, and study something really important and write brilliant papers about it and become the world's expert in my field.

I'd make this list much, much longer but it's probably boring you already. Instead of my list, type in your own list of what you still want to accomplish today, this week, and in this life. Risk looking like a fool!

These three "paragraphs" have only one Return between them.

Robin Williams
Santa Fe
New Mexico

Yes, type this letter "t." t

Format the text

Format the text with bold and italic words; align the text as shown. This example uses **TextEdit,** but the process is similar in any word processor.

To see the page outline, as shown below, go to the Format menu and choose "Wrap to Page." *Or* press Command Shift W.

To show the ruler, go to the Format menu, choose "Text," then choose "Show Ruler." *Or* just press Command R. ***Anything you choose in the ruler applies to the entire paragraph that is selected.***

To show the Font panel, as you see below, go to the Format menu, choose "Font," and then choose "Font Panel…." *Or* press Command T.

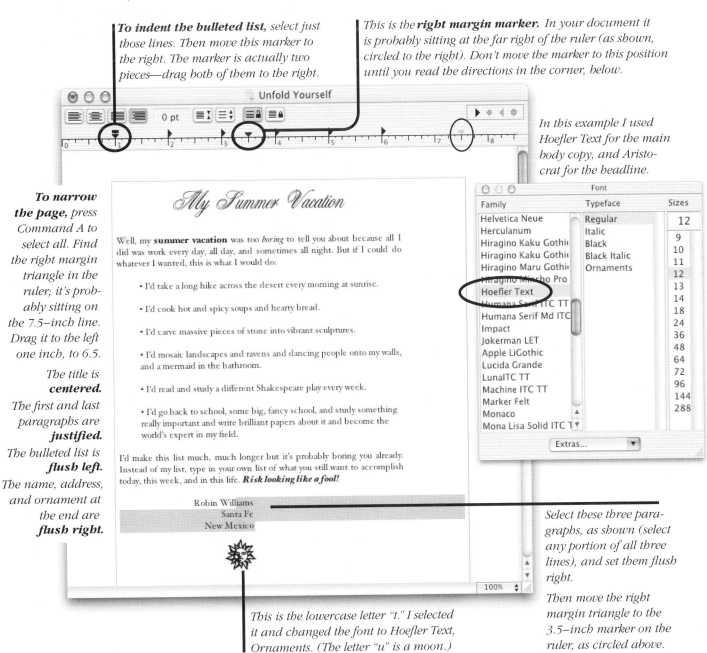

To indent the bulleted list, select just those lines. Then move this marker to the right. The marker is actually two pieces—drag both of them to the right.

*This is the **right margin marker.** In your document it is probably sitting at the far right of the ruler (as shown, circled to the right). Don't move the marker to this position until you read the directions in the corner, below.*

Unfold Yourself

0 pt

In this example I used Hoefler Text for the main body copy, and Aristocrat for the headline.

To narrow the page, press Command A to select all. Find the right margin triangle in the ruler; it's probably sitting on the 7.5–inch line. Drag it to the left one inch, to 6.5.

*The title is **centered.***
*The first and last paragraphs are **justified.***
*The bulleted list is **flush left.***
*The name, address, and ornament at the end are **flush right.***

My Summer Vacation

Well, my **summer vacation** was too *boring* to tell you about because all I did was work every day, all day, and sometimes all night. But if I could do whatever I wanted, this is what I would do:

• I'd take a long hike across the desert every morning at sunrise.

• I'd cook hot and spicy soups and hearty bread.

• I'd carve massive pieces of stone into vibrant sculptures.

• I'd mosaic landscapes and ravens and dancing people onto my walls, and a mermaid in the bathroom.

• I'd read and study a different Shakespeare play every week.

• I'd go back to school, some big, fancy school, and study something really important and write brilliant papers about it and become the world's expert in my field.

I'd make this list much, much longer but it's probably boring you already. Instead of my list, type in your own list of what you still want to accomplish today, this week, and in this life. ***Risk looking like a fool!***

Robin Williams
Santa Fe
New Mexico

Font

Family	Typeface	Sizes
Helvetica Neue	Regular	12
Herculanum	Italic	9
Hiragino Kaku Gothic	Black	10
Hiragino Kaku Gothic	Black Italic	11
Hiragino Maru Gothic	Ornaments	12
Hiragino Mincho Pro		13
Hoefler Text		14
Humana Serif ITC TT		18
Humana Serif Md ITC		24
Impact		36
Jokerman LET		48
Apple LiGothic		64
Lucida Grande		72
LunaITC TT		96
Machine ITC TT		144
Marker Felt		288
Monaco		
Mona Lisa Solid ITC T		

Extras…

100%

Select these three paragraphs, as shown (select any portion of all three lines), and set them flush right.

Then move the right margin triangle to the 3.5–inch marker on the ruler, as circled above.

This is the lowercase letter "t." I selected it and changed the font to Hoefler Text, Ornaments. (The letter "u" is a moon.)

1. What is Rule No. 2 on the Mac?

_____

2. Draw an I-beam, an insertion point, and a pointer.

_____

3. Which of the three items mentioned above do you use to select text?

_____

4. When you press the Delete key, which of the three items above backs up?

_____

5. Name the two ways that an insertion point knows which typeface, size, and style to type in.

_____

6. What is the keyboard shortcut to make selected text bold? Italic? Underlined?

_____

7. How can you make the next word you type appear in bold, without going to the menu? After you type it in bold, how do you make the next word you type appear in plain text?

_____

8. If you decide you want the last paragraph in your document to be the first paragraph, what are the four steps you must take to make that happen?

_____

_____

9. What are the keyboard shortcuts for cut, copy, and paste?

_____

10. What is the difference between "cut" and "clear"?

_____

Extra Credit (50 points):

How many spaces should you type after a period?

_____

Answers on page 731.

218

Saving Your Documents

While you are in the process of creating a document of any sort within any program, the information you put into that document is floating around in the computer's *memory,* which is only a temporary storage place. If you were to turn off the computer, that document would disappear. In fact, if there was a power flicker, the document would disappear. If your computer crashed, the document would disappear. You probably want to keep a permanent copy of it, right? So you need to **save the document** onto your hard disk. Later you can save a backup copy onto a removable disk such as a Zip or Jaz cartridge or a CD or DVD.

Contents of this chapter

RAM: Random Access Memory

Until you actually go through the process of naming a document and saving it, the document hangs around in **RAM,** which stands for **Random Access Memory.** RAM is sort of like the top of the desk in your office, where you spread your stuff out as you work. Your *hard disk* acts more like a filing cabinet where you store all your folders of information.

The metal filing cabinets in your office are very much like the computer's hard disk—a permanent storage space.

Your oak desk is very much like your computer's RAM— a temporary working space.

When you are working on a project, you don't keep running to the filing cabinet every time you need a little piece of information, do you? No, you take all the applicable info out of the filing cabinet and put it on your desk, then when you're finished you put it all away again and take out something else. RAM is sort of like that: when you open an application the computer puts a copy of that application into RAM, also called *memory.* This way the computer doesn't have to keep going into the filing cabinet (the hard disk) to do its work and it can operate much more efficiently.

When you quit that first application and open another one, the Mac puts the first one back where it came from and puts the new application into RAM. If you have lots of RAM, you can open lots of applications and leave them open, as discussed on page 258.

When you create a document, it sits in RAM, too, until you put it in the filing cabinet—your disk. You put the document on your disk by **saving** it. Once it's on a disk, it will stay there until you trash it yourself.

All that time your document is in RAM, it is in **danger.** At any moment, if there is a power failure, even for a split second, or you accidentally hit the wrong button, have a system crash, the screen freezes, your child pulls out the power cord, or any other catastrophe of considerable dimension happens to befall, then everything in RAM *(memory)* is gone. Just plain gone. No way on earth for a mortal person to get it back. Not even the software that can get files out of the Trash after you've emptied the Trash basket can bring back information that only existed in memory.

Danger!

The prevention? **SOS:** Save Often, Sweetie. Save Save Save. Every few minutes, when you're just sitting there thinking about your next marvelous move, Save. In every application it's this easy: just press Command S. Then if there *is* a catastrophe, you will have lost only the last few minutes of your work. Of course you won't listen to me until you have experienced a catastrophe of your very own.

Rule #1: Save Often!

To save a document for the first time, it must be given a name. Under the File menu are the commands **Save As...** and **Save.** At first the subtle difference can be confusing.

Save As... vs. Save

    Save As... is the command you use *first* to give the document a name (every file must have a name). "Save As..." gives you a dialog box such as the ones shown on the following pages (they're slightly different from program to program).

Save As...

    Save is the command to use *after* you have named the document and you want to save the new changes onto that same document. *Save* just goes ahead and does it—you won't get a dialog box, but you will see the Edit menu flash for a quick second. Get in the habit of typing Command S (the keyboard shortcut to save) regularly.

Save

Note: If you have not yet given the document a name, choosing "Save" (or using Command S) will usually give you the "Save As..." dialog box.

The Quick-and-Easy Save

If you are new to computers, all you need to do is this **quick-and-easy save.** This will store your document in the Documents folder, which is in your Home area. When you are ready to learn more about saving and how to save into different folders, then come back and read the rest of this section.

To save your document:

1. From the File menu, choose "Save As..." to open the "Save As" dialog box, shown below.

2. Type the name of your file.

3. Click the Save button (or hit the Return or Enter key).

Tip: Give your document a name you will remember! A name like "Photo 1" is going to confuse you when you have a folder of thirty photos.

Practice: If you've been following along in the practice exercises and have a document open, **save it now** (if you haven't already).

Just go to the File menu and choose "Save As...."

Type the name of the document.

Hit the Enter key or click the Save button.

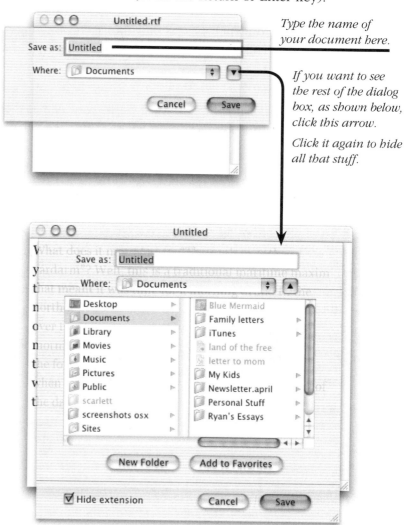

Type the name of your document here.

If you want to see the rest of the dialog box, as shown below, click this arrow.

Click it again to hide all that stuff.

If you want to know all about the Save As dialog box and how to use it, read on. It will give you more control over where you are saving files. It's not as scary as it looks. Drag the bottom-right corner of the dialog box to enlarge it so you can see more of the directory at once.

The Entire "Save As" Dialog Box

*Type here to **name** the document (1). The highlight is a **visual clue** telling you that this current name, "Untitled," is **selected**—just type, and this highlighted text will be replaced (that is, you don't have to delete the existing text first).*

If you don't see the directory below, as shown here, click this button.

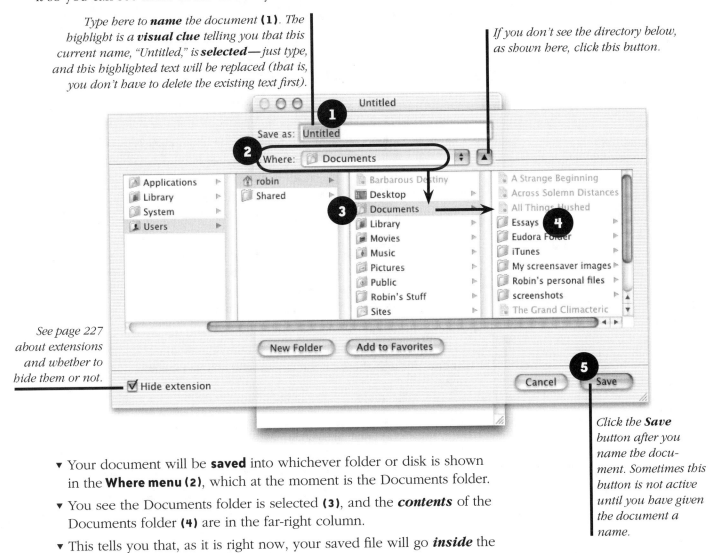

See page 227 about extensions and whether to hide them or not.

*Click the **Save** button after you name the document. Sometimes this button is not active until you have given the document a name.*

▼ Your document will be **saved** into whichever folder or disk is shown in the **Where menu (2)**, which at the moment is the Documents folder.

▼ You see the Documents folder is selected **(3)**, and the **contents** of the Documents folder **(4)** are in the far-right column.

▼ This tells you that, as it is right now, your saved file will go **inside** the Documents folder along with the rest of the Documents folder contents.

▼ **To save into a different folder,** single-click any folder name in any column to **select that folder.** That folder name will appear in the "Where" menu and its contents in the next-right column. If you then click the Save button **(5)**, your file will be saved into *that* folder.

See the following page for an explanation of the "Where" menu, how to make and save into new folders, and how to add a folder to your Favorites so you can easily save into it.

Advanced Tip: Drag any folder from the Desktop or from a Finder window and drop it anywhere inside the Save As dialog box. This will automatically choose that folder as the destination for your saved file. Try it!

Using the Where Menu

Take advantage of the **Where menu** to save into folders that you use often.

▼ **The very first item** in the "Where" menu is the currently selected folder; if you hit the Save button, you will save the document into the folder that is at the top of this list. In the example below, that would be the Documents folder.

▼ Choose **Desktop** to save the document directly to your Desktop.

▼ Choose **Home** to save the document into your Home folder, or to open any of your Home folders.

▼ Choose **iDisk** to connect to the Internet and save documents directly onto Apple's server (see pages xxi–xxii for information about iDisk).

▼ **Favorite Places** are those *folders* you have previously put in your Favorites folder. Your Favorites folder holds other kinds of items besides folders, but the folders are the only items that show up in this "Where" menu so you can save into them.

To add a folder to the Favorites list so you can get to it easily, find the folder in the directory of the dialog box, select the folder, and click the button in the bottom-right, **"Add to Favorites."** *Or* at the Desktop, put the folder or copy of the folder directly in the Favorites folder (drag it to the Favorites icon in the Toolbar), and then it will appear in this menu. See Chapter 24 for details about Favorites.

▼ **Recent Places** are the most recent folders and disks you have used while working on your Mac. You control how many items are in this menu through the General preferences pane (see page 136).

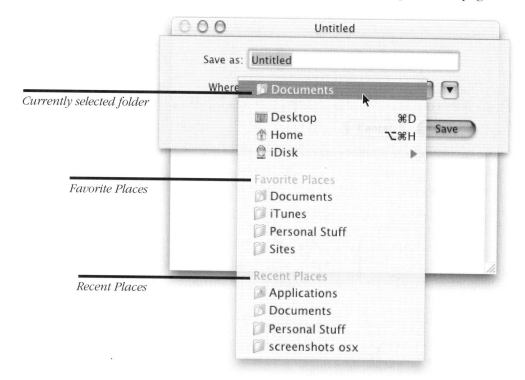

Currently selected folder

Favorite Places

Recent Places

One of the best ways to keep your work organized is to **create a specific new folder** for a new project *before* you create the documents for the project, and then save the documents right into their own folder. For instance, if you are about to create a newsletter in which there will be ten to twelve separate stories, it's best to store all these files in one folder with a recognizable name. If you didn't create a new folder before you started a document, you can always create it here in the Save As dialog box.

Creating a New Folder to Save Into

To create a new folder in the Save As dialog box:

1. Decide where you want to store the new folder and make sure that location is what you see in the "Where" menu. For instance, in the example on the opposite page, "Documents" is the location; if you click the "New Folder" button in that dialog box, the new folder will be placed inside the Documents folder. If you want the new folder on the Desktop, choose "Desktop" from the "Where" menu.

No matter where you store the folder at the moment, you can always move it later.

2. Click the button "New Folder." If you don't see that button, click the single, blue, downward-pointing arrow at the end of the "Where" menu.

3. In the little window that appears, as shown below, type the name of your new folder, then click the "Create" button.

You don't have to delete this text first (on the left)—just type the new name and it will replace whatever is selected (shown to the right).

4. Your new folder will appear in the directory, as shown below, already selected and waiting for you to name your document and save it directly into this folder.

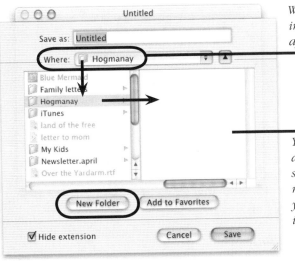

Whenever you save a file, it is ALWAYS saved into whichever folder or onto whichever disk appears at the top of the "Where" menu.

Your document, after you name it and click the Save button, will be stored right in this folder and the next time you see this dialog box, your new document will be listed in this right-hand column.

Visual Clues and Navigating in the Dialog Box

As is typical on the Mac, the dialog box has many **visual clues** that tell you what to do or what to expect, as well as clues to navigating (moving around and selecting files in the dialog box).

Look carefully at the two dialog boxes below. The most important visual clue, one that you should become accustomed to noticing, is the **selection** in each box.

▼ On the left, the edit box is selected, where it says "Untitled," waiting for you to type the name. Notice the border around the edit box.

▼ On the right, the folder "Documents" is selected. Notice the border is around the directory now, instead of around the edit box.

This is important to notice because when you start to type, your typing will **either** change "Untitled" **or** it will select a folder. That is, if the edit box is selected, what you type will be the name of your new document. But if the directory is selected, what you type will select a folder.

To select the edit box or the directory, hit the Tab key. Whichever one is selected at the moment, the Tab key will select the other. Try it.

To navigate through the directory, hit the Tab key to select the directory, if it isn't already. Then use the arrow keys to move left and right from column to column, and up and down within one column.

*In this example, **the edit box is selected,** as you can see by the border, and the current title, "Untitled," is highlighted.*

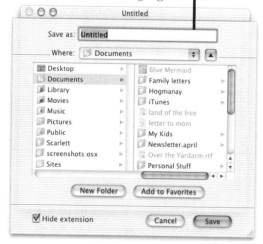

*In this example, **the directory is selected,** as you can see by the border, and the folder, "Documents," is highlighted.*

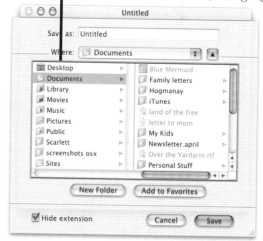

*When a file name is gray, it is a **visual clue** that the file itself is in the folder, but you can't do anything with it because this is the Save As dialog box. But you can see what other files are already stored in a particular folder.*

*Folder names are black, which is a **visual clue** that you can select them (single-click) to store documents inside.*

*As everywhere else on the Mac, there are all the standard **visual clues** such as scroll arrows and scrollers (or lack of), menu arrows, a disclosure triangle, a pulsing button, and the insertion point (when you are typing the file name).*

In Mac OS X, every file name has an **extension** (whether you see it or not), which is a short abbreviation at the end of a file name, preceded by a period, such as *.jpg*. This extension tells the Mac what to do with the file.

You can add your own extension to the end of a file name, if you know the exact characters for your document, or you can just let the Mac add the correct one for you; what you *don't* want to do is add an extension without knowing that the *Mac* has added an extension to your extension. To make sure that doesn't happen, or to make sure you get the extension you want, you can choose to see the extensions on a file-by-file basis, or you can choose a global setting to *always* see the file extension or *never* see it.

robin's story   robin's story.rtf

The extension is so important to some files that if you take it off, the Mac doesn't know what to do with the file when you try to open in. In the example above, the Mac cannot open the file on the left, even though it is exactly the same as the file on the right, minus the .rtf extension.

chapter8   chapter8.dock

Adding an extension of .dock to this folder in which I stored files for the Dock chapter turned the folder into a "dockling." Unfortunately, Apple does not provide a list of extensions that you should avoid.

To make the extensions visible or invisible on an individual basis, use the Info window: Click once on an icon to select it (or select a number of icons), then go to the File menu and choose "Get Info," or press Command I. Click the triangle for "Name & Extension." Check or uncheck the box to "Hide extension."

Notice when you hide the extension, it is hidden from the file name you see on the Desktop (shown at the top of the Info window), but the system name that the Mac uses retains the extension.

To hide or show extensions globally, from the Finder menu, choose "Preferences...." Check or uncheck the box to "Always show file extensions." If you choose to always show them, you won't inadvertently add your own extension as well.

Illegal characters in file names: Do not start file names with a hyphen or period. Do not use a colon (:) or a slash (/).

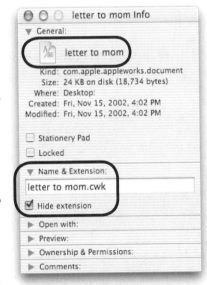

Naming Your Files and Extensions

Below is a list of some (not all) common file extensions you might run across.

Document extensions

.doc	Word document
.txt	Plain Text
.rtf	Rich Text Format
.rtfd	Rich Text Format Directory
.pdf	Portable Document Format
.psd	Photoshop file
.idd	Adobe InDesign file
.qxp	QuarkXPress file
.pps	PowerPoint Show
.xls	Excel spreadsheet
.mov	QuickTime movie

Graphic file format extensions

.gif	Graphic Interchange Format, ideal for web graphics
.jpg, jpeg	Joint Photographic Experts Group, photos, ideal for web
.tif, tiff	Tagged Image File Format, graphic for printing
.eps	Encapsulated PostScript, illustration graphic

Compression extensions

.sit	StuffIt Deluxe
.sea	self-extracting archive
.zip	stuffed file from a Windows machine; your Mac can open it with StuffIt Deluxe
.exe	executable file, which is a Windows application that you can't use on your Mac
.smi	self-mounting image for disk images
.dmg	disk image

Encoding extensions

.bin	MacBinary for newer systems
.hqx	BinHex for older systems

Reverting to a Previously Saved Version

Sometimes you might make a bunch of changes to a document and then decide you don't like the changes. In that case, check the File menu to see if your application has a command called **Revert.** If so, choose it and the document will revert *to exactly how it was the last time you **saved** it.* So if you haven't saved it yet, you can't revert. (I recommend saving a file even before you begin typing, although some applications won't let you save until you have at least typed one character.)

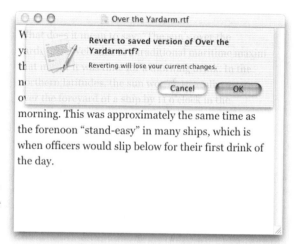

Choose "Revert to Saved," then click OK in the dialog box to revert the document back to the last time you saved it.

If there is no Revert command, then *close* the document. When you see the box that asks if you want to save the changes (shown below), click the button that says "Don't Save" or "No." Reopen the document and everything will be exactly the way it was *the last time you saved it.* This means, of course, that anything you did since you last saved it, *the good stuff as well as the bad,* will be gone.

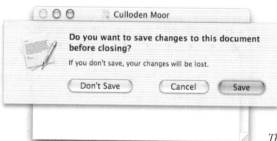

These are two examples of the message you get when you close. In many applications, you can press Command D instead of clicking the "Don't Save" button.

Sometimes you might want to create changes in a document, but you still want to keep a **copy of the original without the changes.** For instance, let's say you write a witty letter to Uncle Jeff, then decide you also want to write to Uncle Cliff. You have a few things to tell Cliff that Jeff isn't interested in, but you don't want to retype the entire letter. That's when you'll use *Save As...* a *second* time to give the document a *new* name, which actually creates a new, separate file and leaves the original file intact.

Making Several Versions

To make a version separate from an original:

1. Save the original document. Let's say you've named it "Witty letter to Uncle Jeff." Don't close the document.

2. While that document is still open on the screen, from the File menu, choose "Save As...."

3. Change the name, say from "Witty letter to Uncle Jeff" to "Witty letter to Uncle Cliff."

This automatically puts the original document (to Uncle Jeff) safely away on your disk and opens a new one (the copy to Uncle Cliff) right on the screen. You'll notice the name in the title bar of your document changes to what you renamed it. Any changes you make to *this* document (Uncle Cliff's) will not affect the original (Uncle Jeff's).

Witty letter to Uncle Jeff   Witty letter to Uncle Cliff

Witty letter to Uncle Lloyd   Witty letter to Uncle Merwyn

All of these letters are based on the original letter to Uncle Jeff. I just kept choosing "Save As" and giving the new ones new names. The information, layout, type choices, etc., all stayed the same, but now each letter is separate and I can add or delete details in each.

Templates and Stationery

Another way to make several versions of the same letter, or to keep a master copy of your newsletter or budget report, etc., is to make a **template** or **stationery pad** of the document. Once you turn a document into a template, the original file doesn't open anymore—when you open the template you get a brand new, untitled *copy* of the original. (Well, you *can* open the original file if you need to; see the note on the opposite page.)

Depending on your project, you might want to make a *copy* of the original, then turn the *copy* into a template.

Take a look in the "Save As" dialog box in your application—some applications have a button or a menu choice to create a template, as shown below. If your application can't make a template (or even if it can), you can always use the Get Info window, as explained on the opposite page.

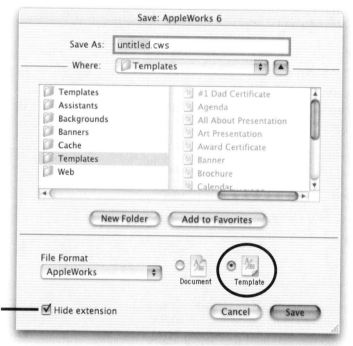

See page 227 about extensions.

In AppleWorks, as soon as you click the "Template" button, the Templates folder is selected (on the left and in the "Where" menu), waiting for you to save your new template into the folder. (You can choose to save the template anywhere you like.)

letter to mom template

*AppleWorks creates a new icon for you with a **visual clue** that this is a template: the bottom-right corner is turned up (a regular document has the top-right corner turned down).*

To make a template (stationery pad) of a document using Get Info:

1. Select the document on the Desktop or in a Finder window (click once on the document icon to select it).

2. From the File menu, choose "Get Info," or press Command I.

3. Click the checkbox for "Stationery Pad" (circled, below). Now the selected document is what the Mac calls a "stationery pad," also known as a "template." It contains all the fonts, formatting, information, etc., that was in the original document.

There is no longer a visual clue in the icon that tells you a file is a Stationery Pad. This is a really lame implementation of a template file because when you change the name of the copy to something useful, you now have the copy still on your hard disk, which you'll most likely just throw away. And although you can select any file and click the Stationery Pad box, not every file can really be a Stationery Pad—it's lying to you.

letter to family

Select a file and press Command I (or go to the File menu and choose "Get Info").

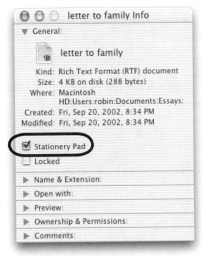

Check "Stationery Pad."

letter to family copy

*When you double-click the Stationery file, a **copy** instantly appears and opens in the application.*

To change its name while in the application, go to the File menu and choose "Save As...."

To open the original document again, instead of the template, select the document icon, press Command I to Get Info, and uncheck the "Stationery Pad" box. Then you can double-click the document icon and it will open the original file.

Use the dialog boxes shown below (A or B) to answer the first five questions.

1. Which dialog box has the directory, or list, selected?

_____

2. Which dialog box is ready for you to name the document?

_____

3. If you were in dialog box **A** and typed the letter "P," what would happen?

_____

4. In dialog box **A,** what would happen if you were to click on the folder named "Hogmanay"?

_____

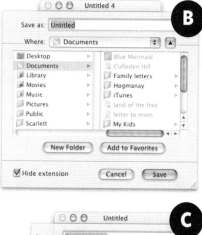

5. If you were in dialog box **A** and you wanted to name the document, which key would you press to select the edit box?

_____

6. What would you press to get the menu, **C,** shown to the left?

_____

7. What would happen if you were to choose "Home" from this menu, **C**?

_____

8. Briefly describe two ways to avoid saving your changes.

_____

9. Where is the document before you save it?

_____

10. Which command would you use to save another copy of a document, but with a new name?

_____

Answers on page 731.

Printing Documents

Printing is usually the point, right? It's well and good to create all these great things on the computer, but most of the time we need to actually *print* our creations to make them useful. In this chapter I'll walk you through the printing process, but keep in mind that each of the hundreds of printers for the Macintosh has its own software, so details might look different from what I show here. Please read the documentation that came with your printer!

Also, different applications often create their own Page Setup and Print dialog boxes, so the ones you use might not exactly match the ones I show in this chapter—but they're all similar.

Contents of this chapter

Printers

First of all, it's a good idea to know whether you have a **PostScript printer** or a **non-PostScript printer.** Here's an easy way to tell: If your printer cost less than $1,000, it's non-PostScript.

It's also good to know whether your printer is **USB** or **serial.** You can tell by the connector on the end of the printer cable, the end that plugs into the computer. If it's small and rectangular, it's USB. If it's round, it's serial. Most people at home or in a small office today have USB printers, especially if it's plugged directly into your computer rather than on a network.

See Chapter 37 if you care to know about "USB" and "serial" in reference to printers.

You don't need to read the rest of this page—it's here if you want to come back to it later. If ever.

Non-PostScript printers

Most printers with the word "inkjet" in their names are examples of **non-PostScript printers,** with "resolutions" ranging from about 75 to 600 dots per inch (the higher the resolution, the smoother the printed image). Inkjet cartridges typically are small (they fit easily in your hand) and you have one small cartridge for black and another one for the colors (cyan/blue, magenta/red, and yellow). The ink tends to smear easily on the page. Printed images can look vastly different depending on the paper used. Inkjets usually have only one paper tray.

PostScript printers

PostScript is a "page description language," a programming language, that a **PostScript printer** can interpret. Black-and-white desktop PostScript printers are laser printers, not inkjet (though not all laser printers are PostScript). They create high-quality, very clean type and images. Personal PostScript printers are rather expensive, typically around $1,000 to $3,000 for black-and-white (color printers often run above $4,000). They're expensive because they have a powerful computer inside, complete with memory and a specialized CPU (central processing unit, the tiny chip that runs the entire process). They're relatively large printers, and a typical black toner cartridge is about the size of a bread loaf that costs around $100. Although they're expensive, they are workhorses and will print many thousands of pages for years and years and years. You can highlight text on the page and it won't smear.

Imagesetters

There are also *very* expensive (like $100,000), very high-end PostScript printers with resolutions of around 1270 or 2540 dots per inch, such as the Linotronic. These machines, called **imagesetters,** output (print) onto resin-coated film, not plain paper, and the hard copy looks virtually like traditional phototypesetting, limited only by the professional expertise of the person who input (typed in) the text.

Service bureaus

Since the high-resolution machines are so expensive, you only find them in **service bureaus** — shops where they offer the "output" (the hard copy, the printed pages) as a service. You take the disk containing your document to them, leave it there, and they print it up for you. It usually costs from $4 to $10 a page, but it's beautiful. Then you take those pages to a print shop for reproductions.

Here are the briefest of directions for **printing your pages.** If it works, *then you can skip the rest of this chapter,* unless you want to understand what all the options are. For this very quick start, I have to assume you have the printer plugged in to both the wall and the computer with the appropriate cables, there is paper in the printer, and the printer is turned on and warmed up. If so:

1. Open the document that you want to print.
2. From the File menu, choose "Print…."
3. Click the "Print" button (or hit the Return key).

   That's all. **If it worked,** skip to page 241 to learn about the various printing options.

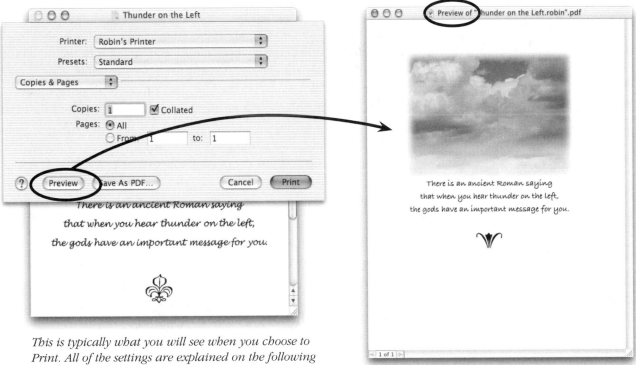

This is typically what you will see when you choose to Print. All of the settings are explained on the following pages, but if you just want to print the page or pages in your document to make sure printing works, you can safely hit the "Print" button without bothering about anything else.

Click the "Preview" button in the Print dialog box to see what your document will look like when printed on the page. The Preview button actually creates a PDF file, which then opens in the application Preview. Check out your menu options in Preview, and see pages 440–441.

IF THE STEPS ABOVE DIDN'T WORK, the only thing you probably need to do is add your printer to the list so the Mac knows it's there, or maybe you need to turn on AppleTalk. Both are explained on the following pages.

Making Sure Your Printer is Connected and Turned On

If you just need to "add" your printer to the printer list, skip to the following page. If something else seems to be wrong, check the list below.

If your printing didn't work automatically, **check** the following:

▼ I'm assuming that if you bought a printer, you made sure it was **compatible** with your Macintosh; for instance, if your computer uses USB ports (which it does if it was built since late 1998), you must get a USB-compatible printer and a USB cable.

Even though there is a USB port in your keyboard, don't plug your printer into that port—your printer will usually work more reliably if you plug it directly into your computer, or at least into a "hub" with a power source. (See Chapter 37 for some information on ports and hubs and the things that plug into them.)

▼ You also need the correct **cable** to connect your printer to your Mac. Many printers don't come with a cable to connect it to the Mac (you have to buy it separately), so if you brought your printer home without one you will have to go back to the computer store or catalog and get one before you can print. This cable connects the printer to the Mac.

▼ Make sure your printer is plugged into a **power** socket in the wall or into a "surge suppressor" (an outlet strip that you can buy at any office supply store; it protects your printer and your computer from daily power spikes).

▼ **Wait** several minutes after you turn on the printer before you try to print; wait until all printer noises have stopped.

▼ When you bought your printer you got a disk with **software** on it. If you went through the steps on the previous page and your printer didn't work automatically, follow the directions in the printer's manual to install the software. Besides helping your Mac connect to the printer, the software will often provide more options in the print dialog boxes.

If you are trying to connect an old printer to your new Mac, you might need to go to the web site for your printer and find a new "driver." Download that driver and install it (see Chapter 21) and try again.

If these things are all okay, you probably need to add your printer to the printer list, as described on the following pages.

Adding a Printer to the List

Your Mac needs to put your computer in its **Printer List** so you can choose to print to it and so the computer knows what that particular printer is capable of doing. For instance, if you choose to print to a color inkjet, the Print dialog box will provide color options, but not paper tray options. If you choose to print to a black-and-white PostScript laser printer, you won't have any color options, but you will have paper tray options.

To add a printer to the List, you can either go back to the Print dialog box in your document, or you can open the Print Center directly. Either way is exactly the same, as follows:

1. Turn on the printer(s) you want to add to the List. Wait until it is fully warmed up (wait until it stops making noise and the green light is not flashing).

2. **Either:** At the Desktop, open any Finder window. Click on the Applications icon in the Toolbar. From inside that window, open the Utilities folder. Inside the Utilities folder, find the **Print Center** icon, as shown to the right.

   Print Center

   Double-click on the Print Center icon.

   Go to Step 3 on the following page.

   Or: While your document is open, go to the File menu and choose "Print." In the Print dialog box, click on the "Printer" menu and choose "Edit Printer List...," as shown below.

   Go to Step 3 on the following page.

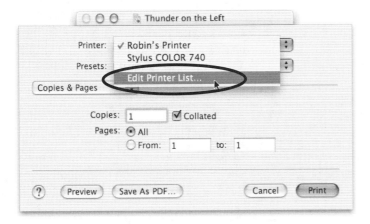

3. Both of the methods described on the previous page will open the Printer List, as shown below. This List shows you the printers the Mac knows about already. The bold printer name is the default printer.

To add another printer to the list, click the "Add" icon.

To change the default printer, select one of the printers in this List, then click the "Make Default" icon in the toolbar.

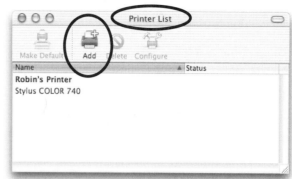

4. A dialog "sheet" will slip down from the title bar, as shown below. Click on the menu circled below to see your options.

To add a USB printer to the list, choose "USB" from the menu.

To add an AppleTalk printer, which is probably on a local network, to the List, choose "AppleTalk." If your printer is a PostScript laser printer, it is probably on an AppleTalk network whether you realize it or not.

If you have the DNS name or IP address of a **line printer** you can connect to through the Internet, choose "IP Printing."
If that doesn't make sense to you, you're probably not using a line printer; if you think you may be, talk to your network administrator.

If you have an **Epson printer** that you connect with an Ethernet cable, choose "EPSON AppleTalk." If it connects with a FireWire or USB cable, choose that appropriate option.

If your computer is at home or in a small office, you won't use ***Directory Services.*** *If you are in a large corporation or school with a large network, talk to your network administrator about Directory Services.*

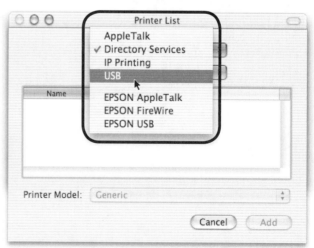

5. If you chose "AppleTalk," you might get a message that you have to turn AppleTalk on—*if you don't get this message, skip this step.* If the message shown below appears, go ahead and click the button, "Open Network Preferences."

The Network preferences pane will appear. ***If you don't see the AppleTalk tab,*** as circled below, check the "Show" menu to make sure "Built-In Ethernet" is selected, not "Internal Modem."

Click the checkbox to "Make AppleTalk active," click the "Apply Now" button at the bottom, and close the Network preferences. Go back to the Printer List dialog box.

Go to Step 6.

Note: If the entire pane is gray, you are not the administrator of this machine and you cannot make these kinds of changes. Find the administrator and ask for help.

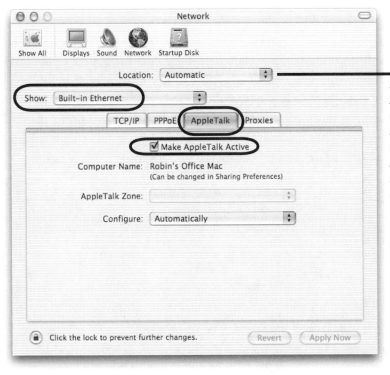

If the Mac still yells at you about AppleTalk, perhaps you have the wrong "Location" chosen. Check to see if there are any other Locations in the menu, and try changing the AppleTalk checkbox in the other Locations. For more information about Locations, see Chapter 36.

6. After you choose the type of printer, you will get a list of those printers *that are turned on and available for you to use.* You can't add a printer that is not turned on!

If you don't see your printer in the list, click on the "Printer Model" menu and choose the model you know is attached and turned on. This should make it appear.

7. Click on the printer name in the list, then click the "Add" button.

8. You will automatically go back to the Printer List, which can be confusing because it makes you think you should click the "Add" button again—*don't.* (Well, you can if you want, but it will just take you back to the dialog box above.)

Just click the red close button in the upper-left corner of the window. That printer is now added to the list and you will be able to choose it in the main Print dialog box.

Close this box with this button.

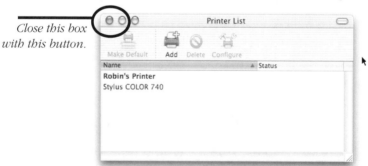

*The default printer (the automatic choice) is the one shown in **bold text.** If you have more than one printer in this list and you want a different printer to be the default, do this: Click once on the printer name, then click the "Make Default" icon that you see in the toolbar.*

Page Setup

You should get in the habit of checking the **Page Setup** command in the File menu. Page Setup opens a dialog box where you can set specifications for printing the document—use these in conjunction with the individual Print dialog box specifications, as shown on the following pages. Below are sample Page Setup boxes, but your particular application may have added other features of its own.

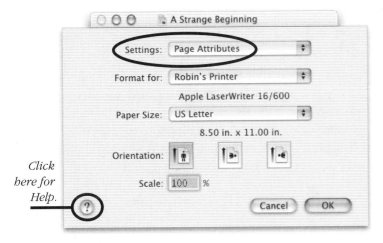

Click here for Help.

See below for the "Summary" option that is also available in this menu.

If you have different printers in your list, use the "Format for" pop-up menu to choose the one you plan to print to so the Mac will find the specific details about it, like how many paper trays it has, what kinds of color options, etc.

▼ **Paper Size:** This refers to the size of the paper that the document will be printed on, not the size of the page you are typing on. For instance, you might be creating a business card, but you can't put paper sized 2 x 3.5 through your printer—usually, the cards will be printed on regular letter-sized paper. If you have other-sized paper to use, choose it from this menu.

▼ **Orientation:** The Mac wants to know if the document should print upside right or sideways (8.5 x 11 or 11 x 8.5); also known as Tall or Wide, Portrait or Landscape.

▼ **Scale:** Enter a number here to enlarge or reduce the printed page. For instance, enter 50% to print your work at half size. Remember, half of an 8.5 x 11 is 4.25 x 5.5—you must halve both directions. On paper, this looks like the image is ¼ the original size; it isn't— it's half of both the horizontal and the vertical.

Reducing an image reduces it in both directions, not just one.

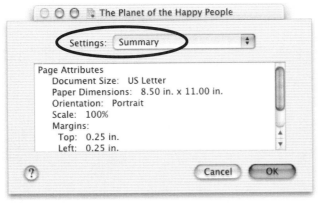

*This is a **Summary** of the specifications chosen in this dialog box, as well as those chosen in the document itself, such as the margins.*

*Adobe InDesign is the
page layout application
I designed and produced
this book with.*

The more sophisticated an application is, the more it might change the Page Setup to suit itself. For instance, when I choose to print in **Adobe InDesign,** there is a "Page Setup" button on InDesign's professional print dialog box, but InDesign doesn't like me to use it—it prefers that I make all those settings within its own options.

Print Specifications

Once you have successfully added your printer to the list, you can print merrily away. On these next few pages are explanations of the various printing options you have. You may see different print dialog boxes depending on which printer you are connected to, and the dialog boxes within different applications may look slightly different from what you see here, but basically all you need to do is answer the questions they ask.

*Click on this menu to see
your list of options. Choose
one of these options to get
a pane where you can
customize this print job.*

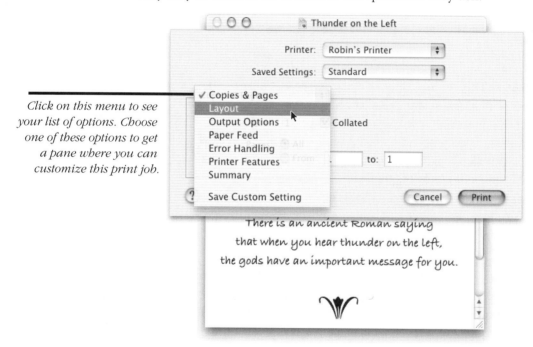

Very often you will not need to go beyond this first dialog box, where you can choose the **pages** to print and **how many.**

Copies & Pages

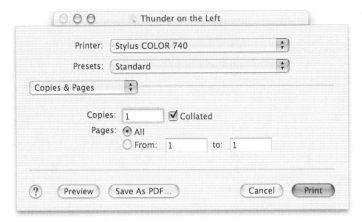

▾ **Copies:** Type in the number of copies you want to print.

▾ **Collated:** If you're printing more than one copy of a multi-page document, you can make the printer collate the copies—it will print all the pages of one set, then print the next set. If you *don't* click collate, you will get, for instance, 5 copies of page 1, 5 copies of page 2, 5 copies of page 3, etc. But keep in mind that it takes longer for the printer to collate than to print multiple copies of one page at a time.

▾ **Pages: All** or **From __ to __:** You can choose to print *all* of the pages contained in your document, or just pages 3 through 12 (or whatever your choice is, of course). If you don't know the number of the last page, enter something like "999" and the printer will print to the end.

Choose **All** to override any numbers in the **From/To** boxes.

In this dialog box, you cannot print non-consecutive pages, such as pages 3, 7, and 11. If you use a page layout or other sophisticated application, you will have the option to print non-consecutive pages.

Layout Choose **Layout** when you want to print multiple pages on one sheet of paper. This is handy when you have, for instance, a presentation to give and you want to create handouts for your audience or students so they can follow along. Or it can help you see your overall project at a glance so you can get a better idea of how things are working together (or not).

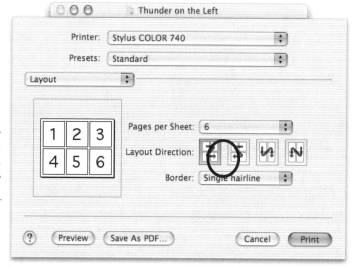

In this example, I have chosen six pages per sheet, a layout direction of left to right, and a single hairline border around each individual miniature page.

▼ **Pages per Sheet:** Choose how many pages of your document you want to see on each printed sheet of paper. Every page will be reduced to fit, of course.

▼ **Layout Direction:** Click on a layout to determine how the pages are arranged on the sheet. As you click each button, the display on the left will show you how your pages will be arranged. In the example above, the first button is clicked.

▼ **Border:** Choose a border so each page will be clearly defined on the printed sheet. The display to the left will give you an idea of what to expect with each border option as you choose it.

Output Options

In the **Output Options** pane you are not *printing* the file—notice the "Print" button has changed to a "Save…" button. In this pane you can choose to **save** your document as a **PDF file.** PDF stands for "portable document format" and is especially designed to save your document in a format that you can send to anyone on any kind of computer and they will see it exactly as you do. For instance, maybe you created a nice invitation to your sister's birthday party and you want to send her a copy to make sure she likes it. You can save it as a PDF, then email the PDF to her for approval, knowing she will see it exactly as you do even if she doesn't have the fonts, the graphics, or the application you created it in.

If the person receiving the file is using Mac OS X, she already has the software application Preview that will open and display PDF files—she just needs to double-click on the PDF file icon.

If the person receiving the file is using an older Mac or a PC, she needs the free software "Acrobat Reader," which is probably already installed on her computer. If not, send her to **www.adobe.com** to download and *install* the Reader.

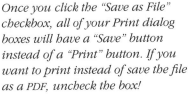

Once you click the "Save as File" checkbox, all of your Print dialog boxes will have a "Save" button instead of a "Print" button. If you want to print instead of save the file as a PDF, uncheck the box!

Thunder.pdf

If you are connected to a PostScript printer (as explained on page 234), you can make a **PostScript file.** You see, when you make a *PDF* file through this Print dialog box, you don't have any options to adjust the PDF for its intended use. But if you have the full (not free) Adobe Acrobat application with the "Distiller," you can drop a *PostScript file* on the Distiller and have options to make the file low-resolution so it looks good on the screen, but still emails quickly. Or you can make it a high-resolution file so it can be printed on a high-quality press, or a mid-resolution file for desktop printers.

Thunder.ps

Tip: If you don't have a PostScript printer but need to make a PostScript file, make a "virtual PostScript printer." See page 254.

Print Settings

Your Print Settings might not look exactly like the ones shown. Read the manual for your particular printer to learn all the details about every option.

The dialog boxes on these two pages only appear in color printers. In color inkjet printers, the type of paper that you specify and put in the printer makes a remarkable difference in the finished image. A low-quality mode with cheap paper makes an image look worse than in the newspaper comic strip. Photo-quality paper with a high-quality mode can make the same image look like a photograph you had enlarged at a photo studio. Use the **Print Settings** to specify the paper ("Media Type") you have ready in the printer, plus the "Quality" of your finished product.

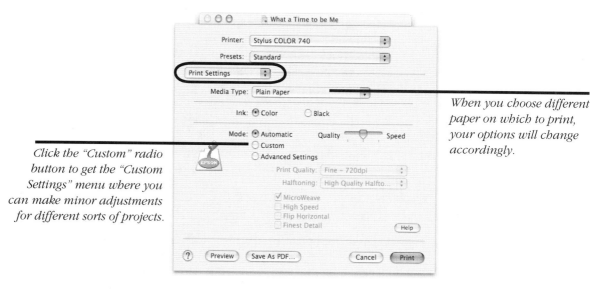

Click the "Custom" radio button to get the "Custom Settings" menu where you can make minor adjustments for different sorts of projects.

When you choose different paper on which to print, your options will change accordingly.

Color Management

If you are experienced with printed color, you can make some adjustments in the **Color Management** dialog box—if your printer displays this one. Even if you're not experienced, you can adjust the brightness and contrast of the printed page, and maybe take out some of the magenta if your brother's face looks too red in the photo, etc.

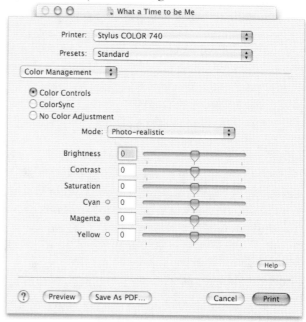

Error Handling will print you a special report telling you what the problem is (as long as the problem doesn't involve the actual printing or how could it print you a report?). Chances are you won't understand what the report is talking about anyway, but you can click this button when you get desperate and hope to find some kind of clue about why things aren't working properly. Good luck.

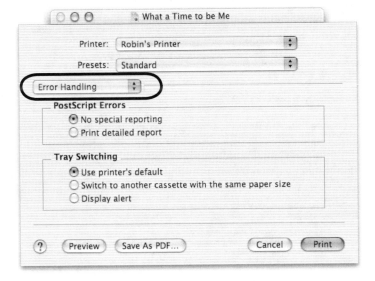

The **Paper Feed** pane only appears if you have a big printer with several paper trays (the Mac discovers this from talking to your printer). Generally you'll just print from the main paper tray, but there might be times when you want to do something special, like print the cover of a report on heavier red stock, and the rest of the report from a tray that holds nicer paper than the regular cheap stuff. So you can set up the dialog box as shown below: You'll manually feed in the heavier red stock for the cover, then let it take the rest of the pages from the tray you specify.

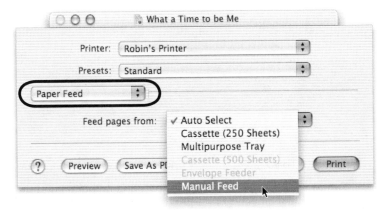

Printer Features

The **Printer Features** menu may change and might not even be there for you, depending on your chosen printer. You can see below that the same dialog boxes for two different PostScript Apple laser printers are different.

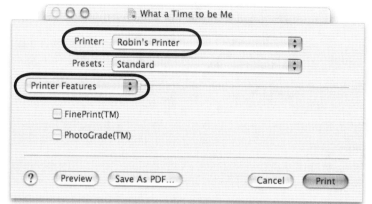

"FinePrint™" and "PhotoGrade™" are technologies built into certain Apple laser printers that are designed to improve the printing of type and line art (FinePrint) as well as photographs and paintings (PhotoGrade).

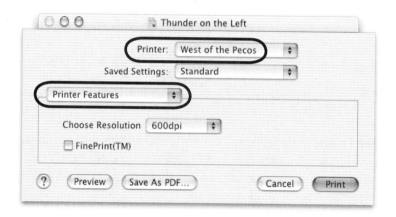

Most applications will have a menu with features **specific to the application,** as shown below. Always check these out.

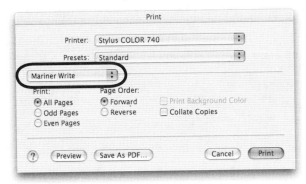

The web browser **Internet Explorer** has features that will put "headers" and "footers" on each printed page. A header is a line of information at the top of the page, and a footer is a line of information at the bottom on the page. Typically this information tells you the web address, the date, the time, etc. To see exactly what will print, click the "Preview" button. If you use the browser **Netscape,** you have even more control over what prints; check its Page Setup to control exactly what is displayed in the headers and footers.

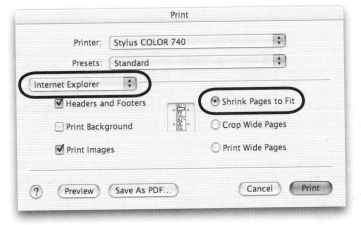

Rarely do you want to **print the background** of a web page because it will use up your entire (expensive) ink cartridge. The one exception is when the text is white on a dark background. But rather than do that, try this: Select the text you want to print, copy it, paste it into TextEdit, then select and change the text to black (if necessary), and print from TextEdit.

Have you ever printed a poorly designed web page that prints twice as many pages as you need because it is about half an inch too wide for the paper? If so, click **Shrink Pages to Fit** to force pages to shrink just enough to fit on the page.

In some versions of **Netscape,** however, the default is checked on to "Fit to page," which prints web pages about an inch big. To fix this, go to Page Setup, choose "Netscape" from the pop-up menu, and uncheck that box.

Summary   The **Summary** pane displays a list of the options you have selected for print-ing this particular document. It's a good idea to skim through this list and make sure there are no leftover options chosen in dialog boxes that don't apply to this document.

Check this out before you print.

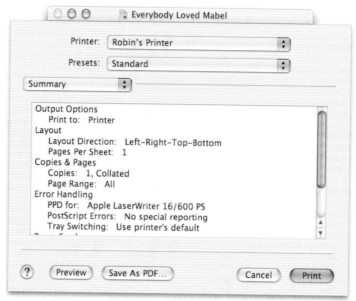

Save a Custom Setting   If you are working on a document and every time you go to the Print dialog box you choose "2 to 7 pages" and you print it in a layout with six miniature pages on a printed sheet with a thin line around each page, you can choose to save these options so you don't have to make the same choices every time you go to print. In fact, you can use these same options on any other documents as well. Just make all of your selections, then from the "Presets" menu, choose **Save As....** Now in the "Presets" menu, you'll be able to choose the setting you saved. You can make other custom settings, rename existing ones, or delete them.

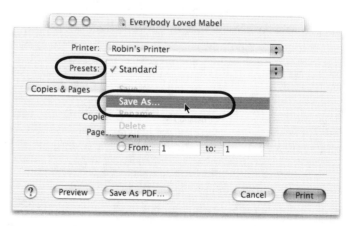

Using the Print Center

The **Print Center** just works away without you having to do anything about it until you have a problem. Or until you decide you want to do something like get a bunch of documents ready to print so you can go to lunch and have them all print while you're gone. Generally, when you are in your application and choose to print, the Mac opens the Print Center (you'll see it appear in the Dock) and it does its business; when it's done, the Print Center disappears from the Dock and you never have to worry about it. But there are a number of things you can do in the Print Center, should you find the need. If the Print Center is not in the Dock and you need it, follow the steps below to open it directly.

To open the Print Center directly:

1. In any Finder window, click on the Applications icon to open the Applications window.

2. Inside the Applications window, find the Utilities folder (type the letter U to select it and put it in front of you) and open it (press Command O or double-click the folder).

3. Inside the Utilities window, find the Print Center (type the letter P to select it and put it in front of you) and open it (press Command O or double-click the icon).

Print Center

This is the Print Center icon in the Utilities folder.

This is the Print Center icon in the Dock. The little number tells you how many pages in the document are left to print.

Keep the Print Center in the Dock

While you're printing, the Print Center icon will appear in the Dock, as shown above, then disappear when the job is finished. If you print regularly, though, it comes in handy to have the Print Center more easily accessible—I like to keep mine permanently in the Dock. To do this, drag the icon from the Utilities folder and just drop it in the Dock. *Or* when you open the Print Center and its icon is already in the Dock, click once on that icon and you'll get the menu shown below, left. Choose "Keep in Dock," and it will stay there even after the printing is done.

You can do this with any application in the Dock.

Depending on what the Print Center is doing at the moment, you'll have different options in the Dock menu.

Control your print jobs   When you open the Print Center directly, you'll probably see the Printer List, as shown below. This is exactly the same Printer List that appeared when you added a printer on pages 237–238. When the Printer List or the Jobs window (also shown below) is visible, you have new menu items. These are things you can do using the menus and the windows.

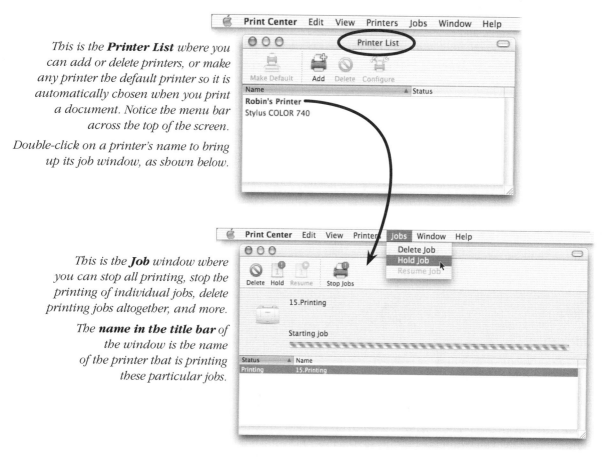

*This is the **Printer List** where you can add or delete printers, or make any printer the default printer so it is automatically chosen when you print a document. Notice the menu bar across the top of the screen.*

Double-click on a printer's name to bring up its job window, as shown below.

*This is the **Job** window where you can stop all printing, stop the printing of individual jobs, delete printing jobs altogether, and more.*

*The **name in the title bar** of the window is the name of the printer that is printing these particular jobs.*

To control printing of individual documents and also of the entire printer:

▼ **Show Jobs:** Choose "Show Jobs" from the "Printers" menu to see which documents are lined up waiting to print (shown directly above and on the following page), or double-click on the name of your printer in the Printer List. You can also click on the Print Center icon in the Dock and choose "Show Jobs" from the pop-up menu. Each printer has its own jobs window. The line of documents waiting to print is called a **queue.**

(If you tell a document to print and it doesn't print and you keep telling it to print over and over again, eventually you'll come to this window and see all of those documents waiting in line to print, just like you told them. Just select their names and click the "Delete" button.)

▼ **STOP ONE JOB from printing:** In the job window, click once on the name of a document in the list, then either click the "Hold" button or go to the Jobs menu and choose "Hold Job." This does not *delete* the job from the queue—it just puts it on hold.

▼ **RESUME printing one job:** If a job has been put on hold, select its name in the job window. Then click the "Resume" button, or go to the Jobs menu and choose "Resume Job."

▼ **STOP ALL THE DOCUMENTS from printing:** If the jobs are in the process of printing, the printer icon in the toolbar is "Stop Jobs." This stops the entire line-up of documents waiting to print. While it is stopped, you can delete jobs, print an individual job, go to lunch, etc.

If you try to print several times and nothing goes through, check to make sure the jobs have not been stopped! You'll know the queue has been stopped because the printer icon in the toolbar will be "Start Jobs." Plus, if you see an exclamation point in the Print dialog box, as shown to the right, that means the queue has been stopped.

▼ **START ALL THE DOCUMENTS to print:** If the queue has been stopped, the icon in the toolbar is "Start Jobs," as shown below. Click this icon to start the printing process for the entire line-up of documents. Or select one or more documents, go to the Jobs menu, and choose "Resume Job."

This exclamation point means the print queue has been stopped and your print job will not print.

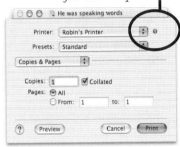

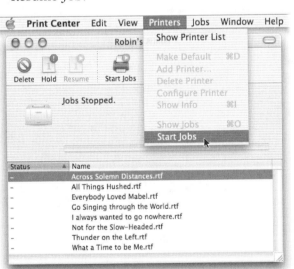

▼ **CANCEL a print job:** In the job window, click once on a document name to select it, then hit the Delete button, or go to the Jobs menu and choose "Delete Job."

You can select more than one job to delete: hold down the Command key and click on each document name you want to delete.

Collect Files to Print Later

It's possible to put a bunch of documents in a queue, then **print those jobs later,** like during lunch. Just open the Print Center, open the Jobs window, and click the icon to "Stop Jobs." Yes, you are stopping the queue before you even begin to print. Open each of your documents and tell them to print; you might get the message shown to the left, which sounds like they are going to print. They're not. Later, click the "Start Jobs" icon in the Jobs window and the files will print in the order you sent them.

Create a Virtual PostScript Printer

If you need to make a PostScript file but you don't have a PostScript printer, you can make a "virtual" (pretend) PostScript printer that will work.

To make a virtual PostScript printer:

1. Open Print Center (as explained on page 251). If you don't see the Printer List, go to the Printers menu and choose "Show Printer List."
2. Click the "Add" button.
3. In the menu at the top of the dialog box, choose "IP Printing."
4. In the new dialog box you get, enter the information shown below, then click the "Add" button.

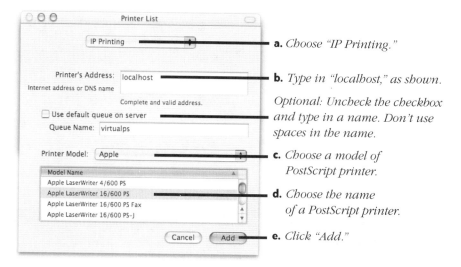

a. *Choose "IP Printing."*

b. *Type in "localhost," as shown.*

Optional: Uncheck the checkbox and type in a name. Don't use spaces in the name.

c. *Choose a model of PostScript printer.*

d. *Choose the name of a PostScript printer.*

e. *Click "Add."*

5. In your document, press Command P to Print. Choose the virtual printer, go to the "Output Options" menu, check "Save as File," and choose the "PostScript" format, as shown below. Click "Save...."

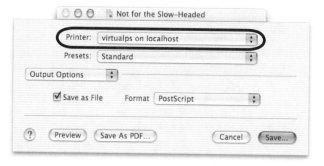

If you have a color printer, you would probably like to **access the tools** to clean the nozzles, align the printer head, etc. This is how to do it:

Use your Color Printer Tools

Print Center

To access the tools for your color inkjet printer:

1. Turn on your printer and let it warm up.

2. Open the Print Center (it's in the Utilities folder, which is in the Applications folder; double-click the icon).

3. If the Printer List doesn't automatically appear, go to the Printers menu and choose "Show Printer List." You will get the dialog box shown below.

4. Select your color printer (single-click on its name). If your printer's name doesn't appear, make sure it's turned on and warmed up. If it still doesn't appear, see pages 236–237.

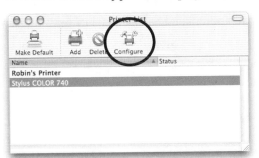

Choose your printer, then click the Configure icon.

5. After you select the printer, click the "Configure" icon in the Toolbar, and you'll get a dialog box similar to the one shown below.

    If the Configure icon is not available (it's gray), that means there are no tools you can access for the selected printer.

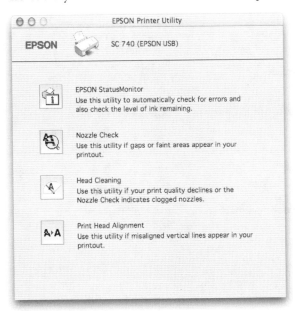

When you are finished with this, click in the red Close box to put it away.

1. Is the printer that you print to PostScript or not?

    _____

2. Is your printer USB or serial?

    _____

3. Explain how to make a printer the default printer.

    _____

4. Where would you (generally speaking) tell the printer to print
    your job "sideways"?

    _____

5. How could you tell the printer to print a number of miniature pages
    on one sheet of paper?

    _____

6. How do you open the Print Center to monitor a print job in progress?

    _____

7. What's the difference between putting a job on "Hold" and choosing
    to "Stop Jobs"?

    _____

8. If you have a report of eight pages and you need to pass this report out to five
    people, how could you make the printer collate the report for you?

    _____

9. Describe two ways to put the Print Center in the Dock so it stays there.

    _____

    _____

10. To save a PDF file from your document so you could send it to your boss
    who uses a PC, which Print pane would you choose?

    _____

Answers on page 731.

Closing & Quitting

There is a big and important difference between **closing** and **quitting**. You **close** *a document,* but you **quit** *an application.* This is a vital concept to understand, so don't skip this short chapter.

16

Contents of this chapter

Quit vs. Close

At first it seems a bit confusing—what's the big deal, **quitting** or **closing**. Either way, you're finished, right? Wrong.

Essentially, this is what happens: Say you open an *application* like your word processer—that is comparable to putting a typewriter on your desk. Then you start a new *document*—that is comparable to putting a piece of paper in the typewriter.

When you choose "Close" from the File menu, that is comparable to taking the piece of paper (the *document*) out of the typewriter. The typewriter, though (the *application*), is still on the desk! On a computer, both the desk and the "typewriter" are rather invisible so you might *think* the typewriter (the application) is gone.

But the typewriter—the word processor—stays on the desk (in the computer's *memory,* called *RAM*) until you physically put the word processor away. When you choose "Quit" from the File menu, that is comparable to putting the typewriter away.

If you leave too many applications open without quitting or too many large documents open without saving, the memory on your Mac gets full and you'll get errors, you might not be able to print or copy files, and you might hear your hard disk "thrashing," or clicking continuously. If you have a huge amount of memory, you can get away with leaving applications and documents open and not worry.

How much memory is a "huge" amount, and how do you know how much you have? Go to the Apple menu and choose "About This Mac." The little window that appears tells you how much memory is installed. Apple recommends a *minimum* amount of 128 megabytes. A good-sized amount is at least three or four times that, and if you can afford a gigabyte or two, that's excellent.

Note: A gigabyte is a 1024 megabytes, and a megabyte is a 1024 kilobytes, and a kilobyte is a 1024 bytes, and it takes 1 byte to make a standard character on the screen, like the letter "A." And because I know you're dyin' to know, 1 byte is made of 8 bits. And that's as small as it gets.

This says I have 1.25 gigabytes of memory (RAM) in my big Mac. That's a nice big chunk, but my friend Bob LeVitus has over 2 gigabytes.

When you are finished working on a document, you can **close that document window** in a number of ways:

Closing a Document Window

▼ **Either** click the red button in the upper-left of the window.

▼ **Or** choose "Close" from the File menu.

▼ **Or** in most applications, the keyboard shortcut to close a document is usually **Command W,** just like closing a Finder window.

Whichever method you use, you are simply *closing the document window* (putting away the paper) and *the application (the software program) is still open and taking up memory.* You still see the menu belonging to the application, even though the rest of your screen may look just like your Desktop, and even if you see windows that belong to other applications or to the Desktop!

Close a window when you are finished with a document and perhaps want to start another. If you know you are going to come back to this application later, you don't really need to quit (if you have enough memory).

If a document window has a dot in the middle of the red button, that means it has **unsaved changes,** meaning you made changes to the document since last time you saved it (if ever). Perhaps you wrote more, fixed a typo, or changed the typeface. If you don't save those changes before you close, you'll get a message warning you, as shown on the following page.

Unsaved changes

When the red Close button has a dot in it, you need to save the file.

> It was a long way to Tipperary. It was an especially long way to Celia because she had no idea where Tipperary was. She couldn't even positively state that it was in America. It could be in Timbuktu for all she knew. And if it was in Timbuktu, well, how on earth was she going to get there? She certainly didn't have a boat. My goodness, Celia barely had shoes.

To Tipperary

Quitting an Application

The item "Quit" is always the last command in the Application menu. If you don't see Quit in this menu, you are probably at the Desktop/Finder.

To quit an application, you must choose the Quit command. This command is always in the Application menu, and "Quit" is always the very last item. In every application you can use the keyboard shortcut instead: **Command Q.**

If you haven't saved all of your changes in any of the open documents, the Mac will politely ask if you want to save them at this point (it also asks when you *close* an unsaved document). Thank goodness.

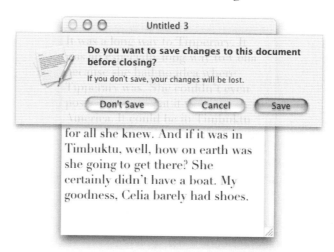

▼ Click the **Don't Save** button if you decide at this point you don't want the changes (or the document, if you've never named it). Often you can use the keyboard shortcut Command D instead of actually clicking the "Don't Save" button. In some applications, you can just hit the letter D.

▼ Click **Cancel** to return to your document without saving any changes or quitting. You can always press Command Period to cancel.

▼ If you click **Save** and you haven't yet even saved the document with a name, you'll get the "Save As…" dialog box (page 221) to name the document before quitting because nothing can be saved without a name. You can hit the Return or Enter key instead of clicking the Save button, and in some applications you can press S.

Quit when you are finished working in the application for the day (or if you are having memory problems—see page 258). Once you quit, the application is removed from the computer's memory.

Shortcut

Press on an application icon to get this menu.

There is a sweet little **shortcut to quit.** You don't even have to open the application to do this. Just press (don't click) on the application's icon in the Dock. In the pop-up menu that appears, choose "Quit."

If you're not sure if you have quit your application or not, check the Dock. Any application icon that appears in the Dock with a **triangle** beneath it is still open and taking up memory. If you want to quit that application, click once on its icon, then press Command Q to quit, even if you don't see the application anywhere! Trust me. (You can't quit the Finder, however.)

Remember, applications are only on the *left* side of the Dock, to the left of the dividing line. That's why you never see triangles on the right side, even if a folder in the Dock is open.

Check to see if applications are open

The Finder is always open because it runs the Desktop.

You can see that four other applications are still open. If you have lots of memory, you can leave lots of applications open.

When you choose to Log Out, Restart, or Shut Down, the Mac will **automatically quit** all open applications for you. If you have documents still open that need changes saved, you'll get a message for each one, giving you the opportunity to save them. This is a great option for anyone who tends to leave lots of applications open—at the end of the day, instead of taking the time to make each application active one at a time and quit it (as described above), just Shut Down and they will all quit anyway.

Quit applications upon Log Out, Restart, and Shut Down

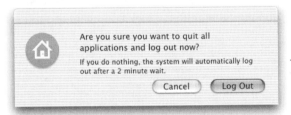

This is the message you'll get if you choose to Log Out (from the Apple menu) while applications are still open.

Tip: If you have a lot of applications open, don't choose "Shut Down" and then walk away from your computer! Wait until you see the blue screen because if there is an unsaved document anywhere on your Mac, a message will pop up asking you to save it. If you aren't there to deal with it, the Shut Down process (or Logout or Restart) times out and your computer just sits there, patiently waiting for you to come back.

Force Quit

Sometimes an application gets a little screwy and you have to force it to quit. You might not be able to get to the application's File menu to choose "Quit," but there are several other things you can do. You can also use these techniques to **force quit** applications that you're not using at the moment.

In Mac OS X when one application goes down, it doesn't take the rest of the computer down with it, as happened in previous operating systems. And if you're a Mac user from way back, you'll be happy to learn that force quit in OS X actually works.

To force quit an application, either:

1. From the **Apple menu,** choose "Force Quit...."

2. In the dialog box that appears, click once on the name of the application you want to quit.

3. Hit the Return or Enter key, or click the "Force Quit" button.

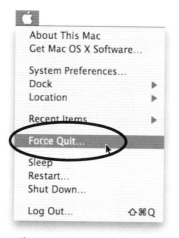

Choose "Force Quit..." from the Apple menu to get the dialog box.

Choose the application you want to force quit, then click the button.

Or:

▼ Instead of going to the Apple menu, you can press **Command Option Escape** to get the "Force Quit Applications" dialog box. (Remember, *hold down* Command and Option, then *tap* the Escape key. The Escape key is in the upper-left corner of your keyboard, and it has "esc" on it.)

Or:

▼ Hold down the **Option key and press** on the application's icon in the Dock (don't click—*hold* the button down). The menu that pops up typically says "Quit," but with the Option key down it changes to "Force Quit." Choose that item and it will force quit the selected application.

The Dock menu for TextEdit (the selected application) shows a window that is open in that application, the command to "Show In Finder," which will open the window that this application is stored in, and "Quit," which will quit just this one application.

With the Option key down (either before or after you choose this menu), "Quit" changes to "Force Quit."

Relaunch the Finder

If you have trouble in the **Finder** (at the Desktop), you can't *quit* the Finder. But you can **relaunch** it which might clear up any weird little problems you may be having. Relaunching the Finder does not affect your other applications or open windows.

To relaunch the Finder:

1. From the **Apple menu,** choose "Force Quit…," or press Command Option Escape.

2. In the dialog box, click once on "Finder."

3. Click the Relaunch button.

Circle the correct answer to these questions:

close	*quit*	**1.**	To put away a document.
close	*quit*	**2.**	To put away an application.
close	*quit*	**3.**	Press Command W.
close	*quit*	**4.**	Press Command Q.
close	*quit*	**5.**	Take the "paper" out of the "typewriter."
close	*quit*	**6.**	Put the "typewriter" away.

Use this illustration of the Dock to answer the rest of the questions:

7. How many applications (besides the Finder) are open at the moment?

_____

8. Describe how to quit Sherlock (the icon with the Sherlock Holmes hat).

_____

9. If you have a dozen applications open and you're ready to leave your Mac for the day, what is the fastest way to quit all of the applications?

_____

10. Describe three ways to force quit an application.

_____

_____

Answers on page 731.

Using the Trash

The **Trash basket** on the Mac works just like the trash can in your yard—you put things in it you don't want anymore and the garbage collector comes and takes it away and you never see it again. The Trash basket is kept in the Dock, as shown below. Since the Trash is such an important part of working on the Mac, it gets its own chapter with tips about using it.

If your machine has **multiple users,** each user has their own personal Trash basket: no one but that user can empty that basket, and no user can see what any other user has in their Trash.

This is the Trash, the waste basket.
Right now it's empty.

Contents of this chapter

Putting Something in the Trash

*The paper in the basket is an obvious **visual clue** that there is something in the garbage.*

To put something in the Trash, press-and-drag an icon over to the Trash can (actually, it looks like a wastebasket). *When the basket turns black,* let go and the file will drop inside. Don't let go of the file before the basket turns black! If you find a bunch of garbage hanging around outside the Trash or sitting in the Dock, *it's because you didn't wait for it to turn black*—you just set the trash down *next* to the basket.

The trick is that the **tip of the pointer** must touch the Trash basket! Whether you are putting one file in the Trash or whether you have selected several icons and are dragging them all together to the Trash, **the tip of the pointer** is the thing that selects the wastebasket. The shadows of the objects have nothing to do with it—forget those shadows trailing along behind—just make sure the tip of the pointer touches the basket and turns it black. Then let go.

*You can see the original file (the top one), plus the shadow that is pulled by the pointer (over the Trash basket). When the **pointer** touches the basket, the basket turns dark. That means you can let go.*

Here you can see I selected three files (I held down the Command key and clicked on each one.)

*Then I **let go** of the Command key, dragged **one** of those selected files to the Trash, and the rest followed.*

*You can see all three shadows of the files, but notice where the pointer is. It's that **tip** of the pointer, not the shadows of the icons, that selects the Trash so the files can drop in.*

You might have chosen to **hide your Dock** (as explained on page 123). If so, you can't see the Trash basket. But don't worry—as you drag a file down toward the Dock, it will pop up, you can drop the file in the Trash, and then the Dock will hide again. Or you can use any of the methods below to throw away a file without ever having to see the basket.

There are several other ways to **move an item to the Trash** besides physically dragging a file and dropping it in the basket.

▼ Select the item (click once on it). From the File menu, choose "Move to Trash."

▼ **Or** select the item (click once on it). Press Command Delete.

▼ **Or** hold down the Control key (not the Command key) and click on a file you want to throw away. A little menu (called a "contextual menu," shown below) pops up and gives you, among other things, the option to move that item to the Trash. Choose it.

This is called a contextual menu, as explained in Chapter 5.

Taking Something out of the Trash

To remove something from the Trash, click once on the basket and you'll find that it opens up to a window, just like any other window. So if you decide you want that item you just threw away, you can go get it. But don't forget—you can only get items back from the Trash if you have *not* emptied the Trash!

▼ If you change your mind directly after you throw something away, press Command Z (the "Undo" command) and the item(s) you just put in the Trash will be instantly put back where it came from.

Keep in mind that Command Z only undoes *the very last action you did;* that is, if you put a second file in the Trash, it is the second file that will be put back, not the first one. Or if you threw away a file and then you made a copy of a different file, Undo (Command Z) will undo the copying, not the trashing.

▼ You can always open the Trash window and drag the file out of the window and put it back where it belongs, as long as you have not emptied the Trash yet.

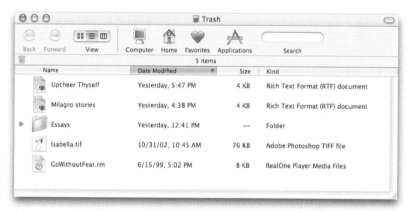

The Trash opens to a window. Drag any file out and put it wherever you want.

Anything you put in the Trash basket will stay there, even if you turn off the computer, *until you consciously empty the Trash*. Once you do that, everything in the basket is gone forever. No amount of crying or pleading will bring it back. Believe me.

Sometimes you throw away files because you want to make space on a disk. Keep in mind that the Trash must be emptied before the space will open up; that is, until you actually empty the Trash, the files continue to take up space on your hard disk or any other disk.

To empty the Trash (you don't have to select the basket first):

▼ If "Finder" is not in the menu bar, click once on the Desktop. Now that the Finder menu is showing, choose "Empty Trash…" from it. The ellipsis (three dots …) after this command indicates you will get a dialog box. **You will get a warning** asking if you really want to throw those files away. Click OK.

To avoid this warning, hold down the Option key when you choose "Empty Trash…," *or* turn off the warning altogether; see the following page.

▼ **Or** instead of going to the Finder menu, press (don't click) the mouse button directly on the wastebasket and hold it for a second or two; a little menu will pop up. Choose "Empty Trash," then let go of the mouse button. **You will NOT get the warning message.**

▼ **Or** instead of going to any menu, use the keyboard shortcut Command Shift Delete. **You WILL get the warning message** unless you have turned it off; see the following page.

Emptying the Trash

Well, if you empty the Trash and tragically realize that you threw away your only copy of something very important, there is software and there are technicians who can often bring back your information, so if you lose something important, call your local guru, power user, or user group. In the meantime, don't turn off your computer or create new files.

In general, to be safe, when you toss something in the Trash, consider it gone.

Stop the Trash Warning

Some people appreciate having a **warning** that items in the Trash will be forever deleted if they empty it, but it makes others crazy to have to click the button every time they want to empty the Trash. As mentioned on the previous page, there are a couple of ways to avoid the Trash warning temporarily, but you can also turn it off permanently (until you want to turn it back on again).

To turn off the Trash warning:

1. At the Desktop, go to the Finder menu and choose "Preferences...."

2. Uncheck the box, "Show warning before emptying the Trash."

3. Close the Finder Preferences.

When there is a checkmark, you will get a warning.

Uncheck the box (click once in it) to disable the warning.

Note: When the warning is disabled, you'll see a subtle **visual clue** in the Finder menu. The command "Empty Trash" will no longer have the ellipses (three dots), which means you won't get a dialog box—the command will be carried out instantly.

If a file is **locked,** you cannot **throw it away;** if you try, you'll get a message telling you that you don't have "sufficient privileges" to trash the item. This warning, "sufficient privileges," covers a lot of ground—it might mean the file is simply locked in the Get Info box and you can go unlock it (explained below), or perhaps it belongs to some other user, or perhaps only the administrator of the computer can throw it away because the file is some sort of important system file.

Throwing Away Locked Files

Upcheer Thyself

This is a locked file—you can see the tiny lock on the bottom-left corner of the icon. You can unlock most files in the Get Info box.

You'll probably see this message more often than you care to.

If the file is yours and you created it and it doesn't have anything to do with operating the Macintosh, you can usually unlock it using Get Info.

To unlock a locked file:

1. Click once on the file that you think may be locked.

2. From the File menu, choose "Get Info," *or* press Command I.

3. If there is a checkmark in the "Locked" checkbox, click once in the checkbox to remove the mark. Close the Get Info window.

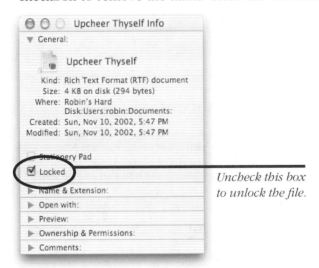

Uncheck this box to unlock the file.

If the file is not locked and you still can't throw it away, perhaps you locked this particular file when you were working in Mac OS 9. If you think that might be so, you'll need to restart using OS 9 and unlock the file from there. If that does not solve the problem and you know the file is yours and you are the administrator of the Mac, see Chapter 20.

1. What does it indicate when the Trash basket icon appears to have wadded paper in it?

   _____

2. When do the files in the Trash disappear?

   _____

3. Describe four ways to move an item to the Trash.

   _____

   _____

4. What happens if you click on the Trash basket?

   _____

5. If you decide a file should not be in the Trash after all, how do you get it out?

   _____

6. What is the keyboard shortcut that can put a Trashed file back where it belongs, if you think fast enough?

   _____

7. If you have emptied the Trash, can you get your file back?

   _____

8. How can you avoid the Trash warning temporarily, and how can you avoid it permanently?

   _____

9. How can you throw away a locked item?

   _____

10. How can you drag a file into the Trash if the Dock is hidden?

   _____

Answers on page 731.

Ejecting Disks 18

Disks go in and disks come out. Sometimes they don't come out. Sometimes they get stuck. Sometimes they won't "mount," which means their icon doesn't show up on the Desktop. This short section covers all the tricks to getting removable hard disks, CDs, DVDs, and even floppy disks in and out of your Macintosh.

Contents of this chapter

Mounting and Unmounting

You may hear talk of **mounting** and **unmounting** disks, rather than inserting and ejecting them. The terms *mount* and *unmount* refer to hard disks (internal or external), removable hard disks such as Zips and Jaz, CDs and DVDs, as well as floppies, if you have a floppy drive.

It is possible and very common to have more than one hard disk attached to your computer. You probably have removable hard disks that you insert into a cartridge drive sort of like inserting a video tape into a VCR (Zip or Jaz). But even though that hard disk is attached to the computer or you have inserted a disk into a drive, that does not guarantee that its icon will show up on the screen. If the icon does not appear (which means the computer cannot "read" the disk), we say that the disk did not *mount*.

Someone might ask you to *unmount* a disk, which is to remove it from the computer's grasp. If you have a CD/DVD tray, you'll find that you cannot open the tray by pushing its button until you first *unmount* the CD or DVD; that is, you have to drag the disk icon to the Trash basket or press Command E (for eject) before the button will open the CD tray. Or press F12 to open and close the tray, even if a CD or DVD is still mounted. Make sure you quit everything you were using on the CD/DVD before you eject the disk.

Ejecting a Removable Disk

You may sometimes need to eject a floppy disk or removable hard disk to trade it with another, or simply to take your disk and go away. There are actually several ways to **eject a removable disk.** These techniques work for any removable disks you might use, such as Zip, Jaz, CDs, DVDs, or floppies. Except for using the Media Eject key, as explained on page 276, all of these techniques require that you be at the Desktop.

Always make sure before you eject a disk that you have closed any documents and quit any applications you used from that disk. If you don't, you'll get this message when you try to eject:

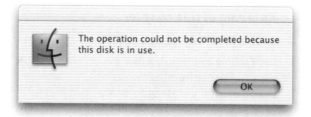

If you get this message, check to see if you opened a ReadMe file or some other document from that disk and maybe it's still open. Check the Dock to see which applications are still open; select any application you might have used from the disk, then quit that application. Or did you load fonts directly from the disk? If you loaded fonts, close them. (If you don't know how to open or load fonts, you didn't.)

One easy and obvious method to eject a disk is to use the command in the File menu.

1. Select the disk (click once on it).

2. From the File menu, choose "Eject." (If "Eject" is gray, it means you did not select a removable disk.)

   Or use the shortcut **Command E.**

Another simple and effective method is to eject the disk through the Trash. Aack, you say! Yes, that's a frightening thought, but calm down; it's quite all right. *The Trash doesn't erase anything off your disk.*

1. Simply **press on the disk icon, and drag it down toward the Trash.**

2. As soon as you press on the disk, take a look at the Trash basket— it has turned into an "Media Eject" icon, as shown to the right. Drag the disk down to this new icon **and drop it directly on top.** The disk will pop out safely.

Yet another easy method to eject a disk is with a contextual menu.

1. Hold down the **Control key and click** on the disk.

2. A contextual menu pops up—choose "Eject."

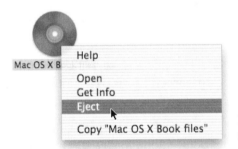

This contextual menu pops up when you Control-click on a disk.

Ejecting from the menu or the keyboard shortcut

Ejecting a disk through the Trash

The Trash icon changes to the Media Eject icon when you select a disk.

Ejecting a disk using a contextual menu

Tip: If your hard disk is partitioned into separate volumes, it's possible to eject an individual partition using any of these methods. If you want that partition mounted again, you must restart the computer. Go to the Apple menu and choose "Restart."

Ejecting multi-session CDs   If you have a **CD** on which there are **several sessions,** which the Mac thinks are individual *volumes,* you can eject all of the volumes at once using any of the methods explained on the previous page. You do *not* need to select every volume on the disk—you only need to select one. Also read about the Media Eject key, below.

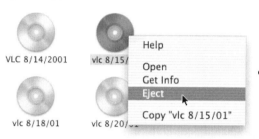

VLC 8/14/2001   vlc 8/15/

vlc 8/18/01   vlc 8/20/

| Help |
| Open |
| Get Info |
| Eject |
| Copy "vlc 8/15/01" |

*Select one of the volumes on a CD, then press Command E, **or** drag it to the Trash, **or** use the contextual menu, and all volumes will unmount and eject.*

Media Eject Key

This is the symbol for the Media Eject key, if you have one on your keyboard.

Some keyboards have a **Media Eject key.** If you have it, it's in the upper-right of the keyboard, the most upper-right key there is at the top of the numeric keypad. It has the symbol shown to the left. The great thing about this key is that you don't have to select the disk—just hit the key and the CD or DVD will eject. In fact, you don't even have to be at the Desktop—you can hit the Media Eject key while you're working in another OS X application and the disk will eject. Just make sure you first close any documents and quit any applications that opened documents from that CD before you eject the disk.

F12 Key

If you don't have an Media Eject key, use the **F12 key** (it's just above the Delete key). This will not only eject a mounted CD or DVD, but if you have a CD tray, it will open or close the tray. Try it. You might need to press firmly.

Eject on Shut Down or Restart

When you restart your Mac or when you are done for the day and **shut down** the whole computer (from the Apple menu choose "Shut Down"), most of your disks will automatically eject, except CDs and DVDs. If you're having trouble getting rid of CDs or DVDs, see the tips on the opposite page.

For details about shutting down, restarting, and logging out, please see Chapter 19.

If for some reason, perhaps because of a power outage or a system error or a bug on the disk, your CD or DVD is stuck in the computer, try the good ol' **mouse trick:**

> Hold down the mouse button. *Keep holding it down* and turn the computer back on; your disk(s) should pop out like toast.

The Mouse Trick

If you have a **Media Eject key** on your keyboard, in the upper-right, you can use a similar trick as described above. Restart your Mac, and right after you hear the start-up sound, hold down the Media Eject key until the CD ejects.

The Media Eject Key Trick

If all else fails, notice that tiny hole next to the CD slot, internal Zip drive, or floppy drive? That hole is **paperclip** size. Unbend a paperclip and push it in. It's very safe as all you're doing is releasing the mechanism that holds the disk in place—push firmly. You can even do this if the computer is turned off or unplugged and stored in a closet.

If you have an internal Zip drive, you might discover that the paperclip hole in the outer plastic casing does not exactly line up with the release mechanism on the drive inside. If you have trouble, pop the front off of the Mac (if that's possible on your machine) and stick your paperclip directly into the hole on the front of the drive.

The Paperclip Trick

New machines might not have a paperclip hole! Use the mouse trick instead.

1. What are four easy ways to eject a disk?

_____

2. Say you inserted a CD and opened the ReadMe file that was on the CD. Now when you eject the disk you get a message telling you that operation could not be completed because something is still in use. What do you do?

_____

3. What does it mean to say a disk didn't "mount"?

_____

4. If a CD or Zip is stuck in an internal drive and won't come out, describe two emergency measures to get it unstuck.

_____

_____

Answers on page 731.

Restart, Shut Down, or Log Out

19

If you've been working your way through the practice exercises in this book, you're probably ready to **Shut Down.** Shutting down is the computer's process of tying up all the loose ends inside of itself and "parking" the hard disk before it's turned off. It is certainly possible to turn the computer off without going through the Shut Down process, but you run the risk of losing data and possibly damaging mysterious but important elements. At the very least, turning off your Mac without choosing Shut Down leaves your computer in an unstable state. So follow this simple ritual when you are finished for the day!

Sometimes you don't want to completely shut down, but **Restart** or **Log Out.** And sometimes you want to leave it on for a week or two at a time. This chapter covers all those bases.

Contents of this chapter

The Options

All four of these commands are in the Apple menu, but you can also accomplish any of these tasks without opening the Apple menu.

In the Apple menu the last four options are **Sleep, Restart, Shut Down,** and **Log Out.** Here is a brief description of when you might use each of these options.

▼ **Sleep** does two things: 1) It turns off the monitor display so your screen goes black, and 2) it stops the hard disk from spinning. Both of these features save energy. You can control when your Mac goes to sleep; for instance, you might want it to automatically sleep whenever you haven't used it for twenty minutes. You can tell the monitor and the hard disk to go to sleep at two different times, since it takes longer for the hard disk to wake up than the display (some people get annoyed waiting for the hard disk to start spinning again, so you can have the display sleep but not the hard disk, if you like). On some models of Mac, you can push the flat Power button in for one second to put the machine to sleep. For all the details, see page 340.

▼ **Restart** shuts your Mac down and starts it up again without ever turning off the power. This is easier on the computer than turning off the power and rebooting (turning it back on). You often have to restart after installing new software or anytime things just start acting weird. See page 282 for details.

▼ On **Shut Down,** the Mac takes care of internal business, cleans up everything, and turns itself off (it actually turns off the power). Shut Down when you are done for the day or longer. Actually, you rarely have to Shut Down in Mac OS X—you can leave your machine on for weeks at a time, setting it to sleep automatically after a certain number of idle minutes. My partner John leaves his computer on for days on end; I shut mine down most nights. See page 284.

▼ Use **Log Out** to switch between multiple users. If you are the only user, you can use it as a safety precaution. See page 283 for details.

Keyboard Shortcuts

Newer keyboards have an **Eject Media Key** in the upper-right of the keyboard, with this symbol: ⏏ . If you have this Eject key, here are **keyboard shortcuts** that will *instantly* Sleep, Restart, or Shut Down your Mac (unless you have unsaved documents):

Sleep:	Command Option Eject
Restart:	Command Control Eject
Shut Down:	Command Option Control Eject

To display the **dialog box** with options to Restart, Sleep, Shut Down, or Cancel, press Control Eject.

Unsaved Documents

Several times in this chapter I mentioned **unsaved documents.** If you try to Restart, Shut Down, or Log Out and the Mac finds documents that you haven't saved yet, or that have had changes made that you didn't save, a message will appear asking if you want to save them, as shown below.

Now, if you hit the button to Log Out, for instance, and then you walk away from your computer and the Mac finds an unsaved document, it will wait several minutes for you to respond. **If you don't respond** because you've done something like left the building, then the Log Out (or Restart or Shut Down) process times out and your computer goes back to normal without logging out, restarting, or shutting down. **If you click the Cancel button,** you don't just cancel saving the document, you cancel the entire Log Out, Restart, or Shut Down process.

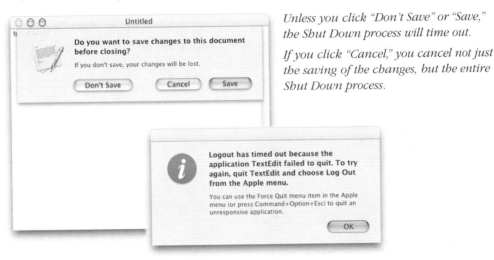

Unless you click "Don't Save" or "Save," the Shut Down process will time out.

If you click "Cancel," you cancel not just the saving of the changes, but the entire Shut Down process.

Good Housekeeping

When you've finished working for the day, it's good housekeeping to close up all your windows on the Desktop because any window you leave open will reappear in front of your face when you turn your computer back on. It's kind of like walking into the kitchen in the morning and finding last night's dinner dishes still on the counter. Press **Command Option W** (or Option-click on a red close button) and every open Finder window will tuck itself away where it belongs. Wish the dishes did that.

However, you can take advantage of these windows staying where you left them and perhaps leave open your nice, neatly organized Home window and perhaps your favorite project folder so when you return to the Mac they are ready and waiting for you.

Restart

Restart does exactly that: it restarts your Mac, but without turning the power off. It's sort of like turning your Mac off and then turning it back on again, but without the stress of powering completely down and up. You occasionally have to restart after installing some software. And sometimes when things are just acting goofy, Restart can clear up the problem.

You can choose "Restart" from the Apple menu, obviously, but occasionally your Mac is acting so weird you can't get to the Apple menu. So there are several other ways to Restart, depending on what kind of Mac you have.

- ▼ On most **G3 and G4 towers,** there is a tiny Restart button (and programmer's switch) right below the Power button on the front of the tower. The Restart button has a solid black triangle on it.

- ▼ If you have an **Eject Media Key** in the upper-right of your keyboard, hold down the Command and Control keys, and press the Eject key.

- ▼ If you turn on your **Mac with a big Power Key** on the keyboard, the one with a triangle outline on it (not the flat, round button with the circle on it), hold down the Command and Control keys, then press the Power Key.

- ▼ If you have a colorful **iMac,** press the Power button on the keyboard (not the one on the monitor) and you should get the message shown below where you can choose to Restart.

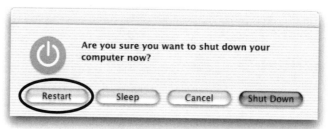

Are you sure you want to shut down your computer now?

Restart   Sleep   Cancel   Shut Down

Instead of the Shut Down option, you can choose to Restart.

- ▼ Also on a colorful **iMac** (as opposed to the flat-panel Macs), look in the little panel on the right side of the computer. You'll see two tiny buttons, one with a tiny, solid triangle. That's the Restart button; push it to Restart. Don't push the other button—that's a programmer's switch (it's actually indented a little to make it difficult to hit accidentally). But if you do accidentally push the programmer's switch and you get weird stuff on your screen, go back and push the Restart button this time.

   On **older iMacs,** it's not a button, but a solid triangle above a tiny hole—unfold a paperclip and push it in the hole to Restart. Don't stick the paperclip in the programmer's switch!

- ▼ When you **install software** that needs your computer to Restart, they'll provide you with a Restart button in a dialog box.

- ▼ You can choose to **Restart Classic** separately from OS X using the Classic preferences pane; see Chapter 39.

Log Out

Choose to **Log Out,** even if you're the only user on the whole machine, when you are going to be away from your Mac for a while. Once you are logged out, no one else can get to your personal documents, fonts, applications, or even your Trash basket.

For extra protection, you can hide the Restart and Shut Down buttons that appear on the login screen (although I'm not clear on what good that does because anyone can just restart with the Restart button). Go to the Accounts system preferences and click the "Login Options" tab to hide the Restart and Shut Down buttons.

Log Out does not turn off the power to the computer, as Shut Down does, although it does go into a low-power mode. See Chapter 20 for details about multiple users and logging in and out.

▼ Command Shift Q will give you the dialog box shown below.

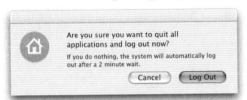

Shut Down   From the Apple menu, choose **Shut Down.** All open applications will quit, any extra hard disks will unmount, you will be disconnected from any servers you were connected to, and the Mac will automatically turn its own power off.

There are several ways to Shut Down, depending on the Mac you have.

▼ If you have a **G3 or G4 tower,** you can usually push the Power button in and hold it to the count of five to Shut Down. You won't get any warning message unless you have unsaved documents still open. (Push this button for one second to put the Mac to Sleep instead of Shut Down.)

▼ This works on Macs that have an **Eject Media key** in the upper-right of the keyboard, including laptops: Hold the Control key and press the Eject Media key. You'll get the message shown below.

Most Shut Down methods will display this alert message. You can hit the Return or the Enter key instead of clicking the "Shut Down" button.

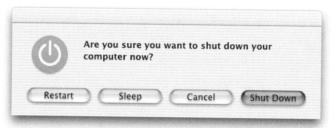

▼ On a newer laptop, press the Power button for five seconds to Shut Down. On an older **laptop,** this combination usually works: hold down Control Shift fn, then press the Power key. You won't see any message unless you have unsaved documents.

▼ If you have a keyboard with a **flat, round, green-glowing Power button on the keyboard,** you can push that to Shut Down and you will get the message shown above.

▼ If you have an older, colored **iMac** with a Power button on the keyboard *and* a Power button on the monitor, push the button on the **keyboard** to get the message shown above.

The Power button on the **monitor** will do one of two things: it will either put your Mac to sleep, as described on page 280, **or** it will instantly quit all open applications, Shut Down, and turn off your Mac without any warning UNLESS you have unsaved documents.

▼ If you turn on your **Mac with a big Power Key** on the keyboard, the one with a triangle on it (not the flat, round button with the circle on it), you can usually push that key again to turn the Mac off.

You can **lock your Mac** while you're away from it. When you lock the computer, your screen saver instantly appears, and it won't go away until you enter your login password.

Of course, you can set your screen saver so if it comes on, you need a password to make the screen saver go away, as descibed on page 332. But the advantage of locking your Mac with this technique is that the screen saver will only lock you out when you choose, not every time it comes on.

Lock People out of your Mac

To lock your Mac with a click:

1. Open Keychain Access (it's in the Utilities folder, which is inside the Applications folder).

2. From the View menu across the top of the screen, choose "Show Status in Menu Bar." Quit Keychain Access.

3. Back at the Finder, you'll now see a tiny padlock icon on the right side of your menu bar, across the top of your screen. Click that padlock icon to get the menu shown below.

   Choose "Lock Screen" and your screen saver will start and no one can access your Mac unless they know your login password.

If you choose "Lock 'name,'" the Keychain Access for that user will be locked.

1. Of the four options in the Apple menu (Sleep, Restart, Shut Down, and Log Out), which is the only one that turns off the power?

   _____

2. Of these four options, which is the only one that helps protect your Mac from snoops?

   _____

3. What symbol does a Restart button have on it?

   _____

4. What will happen to open applications if you choose "Shut Down" before you have quit each application?

   _____

5. What is the keyboard shortcut to close all of your Finder windows at once?

   _____

Answers on page 731.

Multiple Users & their Homes

20

Mac OS X is specifically built for what's called a **multiple user environment;** that is, Apple expects that more than one person is probably using the same machine, whether it's in a school, office, or home.

If you are the only user who ever has or ever will use this computer, skip this chapter altogether. But are you really the only user? Perhaps your grand-kids come over and want to use your Mac. Or maybe your husband uses your machine from time to time. Or sometimes you have relatives staying for a week who just want to use your Mac to get their email. In all of these cases, you can set up another user so no one else can access your personal letters, change the sound level, poke around in your financial files, put up a dorky picture as the Desktop background, or change any of your settings.

Contents of this chapter

Advantages of having Multiple Users

First, let me explain the **concept and advantages of having multiple users** set up on your Mac so you can decide if you need or want to create other users. You already have one user, you, which was automatically created when you first turned on your Mac and went through the setup process.

You might not have noticed that you are a "user" because Apple sets a default so when you turn on your Mac, you are automatically "logged in" without having to type in a password. Once you have other users set up, you can change this default so everyone must log in with a password. If others use your Mac only occasionally, like your grandkids, you can set it to automatically let you in daily; then when the kids come over, all you have to do is log *out,* which means they must then log *in* with their own settings and yours will be protected. I'll explain how to do that—it's so easy.

One user, the first (which was you, if it's your own Mac), is automatically created as the original, main **Administrator (Admin)** of the computer (if you are the *only* user, you are still the Administrator). All other people are "users" and are limited in certain ways:

▼ Applications can be made available to everyone, or limited to specific users. This means you could install a game in your child's Home folder and it won't clutter up your own Applications folder. If the game has to change the resolution of the monitor and the number of colors and your child cranks the volume way up, it won't affect what you see and hear when you log back in.

Also for kids and grandkids, you can customize their Dock so they have easy access to their own programs, and you can eliminate from the Dock the icons they don't need.

It also means you can install your financial program in your own Home folder so others cannot use it nor access your files.

▼ Even if an application is available to everyone who uses the machine, individual users can set their own preferences because the preferences are stored in the user's personal Library folder.

▼ Every user can customize the Mail program, and all of the email is privately stored in each user's personal Library folder.

▼ Every user can set up her own screen effects. Favorites, fonts, window and Desktop backgrounds, and Dock placement and preferences are individually customizable. Preferences are also individual for the keyboard, mouse, Internet, web browser bookmarks or favorites, international keyboard settings, Classic, applications that startup on login, and QuickTime.

▼ The features that make the Mac easier to use for people with challenges can be customized by user. This includes the Universal Access settings, full keyboard access, Speech preferences (talking to your Mac to make it do things), etc.

▼ Users who need international settings, such as for date, time, numbers, or for typing other languages, etc., can customize the Mac without bothering other users. If you have a laptop that you travel with, you can set yourself up as another user, such as "Carmen in Belize," and customize those settings for that country without affecting all your settings for home.

▼ Users *cannot* change the date or time (except for the menu bar settings), nor can they change the preferences for energy saving, file sharing, networking, or the startup disk. They cannot add new users nor change certain parts of the login process.

As the Administrator, you can **assign Admin status to any other user** (see page 295). When that user logs in, he can make system-wide changes that regular users cannot, he can create and delete other users, and do most of the things you can do. But your personal Home files are still protected from everyone else, including other Admins.

Can be more than one Admin

**Logging Out
and Logging In**

Automatic login allows *one* selected user to use the Mac without having to enter a password. If automatic login is enabled (pages 295–296), then to switch to another user you must make sure to **Log Out** instead of shutting down or restarting (because when the machine starts up again, it will automatically log in the selected user).

If automatic login is *not* enabled, then it doesn't matter how you turn off the Mac—it will always display a **Log In** screen where every user, even Admins, will have to enter a password.

This is a typical login screen with a number of users. In the Login preferences pane, shown on page 295, this is the "list" option.

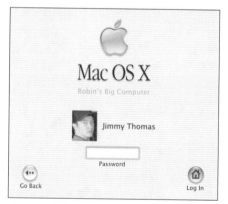

A user clicks on his name, above, and another pane appears where he enters his password and clicks the Log In button.

If you are the Admin (as explained on the previous pages), you can create new users. There are two preference panes you'll work with, **Accounts** and **Login Items;** users themselves can make some adjustments settings in **My Account.**

In the Accounts pane, you'll create the new user, plus assign them a login picture and password. In the Login Options pane, you can make adjustments to the login window and provide the password hint.

Creating New Users

Accounts

Login Items

My Account

To create a new user:

1. Open the System Preferences: either click on the icon in the Dock, or go to the Apple menu and choose "System Preferences...."

2. In the System Preferences pane, click once on "Accounts." You'll get the dialog box shown below, except it probably has only one user listed, you. The one user is also the Admin.

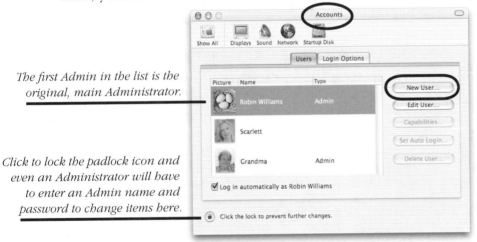

The first Admin in the list is the original, main Administrator.

Click to lock the padlock icon and even an Administrator will have to enter an Admin name and password to change items here.

3. Click "New User..." to get the dialog box shown on the next page.

Type in the full **name** (or anything else you prefer) in the "Name" edit box. A **short name** will be automatically created for you, but you can edit it. The short name should be short, you can't use capital letters or spaces, and it's best to avoid any non-alphabet characters (like *, !, ? or /).

Mac OS X can use either the short name or long name. But the short name is necessary if you ever use FTP, Telnet, or other applications that let you log in to your Mac from some other location.

You will never be able to change the short name after you click Save! The only way to "change" it is to delete the entire user and make a new one! (To do this, first create a new user with the correct short name, transfer all necessary files/folders, such as Documents, into the new user's account [through their Drop Box], *then* delete the first user whose short name you didn't like.)

Tip: If you have a very young user or two, you can set them up as a user with no password so all they have to do is click on their picture to log in. Or make the password something like "xxx" so it's really easy for them.

4. Enter a **password** for the user. As you've probably seen before, you need to type in the password twice to make sure you've spelled it right, since you can't see it.

Passwords are "case sensitive." That means capital or lowercase letters **change the password:** "ChoCo" is *not* the same password as "choco." So be darn sure when you write your password down somewhere that you make note of any capital letters.

Use up to eight characters or numbers, no spaces, no apostrophes or quotation marks or other non-alphanumeric characters, and don't use a word that can be found in the dictionary. (You can type in more than eight characters, but the Mac only checks the first eight in this case).

It is possible to leave the password blank, but that makes that user's Home easier to break into.

The password you provide here is the same one that will be used with the **screen effect** to protect your Mac when you walk away— you leave the computer, the screen saver starts, and the password must be entered to get back to the Desktop. See page 332 for details.

You can, if you like, enter a **password hint.** On login, if a user enters the wrong password three times, a message appears with this hint. But make sure the checkbox is checked in the Login Options pane to tell this message to appear! (See page 297.)

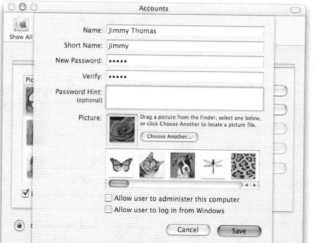

—continued

Do not *use the word "root" as a short name.*

To add a photo, see the following page.

When you see the bullets that are hiding your password, you'll sometimes notice there are more bullets than the characters in your password. This is a protective device to help prevent snoops from trying to guess your password. Don't worry that maybe it's a different password from what you remember!

5. Choose a **login picture.** There are three ways to do this.

   a. Either click once on any picture in the sliding pane shown at the bottom of the dialog box.

   b. Or click the "Choose…" button, which will open the standard Open dialog box where you can select any photo or graphic image on your Mac.

   c. Or open a folder that contains the photo or image you want. Position the folder window to the right of your screen. Drag a photo from that window and drop it onto the picture "well" in the Identity pane, as illustrated below.

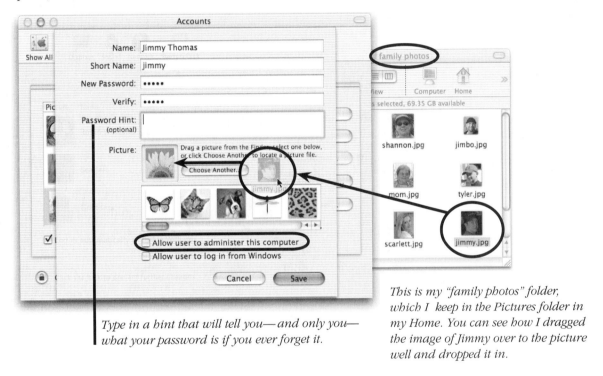

Type in a hint that will tell you—and only you—what your password is if you ever forget it.

This is my "family photos" folder, which I keep in the Pictures folder in my Home. You can see how I dragged the image of Jimmy over to the picture well and dropped it in.

6. This pane is also the place where you can **change a user's status to Admin:** Check the box to "Allow user to administer this computer." You can have as many Admin users as you like, but that means your Mac would not be very well protected.

   The option to "Allow user to log in from Windows" is explained in Chapter 35. You can set up a user here on your Mac, set up another user on a PC, and they can share files back and forth.

7. Click Save. Continue to the next page.

8. Back at the **Accounts** pane, you can assign a user to **automatic login,** as explained below.

I just set up several new users, but my Mac is set to automatically start up with "Robin Williams," meaning I do not have to go through the login screen and enter a password whenever the Mac starts or restarts. This is good for me. Because the Mac will automatically log me in, the only way the other users can get to their Home folders is if I go to the Apple menu and choose "Log Out...," or if I turn off the automatic login for myself. Which one you choose depends on how often the other user will need your machine; if it's infrequent, you can let yourself automatically log in daily, then log out when the other user arrives to log in.

Only one user can be assigned the automatic login. Any time you like, open this pane, select another user, and click the button to give them the automatic login privilege.

9. If you want to limit what the new user can access, see pages 298–300. Otherwise, **close** the Accounts preferences pane (click in the red Close button).

This is Jimmy's new Home. He has exactly the same folders as you have in your Home. Everything in his Home is private except for the files he has added to his Public folder—any other user can read and copy those files.

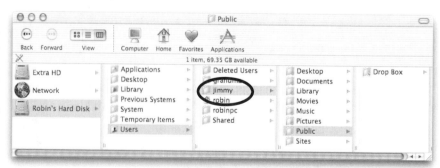

The other pane in the Accounts preferences, the **Login Options,** is accessible only to Administrators. Here an Admin can set a number of preferences for the Login window, as shown on page 292:

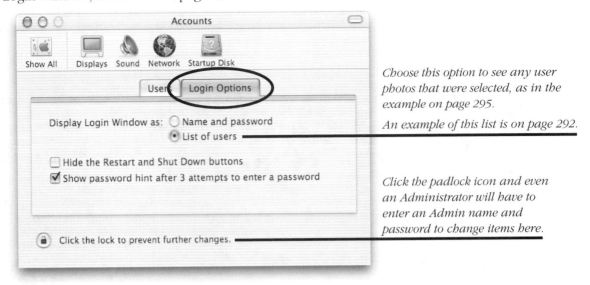

Choose this option to see any user photos that were selected, as in the example on page 295.

An example of this list is on page 292.

Click the padlock icon and even an Administrator will have to enter an Admin name and password to change items here.

▼ **Display Login Window as:** "Name and password" displays a small window with two edit boxes: one for the user name and one for the password. A user will have to type in both name and password.

"List of users" displays list of all accounts. The pictures that were chosen in the User pane (page 295) appear next to the names of the users. It's really cute. Click a picture, then type your password.

▼ **Hide Restart and Shut Down buttons:** This adds a wee bit more security to your Mac. See, when you log out, your computer does not turn off. It sits there with a little window where you can log back in again, and there are two buttons, one to "Restart" and one to "Shut Down." If your Mac is set to automatically log you in on startup, then an unauthorized user can walk by after you have logged out, click the Restart button, and your Mac will restart and automatically log you in. Or someone could shut down your Mac, insert an OS X CD, and boot up the Mac and get access to your whole computer. By disabling the Restart and Shut Down buttons, an unauthorized user cannot click them, which would make your Mac one step closer to being protected.

However, there is nothing to prevent anyone from pushing the Restart button on the Mac, so if you really don't want people getting into your Mac, do not enable automatic log in, and don't leave your OS X CD laying around.

▼ **Show password hint:** If the user types in the wrong password three times, the hint provided (as shown on page 294) will appear.

Limit a User's Access

Simple Finder is not something you would use for yourself, but you might apply it to another **user** of your Mac. It limits what the other user has access to. Previously, it was possible for you to limit a user from getting at files on your main hard disk, but if you had other partitions, another user could access (or destroy) just about anything on those other partitions. Simple Finder *seriously* limits what the other user can even see—you have total control over what she can access, as you can see below.

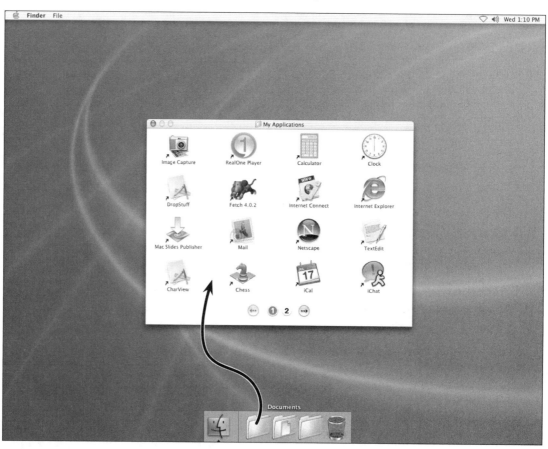

The three folders in the Dock are Applications, Documents, and Shared. See the tip about the Shared folder on the following page.

This shows what a user logged in using **Simple Finder** might see.

- The Applications and Utilities are limited to what you choose to allow.
- The user has no access to a Desktop or other partitions.
- The user has three folders in their Dock: Applications, Documents, and Shared. The Shared folder contains items placed in it by other users of the computer, as explained in Chapter 34.
- The Finder windows have no Toolbars.
- Not a single hard disk or partition is available.

To set up a user with Simple Finder:

1. Open the System Preferences (click the icon in the Dock, or go to the Apple menu and choose "System Preferences…").

2. Click the "Accounts" icon, which is in the bottom-left corner of the System Preferences pane. The Accounts pane will appear.

This is the Accounts icon.

3. If you don't have a user yet, click the button "New User…" to set one up (see the previous pages).

4. Click the "Capabilities…" button; you'll see the sheet shown below.

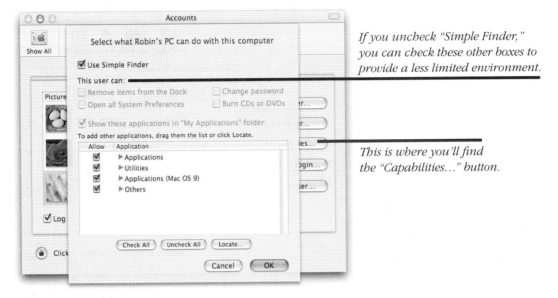

If you uncheck "Simple Finder," you can check these other boxes to provide a less limited environment.

This is where you'll find the "Capabilities…" button.

5. Check the box to "Use Simple Finder." Click the triangles next to "Applications," "Utilities," "Applications (Mac OS 9)," and "Others" to choose which of those items you will allow this user to access.

   Notice, **alternatively,** that when the "Use Simple Finder" box is *un*checked, you can put limitations on the user without going to the extreme of the Simple Finder.

6. Click OK. When that user logs in to their account, their use of your Mac will be extremely limited.

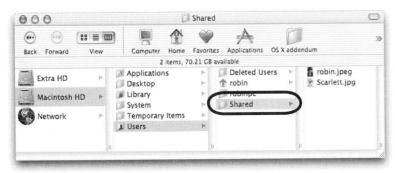

Tip: Anything anyone puts into the "Shared" folder, shown to the left, will be available even to users running Simple Finder.

Setting up a User's Login

Login Items

In **Login Items,** any user (including yourself) can choose to have certain items automatically open during the login process (this window applies only to the user who is currently logged in). You can have your favorite applications open, or utilities, documents, even movies or music. If you choose to have a document open, the application it was created in will have to open, as well, even if you don't have it in the list.

The files will **open in the order they are listed.** Drag any file in the list up or down to change the order.

If you don't want to see a certain application right away, click in the box to **hide** it. It will still open, but its windows won't be visible on the screen. The application icon in the Dock will have the triangle, though, so you know it's open and you can access it at any time.

It doesn't work very well to add Classic applications to the Login Items.

Once you or any user is logged in, you can adjust some of the login settings, even if you're not the Administrator. In **My Account** preferences, you can change your password (you have to know the current password before you can change to a new password). You can also change your image and go straight to your vcard (virtual card) in the Address Book (see Chapter 32 about the Address Book).

Users Can Adjust Their Own Settings

My Account

Any user can change these preferences.

Folders for Sharing Files with Others

Once a user is set up, the default is to allow **access** only to the Public folder, the Sites folder, and the Drop Box. The Shared folder (which is in the Users folder, which is on your main hard disk) belongs to everyone who uses the Mac. If you plan to share files between users on this one computer, please see Chapter 34, which explains all this in detail (the Sites folder is explained in Chapter 36). Here are very brief explanations:

▾ Put files in your **Public** folder that you want others to be able to read, copy, or print. They have to open your Public folder to do so.

▾ Other users can put files for you into your **Drop Box,** which is located inside of your Public folder. They cannot open your Drop Box, not even to see if their file successfully transferred.

▾ Put files in the **Shared** folder that you want everyone who uses the Mac to have access to. This is a good way to distribute something to everyone on the Mac without having to copy it to each individual user's Drop Box.

▾ The **Sites** folder is where you can store a web site or files that you want people to access through the Internet. See Chapter 36.

You can also change the sharing "privileges" for any folder in your Home. That is, you can turn *off* the sharing privileges for the Public folder and the Drop Box so no one can access them, and you can also choose to share *any* or all of your other folders, with varying levels of access. Please see Chapter 34 for details.

Any Admin can **delete a user.** When a *user* is deleted, their *files* are not really deleted, but are compressed into a "disk image" and put into a folder named "Deleted Users." This gives you an escape in case you decide it was a drastic mistake to remove a user—at least you have the important files.

Deleting Users

To delete a user:

1. Open System Preferences, click "Accounts," then click "Users."

2. Click once on the name of the user you want to delete.

3. Click the button, "Delete User...."

4. You will be asked if you really want to delete this user. Click "Cancel" if you change your mind, and click "OK" if that's what you really want to do.

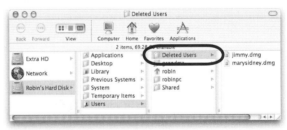

Once a user's account has been deleted, you'll see it in the Users folder, in the "Deleted Users" folder. All of the folders are compressed into a disk image and are accessible to the Administrator (double-click the .dmg file; see Chapter 21).

5. Now you are stuck forever with the "Deleted Users" folder. You can throw away all the files inside the "Deleted Users" folder, but you can't throw away the actual folder itself. To get rid of it, you have to log in as the "root" user. See the directions on pages 458–459 if you need to do that.

1. Can there be more than one Administrator on one Mac?

_____

2. Can regular users create more users?

_____

3. Why is it important to make sure the short name is the one you really want before you click Save?

_____

4. How do you know which Administrator is the main, original one?

_____

5. Why is "dog food" not a good password?

_____

6. If the password is "2002mtxlpk," would "2002MtxlpK" get you in?

_____

7. Which preferences pane do you use to assign Admin status?

_____

8. If you delete a user, do you delete all of their files?

_____

9. Which option would you choose to limit a user to the most basic features?

_____

10. How you could have Mail and your browser open for you automatically?

_____

Answers on page 732.

Downloading & Installing

Downloading and installing files can be rather confusing because a variety of files appear on your Desktop (or disappear and you can't find them) and then you're not sure what to do with which one and you're not sure if you can throw any of them away because they might be important. So I hope this chapter will sort most of this out for you.

Note: You will always be asked for an administrator's **name and password** before any new applications or utilities can be installed, so make sure you have those handy. If you've forgotten them completely, see pages 322 and 323.

Contents of this chapter

Downloading Software

When you **download** a file from the Internet (copy it from another computer to yours), it might be in any number of different "formats," which are explained on the following pages. For right now, let's walk through the process of actually downloading something, then we'll look at what to do with the file you downloaded. If you've done this before, skip to the next section.

Practice downloading software from the Internet:

In this example, we'll go to Apple's web site and download the demo version of a game. The process is basically the same no matter where you download software, even if you buy it at an online store.

1. Make sure you are connected to the Internet. If you're using AOL, log on to AOL, then follow these same directions in your browser.

2. Go up to the Apple menu and choose "Get Mac OS X Software…." This opens your browser and takes you to a page on Apple's site where you can download files for OS X, as shown below.

The software on this page will change as time goes by, but you'll always find things to download here.

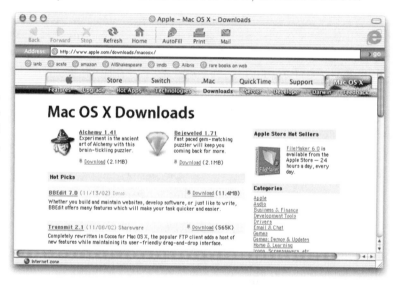

3. As I write this, the games called Alchemy and Bejeweled are at the top of the web page—it will be something different by the time you go there! Choose something else, if you like, or just read along to get an idea of the process.

   The two downloads in this example are "demo" versions, which will only work for a short time. If you like them, you can buy them both as one package for $19.95 right here on Apple's site.

   If you click on the *name* of the file (Alchemy 1.41, in this case), you'll get a web page describing the item in more detail, plus a link to download the file (or buy it).

   If you click on the "Download" link you see above, you'll start downloading the file immediately.

4. The Download Manager, as shown below, might or might not appear in front of you. If it doesn't and you're using Internet Explorer, go to the Window menu and choose "Download Manager." You don't have to do this, but it's comforting to be able to see the progress of your download.

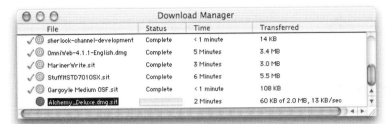

Take note of the name of this file in case you have to search for it later!

5. Once your file has downloaded to your computer, the Mac automatically goes to work taking care of it. In this particular case, you'll see this dialog box appear on the screen for a minute or two—it's "unstuffing" the file for you:

If your Mac doesn't unstuff the file automatically, double-click the icon that is now on your Desktop, the icon you saw downloading in Step 4. In this case, it is a file ending with the extension ".dmg.sit."

6. In this case, once it has been unstuffed (uncompressed), your Mac "mounts" this particular file for you. You'll be asked to agree with the License Agreement. Just click the "Agree" button.

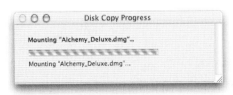

After unstuffing the file, as above, your Mac will mount the downloaded file. This will only happen with certain files called "disk images," as explained on the following pages. If your file did not mount, see the caption in the next step.

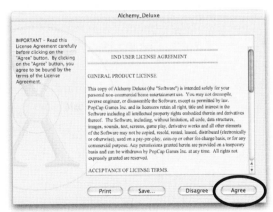

Alchemy Deluxe

This is called a "disk image." If you double-click this icon, it opens the window shown to the right. But the Mac automatically opens the window for you.

Save and throw away
Unmount the disk image:
Click on it, then press Command E to eject it, or drag it to the Trash.

***If** you want to save a backup of the application, **save the .dmg** file onto a CD or Zip disk.*

*Now you can **throw away the .dmg** file.*

7. Now, what your Mac did is "mount" a disk image and automatically open that disk image so you see the window shown below. Double-click the "Alchemy Deluxe" file to open and play the game.

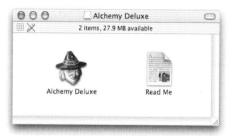

The Read Me file gives you directions on how to play the game, and there is an excellent tutorial in the game itself.

8. This particular game is only a demo version. In this case, you can only play the game as long as the disk image (shown to the upper-left) is on your Mac. You'll find that disk image on your Desktop, or if not, it will be in your Computer window.

To delete this demo game, find that disk image. Select it (click once on it), and press Command E to eject it.

To buy this game, go back to the web site, click the name of the game, and follow the directions to buy it. When you download the paid-for game, the steps above will have one more step—install it into your Applications folder.

Practice downloading and installing software from the Internet:

In this next example, let's go to a web site where you can download and install a working version of a great word processing program called **Mariner Write.** The download is free; after thirty days, if you like the program, you can pay the $69.95 fee and legitimize your copy.

1. Connect to the Internet, if you're not already, and open your browser.

2. Go to the page **www.MarinerSoftware.com,** then click the "download" link (circled in the illustration on the next page). You will be asked to log in with your name, plus make up a password. Do that (and write it down somewhere), then click the "Send info" button. You will arrive at the web page shown on the next page.

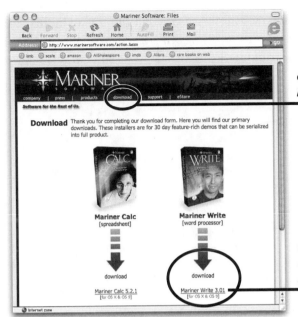

Click the "download" link to get to this page.

3. To download either Mariner Write word processor or Mariner Calc spreadsheet, click once on the download link for that application.

Click either underlined link to download the software of your choice.

4. The Download Manager in your browser will open, as shown below. Take notice of the name of the file that is being downloaded just in case you have to go looking for it. (The default for your Mac is to put downloaded files directly on your Desktop, although you can change that in your browser preferences.)

5. Notice in the Download Manager that the file you're downloading has the extension (letters at the end of its name) of ".sit." A .sit file is "compressed," or made smaller so it will go through the Internet faster. Your Mac will automatically uncompress this .sit.

MarinerWrite.sit *This is the .sit file that you downloaded.*

—continued

309

6. Your Mac automatically uncompresses the .sit file. Now, in this case, the .sit file uncompressed to an ".img" file, as shown below. Also in this case, this .img file automatically opens to a window, also shown below, right.

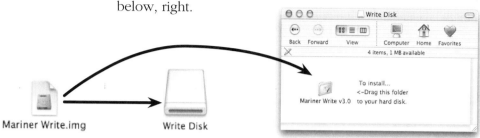

Technically, this .img file opens to a disk image, as shown to its right. But often your Mac will open the disk image, then immediately open the disk icon to its window.

This is the disk image from the .img file. You'll find it either on your Desktop or in your Computer window.

This is the window that your Mac probably automatically opens. If it doesn't, find the disk image in your Computer window and double-click it.

7. To actually **install** Mariner Write or Mariner Calc, drag the icon in the window—*not to your hard disk, as it says*—to your Applications icon in the Toolbar (just drop it on the icon). This will painlessly install the software on your Mac.

Save and throw away

Unmount the disk image:
Click on it, then press Command E to eject it, or drag it to the Trash.

***If** you want to save a backup of the application, **save the .img** file onto a CD or Zip disk.*

*Now you can **throw away the .img** file.*

Mariner Write

This folder icon will be in your Applications folder.

Mariner Write

Inside the folder is the application icon for Mariner Write. Drag this icon to the Dock so it's easily accessible.

8. So now there's just one thing left to do. You've got two icons still on your hard disk: the *disk image* in your Computer window and the original *.img* file.

▾ First, click once on the disk image, then either drag it to the Trash or press Command E to eject it (it thinks it's a real hard disk). This **unmounts** the image.

▾ After you unmount the disk icon, you can throw away the .img file if you like. If you paid for the software, it's a good idea to copy it to a removable hard disk in case your computer crashes or you get a new Mac—you'll have an important backup copy. Then you can **throw away** the .img that's still on your hard disk.

What are all those Files?

When you **download software from the Internet,** it can be mighty confusing. Several files will probably appear during the process. They have "extensions" at the ends of their file names that give you a clue as to what they are—some extensions indicate a file is "compressed" so it goes through the Internet lines faster; some indicate the file is "encoded" so it arrives on a particular type of computer with all of its data intact. Here is a list of the most common extensions you will see, plus brief explanations.

You don't really need to know all this, though, to be able to install files correctly. You can just skip to the appropriate page for the type of file that appeared on your computer, and I'll tell you specifically how to install it. But if you're curious:

.dmg   **disk image.** *OS X only.* When you double-click this icon, it automatically opens with Disk Copy (a utility in your Utilities folder). What looks like a removable hard disk appears in your Computer window.

.img   **disk image.** *OS X only.* When you double-click this icon, it automatically opens with Disk Copy (a utility in your Utilities folder). What looks like a removable hard disk appears in your Computer window.

.smi   **self-mounting disk image.** *OS X only.* When you double-click this icon, it opens itself without using Disk Copy. What looks like a removable hard disk appears in your Computer window.

.sit   **stuffed file** (compressed) made with Aladdin software. *OS X or OS 9.* A stuffed file is generally not as large as a disk image. When you download a .sit file, typically it automatically opens in StuffIt Expander (a utility in your Utilities folder) and unstuffs. Sometimes a .sit will unstuff to a disk image.

.bin   **BinHex encoding.** *Best for OS X.* A .bin file might open directly to an installer, or it might open to a stuffed file or disk image.

.hqx   An older form of **BinHex encoding** that is compatible with older versions of the operating system. *Best for OS 9.* You might have a choice of downloading a .bin or a .hqx—choose .bin because you're using OS X.

You might see a file with the extension of *.sit.hqx,* which indicates the file was encoded (hqx), then stuffed (sit). The hqx will *unencode* and you'll get a .sit file, which will *uncompress* and give you the actual file itself.

.zip   **compressed file.** Generally this indicates a file from a Windows machine. If your Mac doesn't automatically unzip the file, drag it on top of StuffIt Expander, which is in your Utilities folder (which is in your Applications folder).

Visual Examples of all those Files and What They Do

Here are examples of the **most common files** you will download and some of the possible scenarios for installing them. Many files might act differently from what's described here, but they're all pretty similar.

The simple .sit

Below is a good old-fashioned **.sit** (dot sit) file, the kind that's been around forever. You can make a .sit file with the program StuffIt Lite or StuffIt Deluxe. Every Mac for the past several years has had a utility called StuffIt Expander included, so when you double-click a .sit, it automatically unstuffs.

Your browser is already set up so when you download a .sit, StuffIt Expander automatically unstuffs it before you even notice. What you will notice is a .sit file probably sitting on your Desktop. Before you double-click it, look around your Desktop and see if you can find the file that the .sit unstuffed into. It might be a folder, a disk image (such as an .img), or a document.

For instance, here is a simple example: At one of my favorite web sites, **www.Veer.com**, I downloaded a free font. The .sit file landed on my Desktop and was immediately unstuffed. So by the time I noticed, I had both of the files below on my computer.

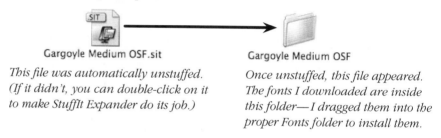

Gargoyle Medium OSF.sit

This file was automatically unstuffed. (If it didn't, you can double-click on it to make StuffIt Expander do its job.)

Gargoyle Medium OSF

Once unstuffed, this file appeared. The fonts I downloaded are inside this folder—I dragged them into the proper Fonts folder to install them.

The more complex .sit

Here is an example of a slightly more complicated process. Follow along with the icons and dialog boxes to see how it works.

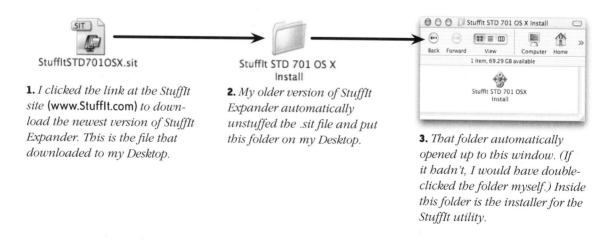

StuffItSTD701OSX.sit

1. *I clicked the link at the StuffIt site (www.StuffIt.com) to download the newest version of StuffIt Expander. This is the file that downloaded to my Desktop.*

StuffIt STD 701 OS X Install

2. *My older version of StuffIt Expander automatically unstuffed the .sit file and put this folder on my Desktop.*

3. *That folder automatically opened up to this window. (If it hadn't, I would have double-clicked the folder myself.) Inside this folder is the installer for the StuffIt utility.*

4. *I double-clicked the installer icon that was inside the folder. It started the installation process, as you can see here. I clicked the "Install" button.*

5. *The installer asked me where I wanted to put the utility. I chose my Utilities folder, as you can see above. Then I clicked "Choose."*

7. *Installation was successful, so I clicked the "Quit" button.*

6. *This tells me the file is being installed on my Mac. I don't need to do anything but sit here dumbfounded.*

8. *Now in my Utilities folder I have this wonderful suite of tools.*

I keep DropStuff in my Dock so when I need to stuff a file to send to someone else, I just drop the file on DropStuff and it creates a .sit for me.

Save and throw away

*If you want to save a backup of these utilities, **save the original .sit** onto a removable disk. Then you can throw away the .sit file.*

*You can **throw away the Install** folder (shown in Step 2).*

The .sit to .img   This is the same example I showed on pages 308–310, but briefly. If you've been reading along, you've noticed that .sits might open to a variety of other files. This one opens to a **.img,** which is a **disk image file** that opens to *another* file that looks and acts like a hard disk.

The final disk image icons never have extensions at the ends of their file names. Because they think they're real disks, you'll find their icons in your Computer window (click the Computer icon in any window Toolbar). If you have set your Finder preferences so that hard disk icons appear on your Desktop (see page 131), then you'll see the same icon on your Desktop that is in your Computer window.

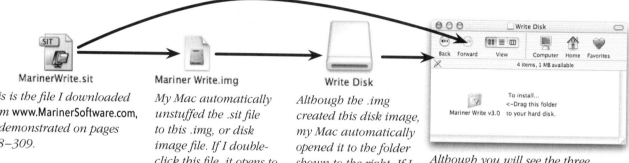

MarinerWrite.sit

This is the file I downloaded from www.MarinerSoftware.com, as demonstrated on pages 308–309.

Mariner Write.img

My Mac automatically unstuffed the .sit file to this .img, or disk image file. If I double-click this file, it opens to the actual disk image shown to the right.

Write Disk

Although the .img created this disk image, my Mac automatically opened it to the folder shown to the right. If I double-click this disk icon myself, it opens to the same folder shown.

Although you will see the three intermediary files on your hard disk, sometimes the process is so automatic that you won't have to double-click anything—this folder will just appear in front of you and you'll wonder what those three other files are doing on your Desktop.

Save and throw away

Unmount the disk image: *click on it, then press Command E to eject it, or drag it to the Trash.*

If *you want to save a backup of the application,* ***save the .sit*** *file onto a CD or Zip disk.*

Now you can ***throw away the .img*** *file and the* ***.sit*** *file.*

A **.dmg** is a **disk image file** that opens *another* file that looks and acts like a hard disk.

The final disk images never have extensions at the ends of their files names. Because they think they're real disks, you'll find their icons in your Computer window (click the Computer icon in any window Toolbar). If you have set your Finder preferences so that hard disk icons appear on your Desktop (see page 131), then you'll see the same icon on your Desktop that is in your Computer window.

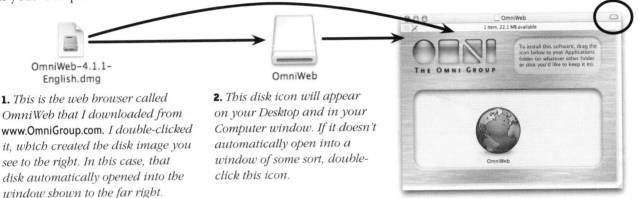

OmniWeb-4.1.1-English.dmg

OmniWeb

1. *This is the web browser called OmniWeb that I downloaded from* www.OmniGroup.com. *I double-clicked it, which created the disk image you see to the right. In this case, that disk automatically opened into the window shown to the far right.*

2. *This disk icon will appear on your Desktop and in your Computer window. If it doesn't automatically open into a window of some sort, double-click this icon.*

3. *The directions in the top portion of this window tell you to drag the OmniWeb icon into your Applications folder. Well, that would be easier if your Toolbar was showing: click the tiny, clear button in the upper-right corner to make the Toolbar appear, as shown below, left.*

4. *Now that the Toolbar is showing, drag the big globe icon and drop it on the Applications icon.*

OmniWeb

5. *This is the installed browser in your Applicaions folder. Drag it to your Dock for easy access.*

Save and throw away

Unmount the disk icon: *click on it, then press Command E to eject it, or drag it to the Trash.*

If you want to save a backup of the application, ***save the .dmg*** *file onto a CD or Zip disk.*

Now you can ***throw away the .dmg*** *file.*

The .dmg to .pkg   A **.dmg** is a **disk image file** that opens *another* file that looks and acts like a hard disk.

The final disk images never have extensions at the ends of their file names. Because they think they're real disks, you'll find their icons in your Computer window (click the Computer icon in any window Toolbar). If you have set your Finder preferences so that hard disk icons appear on your Desktop (see page 131), then you'll see the same icon on your Desktop that is in your Computer window.

In this example the disk icon opens a window that contains a **.pkg,** a package file, which is a self-contained unit. Double-click a .pkg to open and run the installation.

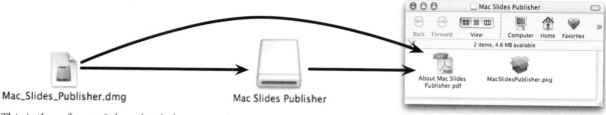

Mac_Slides_Publisher.dmg

Mac Slides Publisher

1. *This is the software I downloaded from the Mac.com site so I could make and publish slides shows as screen savers (see pages 333–336).*

2. *This disk image will appear on your Desktop and in your Computer window. If it doesn't automatically open into a window of some sort, double-click this icon.*

3. *In this particular case, the .dmg file automatically opened this window. Now I can double-click on the .pkg to start the installation.*

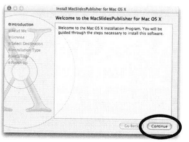

Mac Slides Publisher

4. *This begins the installation. Just click "Continue" and carry on.*

5. *This is the file that gets installed into your Applications folder.*

Save and throw away

Unmount the disk icon: *click on it, then press Command E to eject it, or drag it to the Trash.*

*Now you can **throw away the .dmg** file, **unless** you want to back it up first onto a CD, Zip, or Jaz disk. After you back it up, then you can throw away the one on your Desktop.*

You don't need to save any files at all if the file you downloaded was free and you can download it again if your computer crashes or you get a new one.

An **.smi** file is a "self mounting image," which means it doesn't need to open through the utility called Disk Copy, like .img and .dmg files do. But it does uncompress to what looks and acts like a hard disk icon.

The .smi file

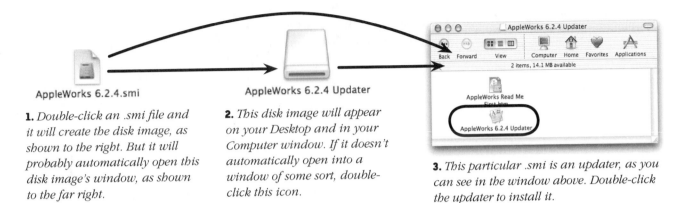

AppleWorks 6.2.4.smi

AppleWorks 6.2.4 Updater

1. *Double-click an .smi file and it will create the disk image, as shown to the right. But it will probably automatically open this disk image's window, as shown to the far right.*

2. *This disk image will appear on your Desktop and in your Computer window. If it doesn't automatically open into a window of some sort, double-click this icon.*

3. *This particular .smi is an updater, as you can see in the window above. Double-click the updater to install it.*

If you have a choice between downloading a **.bin** file or a **.hqx** file, choose the .bin file because it is created specifically for newer operating systems, like Mac OS X. Generally you can just double-click a .bin and it will open either to the final file or to an installer that you can double-click to install the software.

The .bin file

AcroReader51_ENU.bin

Acrobat Reader Installer

1. *Double-click a .bin file to open the compressed file.*

2. *If this is an installer of some sort, double-click it to start the installation process.*

Save and throw away

Unmount the disk icon: *click on it, then press Command E to eject it, or drag it to the Trash.*

If you want to save a backbup, ***save the .smi or the .bin*** *file.*

Now you can ***throw away the .smi or .bin*** *file.*

Installing Applications

On a corporate network, applications can also be installed on the main network server so all users can access them. Talk to your system administrator.

Sometimes you need to make a decision about *where* to install a file. Usually the Mac will automatically install applications into the main Applications folder (provided you can supply an Administrator name and password) where **all users** have access to them.

If you want to be the **only one** who can use an application, create a new folder in your Home folder, as circled below, right, and call it something like "My Applications" or "Applications for Lew." Install the application inside this folder.

Any user can install an application into their own Home folder. They still need to know their own password.

Install into this folder so all users of this Mac can open and use the application.

Create your own personal applications folder and install into it so only you can use the application.

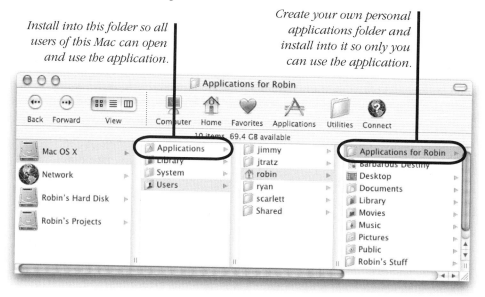

Installing Classic applications

If you have to install **applications that will only run in OS 9,** they need to go into the folder called "Applications (Mac OS 9)." This folder is in the same folder in which your OS 9 system folder is stored.

To install some older applications, you may have to actually start up your computer in OS 9, install the software, then boot up again in OS X. Although you had to install it in OS 9, it should work just fine in Classic while running OS X. If you use the application often, put its icon in the Dock for easy access. Be forewarned that new Macs made after January, 2003, will no longer boot in OS 9, and so it will be impossible to install old software. They will still run Classic—you just won't be able to start up in OS 9.

Install from a CD

One of the most common ways you'll get new software is on a **CD.** This kind of CD almost always has an "installer" file that will do the installation with very little help from you. It's great. Generally you should quit all other applications while you install new software.

To install an application from a CD:

1. Insert the CD into the drive, label-side upwards. It takes a few seconds for the CD icon to appear on your Desktop. (If you changed the Finder preferences so "removable media" does not show up on your Desktop, click the Computer icon in a Finder window to see the CD icon.)

   The install window often pops open automatically, as shown below. If it doesn't, double-click the CD icon.

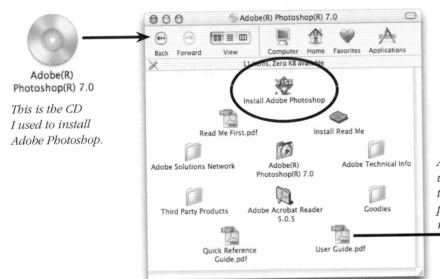

Adobe(R)
Photoshop(R) 7.0

*This is the CD
I used to install
Adobe Photoshop.*

*After you install, you might
want to see if there is documentation on this CD that you can
print, or other useful tools that
need to be installed.*

*An install CD typically has an "installer" icon at the
top of the window. There are lots of other files on the
CD, but you can ignore them all for now except the
installer and the "Read Me" file (read it!).*

2. Double-click the installer icon. You will be asked for an Administrator name and password, and you'll need to agree with the license agreement.

—continued

3. The installer suggests where to put the application; if it is an OS X application, it automatically chooses the Applications folder. If you want to put it somewhere else, based on the restrictions mentioned on page 318, click the button circled below and choose a new destination.

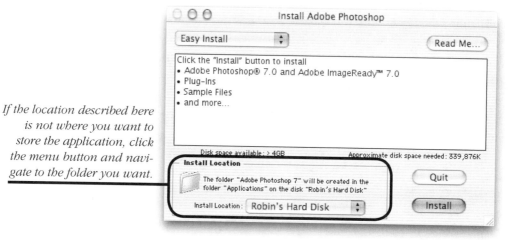

If the location described here is not where you want to store the application, click the menu button and navigate to the folder you want.

Tip: *You'll find the registration number with the documentation that came with the CD. The number is typically a combination of numbers and capital letters. Press the Caps Lock key down, and then you can type both letters and numbers without having to hold the Shift key down.*

4. You will usually have to enter your registration number to install software packages. Once you do that, the installer will whiz merrily along. Sometimes you must restart after installing new software; if you do, the software will tell you so.

Adobe Photoshop 7

When the installation is complete, you'll find something like a folder or an application icon in the folder you chose above.

If a folder was installed, double-click the folder to find the application icon inside. Drag the application icon to the Dock so you can access it easily.

Install by Dragging

If you have software already installed on a Mac running OS X, it is sometimes possible to **drag** that software folder to another Mac through your file sharing connection, or drag it from a Zip disk or a CD onto another Mac. This isn't the best way to install most software because some applications put files in various Library folders as they go through the installation process, but it will usually work. Remember, though, that when you buy software, you don't really buy the *software*—you buy the *right* to use that software on *one* computer, so you can't be dragging your $600 version of Photoshop onto all your friends' computers. You can, however, give all your friends a copy of **freeware** (such as Acrobat Reader) or **shareware** programs, provided your friends know where to send their small shareware fee.

There is one important thing to know about dragging software files or folders from one Mac to another. Every file or folder, when dragged to another computer, comes along with its **access privileges.** These access privileges can limit who uses the software. If it's an extremely useful freeware product such as Acrobat Reader and you plan to install it into the general Applications folder so everyone can use it, you want to make sure it is accessible to everyone who uses that Mac. You must be the Admin user to change the privileges.

Shareware is software that is distributed freely. If you install it, use it, like it, and decide to keep it, you have a moral obligation to check the ReadMe file that came with the software and send its author their small fee, usually something like $5 to $20.

To make sure all users have privileges to use an application:

1. Click once on the folder that stores the application. If the application does not come in its own folder, click once on the application itself.

Click on the application folder to check the privileges.

2. Press Command I to get the Get Info box. Click the tiny triangle next to "Ownership & Permissions," as shown to the right.

3. Make sure the "Access" and "Others" permissions are set to "Read & Write."

4. Click the button to "Apply to enclosed items…" so the application has no trouble accessing its dictionary, templates, and other folders as it works.

For details about privileges and what they all mean, see Chapter 34.

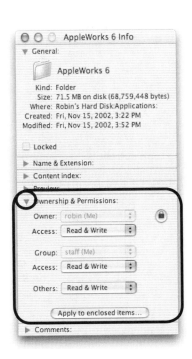

If You Forgot a Password

After you **forget your password** for this or for that a few times, you get in the habit of writing it down. By the time you read this page, it's probably too late and you've totally and utterly forgotten your password, or one of the users on your Mac forgot hers.

Change a user's password

The main Administrator of the computer (the first Admin, the one who first turned on the machine and set it up) can change the password of a user or of a secondary Administrator.

To change a user's password:

1. You must be the main Admin of this computer, or have the name and password of the Admin so you can log in as Administrator.

2. Open the Accounts preferences (from the Apple menu, choose "System Preferences…," then click "Accounts").

3. Click once on the user's name, then click the "Edit User…" button.

4. Delete the existing password, then type in the new password in both edit boxes ("Password" and "Verify").

5. Click the "Save" button.

After you click the "Save" button, you may get the message shown below:

If you have never used and never plan to use Keychain Access, this doesn't matter anyway. If you have no idea what Keychain Access is, you're not using it. See pages 466–473 if you want to know and need to change the Keychain password.

It's not quite so easy to **change the main Administrator's password.** You need the original Mac OS X installer CD, not an update CD. You don't need to be the Admin to do this, which means anyone with the original CD can change the Admin password, so protect your copy of the CD from unauthorized hands.

To change the original Administrator's password:

1. Start up the Mac with the original installer CD for Mac OS X: put the disk in, restart, hold the C key down.

   If you put the CD in and see the icon called "Install Mac OS X," don't bother to double-click it because it will ask for your password.

2. When the first install window finally appears, ignore it. Notice in the upper-left corner, next to the Apple, there is a menu item called "Installer." From that Installer menu, choose "Reset Password...."

3. In the dialog box that appears, click once on the hard disk icon that stores your OS X system.

4. Below the icons of the hard disks, there is a menu that lists all the users of your Mac. Choose "System Administrator (root)" from that menu.

5. Enter the new password in both of the edit boxes. And this time, *write down your password!*

6. Click the Save button.

7. Go back to the Installer menu and choose "Quit Installer," or press Command Q. You will be given an option to Restart your Mac. Go ahead and restart.

Change the main Admin password

I have so many passwords I keep a small Rolodex file just for them. It has saved my boompah a number of times. Sometimes I go to a web site I swear I've never seen before and so how could I have a password, and then I find my password for that web site in my Rolodex. sheesh.

1. Which utility automatically uncompresses .dmg and .img files for you?

_____

2. In Mac OS X, should you choose a .bin file or a .hqx if you have a choice?

_____

3. Which utility automatically uncompresses .sit files for you?

_____

4. Let's say you downloaded and unstuffed a .sit file, which opened an .img file, which mounted a disk image, which allowed you to install a software application. When you're done installing, which files can you throw away?

_____

5. How is an .smi file different from an .img or .dmg file?

_____

6. Why would you want to save a downloaded file after you've installed it?

_____

7. How is a disk image like a real disk?

_____

8. Who can change a user's password?

_____

9. If you want all users of this Mac to be able to use an application, where should you install it?

_____

10. If you want only a specific user to have access to a certain application, where should you install it?

_____

Answers on page 732.

Customizing Your Mac with
System Preferences

The **System Preferences** allow you to change the settings of a number of features on your computer. This will become a familiar process to you as you work with your Mac. You might want to skim through this chapter to learn what each of the various preferences offer, then come back when you decide you want to change something.

Contents of this chapter

System Preferences

The **System Preferences** pane holds all of the individual preferences. If you are an experienced Mac OS 9 user, you'll recognize these as the replacements to the control panels.

This is the System Preferences icon that is probably in the Dock.

To open System Preferences:

▼ The icon shown to the left should be in your Dock. Click once on it.

▼ You can always go to the Apple menu and choose "System Preferences…."

The "favorites toolbar" across the top can be **customized:**

▼ **To add** a preference to the toolbar for easier access, drag any icon from the pane up into the toolbar.

▼ **To remove** a preference from the toolbar, drag any icon off of the toolbar and drop it on the Desktop.

▼ **To hide the Toolbar** altogether, go to the View menu and choose "Hide Toolbar," or click the Hide/Show Toolbar button in the upper-right of the window.

This is the Favorites toolbar. Many Mac OS X applications have their own favorites toolbar like this, and they can always be customized.

*Single-click any icon to open its preference pane. The new pane will **replace** the one you see. **To come back to this pane,** single-click the "Show All" button in the upper-left of the window, or press Command L.*

Once System Preferences is open, you can use the "View" menu to choose different preference panes, even if the main pane is closed.

Personal

The **Personal** set of System Preferences are those that change the look of your screen and its various parts, which include the *Desktop, Dock, General,* and *Screen Effects* panes. This is also where you access the *Login Items* preferences for multiple users. The *International* preferences can change the language that appears in all the menus, dialog boxes, and even on the keyboard. These are either explained below, or there is a note telling you where else in the book you will find detailed information.

Desktop

Use the **Desktop** preferences to change the color of your background on the monitor. Instead of a color, you can choose a photograph or an abstract image. You can also use any photo or graphic image of your choice. Just put that photo or image in your Pictures folder, then choose "Pictures Folder" from the Collection menu (circled, below) to add the photo. For details on how to use these Desktop preferences, see pages 127–128.

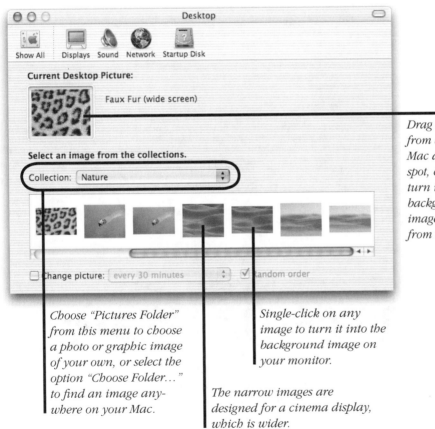

Drag a photo or graphic from anywhere on your Mac and drop it into this spot, called a "well," to turn it into your monitor's background. The original image will not be removed from its storage place.

Choose "Pictures Folder" from this menu to choose a photo or graphic image of your own, or select the option "Choose Folder..." to find an image anywhere on your Mac.

Single-click on any image to turn it into the background image on your monitor.

The narrow images are designed for a cinema display, which is wider.

Dock

Dock

The **Dock** preferences pane lets you control several features of the Dock, including its size, whether it enlarges as your mouse rolls over it, where the Dock appears on your screen, and more. For explanations and illustrations of each feature, please see Chapter 8.

You can also access the Dock preferences two other ways:

▼ **Either** from the Apple menu, choose "Dock."

▼ **Or** hold down the Control key and click on the dividing line in the Dock.

Both of the techniques mentioned above give you a menu where you can choose several of the options you see in the preferences pane. Also in those menus you can call up this entire pane.

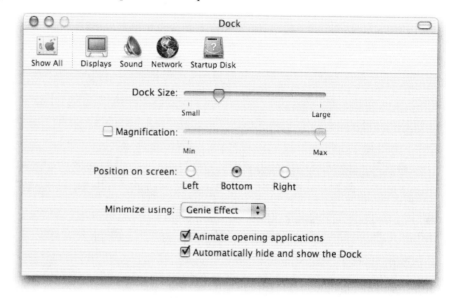

The "Magnification" setting, for example, adjusts how large these icons become as your mouse moves across them. If you leave the box unchecked, they do not enlarge at all.

The **General** preferences pane offers a variety of options, all of which have been discussed at other places in this book. If something in the pane doesn't make sense to you, please check the reference page for that item.

General

See page 136.

See page 72.

See page 136.

See page 136.

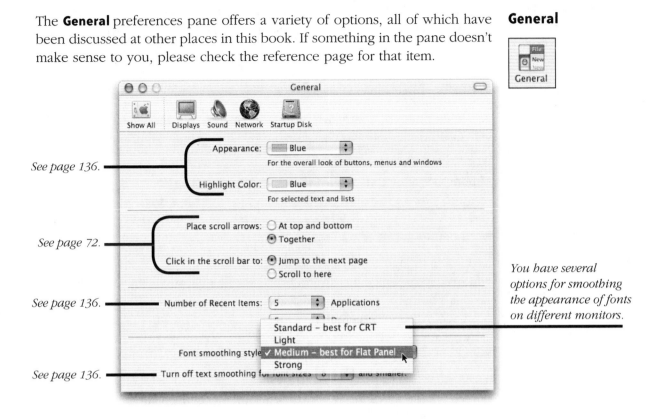

You have several options for smoothing the appearance of fonts on different monitors.

The **International** preferences pane actually allows you to change the menu bars, menus, and dialog boxes into other languages, as well as change the keyboard layout so you can type appropriately. You can also choose options to display the time, date, and numbers in the particular style of other languages. See Chapter 4 for full details.

International

The **Login Items** preferences pane is where you can choose files that will open automatically whenever you log in. See Chapter 20 for all the details.

Login Items

Screen Effects

Screen Effects

The **Screen Effects** preferences let you set up a series of images that will automatically appear on your screen. The basic function of a screen saver is to prolong the life of your monitor and to prevent static images from being "burned" into the screen. But if you have a monitor that's newer than five years old (which you most probably do because monitors rarely live longer than five years), an image is not going to get burned into your screen even if you left it on for a month. To prolong the life of your monitor, especially flat screen displays, you should probably use the Energy Saver monitor option (see page 340).

Although Screen Effects is not necessary to protect the *monitor*, you can use it to protect the *data* on your computer by **requiring a password:** After Screen Effects automatically activates, a person would have to enter a password before the screen effect would go away.

And even though it's not necessary, Screen Effects is really quite lovely and makes for a nice look in an office with all the monitors dissolving into various photos of beaches and forest and the universe. If you are a web designer, make screen shots of your web sites (see page 476) and use them as the screen effect to impress your clients. If you're an illustrator or photographer, user your own images as the screen effect.

If you want your Mac to go to sleep to save energy after a certain amount of time, use the Energy Saver, described on page 340. It will go to sleep even if the screen effect is active.

To turn off the screen effect so you can work again, click anywhere, tap a key, or wiggle the mouse.

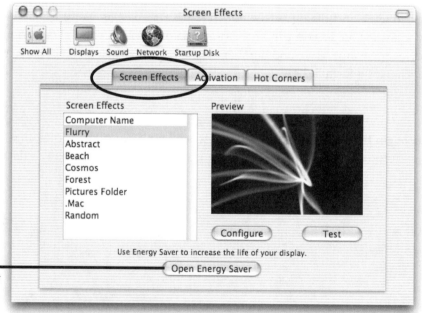

See page 340 for information about the Energy Saver preferences pane.

Below are explanations of the screen effects that are prepared for you.

▼ **Computer Name:** This displays a dark gray screen with an Apple logo and the computer's "name." For instance, mine says "Robin's Friend." If you want to change the name that is displayed, go to the Sharing preferences pane and change the "Computer Name."

▼ **Flurry:** This creates undulating colored streams of light. Click the "Configure" button to set parameters that affect its appearance.

▼ **Abstract, Beach, Cosmos, Forest:** These are photos supplied by Apple for your enjoyment. You cannot configure anything with these sets.

▼ **Pictures Folder:** This creates a slide show using any images you have stored in the Pictures folder in your Home area. If you want to use a select few of your images as your screen effect, do this:

   1. Go to the Desktop and make a new folder by pressing Command Shift N.

   2. Name the new folder something like "My Screen Saver."

   3. Put the images (or copies of the images) you want to appear in the screen saver inside this new folder.

   4. Go back to the Screen Effects preferences pane and click once on "Pictures Folder."

   5. Click the "Configure" button. Drag your new folder into the square well in the top-left corner of the drop-down panel, select the "Display Options" you prefer, then click OK.

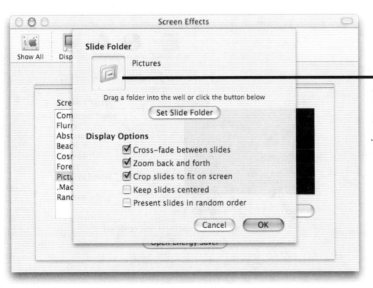

*Drag any folder of photos into the well, **or** click the "Set Slide Folder" button, then select a folder of photos from the "Open" dialog box.*

▼ **.Mac:** See pages 333–336.

▼ **Random:** The Mac will randomly select from one of the various screen effects in the list. Every time Screen Effects turns on, you'll get a different one.

—continued

Screen Effects Activation   You can determine **when** you want the screen effects to automatically appear, and whether or not to require a **password.** The password that will wake the screen saver is the password for the current user.

If you are the only user, you were asked to provide a password and a hint when you first set up your Mac. If you've *forgotten* your password and need a hint, see page 292. If you *don't know* the password even if someone gave you a hint, see pages 322 and 323.

Drag the slider bar to one of these time slots. When you don't use your Mac for that period of time, the screen saver will automatically start.

Choose whether or not to require a password to turn off the screen saver.

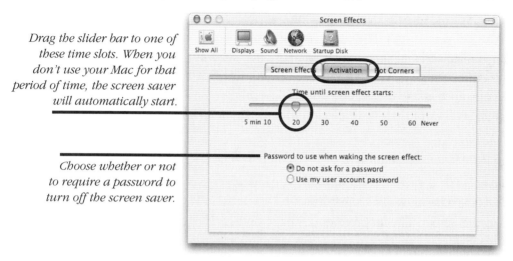

Screen Saver Hot Corners   The **Hot Corners** pane lets you select a corner that will **turn on** your screen saver when you shove the mouse into it. For instance, in the example below there is a checkmark in the upper-right corner of the screen image. If you push your mouse into that corner (*without* pressing the mouse button down), the screen saver instantly activates without waiting for the pre-scribed period of time, as chosen above. If you set a hot corner with a minus sign, you can shove your mouse into that corner and the screen saver **will not activate** as long as the mouse stays in that corner, even if the time's up.

To check the boxes:

If a checkbox corner is empty, click once to put a check in it.

Click once again to change the check to a minus.

Click once again to clear the checkbox.

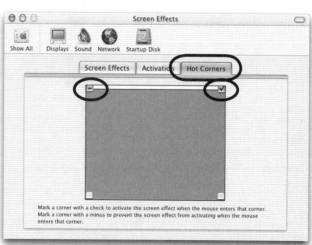

In the **Screen Effects** preferences, there's an interesting feature called a **.Mac slide show.** .Mac, pronounced *dot mac,* is a membership suite of features; see pages xxi–xxii.

If you are a .Mac member, you can download a piece of software from **www.mac.com,** then instantly "publish" a collection of personal images as a public slide show for others to use. If you are *not* a .Mac member, you (or anyone running Mac OS X version 10.2) can "subscribe" to any .Mac member's slide show—and you don't have to download any software first to do it.

To download the software so you can publish a slide show for others to use

(you must be a .Mac member)**:**

1. Go to **www.mac.com.**

2. Log in with your screen name and password.

3. Click the button called ".Mac Slides Publisher."

4. This takes you to another web page, shown below. Click "Download .Mac Slides."

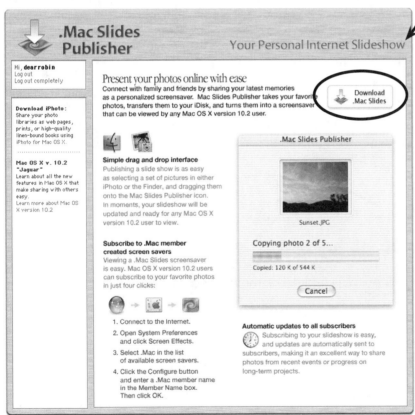

As time goes by, the software might be moved to another part of the website or its name might change! If you don't find it here, poke around the .Mac site.

5. This opens the web page with a link for the download, as shown on the following page.

— *continued*

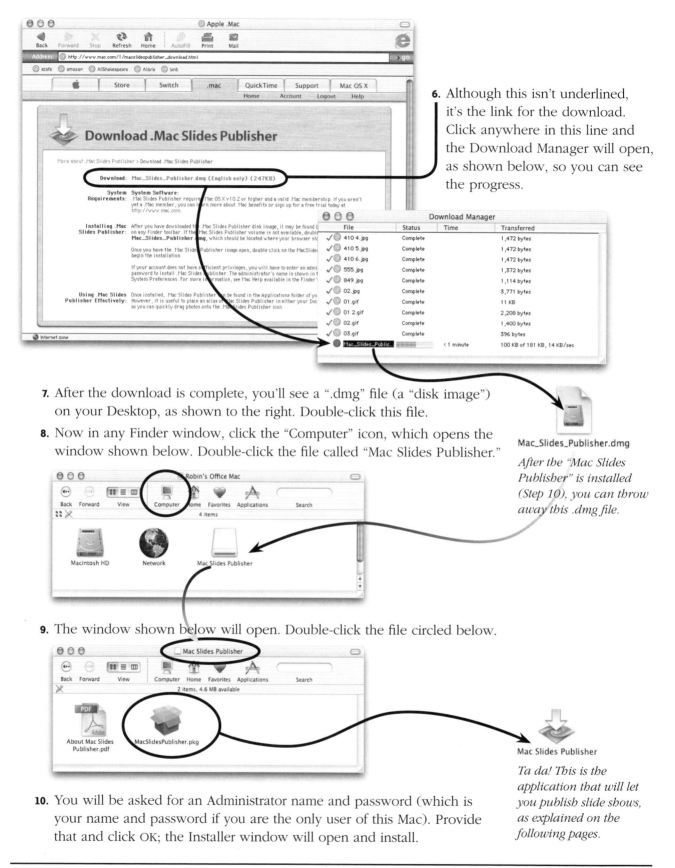

6. Although this isn't underlined, it's the link for the download. Click anywhere in this line and the Download Manager will open, as shown below, so you can see the progress.

7. After the download is complete, you'll see a ".dmg" file (a "disk image") on your Desktop, as shown to the right. Double-click this file.

8. Now in any Finder window, click the "Computer" icon, which opens the window shown below. Double-click the file called "Mac Slides Publisher."

Mac_Slides_Publisher.dmg

After the "Mac Slides Publisher" is installed (Step 10), you can throw away this .dmg file.

9. The window shown below will open. Double-click the file circled below.

Mac Slides Publisher

Ta da! This is the application that will let you publish slide shows, as explained on the following pages.

10. You will be asked for an Administrator name and password (which is your name and password if you are the only user of this Mac). Provide that and click OK; the Installer window will open and install.

To publish a slide show for others to use (you must be a .Mac member)**:**

1. Follow the directions on the previous pages to download the software.

2. Connect to the Internet, if you're not already.

3. Position the icon for the "Mac Slides Publisher" where you will be able to see it when you have pictures accessible or iPhoto open. You can drag the application icon to the Dock, into a Toolbar, or make an alias on the side of your Desktop (to make an alias, hold down Command and Option, then drag the application icon to the Desktop).

Mac Slides Publisher

This is the application icon. It's in your Applications window after you download and install it.

4. To publish a slide show, simply drag photographs or other image files to the "Mac Slides Publisher" icon and drop them on top.

    ▼ The only files that will work are .jpg or .jpeg files (same things). This is the format a digital camera automatically shoots pictures in.

    ▼ You can drag .jpg files from a Finder window (shown below) or from the iPhoto window (shown on the following page).

    ▼ You must drag over all the files you want in the slide show at once—that is, you cannot drop two photos on the icon, then go get three more, etc. You must select every photo you want in the slide show and *drag them all at once to the icon.* (You cannot drop a folder on top of the publisher icon.)

    To select more than one photo, hold down the Command key and click on the images you want to use. Then *let go* of the Command key and drag *one* of the selected files—they will all follow along.

*Note: Everytime you drop photos on the publisher icon, you **replace** the existing slide-show with the new photos!*

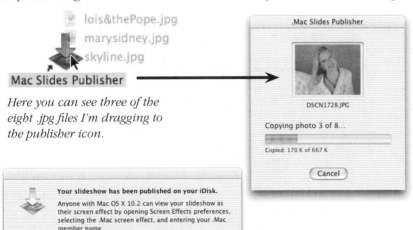

Here you can see three of the eight .jpg files I'm dragging to the publisher icon.

As soon as you "drop" (let go of) the images, a window opens to display the progress.

When the process is complete, you'll get this opportunity to announce your slide show.

—continued

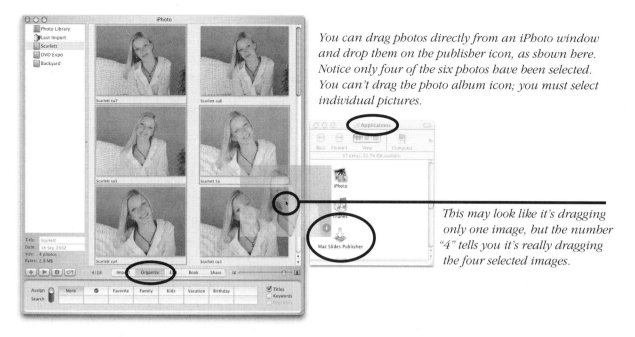

You can drag photos directly from an iPhoto window and drop them on the publisher icon, as shown here. Notice only four of the six photos have been selected. You can't drag the photo album icon; you must select individual pictures.

This may look like it's dragging only one image, but the number "4" tells you it's really dragging the four selected images.

To subscribe to a slide show that someone else has published
(you do *not* need to be a .Mac member):

Tip: Your Mac will go online to the .Mac member's slide show every time you connect to the Internet. If it finds new photos, they will be automatically downloaded to your Mac. This means if you connect with a dial-up modem, you might not want your computer downloading files without you knowing it! **To prevent automatic downloading,** uncheck the box after you have played the selected slide show at least once.

1. Connect to the Internet, if you're not already.

2. Open the Screen Effects system preferences (see page 330).

3. In the list on the left side of the pane, single-click ".Mac."

4. To the right, single-click the button "Configure." You'll see the "sheet" (as shown below) slide down from the top of the window.

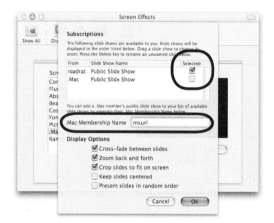

5. In the center of this sheet, type the screen name of the .Mac member who has published a slide show.

6. Choose the "Display Options" you'd like, then click OK. As you click OK, the screen name will go to the area at the top of this sheet and its checkbox will be automatically checked.

7. It will take several minutes for the slide show to download to your Mac. Once it has, you do not have to be online to view the slide show.

Hardware

The **Hardware** preferences include *ColorSync, Displays,* and *Energy Saver,* which all have to do with your monitor. You can also customize the *Keyboard* and *Mouse,* set your *Sound preferences,* and tell your *CDs & DVDs* what to do.

ColorSync

ColorSync is an industry-standard color management technology that creates "profiles" embedded in color files. The profiles contain information used by scanners, monitors, presses, high-end copiers, and other hardware. In the process of creating catalogs, web pages, magazines, books, videos, Quick-Time movies, transparencies, and other creative media, this standard helps to ensure that the color you or anyone in the entire workgroup sees on all machines and output on all projects is as similar as possible.

Exactly how to use ColorSync is beyond the scope of this book. If you are a professional who needs to take advantage of this technology, you'll find lots of information at www.apple.com/colorsync.

Displays

The **Displays** preferences give you various controls, depending on the type of monitor you have. If you don't see some of what's shown here, like the "Geometry" section, you probably have those controls built into your monitor somewhere else—check your monitor manual.

You will certainly have the options to change the colors and the resolutions of your monitor display. Here are explanations of typical settings you might find in your preferences pane.

> **Resolutions:** You may be accustomed to working with the resolution of a printer or output device, where more dots per inch make an image look better. But the term resolution as applied to a monitor is something completely different. The measurements here are pixels per inch; a pixel is a tiny unit on your monitor, like a tiny square. The more pixels you display on the screen, the *smaller* everything looks, so if you want to fit more stuff on the screen, choose a higher resolution (1024 x 768). If you want everything to look *larger,* choose a lower resolution (800 x 600).

> **Colors:** Switch between thousands and millions of colors. The more colors, the more "resolved," or better-looking, photographs and other digital images will appear. If you don't have much RAM (memory), use thousands because it takes more memory to create millions of colors. Using thousands of colors instead of millions can also make everything in the Finder work a little faster, especially if you have a larger monitor.

Refresh Rate: CRT displays (not flat-panel displays) redraw the entire screen many times per second; this is called the "refresh rate." If your refresh rate is too slow, it makes the screen appear to vibrate (and gives me a big headache). Flat-panel displays do not refresh.

Show modes recommended by display: It's possible to have a long list of resolution options, but that doesn't necessarily mean your monitor can actually display all of those various options. To see only the resolutions that your particular monitor can display, check this box.

Show displays in menu bar: Check this box to put a small icon on the right side of your menu bar that gives you a menu with the choices of colors and resolutions. You can also open the Displays preferences from this menu.

Notice the title bar does not say "Displays." Instead, it tells you which color profile is selected at the moment for this monitor, as shown on page 339.

If your display supports "Theater Mode," you'll have an "Auto" checkbox. Click "Auto" before you watch a video on your monitor because it will make the screen brighter for the presentation.

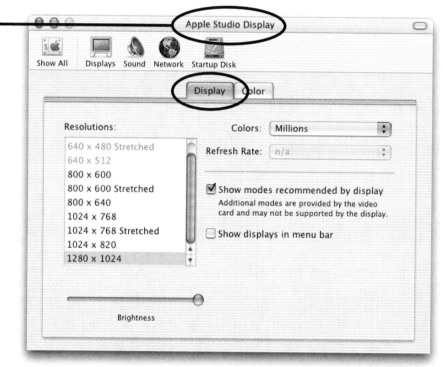

With this Brightness control, you can obviously adjust the brightness. If your Displays pane doesn't have this, your monitor probably has its own controls (read the manual for your monitor).

—Displays continues

If you have a **Geometry** tab, experiment with the buttons and arrows—if you mess things up, just press the "Factory Defaults" button to take the monitor back to its original state. You can move the monitor image up or down or left or right, expand or contract it, rotate it, fix a keystone (where the image appears wider or narrower at the top than at the bottom), and more. If you find that the black edges are slowly encroaching upon your image area, use the "Height/Width" button and arrows to fix it.

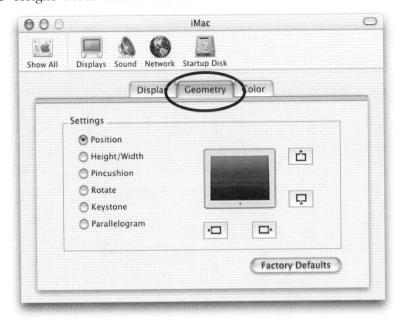

The **Color** tab lets you choose a ColorSync profile, if you know what that is and why you might need to do it sometimes. Only rare graphics professionals need to change the profile. If you're one of those, you know what to do here. If you don't have a clue what color profiles are, never mind. If you want to know more, go to **www.apple.com/colorsync.**

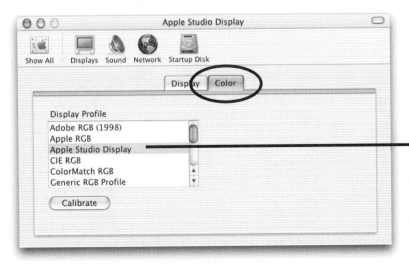

The color profile selected here is the one that all of these settings will affect, as shown by its name in the title bar.

Click "Calibrate" to adjust the color settings. Most of it is self-explanatory.

Energy Saver

Energy Saver

You can always choose to put the Mac to sleep instantly: from the Apple menu, choose "Sleep," or press Command Shift 0 (zero).

Note: Sleep will kick in even if the screen effect is active.

The **Energy Saver** preferences let you determine when or if your Mac goes to sleep to save energy. When it goes to sleep, the screen turns completely black. **To wake it up,** hit any key or click the mouse.

There are actually two different pieces of your Mac that go to sleep: the monitor (display) and the hard disk. The monitor wakes up pretty fast, but if the hard disk goes to sleep, it can be mildy irritating waiting for it to spin back up again (gosh, it could take a whole minute). You might want your monitor to go to sleep after ten minutes of inactivity, which would kick in when you go for a short break. But you might want the hard disk to keep spinning until at least twenty minutes has gone by just to make sure it doesn't go to sleep every time you run down the hall.

Many people prefer to let their machine go to sleep at night instead of shutting it down. You might want to set it to sleep after one hour of inactivity so after you leave work, you can rest assured that your Mac will sleep even if you forgot to tell it to.

If you use an Apple laptop (PowerBook), the Energy Saver preferences change to allow separate settings for "Battery Power" and "Power Adapter."

*You can set the sleep timing separately for the monitor and the hard disk, but neither one can be **more** than the top bar.*

If the "display sleep" time setting is shorter than the Screen Effects activation time setting, a warning appears, along with a "Screen Effects…" button so you can switch to Screen Effects preferences and change its activation time setting.

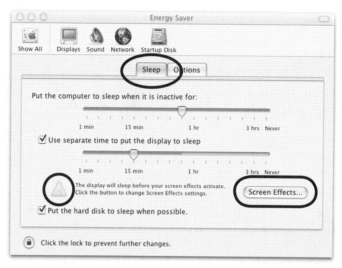

CDs & DVDs

CDs & DVDs

Use the **CDs & DVDs** pop-up menus to instruct your computer what to do when different types of disks are inserted in a CD or CD/DVD drive.

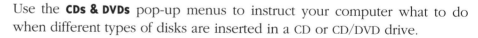

The **Keyboard** preferences let you decide how fast keys will repeat when you hold them down, and how long it takes before they start to repeat. This is useful if you tend to be heavy on the keys—if you find you often type more than one of the same character in a row, or too many spaces between words, go to the Keyboard preferences. You can also choose to turn on Full Keyboard Access, which lets you select and activate items using the keyboard, without having to pick up the mouse. Details of all these features are explained on pages 42–44.

Keyboard

The **Mouse** preferences are explained in detail on pages 28 and 29, along with the **Trackpad** preferences on page 30, if you're using a laptop. You can make the mouse move "faster" along the screen as you move the mouse across a mouse pad—when it moves "faster," you don't have to move your hand so far to make the mouse move across the screen.

Mouse or **Trackpad**

If you find you have trouble making the mouse double-click because your hands are a little slow, slow down the double-click speed. See Chapter 3 if you need more details.

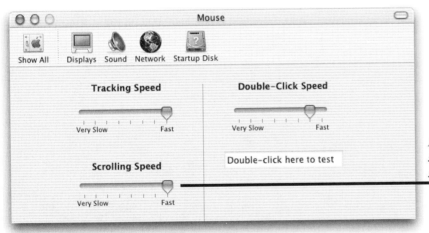

If you find that windows scroll past you too quickly, slow them down here.

If you're doing precise work in a photo-editing application, for instance, you might want to make the mouse move slower. If you use a drawing tablet, you'll probably find that a slower mouse speed works better because it is in more direct proportion to your hand movements.

If you use an Apple PowerBook (laptop), the Mouse preferences panel contains two tabs: a **Mouse** tab and a **Trackpad** tab. All the settings are the same as above, except for some special Trackpad options that enable you to use the trackpad to click, drag, or drag lock.

▼ Select "Ignore trackpad while typing" to prevent typing errors caused by accidently dragging your fingers across the trackpad while typing.

▼ Select "Ignore trackpad when mouse is present" to prevent competing commands between an attached mouse and the trackpad.

Sound

The **Sound** preferences let you choose an alert sound (the sound you hear when the Mac wants to yell at you about something), how loud that alert is, and how loud the general sounds on your Macintosh are, like music and video. You can also choose to put a sound volume icon in the menu bar so you don't have to open this preferences pane to change the volume.

Notice you have **two volume settings!** One is for the alert sounds, and the other is the main volume control on your computer.

As you click each of these, you'll hear its sound. The last one you choose is the one that will be your new alert sound.

If you have external speakers attached, you can choose them to play alerts and sound effects.

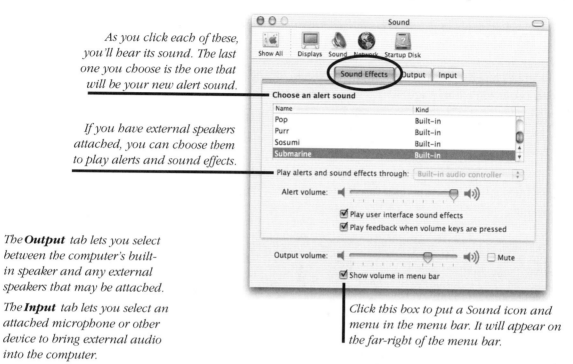

*The **Output** tab lets you select between the computer's built-in speaker and any external speakers that may be attached.*

*The **Input** tab lets you select an attached microphone or other device to bring external audio into the computer.*

Click this box to put a Sound icon and menu in the menu bar. It will appear on the far-right of the menu bar.

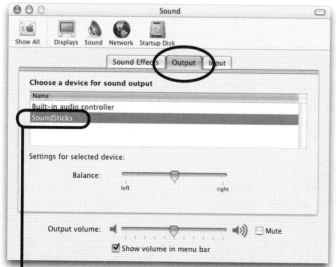

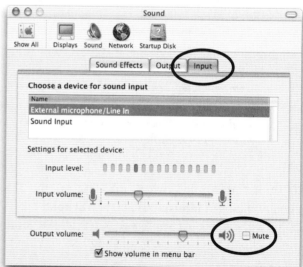

If you have installed extra speakers for your Mac, you can choose to have all of your sounds, such as from video, music CDs, etc., come out of your fancy speakers instead of the Mac's built-in audio controller.

*The Mute button will mute **all** sounds on your Mac. When you press the Mute key on your keyboard (pages 34 and 39), it checks this button.*

Internet & Network

The **Internet & Network** preferences cover the settings for connecting you to the *Internet,* for connecting *(networking)* the computers in your office, for *sharing* files between local computers once they're connected, and for using *QuickTime.*

Internet

The **Internet** preferences are explained in Chapters 30 through 36 (check the index for a particular feature). Here is where you can sign up for a .Mac account (pronounced "dot Mac"), if you haven't already, which gives you access to Apple's WebMail, storage space on their servers so you can share files with other Mac users, and more (see pages xxi–xxii). This is also where you'll set up your email specifics, some of your web preferences, plus an iDisk panel to monitor your storage and manage your Public Folder access.

Network

The **Network** preferences apply to both your Internet connection (sometimes) and to your local area network (LAN) that you might have in your small office or home office. If you are on a big network, you'll probably want to talk with your network administrator before changing anything in these panes.

Everything in this preferences pane has been explained elsewhere in the book, in context to networking and connecting. Please see Chapter 35 about networking several computers together in a small office to share files, and Chapter 30 about connecting to the Internet.

The **Location** pop-up menu lets you create custom sets of network configurations to be used in various locations that you regularly take your laptop computer. The **Show** pop-up menu lets you choose between different types of networks, such as Built-in Ethernet or wireless Airport networks.

The **TCP/IP** pane contains your settings for connecting to the Internet.

The **PPPoE** (Point to Point Protocol over Ethernet) pane refers to a type of network sometimes used by large offices or apartment complexes. If you use a PPPoE network, ask the network administrator to help with these settings.

The **AppleTalk** pane lets you turn AppleTalk on or off. AppleTalk should be active (on) in most cases.

Proxies are used by some networks for added security. Ask the network administrator for this information if proxies are needed on your network.

If you have an AirPort card and are within range of a wireless AirPort network, you can choose "AirPort" from this pop-up menu; the PPPoE tab disappears and an AirPort tab appears.

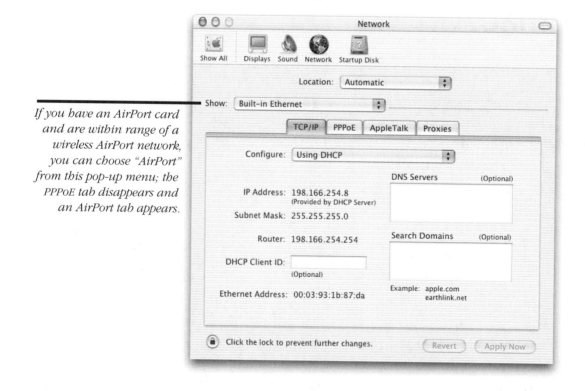

QuickTime, briefly, is software that plays audio and video files on your computer. QuickTime is also a technology standard for delivering "streaming" audio and video. Ordinarily, an audio/video file has to completely download to your hard drive before it will play. If the media file is streaming, data is displayed as it arrives, but does not remain on your hard disk.

QuickTime

The **Plug-In** settings affect the behavior of QuickTime in your web browser.

QuickTime Plug-In

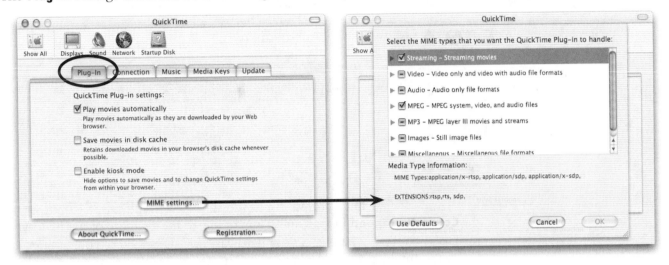

Play movies automatically: This is checked for you.

Save movies in disk cache: As explained, this option will keep downloaded movies in your browser's disk cache "whenever possible," making instant replay of downloaded movies possible instead of having to reload them. If you want to use this feature, you may need to find your browser's preferences and assign more space to your browser's cache.

Enable kiosk mode: When you're viewing a movie in a browser, you get a pop-up menu with various settings you can adjust. This checkbox disables that pop-up menu and hides options to save movies (including drag-and-drop copying of movies). This is useful in a classroom setting or when your grandkids are over so they don't fill your hard disk with big files.

MIME settings: MIMEs (Multi-purpose Internet Mail Extensions) identify different types of data so they can be handled appropriately by a server or by your own computer. The "MIME types" drop-down pane lists general data type categories that you can choose to have QuickTime handle. Click the triangle to the left of the checkboxes for submenus of various file types that are included in each general category, plus each file's possible MIME types. Below each file type are extensions that are common to that kind of file. You can customize which file types you want handled by QuickTime by selectively clicking the main category checkboxes or the submenu boxes. To return to the default settings, click "Use Defaults." The "OK" button becomes available after changes have been made to the scrolling list.

*The **QuickTime Player** application can play slide shows, audio and video files, live streaming content, virtual reality files, and 3D media. The "Pro" version of QuickTime is an authoring environment for creating and editing multimedia content. QuickTime Pro can also be used to convert many different multimedia file types to various other file types.*

QuickTime Connection   The **Connection** settings affect the download speed and quality of QuickTime media playing in your web browser.

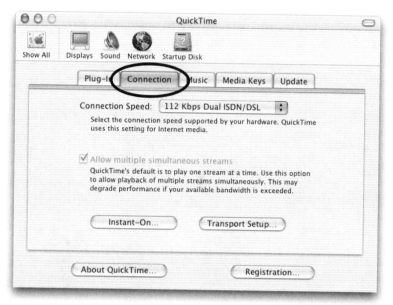

Connection Speed helps QuickTime optimize the delivery of media to you, based on the limitations of your hardware and the speed of your connection to the Internet. From the menu, select the option that best describes your Internet connection.

Allow multiple simultaneous streams: This option is only available when the Connection Speed is set on one of the two modem (slowest) options. Unless you're really getting 56K from your modem connection (unlikely), you'll probably want to leave this option unchecked.

Transport Setup: This opens the "Streaming Transport Setup" window. These settings tell QuickTime which *protocol,* or set of rules, to use for getting data from one computer to another. UDP (User Datagram Protocol) and HTTP (HyperText Transfer Protocol) are communication protocols.

> *Auto Configure* will check your system and automatically make the selections for you.
>
> *RTSP* (Real-Time Streaming Protocol) insures the best performance of streaming data.
>
> *Port ID* is an identification number attached to the header of a streaming file, identifying the file type and enabling its identification and handling.

If your Internet connection is protected by a firewall, RTSP may not work. If not, select HTTP from the Transport Protocol options, then click "Auto Configure." If your computer cannot configure itself to your firewall, you may be able to use proxy server software to work around this problem. Apple provides proxy servers for most popular firewalls. Contact your network administrator for assistance.

If you have installed third-party **music** synthesizer software, it will appear in this list. To have music files handled by your favorite synthesizer, select its name in the list, then click "Make Default." Most people will have only the QuickTime Music Synthesizer that appears here.

QuickTime Music

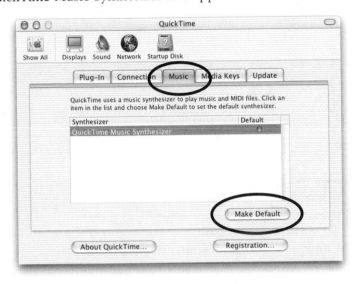

QuickTime files are sometimes encoded by their creators with a password, or **media key,** that locks the file. To play secured media files such as this, you need to obtain the media key and file category information from the creator of the file and enter that information into the Media Keys pane. This will authorize your access to the file, allowing it to play.

QuickTime Media Keys

To add media key information, click the "Add…" button. **To edit** existing media keys, click one in the list, then click "Edit…."

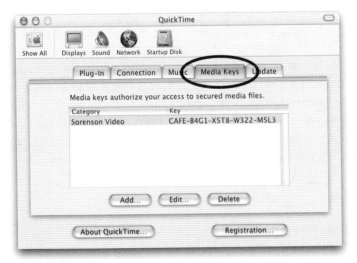

QuickTime Update   The **Update** pane makes it easy to check online for QuickTime software updates and to install QuickTime or third-party software.

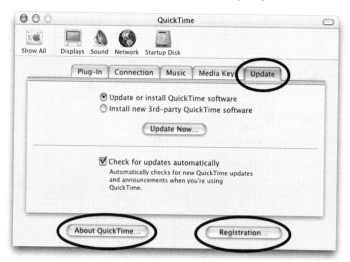

Click the **Update Now...** button and your computer will connect to the QuickTime web site to check for updates or to install new software from third parties (if you don't have a permanent connection, QuickTime will ask if you want to connect through your phone line). You can also choose to update anytime the QuickTime Player is open—use the application menu (the one that says "QuickTime Player").

Check for updates automatically checks for new or updated software anytime you're connected to the Internet and using QuickTime.

About QuickTime is simply a slide show of QuickTime developer logos and their web site address information.

The **Registration** button opens a window where you can enter your name and registration number, if you already have one. If you haven't registered your copy of QuickTime, click the "Register Online" button to go to the QuickTime web site where you can register and choose to upgrade to the Pro version for a small fee. When you register online and pay the Pro upgrade fee, you'll receive an email with a "key." The key is a number that you enter into the Registration pane to unlock the Pro features of QuickTime. If you just want to use the Player and don't think you'll need the content creation and editing features of the Pro version, don't register and pay for the upgrade. You can always do it later if you change your mind.

Sharing

The **Sharing** preferences combines several different aspects of file sharing into one pane. Some of these preferences allow access to the other people in your home, school, or office who are connected through a *local area net-work,* where you are physically connected with cables or perhaps through a wireless network such as AirPort. Other preferences are for sharing your files with people anywhere in the world over the *Internet.* The different services are explained on the following pages.

Personal File Sharing gives other computer users on your *local* network access to the Public folder on *your* computer (or any other folder, depending on how you log in to the other computer). To do any kind of file sharing between computers, you need to check this box. See Chapters 34–35 about file sharing; see page 642 for hints on using the Public folder; see the first half of Chapter 20 for all the details about the Public and Drop Box folders.

Windows File Sharing lets you allow certain Windows users on your *local* network to log in to your Macintosh and access your files, and you can send files to that Windows user. See pages 650–655 for full details.

Personal Web Sharing allows computer users to view the web sites that you have posted in your own Sites folder in your Home. See pages 658–663 in for details on how to use this.

Remote Login allows you or someone else to log in to your computer from somewhere else in the world, if you know how to use an SSH (Secure Shell) client (Telnet won't do it). On another Mac running OS X, you can use the Terminal application, found in the Utilities folder. See the Mac Help file or Sherlock's AppleCare for more details.

FTP Access sets up your Mac as an FTP (file transfer protocol) server, which means anyone can use a browser and download (copy) files from your computer to theirs. Detailed directions for setting up and using FTP access are on pages 664–667.

Remote Apple Events lets people on other computers on your local network send "Apple Events" to your computer. An Apple Event is a command to do something, such as open a file or get data.

Printer Sharing is particularly great. If you have a network in your home, school, or office, click this button (shown on the previous page) to instantly allow anyone on the network to print to the printer that is connected to your computer, even if it is not a "networkable" printer (printers that can network generally cost more). That is, you can even share your little $50 color inkjet with anyone else. Just check this button and the printer you are plugged into will be one of the options in the "Printer" menus on the other computers on your network.

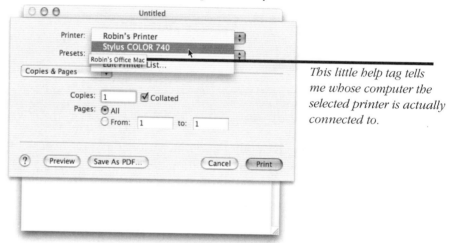

This little help tag tells me whose computer the selected printer is actually connected to.

The **Internet** pane is useful if you have an AirPort card installed in your Mac—when your Mac is connected to the Internet, your Mac can act as a base station for other computers on your network. That is, you can *share* your connection with other nearby Macs if **1)** they also have AirPort cards installed, or **2)** if the other Macs are connected to yours with an Ethernet connection. If you restart your Mac or if it goes to sleep (or if you lose your Internet connection), you'll need to come back to this pane and restart Internet Sharing.

The **Firewall** pane provides an extra security measure by putting up a virtual "firewall" so intruders cannot get into your Mac through the network or the Internet. You don't need to do anything in this pane because the firewall is automatically enabled and disabled as you check items on or off in the Services pane. If you understand ports and firewalls, you can add a new port and control its firewall through this pane.

System

The **System** section includes preferences that control a number of software features on your Mac, including *Accounts, Classic, Date & Time, Software Update, Speech, Startup Disk,* and *Universal Access.*

Classic

Classic is the Mac OS 9 operating system you'll need for the next year or two until all of the software you use has been updated for OS X. When you open an OS 9 application, it will automatically open in Classic. Essentially, you will be switching between two different operating systems. If you have no OS 9 applications, you will never need to use Classic and you don't even need to install it.

If you do use Classic, I recommend you go to the preferences pane and tell it to automatically start up when you log in to your Mac. For all the details about working in the Classic environment, see Chapter 39.

Date & Time

The **Date & Time** preferences obviously allow you to set the date and time. This is important even if you personally don't care what the date is because your Mac uses these settings to do things like time-stamp all of your documents, make decisions about when to show you alerts you might have programmed in various applications (like when to pay bills), and when to time-out software you have downloaded.

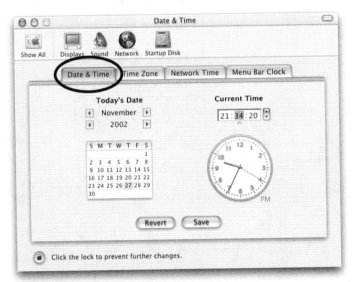

Tip: You can also use the Clock feature to make an actual clock appear, either analog or digital as shown below. It can sit in the Dock or float around the Desktop. See page 432 for details.

To change the date, *click the month and year arrows up or down, then click on a date in the month.*

To change the time, *click on the hour, minutes, or seconds, then either type the new number or use the arrow buttons. Or you can drag the hour and minute hands around the clock.*

When everything is correct, click the "Save" button.

If you cannot change the date or time (and you want to), go to the "Network Time" pane, and uncheck the box, "Use a network time server," as shown on the next page.

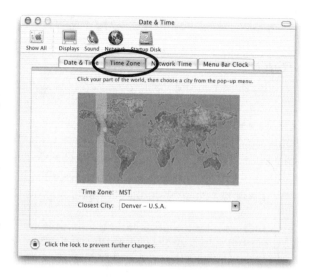

I guarantee you'll learn some interesting things about the world as you click on different areas. Do you know which small country has its own time zone? (IRT)

If you are in a time zone that switches between daylight savings time or not, your Mac will automatically make the switch for you.

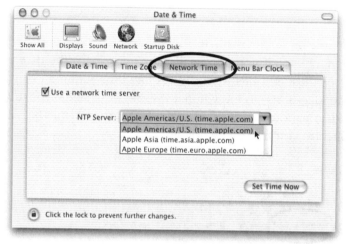

If you have a full-time connection, such as DSL, cable, satellite, ISDN, T1, or similar, you can choose to connect to a network time server that will always make sure your computer displays exactly the correct time. Once you check this box, you will not be able to change the time in the "Date & Time" pane.

If you have a dial-up connection, don't check this box.

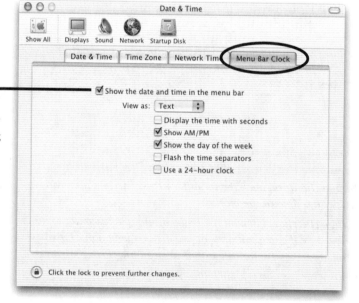

If you don't want the time showing in the menu bar, uncheck this box.

If the time is visible in the menu bar, you can click on it to see the entire date, and you can choose to open this preferences pane from its menu.

The **Software Update** preferences let you determine when your computer will go to the Internet and check to see if any of your **Apple software** has downloadable versions of free updates. If you have a permanent connection, such as ISDN, DSL, T1 , cable, etc., then it is safe to tell your Mac to automatically check for updates.

If you have to dial-up to connect to the Internet, check the "Manually" option, then when you have time to let the computer go do its updating, log on through your dial-up and click the "Update Now" button.

Software Update

Software Update

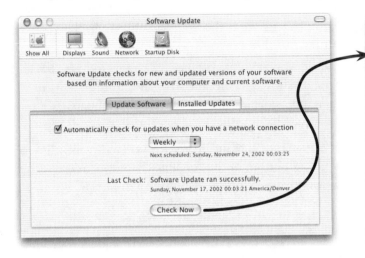

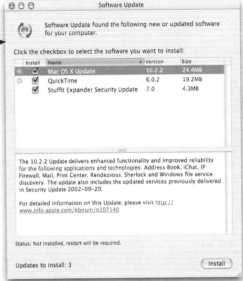

In this dialog box you can put a checkmark next to the items you want to update.

If you don't want to install something *and it keeps showing up, highlight the item, then go to the Update menu and choose "Make Inactive…." Later, when you decide to install it, choose "Show Inactive Updates" from the Update menu.*

From the Apple menu, you can choose "Get Mac OS X Software…." This command automatically opens your browser and takes you to an Apple web site where they keep track of software that is available for Mac OS X. You can choose to download these files. Many are free. See pages 306–308 for a mini-tutorial on how to download software from this page.

Speech

Speech

In the **Speech** preferences you can arrange to talk to your computer. Using your voice, you can open and close applications and windows, copy and paste, get your mail, ask the date or time, and more. You can make other applications listen to you, and if you know how to write AppleScripts, you can write new commands for applications. You can add spoken commands for any keyboard shortcut you see in the menu. The Mac will even tell you jokes. To teach you how to use Speech effectively would take a small book, so I'm afraid I'll just be able to give you a few tips here. You can find a lot of information in the Help files.

▼ The **voice** the computer uses is the one you choose in the Spoken User Interface pane, shown on page 355.

▼ Once you turn on "Apple Speakable Items," the round **feedback window** appears, as shown to the left. To make it listen to your voice commands, press the Escape key on your keyboard.

To send this window down to the Dock, double-click it.

To get a list of commands that are ready for you to speak, click on the tiny arrow at the bottom of the feedback window and choose "Open Speech Commands window" (shown to the left).

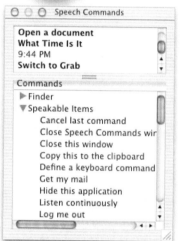

Above is the round feedback window, and below that is the list of commands already built in and ready for you to speak.

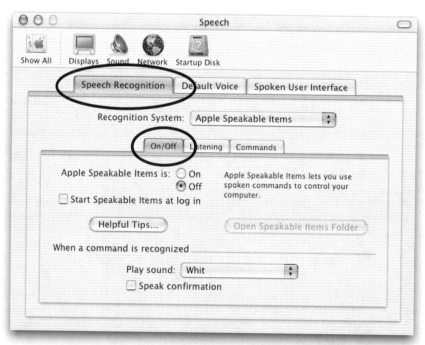

Unlike other voice recognition packages, you don't have to train Apple Speakable Items to learn your voice.

—continued

You can choose that your Mac listens and responds to you only when you activate it with the "listening key," or you can make it stay on all the time so you can speak commands without having to hold down a key. The default listening key is the Escape key (esc).

Listening

When you choose the "Listening Method" to **Listen only while key is pressed,** that means you need to hold down the Escape key for about half a second to let the Mac know you are about to give a command (you don't have to hold it down the whole time). You hold Esc, let go, speak your command, and the computer will either activate your command or speak back to you.

If you plan to play the Chess game included in your Applications folder or you have other speakable applications you use throughout the day, you might want to change the "Listening Method" to **Key toggles listening on and off.** In this case you hold down the Escape key for about a second, which turns listening on *until* you hold down that key again. While listening is on, you must call the computer by name so it knows you are about to tell it some-thing. The default name is "Computer." For instance, you would say, "Com-puter. Tell me a joke." Try it.

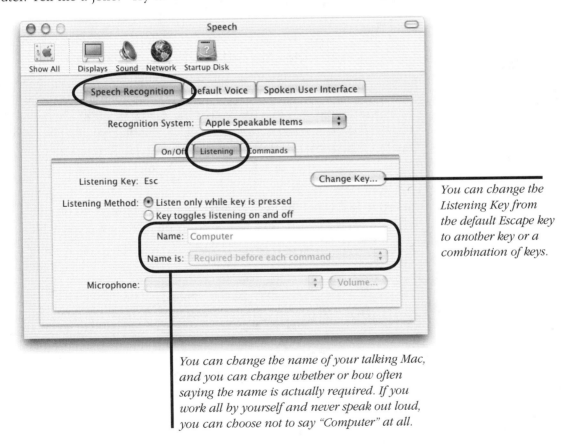

You can change the Listening Key from the default Escape key to another key or a combination of keys.

You can change the name of your talking Mac, and you can change whether or how often saying the name is actually required. If you work all by yourself and never speak out loud, you can choose not to say "Computer" at all.

Spoken User Interface   In the **Spoken User Interface** pane you can set specific **Talking Alerts**.

▼ **Speak the phrase** offers several different alert phrases which can be constant, played in order, or played randomly. Click this menu to choose "Edit Phrase List…" where you can type in your own alert (or naughty) phrase.

▼ Choose **Speak the alert text** to have your computer speak the text in alert windows that occasionally appear on your Desktop.

▼ Click the **Talking Alerts voice** menu to choose the voice for speaking. The default voice is the one last chosen in the Default Voice pane.

▼ The **Wait before speaking** slider sets a delay before the default voice starts speaking.

▼ Click the **Demonstrate Settings** button to hear a demonstration of your settings, including the delay setting. If you don't hear anything, your delay setting may be set for a long delay.

The **Other spoken items** section of this pane contains three more options.

▼ **Announce when an application requires your attention** speaks an alert when necessary.

When you choose the "Text under the mouse" option, this alert drops down. Click this button to open Universal Access preferences and enable assistive devices.

▼ **Text under the mouse** speaks the Finder text that appears under your mouse pointer, such as file and folder names, menu commands, some application commands, and more. When you click this checkbox, an alert tells you to turn on "assistive features" in Universal Access preferences. Click the "Universal Access" button, then click the "Universal Access" button and select "Enable access for assistive devices." Now try selecting some text in a document, then press the default key (Escape) or whatever key you may have assigned by using the "Change Key…" button.

▼ **Selected text when the key is pressed** enables your computer to speak selected text in text and desktop publishing files, PDF files, email messages, or the Address Book.

In the **Default Voice** pane, choose a voice for the computer to use. As you choose each one, it will say something out loud. You can adjust the speed at which most of them talk. You'll hear this voice whenever an application can speak to you, including the built-in voice recognition explained on the previous pages. Try this experiment:

Default Voice

1. Open TextEdit.

2. Type something (it's really fun to type something naughty).

3. From the Edit menu, slide down to "Speech," then out to "Start speaking." If no text was selected, the speaker will read the entire page to you. If text was selected, just the selected text will be read.

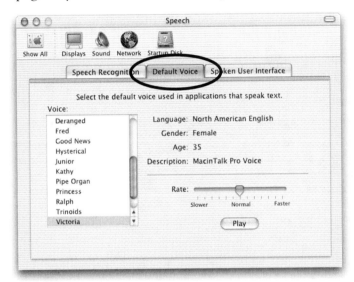

Click on a voice and it will automatically speak something. The last one you choose is the one that will be the voice used for all speaking applications.

Startup Disk

The **Startup Disk** preferences pane lets you choose which disk you want your computer to start up from next time you restart or turn it on. If you have a CD inserted that holds an operating system, that CD will also appear in this pane. You might need to restart from a different operating system so you can update the system, fix problems, use Mac OS 9 instead of OS X, or other reasons.

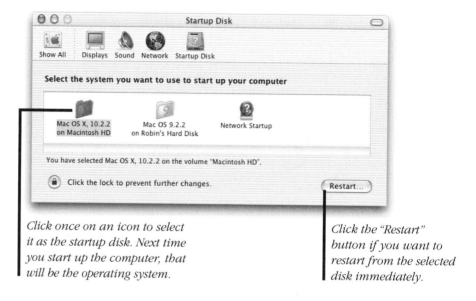

Click once on an icon to select it as the startup disk. Next time you start up the computer, that will be the operating system.

Click the "Restart" button if you want to restart from the selected disk immediately.

The **Users** pane of **Accounts** preferences is where you can create the special Home areas for multiple users of your computer. All users have their own Homes, their own Trash baskets, and can set their own preferences. You can even create login buttons with their photos. See Chapter 20 for all the details about using these preferences.

Accounts

This shows there are two users of this computer at the moment.
You can edit the preferences for each user at any time, and add
new ones. You can delete any user except the Administrator.

The **Login Options** pane lets you set the Display Login Window as simply "Name and Password" or as a "List of users."

▼ Select "Hide the Restart and Shut Down buttons" to remove those buttons from the Login window and prevent other users from shutting down your computer.

▼ Select "Show password hint after 3 attempts to enter a password" if you have trouble remembering all your passwords. Leave this unchecked if you don't want other people to possibly see your password hint.

Universal Access

The **Universal Access** preferences pane makes using keyboard shortcuts and the mouse easier for people who find it difficult. For instance, keyboard shortcuts often require that two or three keys be held down at once, and then tap yet another key. This can be impossible for many users. Also, some people cannot use the mouse for one reason or another. In the Mouse pane of Universal Access, you can switch to using the numeric keypad to move the cursor up, down, left, or right. If you or anyone you know needs to have their Mac adjusted for these issues, use these preferences.

Universal Access Seeing

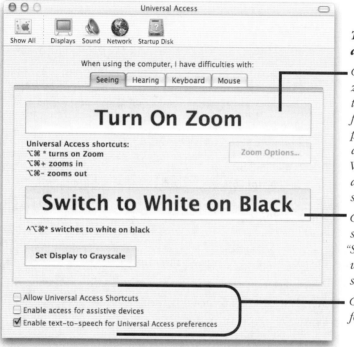

To access helpful options for visual difficulties, click the "Seeing" tab.

Click "Turn On Zoom" to enable powerful zooming of the Desktop screen. With Zoom turned on, click the "Zoom Options..." button for more control, where you can click "Show preview rectangle when zoomed out" to display a black rectangle on the screen. When you position the preview rectangle on an area of the screen, the Zoom keyboard shortcut zooms in on the selected area.

Click "Switch to White on Black" to show the screen as a negative image, but first click "Set Display to Grayscale" to show a purely white-on-black effect without introducing strange, negative colors to the screen.

Choose the options you want to activate for all Universal Access preferences.

Universal Access Hearing

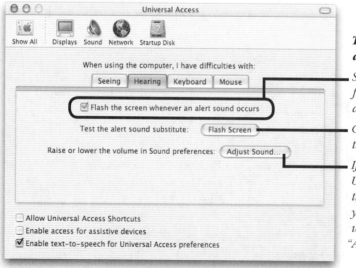

To access options in case of hearing difficulties, click the "Hearing" tab.

Select this checkbox to make the screen flash to white when an alert sound, such as a beep, occurs.

Click the "Flash Screen" button to test the visual flash alert.

If you click "Adjust Sound..." now, the Universal Access window is replaced with the Sound system preferences window. So you might want to customize your settings under the other tabs before you click the "Adjust Sound" button.

Keyboard: "Sticky Keys" has been on the Mac for almost forever. This is what it does: You press the Shift key five times in a row. It doesn't matter how fast or slow you press it. After five times, you'll hear a little beepy musical that tells you Sticky Keys is now activated. Then, let's say you want to make a new folder in a Finder window; the keyboard shortcut is Command Shift N. Just tap the Command key, then tap the Shift key, then tap the N key.

Tap the Shift key five more times when you want to turn off Sticky Keys.

If you have the two checkboxes shown below checked, to **beep** and to **show pressed keys,** then you will hear a small beep when the modifier key has been tapped, and you will see an image of the key(s) appear in the upper-right corner of the monitor (shown to the right).

If keys are repeating across the page and you don't want them to, turn on **Slow Keys** and adjust the "Acceptance Delay" slider to a longer delay. Or you can click the "Set Key Repeat…" button, which opens the Keyboard preferences. On the right side of that pane, slide the "Delay Until Repeat" bar over to the left, all the way to "Off," as shown on page 42.

Universal Access Keyboard

You'll see images of the modifier keys as you type them.

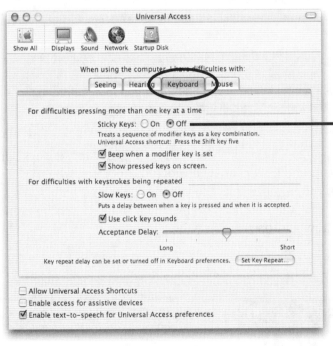

The "Off" button is selected by default. If you click the "Allow Universal Access Shortcuts" checkbox in the bottom left of the window, you can press the Shift key five times to turn Sticky Keys on, five more times to turn Sticky Keys off.

—continued

Universal Access Mouse   If you or someone you know has trouble using a mouse, you can turn on the Universal Access features (see page 360) and use the numeric keypad to guide the mouse pointer. You can even select items and drag things around.

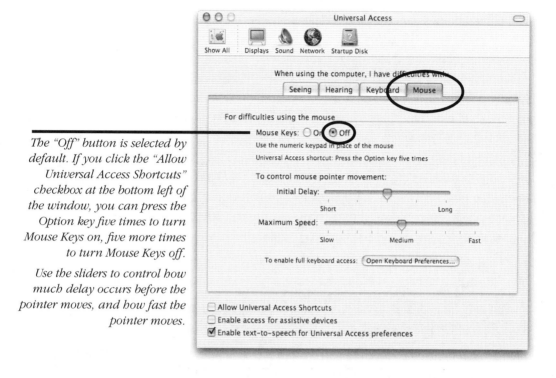

The "Off" button is selected by default. If you click the "Allow Universal Access Shortcuts" checkbox at the bottom left of the window, you can press the Option key five times to turn Mouse Keys on, five more times to turn Mouse Keys off.

Use the sliders to control how much delay occurs before the pointer moves, and how fast the pointer moves.

Mouse Keys: Tap the Option key five times to turn "Mouse Keys" on. Now tapping on the numeric keypad will move the pointer around the screen. If you think of the number 5 as the center of a wheel with spokes radiating out, that is how the numbers around the 5 in the keypad will move the pointer. See below and on the following page.

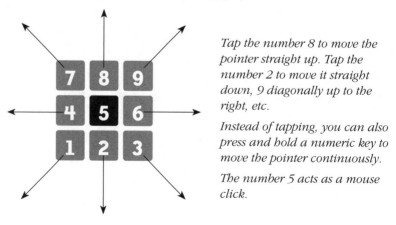

Tap the number 8 to move the pointer straight up. Tap the number 2 to move it straight down, 9 diagonally up to the right, etc.

Instead of tapping, you can also press and hold a numeric key to move the pointer continuously.

The number 5 acts as a mouse click.

To click the mouse: Tap the number 5.

To select an item to drag it: Position the pointer on the item you want to drag. Then tap the 0 (zero) key. Use the number keys to drag the item. This works to drag windows around, to move the scroll slider bars, to access and select from menus, and even to select text, as explained below.

To let go of an item you're dragging: Tap the decimal point (.).

To select a command in a menu:

1. Use the number keys to position the pointer on the menu name.
2. Tap the 5 key to select the menu, which pops it open.
3. Use the number keys to slide the pointer to the command you want.
4. Tap the 5 key to activate the command.

To select text:

1. Use the number keys to position the pointer in the text.
2. Tap the 5 to set the insertion point down.
3. Tap the 0 (zero) so you can start dragging/selecting.
4. Use the number keys to move the insertion point over the text; you'll notice the text highlights as the insertion point moves.
5. When you have selected the text you want, tap the decimal point (.). Now you can use the pointer to change the font, the size, delete or replace the text, etc.
6. To deselect the text, tap 5.

The other two options in the Mouse pane of Universal Access let you control the **initial delay,** or how long it takes after you tap the number key to actually make the pointer move. If your hands are quick, make it a short delay so as soon as you tap the key, the pointer takes off. If you have trouble tapping the numbers very quickly, then give it a longer delay so the pointer doesn't run away before you know where it's going.

Set the **maximum speed** that you want the pointer to whiz across the screen. Again, if your hands are quick and confident, let it speed along at a fast pace. If you want it to move more slowly so you have more time to react, set a lower speed.

Which preference pane would you use to accomplish each task below?

1. Make the mouse move more quickly over the screen without your hand having to move much at all.

    _____

2. Change the pattern of your Desktop.

    _____

3. Start file sharing between several computers.

    _____

4. Change the rate of how fast a keyboard character will repeat across the page when you hold the key down.

    _____

5. Enlarge or reduce everything you see on the screen.

    _____

6. Change the time that shows up in your menu bar.

    _____

7. Create a separate and private area on your Mac for someone else who will be using the computer.

    _____

8. Set up a new .Mac account.

    _____

9. Change the settings for your Internet connection.

    _____

10. Choose special preferences to make the mouse and keyboard easier to use for people with challenges.

Answers on page 732.   _____

Using Aliases

Aliases are one of the greatest features of the Mac. An alias is an icon that represents the real thing—you double-click the alias and it goes and gets the real thing and opens it. This can make your life so much easier because you can put the aliases in easy-to-access places and so get to your most-used files very quickly without having to dig down into folders.

For instance, let's say you're working on a newsletter for your greenhouse enterprise and you have an "April Newsletter" folder. Inside this folder is a PageMaker file for the newsletter itself, plus all of the word processing stories and all of the photographs that will be dropped into the newsletter file. This "April Newsletter" folder is stored in your Home area, inside the Documents folder, inside the "Greenhouse" folder. Instead of having to dig down into all of those folders to get to the PageMaker file, make an alias of the PageMaker file and put the alias right on your Desktop. Then you'll just double-click the alias to open the newsletter and get right to work.

Aliases are very easy to create and work with, so take advantage of them!

Contents of this chapter

What is an Alias?

An **alias** is an "empty" icon that represents the real thing. Aliases are especially useful for applications. You see, most applications must stay in the folder they were installed into because when the application opens, it calls upon resources within its folder. If you store the application icon itself (without all of its resource files) in a different folder or on your Desktop, you run the risk that the application won't be able to function properly. That's where the alias comes in: You make an alias, which *represents* the application, and you can put that alias anywhere. In fact, you can make a dozen aliases of the same application and store them in all sorts of handy places. When you double-click an application alias, it goes into the original folder and tells the real application to open.

Let's say you have an application you use frequently—your word processing program, for instance. You can make an alias of AppleWorks or Quicken or whatever you use and put it just about anywhere. You might want to put it right on your Desktop, in a folder full of application aliases, or in your Home folder. Since you can have many aliases of the same file, you can put aliases to the same item in several places!

Aliases only take up about 2 or 3K of disk space (which is a really tiny bit), so you can make lots and store them all over the place, wherever they come in handy.

You can make aliases of applications, documents, partitions, folders, utilities, games, etc. Aliases are wonderful tools for organizing your work—anything you want to use is only one double-click away from wherever you are. Remember, an alias is just a picture that goes and gets the real file.

Using Aliases

Before I tell you *how* to make them, here are ideas for **using aliases** so you will *want* to make them (how to make an alias is on the following page).

▼ Store aliases of documents in two or three places at once, including right on your Desktop. For instance, you may want to keep budget reports in folders organized by months, as well as in folders organized by projects. When you update the real document, every alias will open the updated document.

▼ Leave aliases of applications neatly organized directly on your Desktop. This makes your applications available to you for the **drag-and-drop trick of opening files,** including files from other applications. (As explained in Chapter 12, you can drag any document onto the icon of the application to open the document. Many applications can open files created in other programs, so if you come across a file from a program you don't have or perhaps you don't know where it came from, you can drag the unknown file over the top of all these aliases that are sitting on your Desktop. Any icon that changes color when you drag the document on top of it will try to open that document. You can do this with application icons in the Dock as well.)

▼ You might find you use a particular utility regularly. If so, put an alias of that utility right on your Desktop. (Utilities are stored in the Utilities folder, which is in the Applications folder.)

▼ Put aliases of your favorite applications in a folder, then put that folder in the Dock. When you want to open an application, no matter where you are (meaning you don't have to go back to the Finder), just press on that folder icon in the Dock to get the pop-up menu and choose your application from that menu. This is particularly useful if you have applications that need to open in Classic, because their icons are not in your Applications folder.

Automatic Aliases

There are a several places on your computer where the Mac **automatically creates an alias** for you: When you drag an item into the **Dock,** the original item doesn't actually *move* to the Dock—the Mac puts an alias in the Dock. That's why you can delete the icon from the Dock in a puff of dust and you still have the original file in your folder. The same thing happens when you drag an item into any Finder window **Toolbar**—the Mac puts an alias in the Toolbar. The **Recent Places** menu that appears in "Save As" and "Open" dialog boxes, as well as the Apple menu, uses aliases that are automatically created for you.

When you drop a file on the Favorites icon in the Toolbar, *or* when you select a file and use the Favorites command in the File menu ("Add to Favorites," or press Command T), the Mac automatically puts an *alias* of the file in the **Favorites folder.** (See Chapter 24 about Favorites.)

Making an Alias

jimmy.jpeg

An alias looks just like the original icon, but there's a tiny arrow in the bottom-left corner. Unfortunately, the arrow is too dang tiny to be a very good **visual clue.**

Making an alias is so easy:

1. Select the item you want to make an alias of (click once on it).

2. Then choose one of these four easy ways to make an alias:

   a. **Either** from the File menu, choose "Make Alias."

   b. **Or** press Command L instead of going to the File menu.

   c. **Or** hold down the Control key and click on the item you want to make an alias of. A contextual menu will pop up, as shown below; choose "Make Alias."

After you choose "Make Alias," the new alias will be sitting right on top of the original file. Just drag it to where you want to keep it.

   d. **Or** hold down Command Option and drag the file—if you drag it to a *different* folder or to the Desktop, when you let go you'll have an alias with the word "alias" removed from its name; if you drag to somewhere else in the *same* folder, you'll have an alias with the word "alias" at the end of it.

You can also **make an alias of any open document:**

1. Save the open document.

2. Drag the tiny picture in the title bar and drop it on the Desktop or in any folder. You'll notice as you drag that the pointer has a tiny arrow attached to it, which is a **visual clue** that you are in the process of making an alias.

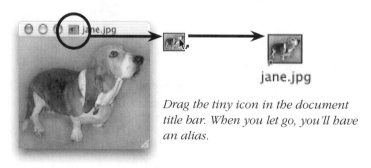

jane.jpg

Drag the tiny icon in the document title bar. When you let go, you'll have an alias.

The **new alias icon** will look the same and will be named the same, with the word *alias* added (unless you used the Command-Option–drag trick). If you want to remove the word "alias" (it makes the name too long) first move the alias out of the folder the original file is in because you cannot have two files with the same name in one folder.

Drag the icon to wherever you want to keep it. Rename it if you like. The new file does not have to have the word "alias" in its name. *And it doesn't matter if you move the original file*—the alias can always find it.

Important note: An alias is not a copy of a file—it is just a pointer. Although you can throw away any alias, do not throw away the original file!

Details of Aliases

Making aliases is easy, but here are some **details** you should understand.

▼ An alias isn't a *duplicate* of anything; it's just a **pointer** to the real thing. If you double-click an *alias* of Quicken, you'll open your *original* Quicken application, even if the original Quicken is stored in a completely different folder.

▼ If you **delete** an alias, you don't delete the original—the original is still stored on your hard disk. So you can keep revising your filing system as your needs change. Don't want that alias of Budget Charts cluttering up your Project Plans folder any more? Fine; throw it away. The original Budget Charts is still where you stored it.

▼ If you put an item into an *alias* of a **folder,** the item actually gets put into the *original* folder.

▼ You can **move** an alias and even **rename** an alias. The Mac will still be able to find the original and open it whenever you double-click on the alias.

▼ Even if you move or rename the **original** file, the alias can still find it.

▼ If you **delete** the *original* file, the Mac does *not* automatically delete any of the aliases you created for that file. When you double-click on an alias whose original has been trashed, you will get a message telling you the original could not be located. See the following page.

Finding the Original File

Sometimes you want to find the original file that the alias is linked to. For instance, maybe you need to get something from an application's folder, but you don't want to dig down through all the other folders to get there.

To find the original file belonging to an alias, follow these simple steps:

1. Click once on the alias to select it.
2. From the File menu, choose "Show Original," **or** press Command R.

The original file will appear in front of you, selected.

Linking an Alias to a New Original

If necessary, you can **link an alias to a different original.** It doesn't even have to be the same sort of file; that is, if the alias is a folder icon and you now link it to a document, the alias icon will change to a document icon. The *name* of the alias, however, will not change to the name of the file you now link it to—you'll have to change the alias name yourself.

1. Click once on the alias to select it.
2. Press Command I to get the Get Info box.
3. Click the button, "Select New Original...."
4. You'll get a dialog box, which is actually the same as the "Fix Alias" dialog box that you see on the opposite page. Find the file you want to link to this alias, and click OK.

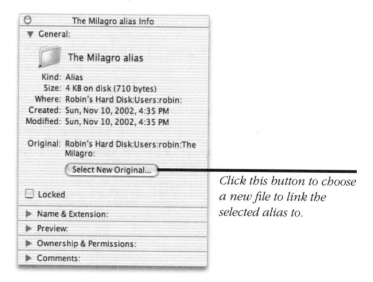

Click this button to choose a new file to link the selected alias to.

If something happened to the **original file,** like it got thrown in the Trash and the Trash was emptied, or maybe the original is on a removable disk, you'll get the message shown below.

If you think the file is just lost on your Mac, you can try the "Fix Alias…" button. This takes you to a dialog box exactly like an "Open" dialog box, and you can choose a file to link to the alias. But if the computer couldn't find the original, don't count on finding it yourself. Unfortunately, the original is probably gone and all that "Fix Alias" will do is let you link this alias to a different file.

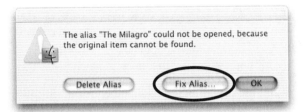

*If you click the "Fix Alias…" button, you'll get a dialog box, as
shown below, where you can navigate to the original item or
to a new item. If you don't know how to navigate yet, just click
"Delete Alias" and then make a new alias from the original item.*

Select the file of your choice to link to the alias.

1. What is an alias, anyway?

   _____

2. How large, in file size, is a typical alias?

   _____

3. Name at least four ways to create an alias.

   _____

   _____

4. What is the quickest way to put an alias into the Apple menu?

   _____

5. If you throw away an alias, what happens to the real item?

   _____

6. If you throw away the real item, what happens to all of its aliases?

   _____

7. What is the easiest way to find the original of an alias?

   _____

8. If you use the Calculator utility several times a day, where would be a good place to keep an alias of it?

   _____

9. If you put a file into an alias of a folder, what happens to that file?

   _____

10. What happens if you make an alias, then rename the original?

   _____

Answers on page 732.

Making & Using Favorites

Favorites are files that you have chosen to have easy access to. For instance, maybe you have a folder you save your research papers into, and it's stored inside several other folders which are inside the Documents folder. If you make the research folder a Favorite, you can save files into it, open it on the Desktop, and even open the folder inside of Open dialog boxes in applications—all with just one or two clicks, instead of having to dig down through the directory. This chapter explains how to use and create Favorites.

The term "favorites" on the Mac also refers to the icons that appear in toolbars across the tops of application panes, such as System Preferences or Mail. (I hate it when they give the same name to two completely different things!) Internet Explorer uses the term "Favorites" to describe their bookmarks. America Online lets you select "Favorite" places, also designated with a little red heart. All of these "favorites" are similar in that they make it easy for you to open and use files and settings that you need often. *But this chapter is only concerned with Favorites as it applies to the Favorites window in the Macintosh Finder.*

Contents of this chapter

What are Favorites?

*Briefly, to make an alias: Click on a regular file icon and press Command L. This makes a **copy** of the **icon** (not of the file itself), and you can put that copy, that alias, anywhere on your computer. When you double-click the alias, it will go find and open the original file.*

You've most likely opened the **Favorites** window by now—click once on the red heart in any Finder window Toolbar. If you haven't put anything in this folder yet, it probably has only one icon in it, an "alias" of the Documents folder. Favorites use the alias concept quite a bit, so if you don't know what aliases are, please skim Chapter 23 before you work with Favorites.

Most files in the Favorites folder will be aliases, although you can certainly store original files in here as well. All sorts of files can become favorites: folders, applications, documents, servers, partitions, and even web sites. (Do you see the one file in the window below that is *not* an alias?)

Anything that you want to be able to get to easily, either to open it or to save into it, you can turn into a Favorite. Because most Favorites are aliases, you can safely delete them (the aliases) when you don't need them anymore.

Favorite folders will be available in the Open and Save As dialog boxes. The last folder in this row, "Robin's favorite sites," is not an alias.

These Favorites are applications.

These Favorites are documents.

These two Favorites are servers. They act as shortcuts to connect.

These Favorites are web locations.

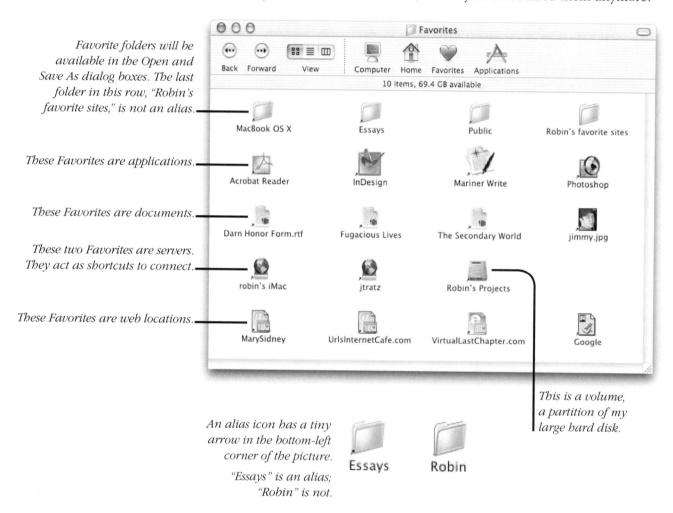

This is a volume, a partition of my large hard disk.

An alias icon has a tiny arrow in the bottom-left corner of the picture.

"Essays" is an alias; "Robin" is not.

Favorites can make it much easier to access your favorite folders, documents, web pages, etc. Here are some ways to **take advantage of Favorites.**

Taking Advantage of Favorites

▼ Rather than go hunting for **the folder you are using most often this week,** make it a Favorite. Then you can go to the Favorites submenu or Favorites folder to open it quickly, rather than having to dig through the Finder windows. For instance, at the moment I need to get to my folder that stores all of the chapters for this book. It resides in a "partition" (a separate section of my hard disk), which means to get to it I have to open that disk partition from the Computer window and open another window or two to get to my book folder. Instead, I made the folder a Favorite. Now from the Go menu I can open the folder directly, or open my Favorites folder with a click on the icon, then open my book folder.

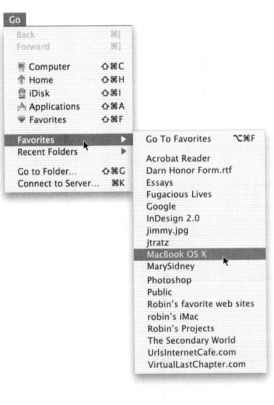

*A problem with the Favorites submenu is that there are **no visual clues** as to whether a file listed is a folder, application, document, web site, server, etc. You have to be very familiar with the files you put in here.*

Notice that Favorite folders have no submenus—you can't go straight to a document in a folder, but you can open the folder.

Notice also that if you have a large number of Favorites (as shown here), it sort of defeats the purpose of making things easy to find and open. There are other ways to make files accessible, so use Favorites as a rotating collection of the files you need the most at this particular moment.

▼ Another advantage to putting my book folder in Favorites is that when I need to **open** another book chapter, the folder is listed in my menu in the **Open dialog box,** as shown below. I don't have to hunt around the directory to find it. I love this feature.

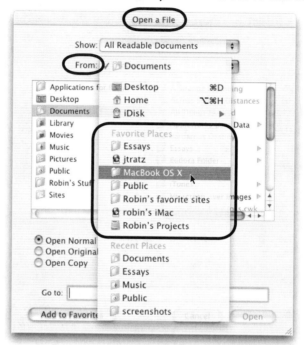

In some applications' Open dialog boxes, only the folders, partitions, and servers in the Favorites folder appear in this "From" menu.

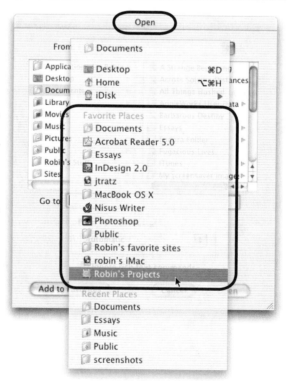

*In other Open dialog boxes, the Favorite applications also appear in this list. However, if you select a Favorite application, the dialog box opens the **folder** that the application is stored within, not the application itself.*

▼ Yet another advantage to putting my book folder in Favorites is that when I need to **save** a new chapter, the folder is listed in the "Where" menu in the **Save As dialog box,** as shown below. I don't have to hunt around the directory to find it. I love this feature, too.

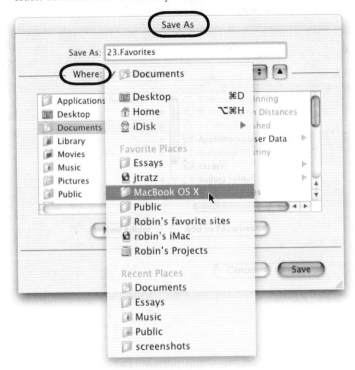

▼ If you are on a network, either a small one in your home office or a larger corporate network, you can **make a Favorite of a server icon** (directions are on page 382). Then when you need to connect, you can just double-click the server Favorite.

If you originally logged on to that server as "Guest," you won't see any dialog boxes when you connect with the alias—the server will just appear almost instantly. If you originally signed on with a name and a password, you will have to type the password.

Server Favorite icons are automatically named with the volume they are connected to, but you can change their names to anything that helps you remember which ones are which.

robin's iMac   **jtratz**

Making Favorites

There are several ways to create Favorites. Which one you choose depends on what you are selecting as a Favorite and where you are. Below is a list of techniques.

To make a Favorite using the menu command:

1. Select a file in a Finder window or on the Desktop (click once on it).
2. From the File menu, choose "Add to Favorites."

To make a Favorite using the keyboard shortcut:

1. Select a file in a Finder window or on the Desktop (click once on it).
2. Press Command T.

To make a Favorite of a file using drag-and-drop:

1. Open any Finder window and make sure the Toolbar is visible, with the Favorites icon showing.
2. Drag a file from any Finder window or the Desktop and drop it on the Favorites icon in any window Toolbar, as shown below.

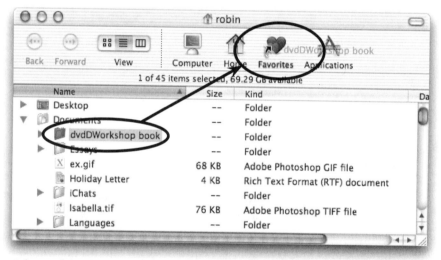

*I dragged this file up to the Favorites icon in the Toolbar. If you look carefully, you can see the shadow of the file name in the Toolbar, and you can see the pointer has turned into a curved arrow. That is my **visual clue** that the file I am dragging is about to become an alias. The original file will stay right where it is.*

Important Note: If you drag a file to the Favorites icon in the Toolbar, the Mac will always make an ***alias*** for the file. But if you drag a file icon directly into the open Favorites window, that will simply ***move*** most original files into that window, *not* make an alias. Be aware! (Servers and disks will always appear in the Favorites folder as aliases, no matter how you drag them in.)

To make a Favorite of an open document using drag-and-drop:

This only works in applications that were written specifically for Mac OS X; that is, this technique won't work from Classic applications, or even those programs that are written to be used in both Mac OS 9 and OS X.

1. Open a document. If it hasn't been saved recently, save it now. There are two visual clues that tell you the changes have not been saved: There is a dot inside the red button, and the tiny document icon in the title bar is a shadow.

The red Close button has a dot in it.

The document icon in the title bar is a shadow.

2. After you've saved the file, drag the tiny document icon and drop it onto the Favorites icon in the Toolbar, as shown below.

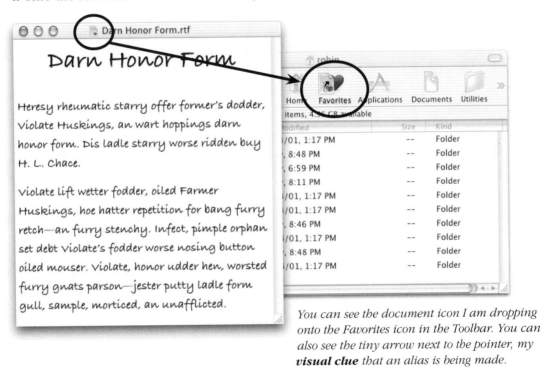

*You can see the document icon I am dropping onto the Favorites icon in the Toolbar. You can also see the tiny arrow next to the pointer, my **visual clue** that an alias is being made.*

To make a Favorite of any folder while in Save As or Open dialog boxes:

You've probably noticed the button "Add to Favorites" in the Save As and Open dialog boxes. Once you have fumbled around the directory and found the folder you need, you can add it to your Favorites instantly so it will appear in the "From" and "Where" menus, as shown on pages 376 and 377. You can only add *folders* and disks, including partitions, this way (not documents or applications or anything else).

1. In your application, Save As (Command S) or Open (Command O).

2. If you don't see the full directory and "Add to Favorites" button, click the triangle button circled below.

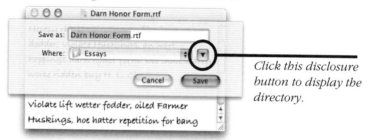

Click this disclosure button to display the directory.

3. Click once on a folder name to select it, then click the "Add to Favorites" button. The folder will instantly appear as the selected folder at the top of the "Where" or "From" menus, as well as in the Favorites section of the menu list.

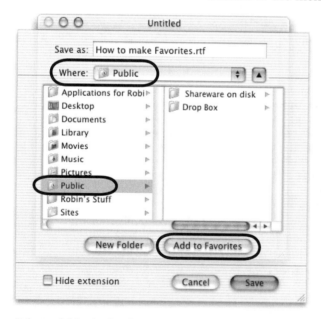

Select a folder in the directory list, then click the "Add to Favorites" button. If you don't know how to find your way around the directory, see pages 223–226.

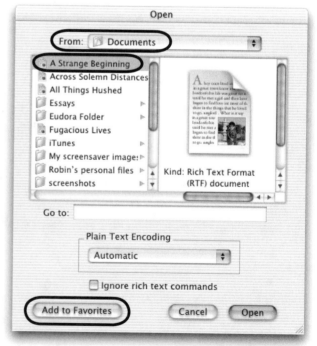

*Notice a document is selected here, not a folder. This gives you the impression you can add a document to Favorites, but when you click the button, it actually adds the **folder** that this document is stored within.*

To make a Favorite of a web page:

You can't directly make Favorites of web page addresses, but you can make "Web Internet Location" files of web pages and add those to your Favorites folder. Then when you choose that Favorite, it will open your default web browser and display that page. You can also drag any location file, whether it's a Favorite or not, and drop it right in the middle of any web page (not in the address bar)—the browser will go to that page.

1. Open your web browser and go to a page you like.

2. In the address bar, where you type in a web address, you see a little icon (shown below). Grab that icon and drag it to the Desktop or directly into any folder. You cannot drag this icon onto the Favorites icon in the Toolbar—you'll have to drag it directly into the folder.

*The web browser Internet Explorer (IE) has something called "Favorites" which are not the same as the Favorites we're talking about here. Internet Explorer Favorites are essentially bookmarks to web pages you want to find again easily. Anything you save as a Favorite in IE will **not** appear in the Favorites folder on your Desktop. Nor will anything in the Favorites folder on your Desktop appear in IE.*

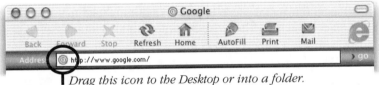

Internet Explorer

Drag this icon to the Desktop or into a folder.

OmniWeb

Drag this icon to the Desktop or into a folder.

3. When you drag the little icon to the Desktop or a folder and let go, you'll get a new file, as shown below. Each of these shown is an Internet Web Location.

www.ratz.com/
From OmniWeb.

Virtual Last Chapter .url
From Internet Explorer.

Google
From Netscape.

4. You'll notice if you drag the browser icon directly into the Favorites folder, it does not make an alias—it is still an original location file. This is perfectly fine, as long as you remember that if you ever want to throw this file away, you are throwing away the original.

If you want only aliases in your Favorites folder, make another folder in which to store all of your Internet Web Location files, then drop just the locations you want to use as Favorites onto the Favorites icon in the Finder window Toolbar.

Tip: In web browsers developed for Mac OS X, you can drag that tiny location icon and drop it directly in the Dock, on the right-hand side. It becomes a little spring icon with an @ symbol, as shown above; click once on this Dock icon and it will open the web page it came from. Unlike most other items in the Dock, however, if you remove this web address from the Dock, it is really gone because you have no other file for it.

To make a Favorite of a server connection:

Information about connecting to servers (other computers on your local network) is in Chapter 35.

Once you have a Favorite of a server connection, you need only select the Favorite from the Go menu or double-click its icon in the Favorites window, and you will be connected automatically.

If you originally logged on to that server as "Guest," you won't see any dialog boxes when you connect with the alias—the server will just appear almost instantly.

If you originally signed on with a name and a password, you will have to type the password. If you originally chose a volume when you connected, you won't have to select the volume when you use the Favorite because the volume choice is part of the server Favorite.

1. Connect to the server as usual. You'll see your server icon in the Computer window and/or on the Desktop, as usual.

2. Drag the server icon either directly into the Favorites open window, or drop it on the Favorites icon in any Finder window Toolbar. Either way will make an alias in the Favorites folder.

   You could also click once on the server icon to select it, then press Command T.

Even after you disconnect from the server, log out, shut down, or restart, your server Favorite will stay in the Favorites folder and you'll have a short-cut for connecting (until the IP address of that computer changes, which sometimes it does).

To make a Favorite of a partition or other volume:

1. Open the Computer window.

2. Click once on the volume you would like as a Favorite.

3. Drag it up to the Toolbar and drop it on the Favorites icon, *or* press Command T.

If you make a Favorite of a removable hard disk, CD, or DVD, the disk will appear in the Save As and Open dialog boxes as long as the disk is in the computer. When you take the disk out of the computer, the alias link will be broken; when you reinsert the disk, the link will connect once again.

Deleting Favorites is easy. Just remove them from the Favorites folder.

Most Favorites, *but not all,* are aliases, so it's important to check before you throw away a file from the Favorites folder. For instance, if you dragged a folder, document, application, or web location directly into the open Favorites window, the Mac did not make an alias—the original file was *moved* into the folder. (When you drop a file on the Favorites icon in the Toolbar, it always makes an alias.)

So you can *remove* files from the Favorites folder to delete them as Favorites, but check the icon before you actually *delete* files!

Deleting Favorites

*Do you see the two files in this folder that are **not** aliases?*

1. Are Favorites always aliases?

_____

2. Name at least six sorts of files that you can make Favorites of.

_____

3. If you want an easy way to access all of your applications on the Mac, is making Favorites of all of them the best solution?

_____

4. Can you change the name of a Favorite?

_____

5. If you drag a file into the open Favorites window, what happens?

_____

6. If you drop a file onto the Favorites icon in the Toolbar, what happens?

_____

7. Describe how to make a Favorite of an open document.

_____

8. In the Open and Save As dialog boxes, what sort of files can be selected and made into Favorites?

_____

9. Can you make a Favorite of a removable disk? Is that useful?

_____

10. Can you safely delete every Favorite in the window?

_____

Answers on page 732.

Find Files on Your Computer

As you work on your computer, you'll create more and more files and more and more folders in which to store those files. Sometimes you need to find a document whose name you've forgotten, and it can be a chore to start looking through all those folders. Well, the Search feature can do that for you. It can find files whose names you only slightly remember, or maybe you don't remember the name at all but you have an idea of the time frame in which it was created, or maybe you don't remember anything about creating the file but you know what it was about—Search can even look at the contents of your documents to find it for you.

Contents of this chapter

The Search Box The **Finder windows** all have a "Search" box in the upper right, as you can see below. You can type a word or phrase into this Search box, hit Return, and the Mac will search for a file of that name, as explained in more detail on the following pages.

If you don't see the Toolbar at all, click once on this tiny button in the right corner.

If you see a Toolbar but it does not display icons and text, as shown here, you won't see the Search box either.

So do this: Control-click on the Toolbar and from the menu that pops up, choose "Icon & Text Mode."

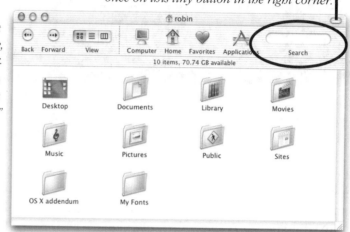

No matter what shows or does not show in your Toolbar, or even if there are no Finder windows open at all, **you can always press Command F** to bring up the Search window, as shown on page 368.

If your window is sized a bit too small for the Search box to appear, you'll see a double arrow on the right side, as shown below. Single-click the double arrow and a menu appears that includes "Search." When you choose this item, you'll get the Search window, as described on the following pages.

If you don't want the Search box in your Toolbar at all, hold down the Command key and drag the Search box out of the Toolbar; drop it on the Desktop and it will disappear.

If you want the Search box back in your Toolbar, Shift-click on the Hide/Show Toolbar button (upper-right of the window) to show the "Customize" window, and drag the Search box back into the Toolbar.

To do a quick-and-easy search, follow these two steps:

1. Your Mac will search in **whichever window you have open at the moment.** For instance, in the example below, the search will take place only in my Home window, "robin." It will search every folder in this Home window, as well as all folders inside any of those folders.

   To search your entire computer, click the "Computer" icon in the Toolbar.

   To search a particular folder within a window, click once on the folder (you don't have to open it); the Mac will search that folder and every folder that's stored inside of it.

2. Type the name of the file you're looking for into the Search box, then hit Return or Enter.

Quick-and-Easy Search

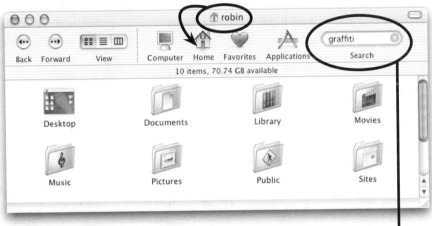

Type your file name or phrase in here.
To **delete** everything in that box, click the **X**.

Tips: It doesn't matter whether you type capital or lowercase letters—the search will find "Love Letter" even if you search for "love letter."

Spaces, however, *do* matter. That is, "love letter" will not find "loveletter."

If you don't know the exact name of the file, just type any part of it that you think is in the file name, such as "love."

3. Search will open a window displaying the results of what it found, as shown and explained on the following page.

—continued

*This tells you **what** you searched for and **where** your search took place.*

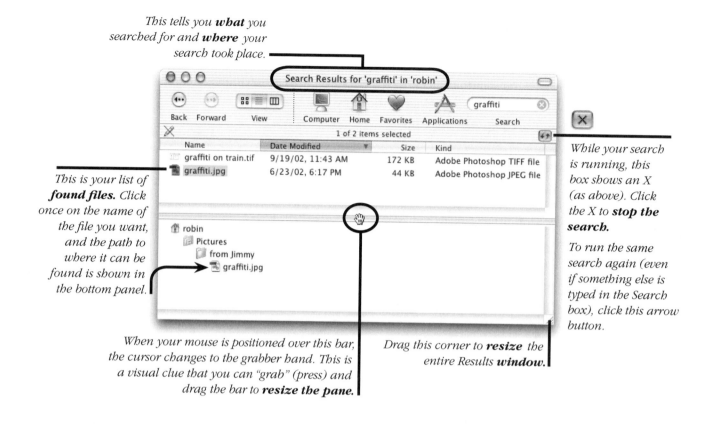

*This is your list of **found files.** Click once on the name of the file you want, and the path to where it can be found is shown in the bottom panel.*

*While your search is running, this box shows an X (as above). Click the X to **stop the search.***

To run the same search again (even if something else is typed in the Search box), click this arrow button.

*When your mouse is positioned over this bar, the cursor changes to the grabber hand. This is a visual clue that you can "grab" (press) and drag the bar to **resize the pane.***

*Drag this corner to **resize** the entire Results **window.***

Once Search has located the file you want, there are several things you can do. First, click once on the file name in either the middle or the lower panel to select that file. Then do one of the following:

▼ **To open the file,** double-click the file name, or single-click the file name to select it and press Command O. This will, of course, also open the application that the file was created in.

▼ **To open the folder** in which the file is stored, press Command E.

▼ **To print the item** (if it's a document), press Command P.

▼ **To move the item,** drag it to wherever you want, outside the window.

▼ **To copy the item,** hold down the Option key and drag the file somewhere outside of the Search window.

▼ **To delete the item,** drag the file from the window to the Trash basket, *or* select the file and press Command Delete.

▼ **To find the original of an alias,** select its icon and press Command R.

For the following technique, you must select the file in the *middle* panel—it won't work if you select the file in the lower panel.

▼ **To make an alias of the file,** hold down the Command and Option keys and drag the file to the Desktop or into a folder; let go and an alias will appear (see Chapter 23 for information about aliases).

You can also do a **more detailed search** of your hard disk, called a "narrower" search. You need to open the actual Search window for this; you can't do it in the Search box in the Toolbar.

More Detailed Search

To open the "Find" window:

- **Either:** Single-click the word "Search" directly below the Search box.
- **Or:** In the Finder, press Command F.
- **Or:** In the Finder, go to the File menu and choose "Find...."
- **Or:** If your Search box is not visible in the Toolbar, single-click the double-arrows at the end of the Toolbar and choose "Search."
- **Or:** Customize your Toolbar (see page 15) and replace the Search box with the "Find" icon, which looks like a magnifying glass. When you click on the Find icon, it brings up the dialog box shown below.

In the Find window, **1)** choose exactly where you want to search (shown below), and then **2)** apply specific criteria to the search "string," or phrase (next page).

First, decide where you want to search

Local disks: *Choose this to find files on any of your internal or attached hard disks, as well as any Zip disks or CDs that are inserted into their drives.*

Home: *Choose this to search just your Home window and all folders inside Home.*

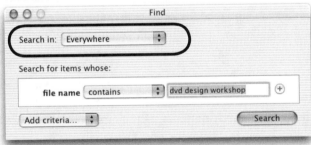

Everywhere: *Choose this to search not only your entire hard disk and all other disks that are "mounted" (showing in your Computer window), but it will also search any disks on your network **that you have mounted.** That is, it won't go looking on everyone's computer who is on your network; it will only search on those hard disks that you are connected to and whose icons you can see either on your Desktop or in your Computer window.*

Specific places: *Choose this to limit the search to specific disks or folders. Here you see my two internal hard disks. Only the disks or folders whose boxes are checked will be searched.*

See the following page for details on how to add specific folders.

Search a specific folder

Sometimes you want to **search one particular folder** or several folders instead of every disk. That's easy to do.

First, make sure the "Search in" choice is "Specific places," as shown below. Then either click the "Add" button to choose a folder in the dialog box, or just drag a folder from your Desktop and drop it in the Search window.

Even if a folder name is in this pane, it will only be searched if you check the box.

Click the "Add" button to display the standard Open dialog box, where you can choose a folder.

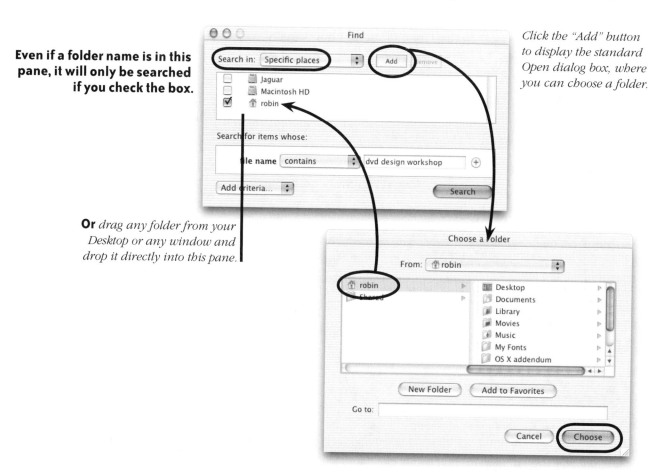

Or *drag any folder from your Desktop or any window and drop it directly into this pane.*

To delete a folder from the Search pane, select it and click the "Remove" button. Or you can leave the folder there and just uncheck its box—it will not be included in the search if its box is unchecked.

Once you have chosen a place within which to search, **choose your criteria** for the search. Check the menus for the various options; click the **+** sign to add more fields to narrow the search; click the **−** sign to delete the fields you don't need.

Second, choose your search criteria

You can search the same criterion more than once. That is, you can search for "file name contains dog" AND "file name contains rover."

You can get up to three fields with these buttons (they are plus signs until you click them). If you need more options, use the "Add criteria..." menu, as shown below.

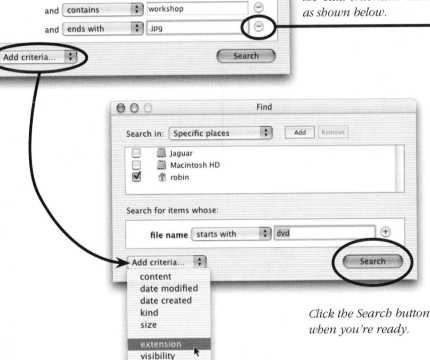

Click the Search button when you're ready.

To search the contents of documents,
choose "content" from this menu. See the following page for details.

This feature has been greatly improved— it will now search things like InDesign files, PDF files, HTML pages, and more. See the tip on the following page regarding indexing, which helps find the contents.

Third, click "Search" and get the Results

When you've chosen where to search and with what criteria, click the **Search** button.

Each search you do will create a **separate Results pane,** one of which is shown below. See page 388 for a list of the things you can do from the Results pane: select a file to delete it, open it, move it, make an alias, print it, and more.

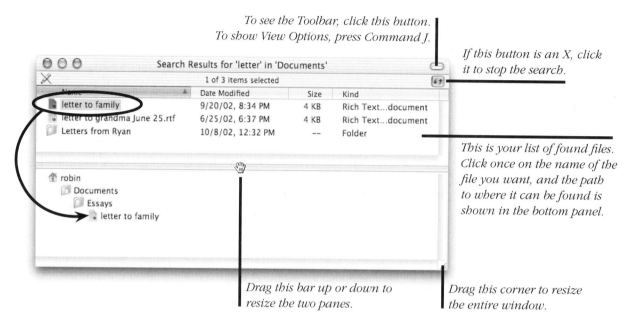

To see the Toolbar, click this button.
To show View Options, press Command J.

If this button is an X, click it to stop the search.

This is your list of found files. Click once on the name of the file you want, and the path to where it can be found is shown in the bottom panel.

Drag this bar up or down to resize the two panes.

Drag this corner to resize the entire window.

Indexing Files for Content Searches

As noted on the previous page, Search will look through the **contents** of most text files. For instance, maybe you're working on a research project and you've created dozens of files on the topic of chess. You want to find all the papers in your collection that mention "en passant." That's when you click the "Contents" button; instead of searching for just the *name* of a file, Search will actually read the *contents* of files. For instance, you might have written an article that you titled "Special Moves in Chess," and in the article itself you wrote about the en passant move, but you also mention en passant in three other articles that have different titles—Search will find every file that includes the phrase "en passant" in the text.

BUT Search cannot search the contents of your files *until* it has first **indexed** every file. That is, Search has to read every file on your computer and then organize every word into a database that it can search when you request it. Logically, if you write more articles after Search has indexed the files on your hard disk, Search has to index things again to update and add those new files to its database. Fortunately, it indexes folders and disks constantly.

As you create and install more and more files that get added to the index, the index database can become huge, which means it uses a large chunk of your hard disk to store the index. If you need to, you can delete the index file for selected disks or folders. (If you have a huge hard disk and are not worried about space, don't worry about eliminating the index file. If you eliminate it, of course, you cannot search by content.)

Delete content indexes

1. Click on any folder or disk whose contents you want to index, or whose index you want to delete.
2. Press Command I to get the Get Info box.
3. Click the triangle next to "Content index."
4. Choose to "Index Now" or "Delete Index."

The list of **languages** that Search uses when **searching the contents** of files is buried in the Finder Preferences (from the Finder menu when you're at the Desktop). Uncheck all the languages except those which you might use.

Language preferences for indexing

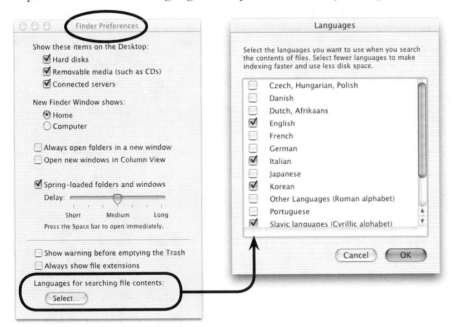

1. To search for a file, do you have to type in the exact and entire name of the file you're looking for?

_____

2. Do you have to type capital and lowercase letters exactly as in the file name?

_____

3. Do you have to type spaces in exactly the right place?

_____

4. How do you tell Search to limit the search to certain disks?

_____

5. How would you find a file you wrote sometime in March '03 that you know had the word "budget" in the file name? You have hundreds of reports with the word "budget" in the names.

_____

6. Once Search has found a file you want, what is the easiest way to open that file?

_____

7. In what utility can you tell Search to delete an index?

_____

8. What keyboard shortcut can you press to open the folder that contains a file found on your Mac?

_____

9. How can you trash a file that's displayed in the Search results list?

_____

10. Search found lots of files for you. How can you organize them in the Results window so they're grouped according to what kind of file they are?

_____

Answers on page 732.

Fonts on Your Mac

If you don't know much about fonts, or typefaces, you probably get frustrated looking at the font list in Mac OS X because you have no idea what all those names represent. So the first half of this chapter shows you what all of your fonts like. Even if you're a new user you might like to then customize the font panel in TextEdit.

For experienced font users, the last part of the chapter provides the basic technical information about the font changes in Mac OS X and what to do about your font management utilities.

Contents of this chapter

What Your Fonts Look Like

You have quite a few **fonts (typefaces)** available in Mac OS X. On these next several pages are examples of what is installed at the moment I write this, including the fonts that come with AppleWorks on iMacs (Apple always seems to add and remove a few fonts with every system upgrade). I've divided them into categories so it's easier to find the sort of font you need.

Many applications automatically install their own fonts in a separate place so they are only accessible when that application is open, so you may find fonts in your font list that you don't see here.

You'll see there are a number of typefaces that you will probably never use, so to clean up your font list, you should probably sort them into collections, as explained on pages 414–416. It will only take a couple of minutes (and it will only apply to certain applications).

If you are a font collector, you really need a font management program, which you probably already have. See pages 422–423 for current information about font management programs for Mac OS X.

Print up your own list

Apple has provided you with a "script" that will open TextEdit, type dozens of sentences (the same sentence over and over), and change each sentence into a font sample, labeled with that font name. Then you can print that up and have it next to you. It only prints the fonts in its list, not every font you have installed on your Mac (although if you know how to edit an AppleScript, you could add your font names to the list).

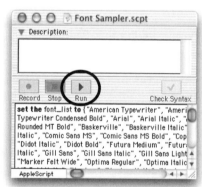

This is the Script Editor that will open. Just click "Run" and it will do what it's supposed to do.

To open and run the Font Sampler script, do this:

1. Press Command Option A to open the Applications folder, or click on the Applications icon in any Finder window.

2. Double-click the "AppleScript" folder.

3. Inside that folder, double-click the "Example Scripts" folder.

4. Inside that folder, double-click the "Info Scripts" folder.

5. Inside that folder, double-click on the file named "Font Sampler.scpt." The Script Editor will open, as shown to the left.

6. Click the "Run" button.

   The script will do as I explained above, then you can print those pages. Quit the Script Editor when you're done.

A **serif typeface** (pronounced *sair´ if,* not *sa reef´*) has small bits on the ends of the strokes, called serifs. This kind of typeface works better than most others when you need to set lots of text in print. This is the kind of type you are most likely to see in a book, such as this one, or any novel. The more distinctive the typeface, like Humana Serif, the more difficult it is to read in long blocks of text, although Humana Serif's distinctive look is perfect for something like a brochure.

Baskerville Regular, *Italic*
SemiBold, *SemiBold Italic*
Bold, *Bold Italic*

Georgia, *Italic,* **Bold,** *Bold Italic*

Hoefler Text Regular, *Italic*
Black, *Black Italic*

Humana Serif Light, *LightItalic*
Humana Serif Medium, Medium Italic

Palatino, *Italic,* **Bold,** *Bold Italic*

Times, *Italic,* **Bold,** *Bold Italic*

Times New Roman, *Italic,* **Bold,** *Bold Italic*

Serif faces

Several of the serifs are circled above.

Hoefler also has a set of ornaments, shown on page 407.

*These two versions of **Times** are basically the same typeface. The reason you have both is because Windows uses Times New Roman instead of Times, so if you are creating a document that will be used on or sent to a Windows machine, use Times New Roman.*

All caps Several fonts are **all caps** (capital letters) and so their use is limited. Words in all caps are much more difficult to read. But these are great for short bursts of text or a distinctive touch here and there.

BLAIRMdITC

CAPITALS

COPPERPLATE LIGHT, REGULAR, BOLD

Specialty serif faces The typefaces shown below are **serif faces** that have special uses. All of these are particularly elegant at large sizes of type, but difficult to read at small sizes.

Didot is what's considered a classic Modern typeface, with strong contrasts between the thick and thin parts of the letters. Use it nice and large where you want a classy look.

Didot Regular, *Italic,* **Bold**

Bodoni SvtyTwo Book 1234567890, *Book Italic,* **Bold**

Bodoni SeventyTwo and Big Caslon are both specially designed to be used at very large point sizes, as you can see in the examples on the opposite page. Compare the numerals in the two Bodonis.

Bodoni SvtyTwo OS Book 1234567890, *Book Italic,* **Bold**

Big Caslon

The "OS" you see in some typefaces stands for OldStyle. These faces give you the beautiful numerals shown in the example to the far right.

The 58 Times of Day
1564 Noon Square
Beloxi, MI 98765
505.438.9762

This is Bodoni SeventyTwo with the regular (called "lining") numerals. They appear too large.

The 58 Times of Day
1564 Noon Square
Beloxi, MI 98765
505.438.9762

This is Bodoni SeventyTwo OS with the oldstyle numerals. So pretty!

This is Bodoni SeventyTwo os set in 72 point.

These two examples, above and below, compare a typeface that is specifically designed for large print with a regular typeface that is designed to be used in body copy. Notice how the Palatino face looks so heavy and horsey because the thicker lines that make it readable in smaller sizes are too large for this size of text.

The typeface above looks great in the large size, but those thin strokes that look so good when set large will disintegrate when printed at small sizes.

This is Palatino set in 72-point type.

Sans serif faces   The word "sans" is French for "without," so **sans serif faces** are those without the serifs. Sans serifs are best for headlines, signage, and emphasis, as you see throughout this book. Many of them are also good for faxing, copying, and printing on cheap paper because they hold up very well.

Arial Regular, *Italic*, **Bold**, ***Bold Italic***
Arial Black
Arial Narrow, *Italic*, **Bold**, *Bold Italic*
Arial Rounded Bold

Futura Medium, *Medium Italic*, Condensed Medium, **Condensed ExtraBold**

Gadget

Helvetica Regular, *Oblique (Italic)*, **Bold**, ***Bold Oblique (Italic)***

Helvetica Neue Regular, *Italic*, ***Bold, Bold Italic***
Helvetica Neue Light, *Light Italic*
Helvetica Neue UltraLight, *UltraLight Italic*
Helvetica Neue Condensed Bold, Condensed Black

Lucida Grande Regular, **Bold**

Optima Regular, *Italic*, **Bold**, *Bold Italic*, **Extra Black**

Skia Regular

Stone Sans Semibold, *Semibold Italic 12345*
Stone Sans Bold 12345
Stone Sans Semibold Italic OS 12345
Stone Sans Semibold OS 12345
Stone Sans OS Bold 12345
Stone Sans Semibold SC (small caps) 12345

Here are three more fonts with oldstyle numerals, as well as a SMALL CAPS face (SC).

Trebuchet Regular, *Italic*, **Bold**, *Bold Italic*

Verdana, *Italic*, **Bold**, ***Bold Italic***

On the chance that you need text that lines up in columns, emulates a typewriter look, or is necessary in some techy terminal stuff, you have several **monospaced fonts.** Monospaced, also called fixed-width, means every character takes up the same amount of space, as on typewriters. As shown below, a comma takes up the same amount of space as a capital M.

Typefaces that are not monospaced are called **proportional,** or sometimes variable width.

The typeface American Typewriter, shown on page 404, emulates the look of a typewriter, but with the professional typesetting features in regard to letterspacing, character shape, and other features. But American Typewriter is not monospaced like a real typewriter.

Monospaced faces

Andale Mono

Courier, *Oblique,* **Bold,**

Bold Oblique

Courier New, *Italic,* **Bold,**

Bold Italic

Monaco

VT100 Roman, **Bold**

Script faces   **Scripts** are wonderful for that elegant, casual, party, or personal accent.

Apple Chancery

Aristrocrat—oh yes, we are!

Brush Script

Bickley Script—a casual affair

For directions on which keys to press to type all of the great little drawings built into the Party font, see page 408.

Party—Let's Whoop it Up!

Zapfino is a very elegant face.

Same with **handlettered** fonts.

Handlettered fonts

Bradley Hand

Comic Sans Regular, **Bold**

Marker Felt Thin, **Wide**

Sand

Papyrus

Textile Regular

Decorative fonts   **Decorative faces** are the most fun to use. They're just irresistible. Use them big and bold—don't be a wimp!

American Typewriter Light, Regular, **Bold**
Condensed Light, Condensed Regular, **Condensed Bold**

BERTRAM—WHAT A CLOWN

Bordeaux Roman Bold

HERCULANUM

Impact—boy does it have one

Jokerman—you are one

Luna—as in Lunatics of the Moon

MACHINE —MADE IN USA

Mona Lisa Solid

PORTAGO   —EXPEDITE

Techno Regular

Tremor —hey, it looks like California

Wanted   —Alive and Well

One of the big deals about Mac OS X is that it uses **Unicode.** See, most computers and fonts use ASCII, an international standard of character encoding. ASCII uses one electronic "byte" of information per character. One byte of information is eight bits. Each of these eight bits is either a one or a zero, an on or an off signal. If there are two options (on or off) for each of the eight bits, that's 2^8, which is a total of 256 different characters that can be created. This is okay for English, but is totally inadequate for many **non-Roman languages** such as Japanese, Chinese, Korean, etc.

Well, Unicode uses *two* bytes (16 bits), so that's a possibility of 2^{16}, or over 65,000 different characters in a font. Unicode, combined with the International and Keyboard preferences built into the Mac, makes your computer truly international. To that end, Apple has supplied several OpenType fonts that will type various languages, once you have activated those languages as explained on pages 47–51. The OpenType format is the only font format that can take advantage of Unicode.

Type for non-Roman languages

Apple Gothic

Apple LiGothic Medium

Hei Regular

Hiragino Kaku Gothic Pro W3
Hiragino Kaku Gothic Pro W6
Hiragino Kaku Gothic Std W8
Hiragino Maru Gothic Pro W4

Hiragino Mincho Pro W3
Hiragino Mincho Pro W6

Osaka Regular, Regular-Mono

WebDings These are just a few of the characters available in **WebDings.** Also try typing any character with the Option key held down, then with both the Option and the Shift keys down. Each time you'll get different characters.

Below are the available ornaments in the font **Bodoni Ornaments** which you might or might not have on your Mac. Either select the Bodoni Ornaments font and then type the character shown below to get the ornament you want, or type the character first and then change the character's font to Bodoni Ornaments.

Bodoni Ornaments

Hold down the Option key and press:

 Party ☆ Ornaments   Follow the directions as explained on the previous page.

=

hold down the Shift key and press:

` 1 2 3 6 + , .

hold down the Option key and press:

1 2 6 7 r t g /

5 9 0 = w d b . h j   Shift Option p

hold down the Shift and the Option keys and press:

7 8 = g

Hoefler Ornaments

Follow the directions as explained on page 407.

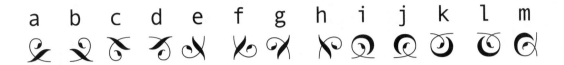

a b c d e f g h i j k l m

n o p q r s t u v w x y z

A B C D E F G H I J K L M

N O P Q R S

1 2 3 4 5 6 7 8 9 0 - =

, . / [ ] \ { } |

This is the character }
typed over and over.

Using the Font Panel

Many applications that are built specifically for Mac OS X, including TextEdit and Mail, use a **font panel.** Professional design applications will use their own version of the font panel, but there is a lot you can do with this built-in version. The most useful task is to organize your font list so you don't have to scroll through so many fonts you don't need.

To open the font panel in TextEdit:

▼ Press Command T.

You can also go to the Format menu, choose "Font," then slide out to the right and choose "Show Fonts...."

In applications other than TextEdit, you might find the font panel in another menu, but its command is usually always Command T.

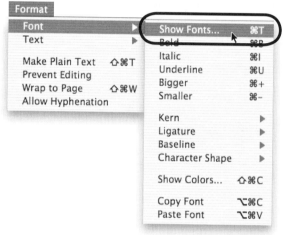

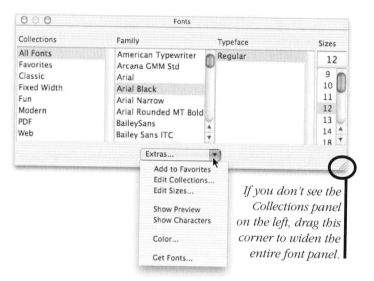

If you don't see the Collections panel on the left, drag this corner to widen the entire font panel.

Switch to a Size slider

This is not terribly important, but a nice feature: you can change the **Sizes** control so you can drag a slider to resize your seleted text. As you drag, the text grows bigger or smaller. This is nice if you don't know exactly what point size of type you want, but you'll know it when you see it.

The font panel shown above uses the "Fixed List." You can add specific fonts to that list in this little dialog box.

Click the "Adjustable Slider" button to change that fixed list to an adjustable slider, as shown here. Or choose "List & Slider" to see them both.

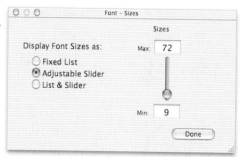

Not all typefaces have the same number or types of **styles** available. For instance, in the font panel shown below, on the left, you see the "Family" name Arial chosen, and in the column next to it, you see four "Typeface" (or style) choices: Regular, Italic, Bold, and Bold Italic. This means the designer created four typeface variations of Arial, and if you choose the keyboard shortcut or click the button or menu command to make the selected Arial text italic or bold, you will get the designed style.

But you will only get the designed style *if* the designer built it into the font in the first place, and *if* that style variation is installed in your Mac. For instance, in the font panel shown on the right, you see "Arial Black" is chosen, and the "Typeface" column only lists "Regular." This means there is no italic or bold italic of this font installed in your Mac (it might not have ever been designed). If you try to make the Arial Black font into an italic or bold version, you will either hear a beep, which tells you it's impossible, or the application will apply a fake italic or bold, which is a bad thing—not only does it look bad, but it can cause printing problems.

Choosing the right style

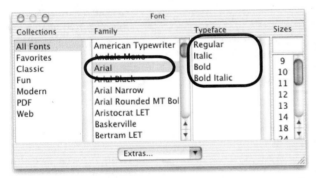

Arial has the same four standard variations as most of the basic fonts.

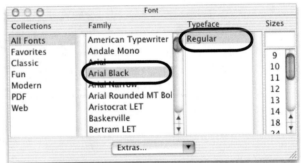

Arial Black is a special font, a very heavy addition to the Arial family. It is so heavy it does not need a bold, nor would it work very well in italic, so they were not included in the family. Don't try to make it italic.

View any font

You can **view any font** on your Mac that is installed in either the System fonts folder or in your user fonts folder. If you're accustomed to using Adobe Font Reunion, this feature is not as useful, but it will do in a pinch.

To see what your installed fonts look like:

1. Open an Apple OS X application such as Mail, TextEdit, or iChat.
2. Press Command T to open the "Show Fonts" window.
3. At the bottom of this window, there is a menu labeled "Extras...." Click on this menu and choose "Show Preview." Your dialog box will change, as shown below.
4. Choose any font and a size and the top section will display it.

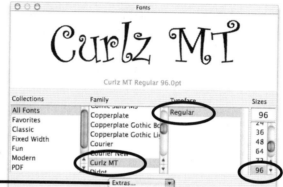

Choose "Show Preview" from this menu.

Choose a family font name, the typeface style, and the size you want to see.

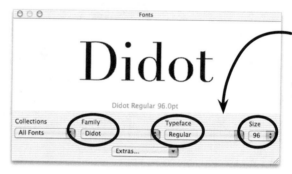

Grab this edge and drag it down, if you like, so you have a full display area. All of the font choices turn into menus, as shown.

Character Palette

You can also use the **Character Palette** to see all of the available characters in a particular font, which might include dingbats, swash characters, pictures, fractions, etc.

To open and use the Character Palette:

1. Follow Steps 1 and 2 above.
2. From the "Extras..." menu, choose "Show Characters." You'll see the Character Palette, but it probably won't look quite like the window shown on the opposite page.

3. From the View menu in the upper-left of the window, choose "All."

4. Click on the "Glyph Catalog" tab. Now your window looks like the one shown below.

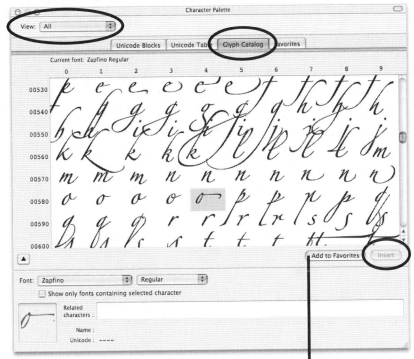

Zapfino is a font that takes advantage of Unicode and has more than 1,400 different characters in it.

Notice to the left how many different forms there are for each character.

Characters you use regularly can be added to a Favorites page for easy access. Select a characer, click this button, then use the "Favorites" tab to quickly access them whenever you want.

5. In the bottom-left of the Character Palette, choose the font and style you want to see.

6. Use the scroller on the right to view all of the available characters.

7. **To add a selected character to your document** (it will appear where the insertion point is flashing), **either** double-click the character **or** single-click it and then click the "Insert" button.

   The font on your document page might not look like the correct character—if not, select the character on your document page and change it to the same font you used in the Character Palette.

Font panel collections

The font panel allows you to create **collections,** or subsets of the list of fonts. Several collections are made for you, and you can make as many others as you like. You might make a collection of the four fonts you want to use in a particular report, or the six fonts you use in your monthly newsletter. You can add the same font to any number of collections. When you click a collection name, all of the other fonts in the list disappear temporarily, which makes it much easier to choose the fonts you need. The fonts are not gone, disabled, or removed—they just don't appear in the collection's list. Below you see the font panel with a collection in use.

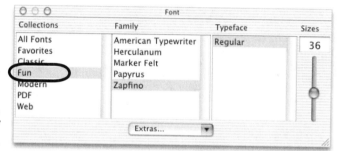

Whoever made up the names of these collections certainly didn't know anything about type. Don't be fooled into thinking these "Fun" fonts are the most "fun" ones you have on your Mac, or that the "Classic" fonts or "Modern" fonts are actually classic or modern.

With a collection chosen (in the left panel), the list of fonts in the "Family" column is limited to just those in the selected collection. This is much easier to work with than scrolling through the long list in "All Fonts."

To see the entire list of fonts again, *choose the collection "All Fonts."*

Add or delete fonts from the Favorites collection

In the **Favorites collection,** you can add not just a font family, but a specific style ("Typeface") and point size.

To add fonts to or delete fonts from the Favorites collection:

▼ **To add a font:** In the font panel, click once on any font "Family" name, plus any "Typeface" style you want, plus a point size.

From the "Extras…" menu at the bottom of the font panel, choose "Add to Favorites."

▼ **To delete a font,** select it, then from the "Extras…" menu, choose "Remove from Favorites."

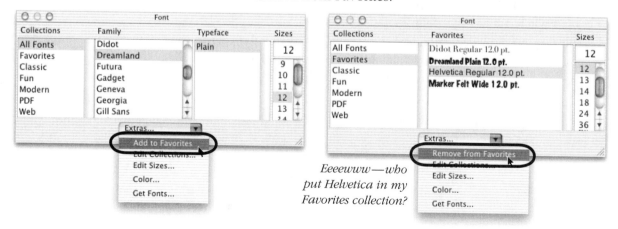

Eeeewww—who put Helvetica in my Favorites collection?

You can **create new collections** for yourself. These might be project-specific collections, or category specific. For instance, you might want a collection that displays all of the available script faces so when you want a script, you don't have to scroll through the entire list. You might want a collection that eliminates all of the fonts you don't need at the moment, like the ones designed for non-Roman characters, math and science characters, and the terminal application fonts. Remember, it is impossible for you to remove fonts from your Mac in this way—you are merely removing them from the list subset.

Create your own collections

Any new collections you make in the font panel will appear in all other applications that use the font panel the next time you open the application.

To create a new collection:

1. From the "Extras…" menu at the bottom of the font panel, choose "Edit Collections…."

2. Click the **+** symbol in the bottom-left of the window.

3. A new collection name appears in the left column, named "New-1."

4. Click the "Rename" button, then select the text "New-1" and replace it with your own word or words.

5. Now add (or delete) fonts to your new collection as described on the following page.

   Note: *In the current version of font panel, once you quit the application, you cannot edit your own collection! You cannot add or delete fonts from it. This must be just a bug and will surely be fixed in a future version.*

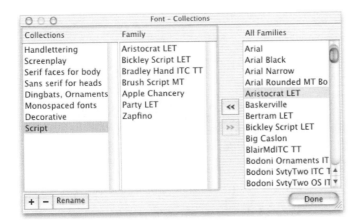

I created more reasonable and typographically correct collections for myself.

To delete an entire collection (which does not delete any fonts), select the collection in the left column, then click the **–** button.

Add a font to an existing collection

You can **add** fonts to your new collections. In fact, you can add the same font to as many collections as you like. (To add to the Favorites collection, see the previous page.)

To add fonts to a collection:

1. From the "Extras..." menu at the bottom of the font panel, choose "Edit Collections...."

2. Click once on a collection name.

3. In the column on the far-right labeled "All Families," click on the name of the font that you want to **add** to the collection.

4. The double-arrow button that points to the left will appear. Click it to move a copy of the selected font over to the list of fonts in the collection.

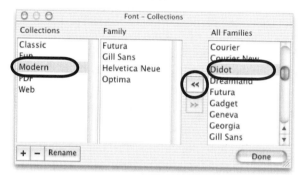

Delete a font from an existing collection

You can **delete** fonts from your new collections, or delete a collection altogether. Deleting fonts from a collection does not delete them from your Mac, or even from the "All Fonts" or "Family" list.

To delete fonts from a collection:

1. From the "Extras..." menu at the bottom of the font panel, choose "Edit Collections...."

2. Click once on a collection name in the far-left column.

3. Click on the name of the font in the middle column, labeled "Family," that you want to **delete** from the collection.

4. The double-arrow button that points to the right will appear. Click it to delete the font name from the collection.

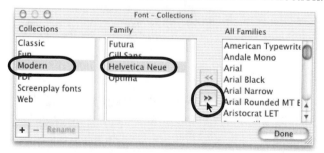

If you love using type and learning about type or maybe you teach typography and so you've created a lovely **assortment of collections** to keep your fonts organized, you can spread your affection to those who care less. That is, if you've taken the time to organize your fonts into collections, you can give those collection files to others (like students) so their font panels are as neat as yours.

In the illustration below, you see where the collections files, called **.fcache,** are stored. Just copy them from your folder, give them to another user, and he should put them into his own personal FontCollections folder.

If the other user has never made a collection, he won't have a FontCollections folder. In this case, go ahead and copy your entire FontCollections folder into his Library folder.

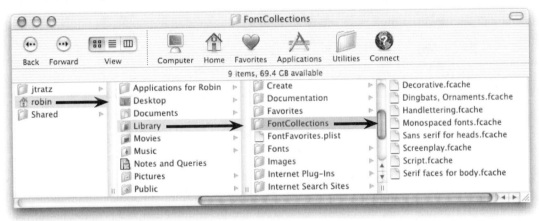

The .fcache files are stored in each user's personal Library folder, in the FontCollections folder.

You've probably noticed the menu option in the "Extras…" menu called **"Get Fonts…."** If you haven't clicked it already, here's what it does *not* do: it does *not* take you to a place on your Mac where there are extra fonts just waiting for you to install. It does *not* take you to a place online where someone is giving away free fonts to add to your system.

This menu option *does* take you to an Apple web site where you can choose to *buy* more fonts (the menu choice should be "Buy Fonts…," not "Get Fonts…"). If you have a broadband connection (a very fast connection that is "on" all the time), this automatic connection might be nothing more than an inconvenience. But if you have a dial-up account (you have a telephone modem that dials the phone to connect to the Internet), this can be a pain in the wazoo because you have to wait for either the connection to be made, or a message telling you the connection couldn't be made for one reason or another (maybe because someone else is already using that line). If you have a dial-up Internet account and want to check out this web page, I suggest you connect to the Internet first, *then* choose this command.

Installing New Fonts

If you are the system administrator for a corporate network, you can install fonts in the Network Fonts folder as well.

Installing new fonts that you have bought or acquired is quite simple. Fonts are stored in several places on the Mac, but as a regular user, you are really only concerned about two of these places, as described below.

1 If you want the newly installed fonts to be **available to everyone** who uses the Mac, install them in the System's Library Fonts folder, as shown in **1,** below. You must be logged in as the Administrator or have the Administrator name and password to install into this folder.

2 Fonts can also be installed into the Fonts folders in individual users' Homes, as shown in **2,** below. The fonts will only be **available to that one user.**

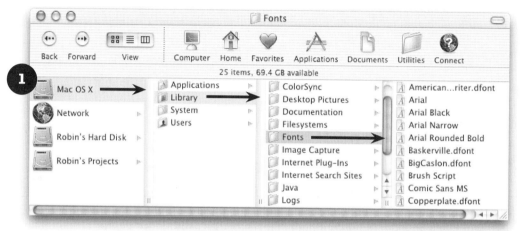

To make fonts available to all users, install them into the folder shown above: On your main hard disk, the one that has Mac OS X on it, open the Library folder, then open the Fonts folder.

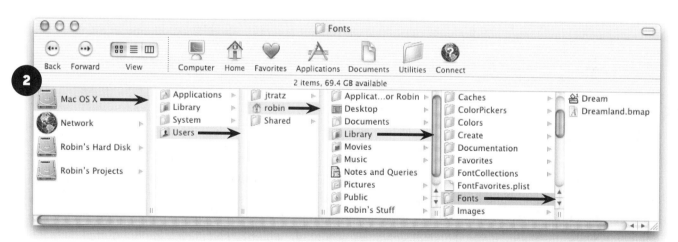

*So fonts will be **available to a single user** (you must be logged in as that user), install them into the folder shown above: On the main hard disk, the one that has Mac OS X on it, open the Users folder, then open that user's Home folder, then open her Library folder, then open her Fonts folder.*

DO NOT put fonts in the **main System** Library Fonts folder. Actually, it's impossible for you to put fonts in there, to remove fonts, or to rename anything in that folder, so don't worry. If you are trying to install fonts and you get the message shown below, you're putting them in the wrong place. Check the screen shot **#1,** on the opposite page, to make sure you've got the correct folder.

DO NOT try to install fonts in the System itself

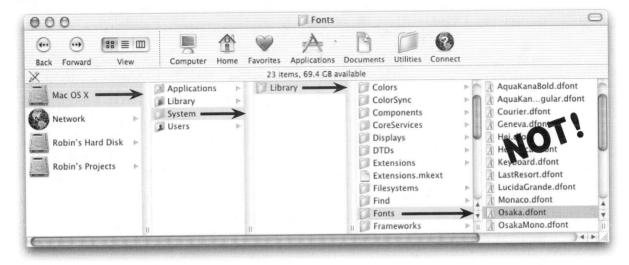

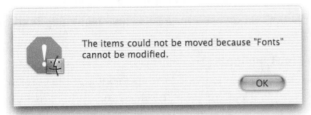

If you're trying to install fonts for everyone and you get this message, you've got the wrong folder. Go through the first "Library" folder, as shown on the opposite page, not the "System" folder shown above.

There is **one more place** where any user can **install fonts,** and that's in Mac OS 9. If you use a lot of Classic applications (applications that have not been rewritten yet to work in Mac OS X), you can install fonts as usual into the Fonts folder inside the System Folder (or use your favorite font manager).

There's one more place . . .

Classic applications cannot access the Mac OS X fonts—the applications call on the fonts that are installed in the Mac OS 9 System Folder or from your font manager, if you use one.

If you're a Type Hawg, like me, and have so many fonts that you use a font manager such as ATM Deluxe, Extensis Suitcase, Alsoft MasterJuggler Pro, or DiamondSoft's Font Reserve, you can still use those managers just fine with your Classic applications. For instance, I wrote the entire first edition of this book in Adobe InDesign 1.5 in the Classic environment, using ATM Deluxe as my font manager with fonts installed in Mac OS 9, while running Mac OS X. (Now InDesign 2.0 and Photoshop 7 both work in OS X so I don't use Classic anymore.)

Technical Font Stuff

The **technical font stuff** is changing once again. Mac OS X uses a new font technology, actually a couple of new font technologies, but hasn't abandoned the ones we've been using for years. Because I've written entire books and chapters in other books (including a chapter in all of the previous editions of *The Little Mac Book*) about font technology, I'm not going to explain all the details here. Most people don't care anyway. I'll just tell you the important stuff.

These are the sorts of fonts you can install in Mac OS X:

▾ **PostScript Type 1:** You must install both the printer fonts and their matching screen fonts, as usual. They don't always have extensions.

▾ **Mac TrueType:** The font name usually has a **TT** in it, but not always.

▾ **Mac .dfonts:** The extension is **.dfont**. These are basically TrueType fonts with all of the information contained in the data fork, instead of in the separate resource fork. They are binary files that can be used on other platforms.

▾ **Mac OpenType fonts:** The extension is **.otf**. OpenType fonts can contain over 65,000 different glyphs (characters), as explained on page 399, which allows type to be set in non-Roman languages such as Japanese and Korean. It also allows lots of extra characters in Roman fonts for truly professional typesetting. Applications must be specially written to use OpenType and Unicode; TextEdit and Adobe InDesign are both ready.

▾ **Windows TrueType fonts:** The extension is **.TTF**. This is true—you can install and use Windows TrueType fonts, as shown on the opposite page. This is great for cross-platform work because you can use the exact same font on both platforms. But be careful—not every font works perfectly. For instance, in the example on the opposite page there are three Windows TrueType fonts installed in my Fonts folder. One file, ITCEdscr.TTF (love those Windows filenames), is an elegant Edwardian script that shows up on the screen, but would not print nor convert to outlines (although the Mac version works fine, as you can tell by the chapter headings in this book. So before you create an entire project using a Windows font on your Mac, make sure it really does work on both platforms, looks exactly the same (same line breaks, etc.), and will print to your final output device.

▾ **Windows OpenType fonts:** The extension is **.OTF**. Same as above.

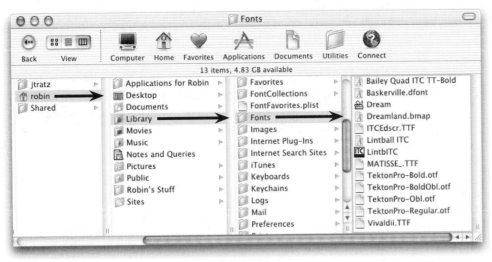

This is my user Fonts folder.
In it you see these font formats
in order:

Mac TrueType

Mac .dfont

*Mac PostScript Type 1
(printer font and screen font)*

Windows TrueType

*Mac PostScript Type 1
(screen font and printer font)*

Windows TrueType

*Mac OpenType family
(four members)*

Windows TrueType

THIS IS MATISSE. THIS PARTICULAR VERSION IS A WINDOWS FONT.

Vivaldi has always been a favorite.

*These two examples are fonts I borrowed from my PC and installed
in Mac OS X, as you can see above. They appeared in the font list,
rendered nicely on the screen, and printed just fine. Amazing.*

ATM and Mac OS X

Many of us are accustomed to using **Adobe Type Manager (ATM)** to make
PostScript fonts look clean and smooth on the screen. In Mac OS X, the font
rendering on the screen and to the PostScript printer is taken care of by the
system so you don't need to install ATM. In fact, Adobe is not updating ATM
or ATM Deluxe, the font manager, for OS X.

Font Management

Making collections of typefaces in the font panel (if the application has one) is fine for a small number of fonts. But I happen to have over 150 megabytes of them, which is probably over 3,000 fonts, and those are just the ones I have installed. There's no way I can drop all of those into my Fonts folder—my font list would be 12 feet long and my computer would probably drop dead. So I use a **font management** utility, which you probably do too if you're reading this paragraph.

If you haven't used a font management program yet, this is what it does: Instead of installing all of your fonts into the Fonts folder, which makes every font open all the time, you can store your fonts in a separate folder anywhere in your Home area that you like. For instance, you could have a folder called "My Fonts" in your Home folder. Then your font management utility lets you create **sets of fonts** from this folder so you can open just the ones you want when you want them. Sets are sort of like the font collections in the font panel, except all of the fonts that you're not using at the moment are actually "disabled" and *do not* take up memory or processing power at all. The unused fonts are just sitting in their folder doing nothing, like all other files that are not open. In your application's font list, you see only the fonts you need for that particular project.

Current status of font managers

If you currently use **Adobe Type Manager Deluxe,** you're going to have to switch to another font manager because Adobe is abandoning this product. It still works fine in the Classic environment, so until you switch over your main application to an OS X version, ATM Deluxe will continue to work for you. If you plan to use OpenType fonts, you might want to upgrade to ATM Deluxe version 4.6.

DiamondSoft **Font Reserve** has a Mac OS X version. Font Reserve is a fabulous font management program, very powerful. If you already use it in OS 9, buy the upgrade for OS X. www.fontreserve.com

According to their web site, Alsoft's **MasterJuggler** is not quite ready for Mac OS X, but they're working on it. www.alsoft.com

Extensis **Suitcase** is available for Mac OS X. The latest version actually works in both OS 9 and OS X. As shown below, it's lovely, powerful, and easy to use. As with Font Reserve, you can activate or deactivate entire sets or individual fonts with the click of a button, view individual fonts or entire sets, get information about what type of font and who the vendor is, collect fonts for output, and many more features. Suitcase is dedicated to supporting the new font formats. **www.extensis.com**

You can turn sets on and off right from the Dock. Fabulous.

1. What sort of type family is best for lots of body copy, like in a book?

_____

2. When would you use a typeface like Big Caslon?

_____

3. What does it mean when a typeface name has the abbreviation "OS" in it?

_____

4. If you want to install fonts for your own personal use, where would you put them?

_____

5. If you want to install fonts for every user of the Mac to use, where would you put them?

_____

6. What is a monospaced font?

_____

7. If a font is not monospaced, what is it?

_____

8. From the fonts automatically installed on your Mac, can you type Comic Sans in italic or Brush Script in bold? If not, why not?

_____

9. Can your Mac use Windows fonts?

_____

10. Are you a Font Hawg?

_____

Answers are on page 732.

Applications on Your Mac

Mac OS X includes a number of small but useful **applications.** This chapter explains what each of these does and when to use it.

If you're an experienced Mac user, you might notice that some applications written specifically for Mac OS X do not come in folders—they come in one file called a "package." For instance, you know that iMovie must have hundreds of supporting files, yet you only have one icon for iMovie—no folder full of stuff. These packages have a file name extension of .app. If you get special plug-ins and other files to customize your application, they will be stored in your user's Library folder (or the main Library folder, if everyone on the Mac has access to the customized tools).

To open a window displaying what is in a package, Command-click on the icon (such as iChat), then choose "Show Package Contents."

Contents in this chapter

iTunes, iMovie, and iPhoto are so great and important that they are now in a separate, companion book to this one, called The Little Mac iApps Book. *That book also includes iDVD, iCal, iSync, Bluetooth, Ink, .Mac, iDisk, Backup, and others.*

Acrobat Reader

Acrobat Reader

The **Acrobat Reader** will open and display PDF files for you. You'll find PDF files everywhere. Often the manual for new software is a PDF file on the CD—double-click the manual and it will open in Acrobat Reader; you can search for terms, read it on the screen, or print it up. Many information files on the web are PDF files that you can download, like your tax forms, requirements for entering the Bodleian Library, job application forms, or syllabi from your instructors.

PDF files are documents that contain all of the information for all of the graphics, fonts, and the layout, compressed into one package that any computer can open and display—even if it doesn't have the application you created the document in, or the fonts, or the graphics. For instance, let's say you use your favorite page layout application to create an eight-page newsletter for your beloved dog shelter, export it as a PDF, then email that PDF to your clients. They get the PDF, double-click it, it opens in the Acrobat Reader, and what your clients see on their computer looks exactly like what you see on your computer, even if they use PCs.

You can create PDFs in any Mac OS X application that uses the OS X Print dialog boxes, even TextEdit:

1. In your open document, press Command P to print.

2. Click the "Save as PDF" button and give this file a name.

   The file will not print at this point—you will be returned to your original document, and your saved PDF will be in the folder. You can send the PDF by email to anyone you like.

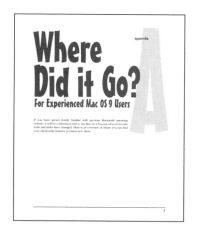

Months before the first edition of this book was published, I created a PDF of the appendix to this book, shown above, and posted it on the Santa Fe Mac User Group web site for anyone to use. I wrote and designed the chapter in Adobe InDesign and used a number of fonts, but anyone can download the file, open it in Acrobat Reader, and print it up. It looks exactly like the chapter in the book. Amazing.

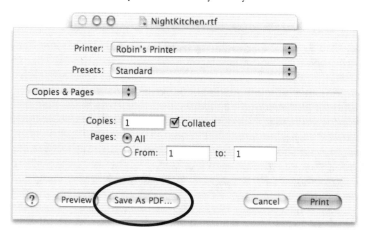

The **Address Book** works with the Mail program. Use it to store your email addresses and other contact information. Full details of how to use it are in Chapter 32.

Address Book

Address Book

An **AppleScript** is a series of commands written in the AppleScript language that tells your Mac to do something for you. AppleScripts can perform repetitive tasks for you, such as change all of your .tiff file names to .tif, or number all of the items in a folder. Or let's say you get lots of files from PC users who name files with all caps and it makes you crazy—you can write a script that will change all of the file names to lowercase; once you write the script, you can run it anytime.

AppleScript

AppleScript

Actually, all of the scripts described above are already written for you and are in the AppleScript "Example Scripts" folder. To see how a script works, run the "Current Temperature by Zipcode" script, as described below. To run this script, you have to be connected to the Internet.

To open and run the "Current Temperature" script, do this:

1. Press Command Option A to open the Applications folder, or click on the Applications icon in any Finder window.

2. Double-click the "AppleScript" folder.

3. Inside that folder, double-click the "Example Scripts" folder.

4. Inside that folder, double-click the "Internet Services" folder.

5. Inside that folder, double-click on the file named "Current Temperature by Zipcode.scpt," shown to the upper-right.

6. The Script Editor will open, as shown to the right.

7. Click the "Run" button.

8. You will be asked to enter a zip code. Do so, then click the "OK" button. The current temperature will appear.

9. Quit the Script Editor. You will be asked if you want to save changes—you don't need to.

   If you want this script to always open with your zip code, find the line in the code that starts with "set," find the zip code in that line, and change that zip code to the one of your choice. Save the changes.

Current Temperature by Zipcode.scpt

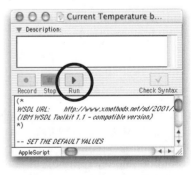

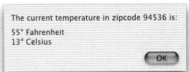

To learn how to write AppleScripts, go to Apple's site and use the tutorial (www.apple.com/applescript). Also, open the Script Editor and then go to the Help menu to get help specific to AppleScript.

Calculator

Calculator

The **Calculator** has finally grown up! You can still use your mouse and pointer to enter numbers, or use your numeric keypad. The asterisk (*) is the multiplication symbol, and the slash (/) is division. And you can copy and paste numbers into and out of the window.

But now you can do lots more. Click the "Advanced" button to display the scientific functions. Click the "Paper Tape" button to see your calculations as you enter them, then hit Command P to print that "tape" for your records, complete with time and date. Press Command Shift S to save the tape as a TextEdit file.

Use the Speech menu (you'll see it in the menu bar when you open the Calculator) to hear a voice tell you what numbers and functions you are entering. Use the Convert menu to convert the number in the Calculator from inches to square feet, from Fahrenheit to Centigrade, from atmospheres to inches of mercury, from miles per hour to kilometers per hour, and many other conversions. It will even convert currency at today's exchange rate (connect to the Internet and choose to "Update Current Exchange Rates" from the Convert menu). Amazing.

Chess

Chess

Chess is just what it appears to be—an electronic chess game between you and the computer, or you can watch the computer play against itself. From the Window menu in Chess, you can choose to play on a three-dimensional or two-dimensional board, as shown on the opposite page.

Before you begin a game, get the Chess Preferences (from the Chess menu) and determine how difficult you want the game to be, who is playing and what color you each have, and whether to use speech recognition or not. You can't change these settings once you begin a game.

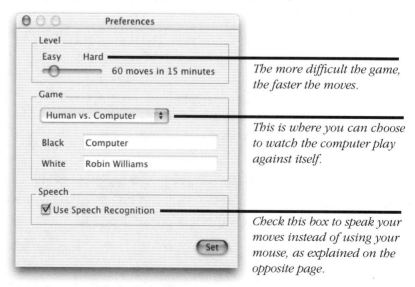

The more difficult the game, the faster the moves.

This is where you can choose to watch the computer play against itself.

Check this box to speak your moves instead of using your mouse, as explained on the opposite page.

This is the three-dimensional board.

This is the two-dimensional board.

If you choose to use **Speech Recognition,** a round microphone will appear on your screen; in fact, if you take a break (like go back to work) in another application, this microphone will still be sitting right in front of your face. See pages 354–356 for details about how to work with this particular speech recognition software. (If you don't want to bother reading that, just try this: Hold down the Escape key, and wait one second. Keep holding the key down, then speak your move, as explained below. Have your move ready before you start speaking so you don't have to stumble. Let go of the Escape key when you're finished. If that doesn't work, go read those pages.)

This is the speech recognition microphone.

Use the modern coordinate notation system when speaking to the microphone. For instance, speak "g1 to f3" to move your knight into the position shown above. The computer also understands if you say the name of the chess piece, as in "Bishop f1 to b5," but you don't need to. Tell it to "Take back move" if you don't like what you just did.

This is the Controls window.

Sometimes the computer takes longer than you would expect to make its move. From the File menu, choose "Controls…" to get the window shown to the right. Then you can "watch" the computer as it thinks (the bar turns progressively white). If it takes too long, click the button at the bottom, "Force Computer To Move."

The button on the bottom, "Start Computer vs. Computer Game" is only available if you have chosen to play "Computer vs. Computer" in the Chess Preferences, as shown on the opposite page.

DVD Player

DVD Player

The **DVD Player** plays DVD (digital versatile disc) movies on your computer. It includes the Viewer (a window in which a movie plays) and the Controller (the device that controls the movie playback). Insert a DVD in your computer's DVD drive and the Player will automatically open. You'll see something like the example below.

The DVD Player plays commercial DVDs and home-movie DVDs, such as this one created with Apple's iDVD software.

The Controller

You can use either a horizontal or vertical **Controller.** From the Controls menu, choose "Controller Type," then choose "Horizontal" or "Vertical."

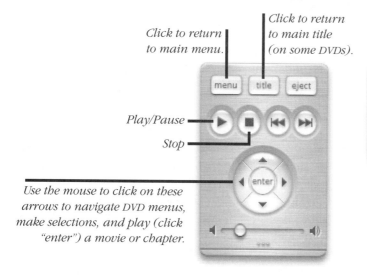

Click to return to main menu.

Click to return to main title (on some DVDs).

Play/Pause

Stop

Use the mouse to click on these arrows to navigate DVD menus, make selections, and play (click "enter") a movie or chapter.

Click to go to Previous or Next Chapter.

Press the buttons circled above to forward or reverse at the default speed set in the Controls menu in the menu bar across the top of the screen: From Controls, choose "Scan Rate," then choose 2x, 4x, or 8x.

Click the small bumps near the edge of the Controller to reveal a number of **additional controls,** as shown below.

Additional controls

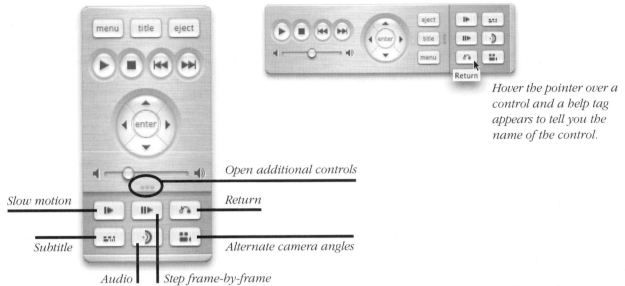

Hover the pointer over a control and a help tag appears to tell you the name of the control.

Open additional controls

Slow motion   *Return*

Subtitle   *Alternate camera angles*

Audio   *Step frame-by-frame*

Slow Motion: Click to cycle through speeds of ½ speed (slow), ¼ speed (slower), and ⅛ speed (slowest).

Click the Play button to resume normal playback speed, or tap the Spacebar.

Step frame-by-frame: Click to advance the playback one frame at a time.

Click the Play button to resume normal playback, or tap the Spacebar.

Return: Click to return to a previous DVD menu. The DVD that you play may have a different function applied to this button, or none at all.

Subtitle: Click to turn subtitles on or off. Language settings for subtitles can usually be set in the DVD movie's menu, or in the Preferences, as explained on the following page.

Audio: Some DVD videos (not all) include additional audio tracks, such as director's comments, that you can select with this button. You can also use this button to switch to alternate languages.

Angle: Some DVDs have alternate scenes that were filmed from different angles. The Angle button lets you select these alternate angles, if they're available.

Keyboard shortcuts:

Play/Pause	Spacebar
Stop	Command Period
Scan Backward	Command LeftArrow
Scan Forward	Command RightArrow
Next Chapter	RightArrow
Previous Chapter	LeftArrow
Display DVD menus	Command ~
Highlight menu items	Arrow keys
Activate menu items	Return or Enter
Volume Up	UpArrow
Volume Down	DownArrow
Mute	Command K
Full Screen Viewer	Command 0 (zero)
Half Size Viewer	Command 1
Normal Size Viewer	Command 2
Maximum Size Viewer	Command 3
Close Windows	Command W
Show/Hide Controller	Control C
Show/Hide Viewer Window	Control V
Horizontal Controller	Shift Command H
Vertical Controller	Shift Command V
Show Info Window	Control I
Eject Disc	Command E
Quit	Command Q

Clock

Clock

If the time display in your menu bar is not enough (or if you prefer to turn off the menu bar display altogether), you can choose to have a nice **Clock** sitting right in the middle of your screen.

After you open the Clock, go to the Clock menu and choose "Preferences…" so you can adjust it to suit yourself. You can choose to display an analog or digital clock, as shown below, with some variations in the digital version. If you display the clock in a floating window, you can adjust its transparency. Even if you choose to see the clock as a floating window, it will still appear in your Dock.

If you have trouble making the Clock go away because its menus have disappeared, click on the Clock icon in the Dock, and choose "Quit."

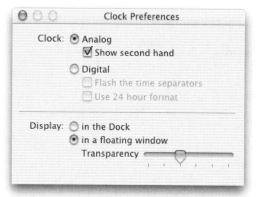

Move the "Transparency" slider to the left to make the clock more transparent, to the right to make it more solid.

These examples show the solid and most transparent states.

Image Capture

Image Capture

Image Capture transfers images from supported digital cameras (with USB connections) to your computer. You can choose to download all photos in the camera, or just selected photos. Image capture can build a web page which you can publish on the World Wide Web, and it can build preview sheets in different size formats so you can print them on your printer. Image Capture can also transfer video clips and MP3 audio files if the camera can create those types of files.

To find information about which cameras are supported by Mac OS X, visit the Apple web site at **www.apple.com,** go to the Support section, select the AppleCare Knowledge Base link, then do a search for "Image Capture."

Why use Image Capture instead of iPhoto?

Three reasons you might choose to use Image Capture instead of iPhoto:

▼ Image Capture captures video clips *and* MP3 files (if your camera creates them) and automatically transfers them to your Movies folder and your Music folder. iPhoto ignores movies and MP3s.

▼ Image Capture can create a quick and basic web site on your hard disk that you can use to post somewhere (or server from your own Mac; see Chapter 36). iPhoto can create a polished-looking web site, but you need a .Mac membership ($100) to have access to this feature.

▼ Image Capture lets you preview the images in the camera before you download them. This gives you an opportunity to delete or rotate images before downloading, or choose just a few to download. iPhoto downloads all photos (this may change in new versions).

Default to Image Capture

Your Mac is probably set up to **automatically open** iPhoto when you connect your camera and turn it on (or plug a card into your card reader). If you want your camera to open Image Capture instead, do this:

Click the Applications icon in any Toolbar, then double-click the Image Capture application icon. You'll get a message that there is no camera connected, but ignore that and go to the Image Capture menu and choose "Preferences...." Select "Image Capture from the "Camera Preferences" menu in the dialog box, as shown below.

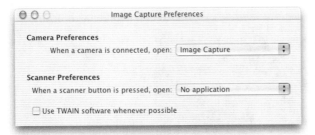

If you're going to use Image Capture, choose to automatically open it when you plug in the camera or your card.

This will change your iPhoto preference, and changing your iPhoto preference will change this one.

Connect your camera or use your card reader

Now you're ready to **connect your camera.** Turn it off, plug in the USB cable to both your camera and the Mac, then turn on your camera. Or plug your card into your **card reader.** This Image Capture panel opens automatically:

This Options button will bring up the Options panel as shown on the following pages. You can also get to that panel in the camera preview window if you click "Download Some...."

Download To: From this pop-up menu, select a download location for your camera's files. The option "Pictures, Movies, and Music folders" means that Image Capture will put the pictures from your camera in the Pictures folder; if you have movies on the same camera, those will go in the Movies folder; and any MP3 files on the camera will end up in the Music folder. If you want to specify another folder, choose "Other..." from this pop-up menu and select the folder of your choise.

An "Automatic Task" actually activates an AppleScript, a series of commands that tell an application what to do. The option of "Other..." lets you choose any other script you may have downloaded to your computer or written yourself.

Automatic Task: Use this pop-up menu to select an automatic task that occurs after the image files are downloaded to your computer:

Build Slide Show: This option automatically creates a full-screen slide show with dissolve transitions, pan, and zoom effects. The slide show starts playing immediately. To access the slide show later, go to the Screen Effects system preference (see page 330), and you'll see a new option to use "Recent Photos."

Build Web Page: If you choose this automatic option, Image Capture automatically builds a web site consisting of a home page with thumbnail versions of your photos, and a separate web page for each full-sized photo. All the photos and web pages are put in the Pictures folder, in a folder named "Index." The page design is stark, but it works. If you're familiar with web design or HTML, you can open the files and make changes, or at least change the name beneath the photos.

See Chapter 36 for details on how people can view your web pages that are served from your own Mac!

Format: Choose one of the "Format" options (3x5, 4x6, 5x7, or 8x10) to automatically create image preview pages that are built in HTML code and that open in your browser for viewing or printing. The size refers to the size the downloaded images will appear in the browser preview, as well as the size they will print.

Preview: If you select "Preview" as the automatic task, Image Capture opens the downloaded images in your Preview application (see pages 439–442). All of the images are shown in the thumbnail drawer; click on the one you want to display in the main Preview window.

Now click the **Options** button for even more customization options. If you have already selected "Download Some...," the Options button is in the bottom-left corner of the camera preview window, as shown on the next page. Here in the **Download Options** pane you'll find:

Options

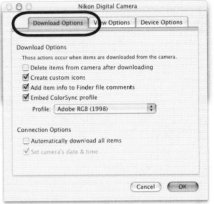

Delete items from camera after downloading: Erases all items from the camera as soon as they are transferred to your computer. Uncheck it if you want to keep the images on the camera.

Create custom icons: Creates an icon for each image that looks like the photo, rather than using a generic JPEG icon.

Add item info to Finder file comments: Adds information about an item to the Comments section of the item's Get Info window, such as width/height pixel measurements and image resolution.

Embed ColorSync profile: Attaches color profile information to an image file for color management; choose a color profile from the "Profile" pop-up menu. Color management strives to accurately capture, display, and output color by using standard color protocols. Located in System Preferences, Apple's ColorSync lets you set profiles for Input, Display, Output, and Proof devices.

Automatically download all items: This will download items from the camera without giving you a chance to preview them. If you want to preview items so you can delete or rotate some images before downloading them, uncheck this box. I prefer to uncheck this option so I can see an immediate preview window of the images, then select and download only the images that look good.

Set camera's date & time: Adds the date and time that an image was created to the camera preview window. You'll see this information in the List View if "Date" is selected in the View Options pane, as described on the following pages. You have to set the date and time in your camera, of course, before this feature can work.

Tip: When you download photos from your camera, keep the camera plugged into its AC adapter so you won't use up all the battery juice.

In the Options window for your camera (as explained on the previous page), click the **View Options** tab to get setting for the Icon and List Views. These settings do not apply to the regular Finder window, but to a special camera preview window, as explained below.

In the Download Options pane (as described on the previous page), you could choose to have the camera "Automatically download all items." If you did *not* choose to do this, then when you plug in your camera to the Mac a window opens that lets you choose to either "Download Some…" or "Download All" of the images in the camera.

If you choose "Download Some…," a camera preview window opens in which you can preview images in the camera before they're downloaded. The window's title bar will show the name of the attached camera.

Click the "Icon View" or "List View" button, circled on the opposite page, located at the upper-left corner of the *preview window* to select a view. This special window is where you'll see the effects of the View Options settings shown below.

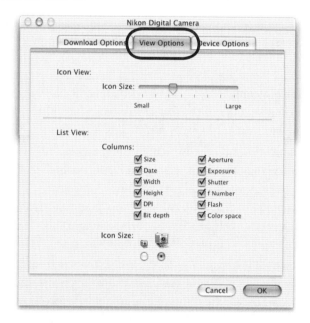

Icon View: Use the "Icon Size" slider to determine the size that an image file's icon will appear in the camera preview window when "Icon View" is active.

List View: From the "Columns" list, choose which columns to show in the camera preview window when "List View" is active. Also choose an "Icon Size" to display.

*Preview the images in
Icon View or List View.*

Select a picture, then rotate or delete it.

*The Camera Preview window shows a preview of the images in the
camera before you download them to your computer. This enables
you to rotate or delete images before downloading. The window's
pop-up menus let you select a Download folder and select an
Automatic Task, as explained on the previous pages.*

Internet Connect

Internet Connect

If you connect to the Internet through a telephone modem, then you'll use **Internet Connect** to tell your modem to dial up your service provider and connect you. This is explained in detail in Chapter 30. If you have an "always on" broadband connection to the Internet, such as cable, DSL, ISDN, satellite, or T1 line, you won't ever need to use Internet Connect.

Internet Explorer

Internet Explorer

Internet Explorer is Microsoft's web browser that is installed on your Mac and has an icon in your Dock. The basics of how to use it are in Chapter 31. If you prefer not to be part of Microsoft's Domination of Society, you can install any other browser of your choice, such as Netscape, OmniWeb, iCab, Opera, or others. I personally keep a Microsoft-free environment.

iPhoto

iPhoto

In iPhoto you can organize all of your digital photographs and clipart, edit them, send them through email, upload them to the web, and much more. So much more that all of the details about iPhoto have to go into another book, *The Little Mac iApps Book,* or this book would be 1,500 pages.

iTunes

iTunes

All of the information about all of the "iApps" from Apple are in The Little Mac iApps Book, *from Peachpit Press.*

With the application **iTunes,** you can play not only music or other audio files on your Mac, you can create a *Playlist* of selected songs from any number of your own music CDs or downloaded MP3 files. iTunes will go to the Internet and find all the information about each song on your CD (like artist, title, length of song, etc.), then add that information to your Playlist. Use iTunes to manage your music collection, play wild visuals on the screen in time with the music, encode music files from one format to another, burn music CDs of your selected collection of music that you can then use anywhere, and copy MP3 files directly to your MP3 player or iPod. If you don't have iTunes, it's a free download from the Apple site at **www.apple.com.**

Mail

Mail

With **Mail** you can send and receive email. You don't have to have a .Mac account to use it—you can use your existing email account from anywhere (except AOL). The **Address Book** is used in conjunction with Mail.

If you have more than one email account, Mail can check them all at once and send mail back out from each account, even if your accounts are on different servers. You can create "rules" that let you filter messages into different mailboxes; for instance, perhaps you want all email from "John" to go into a mailbox named "My LoverMan" so it doesn't get mixed in with the business mail. Or maybe you want all email with the word "free," "enlargement," or "mortgage" in its subject to go straight to the trash. And best of all, Mail has a really great junk mail filter that lets hardly any junk into your mailbox at all! See Chapter 32 for all the details.

Preview

Preview

Preview is a great little application that not only displays your photos and PDF files, but has quite a powerful image-conversion feature built in.

First of all, you've probably already noticed that when you double-click on many photos and other images, they automatically open in Preview, as shown directly below. You can zoom in on an image (enlarge it) and zoom out. You can flip it vertically or horizontally and then save it in that new rotation. You can copy images in Preview and then paste them into an icon's Info window to change the icon image (see page 117 for details on that).

jane.jpg

This is the icon that indicates a file will automatically open in Preview when you double-click on it.

This is an open Preview window.

Robin's Stuff

This is actually a folder whose icon I customized by copying the image from Preview.

You can open multiple images of various formats in one window and use thumbnail images to choose which one to show in Preview's window.

Thumbnail drawer

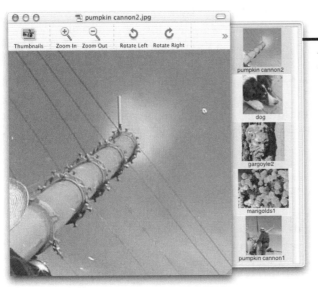

*If you don't see this thumbnail drawer, press Command T, **or** go to the view menu and choose "Thumbnails," **or** just click the "Thumbnails" icon in the toolbar.*

To open one or more images in Preview:

▼ Select one or a group of images from your hard disk and drag them onto the Preview icon in the Dock.

▼ **Or** from the File menu choose "Open...," then locate the image files you want to select. **To select more than one file,** Command-click files to add them to the selection, as shown to the right. Then click "Open."

The toolbar

The **toolbar** across the top of the Preview window is pretty self-explanatory, but here are some quick tips. All the commands available in the toolbar can also be found in the View menu.

Thumbnails: If you opened multiple images, you'll get thumbnails of the images stored in a "drawer" that slides out from the side of the Preview window. To open or close the drawer, click the "Thumbnails" icon in the toolbar. Click on a thumbnail in the drawer **to display that image** in the Preview window. To adjust the size of the thumbnails, use the preferences (from the Preview menu).

Zoom In and **Zoom Out:** Enlarge or reduce what you see in the window. Or use the **keyboard shortcuts:** Command UpArrow to enlarge; Command DownArrow to reduce.

To display an image at 100 percent of the original size, from the View menu choose "Actual Size." Keep in mind that "actual size" can vary on your screen, depending upon the resolutions of both your screen and the image. You can force the actual size to be closer to real actual size if you go to the Preview Preferences (from the Preview menu) and choose, "Ignore DPI for 'Actual Size.'"

Rotate Left and **Rotate Right:** Rotate an image in the Preview window. This does not affect the original file unless you save or export the file.

Backward and **Forward:** Navigate through image thumbnails or through pages of a PDF document.

Or use the **keyboard shortcuts:** DownArrow to go forward to the next image or the next page; UpArrow to go to the previous image or page.

When viewing a **multiple-page PDF document,** you can choose how you want pages to scroll: continuously or page-by-page, as described below. From the View menu, you can turn "Continuous Scrolling" on or off.

- ▾ With "Continuous Scrolling" **turned on** (choose it from the View menu), the scroll bar in Preview will scroll through the entire PDF document, sliding past page after page.

- ▾ With "Continuous Scrolling" **turned off** (choose it again from the View menu to toggle it off), the scroll bar will scroll through the currently displayed page *only*. This is helpful when you've zoomed in on a page, as shown below.

    Use the UpArrow and DownArrow keys to jump to the previous and following pages.

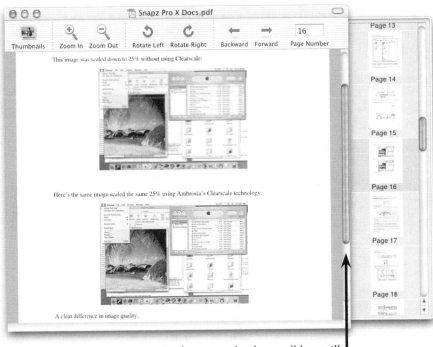

In this example, the scroll bar will scroll through just this one page.

The **Page Number** field in the upper-right of the Preview toolbar will display the number of the page that you are currently viewing in a multiple-page PDF document. When viewing a long PDF document, type the page number you want to go to in the Page Number field, then hit Return or Enter.

Convert graphic file formats

Also see the tip on page 449 about previewing a page you are about to print, and then saving it as a PDF in Preview.

Preview can also **convert** a large number of graphic formats into other formats. If you understand graphic file formats and when you might need one over the other, take advantage of Preview's quick and easy conversion feature. You can change the bit depth, the quality level, the compression method, and a number of other specifications, depending on what type of file you are converting into what other type of file. For instance, if you have a Mac TIFF file you want to send to a PC user, you can export it as a TIFF with the "Little Endian" code attached so the PC user is more likely to be able to see it (Macs use Big Endian). If someone sent you a Photoshop file and you want to put it on your web page, you can convert it to a JPEG, and even control the quality level while you're at it.

To convert a graphic:

1. Open a graphic in Preview.

2. From the File menu choose "Export...."

3. In the sheet that drops down, go to the "Format" pop-up menu and choose a file format. Preview automatically applies the correct three-letter extension at the end of the file name—don't change it.

4. Now click the "Options..." button to get a small dialog box where you can choose settings for that particular format.

5. Name the file and choose a location in which to save it. Click "Save."

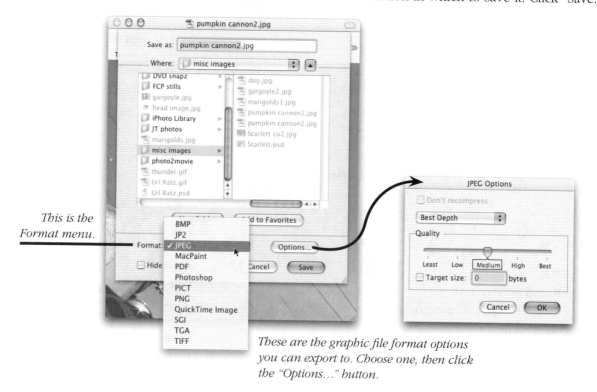

This is the Format menu.

These are the graphic file format options you can export to. Choose one, then click the "Options..." button.

The **QuickTime Player** plays audio, video, and QTVR (QuickTime Virtual Reality) movies. In addition, it can display still image files in almost every mainstream format (JPEG, TIFF, PICT, GIF, PSD, PNG, BMP, and others). Any type of QuickTime file is referred to as a "QuickTime movie."

You can play QuickTime movies in QuickTime Player or in any application that supports QuickTime, such as most popular browsers and some word processors. Use QuickTime Player to play movies that you downloaded to your computer, that you created on your computer, or that exist on the Internet.

There are several ways to **open** QuickTime Player. These three methods open the QuickTime Player with the movie loaded and ready to play.

- ▼ Double-click a QuickTime file on your computer.
- ▼ Click on a QuickTime link on a web page.
- ▼ Drag a QuickTime file's icon on top of the QuickTime application icon, either in the Dock or in the Applications folder.

QuickTime Player

QuickTime Player

Open QuickTime Player

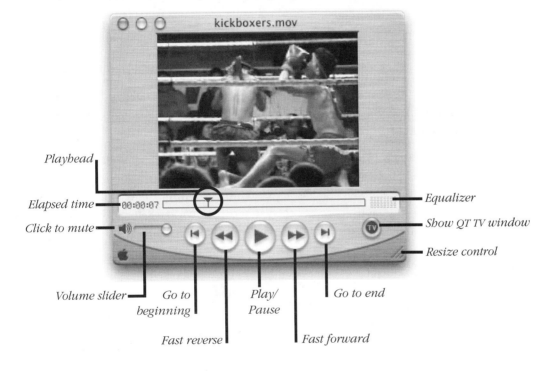

Playhead

Elapsed time

Click to mute

Equalizer

Show QT TV window

Resize control

Volume slider

Go to beginning

Play/ Pause

Go to end

Fast reverse

Fast forward

iMovie is so much fun and so useful—it is literally as easy as writing a letter in your word processor to create your own digital movie in iMovie. We put a great tutorial in *The Little Mac iApps Book,* from Peachpit Press, because this book is too dang large already.

iMovie

iMovie

Sherlock

Sherlock

With **Sherlock** you can search web pages, find shopping bargains, research your paper, find out what time your local movies start, get a map to Grandma's house, print help files from Apple, and more. Please see Chapter 31 for details.

Stickies

Stickies

The **Stickies** application can be very useful. Use it to leave notes to yourself or to others who might use your Mac. Create your shopping list, notes on your upcoming presentation, gossip, snippets for poems you will write later, tidbits to add to your research, interesting stuff from web pages, etc. Below are examples of Stickies and the sorts of things you can do with them.

From the File menu, you can **import** text directly into a Sticky note, import all your notes from Classic, or **export** text from the active Sticky so you can use it in other applications. You can **print** the active note (the one in front with the title bar visible) or all of the open notes.

From the Edit menu, you can **find** certain words that might appear in any of the open notes. You can run the **spell checker** (the "Spelling…" command) on *all* open notes, or ask to **check the spelling** of just the *active* note, in which case each time you choose the command ("Check Spelling") or press Command Semicolon (;), a misspelled word is underlined with dots.

From the Note menu, you can **change the typeface** of selected text, or **change the style** (bold or italic if one is designed into the font). You can **copy the font,** size, and color of a word (*click* inside the typeface example in the note; *do not* select the word; choose "Copy Font"), then select a word in another note (or the same note) and **"Paste Font."** The selected word will take on the typeface, color, and size of the word you copied from.

If you've created a style of note that you like, with the font, size, and color of note, you can make this note's formatting your **default,** so every new note you create will have this look. Just create a note with the formatting you like (only one style of text will apply), then from the Note menu, choose **"Use as Default."** The color of the text will not apply.

Make notes **translucent** so they don't obscure objects behind them.

Drag a **graphic** from any folder and drop it into a Sticky note.

You can **change the color of selected text**—select the text (drag over certain words or press Command A to select all), then choose "Text Colors…" from the Note menu. In the Colors panel that appears, drag the little square around until you find a color you like, then drag the slider bar up or down to make the color darker or lighter.

"Note Info" will tell you the date the note was created and modified.

The Color menu **changes the color of the note,** not the text.

Use the Window menu to **close the active note, miniaturize it,** as shown below, or **deminiaturize** it. You can also use the keyboard shortcut Command M or double-click the title bar to miniaturize and deminiaturize a note ("deminiaturize" is not in my dictionary, and the spell checker in Stickies flags the word as a misspelling). You can choose to neatly arrange your notes (choose **"Arrange in Front"**) whether they are miniaturized or not.

These four notes are miniaturized and arranged in front. Double-click the title bar of any note to open it.

Drag the tiny square around the circle to choose a color, and use the slider bar to make the color darker or lighter.

You can use **Services** to do a number of things with the selected text in a Sticky. For instance, select the text, go to the Stickies menu, and from the Services submenu, choose "Mail" and "Mail Text," as shown below. This will automatically copy the text from the Sticky, open the Mail program, open an email form, and paste this text into the form, ready for you to add the email address and send it.

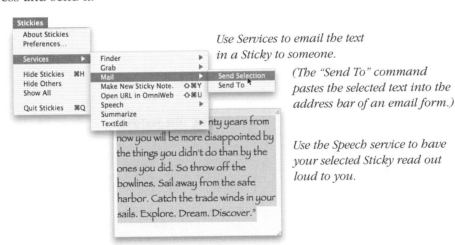

Use Services to email the text in a Sticky to someone.

(The "Send To" command pastes the selected text into the address bar of an email form.)

Use the Speech service to have your selected Sticky read out loud to you.

And in any other OS X application, even from a browser, you can select text, then go to the application menu and use **Services to make a new Sticky** of your selected text.

System Preferences

System Preferences

The **System Preferences** is one "pane" that displays all of the different preferences you can customize. Click one (such as "Date & Time") to select it and its pane will replace the existing one; click the icon "Show All" in the upper-left corner to return to the pane that displays all of the preferences. With System Preferences you can adjust the time that appears in your menu bar, change the picture on your Desktop, choose a language for your menus and dialog boxes to appear in, enter the networking and Internet settings, and much more. See Chapter 22 for details on all of the preferences.

TextEdit

TextEdit

The application **TextEdit** is a small word processor. It can do some surprising things, but is missing enough serious features that you might not want to use it as your only word processor. But here is what it can do:

From the File menu, you can **"Open Recent"** files. This is nice so you don't have to go scrounging around in your hard disk looking for that file you created several days ago.

From the Edit menu, you can do all the basic stuff like **cut, copy, paste, delete** (clear), **undo,** and **select all.** If you don't know how to use those features, please see Chapter 13.

The **Find** command has some fairly robust features. You can *find* words or phrases, and you can *replace* found words or phrases with entirely new words or phrases. For instance, you might have written a novel with a main character named "Peter," then you decide, after 173 pages, that you want his name to be "John." Use the Find panel to "Find: Peter" and "Replace with: John," then click the "Replace All" button. Almost instantly, your hero has a new name.

Position your pointer over a button and wait a second or two—a Help tag appears to tell you what that button will do.

The **Spelling** command gives you three options. "Spelling…" brings up the spell checker for the active document. "Check Spelling" will point out your misspelled words in the active document one at a time; press Command Semicolon (;) to find the next misspelled word. The option to "Check Spelling As You Type" will underline words with red dots as you misspell them.

Use the **Speech** command to have your text read out loud by the voice chosen in the Speech preferences pane (see pages 354–357). If text is selected, that is what will be read. If nothing is selected, the reader will start at the beginning.

From the **Format** menu, use the **Font** and **Text** submenus to format your text, most of which is explained in Chapter 13. To learn to use the Font Panel, see pages 410–413.

The command to **"Make Plain Text"** will turn your document into a "text-only" or ASCII file, which removes all font choices, styles, underlines, etc., and takes the text down to its most basic form. This file is then safe to send through the Internet to any other computer user, regardless of the kind of computer or applications she has on her machine.

If you choose **"Prevent Editing,"** TextEdit will lock the file so it can be read by others, but no one can make changes to it or delete it. Well, they could if they went up to the Format menu and chose "Allow Editing," so it's not a very safe way to protect your document. This command is only meant to prevent accidental damage to the file.

"Wrap to Page" will display the printing guidelines in the window. You can't change the margins—they are stuck at one inch all the way around. But in "Wrap to Page" you are guaranteed that what you see on the screen is what will print, as opposed to "Wrap to Window," explained below.

While in **"Wrap to Window,"** the lines of type stretch to fill the space as wide as you drag your window. When you print, the printer will try to match your line endings, but if your window is wide, it may have to reduce the size of the type to fit your sentences on the same lines of the page that you have on the screen. So if your page of text prints too small, reduce the size of your window and print again.

"Allow Hyphenation" does just what it says—it will allow words to be hyphenated at the ends of lines.

Be sure to go to the TextEdit menu and check the **"Preferences…."** They are pretty self-explanatory. The "Default Font" lets you choose a default font and size so every time you open a new document in TextEdit, you will automatically start to type with your choice of font.

—continued

You can drag **pictures** into your TextEdit documents:

1. On your Desktop, position your open Pictures folder (or whichever folder you store your pictures in) on the right side of your screen.

2. In TextEdit, position your page on the left side of the screen.

3. From the Pictures folder, press-and-drag an image to your TextEdit document—watch carefully to see the insertion point move around the page as you drag the image around! (See page 196 if you're not clear on what the insertion point is and why it is so important.)

4. When the insertion point is flashing in the position you want the image, as shown below, drop it on the page (just let go of the mouse button). The picture will insert itself where the insertion point was flashing.

5. To make more space *above* the picture, position your insertion point to the left of the photo and hit a Return.

   To make more space *after* the picture, position your insertion point to the right of the image and hit a Return.

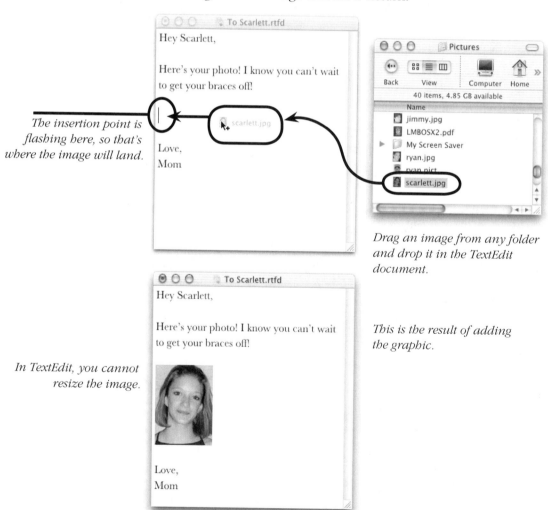

The insertion point is flashing here, so that's where the image will land.

Drag an image from any folder and drop it in the TextEdit document.

This is the result of adding the graphic.

In TextEdit, you cannot resize the image.

When you **save** a text document in TextEdit, it creates what is called a Rich Text Format file with a file name extension of **.rtf**. "Rich Text" means it can include fonts, styles, different point sizes, and other formatting (as opposed to "Plain Text" as described on page 447).

If you insert a photo or other graphic into a TextEdit document, it will become a "Rich Text Format with Attachments" file and must be saved with an extension of **.rtfd** (the "d" stands for "directory" because an .rtfd file is actually a folder, or directory, that bundles the text with the graphics). Don't worry about remembering that—as soon as you try to save a document that has an image in it, the Mac will tell you that you have to change the extension and will actually do it for you. See page 227 for details about file name extensions.

Tip: As discussed in Chapter 15 about printing, you can go to the Print dialog box and click the Preview button. This will make a PDF preview of your document which will open in the application Preview. From there, you can save it as a PDF file so you can email the document to anyone in the world and they can see it just like you created it.

You can also save a file as a PDF simply by going to the Print dialog box and choosing "Save as PDF...."

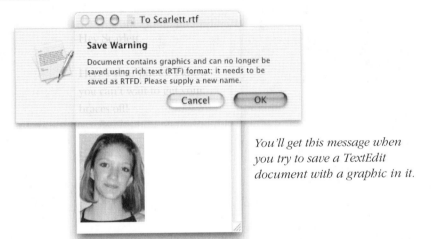

You'll get this message when you try to save a TextEdit document with a graphic in it.

TextEdit does not have a feature that automatically creates real **apostrophes** and **quotation marks,** so you have to learn to type them yourself. Don't ever print your work with typewriter apostrophes and quotation marks—it looks stupid. This is what the marks look like and how to type real ones:

Typewriter apostrophe:	It's Mary's turn.	
Typewriter quotation marks:	"Go get 'em, Mary."	*(Oooh, these are so nasty.)*
Typesetter's apostrophe:	It's Mary's turn.	
Typesetter's quotation marks:	"Go get 'em, Mary."	

To type true typesetter's apostrophe and quotation marks:

apostrophe	'	Shift Option]
opening quotation mark	"	Option [
closing quotation mark	"	Shift Option [

Name the best Mac OS X application to use to accomplish each of the following tasks:

1. Change a graphic image from one format to another.

   _____

2. Find the current temperature of any zip code.

   _____

3. Download all of the photos and movies from your digital camera to your Mac.

   _____

4. Challenge a friend to a game of chess.

   _____

5. Make reminder notes, to-do lists, and snag bits of information and images off the Internet and save them for future reference.

   _____

6. Check the email for all of your email accounts with one click.

   _____

7. Watch commercial or homemade DVDs.

   _____

8. View PDF files that your PC-user friend sent you.

   _____

9. Write letters to your mother and finish your thesis, both with photos in the text.

   _____

10. Make individual playlists of your favorite songs and record them onto a CD.

    _____

Answers on page 732.

Useful Utilities

Mac OS X provides you with a number of **utilities,** which are small applications that perform specific functions, such as help you troubleshoot problems on your computer, manage color, provide security, find special characters in your fonts, and more.

The Utilities folder is stored inside the Applications folder. If you find you get into it often, drag the Utilities folder up to the Finder window Toolbar so you can open it with the click of a button, no matter where you are.

Contents of this chapter

AirPort Setup Assistant

AirPort Setup Assistant

AirPort is Apple's wireless networking technology. You can plug a "base-station" into your existing telephone connection to the Internet, to your cable or DSL modem, or even your T1 connection. Then that base station will send out radio waves to connect any other Mac to the Internet, any Mac that has an AirPort card installed. In fact, the one base station can send the signal out to fifty different Macs. This means you can have an entire classroom or small school connected to the Internet from one connection. The Macs don't have to be plugged into any modem. We have an AirPort installed in our office, and we can surf the Internet on the iMac in the painting studio where there is no physical connection and on the Mac in my library upstairs. (You might see ads showing people connecting while they sit by the pool or at an outdoor cafe, but notice you never see the screen in those ads—that's because you can't *see* the screen in broad daylight. I know this.)

The **AirPort Base Station** looks like a small flying saucer about the size of a danish pastry and costs about $300. An **AirPort card** costs about $100 and can be installed in desktop Macs and newer laptops. When you install Mac OS X, whether you have AirPort or not, you get the **AirPort Setup Assistant** and the **AirPort Admin Utility.** If OS X discovers an AirPort card in your Mac, it automatically puts the AirPort status menu in your menu bar, as shown to the left.

The AirPort Setup Assistant will walk you through setting up your AirPort to connect to the Internet and establish the network.

The darkness of the four stripes in the AirPort menu bar icon indicates how good your signal is. If all four bars are gray, it's not working at all yet—perhaps you need to walk through the Setup Assistant. Or perhaps you turned it off.

When all four bars are black, you've got a great signal.

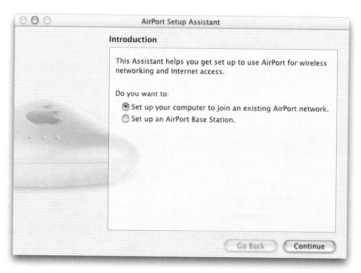

The AirPort Setup Assistant will walk you through establishing your connection and setting up the network.

The **AirPort Admin Utility** lets you change connection settings when necessary. When you installed the AirPort software that came with your AirPort Base Station and card, all of this information was filled in for you.

If you need to make changes, open the AirPort Admin Utility. You will see the first dialog box shown below, which gives you a list of all the base stations that you have access to.

AirPort Admin Utility

To actually get to the administrative utility, as shown below, double-click on the name of the base station in the "Select Base Station" dialog box, shown above. You will have to enter the password that you chose when you set up the base station. So you won't have to enter it again, click the box to add the password to your Keychain (see pages 466–473 about Keychain Access). Once you have entered the password, click OK and you'll get the administrative preferences shown below. You'll need a network administrator to take care of most of these items.

Tip: To remove the AirPort status icon in the menu bar, hold down the Command key and drag it off the bar. If you want to put the status icon back in the menu bar, go to the System Preferences and click on the Network icon. In the "Show" pop-up menu, choose "AirPort." Then click on the "AirPort" tab. Check the box to "Show AirPort status in menu bar."

airportratz

Restart Upload Default Password

| AirPort | Internet | Network | Port Mapping | Access Control | Authentication |

Information in this section is used to identify the base station and configure the wireless network published by the base station.

Base Station

Name: airportratz

Contact:

Location: 192.168.254.14

(Change password...)   ☑ Enable SNMP access on WAN
                          ☑ Enable configuration on WAN

AirPort Network

Name: airportratz

☐ Create a closed network

Channel: 1   ☐ Enable interference robustness
Station density: Low   ☑ Enable encryption (using WEP)
Multicast rate: 2 mb/s   (Change password...)

(Update)

If a microwave or other radio device is near the AirPort, it can cause interference. Check this box to help the AirPort overcome that interference.

Apple System Profiler

Apple System Profiler

The **Apple System Profiler** (in your Utilities folder) is the place to go to find out your Mac's serial number, all the details about your hardware and software, memory chips, every application on your hard disk, and more. You won't need to use it very often, but it's good to check it out so you know what information is available here. If you ever have to call tech support, they will probably ask you to open this.

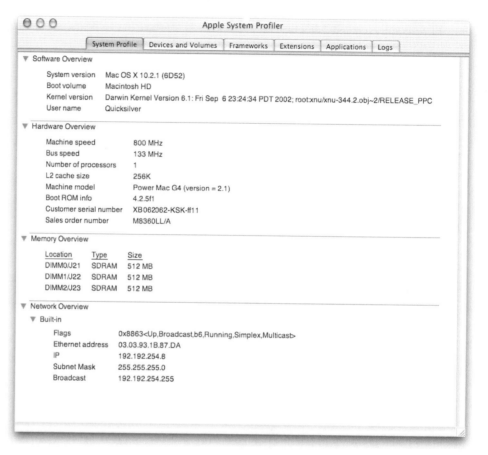

Disk Utility

Disk Utility

The **Disk Utility** provides five different features. Only the Administrator (or someone with the Administrator's name and password) can run Disk Utility.

▼ You can get **Information** on any mounted disk, as shown below, such as its size, how much space is available, and how many files and folders are stored on the disk.

▼ You can run **First Aid** to check for problems and to repair many problems on any mounted disk, *except* the disk that has the operating system on it (the startup disk), CD-ROMs, locked disks, and disks that have open files (quit all applications before you try to run First Aid). First Aid is a good place to start when things start acting weird. It automatically verifies and repairs the startup disk when you first turn on your Mac.

▼ You can **Erase** removable disks and any partitions except the startup disk. Erasing, of course, destroys all the data on the disk. You can erase CD-RW disks, but they may deteriorate if you do it too often.

▼ If you have a very large hard disk, use Disk Utility to **Partition** it into several smaller volumes. Step-by-step directions for how to do this are in Chapter 38.

▼ **RAID** stands for "redundant array of independent disks" and is a professional storage solution involving multiple disks that store the same data in different places (that's why it's redundant). The operating system thinks the array is one hard disk. If you don't already know what RAID is, you won't need this panel of Disk Utility.

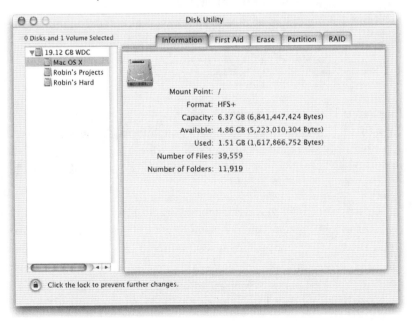

TROUBLESHOOTING UTILITIES

Mac OS X has quite a slew of **troubleshooting utilities.** To use most of these items, you need to really know what you're doing—these are not tools for messing with lightly. All I'm going to do here is provide a brief description of each utility. If you are a typical user who never (or very rarely) needs to use these tools, you might want to store them inside a new folder inside the Utilities folder so they don't get in your way.

Console

The **Console** shows you technical messages from the system software and Mac OS X applications. If you are a programmer or if you need to do some serious troubleshooting, these messages, as Apple says, "may" be useful.

CPU Monitor

CPU Monitor provides a visual representation of what your Mac's central processing unit (the CPU) is doing. If you know what to look for, it can be interesting (and perhaps helpful) to see what the CPU does during video editing, 3D-rendering, and other graphics-intense processes. To see exactly which processes the CPU is working on, open *ProcessViewer* at the same time (you can open it from the CPU Monitor's Processes menu). This is often used in conjunction with "Top" in the *Terminal*, which you can also open from the Processes menu.

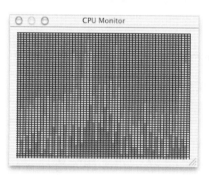

The bars march across the screen constantly, showing you what the CPU is doing.

Directory Access

Directory Setup is a tool for network administrators on campus or corporate networks to set up search policies, attribute mappings, define LDAP data, and select NetInfo domains and other directories. Home and small business users, even those with local networks, won't need to use this.

Terminal

Mac OS X runs on a non-graphical operating system called **Darwin,** which is based on Unix. If you want to access Darwin directly, use the **Terminal** utility. Here in the Terminal window you can use "command lines" to make your Mac do things that you can't do otherwise, like totally destroy your entire computer. Well, of course if you know what you're doing, you won't destroy it, but if you *don't* know what you're doing, leave the Terminal to the programmers.

Network Utility

If you understand basic networking, **Network Utility** can be helpful for finding specific information and for troubleshooting.

Info: Check your computer's network interfaces.

Netstat: Review network performance statistics.

Ping: Test access to specific hosts or IP addresses.

Lookup: Convert between IP addresses and host names.

Traceroute: Trace the route that packets take from one computer to another (type in a web address and see how many times and where the packet stops to ask directions).

Whois, Finger: Find user information (see below for Whois).

Port Scan: Scan the active TCP ports.

If you know how to use Terminal, you can find more information about these tools: type "man" followed by the tool's name, such as **man lookup.**

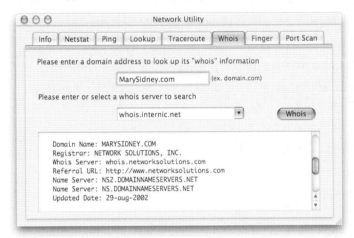

*You can **look up a domain name** to see if it's already been taken by someone. (This does the same thing as going to the Internic web site.) Type in the domain name you want to check, click the "Whois" button, and you can find out if someone already owns the domain. Of course, you must be connected to the Internet to get this information.*

Whois no longer gives you the administrative or other contacts, due to security issues.

ProcessViewer

A "process" is an application of some sort. It might be an application that *you* open and use, or it might be something the Mac opens and uses internally that you never even know is happening. **ProcessViewer** lets you see exactly which processes are running. This is useful to programmers and system administrators in troubleshooting situations. If you call Apple Tech Support, they might ask you to open this and tell them what it's doing.

NetInfo Manager

Your Mac uses a built-in directory service called **NetInfo** to store information about the computer, the users, and the networks that may be connected to it. It's a tool for network administrators that most of us won't need. The one time you might want to open NetInfo is to **enable the root user** so you can throw away perfectly safe files that the Mac won't let you throw away otherwise. Directions for logging in as the root user are on the following pages.

—continued

Log in as Root User

There is another user on the Mac, called the **root user,** or superuser. By logging into this account, you can change any file on the entire Mac, even system files that you as the Admin are not allowed to touch. By default, the root account is disabled in Mac OS X because it is phenomenally easy to destroy your entire system with the click of a mouse. But sometimes you try to throw away items you created or you might try to install software into the Applications folder and the Mac yells at you that it's not possible, usually because you don't have sufficient privileges. And you wonder, "Well, I'm the only person who has ever used this machine—if I don't have privileges, *who on earth does!?*" This is when you might have to log in as the **root user.** It's not something you want or need to do often, and you don't want to leave your computer sitting around with the root user available because as the root user, you (or anyone using your machine) has access to read, write, and destroy any file on the Mac, including all other user files.

But if you need to do it, log in as the root user, do what you need to do, then log out and disable the root user when you're done. You must know the Administrator's short name and password to do this.

NetInfo Manager

This is the NetInfo Manager icon in the Utilities folder.

To enable the root user and log in:

1. Click on the Applications icon in any Finder window, or go to the Go menu and choose "Applications."

2. In the Applications window, open the Utilities folder.

3. In the Utilities window, find and double-click "NetInfo Manager."

4. In the NetInfo Manager window, click the padlock icon in the bottom-left corner.

5. In the dialog box that appears, type in the *short* name of the main Admin of the Mac, plus that Admin's password. It must be the name of the main, original Administrator—not a user who has been granted administrative status. Click OK.

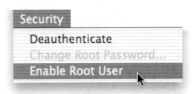

6. From the Security menu, slide down to "Security," and then choose "Enable Root User," as shown to the right.

   (If the root user has already been enabled, this item says "Disable Root User"; skip to Step 9.)

7. If there is not a root password already, you will be asked to create one. Use the standard password guidelines: difficult to figure out, a combination of letters and number, no non-alphanumeric characters, no spaces, etc. Capital letters and lowercase letters are different characters in a password. *Write this password down somewhere!!*

   After you type the password the first time, you'll be asked to type it again to verify it. Click the Verify button.

8. You have now enabled the root user. The padlock in the NetInfo window will automatically shut—you'll get a message that you must "re-authenticate" to make any more changes. Quit NetInfo.

9. Next you need to **log out** so you can **log in** as the root user.

10. From the Apple menu, choose "Log Out...." In the Login window that appears, type "root" as the user name, and type the root password you assigned earlier. Voilà. You can now delete files that you weren't allowed to delete earlier. Be careful.

11. When you're finished doing your root business, log out, log back in as yourself, and disable root access in the NetInfo Manager.

If the Login window shows a list, click "Other," then log in as root.

JAVA UTILITIES

Java is a programming language. Some of the very common things created with Java are applets, or small applications, that can be sent along with a web page. You, as a user, go to the web page and see interactive animations, calculations, live news scrolling across the page, and other tasks. Java also runs more complex actions, such as Internet chats and working with databases. These Java utilities are in the "Java" folder, inside the Utilities folder.

Applet Launcher

Applet Launcher

Applet Launcher lets you run Java applets that are stored on your Mac or on a web site—without having to open a web browser. (You do have to connect to the Internet.)

To run an applet that's on a web site, type the URL in the edit box shown below, including the **http://**. Then click the "Launch" button.

You can also click the "Open…" button to open an html file that contains Java applets. The Applet Launcher will connect to the page and run all of the applets on the page.

When the applet runs, another applet from Sun Microsystems will open and provide you with basic controls for starting and stopping the applets.

Java Plug-in Settings

This is a **Java Plug-in Control Panel** that lets you enable Java plug-ins, clear something called JAR cache, and set other Java-geek options.

Java Web Start

Java Web Start

Java Web Start is attractive to large companies that maintain hundreds of thousands of workstations and have to keep up-to-date software on these computers. Java Web Start applications (which are HTML-based) can be launched securely via any browser on any platform from anywhere on the web. You can try it out: open Java Web Start, click the "Start" button, and walk through the process using the dialog box shown below.

If you are a professional in the graphics field and rely on precise color reproduction, Apple has provided a suite of **color utilities.** Use these in combination with your graphics applications to help you capture, display, and output accurate color. Color gets very complicated, so I'm only going to give you the highlights of these utilities. To learn all about ColorSync and how to really take advantage of it, Apple has provided a tutorial on their web site at www.apple.com/colorsync. At that site you can also find a ColorSync consultant (or become one).

The **Display Calibrator** will adjust your monitor to give you the most accurate color, and these specifications will be made into a color "profile" that you can use in ColorSync. Open the Display Calibrator and walk through the process to adjust your monitor—it's easy.

Use the **ColorSync Utility** and the ColorSync preferences (in the System Preferences) to specify color profiles for the capture, display, proofing, and final output devices you use.

COLOR UTILITIES

Display Calibrator

ColorSync Utility

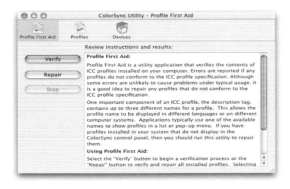

▾ If an ICC profile that you need doesn't appear in the ColorSync pane of System Preferences, it may contain information in a non-standard format. Use **Profile First Aid** to validate and repair the profile.

▾ Click **Profiles** to see which profiles you have installed and to get information about each one, such as what color space it uses, its ICC version, or when it was created. Click the black triangle in the right corner of the list to organize that list by location (which is probably what you see when you open it), by class (which groups them according to input displays, output profiles, etc.), or by color space (such as LAB color, RGB, CMYK, etc.).

▾ Click **Devices** to check the capabilities, contained in its color profile, of a camera, printer, display, or other device you have attached to your Mac. If you don't see a profile for your chosen device, maybe you didn't install the software that came with it. Also check the vendor's web site to see if you can download a profile if you don't have one.

*An **ICC profile** is a standard developed by the International Color Consortium for documenting the color characteristics of input and output devices. These profiles help correct visual data for viewing on different devices.*

*Not all images contain color space information. The World Wide Web Consortium has declared that all colors specified in cascading style sheets and HTML should be in the **sRGB** color space.*

—continued

Once you've got your ColorSync profiles worked out, turn on the color management features of your image capture, editing, and output applications. For example, in Internet Explorer you can more accurately view web images that use profiles: open the Preferences; in the Web Browser list, choose "Web Content"; then click the button to "Use ColorSync™."

DigitalColor Meter

Use the **DigitalColor Meter** to get the hexadecimal colors of any item on your screen, or the actual RGB values, or the percentage values of red, green, and blue. If you have certain Apple monitors, the DigitalColor Meter can translate the RGB values to CIE, LAB, and Tristimulus.

Open the DigitalColor Meter and move your mouse around. The bigger window on the left will display an enlarged view of whatever your mouse is positioned over, and the exact pixel color will appear in the little window to the right. To move the measurement aperture (the tiny square inside the larger window) one pixel at a time, use the arrow keys. To "hold" a particular color in the little window so you can move your mouse somewhere else, get the color you want, then press Command Shift H. Press the keyboard shortcut again to release the hold.

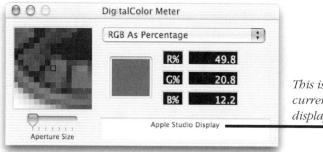

This is the name of the current profile being displayed on your monitor.

OTHER UTILITIES

Disk Copy

Disk Copy

Disk Copy is a utility that will open itself up and do what it needs to do when it needs to; you don't have to go get it. Disk Copy works with "disk images," which are like pretend hard disks that store compressed data. Disk images typically have an extension of **.img** or **.dmg**—double-click one and it will open Disk Copy, extract itself, and create an icon of a disk on your Mac, from which you can install files. See Chapter 21 for information on disk images and how to work with them. You can also use Disk Copy to create your own disk images, a convenient way to store or share files.

Files with the extension of **.smi** are also disk images, but they are "self-mounting" and don't need to use Disk Copy.

Installer

Installer

The **Installer** is another utility that does what it needs to do without you asking it. Whenever you install new software, Installer will take care of the process for you, then quietly disappear.

Grab is a utility that lets you take pictures of what is visible on your monitor, called **screen shots.** This book is filled with thousands of screen shots. If you're a teacher, it's great to include screen shots in your handouts. If you're having trouble with something, you can send a screen shot to your favorite tech support person so they have a clearer idea of the problem. You can even use the Grab service to take a quick screen shot and drop it into an email or a TextEdit document.

Grab

Grab

Note: Grab is the only screen shot utility that let me take screen shots of Classic while running OS X.

To use Grab:

1. Double-click the Grab icon to open it.

2. To capture the **entire screen,** press Command Z.

   To capture a **selected portion** of the screen, press Command Shift A. You'll get a pointer as shown below; press-and-drag to select the area you want to capture.

This is what the pointer looks like as you start to grab a portion of the screen.

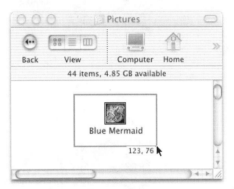

When you let go, the new file will open instantly in Grab, waiting for you to save it.

With the Command-Shift-A procedure above, you cannot grab the **pointer** nor can you grab **active windows** — the windows are always in the background. You can't get **pop-up menus,** either. So to get one of these items, press Command Shift Z; you'll get the message shown below, the "Timed Screen Grab." Hit Return to activate it, then go to the window, pop-up menu, dialog box, etc., that you want a screen shot of, put everything in position, and hold it until the timer goes off. The screen shot will open instantly in Grab.

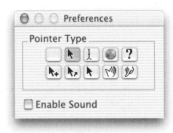

If you need the pointer to show where you've positioned it, or if you want to make sure it doesn't, go to the Grab menu and choose "Preferences..." to get this dialog box. Choose the pointer that you want to appear in the screen shot, then close the box.

Key Caps

Key Caps

You are probably accustomed to the two main keyboard layouts on your Mac, the regular lowercase letters and numbers, and the capital letters and symbols that appear when you hold down the Shift key. But you actually have two more keyboard layouts that give you lots of extra characters, including dozens of accented letters. To find them, use **Key Caps.**

Double-click Key Caps to open it. Once it's open, you have a Font menu from which you can select any font to see the characters it contains. Choose a font, then follow along with the examples shown below.

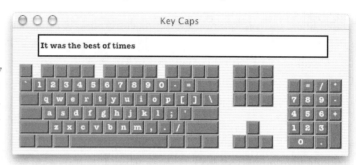

*This is the regular key layout you have when **no keys** are pressed down. You already know this.*

*When the **Shift key** is down, as shown circled, you get the capital letters and the symbols above the numbers. You already know this.*

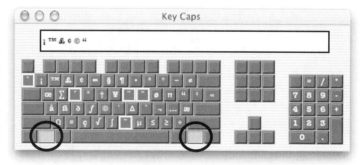

*When the **Option key** is down, as shown circled, you get access to a hidden keyboard. To type these characters, hold down the Option key and press the character key. It's just like using the Shift key to get capital letters or the symbols above the numbers.*

The white boxes around some characters indicate they contain two-step accent marks. For instance, if you press Option e, let go, then press the letter e, you get é. See the chart in Appendix B.

To type the following symbols:

™	Option 2
£	Option 3 (which is also the pound symbol)
¢	Option 4 (which is also the dollar sign)
©	Option G

Hold down both the Shift and Option keys together and you get still another keyboard layout with more characters to choose from.

See the chart in Appendix B.

For instance, to type the following symbols:

±	Option Shift =
Ø	Option Shift O
Ç	Option Shift C
»	Option Shift \ (« is Option \)

*Key Caps is especially useful for fonts that contain **ornaments, dingbats, and special characters.*** *Above you see one of the four key layouts for Bodoni Ornaments.*

You can either type the ornaments you want right into Key Caps, then copy and paste them into your document. Or you can use Key Caps to figure out which combinations of keys creates the character you need, then select the font and type that combination directly in your document.

It's really a pity the Key Caps window does not enlarge.

Keychain Access

Keychain Access

Keychain Access provides a secure place to store information that can only be accessed with a user name and password. Use Keychains to safely store passwords for applications, and passwords to access secure servers or certain web sites. You can also use Keychains for storage of credit card numbers, PINS (Personal Information Numbers used by bank cards and phone cards), or other brief information that you don't want accessible to anyone else.

Keychain Access has been around for awhile, but many of us ignored it, not realizing how useful it can be. Now that Mac OS X automatically creates a Keychain account for you, this is a good time to learn more about it.

Your Keychain account

When you set up Mac OS X and assigned yourself a user name and password, that same information was used to create a **Keychain account for you.** This assures that your Keychain will unlock automatically when you log in. If you're the only user on your computer, Keychain has been working in the background even though you weren't aware of it.

You (and any other users set up on your computer) can set up as many Keychain accounts as you need. You might want one Keychain for work-related passwords, another for online shopping passwords, and another for personal information.

Keychain gives you a secure place to store small amounts of information, like **credit card numbers.** Keychain is not going to enter your card number for you while you shop, but you can keep a list of your card numbers in a locked Keychain account, which is much safer than keeping a list on a Stickie or in a TextEdit document.

Have you collected quite a few **passwords** over the years? Like one for your online banking, another for your teenagers' credit cards, rare book sites, PayPal, PhotoDisc, Amazon, Barnes&Noble, beta software sites, online catalogs, research sites, your Apple Store account, several different email accounts, etc., etc., etc. Make a Keychain account just to store all of your passwords so they are safe and secure, yet you can find out what they are whenever necessary.

Select a Keychain in the drawer on the right to show a list of all the Password Items in that Keychain.

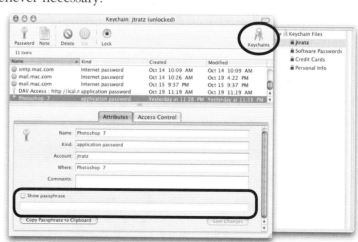

Click the Keychain icon to open the Keychain drawer.

To show an item's password in this box, select "Show passphrase," then enter the Keychain's password in the dialog box that opens.

If an application is "password aware," such as your email client, Keychain can store that information and actually enter your password for you. One **example** of an application that uses a password is Mail, Apple's email client that comes with Mac OS X. In the illustration below, "jtratz" is the default Keychain for my partner John, but it's locked. When John tries to get mail, the "Unlock Keychain" dialog box opens and requests the Keychain password so it can be unlocked.

An example

Once the Keychain is unlocked, all the passwords stored in it are available to the applications that need them, so you won't have to repeat this process over and over. You can, however, set a preference (explained on page 516) that tells Keychain to automatically lock everything again after a certain period of time.

Keychains are **secure** because they're locked. When an application needs the password information that's stored in a locked keychain, as shown above, it asks for your permission and the password. You can either deny permission or you can type in the password and choose to grant permission "one time only" or "always." This gives the application access to the password so it can function normally.

Security

The default Keychain that was automatically created when you set yourself up as a user in Mac OS X uses the same user and password information so that it automatically unlocks when you log in. If you're the only user on your computer, your default Keychain unlocks when you start your computer; if you create other accounts, they are not unlocked automatically. A locked Keychain is, in effect, turned off; an unlocked keychain is turned on.

—continued

Basic Keychain tasks

Keychain Access

Below are the **basic tasks** to get you started using Keychain. You can create as many Keychain files as you need.

To locate and open the Keychain Access application:

Click the "Applications" icon in the Toolbar (or press Command Option A) to open the Applications window. Then double-click the Utilities icon to open its window, then double-click the Keychain Access icon.

To create a new Keychain file:

1. Open Keychain as described above. Then from the File menu choose "New," then choose "New Keychain…."

2. In the New Keychain window that opens, enter a descriptive name for the new Keychain, select a location in which to save it, then click "Create…."

3. When the "New Keychain Passphrase" dialog box opens, enter a password for the new Keychain, then click OK.

4. The new Keychain now appears in the Keychain drawer (click the Keychain icon to open the drawer and see all Keychains). The next step is to add Password Items to the new Keychain.

Tip: Keychain Access sets up your initial Keychain file, the one based on your user name and password, as the default keychain. This default keychain is automatically opened when you start up your Mac or log on.

To make other Keychains more secure, such as your list of credit card numbers or banking passwords, be sure to make *new* Keychain files for these instead of *adding* them to your default file.

To add a new Password Item to this Keychain, click the Password icon in the toolbar.

To add a new Secure Note item, click the Note icon in the toolbar.

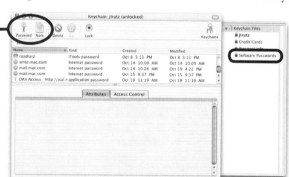

The new Keychain, ready for you to add password items.

To manually add a new password item to a Keychain:

1. Open Keychain (it's in the Utilities folder, which is in the Applications folder).

2. Open the Keychain drawer and select the Keychain to which you want to add a password item.

3. From the File menu choose "New," then choose "New Password Item…" or "New Secure Note…." You can also click the Password icon or the Note icon in the Keychain window toolbar.

*A **Password Item** can be a password, a software registration number, or any other short information.*

*A password item can also be a **Secure Note**: more lengthy information that requires a larger text field, such as a confidential contract that you want to store on your computer.*

4. In the "New Password Item" dialog box, enter a descriptive name for the password item in the "Name" field, a name that will remind you what it is.

5. Enter an account name associated with this password, if there is one, in the "Account" field. For instance, at Amazon.com you have an account name, plus a password. Enter that account name here (not the Keychain account name!). This is sometimes called the User ID. If there is no account name associated with the information you're entering (such as your bike lock combination), enter your user name.

6. Enter the password, registration number, or other type of information you want to make secure in the "Passphrase" field. In this example I entered the registration number for Photoshop.

   The password is displayed as bullets (round dots) unless you check the "Show Typing" checkbox. Check "Show Typing" to see the characters as you type and to proofread the password.

7. Click the "Add" button to add the new password item to the current Keychain file. If the Keychain file to which you're adding an item is locked, enter the password for the associated Keychain in the "Unlock Keychain" dialog box that appears.

Tip: If you make a number of Keychain files, you're going to have more passwords to remember! You can make a Keychain file to store all of your Keychain passwords. Then you must remember that one password.

—continued

To automatically add a new password item to a Keychain:

When you try to access a keychain-aware application, a password-protected server (such as an FTP server, shown below) or a secure web site, see if there is an "Options..." button where you can choose to "Add Password to Keychain." If you do add the account name and password information this one time, then next time you access the same server, or application, Keychain will automatically grant access unless the Keychain is locked at the time (see details of locking and unlocking keychains on the opposite page).

When connecting to a server, type in the account name and password, then click the "Options..." button to get the dialog box shown below. If you add the password to Keychain, the next time you go to this server you'll never even see the password dialog box—you'll just get right in.

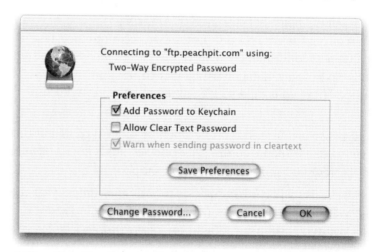

"Allow Clear Text Password" shows the password in less secure (but readable) text rather than encrypted as dots.

"Warn when sending password in cleartext" alerts you that your Clear Text password will be sent in an insecure manner. Make your choices, then click OK.

To see a list of your Keychains, open Keychain Access, then click the Keychain icon in the top-right corner of the window to open the drawer. The drawer contains a list of all Keychains. (See page 466.)

To open a specific Keychain file in a list, click on it in the Keychain drawer.

To take a Keychain file to another computer, copy it from the Keychains folder, which is in your Library folder, which is in your Home folder.

To add a Keychain that you brought to your computer from another Mac, open Keychain Access, then from the File menu choose "Add Keychain." In the standard Open dialog that appears, navigate to the folder where you stored the Keychain file. Select the file, then click "Open."

To lock a Keychain: Even though your default Keychain opens automatically when you start your computer or when you log in, you can lock it (or any other Keychain) whenever you want extra security. Click the "Lock" button in the Keychain window's toolbar to lock it.

To unlock a Keychain: Select a locked Keychain in the drawer, the click the "Unlock" button in the toolbar to open the "Unlock Keychain" window. Type the Keychain's password in the "Password or phrase" field, then click OK.

Client passwords
This is what a Keychain file looks like in the Keychain folder.

If a Keychain file is locked when you try to access a password-enabled item, Keychain opens the "Confirm Access to Keychain" window. Choose if you want to "Deny" access, "Allow Once," or "Always Allow." The "Allow Once" option grants access this one time, then presents these same options next time. "Always Allow" grants access every time.

—continued

Access Control: In this area you can set different levels of security.

Always allow access to this item: Refers to whether applications will have access to the secure information in the Keychain without showing the "Unlock Keychain" window (page 467). If you uncheck this option, every password-aware application will open an "Unlock Keychain" window to get authorization from you.

Confirm before allowing access: If you select this, you decrease the risk of a computer virus or some other cracker software retrieving your passwords.

Ask for Keychain password: Force Keychain to ask for a password, even if the Keychain is unlocked.

Always allow access by these applications: Limit access to certain applications that you know and trust.

To add an application to the trusted list, click **Add**. In the "Open" window that drops down, navigate to an application, select it, then click "Open."

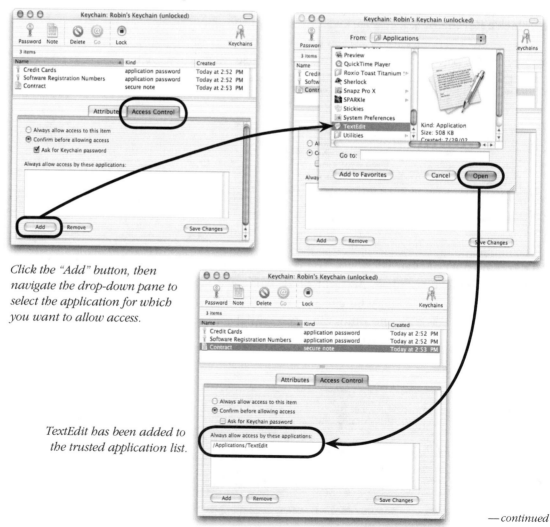

Click the "Add" button, then navigate the drop-down pane to select the application for which you want to allow access.

TextEdit has been added to the trusted application list.

—continued

You can change some of the **Keychain settings** in the "Change Settings" dialog. To get to the settings, select a Keychain in the drawer, then from the Edit menu choose "*Keychain'* Settings." The actual name of your selected Keychain will appear in place of the word "Keychain."

Keychain settings

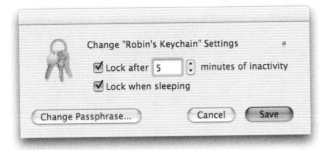

Lock after: Check this box to lock the Keychain after a specified time period. This helps to prevent you from accidently leaving privileged information unlocked and available.

Lock when sleeping: Check this box for extra security. If you've walked away from your computer long enough for it to sleep, you may want to make sure your Keychains are secure.

Change Passphrase: Click this to change the Keychain's password or passphrase. Don't change the passphrase if this is a Keychain that you want to open automatically when you log in as a user or when you start your computer. If you change the password to one that's different from your Mac OS X password, the Keychain will not open automatically when start your computer.

ODBC Administrator

ODBC Administrator

ODBC (Open Database Connectivity) is an open standard API (application programming interface) for accessing databases. ODBC enables you to access files in various databases, including Access, dBase, DB2, Excel, and others. A separate driver is needed for each database you access. This utility is for specially skilled database administrators, not for most of us.

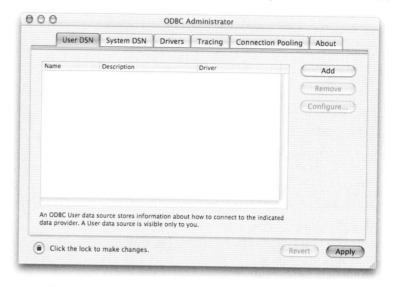

Bluetooth

Bluetooth File Exchange

Bluetooth is a globally compatible specification that enables mobile phones, computers, handheld devices, and (coming soon) even home appliances to communicate wirelessly with each other. A Bluetooth-enabled device contains a transceiver chip (either built-in or as a plug-in module) that transmits and receives data within a range of about 30 feet. A lot of things are planned for Bluetooth, but for now you can wirelessly communicate between two computers, your computer and a handheld device such as a Palm Pilot or iPod, or with a compatible mobile phone. Bluetooth automatically discovers other devices that are within range.

The **Bluetooth File Exchange** utility is the software that enables the discovery and connection of other Bluetooth devices.

To enable Bluetooth, you must plug in a Bluetooth USB Adapter to an available port on your computer. One such adapter is the D-Link DWB-120M USB Bluetooth Adapter (check **www.apple.com** for current information about available adapters). From the Bluetooth menu choose "Preferences..." to set up devices that are discovered within range. Select a device from the list of in-range devices, then click the "Pair" button to connect.

Due to Bluetooth's low bandwidth (2.4 GHz), Apple recommends AirPort wireless networking over Bluetooth for only the smallest of files. Bluetooth is ideal to perform a HotSync operation with your handheld, to send vCards and vCalendars (iCal), or to send small photos and iCards.

The **Print Center** manages printing your files. You can add printers to your list, start and stop printing, put files in a queue for printing later, delete files from the queue so they won't print at all, and more. The Print Center is explained at length in Chapter 15.

Print Center

Print Center

StuffIt Expander works all by itself to uncompress (unstuff) .sit files, as well as a number of other compressed file formats. You rarely have to open it yourself—just double-click a compressed file, StuffIt Expander will open and unstuff the file, and then put itself away. Anytime you like, however, you can drag a compressed file onto the StuffIt Expander icon to unstuff it. I keep it in my Dock so I can drag files onto it whenever necessary.

StuffIt Expander

StuffIt Expander

If you have peripheral audio devices connected to your computer, such as external speakers or a MIDI keyboard, use **Audio MIDI Setup** to set the default input and output devices, choose format settings for audio, add external MIDI devices, and set various controls for managing MIDI equipment and connections.

Audio MIDI Setup

Audio MIDI Setup

OTHER STUFF   There are several other useful features of your Mac that don't fall into the applications or utilities category.

Battery   If you're using a laptop, the **Battery** icon will appear in the upper-right of your menu bar to show you either how much time in hours and minutes you have left, or what percentage of your battery is left. If you don't have the battery icon in the menu bar, go to the Energy Saver preferences and check the box to turn it on.

Screen Shots   As you might have read on page 463, you can take **screen shots** with Grab. But there are lots of times you just want a quick snapshot, in which case you can use one of the tricks listed below. The pointer will not appear in the shot, though, which might or might not be an issue in a particular shot.

Each time you take a screen shot you'll hear the sound of a camera shutter snapping, and an icon will appear on your Desktop called Picture 1. As you create more shots, the files will be named Picture 2, Picture 3, etc.

Double-click any screen shot to open it in Preview. Drag any screen shot to a Photoshop icon to open it in Photoshop.

▼ **To take a screen shot of the entire screen,** press Command Shift 3.

▼ To get a crosshair cursor to take a screen shot of **just a portion of the screen,** press Command Shift 4. Drag over an area.

▼ **To take a screen shot of a selected item,** such as an open window, an icon, or the Desktop, press Command Shift 4, then press the Spacebar. The pointer turns into a camera icon that highlights items beneath it. When the item you want to shoot is hightlighted, click the mouse.

▼ To take a screen shot that will go **straight to the Clipboard** (it will not make a Picture file) so you can then just paste it directly into a document or into something like a Photoshop file. Press Command Shift 4 to get the crosshair, hold down the Control key. Drag over an area. You'll hear a much smaller snapping sound.

Go to your document. If it's a text document, click the insertion point where you want the graphic to paste in. Then press Command V to paste the screen shot onto the page.

Get Info is a small window that gives you pertinent information about any selected file. The kind of information you get depends on what type of file is selected, as shown below and on the following pages.

Get Info

Get **general information** about any file. **Lock** a file (if you have the privileges to do so). Locking a file prevents accidental changes. No one can print a locked file.

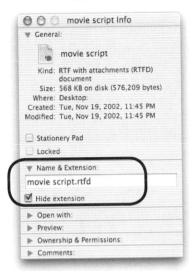

Rename a file. Hide or show the **file name extension** (depends on the setting in Finder preferences). Notice if you hide the extension, it hides it from the name at the top and in your windows, but the "Name and Extension" still holds onto the extension because it is just hidden from public view, not gone.

- ▼ **To open Get Info:** Select any icon, then press Command I. The Get Info window will display information for that one item.

- ▼ **To open Show Inspector:** Press Command Option I. As you click on icons, the information in the Inspector window will change.

- ▼ **Tip:** You can select more than one item, then open Get Info or Show Inspector.

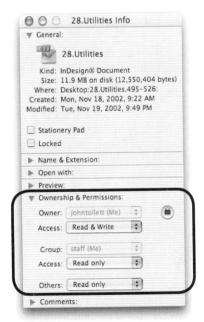

Change the **ownership & permissions,** if you have the privileges to do so. See Chapter 34 for details on sharing privileges.

Tell **Carbon applications** to open in the Classic environment. A Carbon application is one that will work in both Mac OS 9 and OS X.

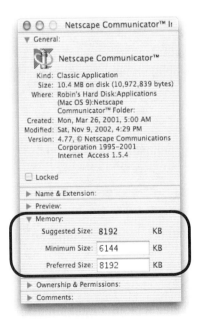

Allocate more memory to a Classic application. See Chapter 39 for more details.

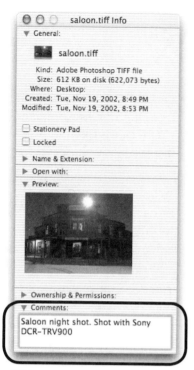

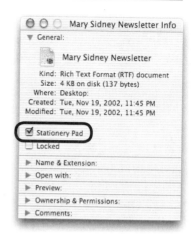

*Change the picture of the **icon:** in a Mac OS X graphics application, copy the image you want to use as the icon for this file. Click on the existing icon in this window; paste.*

Turn a document into a stationery template. See page 231.

*Write **comments** in the Comments box. You can choose to display your comments in the Finder windows: use the View Options (see pages 89–90).*

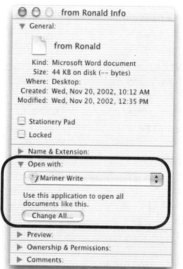

*One of the most important things you can do with the Info window is **assign an application** to open certain file formats. For instance, let's say you keep a Microsoft-free environment, but people often send you Microsoft Word files, which end in an extension of .doc. Using the Info window, you can choose that every .doc file you get will open in Mariner Write (your favorite word processor) instead of looking for Microsoft Word. To do that: Get Info on a .doc file. Click the "Open with" disclosure triangle and from the pop-up menu choose your preferred application. To have all .doc files open with the selected application, click the "Change All…" button.*

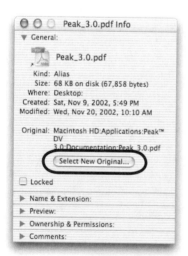

*Select a **new original** for an alias. See Chapter 23 about aliases.*

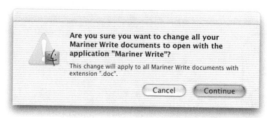

The "Change All…" button opens an alert, which gives you the message shown above. If you're sure, click the "Continue" button.

You can always override this global specification on a per-document basis.

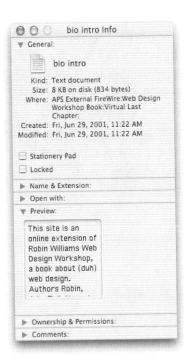

Preview some text documents, PDFs, most images, and most movies right here in the Info window.

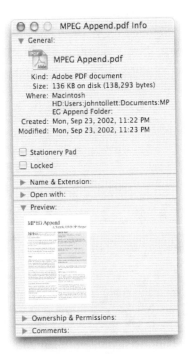

Preview single page PDF files. The preview of a multiple-page PDF file shows the Adobe PDF icon.

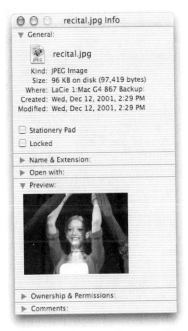

Preview an image file, even if the icon is a generic, such as the JPEG icon above.

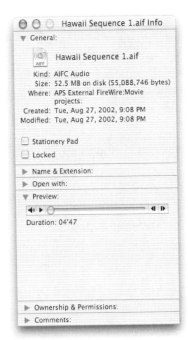

Preview an audio file right here in the Info window. Click the "Play" button (the small black triangle) to hear the file play.

Click the "Play" button to play a movie in the Get Info window.

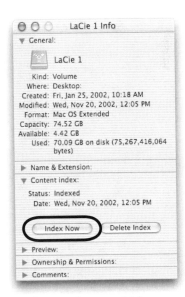

Index *a volume or folder, or delete its index.*

Spelling Checker

Like the *Colors Palette* and *Find and Replace* (explained on the following pages), you'll find the same **Spelling Checker** in a number of Mac OS X applications, including TextEdit, Stickies, and Mail, as well as other applications that follow the Mac OS X specs, such as the great applications from Stone Design (www.stone.com) and OmniGroup (www.omnigroup.com).

To check the spelling in a document or email message, from the Edit menu, choose "Spelling," then choose "Check Spelling..." to open the Spelling window, as shown below.

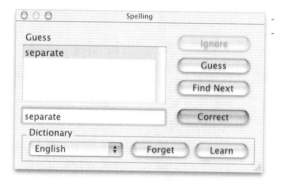

Click the **Find Next** button to find misspelled words.

When an application finds a word it doesn't recognize, the word is highlighted in the document and shown in the text field of the Spelling pane, as you see above. Suggested spellings are listed in the **Guess** pane.

If one of the guesses looks correct, double-click the guess to replace the misspelled word. Or, you can select the correct spelling in the "Guess" pane, then click the **Correct** button.

If the application finds a misspelled word but can't guess the correct spelling, **type** the correct spelling. Now, you have to be careful here and be very conscious of whether the Spelling Checker window is active or your document window—whichever one is **active** is the one where the spelling will be corrected. If the word gets corrected in the document itself, that's fine. If it's corrected in the Spelling Checker window, then click the "Correct" button to make the correction. This might not make sense until you actually use the Spelling Checker.

Often, even though words are not misspelled, they're not recognized by an application because they're not included in the Spelling Checker's built-in dictionary. When an application finds such a word, either click the **Ignore** button, or, add the word to the dictionary: Click in the text field that contains the unrecognized word, then click the **Learn** button.

If you've added a misspelled word to the dictionary by mistake, remove it by entering the word in the text field, then click **Forget.**

Find and Replace

Like the *Spelling Checker* and the *Colors Palette,* **Find and Replace** is a Mac OS X feature that is accessible through a number of applications. You can find a word, any occurrence that includes a part of a word, or find a certain word or phrase and replace it with another. Knowing how to use Find and Replace can help speed up your work; for instance, if you often have to type something like "Santa Fe Community College," you can type "sf" instead, then when you're finished with the report, search for "sf" and replace it with the longer phrase.

To open the "Find Panel," from the Edit menu choose "Find," then choose "Find Panel...."

Find: Search a document or email message for a specific word or phrase. Leave the "Replace with" field empty if you just want to *find* the phrase.

> **Find Options:** Check "Ignore Case" to search without considering if uppercase or lowercase letters are used. This ensures that you find all occurrences of a word, whether they're capitalized or not.
>
> If you want to restrict the search to find occurrences that are "case sensitive" and match exactly your search term, capital letters as typed, uncheck "Ignore Case."

Replace with: Enter text you're searching for in the "Find" text field. In the "Replace With" field, enter the text which will replace found text.

> **Replace All Scope:** Choose "Entire File" to search the entire document or email message. If you selected text *before* you opened the Find Panel, you can choose to search just that "Selection."

Buttons: When your fields are filled in and your Scope and Options chosen, click one of the buttons along the bottom of the Find Panel.

> **Replace All:** This immediately finds all occurrences of your phrase in the entire document and replaces each with the replacement text.
>
> If you prefer to make changes more slowly so you can see each one and make a decision on it, click the **Next** button to find the next occurrence of your text, then click the **Replace** button to change only the current selection.
>
> **Replace & Find:** This replaces the found text, then immediately finds the next occurrence.
>
> To find the previous unchanged occurrence that you skipped over, click the **Previous** button.

Colors Palette

The **Colors Palette** is a simple yet powerful feature. Many applications written specifically for Mac OS X call on this Color Palette whenever you want to change the color of your font, as in TextEdit or Mail, or graphic objects in certain applications (the background of your Finder windows uses a Color Picker which is a little different).

The Colors Palette **toolbar** at the top contains five different color selection tools, which are described below. Click each one to see the various modes of color you can work with.

The Colors Palette also contains these tools:

▼ Beneath the toolbar is a **color box** where the color you create will appear.

▼ Drag the **magnifying glass** anywhere on your screen, then click when the crosshairs of the glass are on top of a color you want to select. The color will appear in the color box.

▼ To save a color for later use, drag the color from the color box to one of the wells in the small **color swatch collection,** located at the bottom of the Colors palette.

▼ When you've found a color you like, click it to apply it to the selected text or object in your document.

Color Wheel: Select a color by clicking or dragging the cursor in the Colors Palette's color wheel. As you move the cursor around the Color Wheel, the color swatch in the bottom-left corner changes.

You can also adjust the value (the lightness or darkness) of the selected color by sliding the vertical slider next to the color wheel.

Image Palettes: You can use the built-in "Spectrum" palette, or select an image from your computer to use as a color palette. Click the "Palette" pop-down menu, then choose "New from File...." Navigate to an image on your computer, then click the "Open" button to display the image. Drag the mouse over any area of the image to select a color from the image. This is a good way to get an exact match of a color for another project.

The "Spectrum" palette name shown in the pop-down menu changes to the name of the image that you select.

Color Sliders: Choose colors from four different standard color spaces: Gray-scale, RGB, CMYK, and HSB. A one-color book like this one uses grayscale. For email, the web, and on the screen, RGB is the preferred color space. For high-quality printing on expensive printing presses, CMYK is the standard. HSB is based on the human perceptions of color, with hue (the color itself), saturation (how deep and true that color is), and brightness (how much white is added to it). It's easier to create a color in HSB than in RGB, so you can create a color in HSB, then click the RGB palette to see how it translated and to actually choose the color (in RGB you're working with colors of light, so red and green make yellow, which can make you crazy). If you know the numeric color values, you can enter those in the boxes of any palette.

To select colors from a palette of Crayons, click the Crayons icon.

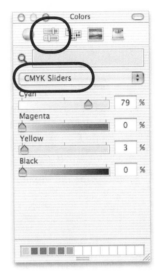
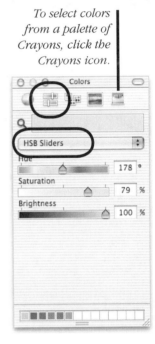

Color Palettes: Choose from a palette of Apple, Developer, or Crayon color swatches, open other palettes you may have, or make your own. **To make your own palette,** click on the "List" pop-up menu and choose "New." Give it a name. Then go to the other color tools, create colors, and put them in the swatch collection. Go back to your new palette and drag each color from the swatch collection into the main palette window. Then click on a color in your palette list, go down to the Color pop-up menu, and choose "Rename…" to give your color a memorable name. To change the name of your new palette from the default name "Unnamed1," to something more descriptive, go back to the "List" menu and choose "Rename…."

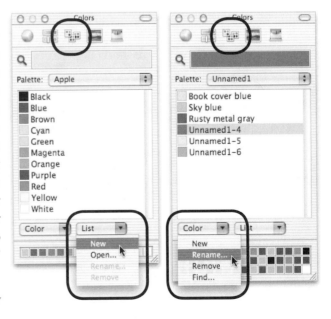

Your custom palette will be available in every application that uses these Mac OS X services.

Name the utility that could accomplish each task listed below.

1. Assign an application to open certain file formats. For instance, assign Photoshop to open all .tif files.

2. Find out who owns an Internet domain name.

3. Log in as the root user.

4. Find the flower ornament in a special font, or the © symbol in any font.

5. Check for and repair problems on a disk.

6. Find out what kind of processor is in your Mac, the speed of your Mac, and the serial number.

7. Take screen shots of what you see on your monitor.

8. Safely store passwords, credit card numbers, bicycle lock numbers, FTP logon account names and passwords, and other important bits of information.

9. Preview a movie file without opening an application.

10. Erase a disk.

Answers on page 732.

What is the Internet?

This chapter explains what the **Internet** is and how the **World Wide Web** is *part* of the Internet. It explains the difference between America Online and the World Wide Web and how they are related. This chapter also clears up a lot of the jargon you probably hear all the time, such as modem, browser, newsgroup, dial up, etc.

Contents of this chapter

The Internet

The **Internet** is a system of computers all over the world that are linked together using phone lines or other sorts of wires or satellites. This linking together of computers is called a "network." It was created by the United States government's Advanced Research Projects Agency (ARPA) in response to the Soviet's Sputnik proj ect. The government wanted to encourage scientists in academic, military, and research institutions to work together to catch up to the Soviet's advances in science. The scientists demanded computers, which were enormously expensive at the time, and ARPA realized they would need fewer computers if the machines were connected by means of a network. So Dr. Leonard Kleinrock and his team established the first ARPANET communication link in September of 1969.

This connectivity now lets regular people like you and me send messages all over the world. The messages bounce from one computer to another along the network until they reach their destination. If one of the computers along the route is down, the message just finds another route.

Modems

Your computer receives these messages through some sort of intermediary **modem,** a piece of hardware that translates the signals coming through the wires into information that your Mac can use.

There are different modems depending on how you connect to the Internet. For instance, you might use the internal modem in your Mac, which is designed to plug into a **phone** jack or telephone in your house. Information goes from your computer, through the modem, over the phone lines to the Internet, and comes back in the same way. This kind of connection is called a **dial up** because the modem dials a phone number to *log on,* or connect to the Internet, and when you are finished with your business online, you *log off,* or hang up. One person at a time can connect through a dial-up account.

Or you might have a box sitting outside of your computer that connects your Mac to a **television** cable, or to a **DSL** line (Digital Subscriber Line, IDSL or ADSL), **ISDN** line, a **T1** or **T3** line, or a **satellite** dish. These connections do not dial up—they are considered *permanent,* or *always on* connections, also known as *broadband.* All of these options are significantly faster than a phone connection, and generally cost from a little more to a lot more. A whole bunch of computers can connect to the Internet at the same time through a broadband connection.

Although the technology is different in each type of modem, they are similar in that **every modem** must translate the information that comes through the cable, say a television signal through a TV cable, into Internet "packets" that your Mac can understand. And the information from your Mac must be translated into a form that the connection cables can understand so they can send it out.

Let's look at a **very simplified version** of how a Mac sends and receives signals through a phone modem, like the one that is built into your Mac. Your computer is *digital,* meaning it can only work with countable, finite information, like ice cubes. The phone lines are *analog,* meaning they can only work with information that is flowing and infinite, like water. So the computer sends the digital info (ice cubes) to the modem, which translates the digital info into analog info (water) so it can be sent over the phone lines. The modem on the other end takes the analog info (water) and turns it back into digital info (ice cubes) so the computer on the other end can understand and use it.

Different types of **connections** process information through to your computer at different **speeds,** which indicate how much information can be sent at a time. The faster the speed, the more "ice cubes" can be translated into "water" and sent through the lines. Below is a chart of the most common speeds at the moment. This will also change, of course.

Connection speeds

The abbreviation **bps** stands for bits per second, and **Mbps** is megabits per second. The **k** stands for kilo, which basically means a thousand. You don't need to worry about exactly how much a bit per second is—just understand that the more, the better.

modem	speed	say it	write it		how is it
phone	2400 bps	twenty-four hundred	2.4	2400	slo-o-o-o-w
	9600	ninety-six hundred	9.6	9600	not much better
	14,400	fourteen-four	14.4		frustratingly slow for the Internet
	28,800	twenty-eight eight	28.8		faster; the Internet is do-able at this speed
	33,600	thirty-three six	33.6		okay for home
	56,000	fifty-six k	56k		very common now for home
IDSL	128,000 bps	one twenty-eight	128k		lower end of DSL, but it's great
ADSL	128,000 to 2,500,000	one twenty-eight k to two point five megabits	128k to 2.5 Mbps		higher end of DSL, really great
cable	1,000,000 bps	one megabit	1 Mbps		cable has a fast download, but uploads are at telephone modem speed
T1	1,540,000 bps	one point fifty-four megabits	1.54 Mbps		generally too expensive for home
T3	45,000,000 bps	45 megabits	45 Mbps		way expensive

Email

For over thirty years people have been using the Internet to send **email,** which is a message typed on a computer and sent over the wires to another computer. The "e" in email stands for "electronic." One of the first things most people use the Internet for is to send and receive email. With all the things we can do on computers, it seems to have evolved that our favorite thing to do is to communicate with other human beings. Far from being an isolating medium, the computer and the Internet have helped develop millions of new relationships between people.

Newsgroups

Another original feature of the Internet is **newsgroups,** which are sort of like online clubs. Each newsgroup is a collection of people with a common interest, such as golf, the Shakespearean authorship question, llama breeding, Zoroastrianism, cancer, Esperanto, children with brain tumors, Wicca, and over 60,000 other topics. Members of newsgroups "post" ongoing discussions on a public "bulletin board," which is similar in concept to tacking notes on a cork bulletin board in the lounge. Whenever you like, you can pop in to the newsgroup, read the messages, and post your own response, question, or opinion. This is a wonderful resource for information about a topic important to you. These groups often form strong communities, since they are people bonded together with a common interest. Go to www.google.com and click "Groups." (I'll tell you how to "go" there in Chapter 31.)

Mailing lists

Mailing lists, or **listservs** (yes, "listserv" is spelled correctly) are another popular feature of the Internet. A listserv is similar to a newsgroup in that it is a collection of people who want to discuss a common interest, but instead of posting messages on a bulletin board, they send email. Piles of email. When anyone sends an email message to the mailing list, it goes to every single person on the list. There are about 49,000 different mailing lists. Go to www.lsoft.com/catalist.html. (I'll tell you how to "go" there in Chapter 31.)

So why does the Internet seem new?

So with all this going on for so many years, why is it that the Internet seems like a fairly new thing? Because all those years the "interface" for the Internet, the way it looked and how you used it, had been pretty ugly and geeky. Only nerds were attracted to it. (Now, don't be offended; "nerd" is not a pejorative term—I'm a nerdette myself. A nerdette in high heels and a hat.) Getting on the Internet was very DOS-like, with command lines and backslashes and codes, and a typical computer monitor displayed yellow text on a black background, monospaced and ugly. No pictures and no music and no color. Then a miraculous event occurred.

The Macintosh was invented.

Now, it's not part of official Internet history, but I do personally believe the World Wide Web would not have happened if the Macintosh computer had not been invented. It was the Mac that changed computing. For the first time, we had a monitor capable of displaying professional type, and it was black type on a white background, so much easier to read. We became accustomed to color, graphics, sound, animation, beautiful text, etc. Microsoft, of course, "borrowed" this technology and soon other computers were able to act (albeit clumsily) like Macintoshes.

As Steve Wozniak, one of the inventors of the Macintosh, says, "Today, essentially every computer is a Macintosh."

This new expectation of computers—graphical and colorful—paved the way for the invention of new software in 1993 that allowed full "pages" to be sent over the Internet and displayed on a computer screen. These pages could have color, graphics, sound, animation, beautiful text, etc. Finally the Internet started to look like something regular people would be interested in. This is the **World Wide Web,** and those pages are called **web pages.** The World Wide Web is a collection of billions of individual web pages displaying text, graphics, sound, and more.

A collection of related web pages about one topic—say, for instance, about your worm farm—is a **web site.** A web site is like a book in that there may be several parts to it, like chapters, and there is a "table of contents" that shows you the organization of the book. On a web site, this table of contents page is called the **home page.** You'll return over and over again to the home page; it's sort of like home base.

So the World Wide Web, then, is one more facet of the Internet. The Internet is sort of like the electrical wiring in your house: the same wiring goes all through your house, but you can use it to do different things, like turn on light bulbs, run a computer, wash your clothes, and power your TV. The Internet network runs all over the world, and you can use it to send email, join newsgroups, discuss matters on a listserv, view web pages, pay your bills, watch video, hear music, and more. Wow.

I don't capitalize the word "web" because in English we don't capitalize any other form of communication, such as television, telephone, or radio.

Web Browsers

Internet Explorer

OmniWeb

Netscape

To see web pages, you need special software that can display them. It's just like anything else on your Mac—if you want to crunch a bunch of numbers, you need spreadsheet software; if you want to write a letter, you need a word processor; **if you want to view web pages, you need a browser.** A browser is simply the software that displays web pages.

Along with your Mac operating system software you got a browser, called Microsoft Internet Explorer. It's not the only browser in the world, though, and some people to use another.

Internet Explorer has an icon in the Dock, as shown to the left, and its application is in the "Applications" folder.

OmniWeb is a great browser that is not included with your Mac, but you can "download" it (copy to your computer) and install it. When you're ready, see Chapter 21 about how to download and install.

Netscape is another great browser. When you're ready, go to www.netscape.com and "download" and install it.

And there are other browsers. For instance, when you use America Online (explained on the following pages), you can view web pages through America Online's special browser, which at the moment is a version of Internet Explorer. There are quite a few browsers, each with loyal fans. You can keep as many browsers as you like on your hard disk. You can switch between them as often as you like. They each display web pages a little differently, and they each have their own special features. I'll show you how to actually use them in the next chapter.

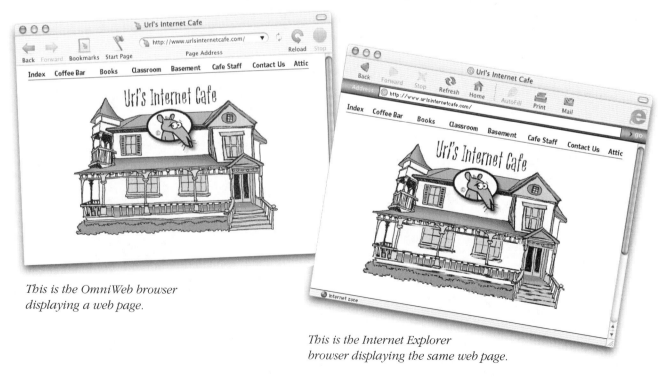

This is the OmniWeb browser displaying a web page.

This is the Internet Explorer browser displaying the same web page.

So how do you get to the Internet and the World Wide Web? You need a computer, a modem, a browser, and an **Internet Service Provider.**

You see, there are many thousands of special computers around the world hooked into the Internet 24 hours a day that act as "nodes," or connection points, that redistribute Internet connections to people like you and me. These companies are Internet Service Providers, or ISPs. From your home or business, you need to pay a provider to provide you with a connection to the Internet. You pay them; they give you any necessary software, instructions for connecting, and if necessary (for phone modems) a local phone number. In the case of a phone modem, you'll have your modem dial the phone number; that puts your computer in touch with your provider's computer and its Internet connection; and you can go anywhere in the world from there, on a local phone call. It's truly amazing.

There are probably several Internet Service Providers in your area. There are also a number of national providers that can set you up with a connection. Ask around your town and at your local Mac user group for the names of the favored providers.

There is an alternative to getting a connection through an Internet Service Provider, as described below.

Another way to get to the Internet and the World Wide Web is through **America Online (AOL).** *America Online is **not** the Internet!* This is how it works: America Online is an online *service* that you join for a monthly fee. If you use a phone modem, your modem dials a local number that AOL gave you and you "log on" (connect) to the service; if you have broadband, you still have to open the AOL application and log on to connect to the Internet.

You are not directly on the Internet—you are safely contained in the AOL "village," where there are clubs and organizations, conferences, chat rooms, a "post office" for sending and receiving email, online magazines, news sources, kids' places, teen hangouts, parent support groups, research resources, romance rooms, your own calendar, and much more. There are live guides to help you figure things out; there are "police officers" who make their rounds and kick out people who act inappropriately; there are classes and interviews; there are friends to make and parties to crash. Everything is nicely organized and easy to find. Wherever you go on America Online, you are still within the village—***until*** you click the button that says "Go to the Web," type in a web address, or click a link that takes you to the web. When you head for the web, you're going out the back door of the village, onto the Internet, straight to the web itself. It opens AOL's own special browser and you can surf the world. There are no guides, no police officers,

Internet Service Providers

America Online is not the Internet!

AOL

When you click this button, a browser opens and takes you to a web site sponsored by AOL.

no maps. You're on your own. You have actually left America Online, even though the AOL menu bar is still there. AOL has integrated the web into its own system so well that it is often difficult to tell when you have left—but don't worry, it's not that important to know when you have left. ***The important thing to know is that AOL acts as your Internet service provider (ISP), so you do not need to get another one.***

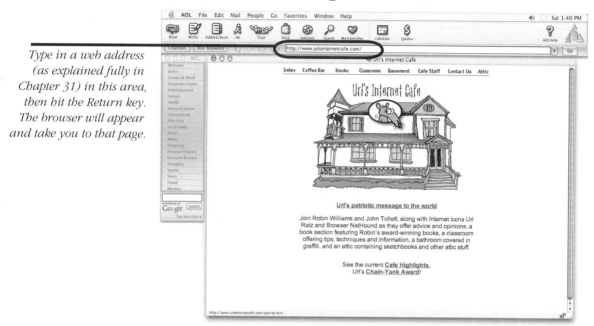

Type in a web address (as explained fully in Chapter 31) in this area, then hit the Return key. The browser will appear and take you to that page.

America Online and other browsers

Using America Online is actually a great way to get to the Internet and the World Wide Web. You pay a monthly fee, something like $20 a month, which is fairly comparable to what you might pay an Internet Service Provider for a phone connection to the Internet.

If you don't like AOL's browser, you can actually surf the web using Netscape, OmniWeb, or **any other browser** of your choice while connected to AOL. This is how to do it:

1. If you don't already have an alias of your favorite browser sitting on your Desktop, make an alias (page 368) and put it within easy reach.

2. Log on to America Online as usual.

3. Then double-click the browser alias on your Desktop.

Et violà! You're on the Internet using your favorite browser to surf the World Wide Web through your AOL account.

America Online is a wonderful service. There are complaints about it, of course, but when you're trying to make forty million ardent users happy, there are bound to be problems here and there. In general, AOL is the easiest, most fun, and least painful introduction to the online world. If you've never been online before, it's not a bad idea to start with AOL. You can explore the Internet and the World Wide Web very easily from America Online. You can have seven separate email addresses, each with its own password, so your whole family can use it. There are parent-controlled features to help keep your kids out of trouble.

If America Online is not already installed on your Macintosh, you can install it from any of the hundreds of CDs you've probably received in the mail, inside magazines, or on airplanes. Just put in the CD and double-click the file called "Install." After it's installed, double-click the AOL icon and it will walk you through the registration process. You're on. *You do not need to sign up with an Internet Service Provider to use America Online,* not even if you want to use a different browser from the one that AOL supplies.

If, however, you have no need for America Online and its services, then you might want to get a "direct" Internet connection from an **Internet Service Provider.** This connection, along with a browser, will get you to the Internet and the World Wide Web, newsgroups, mailing lists, and email.

And it's certainly possible to do **both.** You might have a "broadband" connection (DSL, cable, etc., that is fast and always on), for which you pay a monthly fee, and that broadband connection is your ISP. You can also have AOL at the same time. You will pay *two* monthly fees, but AOL has a separate fee (less per month) for their service if you use a different provider. In my house, for instance, I personally use a direct Internet connection through a service provider, but we also have an America Online account because my kids like to use it.

Should you choose America Online or an Internet Service Provider?

1. What are the four major ways people use the Internet?

   _____

   _____

2. Which is a faster modem speed, 56k or 2.5Mbps?

   _____

3. If you wanted to get a lot of email, would you join a newsgroup or a listserv?

   _____

4. What is a collection of web pages called?

   _____

5. What is the "home page" of a web site?

   _____

6. Why do you need a browser on the World Wide Web?

   _____

7. Explain the connection between America Online and the Internet.

   _____

8. If you use America Online exclusively, do you need to get an Internet connection through an Internet Service Provider?

   _____

9. Explain how to use your favorite browser to surf the web if your connection is through America Online.

   _____

10. What great invention was a critical factor in the development of the World Wide Web?

    _____

Answers on page 732.

Connecting to the Internet & the Web

Your Mac is made for the **Internet.** Not only does it provide you with tools for easy access, Apple fully *expects* that you are connected to the Internet and uses this expectation in many ways—OS X automatically tries to connect to the Internet in Sherlock, iDisk, iTunes, QuickTime Player, with Internet Location Files, the Date & Time server, Software Update, a number of icons in the Dock go to the Internet, many Help files get their information from the Internet, and a number of other features depend on the connection.

In this chapter I'll walk you through getting connected, if you aren't already, and help you manage your Internet features. *If you got yourself all connected with the Internet setup program that ran as soon as you turned on your Mac for the first time, you won't need this chapter at all* unless you want to make changes in settings.

Contents of this chapter

Are ya ratfy for the Net?

Step by Step:
What To Do

Below are the **steps** you'll follow to get yourself connected to the Internet so you can browse the World Wide Web and do email.

If you just turned on your Mac for the first time and it's asking you what to do and you don't know, the easiest option is to plug the phone line into your Mac and into a phone jack, and choose EarthLink. When the screen asks if you want to get set up with a new connection, choose that option and it will walk you through getting connected to EarthLink. You can **skip the rest of this chapter** and be on the Internet in five minutes. You can always change your mind later when you have a better idea of what you want to do.

If you use or plan to use America Online, skip the entire Internet setup process. When the screen asks how you want to connect, say you'll do it yourself later, or never, or whatever the option is today. When you're computer's up and running, insert an AOL disk and go through the simple process. (Read the top half of page 500 regarding America Online and Mac OS X.)

But if you want to plow through all this information, onward . . .

1. Decide on a **provider.** See pages 493–495 and 500–501.
   The only way to get to the Internet is to pay someone money to connect you, as explained in Chapter 29 and again on page 501.

2. Get your **modem** hooked up. See the opposite page.

3. Get the **setup information** from your provider. See page 502.

4. *Either* walk through the **setup process** (pages 502–505) if you're turning on your Mac for the first time.

   Or do it yourself. To do it yourself, you'll use the Network preferences (pages 506–511) and the Internet preferences (pages 512–515).

5. After you've set up the preferences, you're **ready to connect.**

   If you have a **broadband account,** just open your browser or email program; see page 516.

   If you have a telephone modem with a **dial-up account,** use Internet Connect; see pages 516–517.

   Once you're online, see page 518 about how to **disconnect.**

You Need a Modem

Before you can get connected in the first place, you need a **modem** (if you don't know what a modem is, and you care, see pages 488–489). The kind of modem you need depends on how you plan to connect to the Internet.

You have basically two choices. You will connect through:

Either a phone line with the modem that is built into your Mac, as explained below. (If your Mac is older and doesn't have a built-in modem, you'll need to buy one. Go to any office supply store or call MacWarehouse at 800.622.6222 and tell them you need a 56K modem for your Macintosh.)

Or a high-speed, broadband connection such as DSL, ISDN, cable, T1, T3, or satellite. The company that provides your service will sell you a special modem.

If you have a choice, go for the broadband—it's always on, it's fast, and Mac OS X really prefers broadband.

If your Mac is capable of running OS X, it should have a built-in 56K **telephone** modem for connecting through a phone (every Mac built in the past few years has a built-in modem). Look at the back or side of your computer—if you see a phone jack, that's your telephone modem. If you connect through a phone line, you have what's called a **dial-up account** because your modem will dial a phone number to connect to your Internet Service Provider. Only one person at a time can connect through a dial-up account.

This is the modem port on your Mac. It looks just like a phone jack in your house.

If you are going to connect through a high-speed, **broadband,** "always-on" connection such as DSL, ISDN, cable, T1, T3, or satellite, you will still use a modem—but it's not a telephone modem, you don't use the telephone jack in your Mac, and the modem is not built-in to your Mac. The company that provides you with the broadband service will provide you with the modem. You will connect to this modem with an **Ethernet** cable, which you'll plug into the Ethernet port on your Mac. The connectors (the things on the ends) on an Ethernet cable look very similar to a standard phone cable, but a little larger. The Ethernet port looks very similar to the telephone modem port, but a little larger.

This is the Ethernet port on your Mac. If you plug a phone line into this, it won't work.

When you're connected through a broadband modem, you will **not dial** any phone numbers to connect—you will just open your browser and you're on the web. You just open your email application and get your email. More than one computer can connect at the same time with one broadband connection.

Some phone companies that provide DSL (like QWest) might make you go through a little connection process every time you want to get online. That's so cheesy. It defeats half the purpose of having a broadband connection. If possible, don't settle for that. Find a provider who does it right.

*Note: If you have **fax** software so you can fax from your Macintosh, you must plug the telephone cable into the modem port and into a wall jack or telephone, even if you have a broadband connection. Your fax will not go through the broadband connection—it must go through the phone line.*

If You Have an America Online Account

America Online

If you have or plan to have an **America Online** account (AOL), you do not need to do anything to set up your Mac for the Internet—you can skip most of this chapter. You do not need to go through the Internet setup process, find a provider (AOL *is* your provider, as well as an online service, as explained on pages 493–495), or anything. **To sign up for America Online,** just plug the phone line into your Mac, put the AOL CD in your drive, double-click it, and follow the directions to set up a **dial-up** account. If you don't have a CD, call AOL at 1-800-509-7538 and have them send you one.

One issue with Mac OS X and AOL is that Mac OS X loves to go to the Internet. There are dozens of menu commands, icons, buttons, Sherlock searches, even help files, etc., that go to the Internet without asking your permission. This is fine if you're on a broadband connection, but if AOL is your only provider, you cannot connect until you first log on to AOL.

Now, you can have a broadband connection *and* an AOL account. You will have to pay the broadband provider a monthly fee, plus you will pay AOL a monthly fee, but AOL has a significantly lower fee if you use another Internet Service Provider for access (broadband or dial-up).

To log on to AOL, double-click the AOL icon. Drag the icon to the Dock since you'll be using it every day.

If You Don't Have a Provider
and don't want to think about it

EarthLink

If you just brought your Mac home or had it delivered and you want to get connected but you don't want to wait to find out who can get you broadband service in your area or who the local Internet Service Providers are, you can sign up, through your Mac, with the **EarthLink** service over your telephone modem. Later, if you discover a better deal in your area is available, you can cancel EarthLink. Or you might check around and end up deciding that EarthLink dial-up is exactly what you need after all, or you could possibly get a broadband connection through EarthLink, if you live in the right place. The point is that with Apple's set up, you can get started right away without having to make any permanent decisions, and in five minutes you can be on the web.

To sign up with EarthLink, choose the option for a new connection as you go through the Setup Assistant when you first turn on your Mac. This will walk you through the entire easy process of signing up with EarthLink. You will get an account with a password, as well as a several email addresses.

Whether you walk through the connection setup as described on the following pages (which is only available the first time you plug in and turn on your Mac), or if your Mac is already set up and you need to get connected now, first you have to make a **decision** about who is going to be your Internet provider (if you don't already have one). These are your options, summed up from the information on the previous pages:

Dial Up (telephone modem)

America Online: Skip this connection setup and use the AOL CD (credit card or checking account number in hand). You're all done—go to the web. If you don't have a CD, call AOL at 1-800-509-7538 and have them send you one. Skip this chapter.

EarthLink: If you follow the Apple Setup Assistant when you first turn on your Mac, click the button that says you want a new connection. This will lead you to EarthLink, and EarthLink will take care of all the setup—you don't need to worry about a thing. Be sure to check the fine print on the monthly charges to see what applies in your area.

Local provider or national provider: Ask your friends and neighbors, ask your local Mac user group, ask your phone company. Before you can get set up on your Mac, you must call the provider, set up an account, pay them money, and they will give you certain information, such as your user ID/account name, account password, email address, email password, SMTP server, and some other stuff. Write it all down, labeled, and keep it somewhere—I guarantee you will need that information again. Often the provider will walk you through the process, in which case you had better make sure you write down all the names and numbers they give you.

Broadband (high-speed connection)

You need to call a provider and set up an account. Someone will come to your house with a special modem and get you all put together. They will probably get you connected on your Mac, although some broadband providers don't know how to deal with Macs and so you will have to set it up yourself.

There are local and national broadband companies. Ask around your neighborhood to find out who provides the best service. If you are an EarthLink customer, EarthLink can provide DSL if you live in the right area.

AirPort

Whatever your main connection is, that's what the AirPort connection is. If your connection is a dial-up, AirPort serves that dial-up connection. If your connection is broadband, AirPort serves the broadband. All the AirPort does is wirelessly transmit the signal that comes in. AirPort is *not* a provider.

So This is the Decision You Must Make

What You Need Before You Start

Whether you walk through the Setup Assistant the first time you turn on your Mac, or you decide to do it later, there is **information you need to have** from your service provider or network administrator (*unless* you plan to use EarthLink at home or in your small office; see page 500). And remember, if you have or plan to have an America Online account as your only connection, you don't need to go through the Internet setup process at all.

If you have a provider other than EarthLink, before you begin make sure you have the information your provider gave you:

- ▼ User account name and password.
- ▼ Email address and password (which might or might not be the same as your account name and password—often it is not!)
- ▼ If the account is a dial-up, you need that phone number, plus they will probably give you several DNS (domain name server) numbers that look something like this: **198.162.34.8.**
- ▼ If the account is broadband, make sure to ask your provider for the connection type and ask if you'll need a router number.
- ▼ If you are on a local area network (LAN) in a large corporation or school, ask your system administrator for pertinent information.

Write all of this information down! I guarantee you will need it again someday! And don't forget to write down every password as well.

To add an existing email account you will need:

- ▼ Your email address at that account.
- ▼ **Incoming mail server name.** This will be something like mail.mydomainname.com.

  This is not always the same as your provider's name. For instance, I own the domain ratz.com and I get email there so my incoming mail server name is mail.ratz.com. But my provider is actually cybermesa.com.

- ▼ **Outgoing mail server (SMTP).** SMTP stands for Simple Mail Transfer Protocol. This name will be something like **mail.myprovider.com** or **smtp.myprovider.com.**

  This is always the name of your Internet Service Provider because that is where your email gets sent out from.

- ▼ **Account type: IMAP or POP.** Most email accounts are POP (Post Office Protocol) accounts. Services like America Online and Mac.com are IMAP accounts (Internet Message Access Protocol). Ask your provider to be sure. See page 560 if you want to know the difference.

If you choose not to connect to the Internet when you first turn on your Mac, that's okay! You can always do it later. The beginning of the process is just to get your Mac set up with your personal specifications. You will have a number of screens like the first one shown below, with simple questions.

Walking Through the Connection Setup

If you skipped the setup when you first turned on your Mac, you can't go back to it. Use the Network and Internet preferences on pages 506–511 and just fill in the information yourself.

If you click the "Show All" box, you'll see a list of many more countries in the world.

If you have all of your setup information ready, go ahead and follow the process to connect to the Internet. If you don't know the answer to anything that is required (as opposed to the boxes that say "Optional"), call your provider and ask. AOL users: Check the button to sign up later.

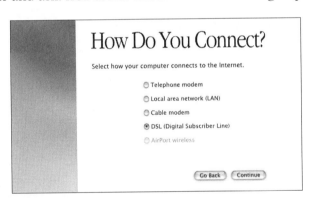

If you are connected through an ISDN, T1, or T3 line, your Mac is not directly connected to that incoming box, so you will choose "Local area network."

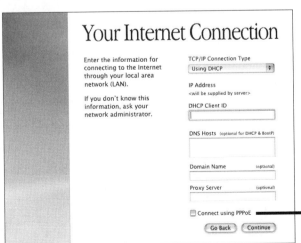

Typically with a DSL connection, all this will fill itself in later—you can usually leave it blank.

PPPoE is Point-to-Point Protocol over Ethernet, generally used in apartment houses or office buildings sharing one DSL so online sessions can be individually monitored for billing purposes.

In the process of getting connected to the Internet, the Mac will ask if you want a **.Mac account.** You can read about .Mac on page xxi–xxii, and/or click the ".Mac" button in the screen that appears to get a little tour from Apple. Or go to **www.mac.com** when you're set up and see if it's something you want. You'll get an email account with Mac.com (although you still need an Internet Service Provider), storage space on Apple's server so you can share files across the Internet, and more. A .Mac account now costs $99 a year.

If, before you started the setup process, you already had a Mac.com account (.Mac), the Mac will set that up for you automatically, as you can see here.

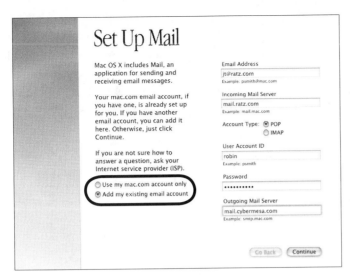

In this example, I chose to add an existing email account.

This is an example of an email account that has a completely different **email** name and password from the **provider** account name and password.

The email address is for my partner, John, at the domain ratz.com, and he has a password for that email address. But the provider account ("User Account ID") is under my name with my account name and password because we use one provider for our home office.

Even if you have one email account, you still might have an account name and password for your email and a different account name and password for your provider.

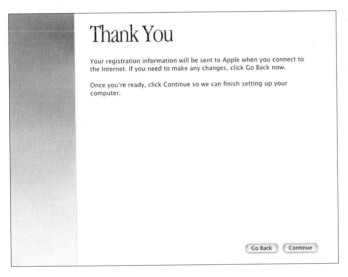

By the time you finish going through the set up, your Mac will be ready to connect to the Internet and Apple will use that connection to send in your registration.

Entering the Setup Information Yourself

Skip this entire section if you already set up your connection with Apple's Setup Assistant, as described on the previous pages.

If you skipped the Internet setup when you first turned on your Mac, it's okay because you can just **enter the information yourself.** You'll use the Network and Internet preferences, as explained below and on the following pages. You will also need to use these preferences when you decide to switch providers, when you upgrade to a broadband connection from a dial-up, when you connect your Macs over Ethernet to share files, when things go wrong, etc.

To open the Network preferences:

1. From the Apple menu, choose "Preferences...," or click on the System Preferences icon in the Dock.

2. Single-click on the "Network" icon. There is probably a Network icon in the toolbar across the top of the System Preferences pane, and there is one in the third row of preferences. They're exactly the same thing.

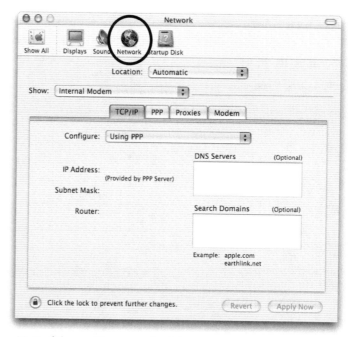

Most of these settings you don't have to worry about, so don't let all this scare you.

If you have a simple situation with your home or office computer in that you have one Internet Service Provider and you won't be switching between your dial-up connection and an AirPort connection and your office network, then **skip** the following information about making a Location. You will be just fine with the "Automatic" Location that Apple will create for you.

Do you need to make a Location?

If you think you're going to add other connections, like an AirPort connection when you take your laptop to your treehouse or a network connection in your office, it's a good idea to make a new **Location.** A Location is simply a collection of your specifications (a "configuration") for that particular connection. If you have several Locations, you can just switch Locations from the Apple menu and all the rest of the changes are made for you.

Making a Location, if necessary

To make a new Location:

1. In the Network preferences, click the "Location" pop-up menu and choose "New Location…." Type in a name and click OK.

2. From the "Show" pop-up menu, choose your method of connection. For instance, if this is a dial-up account through your telephone modem, choose "Internal Modem."

   (If you don't see your connection method in that menu, which is unlikely, choose "Active Network Ports" from the Show menu and make sure all of the ports available to your Mac are checked on. To get back to the main Network pane, from the "Show" menu, choose the port through which you want to connect, such as "Internal Modem.")

3. Follow the steps on the next pages to set up the configuration for this Location. Be sure to click "Apply Now" when you're done.

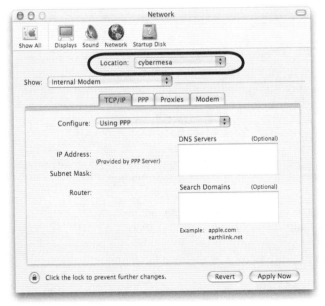

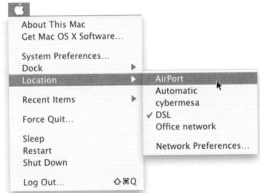

Once you've made a Location, you can go to the Apple menu, choose the "Location" item, then choose the name of your Location. All of your settings will switch immediately and you won't have to go to the Network preferences to change everything.

TCP/IP pane for telephone modem connections

The acronym **TCP/IP** sounds rather intimidating, but it's actually very interesting. If you know basically what it does, it's not so scary:

When we send or receive an email message or request a web page, most of us picture a little letter or a nice, colorful page squeezing itself through the lines, speeding across the country, and landing in someone's computer, unruffling itself just in time.

What actually happens is that the message or web page gets chopped up into little pieces called *packets,* and all these packets go through the lines on different routes, and they're all put back together again at the other end. TCP, or Transmission Control Protocol, is the layer of the TCP/IP program that divides the email file or web page into the individual packets and numbers them. TCP then sends the packets to the IP, or Internet Protocol, layer of the program. The IP sends the packets on their ways, sending each one in a different direction, and the packets stop at all kinds of computers along their paths, asking directions to make sure they're still going the right way. At the computer on the other end, TCP puts all the packets back together again in the right order. Once they are all reassembled correctly, it sends the single file to your mailbox or browser so you can read it. Amazing.

An IP (Internet Protocol) address identifies a computer or device on a TCP/IP network, like the Internet. Networks using TCP/IP route messages based on the IP address of the destination. The format of an IP address is written as four numbers separated by periods, and each number can be from 0 to 255.

Below you see the TCP/IP pane for a **telephone modem connection.** Your "IP Address" will automatically appear after you connect to the server.

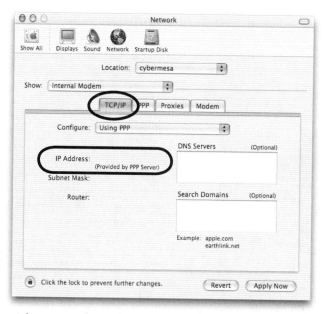

Ask your ISP if you should enter the numbers for DNS (Domain Name Servers). They will be in the same format as the IP address; that is, something like 192.254.10.93.

If you are setting up the configuration for a **telephone modem,** click the **PPP** tab. Enter the name of your service provider, the phone number they told you to dial, and an alternate (if they give you one) in case that one is busy.

The account name and password, in this case, is your account name and password with your service provider. Often it is different from your email name and password! You can change your email password whenever you like, but your account password for your ISP is given to you by your provider and cannot be changed unless you call them up and arrange it.

PPP pane for telephone modem connections

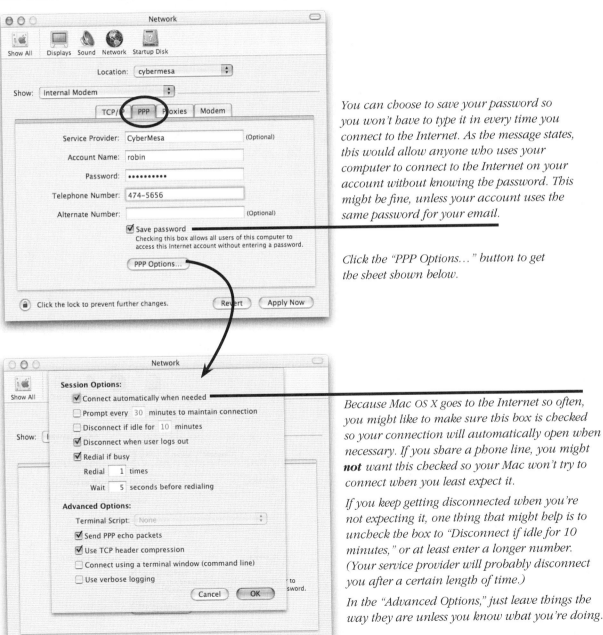

You can choose to save your password so you won't have to type it in every time you connect to the Internet. As the message states, this would allow anyone who uses your computer to connect to the Internet on your account without knowing the password. This might be fine, unless your account uses the same password for your email.

Click the "PPP Options…" button to get the sheet shown below.

*Because Mac OS X goes to the Internet so often, you might like to make sure this box is checked so your connection will automatically open when necessary. If you share a phone line, you might **not** want this checked so your Mac won't try to connect when you least expect it.*

If you keep getting disconnected when you're not expecting it, one thing that might help is to uncheck the box to "Disconnect if idle for 10 minutes," or at least enter a longer number. (Your service provider will probably disconnect you after a certain length of time.)

In the "Advanced Options," just leave things the way they are unless you know what you're doing.

Modem pane for telephone modem connections

In the **Modem** pane, the Mac has already chosen your internal modem for you. If you have a different modem attached to your Mac, you can choose it from the Modem pop-up menu.

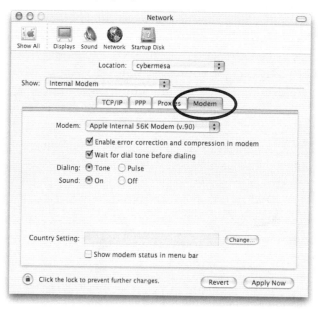

Wait for dial tone before dialing: If you're outside of North America, you might want to uncheck this box because most foreign phone systems use a dial tone that your built-in modem won't recognize.

Dialing: If you have a very old telephone that uses a pulse instead of a tone, choose "Pulse." If you actually dial a round wheel to make phone calls, you've got a pulse phone. If you can play little songs with the musical tones when you punch the buttons to make a call, choose "Tone."

Sound: Annoying as the sound of the modem is, it's a comforting feeling when you hear it connecting. I usually leave it on because then I can instantly tell whether things are working properly or not.

This is the modem status in the menu bar.

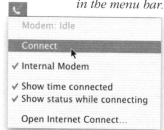

Show modem status in menu bar: Check this box to put a little phone icon on the right side of the menu bar. Choose this modem status menu to connect, change your port, or open Internet Connect (which is shown and explained on page 517). When you want to remove it, Command-drag it off the bar.

If you are a home or small office Mac user, you won't need to bother with the **Proxies** pane. If you work in a large corporation or university, ask the network administrator if you should change any of the Proxies settings. Proxies are designed to work around a *firewall,* which is a system designed to prevent unauthorized access to or from a private network, such as a corporate *intranet* (a private, in-house network). A firewall might be implemented with software or hardware, or a combination of both.

Proxies pane for all connections

If you have a **broadband connection,** you need to choose "Built-in Ethernet" from the "Show" pop-up menu, circled below, because your Mac connects to the special broadband modem with an Ethernet cable.

TCP/IP pane for broadband connections

In the **TCP/IP** pane, the necessary information has probably been filled in by the technician who brought you the modem and set up your connection. If not, you can get the information from your provider (the IP address, the Subnet mask, and the Router number) and fill them in yourself: From the "Configure" pop-up menu, choose "Manually" and fill in the blanks.

If your connection doesn't work, call your provider and go through these settings over the phone to make sure all information is correct and in the right places.

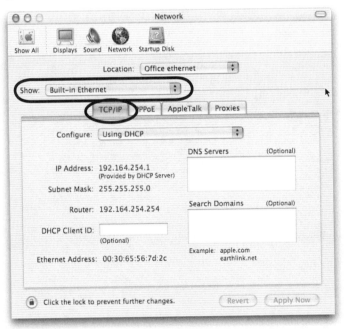

DHCP stands for Dynamic Host Configuration Protocol, which is used for assigning dynamic IP addresses (see page 508 about IP addresses).

PPPoE is Point-to-Point Protocol over Ethernet, generally used in apartment houses or office buildings sharing one DSL so online sessions can be individually monitored for billing purposes. If you use PPPoE, ask your provider what to enter in that pane.

AppleTalk is networking software that allows your Mac to connect with other kinds of networks. You'll use it when you start file sharing.

Internet Preferences

If you went through the Apple setup when you first turned on your Mac, or if you entered all of the information yourself, most of the details in the **Internet preferences** are already filled in for you.

.Mac pane

The **.Mac pane** (pronouned *dot mac*) gives you yet another chance to buy a .Mac membership account, if you haven't already (see pages xxi–xxii). Click the "Sign Up" button and your Mac will connect to the Internet and take you to Apple's web site. If you have an account, your member name and password will be filled in for you in this pane. Apple is not an Internet Service Provider—even though you have a .Mac account, you still have to pay an ISP to connect your Mac to the Internet.

*Click the "Sign Up" button to register for a **free** sixty-day trial membership.*

The **iDisk pane** is only useful if you have a membership with Mac.com (see pages xxi–xxii). Then you have a certain amount of storage space on Apple's server, and you can see how much of it is yet available to you. As shown below, you can also limit access to your Public folder with a password, or open it up and allow people to upload files to you.

iDisk pane

Email pane   The **Email pane** is already filled in for you if you went through the initial setup process as shown on pages 503–505. If not, you can fill in the data here in this pane. See page 502 for explanations of incoming and outgoing mail servers, POP vs. IMAP, and your account names.

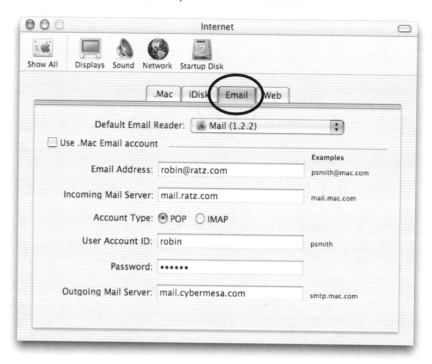

The **Default Email Reader** pop-up menu gives you a choice between the current version of Mail and an older version, or you can select any other email client you have installed, such as Eudora Pro. The default you choose here is what will open when you click on an email link while using Internet Explorer to browse the web.

If you check the box to **Use .Mac Email account,** *any information that was in this pane will disappear and won't come back* so be sure you write down any of this data that you might not have stored elsewhere. The account shown here is what will be used in your chosen default mail program, and it will appear as your return address. You can override this default in your email program's preferences.

The lets you set several default settings, as shown and explained below. But except for the "Default Web Browser" setting, your browser will probably override the browser preferences you set in this pane.

Web pane

To set these same settings in your browser, open your browser and find the menu called "Preferences." If your browser is made for OS X, "Preferences" will be in the application menu; if you use your browser in the Classic environment, "Preferences" or "Options" can usually be found in the Edit menu. In America Online, click the "My AOL" button in the toolbar to find the Preferences command.

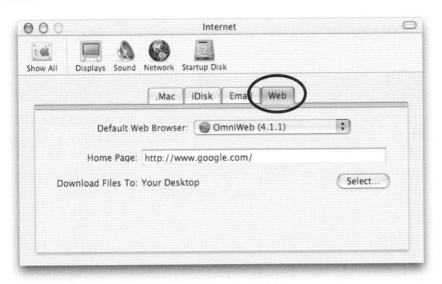

Default Web Browser: Choose a browser that you want to open automatically whenever you choose a Mac OS X command that goes to the web.

Home Page: When you click the "Home" icon in any browser, it will take you to the Home page that you type in here or in your browser preferences.

Download Files To: When you download files from a web page, they will automatically be stored on your Desktop. If you want them stored somewhere else, click the "Select..." button and navigate to another folder. But remember, your browser might override this option and use the folder specified in the browser preferences—check and see, as explained above.

Connect to the Internet with Your Broadband Account

If you have a **broadband account,** *then you are already connected to the Internet.* All you have to do is open a browser or your email application and there you are. It's fabulous. You don't need to disconnect—broadband is an "always on" connection.

Some low-class broadband providers will make you go through a little connection process, like a dial-up, which defeats half the purpose of having a broadband connection. Try to find a company that doesn't do that.

Connect to the Internet with Your Dial-up Account

Okay, you're all set up with your new telephone modem **Internet** account and you want to actually **connect** and go to the web. There are several ways to do this.

Connect automatically

If you checked the box to **"Connect automatically when starting TCP/IP applications,"** as explained on page 509, then you can just single-click on the Mail icon or the Internet Explorer browser icon (or any other browser you choose) in your Dock. The Mac will automatically dial up your connection and log on, then open the application.

If you have any trouble doing that, manually log on to the Internet yourself, as explained below, and then open your browser:

Use the modem status icon

If you have the modem status icon in your menu bar, go to it and choose "Connect." You'll hear the modem start squeaking (if you didn't turn off the sound, as shown on page 510) and the icon in the menu bar will send off "sound waves" to indicate that you are connecting and connected.

Once you are connected to the Internet, open your browser or email application and surf or check your mail.

If the modem icon is not in your menu bar, you can add it; see the opposite page.

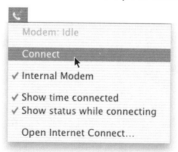

If you choose "Open Internet Connect...," you'll get the dialog box shown on the opposite page.

If you have the modem icon in the menu bar, the animated sound waves give you a visual clue that you are connected.

To disconnect from the Internet, go to the modem status menu and choose "Disconnect."

If you do NOT have the modem status icon in your menu bar, open the Applications window (click on the Applications icon in a Finder window Toolbar or press Command Option A). Then find "Internet Connect" and double-click it. You'll get the dialog box shown below.

Click the **Connect** button to connect to the Internet, and then open your browser or email application and surf or check your mail.

Use Internet Connect

Internet Connect

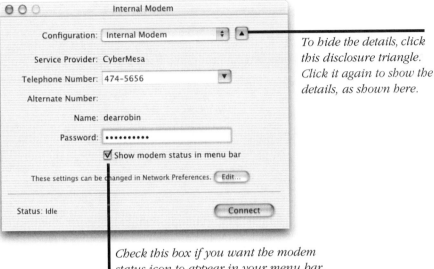

To hide the details, click this disclosure triangle. Click it again to show the details, as shown here.

Check this box if you want the modem status icon to appear in your menu bar.

You will see the connection process in the lower part of this dialog box.

When you open Internet Connect, its icon appears in the Dock. If you want to keep the icon in the Dock so you don't have to open the Application window every time you want to go to the Internet, press on the icon to get the pop-up menu, then choose "Keep in Dock."

Tip: You can close the Internet Connect window while you're online. But then when you make it active again, the dialog box is gone. Choose "New Connection" from the Internet Connect File menu, or press Command N, to get the dialog box back.

To disconnect from the Internet, click the "Disconnect" button.

Here are a few **web addresses** you might find handy. Web addresses have a habit of changing as soon as you print them in a book, so I've tried to give you only well-established sites that won't change. If they have changed and any of these addresses don't work, I apologize!

Macintosh	MacinTouch.com, MacCentral.com, MacMinute.com, MacFixIt.com
Definitions	webopedia.com
Books (retail)	borders.com, amazon.com, bn.com *[Barnes & Noble]*
For writers	bookwire.com *[inside the book world]*
Family	family.com
Movies	imdb.com *[Internet Movie Database]*
Television	gist.com
Sports	espn.com, cnnsi.com *[CNN and Sports Illustrated]*
Travel	LonelyPlanet.com, MapQuest.com
Weather	accuweather.com, weather.com
Music	listen.com, rollingstone.com, allmusic.com
Science	discovery.com, sciam.com *[Scientific American]*
Games	gamesmania.com
Health	ReutersHealth.com, health.com, vh.org *[The Virtual Hospital]*
Money	money.cnn.com
Genealogy	genealogy.com, ancestry.com, genhomepage.com
Recipes	AllRecipes.com, epicurious.com
Stain removal	tide.com
Gardening	gardening.com, OrganicGardening.com, KidsGardening.com
Home improvements, recipes, decorating	bhglive.com *[Better Homes & Gardens]*
IRS	www.irs.gov *[download IRS forms]*
Peachpit Press	peachpit.com

Also go to About.com and type in your passion. As indicated above, you don't need to type "www" on any of these particular addresses.

Using the World Wide Web

The **World Wide Web** is addictively fun to use. That's one of the amazing things about this incredible technology—it's so easy. You just need to know a few things about getting around. This chapter contains only a brief introduction, but it's probably more than many people know who are surfing the web already.

If you're not connected yet, the previous chapter will help you get there. Even if you're not, just skim through this chapter to become familiar with the web, what you can expect, how to type in an address to get where you want to go, and what to do once you get there.

I browse. Deal with it.

Contents of this chapter

What are Web Pages?

Hypertext is a term coined in the 1960s by Theodor Nelson. He explained, "By hypertext, I mean nonsequential writing— text that branches and allows choices to the reader, best read at an interactive screen. As popularly conceived, this is a series of text chunks connected by links which offer the reader different pathways [through the information]."

In the Chapter 30 I explained that the World Wide Web is comprised of several billion individual **web pages.** These pages are literally the same as the pages you create in your word processor—in fact, many of them *are* created in word processors, and the code for any web page can be viewed in a word processor.

The big deal about web pages is that they have "hypertext links"—text you click on to make another page appear in front of you. It's like this: Imagine that you could open a book to its table of contents and touch, say, "Chapter 3," and the book instantly flips to Chapter 3. In Chapter 3, there is a reference to Greek mythology. You touch the word "Greek mythology," and a book about Greek mythology instantly appears in front of you, open to the page you want. As you're reading about Greek mythology, you see a reference to goddess worship so you touch that reference and instantly that book appears in front of you, open to the page you want. That's what web pages do, that's what hypertext is. That is incredible.

If you want to connect right now

You don't have to **connect to the Internet** and the web to read this chapter— just skim through and get the gist of how to use your browser and the web. But if you have a full-time broadband connection (something like a cable modem, DSL, ISDN, or T1 line) and want to connect to experiment, all you need to do to get to the Internet is double-click your browser icon. If your connection uses a telephone modem, please see pages 516–517 for details about connecting. If you're not connected at all or if you have no idea *how* you are connected, please see the previous chapter.

This is the icon for the browser that came with your Mac, called Microsoft Internet Explorer. If you have a full-time connection, just single-click this icon to get to the web.

Practice: If you want to practice using the web, first open your connection:

If you have a full-time connection, just single-click the browser icon in your Dock, as shown above.

If you connect through a phone line and you've never done it before, please see page 516.

Every web page has **links** on it. Single-click on a link with your mouse and a new web page appears. A link might be text or it might be a graphic. If it's text, it almost always has an underline; if it's a graphic, it sometimes has a border around it. Even if the **visual clues** of the underline or the border are missing, you can always tell when something is a link because the pointer turns into a hand with a pointing finger, as shown to the right. Just run your mouse over the page (without pressing the button down) and you'll see the pointer turn into the browser hand whenever you run over a link.

What are Links?

This is a typical "browser hand" that you'll see in a browser.

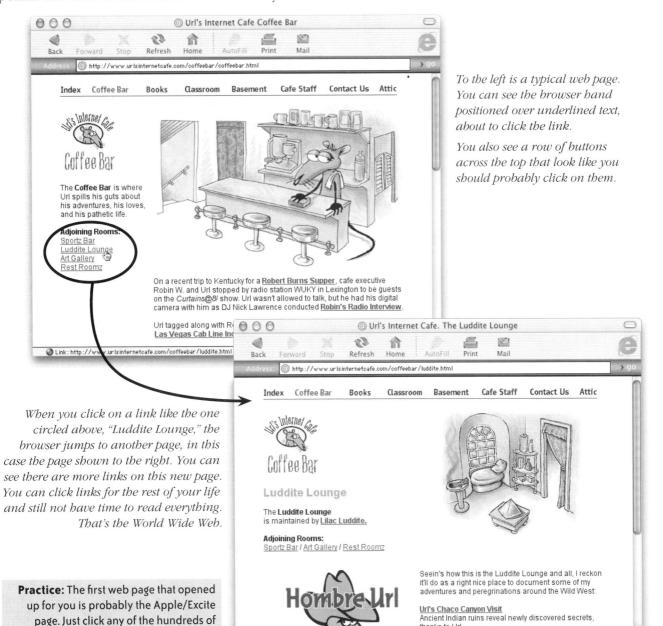

To the left is a typical web page. You can see the browser hand positioned over underlined text, about to click the link.

You also see a row of buttons across the top that look like you should probably click on them.

When you click on a link like the one circled above, "Luddite Lounge," the browser jumps to another page, in this case the page shown to the right. You can see there are more links on this new page. You can click links for the rest of your life and still not have time to read everything. That's the World Wide Web.

Practice: The first web page that opened up for you is probably the Apple/Excite page. Just click any of the hundreds of underlined links on that page that interest you. Poke around for a while!

Web Addresses, also known as URLs

Something you will become intimately familiar with is a **web address.** Just as every home in the country has its own address so you can find it, every web page on the World Wide Web has its own address. The address is also called a **URL** (pronounced *you are ell*), which stands for Uniform Resource Locator (who cares). A typical web address looks like this:

http://www.ratz.com/robin/hats.html

Knowing what a web address represents helps you find your way around on the web. This is what the different parts mean:

http:// These letters stand for hypertext transfer protocol, but who cares. The important thing to know is that the **http** means this address leads to a **web page.** You might also see addresses that start with **news://** or **ftp://**. Those are different from web pages.

www This stands for World Wide Web, of course, but this is not the definitive clue that tells you (and the browser software) that the address goes to a web page! The "www" is just a convention; many addresses don't even include it. (The "http" means it's a web page.)

ratz.com This is the **domain name.** Typically it is the name of the business or vendor. The **com** stands for **commercial.**

The period is pronounced *dot*. So "ratz.com" is pronounced *ratz dot com.*

You can **buy your own** domain name; it generally costs $70 for two years, renewable every year after that for about $30. I bought ratz.com. Ask your service provider to help you buy a domain name.

/robin The slash tells the browser to go down one more level, to look into the next folder (just like the path names on your Mac). So in this address, the slash tells the browser to go to the domain name "ratz.com" and then look inside the folder named "robin."

/hats.html So here's a slash again, which tells the browser to look inside that *folder* (named "robin") and find the *page* that has been saved with the name "hats.html." The "html" is a clue that this is a web page because all *basic* web pages (just about) end with ".htm" or ".html."

Domain names

The domain name gives you a clue to the general type of site. Besides those listed below, many new domain names are now available.

.com *commercial*
.edu *educational*
.gov *government*
.mil *military*
.org *organization, usually non-profit*
.net *network business*

Practice: As you poke around clicking on links and going to web pages, notice the web addresses. Be conscious of what they are telling you.

I'm also known as Url.

The **browser,** as you've learned, is the software that displays web pages on your screen. You enter the address of a web page in the browser, you use search tools through your browser, you watch movies and hear music through your browser, you can print from your browser, and on and on. So it's important to know how to use it. The Help files are usually very good—while you're in your browser, go to the Help menu and choose the command for your application. Right now I'm just going to give you some basic tips that will get you started right away.

Using a Browser

To enter a web address, type it into the "Address," "Location," or "Go To" box (or it might be called something else) at the **top** of the window, in the toolbar. After you type it in, hit Return or Enter to tell the browser to go find that page. Notice carefully in the illustrations below where the Address bar is located!

Enter a web address

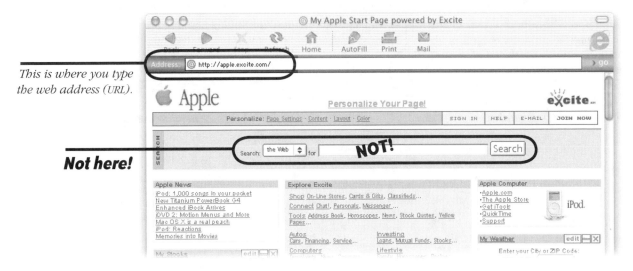

This is where you type the web address (URL).

Not here!

This is where you type the web address (URL).

Not here!

Go back and forth from page to page

You see **buttons** in your **toolbar.** The ones you will use most often are "Back" and "Forward." The Back button, of course, takes you back through pages you have visited. Once you've gone back, then the Forward button appears so you can go forward again.

Use these buttons to go back and forth through pages you have already seen.

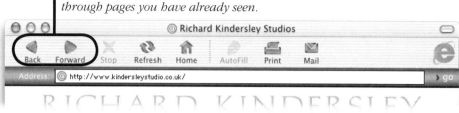

In Internet Explorer, use a contextual menu to get the list of options shown above, including to go back or forward: Hold down the Control key, then click in any blank spot.

Press on the Back button (hold the mouse button down) and you'll get a menu that lists the pages you have been to. Just slide down and choose the one you want to see again.

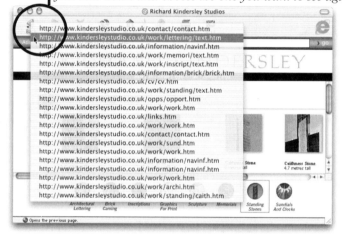

You can also use the **Go menu** to go back through pages you have visited.

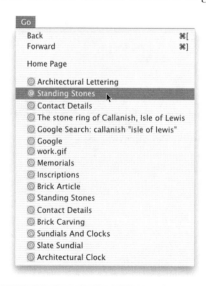

You can have lots and **lots of browser windows open.** This comes in handy when you really like a page, or maybe this page has lots of links you want to follow so when you go to another page you don't want this one to disappear. So instead of *clicking* on the link to get another page, *press* on it (hold the mouse button down). You will get a menu right there in the middle of the page, and one of the options is something like "Open Page in New Window" or "New Window with this Link." Choose that option—a new window with the new page will open, and the previous window will still be open on your screen as well, behind this new one.

The Back button on the new page will be gray because, since this is a new page, it has no where to go back to! Your original page still retains all of the Back pages.

Internet Explorer Help...

Back
Refresh Page
Open Page in New Window
Add Page to Favorites
Add Page to Toolbar Favorites
Track Page with Auction Manager

Set Home Page
View Source

Press—don't click—on a link to get this menu. In Internet Explorer this menu comes up faster if you hold down the Control key and click on the link.

And here's an extra-special shortcut you will love. In most browsers on teh Mac, you don't have to type in the entire ugly web address with the http://and all. For one thing, you never need to type http://. So skip that part altogether. If the rest of the address is in this format, www.**something**.com, all you need to type is **something**. Really. For instance, to get to http://www.**apple**.com, all you need to type is **apple**, then hit Return or Enter. The browser looks for a .com address with the name you entered, and if it finds one, it takes you there. (If the browser cannot find a web site with that domain name, it does a search for that topic and shows you the results of the search.)

If the address uses another top-level domain, such as .org or .net instead of .com, you'll have to type .org or .net, etc. And if the address has other slashes and stuff, you'll have to type everything after the domain name.

Open a new browser window

Practice: On any link on any page, *press* on a link instead of *clicking* on it. Choose the option to open the link in a new page.

(In Internet Explorer, the menu comes up quicker if you Control-click on the link.)

Tip: In some browsers, you can Command-click on a link and it will instantly open that page in a new window. Try it.

Shortcut to enter address

Practice: In your browser, type Command L. This will either open a "Location" box or will highlight the address box where you typically enter an address.

Type "apple."

Hit Return.

Customize your toolbar   You can **customize your toolbar.** One of the first things you might want to do is get rid of the big buttons so you have more room for the web pages. Find your browser's preferences settings—go to the application menu (the one with the name of your browser) and choose "Preferences…." Find the section that controls the toolbar, as shown in the example below. Experiment with different settings to discover what you like best!

In the Preferences dialog box, choose "Show Tool Tips" to display those little clues when you pause the pointer over a button. Or turn them off if they bore you.

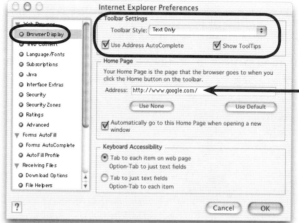

*Whatever address you type in here will become your **"Home"** address. That is, whenever you click the Home button in the toolbar, you will go to this page. So change it from the default to your own favorite page.*

Notice how much smaller this toolbar is than the one on page 523. This means you have more room for the web page.

In the OmniWeb browser, shown to the right, you can customize the browser toolbar just like you customize a Finder window Toolbar.

In Internet Explorer, go to the View menu and choose "Customize Toolbars…" for something similar (but not nearly as elegant.)

The other most important feature to **customize** is **the typeface** you see on most web pages. The default that has been set for you is usually Times, 12 point. On a Macintosh screen, Times is very difficult to read. New York, however, has been designed specifically for the resolution of a monitor. Change your font to New York 10 or 12 point and see what an incredible difference it makes. And use Geneva instead of Helvetica, or try Verdana, which looks lovely on the screen.

Customize your typeface

THE ENEMY CAMP
Dr. Richard Hallmark examines the Apple/Microsoft deal in his editorial "An alliance reborn?" It's a thought-provoking piece that really makes you wonder if Rick's been hanging around with Puff Daddy.

THE INTERFACE POLICE
Lunetta and Howe, fresh from their stint as Honda's ad agency, say--"Here's an idea, Simplify." And we agree! See any old copies of Windows 95 cluttering up your office? Simplify--toss 'em in the incinerator.

THE ENEMY CAMP
Dr. Richard Hallmark examines the Apple/Microsoft deal in his editorial 'An alliance reborn?' It's a thought provoking piece that really makes you wonder if Rick's been hanging around with Puff Daddy.

THE INTERFACE POLICE
Lunetta and Howe, fresh from their stint as Honda's ad agency, say- 'Here's an idea, Simplify.' And we agree! See any old copies of Windows 95 cluttering up your office? Simplify- toss 'em in the incinerator.

PAINTER TIPS AND TRICKS
David Roberts, (who once posed for a famous statue in Rome), says 'Make mine Monet.' David, I hate to tell you this, but any art his brain can tell you Monet did not use Painter. He used Photoshop. (kidding, just a joke!)

The **Coffee Bar** is where Url spills his guts about his adventures, his loves, and his pathetic life.

And this is Verdana, which is particularly clean and easy to read on the screen.

On the left is New York 12 point. On the right is Times 12 point. Which is easier to read, especially on a screen?

Change the font in the Preferences dialog box in your browser: go to the application menu (the one with the name of your browser) and choose "Preferences…." Find the button that opens the Fonts panel (circled, below), then select the fonts that are easiest for you to read. Not all web pages will listen to your choice—many designers create pages that override your choice. But this will help on a large number of pages.

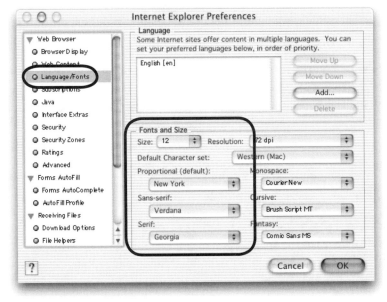

If you don't know your fonts very well, choose the same ones shown in this example. As you become more familiar with your typefaces, feel free to change these preferences whenever you like. Don't forget to choose a size that is easy for you to read on the screen.

Favorites or Bookmarks

The Favorites in Internet Explorer have nothing to do with your Favorites folder or Favorites in general on the Mac.

As you wander around the web, you'll run across web sites you really like and want to come back to. For these sites, make a **Favorite** (Internet Explorer) or **Bookmark** (Netscape and OmniWeb). Once you have a bookmark, the title of the page shows up in your Favorites or Bookmarks menu and you can just choose it from that menu.

As you make lots of bookmarks, you'll need to organize them. Below you see a neatly organized Favorites menu.

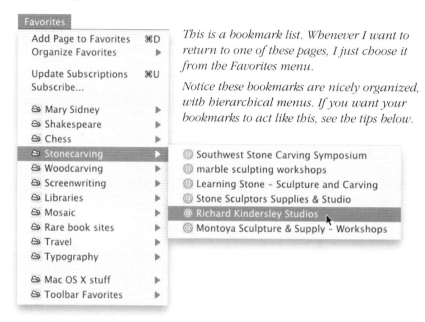

This is a bookmark list. Whenever I want to return to one of these pages, I just choose it from the Favorites menu.

Notice these bookmarks are nicely organized, with hierarchical menus. If you want your bookmarks to act like this, see the tips below.

To make a favorite: Simply view the page you want to save a link to. Press Command D. The title of the page is now in your Favorites or Bookmark menu. If you're using a browser other than Netscape or Internet Explorer, check the menu to see what its keyboard command is.

To organize your favorites: I can't explain how to organize your favorites or bookmarks for every browser, but as I show you how to do it in Internet Explorer, you can use that same information in other browsers.

1. From the Favorites menu, click on the "Organize Favorites" item. I know it looks like you're supposed to go get something from the submenu, but this is a Microsoft product. Don't expect clarity.

*Click right here on the "Organize Favorites" line, **not** in the submenu.*

2. The Favorites window will open, as shown below. This is where you can create new folders in which to store your favorites, delete favorites, rename them, re-order them, add divider spaces, etc.

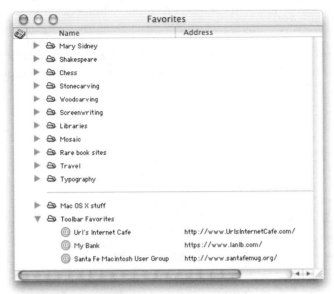

To make a new folder in this Favorites window, go to the Favorites menu, slide down to "Organize Favorites," and choose "New Folder" from the submenu. A new, untitled folder will appear in the window.

To rename a folder, drag over its name, then type, just as you would change any other folder's name at the Desktop.

To move a folder to another position, drag it.

To add a dividing line (which in the Favorites menu will appear as a blank space), go to the Favorites menu, slide down to "Organize Favorites," and choose "New Divider" from the submenu. Drag it to the position you want.

To move an existing favorite into a folder, drag it.

To add a new favorite into a folder, drag the little icon (shown to the right) from the Address bar and drop it into a folder (or directly into the Favorites window, then drag it into the folder of your choice).

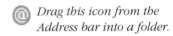 *Drag this icon from the Address bar into a folder.*

To delete a bookmark, select it, then press Command Delete.

You can even **save** your favorites or bookmarks list as a **web page** and then open that page in your browser (open the Favorites window, then from the File menu, choose "Save As"). Each folder will appear as a heading, and each bookmark will be a link! The Mac automatically saves your file in the Documents folder. After you save it, drag the file from the Documents folder and drop it in the middle of any web page, or double-click it. You can give this file to your friends.

Favorites.html

Open this in any browser.

Don't Forget the Help Files!

Y'know why I have a job? Because I **read the directions.** You must be a good direction-reader too, if you've gotten this far. Then I suggest you dive into your browser's Help files. I guarantee that if you actually read the Help files and follow the directions, you will know more than 99 percent of the people using a browser.

As in every Macintosh application, go to the Help menu and choose the application-specific help. Below you see one example of the Internet Explorer Help windows.

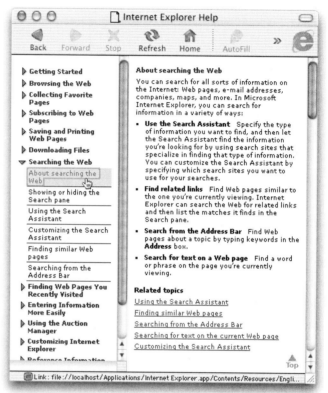

This Help file works like a browser—click links to open new pages of information.

Once you know how to use your browser and start surfing, you'll quickly run up against this problem: There are over a billion web pages out there. How do you find the one you want? You find it with a **search tool,** often referred to as a search engine. You don't have to buy or install search tools—they are just on the web, like any of the other web pages. But they are different from other web pages in that you can type in the names of subjects you want to find, and the search tool will look for it.

Oh, there is so much to tell you about search tools, but that's not the purpose of this book. I can only tell you a couple of important points, and you will have to move on from there.

When you enter a query in a search tool, it does not go running all over the world looking for pages that match your query. **It looks only in its own database** that it has compiled according to its own special criteria. There are many search tools, and they each have their own criteria and their own way of adding sites to their database. So you might ask three different search tools to find "Briards" and come up with three very different lists of web pages about Briards (a dog breed).

Every search tool has different rules for finding information. **Read the Tips or Help section.** It will tell you critical details about how to enter a query so results can be found. As search tools are improved, their rules change a little, so when you see a new look on your favorite search page, check the Tips or Help section again.

Search Tools

Important Point Number One

Important Point Number Two

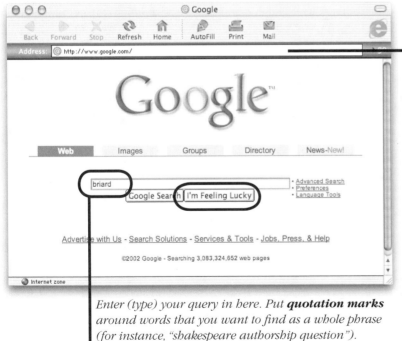

Enter (type) your query in here. Put **quotation marks** around words that you want to find as a whole phrase (for instance, "shakespeare authorship question").

Then press Return or click the "Google Search" button. See the results on the following page.

*This is for the web address (URL). But most browsers will do a **quick search** for you right here. Try this: Type a question mark, then a space, then the text (in quotes, if a phrase) you want to find. Hit Return.*

*The **I'm Feeling Lucky** button is great. Use it in this sort of situation: You want to find a college, but you know the college's web address is some long, obscure .edu sort of name. In that case, type in what you can, using quotation marks where appropriate, such as "santa fe community college" "santa fe" "new mexico," then hit the "I'm Feeling Lucky" button. Instead of getting a list of results, Google will bring up the actual web site for the college. Try it.*

These are the results of the simple search shown on the previous page. Click any link to go to that page. Remember, you can press on a link (or Command-click on it) to get a menu option to open this link in a new window. That way you won't lose this page full of results.

If you want to narrow the search, read the Help or Tips page of the web site! Every search tool gives you tips on how to find specifically the item you want.

*There is a great book from Peachpit Press called **Search Engines for the World Wide Web, Visual QuickStart Guide,** by Alfred and Emily Glossbrenner.*

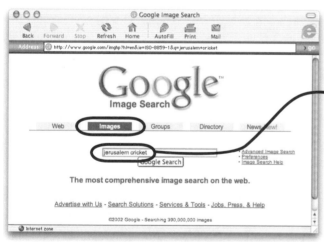

Find a search tool you like and then spend some time getting to know all of its features. In this example, I clicked the button to search for images, typed "jerusalem cricket," and got the results shown to the right.

In Google, as in most search tools, put a + sign in front of a word to make sure your search *includes* that word, and a – sign to *exclude* words. For instance, to search for images of the bird phoenix, but not the city, enter: ***phoenix +bird –arizona.***

Some search tools, called **search engines,** work best by entering words or phrases within quotation marks. The database in search engines is compiled automatically by software "robots." Other search tools, called **directories,** work best by "drilling" down through their selection of web sites. Directories are compiled by human beings who filter out the useless sites.

Use a directory, like the one shown below, to find entire web sites about a topic, such as Sri Lanka or the Wiccan religion. **Use a search engine,** such as the one shown on the previous pages (many search tools include both directories and search engines), when you want to include information that might be contained in web sites about other things, such as people's family vacations or their geneaology research.

You will probably find yourself using the directory called Yahoo, or a similar one called Google Directory, shown below. Instead of typing in a word for the directory to find, try clicking your way down through the list. Click on a category and keep clicking down to narrow your choices.

The Internet itself is the best source of information about how to do things on the Internet. You just have to *find* the stuff. For lots of information, drill down through the Computer category in Google (explained below) until you find the articles on searching the web.

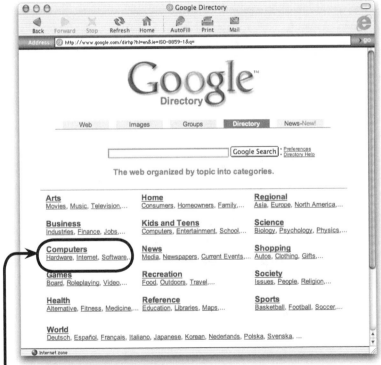

To drill down through a directory, *do something like this:*

Click <u>Internet,</u> *then on the page that comes up click* <u>Searching,</u> *then click* <u>Help and Tutorials,</u> *then choose any of the many articles about searching the web. Try it.*

Other Sorts of Search Tools

URLs for several popular search tools:

google.com

yahoo.com

altavista.com

go.com

excite.com

about.com

hotbot.com

search.com

lycos.com

infospace.com

You might have noticed that Google is my favorite search tool. I love it because it is so clean, the page is not filled with all sorts of junk I don't want, there are no annoying banner ads, it is incredibly fast, and it finds the kinds of things I look for on a daily basis.

*If you're a **New York Times crossword puzzler,** take advantage of Google to fill in just enough letters so you can figure out everything else. You can usually find the answers right in the results page. For instance, let's say you need to find the* Winning *coach of Super Bowl IV. In the Google search engine (not the directory), enter* "winning coach" *in quotes, and* "super bowl IV" *in quotes. Hit Return. Try it: Ta da—Hank Stram. Or you need to find an* ingredient in sealing wax. *Enter* "sealing wax" *in quotes, and the word* ingredient. *Ta da—lac. Amazing.*

Finding Information on the Web with Sherlock

The Sherlock icon in the Dock.

Sherlock is an incredible feature. It's not on the Internet—it's on your Mac, and you can see its icon in your Dock.

Using Sherlock, you can find shopping bargains on the web, track your stocks, get the latest news, research your favorite topics, find out what time the local movie starts, get products and support from Apple, look up definitions and synonyms and spellings of words, and much more. It's not a complete replacement for the search tools you find on the web itself, but it can provide a quick and easy way to locate many things. I'm going to show you a few of Sherlock's features, and you'll have fun exploring it further.

Channels

The different areas of Sherlock are called **channels;** each icon in Sherlock's toolbar represents a different channel, or source of information. Click the Sherlock icon in the upper-left corner to see an explanation of each one.

Each icon represents an available channel.

Click the Sherlock icon to see this pane that explains each channel.

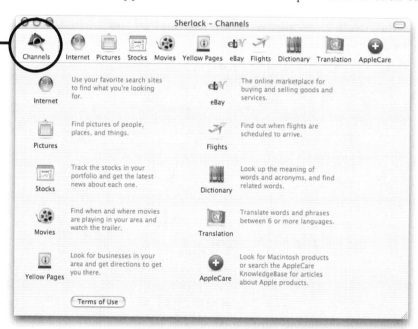

To rearrange the channels, *Command-drag the icons.*

To delete a channel, *Command-drag it off the toolbar.*

To put a channel back that you deleted, *go to the View menu and choose "Customize Toolbar...," then drag the channel back into the Toolbar.*

Note: If America Online is your only email/Internet service, you must first open and log on to AOL before you can use Sherlock to search the Internet!

Some of the channels base their information on where you live, which is called a "location." The **Sherlock preferences** pick up your current location from the information you gave your Mac when you first set it up. But sometimes you want to know information based on another location; for instance, maybe you want to get directions from the airport to your brother's house in Starkville, Mississippi, so when you arrive at the airport you'll know how to get there. To do this, set up another location, then choose it in the appropriate channel when you need it (as shown on page 538).

To add other locations, go to the Sherlock menu, choose "Preferences...," and click the "Locations" tab. Click the "Add" button and fill in the pertinent information.

Preferences

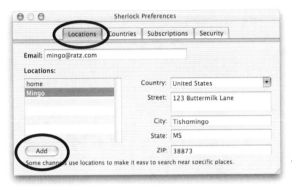

If you happen to be spending a week in Tishomingo with your laptop and want to know what movies are showing nearby, first set up a new location for Tishomingo.

Find web pages with the **Internet channel.** Sherlock searches for results in the databases of a number of online search engines, as displayed at the very bottom of its window.

Internet channel

Enter the information you're looking for here, then click the green magnifying glass.

Single-click a result to see a description in the lower pane.

Double-click a result in this upper pane to go straight to that web page in your brower.

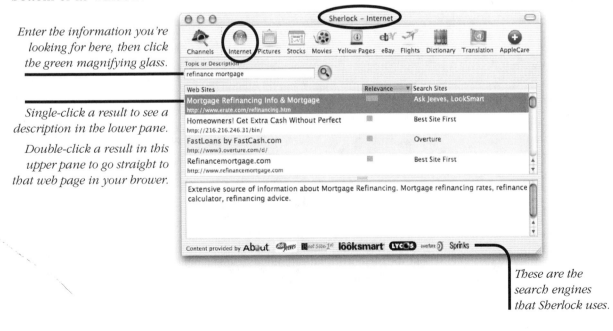

These are the search engines that Sherlock uses.

Pictures channel

In the **Pictures channel,** Sherlock searches the digital library of stock photography of gettyimages, which is owned by Bill Gates. Keep in mind that most of the images you'll find here *are not free*—if you plan to use a photo in a brochure or on your web site, you are expected to pay a royalty.

If you just want to see pictures of what something looks like (for instance, a solpugid), don't use the Sherlock Pictures channel—go to www.google.com; click the "Images" tab, and enter the name of the thing you would like to see (as shown on page 532).

These sorts of images, like the kind you see in advertisements, are called stock photography. Double-click any image to open your browser and display that page, as shown below.

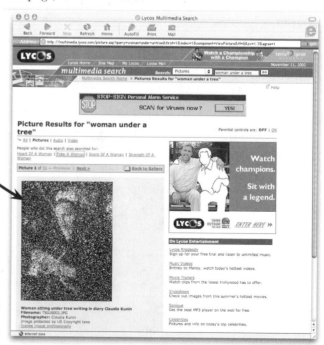

Most of the pages displaying the images are filled with obnoxious flashing ads. (I can't display the image here because I haven't paid for it.)

If you understand stocks and work with them, the **Stocks channel** will make sense to you.

Stocks channel

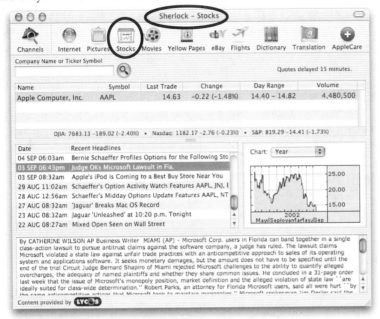

This **Movies channel** is great. And pretty self-explanatory.

Movies channel

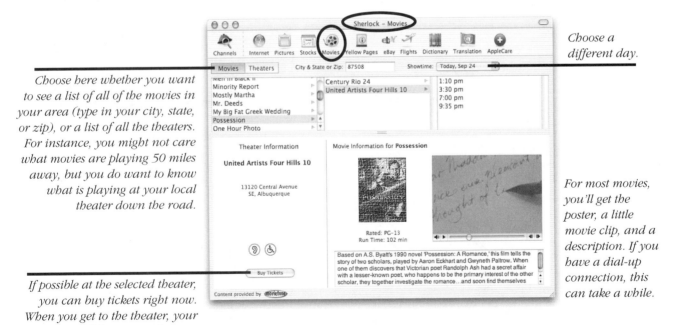

Choose a different day.

Choose here whether you want to see a list of all of the movies in your area (type in your city, state, or zip), or a list of all the theaters. For instance, you might not care what movies are playing 50 miles away, but you do want to know what is playing at your local theater down the road.

For most movies, you'll get the poster, a little movie clip, and a description. If you have a dial-up connection, this can take a while.

If possible at the selected theater, you can buy tickets right now. When you get to the theater, your tickets will be waiting for you.

Yellow Pages channel

The **Yellow Pages channel** is amazing, too. Type in something you're looking for, like "pizza," "vacuum cleaners," "college," "bar," etc. Then enter the city and state or the zip code near which you want Sherlock to look (like your home zip). Click the green button to start the search (or hit your Enter key). Single-click a result to see a map, if available, and printable directions from your house!

Sherlock will only find businesses that have that exact word in the title. For instance, if you type "margarita," you'll get a list of any business with "margarita" in its name, but not a list of bars that sell great margaritas.

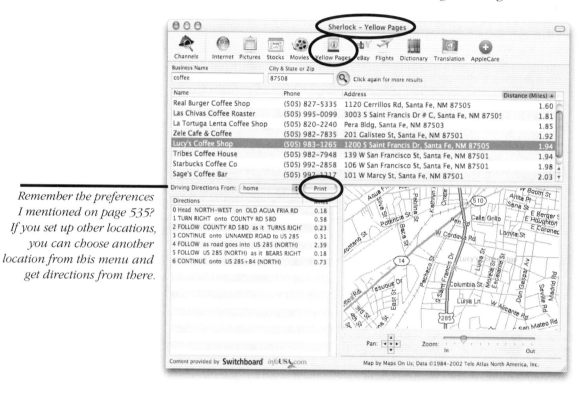

Remember the preferences I mentioned on page 535? If you set up other locations, you can choose another location from this menu and get directions from there.

If you're looking for something to buy, you can use Sherlock's **eBay channel** **eBay channel**
to search eBay instead of going to the eBay web site (www.eBay.com). You
can even track the auction process of selected items.

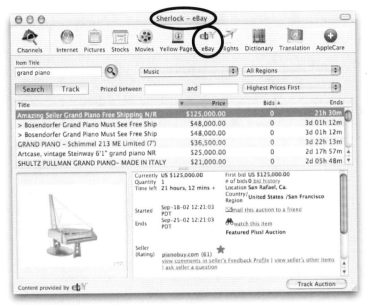

*Make your choices from these boxes
and menus, then click the green
magnifying glass (or hit Return or
Enter).*

*In the Results pane, single-click to
see more information; double-click
to open your browser and go to
that item's web page where you
can make a bid.*

In Sherlock's **Flights channel,** you can choose an airline, enter the flight   **Flights channel**
number and departure and arrival cities, click the green button, and in a
second or two you'll know the status of that flight.

If the flight has more than one leg, choose the segment from the menu
circled to the left, and you'll get lots of details.

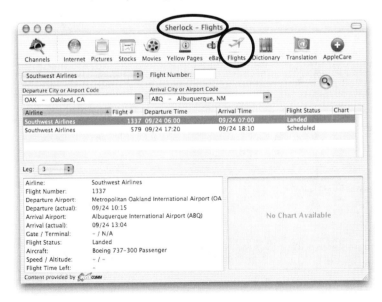

Dictionary channel In the **Dictionary channel,** enter a word you want defined, then click the green magnifying glass. If you spelled the word properly, you'll get the definition, pronunciation, etymology, and even synonyms in the bottom pane.

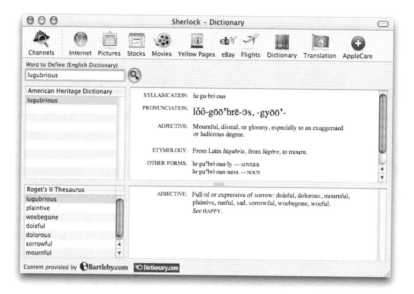

You can use this Dictionary channel as a spelling reference, as well. Type in the word as close as you can figure it out, then click the green button. If you did *not* spell the word properly, you'll get a list of spelling suggestions, as shown below.

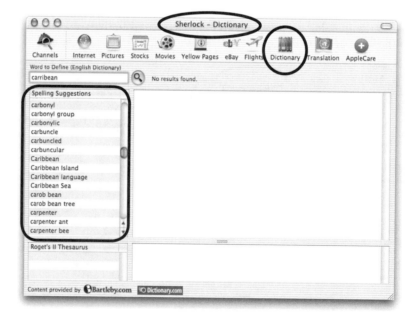

The **Translation channel** works pretty well. In the top pane, type text in any of many languages (you can see the list in the menu, shown below, right). Then choose what you want it translated into (also from that list) and click the "Translate" button. You can see from the example below that it did a pretty good job in this particular case.

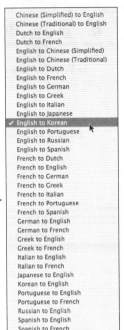

Translation channel

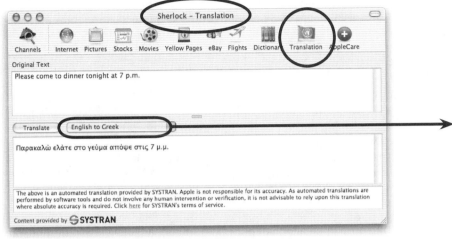

In the **AppleCare channel,** you can access a huge number of articles about all things Mac. Just type in a word or short phrase and click the green magnifying glass. This is a good resource to check if the Help files aren't quite enough.

AppleCare channel

To read an article, single-click its name and the article will appear in the pane below. You can print any selected article.

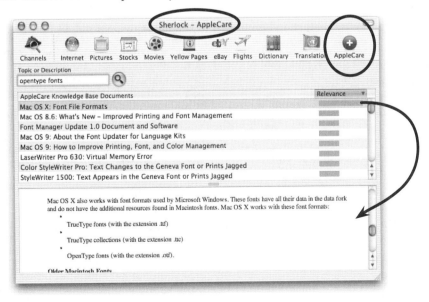

1. **The World Wide Web is made up of millions (or billions) of:**
   a. spiders
   b. individual pages, similar to word processing pages
   c. individual corporations
   d. government troops

2. **You can tell an item on a Web page is a link because:**
   a. it is underlined
   b. it has a border around it
   c. the cursor turns into a hand
   d. any of the above

3. **Hypertext refers to:**
   a. text that branches out non-sequentially, and the reader can choose which path to follow
   b. text on drugs
   c. text you can read really fast
   d. any text on a web page

4. **A URL is a:**
   a. rat
   b. search tool
   c. web page address
   d. domain name

5. **The letters "htm" or "html" at the end of a file name indicate:**
   a. any web page
   b. a domain name
   c. a server
   d. only home pages

6. **To view web pages, you need a:**
   a. search tool
   b. domain name
   c. bookmark or favorite
   d. browser

7. **To find the information you need, use a:**
   a. search tool
   b. domain name
   c. bookmark or favorite
   d. browser

8. **If you want the URL of your web site to be the name of your business, you need to buy a:**
   a. search tool
   b. domain name
   c. bookmark or favorite
   d. browser

9. **To save the location of a page that you want to find again, use a:**
   a. search tool
   b. domain name
   c. bookmark or favorite
   d. browser

10. **In most browsers, to get to a web page with the address** http://www.peachpit.com **what is the minimum you have to type:**
    a. http://www.peachpit.com
    b. www.peachpit.com
    c. peachpit.com
    d. peachpit

11. **In most browsers, to get to a web page with the address** http://www.newmexico.org **what is the minimum you have to type:**
    a. http://www.newmexico.org
    b. www.newmexico.org
    c. newmexico.org
    d. newmexico

12. **Which of these fonts will be the easiest to read on the screen?**
    a. Times
    b. Verdana
    c. Helvetica
    d. Palatino

13. **Which Sherlock channel would you use to find directions to the nearest dry cleaner?**
    a. Stocks
    b. Internet
    c. eBay
    d. Yellow Pages

Answers on page 732.

Mail and Address Book

The Mac OS X application for handling email is called **Mail.** As you'd expect, Mail enables you to write email messages, send messages, and receive messages. Beyond those basic functions, Mail has many useful tools for organizing, formatting, searching, and filtering email.

The **Address Book** is a separate application that works in conjunction with Mail. You can save your favorite email addresses, make a mailing to send a message to a number of people at once, enter an address in a new message with the click of the mouse, and more.

Contents of this chapter

Mail

Mail

The **basic** things you will be doing in **Mail** are checking messages, replying to messages, and composing new messages. On these next few pages are directions for how to do just that, but there is lots more your Mail program can do for you. You can create folders to organize your mail, create "rules" to filter incoming messages and automatically sort them into special folders, spell-check your compositions, search your mail, and add entries to your Address Book.

But since you probably want to get started right away just using email, jump right in. You must have an Internet connection already set up, as explained in Chapter 31, and you must have **already set up your email account** with Mac.com (or any other provider, as mentioned below). If you haven't set up your Mac.com account yet, and you want one (you don't have to have one), see pages xxi–xxii.

You cannot get your AOL mail through any other client except AOL or their web site.

If you have an account with any other provider, you can set that up as an account in Mail so you can use Mail as your email "client"; see pages 561–565. In fact, if you have several email accounts, Mail will check them all for you at the same time, and you can send messages from any account.

The Viewer Window

Mail opens up to the **Viewer Window.** If you open Mail and don't see this window, press Command Option N (or go to the File menu and choose "New Viewer Window").

Customizable Toolbar, see page 558 (you might see different icons).

Activity Viewer hot spot, see page 577.

Status Bar, see page 577.

Customizable columns, see page 548–549.

Message List, see pages 548–549.

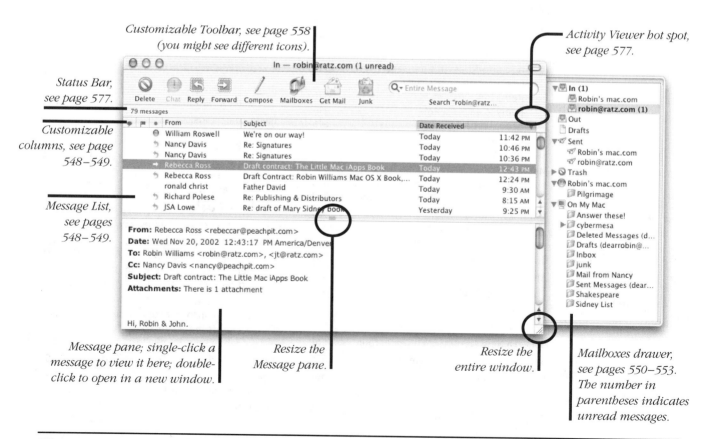

Message pane; single-click a message to view it here; double-click to open in a new window.

Resize the Message pane.

Resize the entire window.

Mailboxes drawer, see pages 550–553. The number in parentheses indicates unread messages.

To compose and send a new message

1. Click "Compose" in the toolbar to open a "New Message" window.

2. Click in the "To" area (called a field) and type an email address.

3. If you want to send a copy to someone, click in the "CC" field and type an address.

   An email address must have an @ symbol, and there must be a "domain name" with a dot, such as "ratz.com," "aol.com," "attbi.net," etc.

   To send to more than one person in either the "To" or the "CC" fields, separate the email addresses with commas.

4. Click in the "Subject" field and type a message description.

5. Click in the blank message area and type a message.

6. Connect to the Internet if you're not already connected.

7. Click the "Send" icon in the toolbar.

   Your copy of the sent message will be stored in the Mailboxes drawer in the "Sent" folder.

If you can't apply formatting to the selected text, perhaps your mail is set up as "Plain Text." From the Format menu, choose "Make Rich Text."

Save As Draft: To finish a message later, click "Save As Draft" in the toolbar, or press Command S. The message will be saved in the Drafts folder within your Mailboxes drawer. **To open the Draft** ("restore" it) later for editing, select the "Drafts" icon in the Mailboxes drawer, then double-click the desired draft in the list.

Mail automatically creates a draft for you whenever you're writing a lengthy letter just in case something happens and your computer goes down, you won't lose the entire letter. But to make sure, press Command S regularly, as you would in any document.

Address: Click the "Address" button in the New Message toolbar to open a limited version of the Address Book. Double-click a name in your list to address your message to that person. Select a number of people and click the "To" button to send the same message to all those people.

To check for messages:

1. Connect to the Internet if you're not already connected.
2. Click once on the Mail icon in the Dock to open Mail.
3. Click the "Get Mail" icon in the toolbar.

   Mail checks any "Accounts" that you've set up (how to set up accounts is on pages 561–565). Any account in the Mailboxes drawer that receives new email displays a notice next to the Inbox that indicates how many unread messages are in the Inbox.
4. Your messages will appear in the Message List. Single-click a message to display its contents in the Message pane.

To reply to the sender of a message:

1. If the message is not already open, select it in the Viewer Window, then click the "Reply" button in the toolbar.
2. A Message window opens which contains the original sender's address in the "To" field, and the original message formatted as a quote. Type your reply above the quote, then click the "Send" button in the toolbar.

To reply to ALL recipients of a message:

Tip: When you select a message and choose "Reply" or "Reply All" from the toolbar, the Reply window that opens also has a "Reply" button in its toolbar. Click the button to toggle it between "Reply" (reply to message sender only) and "Reply to All" (reply to all message recipients).

Mail that you receive may have been sent to multiple recipients, either directly as a Carbon copy (Cc) (or Courtesy copy since it's no longer on carbon paper), or secretly as a Blind carbon copy (Bcc). You can choose to reply to all recipients with one email (the reply will not include anyone in the Bcc list).

1. If the message is not already open, select the message in the Viewer Window, then click the "Reply All" button in the toolbar.
2. Type your reply above the original quoted message, then click the "Send" button in the toolbar.

To send a Bcc (blind courtesy copy):

1. Address and write your message as usual.
2. From the Edit menu, choose "Add Bcc Header." This puts a new field in the address area. Any address(es) you type in this field will *not* be seen by anyone whose address is in the "To" field.

To forward a message:

1. Select or open a message in the Viewer Window, then click the "Forward" button in the toolbar.
2. Type any comments above the original quoted message, then click the "Send" button in the toolbar.

Attach: To attach a file to your message, click the "Attach" button in the toolbar, or choose "Attach" from the Message menu. The standard Open dialog box appears so you can find and select the file you wish to attach. Find the file, select it, then click "Open." (If you don't know how to find files in this window, please see Chapter 12.)

Another way to attach a file to a message is to drag the file's icon from its Finder window and drop it in the "New Message" window. This means you need to go to the Desktop and either arrange an open window to the side of your screen, or drag that file out of its folder and let it sit on the Desktop. Then when you are in Mail and writing your message, you can reach the file to drag it into the message window to attach it, as shown below.

To remove an attachment from a message, select the attachment in the "New Message" window (drag across it), then press the Delete key.

Attach a file

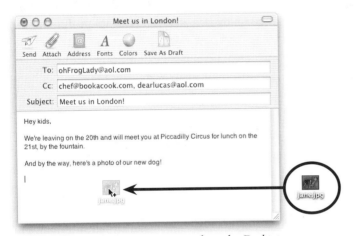

I put the photograph I want to send on the Desktop. Then I opened Mail and wrote my message. Now I can just drag the photo and drop it directly in the message, as shown above.

This is what the attachment looks like once I have dropped it into the message area. The receiver can usually just double-click on the icon to open it. Or drag it to the Desktop first, and then open it.

Depending on the file, you might see the actual image here in the message pane, and the receiver might also see the actual image. She can still just drag it to her Desktop.

Message List

The **Message List** displays a list of all messages in the currently selected Mailbox. The list is divided into several columns. The Message List provides different views of a list, depending on which column is selected.

The columns of information

Besides the default headings that appear in your Viewer Window, you can choose to show a number of additional columns. I explain the ones that aren't so obvious on the opposite page.

Also from the the View menu, you can choose to **hide** any column you don't want to see—just uncheck it from the menu list.

To change the column widths, position the pointer over the gray dividing line in the column headings, then press-and-drag the column left or right.

To rearrange (sort) the list according to the column heading, just click the heading at the top of a column. The column heading that is blue is the one that items are currently arranged by. For instance, I like to keep my email organized by date received, with the newest email at the top of the list, as shown below. But sometimes I want to find an old email from a particular person, so I click the "From" column to alphabetize the names; then I can quickly skim through the collection of email from each person.

These are the column headings. Click a heading to sort the messages by that column.

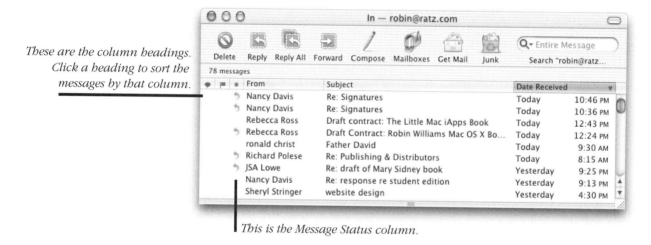

This is the Message Status column.

The **Message Status** column (●) uses different icons to indicate if you've read the message, replied to it, forwarded it, or redirected it. These icons are applied automatically when one of those actions takes place. In addition, you can manually mark an email that you've already read as "unread." You can use this as a reminder to go back and read a message more carefully, or to make a message stand out in the list: Select a message or multiple messages, then from the Message menu, select "Mark As Unread."

Icons in the Message Status column

Click the column heading to group similar categories, such as unread or returned messages, together in the list. Click again in the column heading to reverse the order of the list.

Message Status **icons** give visual clues to the status of messages.

- Blue orb: message has not been read.
- Curved arrow: message was replied to.
- Right arrow: message was forwarded.
- Segmented arrow: message was redirected.

Number column: In a series of email exchanges, it may be useful to know in what order messages were received. The Number column keeps track of the order for you. Click the **#** symbol in the column heading to arrange messages by order. Click again in the column heading to reverse the order of the list.

Flags column: Mark a message as flagged when you want it to stand out in the list, or if you want to temporarily tag a group of related messages. **To search for flagged files** in a list, click the "Flag" column heading; all flagged messages will move to the top of the list. Click the heading again to reverse the order and put flagged messages at the bottom of the list.

Subject column: The Subject column shows the text that the sender typed into the Subject header of their email message. Click the heading of the column to show the subjects in alphabetical order; click again to reverse the order of the list.

Date & Time column: The Date & Time column shows when you received a message. Click the heading of the column to show messages in the time sequence they were received; click again to reverse the order of the list.

Buddy Availability: If you have a Buddy List in iChat (see Chapter 33), this column will display a green orb when a Buddy is online, and a yellow orb when he is online but idle (perhaps his computer has gone to sleep). Supposedly when you see a Buddy is online, you can click the "Chat" icon and start a chat with them. You won't see the Chat icon until you actually start a new message to that person, although you can customize your toolbar (see page 558) and put the Chat button in your Viewer Window toolbar.

Mailboxes Drawer

The **Mailboxes drawer** slides out from the side of the Viewer Window. The drawer might slide out from either side of the Viewer Window, depending on how much screen space is available to the left or right. **To make the drawer appear on one side or the other,** drag a message from the Viewer Window off to the side on which you want the drawer. **To open or close the drawer,** click the Mailbox button in the toolbar, or drag the edge of the drawer.

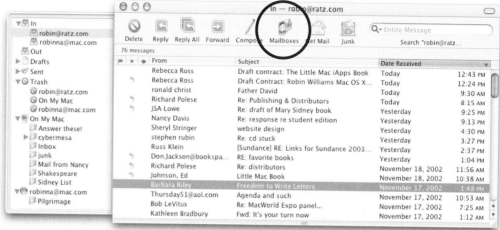

This is the Mailboxes drawer where all of your email is neatly organized.

For explanations of the individual icons, please see the following pages.

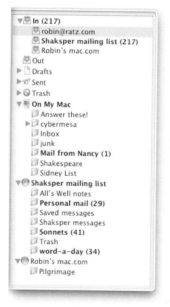

Here you see three email accounts that Mail checks for me (in the In box). Each account has its own Out, Draft, Sent, and Trash folders.

Numbers in parentheses indicate unread messages.

All of the folders (Mailboxes) under "On My Mac" are ones I created myself and in which I store messages. Some of these Mailboxes hold messages that are automatically filtered into them; others store messages I have dragged into them.

The crystal balls indicate messages that are on Apple's servers from my two Mac.com accounts. As you can see, I haven't had a chance to check my Shakespeare mailing list for a while.

Here is an explanation of the various **icons** you might see in your drawer. As you make and delete folders and change your preferences, your arrangement of icons in the drawer will change, so don't worry if you don't see all of these or if you see more than I have listed here.

▼ The **number in parentheses** is the number of unread messages in that folder. The *first-level* folder (the "In" box in the example to the left) shows you the **total** number of messages in all accounts, while the *second-level* folders (for the accounts "jt" and "roadrat" in the example), show you specifically how many messages are in that particular account.

▼ Single-click the main folder (first level) to show a list in the Viewer window of *all* messages of that sort for *all* accounts. For instance, click the "In" box to see all mail in all accounts; click the "Sent" icon to see all messages you have sent from any account; etc.

▼ Click *one* of the individual folders to see messages for just that selected account.

▼ If you have many accounts and want to check for messages from several of them at once, Command-click the accounts.

In box: At the top of the drawer you can tell if you have received any email. Messages contained in these In boxes are stored on your computer.

If you have **more than one email account,** click the triangle next to the In box icon to show the individual In boxes for each account.

Out box: Stores messages temporarily while waiting to be sent. If you're not connected to the Internet at the moment (you're working "offline" or your connection is down), messages you send are stored in the Out box until an online connection is established.

Drafts folder: Stores unfinished messages that you're composing. If you have multiple Mail accounts set up, you'll have separate Draft folders for each account. The messages in the Draft folders are stored on your computer.

Sent folder: Contains copies of messages that you sent to other people. If you have multiple email accounts, the Sent folder contains other Sent folders named for each account you've set up. The messages in the Sent folders are stored on your computer.

Junk folder: Stores messages that have been identified by Mail as junk mail. The number in parentheses tells you how many junk messages have not been read. This Junk folder is automatically created when you change the Junk Mail mode from "Training" to "Automatic" in the Mail menu (as explained on pages 555–557).

Trash (2)

Red circle Trash folder: Contains messages that you deleted. If you have multiple accounts, the main Trash folder contains other Trash folders named for each of your accounts. Messages in the "red circle" Trash folders are stored on your computer—they are not *really* thrown away until you choose to empty the trash.

Use the Mail preferences to set up your Trash to **empty automatically** at certain times: In the Accounts pane, double-click an account name, then click the "Special Mailboxes" tab and make your Trash choice.

If you do not set up Mail to empty the Trash at certain times, make sure to **empty all your Trash mailboxes** occasionally. If you have an IMAP account (like Mac.com), you must empty your Trash or your mailbox on the IMAP server may get too full and you won't get any more mail. **To delete all messages in the Trash,** select the topmost Trash icon in the Mailboxes drawer, then from the Mailbox menu choose "Erase Deleted Messages" (or press Command K).

▼ roadrat@mac.com
  Deleted Messages
  Research
  Sent Messages
  Travel folder

Internet icon: The blue crystal ball indicates this is the Mailbox your Mac.com account (if you have one) and these folders and the files inside of them are stored on Apple's server. You can create new folders in this Mailbox (from the Mailbox menu, make a new Mailbox and choose your Mac.com account), then drag other messages from any account into the folders. You'll have access to everything in this Mailbox from any computer in the world—just open any browser, go to www.mac.com, click the Webmail icon, and sign in. **All messages in these folders are stored in the 15 megabytes of allotted space in your .MAC account.**

In the Mail preferences, you can set up rules (see pages 572–575) that tell certain types of email to go into certain folders, including these.

If you delete all of the folders in this mailbox, the entire Mailbox and crystal ball will disappear. If you want it back, make a new Mailbox as described above, or go to www.mac.com, log in to WebMail, make a new folder online, and it will appear here in Mail.

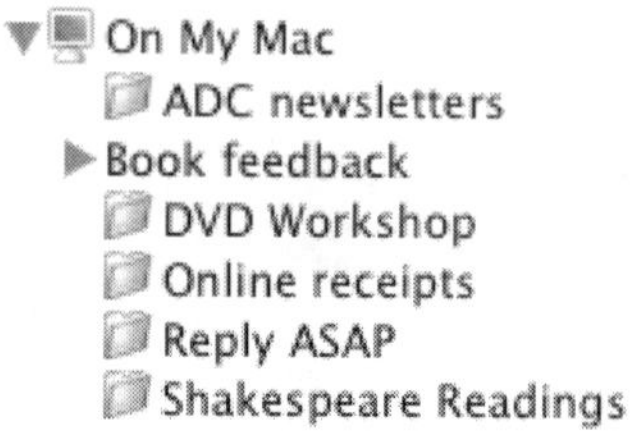

▼ On My Mac
  ADC newsletters
  ▶ Book feedback
  DVD Workshop
  Online receipts
  Reply ASAP
  Shakespeare Readings

On My Mac: Contains custom folders that you create for storing and organizing your messages. If you use rules (see pages 572–575), you can have certain messages automatically sent to one of these folders. **All messages in these folders are stored on your computer.**

You might not see the actual little computer icon called On My Mac unless you also create online folders as described above. But even if you don't see the computer icon, all of these folders are stored on your hard disk.

Important note: If you upgraded from Mac OS X version 10.1 to version 10.2 (Jaguar), you'll find all of your old mail in a folder called "Inbox" located under "On My Mac"!

Tip: to create new folders in this section, Control-click "On My Mac" and choose "New Mailbox." Drag messages in any account from the Viewer Window to any of your new custom folders.

Some people, like me and my partner John, get email at several different addresses, each coming from a different server. **Mail can check all of your email accounts at once.** When you answer mail, you can choose to have it answered from any one of your accounts, no matter to which account the original message was mailed.

If you have more than one account in the Mailboxes drawer, the "New Message" window provides a pop-up **Account menu** that contains the names of any accounts you've created, as shown above. From the pop-up menu, choose the account that you want the message sent from.

To set up your other accounts so Mail can check them all, see pages 561–565.

This is John's Mail. If he received an email to his ratz.com account, he could answer it with a return address from any of his other accounts.

Contextual Menus   Mail makes extensive use of **contextual menus:** Control-click on a message, the toolbar, or an item in the Mailboxes drawer to open a pop-up menu that offers various commands, as shown below. If you have a two-button mouse you can right-click on an item to show a contextual menu.

Using contextual menus is just a convenient way to access menu commands—there is nothing in a contextual menu that you can't find in the main menu bar across the top of your screen.

Hold down the Control key (not the Command key) and click on any message in the Viewer window to get the contextual menu.

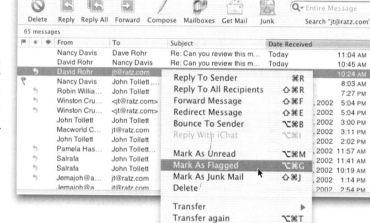

Okay, this is really incredible. You can set Mail so it **automatically deletes junk mail without ever having to see it.** Or if you are a little more cautious, you can have all the junk mail sent to a folder where you can check through it in case something you want accidentally ended up in the junk pile. And this really works—I was getting close to 100 pieces of junk a day in my public email and now I only see two or three a week. The rest are deleted before they even hit my box.

First of all, make sure your viewer window is set up as shown below. This has nothing to do with the junk filter, but it will prevent the following from happening: When you single-click on a junk message to delete it, the message appears in the bottom pane. This does two things—it displays the message, which sometimes can take valuable time, and it often sends back a message to the junk mail sender confirming that this is a valid email address, which means you'll get more email from them and they'll sell your address to other evil junkers! So you don't want to give them the satisfaction of even *opening* a piece of junk mail.

Get rid of the bottom pane, as explained below, and when you want to **read a message,** *double-click* the message name and it will open in its own window.

Junk Mail Filter!

To turn off the Junk Mail feature, *from the Mail menu choose "Junk Mail," then from the submenu select "Off."*

Set up your window

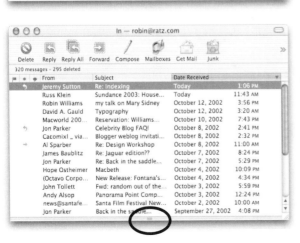

When both panes are showing, as in this example, the entire email appears in the bottom pane when you click on a message—even if you want to delete it.

To prevent this, drag this bar all the way to the bottom.

When the bottom pane is gone, you can select one, several, or all email messages and delete them (hit the Delete key) without having to open them first.

To read a message, double-click it and a separate window will open.

—continued

Automatic junk mail detection
Mail automatically analyzes incoming messages and identifies what it thinks is **junk mail** by highlighting the message in brown. If your "Flags" column is showing in the Viewer window, you'll see a junk mail icon (a brown mail bag) in that column.

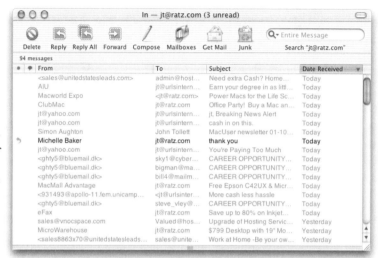

Mail's default is to turn junk mail brown.

This is John's Viewer window. Notice half the junk mail isn't even addressed to him!

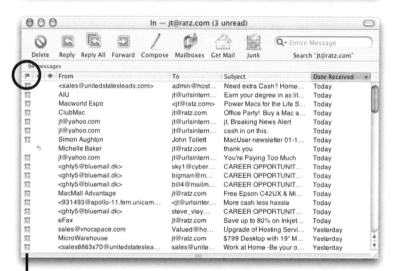

To make the Flags column visible, from the View menu choose "Columns," then from the submenu choose "Flags."

You can **train Mail to be more accurate** in determining whether a message is junk:

1. From the Mail menu, choose "Junk Mail," then select "Training."

2. When you receive a new email message, check to see if Mail has correctly identified it.

   - If the new message is unwanted junk mail, but **Mail did not mark it** as such: Single-click the message, then click the "Junk" icon in the toolbar to mark it as junk mail (*or* from the Message menu, choose "Mark as Junk Mail" *or* press Command Shift J).

   - If **Mail INcorrectly identifies** a message as junk mail, you can correct it: Select the message incorrectly marked and notice the "Junk" icon in the toolbar has changed to "Not Junk." Click the "Not Junk" icon to clear the message's junk designation.

3. Continue training Mail in this way for a couple of weeks, or until most incoming messages seem to be correctly identified.

When you're ready to **let Mail automatically handle junk mail,** go to the Mail menu, choose "Junk Mail," and from the submenu choose "Automatic." Mail will create a Junk mailbox (in the Mailboxes drawer) to store all your unwanted mail. You might want to occasionally review the messages in the Junk mailbox to make sure mail is being correctly identified.

When you're satisfied that Mail is accurately finding junk mail, you may want to change your setting so **Junk mail is instantly deleted.** Be careful with this! If you choose this option, you will never see the mail, nor can you undo the action or find it in any "Trash" mailbox—it's gone. And good riddance.

To delete junk mail before it ever appears in your box:

1. From the Mail menu, choose "Junk Mail," then from the submenu choose "Custom...." This opens the "Rules" pane of Mail preferences, with the "Junk" rules edit sheet available for editing, as shown below.

2. Below you see how I have set up my Mail preferences so Junk is deleted before it ever lands in my box. Remember, you have to be very confident that you're not getting any real mail mixed up in your junk mail (personally, if something gets accidentally labeled as junk and disappears, that's too bad—it's not worth it to me to sort through hundreds of pieces of junk mail to see if there's one good message).

Train Mail to find junk more accurately

Instantly delete junk mail

For more details about making Rules, see pages 572–575.

Click the + sign to create more conditions, the – sign to delete a condition.

Choose options from these menus. Different options will display different parameters—try it!

The Favorites Toolbar   The buttons in the **favorites toolbar** are duplicates of some of the commands that are also available in the menu bar at the top of the screen. You can customize this toolbar just like you customize the one in the Finder window.

To add additional tool buttons to the favorites toolbar, go to the View menu and choose "Customize Toolbar…." A pane of buttons appears that represent various functions, as shown below. Drag any of these buttons to the favorites toolbar for easy access.

To remove a button from the toolbar, Command-drag it off the bar.

To rearrange a button, Command-drag it to another position.

Command-click this button at any time to switch the toolbar between icons, icons with text, or just text.

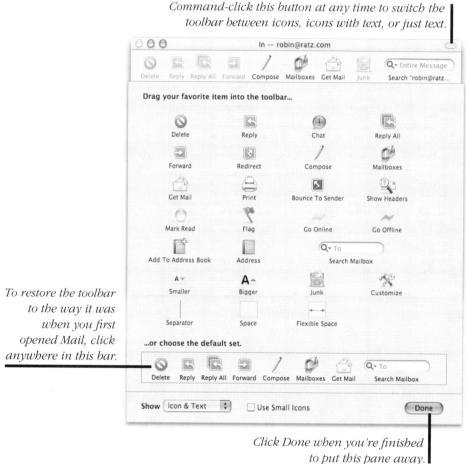

To restore the toolbar to the way it was when you first opened Mail, click anywhere in this bar.

Click Done when you're finished to put this pane away.

Other buttons that don't have obvious functions are "Bounce To Sender" and "Redirect."

The **Bounce To Sender** button is meant to discourage unwanted email: Select an unwanted message in the Message List pane, then from the Message menu, choose "Bounce To Sender" (or click the button in your toolbar, if it's there). The sender will receive a reply that says your email address is invalid and that the message was not delivered. The unwanted message is moved to your "Deleted Messages" folder. The recipient cannot tell if the message has been read. Unfortunately, this does not work for most spam (junk email) because spam return addresses are usually invalid (to prevent spammers from being spammed).

Bounce To Sender

Redirect is similar to "Forward," except that redirected mail shows the original sender's name in the "From" column instead of yours, and shows the time the message was originally composed in the "Date & Time" column of Mail's Viewer Window. When you redirect mail, your name remains in the "To" header at the top of the message so the new recipient will know that you received the message and that you redirected it.

Redirect

You can search a specific account or folder, or all mailboxes at once.

To search a specific account or folder, single-click an account or folder in the Mailboxes drawer, then click the triangle next to the magnifying glass in the Search field. From the pop-up menu, under the heading that identifies the account or folder you selected, choose whether to search entire messages or just one of the header fields (From, To, or Subject).

To search multiple mailboxes and folders, Command-click items in the Mailboxes drawer that you want to search, then set the search criteria as explained above.

To search all mailboxes, from the Search pop-up menu, choose a search criteria under the heading "In All Mailboxes."

Mail Search

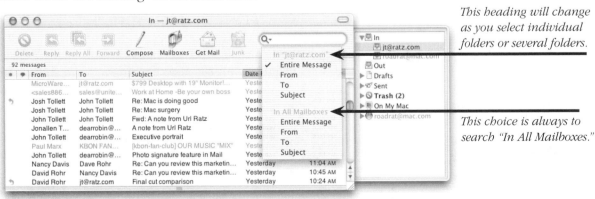

This heading will change as you select individual folders or several folders.

This choice is always to search "In All Mailboxes."

IMAP vs. POP   Apple's Mail program can handle two types of incoming mail "protocol": **IMAP** and **POP** (or POP3, to be specific). A protocol is a particular set of standards or rules having to do with communications between computers.

Email from a POP account is stored "locally," which means on your hard disk.

POP3 (Post Office Protocol 3) is a protocol in which the server automatically downloads the mail to your computer when you check mail, then *deletes* the mail from the server. With POP you cannot read mail until it has been downloaded to your computer. POP works best for users who always use one computer on which the email files are stored and managed. Although Mac OS X uses IMAP to handle Mac.com email accounts, you can also setup POP accounts in Mail just as easily (pages 561–565).

You can choose to leave your mail on the POP server after it has been downloaded to your Mac (see page 563–565), but check with your service provider before you do that—it might make them mad to have all of your email clogging up space on their server.

Email from an IMAP account is stored on a remote server (although you can keep copies on your hard disk).

IMAP (Internet Message Access Protocol) is a protocol that receives and *holds* email on a server for you a certain amount of time, typically thirty days. IMAP allows you to view email before deciding whether or not to download it to your computer.

One advantage of IMAP is that you can manage your email from multiple computers because the email files are kept on the IMAP server for storage and manipulation; this means if you check your mail on one computer while you're away from home, say in Glasgow, then when you come home and check your mail, you can get the same messages at home that you read in Glasgow.

Another advantage is that you can choose *not* to download emails that have large attachments or email from people you don't want to hear from. You can wait until it's convenient, until you know who an attachment is from, or you can just delete unwanted or unsolicited email and attachments before they ever get to your computer.

America Online uses an IMAP server. That's why you can choose whether or not to download a file, and your email disappears automatically after thirty days whether you like it or not.

When you sign up for a Mac.com email service through .Mac, you're assigned a fifteen-megabyte mailbox on Apple's IMAP mail server. All messages within an account, *even deleted messages,* are stored on Apple's server for one month by default, unless you designate a different length of time (see the account preferences on the following pages). If you get more than fifteen megabytes of mail and attachments, people will not be able to send you any more email at that account until you clear it out. (See pages xxi–xxii about .Mac accounts, also called a Mac.com account.)

Use **Mail Preferences** to create new mail accounts, edit existing accounts, and to customize Mail's behavior.

To open Preferences and get the Accounts pane:

1. From the Mail menu, choose "Preferences…," then click **Accounts.**

2. The **Description** list shows all the email accounts you've created.

   To **create** a new account, click "Add Account" and then see the following page.

   To **edit** the preferences of an existing account, select the account in the list, then click "Edit." See the following pages for detailed descriptions of the options.

   To **remove** an account from the list, select it, then click "Remove."

Set Up a New Account or Edit an Account

Accounts

Check for new mail: Set how often you want to check for new mail. This only works if Mail is open (if the triangle is under its icon in the Dock). If you don't have a full-time, always-on connection to the Internet (such as DSL or cable modem), you'll probably want to select the "Manually" option to avoid having your modem dialing and trying to connect when you least expect it.

New mail sound: Choose various sound alerts, or "None," when new mail appears in your In box. If you have various rules set that filter your mail, you can have different sounds for each of the rules so you know exactly when junk mail has been deleted, a letter from your lover has arrived, or mail for your family has gone into the Family mailbox; see pages 572–575.

*Mail cannot get your AOL email. Nothing can get AOL email except AOL (although you can use any browser anywhere in the world and go to **www.aol.com** to get your mail).*

Add or Edit an Account: You may have more than one email account in your life. For instance, you might have one that is strictly for business, one for friends and family, one for your lover, and one for your research. Mail can manage them all for you.

1. From the Mail menu, choose "Preferences…."

2. Click "Accounts" in the toolbar, then click "Add Account" to create a new one, or double-click the name of an existing account.

3. You should see the "Account Information" pane; if not, click the tab.

4. Choose an **Account Type** from the pop-up menu.

Choose ".Mac" if you're setting up an email account that you created using the Mac.com web site.

If you're setting up an account that comes from some other service provider, they can tell you if they use POP or IMAP (most likely POP).

5. In the **Description** field, type a name that will identify the account in the Mailboxes drawer. You can name it anything, such as "Lover Boy," "Research Mailing List," or "earthlink."

6. If you're setting up a Mac.com address, the **Email Address** field will automatically be filled in with your Mac.com email address.

7. **Incoming Mail Server:** If your account type is "Mac.com Account," the host name will automatically be filled in with "mail.mac.com."

If you're setting up another account type, the mail service provider can tell you what name to use. Tell them you need the "incoming" mail server name, also known as the "POP address." (It's probably something like "mail.domainname.com," where "domainname" is the name in your email address, such as mail.ratz.com).

8. If you're setting up a Mac.com account, **User Name** and **Password** are the same ones you chose when you signed up for a Mac.com account. You should have received an email from Apple verifying this information.

   If you're setting up a POP account, your user ID and password may have been assigned by your provider, or they may have been chosen by you. *These are not necessarily the same user ID and password that you use to access your email.* If necessary, ask your provider for the User ID and password information.

9. **Outgoing Mail Server:** No matter where your email account *comes* from, the outoing mail server (the SMTP Host) is always your Internet Service Provider's name, such as "mail.providername.com," because that's whom your email is going *out* through. Your Internet Service Provider is the one you pay monthly to connect you to the Internet. Mac.com is *not* your SMTP host for your Mac.com account.

Next, click the **Special Mailboxes** tab of the window. The items in this tab change, depending on whether you're creating an IMAP account (such as a Mac.com account) or a POP account (most others).

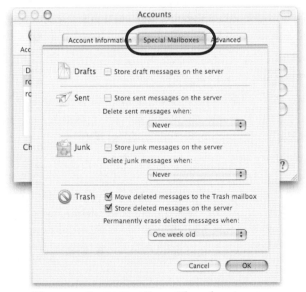

These are the IMAP options. The advantage to storing items on the server is that you can access them from anywhere in the world; they're not stored on your computer. If you have a Mac.com acount, you can go to www.mac.com and log into your account on any computer that has a browser and an Internet connection.

These are the POP options. These refer to the items that are in the Mail program and stored on your Mac, not on a remote server.

—continued

See the opposite page for the POP options.

If you're creating an IMAP account, the following options are shown in the Advanced pane:

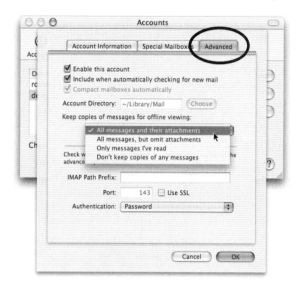

Enable this account: Check to make the account active. Uncheck it to make the account inactive, which does not delete the account—it just tells Mail to ignore it.

Include when automatically checking for new mail: *Un*check this box to prevent Mail from checking email at this address. This is useful if you have several email addresses and you choose not to check some accounts as often as others.

Compact mailboxes automatically: On an IMAP server, when you select and delete messages, they don't really get deleted—they get placed in a "Deleted" folder on the server. The server stores these deleted files for a user-specified length of time before they are erased. Apple doesn't give you a choice about this—the files you delete will be erased immediately when you close the Mail application. This frees up your space on Apple's server.

Keep copies of messages for offline viewing: This menu offers options for copying email messages from an IMAP server onto your own Mac.

"All messages and their attachments" will copy all of your email, plus any attachments you were sent, to your hard disk.

"All messages, but omit attachments" will copy the body of the email messages, but not attachments.

"Only messages I've read" will only copy and store messages if you've read them. You can mark a letter as "Unread" or "Read" whether you really have or not—use the Message menu.

"Don't keep copies of any messages" will not copy any of your mail to your hard disk. This option provides you with extra security and privacy if other people have access to your computer. If you choose this option, be aware that your IMAP server will eventually erase messages whether you've read them or not that have been stored for a user-specified length of time (thirty days at the most, generally).

If you're creating a POP account, the following options are shown in the Advanced tab.

See the previous page for the IMAP options.

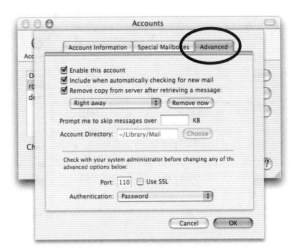

Enable this account: Check to make the account active. Uncheck it to make the account inactive, which does not delete the account—it just tells Mail to ignore it.

Include when automatically checking for new mail: *Un*check this box to prevent Mail from checking email at this address. This is useful if you have several accounts and you choose not to check some email as often as others.

Remove copy from server after retrieving a message: POP servers prefer that you check this so your mail is deleted from the server as soon as it is downloaded to your Mac. Uncheck it only when you need to temporarily keep a copy of your mail on the server. In the pop-up menu you have some options for length of time to store messages.

Prompt me to skip messages over ___ KB: When checking for mail, you can choose to skip over messages that are larger than you want to receive. This can eliminate unsolicited attachments. Enter the maximum file size that you'll permit Mail to download. A typical email message with no attachments is about 1 to 10 KB (kilobytes).

All done? When all the "Accounts" preferences are set, click OK. Your new account will appear in the Mailboxes drawer, under the "In" icon.

See When iChat Buddies are Online

Mail detects when an **iChat Buddy is online** (see Chapter 33 regarding iChat and Buddies) and notifies you: a green dot next to a Buddy's message means she's available and you can send an Instant Message to her computer.

This is the "Buddy Availablity" column. When someone in your iChat Buddy List is online, this green dot will appear. A yellow dot indicates your Buddy is online, but idle; her computer is probably asleep.

If you don't see the "Buddy Availability" column in your Viewer Window, go to the View menu, select "Columns," then choose "Buddy Availability."

Chat with a Buddy

To open a chat with a Buddy:

1. Single-click an online Buddy's email message in the Viewer Window.

2. Press Command Option I, *or* from the Message menu, choose "Reply with iChat," which will open an iChat window, as shown below, right.

OR

1. Double-click a Buddy's email message in the Viewer Window.

2. Click the Reply button as if you were going to write a letter.

3. Click the Chat icon (the blue speech balloon) in the toolbar to open an iChat message window.

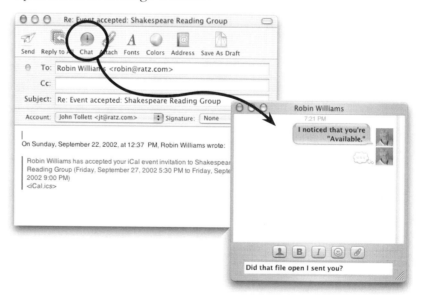

You can select **fonts, font sizes,** and **text colors** for various parts of your email messages.

To open Preferences and get the Fonts & Colors pane:

1. From the Mail menu, choose "Preferences…."

2. The "Mail Preferences" toolbar shows six buttons representing different categories of preferences. Click **Fonts & Colors.**

Fonts & Colors

Fonts & Colors

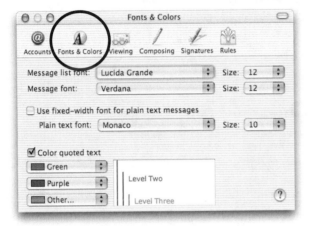

Message list font is the font used in the list of messages.

Message font is the font that you will type your email messages in. If you choose a font that your recipient does not have installed on their computer, it will turn into their default font.

Email replies often contain quotes from previous emails. Color coding and indenting the quotes makes messages easier to read and helps to visually organize the quotes in a hierarchy of responses. To apply color to quotes, check the **Color quoted text** box. Choose colors for up to three levels of quotes from the three color pop-up menus.

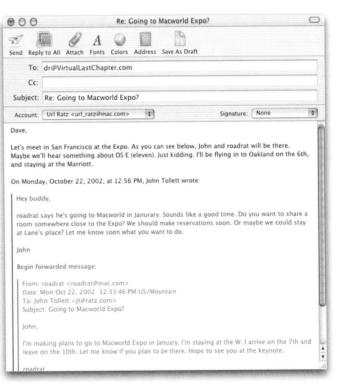

Viewing

Viewing

The **Viewing** preferences affect the information you see in the main window.

To open Preferences and get the Viewing pane:

1. From the Mail menu, choose "Preferences...."

2. The "Mail Preferences" toolbar shows six buttons representing different categories of preferences. Click **Viewing.**

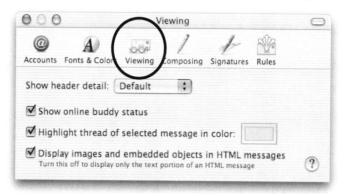

Show header detail: This menu lets you choose how much, if any, header information (all that to/from/date stuff) shows at the top of emails. Choose "Custom..." to customize what information shows in headers. "Default" means the stuff you usually see.

Show online buddy status: Click this to display the Buddy Availability column in your Viewer Window. When someone in your Buddy List is online, a green dot appears in this column; a yellow dot if they are online but idle.

Show thread of selected message in color: If you check this and then click on any message in your Viewer Window, all other messages with the exact same subject will highlight in the color you choose.

Show images and embedded objects in HTML messges: If it makes you crazy when you get big, complex web pages through your email messages, uncheck this box so only the text will appear, not all the fancy graphics.

The **Composing** pane applies to email messages as you write them.

Composing

To open Preferences and get the Composing pane:

1. From the Mail menu, choose "Preferences...."

2. The "Mail Preferences" toolbar shows six buttons representing different categories of preferences. Click **Composing.**

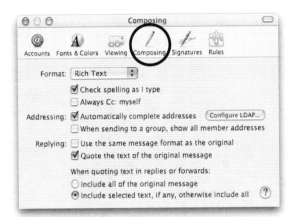

Format: "Rich Text" allows you to stylize messages with fonts and formatting, but not everyone will be able to see these features. "Plain Text" can be seen by everyone, but does not show any color and style formatting. Choose the format you'll use most often as the "Default message format," then change to the other format when necessary (choose it from the Format menu in the main menu bar).

Check spelling as I type: Check this to catch spelling errors immediately. When Mail doesn't recognize a word, it underlines the word with a dotted red line. If you need help with the correct spelling, from the Edit menu choose "Spelling," then choose "Spelling..." from the submenu. For more about checking spelling, see page 480.

Always CC myself to send a copy of outgoing messages to yourself.

Automatically complete addresses: As you type a few letters in the "To" field, Mail will add the rest of the address for you. If there are more than one match, you'll get a list to choose from. If the correct one is in the field, just hit Return. If you get a list, use the DownArrow to move down the list, selecting each one; hit Return or Enter when the proper address is chosen.

When sending to a group, show all member addresses: When you send a message to a group (mailing list, as explained on pages 584–586), Mail will display everyone's address. Unless you have a specific reason to do this, UNcheck this box so the actual addresses are hidden.

The other options are self-explanatory.

Tip: If you select some text in an email message and hit the Reply button, only the selected text will appear in the reply as a quoted message.

Signatures

A **signature** is a blurb of pre-prepared information about you or your company that can be added to the end of a message, either manually or automatically, as shown on the opposite page. You can create different signatures that include different types of information for various types of messages. For instance, in addition to a signature for personal mail that may include your address and phone number, you may want to create a different business signature that doesn't include personal information.

To open Preferences and get the Signatures pane:

1. From the Mail menu, choose "Preferences…."

2. The "Mail Preferences" toolbar shows six buttons representing different categories of preferences. Click **Signatures.**

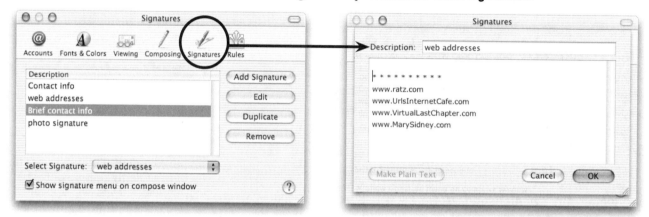

Create Signature: To create a signature, click the "Add Signature" button. In the "Description" field, enter a name for the signature that is descriptive to you. In the big box, enter any information you want to include in the signature. If you want to add a photograph, drag it into the text field. The image format should be JPEG (.jpg) to optimize file size and to minimize translation problems across computing platforms. If your message is going to another Mac, other formats will work, such as TIFF, PICT, or PNG, but JPEG is still the recommended format.

To create a new signature that's similar to an existing signature, select the signature you want to use as a model, then click the "Duplicate" button. This duplicate now shows up in the list of signatures; select it, then click the "Edit" button. Make necessary changes to the signature, change its name in the "Description" field, and click OK.

To edit the information in a signature, choose a signature in the Description list, then click the "Edit" button. Make changes in the signature file, then click OK.

To remove a signature from the list, select it, then click the "Remove" button.

To choose a default signature, select its name in the "Select Signature" pop-up menu. This signature will be used in all messages unless you override it by choosing another signature or "None" from the pop-up menu (discussed below) when you're writing a new email.

Choose signature when composing email: Check this to install a pop-up menu in the "New Message" window that contains all of your signatures. Then in any email message, just choose the one you want to include at the end of that message.

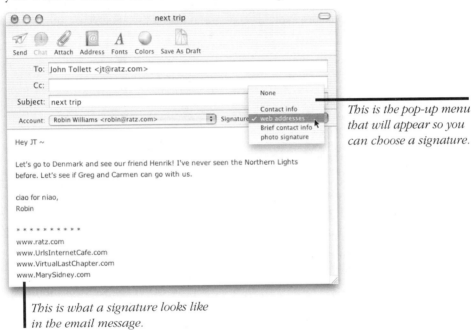

This is the pop-up menu that will appear so you can choose a signature.

This is what a signature looks like in the email message.

Rules

Use **Rules** to manage and organize your messages automatically. Rules act as filters that sift through your messages and put them in their proper mailboxes, delete them, forward them, or follow other actions, according to your directions. You might belong to a mailing list about pack rats, so you can have every email that comes in from that mailing list automatically delivered to the Pack Rat Mailbox. Or you might want to delete every email with a subject that contains the words "mortgage," "enlargement," "babes," "hot," "free," or other obvious junk-mail words.

To open Preferences and get the Rules pane:

1. From the Mail menu, choose "Preferences...."

2. The "Mail Preferences" toolbar shows six buttons representing different categories of preferences. Click **Rules.**

Before you create a new rule: If you want your mail to be automatically organized into different mailboxes, you need to create those mailboxes *before* you make the rule.

To make a new mailbox:

1. If the Mailboxes drawer is not open, open it (click the Mailbox icon in the toolbar).

2. To create a new mailbox that is not inside an existing folder, click once on the "In" icon.

   To create a new mailbox that is inside an existing folder, click on that folder to select it.

3. From the Mailbox menu, choose "New Mailbox...."

4. Choose whether you want this mailbox to be on your hard disk (On My Mac) or on Apple's server, if you have a .Mac account (choose your account name from the Location pop-up menu).

5. Name the mailbox and click OK.

To create a new rule:

1. Click the "Add Rule" button. You'll get the dialog box shown below.

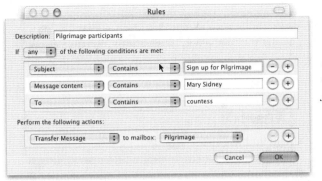

Click the ✚ or ━ to add or delete criteria for the rules.

2. The **Description** field contains a default name, such as "Rule #5." Change this name to something that describes your intended Rule. In the example below, I want all the mail from my son Ryan to go into a special mailbox, so I named it "Mail from Ryan."

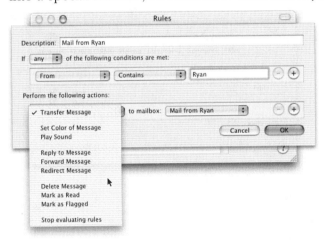

3. In the **following conditions** section, specify which elements of an email message are to be searched and what the subject of the search will be.

   The first pop-up menu contains types of message **headers** that usually are included with an incoming message, such as To, From, Subject, etc., or you can choose to find text in the body of the message. Choose which area to search.

   Then choose a "modifier" from the second pop-up menu, such as "Contains," "Does not contain," or others.

   Type an appropriate word or words into the text field. The rule shown above will search for messages whose "From" field "Contains" the word "Ryan."

—continued

4. **Perform the following actions:** Determines what actions will be applied to messages that match the criteria you specified. You can check as many or as few of these actions as you like.

> **Transfer Message:** Select an existing mailbox (that you previously made according to the directions on page 572) to transfer the messages into.

> **Set Color of Message:** Choose a color for highlighting messages that match the criteria. Then you can quickly identify various categories of filtered email that may appear in a message list.

> **Play Sound:** Choose a sound that will alert you when you receive a message that matches the criteria.

> **Reply to Message:** This opens a text box in which you can type a message that will automatically be included before the original message being forwarded or replied to.

> **Forward to:** To forward targeted incoming mail to another email address, check and enter an email address in the text field that you want the forwarded mail sent to. After you choose this you will get a little button, "Message…"; click it to enter a message that will appear at the beginning of the forwarded email.

> **Redirect to:** *Forwarded* mail shows *your* name in the "From" column of the email, plus the date and time you forwarded it. *Redirected* mail shows the *original* sender's name in the "From" column, and shows the time the message was originally composed in the "Date & Time" column of Mail's message list. When you redirect mail, your name will remain in the "To:" header at the top of the message so the new recipient will know that you received the message and redirected it.

> **Delete Message:** Trash any message that meets the criteria. You can use the header information of mail you suspect to be unwanted email and create a rule that automatically deletes messages like that one.

> **Mark as Read:** Removes the blue dot from the Message Status column (if it's showing) even if you didn't really open and read it.

> **Mark as Flagged:** Puts a little flag marker in the Flags column (if it's showing) to call your attention to this message.

> **Stop evaluating rules:** Just like it says.

5. **OK:** Click OK and the rule is made. All incoming mail will now be searched and sorted using the criteria you just created.

Rules are listed in an order and will be applied in that order. **Change the priority order** by dragging a rule to another position in the list.

Make a rule active or inactive with the checkbox in the **Active** column.

To **edit a rule,** select it in the list, then click the "Edit" button, *or* double-click the rule name in the list.

Duplicate a rule if you want to create a new rule that is similar to an existing one. Select an existing rule in the list, click "Duplicate," then select and edit that new rule.

To remove a rule, select it in the Rule list, then click the "Remove" button or press the "Delete" key on your keyboard.

Rules affect new messages that are received *after* a Rule was created. **To apply Rules to older messages,** select the desired messages from the Message List. From the "Message" menu, choose "Apply Rules to Selections."

News from Apple: The rule is set so these messages from Apple are highlighted in blue. You can change this, delete the rule, etc.

Tips: If you won't be able to respond to your mail for a while, set up an **autoresponder** that will automatically return a message saying you are away and will respond later:

Choose "If sender is in my Address Book," and "Reply to message," then click the button to enter your message. You might say something like, "Thank you for your email. When I return from the Amazon on October 27, I will answer your lovely message."

Or **forward** all of your own email to yourself at another address.

Menu Commands

Following are some of the items in the **menus** that aren't explained elsewhere.

File menu

New Viewer Window: If you've closed the main Viewer Window and realize that you need it back, use this command, or press Command Option N.

Import Mailboxes: Mail can import the mailboxes of many popular email applications. If you have custom mailboxes already set up in another email application, from the File menu, choose "Import Mailboxes...." Select one of the email clients in the list, then click the right arrow button for instructions. Mail will open a directory window so you can navigate to the appropriate mailbox file and import it.

You can't import AOL mailboxes (not because of Mail's limitations, but because of AOL's prohibitions).

To print an email message: Double-click a message to open it. Click the "Print" icon in the open message's toolbar to open the Print dialog box.

Or select a message in the Message List pane, choose File and "Print...."

Make the appropriate selections in the Print dialog box and click "Print."

To print multiple email messages: From the Message List pane, select multiple messages. From the File menu, choose "Print...." All selected messages, including header information, will print out in continuous fashion—it will not print a separate page for each message.

Mailbox menu

Go Offline: If you have a dial-up account that ties up your phone line while you're connected to the Intenret, you can "Go Offline." This disconnects you from the Internet, but leaves mail Open. Before you go offline, transfer any messages you want to read to another mailbox (just drag them over and drop them in). Then go offline, read your mail, compose messages, print them, etc. Messages you compose while offline are stored in the Outbox in the Mailboxes drawer, where you can open and edit them. When you're ready to send mail, from the Mailbox menu, choose "Go Online."

Get New Mail in Account: If you have more than one account in Mail, go to this menu to selectively check the mail in just a single account.

These are some of the items in the **Edit menu** that aren't explained else-where in this chapter or that are not self-explanatory.

Paste As Quotation: Use this command when you want to paste text from another document into an email message as a quotation. In Mail, a quotation is styled with indentation, a vertical bar, and a user-specified color, as explained on pages 567 and 578.

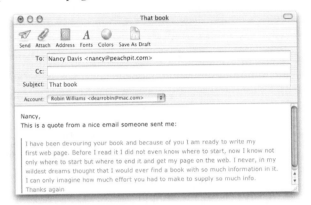

Append Selected Messages: This will add entire email messages you have received onto the end of a message you compose. Compose your message; in the Viewer Window, select the email message you want to append, then choose this command from the Edit menu.

Focus on Selected Messages: Select messages (Command-click to select more than one), then choose this option so *only* those messages will be visible in the Message List. To show all of the messages again, go back to the View menu and choose "Show All Messages."

Hide Status Bar or **Show Status Bar:** The Status Bar is located just below the toolbar. The left side of the Status Bar provides information about your Internet connection when checking for mail, and it displays the number of messages in the current Mailbox. The right side of the Status Bar displays a revolving wheel when connecting to a remote server to send or receive mail. Click that revolving wheel (or click where it would be) to open the Activity Viewer, as shown below, and see what's going on as it connects.

Click the revolving wheel again to close the Activity Viewer (or click the red Close button in the upper-left corner of the Activity Viewer).

Format menu   In the Format menu, under "Font," there is a command to make the selected text **Bigger.** The menu says the keyboard shortcut is Command +, but that doesn't work—use Shift Command +. Sometimes even that doesn't work.

Make Plain Text changes messages from "Rich Text" format to "Plain Text" format, which will strip out all of the formatting, different fonts, colors, etc. If the message is already in Plain Text, this command appears as "Make Rich Text." This will *not* restore any formatting that was removed.

Text Encodings: If you receive email that does not display correctly because it was originally written in a foreign language on a foreign keyboard, it may help to choose "Text Encodings," then select one of the text encoding options from the list.

Increase Quote Level: To format text as a Mail-style quote or to increase the existing quote level, click within a line of text, then choose "Increase Quote Level." Choose the command again to further increase the quote level, as shown below.

The operation is much easier and faster if you learn the keyboard shortcuts: Click within the appropriate text, then type Command ' (that's the typewriter apostrophe, just to the left of the Return key) to "Increase Quote Level," or type Option Command ' to "Decrease Quote Level."

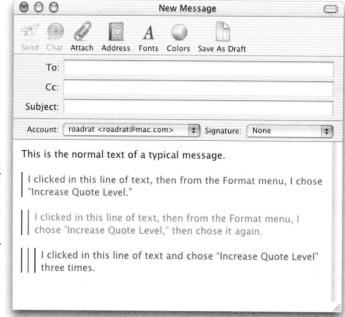

Each of these quoted sections has been increased one more level than the one above it.

The **Address Book** works both independently and with Mail to create Address Cards that store contact information for individuals or groups. When *Mail* is open, you can automatically create an Address Book entry for anyone who sent mail to you. When *Address Book* is open you can automatically address email to an individual or group. You can search the Address Book by name, email address, or by a user-defined Category.

 The Address Book icon is in your Dock, your Applications folder, and in the Mail "Compose" toolbar.

Single-click here to open the dialog box where you can choose an image to apply (TIFF, GIF, or JPG; not EPS format). **Or** *drag an image from your Desktop and drop it in this space.*

Once you add an image, it will appear in a chat session with this person, as shown on page 593.

Switch between views.

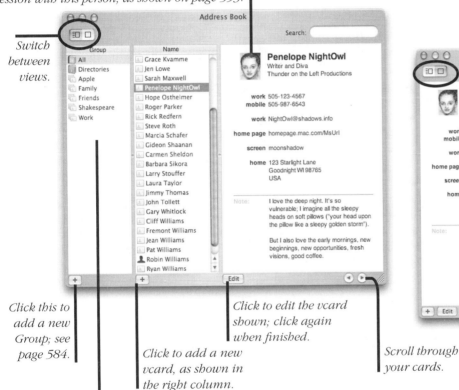

Search for information on any card; enter text and hit Return or Enter.

Click this to add a new Group; see page 584.

Click to edit the vcard shown; click again when finished.

Click to add a new vcard, as shown in the right column.

Scroll through your cards.

Organize *your cards into Groups; see pages 584–586.*

Add *any Name into any number of different Groups; every Name will always appear in the "All" list.*

If you **add** *a Name directly into a* **Group,** *it is automatically added to the All list.*

When you **delete** *a name from a Group, it is not deleted from the All list.*

If you address an **email** *message to the name of a* **Group,** *the message goes to everyone in that Group. See page 586.*

The "card" in the right column is called a **vcard,** *or virtual card.*

A Group of addresses is a **Group vcard.**

Add New Names and Addresses

There are several ways to **add a new vcard of information** or just a name and email address to the Address Book, depending on whether you are using Address Book or Mail at the moment.

To add a new address card while using Address Book:

1. Single-click the **+** sign at the bottom of the "Names" column (or at the bottom of the visible card).

2. This makes a new vcard automatically appear and the name of the person is already selected for you, waiting for you to type, as shown below.

    Type the person's first name, then hit the Tab key. Type the last name, then hit Tab, etc. Continue to fill in all the information you know.

3. If a label is changeable, you'll see two tiny arrows. For instance, maybe you want to change the label "mobile" to "cell." Single-click the tiny arrows and you'll get a little pop-up menu, as shown below. Either choose one of the pre-named labels, or choose "Custom..." and type in the name of the label you want.

Tip: You can use Services to make a Sticky note out of the text in any field.

Just select the text in a field (press Command A to select all of the text, even if you can't see all of it).

From the Apple menu, choose "Services," then choose "Make Sticky."

Or press Command Shift Y instead of going to the menu at all.

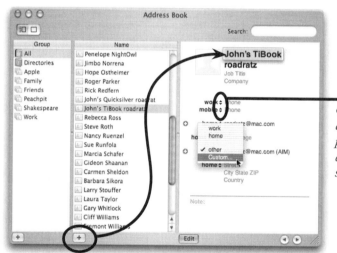

Click the tiny double arrows to get different pop-up menus for different labels, as shown.

Don't forget to put a chunk of dark chocolate in the package when you send Nancy the manuscript!

This is a Sticky note made from the Notes field in the Address Card.

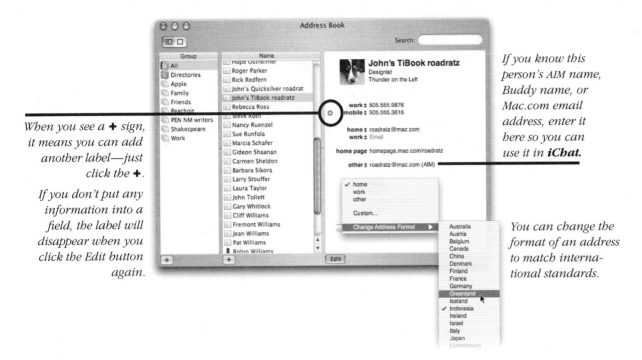

When you see a ✚ sign, it means you can add another label—just click the ✚.

If you don't put any information into a field, the label will disappear when you click the Edit button again.

If you know this person's AIM name, Buddy name, or Mac.com email address, enter it here so you can use it in iChat.

You can change the format of an address to match international standards.

To add a sender's email address to your Address Book instantly:

1. In the **Mail** program, either single-click on an email in your list, or open an email message.

2. From the Message menu in the menu bar across the top of your screen, choose "Add Sender To Address Book," *or* press Command Y. The Address Book will not open, but the sender's address will be added.

    Check on that address later, though, because if a person's first and last name are not included in their own email address, you'll find the new address in your Address Book at the very top of the "Names" column as <No Name>. Edit that vcard to add the person's name so he is sorted in the list properly.

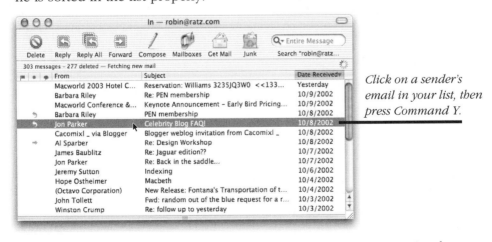

Click on a sender's email in your list, then press Command Y.

—continued

To add someone's address from your History list:

1. In the **Mail** program, go to the Window menu and choose "Address History." This brings up a window, shown below, that has kept track of everyone you have sent email to (not everyone who has sent *you* email because then you'd have thousands of junk mail addresses).

   If an address has a vcard icon to its left, that name and address is already in your Address Book.

2. Single-click the name of someone whom you want to add to your Address Book, then click the button "Add to Address Book." Ta da. You won't see anything happen, but that address has been added.

Note: At the bottom of this list are all the people you have emailed but whose actual names are not shown.

If you add one of those to your Address Book, it will show up in the Names column in your Address Book at the top of the list, called <No Name>.

Select <No Name> to display its vcard, then click the Edit button so you can add the person's name to the vcard.

The various entries in a vcard each have different **options,** as shown below. Single-click on each entry *label* (the bold word on the left, not the entry data) and see what the options are.

Experiment with the options to become familiar with them. If you see pop-up menus that say things like "work" and "home," that means you're still in Edit mode—click the Edit button again to get out of Edit mode.

Label Options

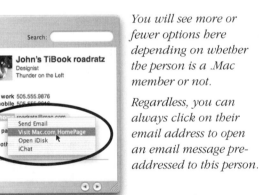

You can choose to see phone and fax numbers in type large enough to fill your screen so you can see it across the rooom when you fax someone. Try it. (Or type a love note instead of a phone number and flash it to your sweetheart on the other side of the room.)

See a fax number across the room

You will see more or fewer options here depending on whether the person is a .Mac member or not.

Regardless, you can always click on their email address to open an email message pre-addressed to this person.

Send an email (or other options)

Go directly to a person's web page, if you included the address in the vcard.

Click on his Instant Message name to open a chat with him (as explained in Chapter 33).

Go to a web page or open a chat

Create a Group   You can make a **Group** in the Address Book, which not only helps organize your address list, but a Group acts as a **mailing list;** that is, you can send an email message to the Group name and the one message will go to everyone in that list.

To make a Group/mailing list:

1. In the Address Book, make sure you see all three columns, as shown below, left. (If you only see one panel, the "Card" panel, click the "View Card and Column" button shown below, right.)

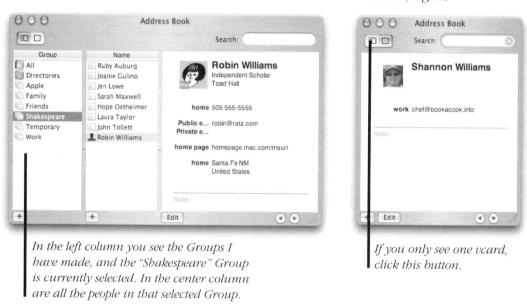

In the left column you see the Groups I have made, and the "Shakespeare" Group is currently selected. In the center column are all the people in that selected Group.

If you only see one vcard, click this button.

2. Under the Group column, click the **+** sign. A "Group Name" will appear in the Group column, selected and ready for you to type a new name, as shown below. Just type to replace the selected name. When done, hit the Enter key.

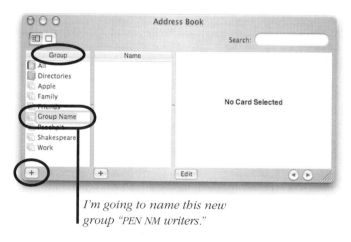

I'm going to name this new group "PEN NM writers."

3. Now you can do one of two things: **Either** in the "Name" column, click the **+** sign and add a new address; this new address will be added to your "All" group *and* to the new Group that you just made (which is still selected, right?).

Or click the "All" Group so you see all of the addresses in your book, then drag an existing address and drop it on the Group name, as shown below.

"All" contains the name of every person in every Group, as well as those who are in no Group at all. Each Group actually contains "aliases" to the one address card.

Now Denise is in the "All" list, as well as in the "PEN NM writers" Group. You can put the same person in any number of Groups.

Here's an **even quicker way** to make a Group: Hold down the Command key and click on all the Names in the list that you want to put into a new Group. Let go of the Command key, go to the File menu, and choose "New Group From Selection." Change the name of the Group, as shown on the previous page.

Shortcut to make a Group

—continued

Send email to an entire Group

To send an email message simultaneously to every person in a Group:

1. You don't have to have the Address Book open. In **Mail,** start a new email message.

2. In the "To" box, type the name of the Group. That's all—write your letter and send it and it will go to everyone in the Group.

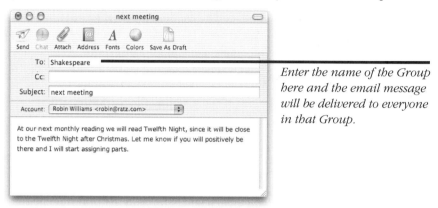

Enter the name of the Group here and the email message will be delivered to everyone in that Group.

Suppress the address list when sending mail to a Group

It's polite to **suppress the address list** when sending to a Group. For one thing, it's *really* annoying to have to scroll through a long list of addresses to get to the message. For another, *some* people don't want their private email address broadcast to everyone else on the list.

To suppress the Group list of addresses:

1. In the Mail program (not the Address Book), open the Mail preferences (go to the Mail menu and choose "Preferences…").

2. Click the "Composing" icon in the Toolbar, as shown below.

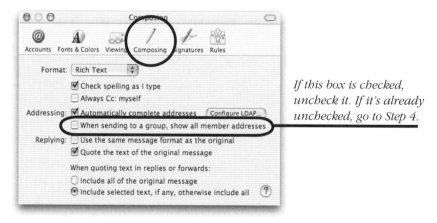

If this box is checked, uncheck it. If it's already unchecked, go to Step 4.

3. **Un**check the box (if it's checked) "When sending to a group, show all member addresses."

4. Put the preferences away (click the red Close button).

Export an Address or a Group of Addresses

You can **export** a single address, a collection of selected addresses, or a Group. Once exported, any other Address Book users can import the addresses into their application. There are two simple ways to export:

▾ Drag a Group, a Name, or a collection of Names from the Address Book and drop them on the Desktop or inside any Finder window. It will make an icon like the ones shown below.

▾ Select the Group, a Name, or a collection of Names in the Address Book. From the File menu, choose "Export vCard(s)…" or "Export Group vCard…." You will be asked where you want to save the exported vcard. An icon like the ones shown below will appear where you chose to save it.

vCards

Drag a selection of vcards to the Desktop and the Mac will create this icon.

Family

Drag a Group to the Desktop and the Mac will create an icon for you with the name of the Group.

Important tip: What you **don't** want to do now is double-click this icon! I know, it's almost irresistible. But if you double-click it, it will look like nothing happened. So you'll probably double-click again. And maybe a third time just to make sure you didn't miss something. Every time you double-click, the addresses in the file are added to your Address Book! So if you double-click three times, you'll have each person's address in your Book four times! So let's say you open your Address Book and delete three of those extra names — if any of those names were in a Group, you could be deleting them from their Group because only one of those four duplicates are actually in the Group — but which one? Sigh. How do you think I know this?

You can **send this file** to anyone with the current version of Address Book—they double-click the file **(once)** and those addresses are now in their Book.

Import Addresses   If you want to **import addresses** from an application *other* than Address Book, first open the other email client and export the address information as a "tab-delimited" file. Then open Address Book, and from the File menu, choose "Import." Use the "Open" window to select the tab-delimited file on your computer, then click "Open."

Keep in mind that if you had information in the other address list that was in a different order from your list in Address Book, data might appear in odd places. It's a good idea to **save a copy** of your original Address Book file in case you need to replace the new one; see below.

You can *export* selected addresses from your Address Book so someone can *add* them to their Mac OS X Address Book; see page 587.

Save your Address Book   If you plan to reformat your hard disk, **save a copy of your Address Book** file so you can place it in the same location after you reinstall Mac OS X. To find the Address Book file, open your Home folder, then open the "Library" folder, then the "Application Support" folder. The address book folder is located here, named **AddressBook**.

This is the AddressBook folder that contains your list of email address and contact information. Before you do anything that might change it, drag a copy of this original file into another folder, like your Documents folder: Hold down the Option key and drag it to another folder.

Email Etiquette

Many people use email everyday without being aware of **email etiquette** and without realizing that they're **1)** annoying co-workers, friends, and relatives; **2)** making themselves look naive and amateurish in the email world; and **3)** turning themselves into junk mailers, albeit well-intentioned.

If no one has complained about your email etiquette, you're probably in good shape. Or it could be that family members and friends do not want to risk embarrassing you. To be safe, consider the following suggestions and see if your email manners are up to date.

1. Get permission before you add someone to a mailing list.

You may be well-intentioned, but most people get so much spam and junk mail that they'd rather not receive the inspirational messages that someone sent you—especially since they probably received five other copies already. Not everyone is a curmudgeon about getting email like this, but it's polite, professional, and considerate to ask for permission before putting someone on your mailing list. And please, don't take it personally if they decline. Privacy on the Internet is hard to come by, and many people try to keep their email address off as many mailing lists as possible. When you add someone's address to your mailing list without their permission, you're publishing private information without permission.

2. Clean up the email headers.

Even if someone wants to be on your mailing list, it's extremely annoying to get email that has dozens (or hundreds) of lines of header information before the message. This happens when you receive an email message that was sent to a list, then someone sent it to their list, then someone else sent it to their list. This kind of email makes the sender look like the clueless amateur they are. Before you send a forwarded message like this, delete all that header stuff so the recipient can see the message at a glance without having to scroll through pages of junk. (To delete the header information, click the Forward button to forward the message, then select all those email addresses and other stuff, and hit the Delete button.)

3. Hide the mailing list addresses.

When you send a message to your mailing list (called a "group" in Mail), you are essentially providing every reader of the message with the email addresses of all your friends and relations. Then if those people forward your message, all of their recipients have the email addresses of all your friends and relations. Not many people appreciate that. Use the tip on page 586 to hide the list of addresses when you send a message. Not only is it neater, it is more polite to everyone involved.

—continued

4. Take the time to personalize your email.

If you send well-intentioned junk email to an aquaintance, friend, or relative, it will be appreciated if you take the time to add a personal note to the forwarded message, such as "Hi Jay, I thought you might enjoy this." To receive an unsolicited, unsigned, almost-anonymous, forwarded email makes me wonder when I can expect to start receiving the rest of the sender's postal service junk mail and Sunday supplements.

5. Identify your email attachments.

When you attach a file to an email message, don't make the recipient guess what kind of file it is or what program might open it. Include a description of the attachment and the file type, or what program is needed to open it. Say something like, "Barbara, the attached file is a photograph that I saved as a .tif in Photoshop 7 on a Mac." Dealing with attachments can be confusing, and any helpful information is usually appreciated.

6. Don't fall for the urban legends and hoaxes that travel around the Internet.

When you get a panic-stricken email from a friend warning you of an apocalyptic virus and to "Please forward this email to everyone you know," do not forward it to anyone you know. This email message usually contains the words "THIS IS NOT A HOAX!" That means that this is a hoax. These messages float around the Internet constantly and some of them are many years old. If there's a deadly virus about to destroy the world as we know it, you're more likely to hear about it from the national news services and online news sites than from your cousin who's been using email for three months.

Also, do not forward the email messages that tell you Microsoft will pay you one dollar every time you use HotMail or visit the Microsoft web site. And don't forward the warning that the postal service is going to start charging us for every email, or that the phone company is going to tax every message, and please stop sending the Neiman Marcus cookie recipe around, and that little boy in the hospital who is waiting for your postcard went home years ago.

And make darn sure your email recipient has *begged* you to send all those messages that say "Send this to at least ten other people. Do not break this chain!"

Tip: If you want to send photographs as email attachments to a wide variety of computer users on all different sorts of computers, follow these guidelines:

Make sure the file is in the *JPEG format.* If you're not sure, open it in Preview and change the format, as explained on page 442.

Name the file with a short name with no special characters such as ! ? / or : .

The file must have the *extension .jpg* at the end; see page 227 for details on extensions, their importance, and how to make sure you don't end up with double extensions.

Chat with iChat

If you've ever used a chat program or "instant messaging" program such as AOL Instant Messenger or ICQ, you'll figure out how to use **iChat** in about four seconds. If you've never used a chat program, it will take you about one whole minute.

With Apple's iChat you can have private written conversations over the Internet with people who already have a .Mac account or an AIM or AOL account; it is not compatible with MSN Messenger, Yahoo Messenger, IRC, Jabber, or ICQ (although it will soon be compatible with ICQ).

Contents in this chapter

Set Up iChat

iChat

If the iChat icon isn't in the Dock, you'll find it in the Applications window.

Note: You must be connected to the Internet to use iChat!

If you are connected to other computers in your office, you can use Rendezvous to chat, even when you're not online. See Chapter 35.

The first time you click the **iChat** icon in the Dock, the Welcome window asks you to enter the information for your iChat account. The "Account Type" pop-up menu lets you choose between using your Mac.com account (if you have one) or an existing AOL Instant Messenger account (called AIM, if you have one; go to **www.aim.com** if you want to sign up; you don't need to have AOL to get an AIM account).

If you don't have a Mac.com account and you want one (see pages xxi–xxii), you can click that button to sign up for it right now. Otherwise, enter your information, and click OK.

Your iChat "Buddy name" (Account Name) is the same as your Mac.com membership name. Your online Buddies will use that name to find you and send Instant Messages or files. You can even have both an AOL Instant Messenger Buddy name and your Mac.com Buddy name and switch between them (only one can be *active* at a time).

This is your "Buddy" name. In the case of a Mac.com account, your Buddy name is your email address.

If you use AOL, this would be your name at AOL (without the "@aol.com" part).

If you have an Internet AIM account, this would be the Buddy name you've been using.

What is it like to "talk" with someone through iChat? Below is a typical iChat window and how it basically works; I'm chatting with my mother, who uses AOL. You type a message to someone; they type back to you.

What is it Like?

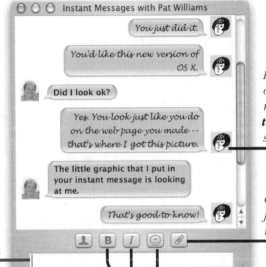

*Each person in the window has her own bubble of talk and an icon that represents her. You can **customize the icon** for yourself or for others; see page 597 and 598.*

Type your message into this edit box and then hit either Return or Enter to send it.

*Click the **paperclip** button to find a file to send (or drag a file into the edit box and hit Return).*

*Use the **B** and **I** buttons to make text bold, italic, or both:*

Either: *Select the text after you type it, as you would in a word processor, then click one or both buttons.*

Or: *Click a button or press Command B or Command I **before** you type—the next words you type will be in bold or italic (or both, if you pressed Command B I). You will continue to type in that style until you either click the buttons again or use the keyboard shortcuts again.*

*Click the **Smiley** button to get a list of Smilies to insert into your message— just click the one you want.*

If you type a standard Smiley, iChat will substitute a real Smiley. For instance, if you type ;-) as a wink, it will automatically turn into a round Smiley icon in the message. Try it.

You can customize the color of your bubble, the typeface, and the color of the typeface for both yourself and your participants. See page 611.

When either you or another participant starts to type, a thought bubble appears to let the other person know.

Click the person-head icon to open this "drawer" on the side that shows you a list of participants.

Instant Message, Direct Message, or Chat?

With iChat, you can communicate with others in **four different ways:** Instant Messages, Direct Messages, Chats, and Rendezvous. I'll explain here how each one is different from the others and on the following pages tell you how to do each one.

An **Instant Message** opens a small window in which you can "talk" back and forth with *one other person,* and your talk is **totally private** (unless someone is looking over your shoulder). You must be connected to the Internet.

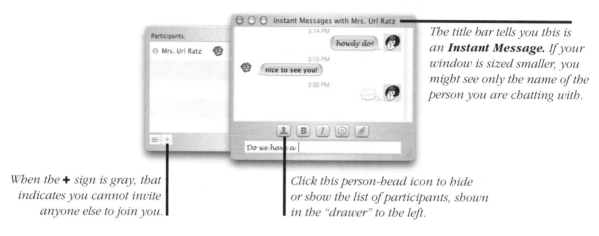

*The title bar tells you this is an **Instant Message.** If your window is sized smaller, you might see only the name of the person you are chatting with.*

When the ✦ sign is gray, that indicates you cannot invite anyone else to join you.

Click this person-head icon to hide or show the list of participants, shown in the "drawer" to the left.

A **Direct Message** looks just like an Instant Message and is even more private. Instant Messages go through a central messaging server on the Internet, while a Direct Message goes directly to *one other person's* computer, bypassing the central server. Some network or firewall security settings will not allow Direct Messages to be sent or delivered. You must be connected to the Internet.

*The title bar in a **Direct Message** also says is an Instant Message, but inside the box you can see you have actually started a Direct Message session.*

A Direct Message is between two people—you cannot invite anyone else to join you.

A **Chat window,** or Chat Room, is a public "room" where you can invite *any number of people.* These people might be spread all over the world, but you can all gab together. People can come and go as they please and the room stays open until the last person leaves. You must be connected to the Internet.

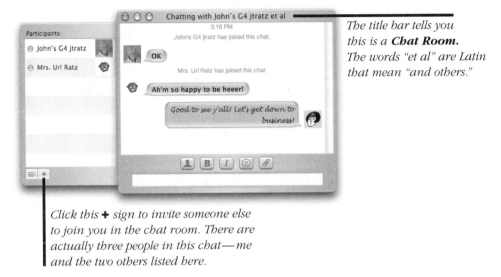

*The title bar tells you this is a **Chat Room.** The words "et al" are Latin that mean "and others."*

Click this + sign to invite someone else to join you in the chat room. There are actually three people in this chat—me and the two others listed here.

A **Rendezvous message** does not go through the Internet—it goes through your local network in your small office or school directly to another computer on the same network. You do not have to be connected to the Internet to send Rendezvous messages. See Chapter 35 for details about Rendezvous.

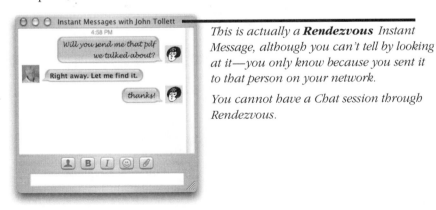

*This is actually a **Rendezvous** Instant Message, although you can't tell by looking at it—you only know because you sent it to that person on your network.*

You cannot have a Chat session through Rendezvous.

Create Your Buddy List

This is a typical Buddy List. The people whose names are in bold are online and you can start a chat with them; the others are offline and unavailable at the moment.

If you plan to **chat often** with certain people, **add them to your Buddy List** so you can easily see when they're online, and with the click of a button you can start a chat or send a file.

To open your Buddy List and add people to it:

1. Click the iChat icon in the Dock, if it's not already open. If you don't see your Buddy List, press Command 1 (that's the number one), *or* go to the Window menu and choose "Buddy List."

2. In the Buddy List window that opens, click the **+** button. A "sheet" will drop down from the top of the window, as shown below.

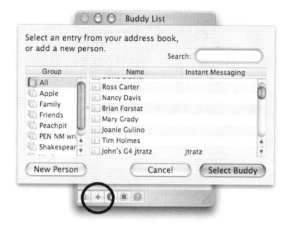

3. The sheet that drops down in front of the Buddy List window contains all of your Address Book contacts (as above).

   If the person you want to add is in your Address Book, select that contact, then click the "Select Buddy" button. The new Buddy can now be seen in the Buddy list. If you have not put that person's AIM name (Buddy name or Mac.com email address) in your Address Book yet, you'll get another sheet like the one shown on the opposite page.

If the Buddy you want to add is NOT in your Address Book, click the "New Person" button in the Address Book panel, which will bring down a different sheet, as shown below.

4. From the "Account Type" pop-up menu, select "Mac.com" *if* the new person uses their Mac.com account for instant messaging.

   Or choose "AIM" if the new person uses an AOL or AIM screen name.

5. Enter the "Address Book Information" if you want this person to be added to your Address Book as well.

6. To make a photo or custom icon appear next to a Buddy's name, drag an image on top of the Buddy Icon window in the New Person panel (the photo or image must be a JPEG, GIF, or TIFF file). This picture will appear in your Address Book, in the Buddy List, and in Chat windows.

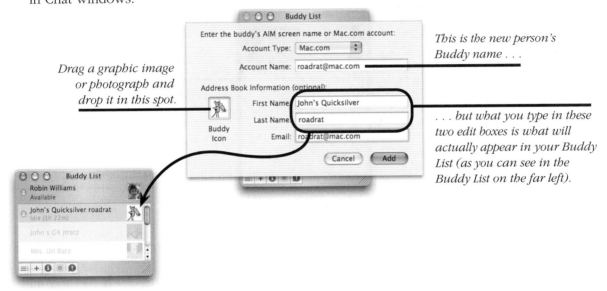

Drag a graphic image or photograph and drop it in this spot.

This is the new person's Buddy name . . .

. . . but what you type in these two edit boxes is what will actually appear in your Buddy List (as you can see in the Buddy List on the far left).

7. Click the "Add" button and that person is added to your Buddy List (and to your Address Book if you entered that information).

Status and messages in Your Buddy List

Your name appears in the top-left corner of the **Buddy List.** The **colored status buttons** indicate the online status of you and your Buddies: green means "Available," red means "Unavailable," and yellow means "Idle," which usually means that person's computer has gone to sleep due to inactivity.

Tip: If you're colorblind between red and green, go to the Preferences (see page 610) and choose to have the availability buttons displayed as squares and circles. They'll still be red and green, but at least you'll be able to tell which is which.

A message indicates your **availability:** "Available," "Away," or any custom message that you can create. *It's not just a message—it actually changes whether people can see you or not.* When you choose any message with a red dot, no one can send you messages.

To change the status message, click the existing message ("Available" or "Away"), then from the pop-down menu (shown below) choose another one.

To create a custom status message, click the existing message ("Available" or "Away"), then from the pop-down menu choose "Custom…" and type your message.

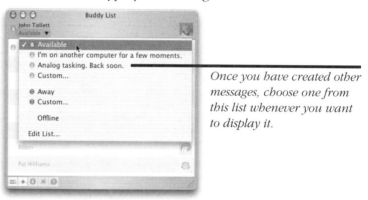

Once you have created other messages, choose one from this list whenever you want to display it.

Photos in your Buddy List

If you have put a **photo or image** for someone (or yourself) in your Address Book, it will appear in your Buddy List and iChat windows. If your AOL Buddy has added a photo or image in AOL or their own iChat application, their photo or image will appear instead of the one you placed.

But perhaps you don't like the image your friend uses. **To override his image,** select his name in your Buddy List, then click the "**i**" button (circled, above), which will give you the box shown to the right. Either add a different photo or leave the "Picture" box blank, and check the box to "Only use this picture." You may have to quit iChat to make the new image appear.

Drag a photo or image (GIF, JPEG, or TIFF) to the "Picture" box.

To remove a picture, *click on the "Picture" box and hit the Delete key.*

*To add or change **your** picture, use the Address Book (see page 579).*

The **iChat File menu** is a little misleading, as explained here:

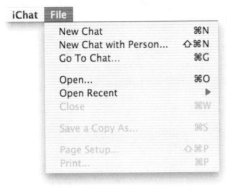

"New Chat" and *"New Chat with Person…"* might open a Chat Room in which you can invite a number of people, **or** it might open an Instant Message or Direct Message in which you can communicate with only one other person. It depends on which "Chat Option" is set for that particular window, as explained below.

"Go To Chat…" really **does** always open a Chat Room in which you can invite a large number of people.

You don't really have to worry about this until you bump into a problem, like not being able to invite anyone into your Chat Room. What makes the difference between whether the first two commands in the File menu open an Instant Message window, a Direct Message window, or a Chat Room window is which of the **Chat options** have been chosen. *Most of the time* these two File commands seem to open an Instant Message window, but you can change the open window to a Direct Message or a Chat Room window *before* you start to talk to someone.

Chat options

To choose between an Instant Message, Direct Message, or Chat Room window:

1. From the File menu, choose "New Chat" or "New Chat with Person…." (as explained above).

2. Before you send a message to anyone, go to the View menu and choose "Chat Options…."

3. Press on the little pop-up menu called "Mode," as shown below. Change the window to a different mode if necessary. Click OK.

You can only change the mode if you haven't yet sent a message. Once you start a dialog, the window is set in the selected mode and can't be changed.

Three Ways to Send an Instant Message

There are three ways to send an Instant Message to someone else. If someone is in your Buddy List and you notice they're online, the third method is the quickest and easiest.

You need to know a person's **AIM name.** It might be someone's Mac.com email address (including the part "@mac.com"), an AOL screen name (without the "@aol.com" part), or an AIM name that a person signed up for at www.aim.com.

To end an Instant Messaging session, just close the window. When either participant closes his or her window, the session ends.

1) Send an Instant Message to anyone whose AIM name you know:

1. From the File menu choose "New Chat." As explained on the previous page, this command *usually* opens an Instant Message (IM) to one other person; you cannot ask anyone else to join the two of you.

2. Click the little person-head icon at the bottom of the IM window; this will pop out a drawer to the side.

3. At the bottom of the drawer, click the + symbol to get the menu, as shown below. Anyone in your Buddy List who is online will appear in this menu; click that person's name to invite him. Or choose "Other…" and enter the AIM name of any person to whom you wish to send an IM.

4. Type a message at the bottom of the IM window, then hit Return or Enter. A message is sent to the other person, inviting him to chat.

5. When he writes back to you, you're on.

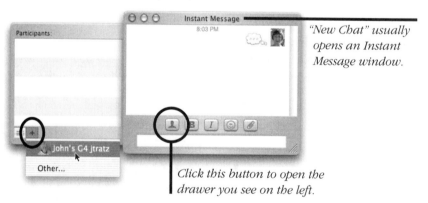

"New Chat" usually opens an Instant Message window.

Click this button to open the drawer you see on the left.

2) Send an Instant Message to anyone whose AIM name you know:

1. From the File menu choose "New Chat with Person…." As explained previously, this command *usually* opens an Instant Message (IM) to one other person; you cannot ask anyone else to join the two of you.

2. In the text field of the panel that drops down, type the AIM name of someone you know. Although it says to type the "address," it really wants the *screen name* of an AOL or AIM member.

   If you are trying to contact a Mac.com member, type their email address, including "@mac.com." Click OK.

3. Type a message at the bottom of the IM window, then hit Return. A message is sent to the other person, inviting him to respond.

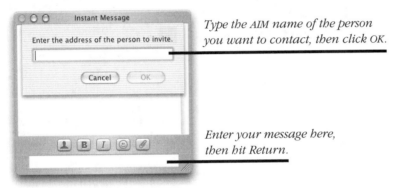

Type the AIM name of the person you want to contact, then click OK.

Enter your message here, then hit Return.

3) Send an Instant Message to someone on your Buddy List:

1. If your Buddy List is not open, press Command 1.

2. Select any Buddy whose name is dark, which means she is online (to select someone, click once on her name).

3. At the bottom of the Buddy List, click the Instant Message (IM) symbol: 🔔 . *Or* press Command Option M.

4. An Instant Message window will open with your Buddy's name in the title bar.

5. Type a message in the edit box, then hit Return or Enter to invite him in.

Select a Buddy who is online, then click the IM symbol.

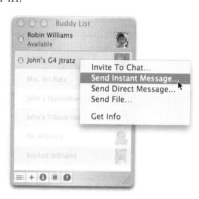

Or Control-click on a Buddy name and choose "Send Instant Message...."

Type something in the edit box, then hit Return or Enter.

Send an Email to Someone on Your Buddy List

Send **email** to anyone on your Buddy List, whether or not that person is online.

1. Select a Buddy in your list (if your Buddy List isn't showing, press Command 1).

2. Click the "Compose email" icon at the bottom of the Buddy List window. It looks like a postage stamp: 🔲 .

3. Mail will open. Compose your email message in the message window that appears, and send as usual.

Instant Messages go through a central messaging server on the Internet. If you have a message to send that requires more privacy, you can use a **Direct Message** that goes directly to another person's computer, bypassing the central server. (Some recipients may have network or firewall security settings that do not allow Direct Messages to be delivered.)

Send a Direct Message

To send a Direct Message to someone in your Buddy List:

1. Select a Buddy in your Buddy List window who is online (if your Buddy List isn't showing, press Command 1).

2. From the Buddies menu at the top of the screen, choose "Send Direct Message...."

   Or Control-click on a Buddy name, then choose "Send Direct Message..." from the contextual menu.

3. Type a message, hit Return or Enter, and wait for a reply.

To END a Direct Instant Message session, either you or the recipient close your window (click the red button).

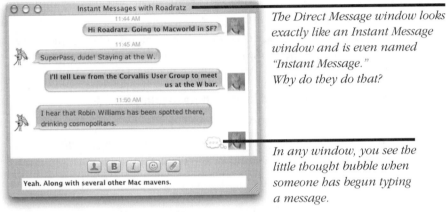

The Direct Message window looks exactly like an Instant Message window and is even named "Instant Message." Why do they do that?

In any window, you see the little thought bubble when someone has begun typing a message.

If there is a pause in the conversation, the time will appear in the window.

To send a Direct Message to someone who is NOT in your Buddy List:

1. From the File menu, choose "New Chat with Person...."

2. Enter the person's AIM name.

3. From the View menu, choose "Chat Options...."

4. Click on the Mode pop-up menu and choose "Direct IM." Click OK.

5. Enter your message in the edit box at the bottom of the window and hit Return or Enter to send it. Although the title bar in your window claims this is an "Instant Message," it is really a Direct Message.

Chat with Several Buddies at Once

A **Chat Room** is different from an Instant or Direct Message in that you can have a number of people around the world in the same "room" (which looks amazingly like an Instant Message window) all chatting at once. Here are your options:

▾ You can **create a new Chat Room** with a unique name and invite a large number of people to join you. Mac.com members, AOL members, and AIM users can all be invited into the Chat Room. (The limit in America Online is 23 people in a room, but I am not sure what the limit is in iChat.) Caps and lowercase don't matter when typing the name of a new Chat Room.

▾ You can **join an existing Chat Room** that another Mac.com member has created if you know the exact name of the room. (You cannot join any Chat Room that an AOL member has created within AOL.)

Note: If you enter the name of a Chat Room that other Mac.com users in the world have already set up, you will land in their room! So you want to be sure to type the correct name of the room you want to join. Caps and lowercase don't matter when typing the name of an existing room.

Create a new Chat Room

Create a new Chat Room and invite others to join you:

1. From the File menu, choose "New Chat."

2. A new message window appears. *Before you type anything,* go to the View menu and choose "Chat Options...."

3. From the pop-up "Mode" menu, choose "Chat," as shown below.

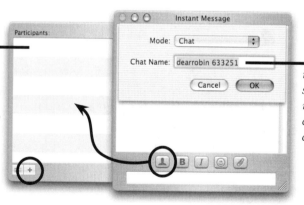

If you don't see this Participants drawer, click the person-head icon at the bottom of the message window, or go to the View menu and choose "Show Chat Participants."

iChat automatically supplies a Chat Room name that no one is currently using. You can change the name.

Tip: You can also start a new Chat Room this way: **Command**-click on each person in your Buddy List whom you want to invite. Then **Control**-click on any selected Buddy in the list, and choose "Invite to Chat...." A Chat Room will open and every selected Buddy will receive an invitation.

4. iChat supplies a unique Chat Room name for you, but you can change it. If you change it, be sure to enter a name that no one else in the world would be using at this moment or you might end up in someone else's Chat Room. (How do you think I know this?) Click OK.

5. **To invite one or more of your Buddies** to the new Chat Room, click the **+** button at the bottom of the Participants drawer, then choose people from your list who are online at the moment. You can also drag names from your Buddy List to the Participants drawer.

   To invite someone who is not on your Buddy List, click the **+** button at the bottom of the drawer, choose "Other …", then type their screen name and click OK. Any invited person must be online already.

6. Once you have added the participants to the list, type a message into the text field at the bottom of the window, hit Return, and that message will go out to everyone on your list.

   You can always add more people at any time, and anyone in the world can enter your Chat Room name and drop in to your window. For instance, if someone is not yet online when you send out an invitation, you can send them an email telling them to join you in that particular room as soon as they are online.

7. All of your participants will get a message on their screens inviting them. As soon as they respond, they will appear in your window.

This is your new Chat Room with three participants, which includes you.

This is the same chat in AOL. Sad but true—it's ugly. And too many commercials.

You can **join an existing Chat Room** that another Mac.com member started if you know its name. You cannot join a chat that an AOL user started in AOL.

1. From the File menu, choose "Go To Chat…."

2. Type in the exact name of the Chat Room you wish to join, then click "Go."

   If a Chat Room by this name exists somewhere in the world, you will appear in it and it will appear on your screen.

   If there is no such existing room, an "Empty Chat Room" will appear on your screen. People can join you there if they know the name, and you can send invitations to other users (as explained on the previous page).

Join an existing Chat Room

Caps and lowercase don't matter in a Chat Name, nor do spaces; that is, "tea room" is the same as "TeaRoom."

Send or Receive Files through iChat

You may want to **send a picture or some other file** to a Buddy in your list. This technique only works if your Buddy is also an iChat user. If he is an AOL user, you'll have to send the file as an email attachment.

To send a file to another iChat Buddy on your list:

1. Drag a file icon and drag it on top of a Buddy's name in the Buddy List.

2. A panel appears on your computer screen to show you the status of the file transfer.

On the recipient's computer (assuming she is an iChat user, not an AOL user), an alert appears warning of an incoming file, as shown below.

1. Click in the alert window (shown below, left) to open the "Incoming File Request" window (shown below, right) which identifies the file and its sender.

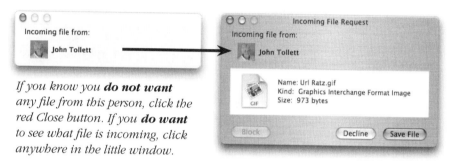

*If you know you **do not want** any file from this person, click the red Close button. If you **do want** to see what file is incoming, click anywhere in the little window.*

2. Either "Decline" the file or click the "Save File" button and download it. If you save the file, it will appear on your Desktop.

You can save a transcript of any chat—Instant Messages, Direct Messages, and Chat Rooms—to document a conversation, read later, or store in your box of love letters.

Save Transcripts of Chats

To save an individual chat:

1. Make sure the chat you want to save is the "active" window on the screen—click once on it to make sure.

2. From the File menu, choose "Save a Copy As…."

3. Name the document and choose a folder in which to store it. Click "Save."

To automatically save all chat transcripts:

1. From the iChat menu, choose "Preferences…."

2. Click the "Messages" icon in the Preferences toolbar.

3. Check the box to "Automatically save chat transcripts." This creates a new folder inside your Documents folder, called "iChats." Every conversation you have in iChat will automatically be recorded and stored in this folder—you don't ever have to choose to "Save."

To read any saved chat, just double-click on its icon; the file will open in a Chat window. If your chats are saved in the iChats folder, you'll find that folder inside your Documents folder.

Customize Chat Background

You can **customize the background** of any chat window by adding a picture or graphic to the background. This comes in handy when you've got several chats going on and don't want to get confused about who is in which window.

This image will appear only on *your* computer—the person you are chatting with will not see it. As soon as you close this chat window, that background disappears and will not automatically re-appear anywhere.

To customize a chat window:

1. Click anywhere in the chat window that you want to customize (this is just to select that window).

2. From the View menu, choose "Set Background…."

3. In the dialog box that appears, select an image file that's on your computer, then click "Open."

   OR you can simply drag any image file from your Desktop and drop it directly into an empty space in the chat window.

Small images will "tile" (repeat over and over) to fill the window space. Large images will display full-sized, cropping off the image where necessary.

As shown by the examples below, a simple or subdued background image increases the readability of the window.

To remove a background, click once in that chat window, then go to the View menu and choose "Clear Background."

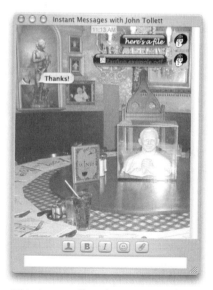

This is actually a large photograph. If I open the Chat window larger, I see my Aunt Lois sitting at the table all by her lonesome.

In addition to your Mac.com account, you can also set up an existing AOL Instant Messenger Account (AIM), another Mac.com account, or use your AOL screen name as a different account. No matter how many different accounts you have, though, only *one* can be *active* at any time. Every account can create a different Buddy List; if you use an existing account, it will pick up your Buddy List from that account.

Set up Additional iChat Accounts

To set up another iChat account:

1. From the iChat menu, choose "Preferences...."

2. Click the "Accounts" icon in the toolbar.

3. Click the "Log Out" button so you can make changes.

4. Type in a new "Screen Name."

   Either: This would be another Mac.com account name you own, which would be your email address including the "@mac.com" part (or click the little arrows to get a menu where you can choose to go to Mac.com and buy a new account).

   Or: Use an existing AIM account name that you got at www.aim.com.

   Or: Use your AOL name. Do *not* include the part "@aol.com."

5. Enter the login password you chose when you set up that particular account.

6. Hit Return to add the new account to the "Screen Name" pop-up menu.

7. Close the Preferences window.

8. From the iChat menu, choose "Log Into AIM" to go online with the currently selected screen name.

To switch accounts,
see the following page.

Switch to a different account

Also see the note about Accounts preferences, below!

To switch to a different iChat account:

1. From the iChat menu, choose "Preferences...."

2. Click the "Accounts" icon in the toolbar.

3. Click the "Log Out" button so you can make changes.

4. From the "Screen Name" pop-up menu, choose a different account that you previously set up (see above). Close the Preferences window.

5. From the iChat menu, choose "Log Into AIM" to go online with the currently selected screen name.

Preferences

Most of the options in **Preferences** are self-explanatory, but here are a few tips:

Accounts: If you have several accounts set up, as described on the previous page, you may want to select a particular account *before* you actually go online. You can save a couple of steps if you do this:

1. Open the iChat Preferences, then click the "Accounts" icon in the toolbar.

2. **Uncheck** the box, "When iChat opens, automatically log in." Close the window.

3. Next time you open iChat, you will not be logged in, so open Preferences and choose an account from the "Screen Name" pop-up menu. Close Preferences.

4. Go to the File menu and choose, "Log Into AIM."

This technique lets you open iChat without being actually logged in, which means no one will know you are online under the previous account.

*You can choose to see the red and green status lights as circles and squares, in case you are **colorblind** between red and green.*

Messages: Use the Messages pane to customize many features of your Chat windows, such as the color of your balloon and the balloons of other people, the font you use and they use, and the colors of the fonts. As you make choices, your choices will be shown in the little window space, as you can see below.

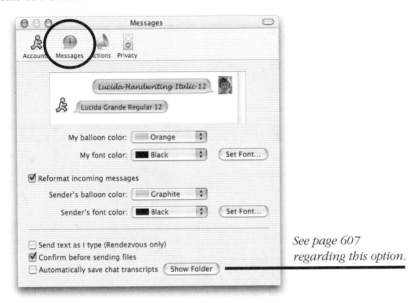

See page 607 regarding this option.

Actions: In the Actions pane, you can have certain actions happen as the result of certain events. For instance, you can make sure your computer tells you how wonderful you look everytime you log in, just in case no one else in your office tells you so.

Choose an event from the menu, then choose the actions you want to happen upon that event.

The text you enter will "speak" in the voice chosen in the Speech system preferences. If you change voices while iChat is open, you'll have to quit iChat and reopen it before the new voice will take effect.

*— continued
from previous page*

Privacy: If you want to be **invisible** to certain people, or you want to be **visible only** to certain people, click the "Privacy" icon in the Preferences toolbar, then from the Privacy Level pop-up menu, choose a setting.

> **To allow or block specific people,** choose "Allow people listed below" or "Block people listed below," then click the plus sign at the bottom of the pane to add a screen name.

> **To remove people from a list,** select the screen name, then click the minus button.

If you choose to "Allow people in my Buddy List," it automatically limits who can see you online to the people you know well enough to have in your List.

Sharing Files on One Mac

Sharing files between multiple users on one Macintosh is useful in homes, schools, and many offices. In homes, for instance, each member of the family can have her or his own Home area, but parents can leave notes and photos for kids in a special folder, or kids can leave school papers for parents to proofread, and no one gets in anyone's way. In schools, instructors can leave files accessible for all students, and students can drop off files for the instructor and no one else. In offices, people can leave important memos, reports, or photos for any other user to access. And best of all, it's really easy.

Contents of this chapter

Permissions

Or if you're not worried about whether other users can change your shared files or not, skip all this permissions stuff and go straight to page 620.

First of all, before you start sharing files on your Mac you should understand what **permissions** are. Every file and folder has an owner (the user who created the file), a group (automatically set unless changed by a system administrator), and a set of permissions (permissions); the various permissions are described below. Unless you are on a big network, you don't need to worry about group permissions—a system administrator can create groups, such as "screenwriters," "readers," and "producers," and assign different permissions for each group so when a document is sent on the rounds, different people are limited as to what they can do with the file.

These permissions are displayed and can be changed in the Get Info window, as shown to the right.

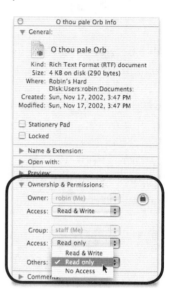

This is the Get Info window. The "Ownership & Permissions" pane is circled below.

Permission options

The owner of each file or folder can determine whether other users can open the file or folder, and in which ways. These are the **permission options:**

▼ **Read & Write:** A user with Read & Write permissions has full access to the file or folder. She can open it, make changes, copy it, read the document, print the document, put files into the folder, etc.

▼ **Read Only:** A user with Read Only permissions can open the document, read it, print it, copy it, or open the folder and see what's inside. He cannot make changes to the document, or add or delete anything in a folder.

If a user copies a Read Only file to his own Home folder, then that user becomes the "owner" and the original owner's permissions automatically switch to the new owner.

Robin's Stuff

A folder displays a red "Do not enter" sign to any user who has "No Access."

▼ **No Access:** A user cannot open a file, copy it, move it, or print it. She cannot open a folder, put things inside of it, copy it, or move it.

▼ **Write Only (Drop Box):** This is for folders only, not documents. If a folder is Write Only, users can put files inside, but they can't open the folder to see what's in it, take things from it, copy it, or move it. The Drop Box in the Public folder is Write Only.

In addition to the permissions assigned to a file or folder, users must have appropriate permissions for the **locations** where they want to copy or move a file to, such as the disk or folder. So if you get confusing messages about not being able to copy or move files around, check the permissions for the file itself, *plus* the folder you are moving it into, *plus* the disk on which the folder is stored.

Location permissions

Now, these permissions **apply only to other users** logged into the computer under a different name from yours—your Mac is not yet smart enough to tell whether the person who sits down at your computer and starts typing is you or not. That is, limiting the permision on a file of yours to "No Access" will not protect the file from anyone while *you* are logged in.

Access files with permissions

Although the limitations for other users sound secure, they're really not. Here are several examples of ways to **get around the permissions** that have been set for a file. I tell you this for two reasons: One is so you understand that files are not totally safe if they are sitting on your Mac, no matter what permissions (or lack of) you apply. And two is because you might need to remove someone's files, like a student's files after the student has left class, or files of an usavory nature that you've found on the Mac.

To access files that have limited permissions:

▾ If you are an Administrator and access another Mac across the network, you will bypass most permissions.

▾ Log in as the root user, as explained on pages 458–459.

▾ Restart in Mac OS 9. None of the permissions set in Mac OS X will apply in OS 9. (Don't be tempted to set permissions in Mac OS 9 because it can cause problems for OS X users using Classic.)

Setting permissions   Don't go randomly **setting permissions** for files and folders until you really have a good reason and know what you're doing. When you're ready, here are the simple directions.

To set or change permissions for a file:

1. Click once on a file to select it.

2. Press Command I to show the Get Info window for the file (or go to the File menu and choose "Get Info").

3. In the Get Info window, click the little triangle next to "Ownership & Permissions" to open the pane.

4. If you are the Owner of the file, you can change the "Access" for the Owner, the Group, and others. You can also click on the padlock and then change the actual Owner or Group, but I wouldn't recommend you do that unless you really know what you're doing.

O thou pale Orb

Select a file or folder, then press Command I to get the Info window.

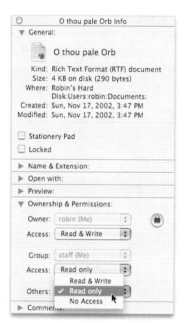

In the open pane shown above, you can see the ownership and permission options. If the selected file is a folder, there is an additional option called "Write only (Drop Box), as shown on page 623.

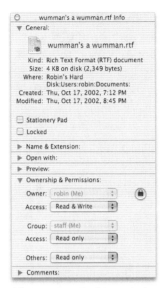

These are typical permissions for a **document.** The owner has full permissions; other users can read, copy, or print the file, but cannot make changes to it.

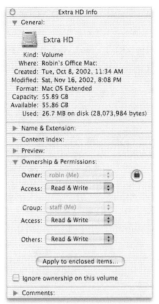

An extra **hard disk** or **partition** offers the option of "Ignore ownership on this volume," which means it will let anyone do anything on the whole disk. You might want to apply this so no one has trouble installing applications on this disk.

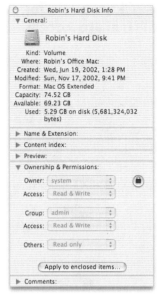

The boot **disk** (the one that has the operating system on it) is completely locked up because you are not the owner. You can't change it.

Folders and disks have an "Apply" button. If you choose to "Apply to enclosed items," you will override any permissions that the subfolders had.

A new folder automatically picks up the permissions of the folder it was created within.

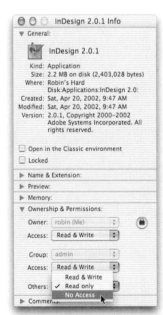

Most **applications** that came with your Mac are owned by the "system" and you cannot change the permissions.

An **application** that you installed belongs to you and you can change the permissions to allow other users to use it or not.

Post a File for All Users to Access   In the Users folder, which is on your main hard disk (if you have more than one partition), you see a folder called **Shared.** Every user on the Mac will see the same Shared folder. So any file that you want everyone to be able to open, copy, or print (depending on the permissions you set), put it in the Shared folder.

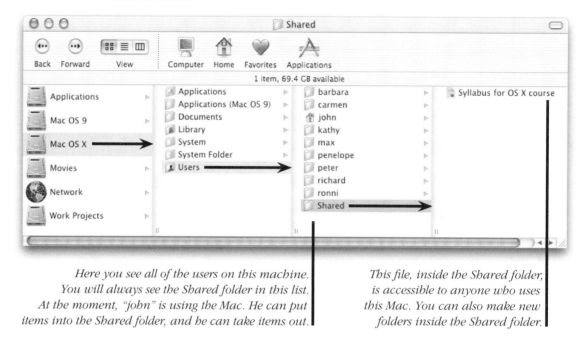

*Here you see all of the users on this machine.
You will always see the Shared folder in this list.
At the moment, "john" is using the Mac. He can put
items into the Shared folder, and he can take items out.*

*This file, inside the Shared folder,
is accessible to anyone who uses
this Mac. You can also make new
folders inside the Shared folder.*

Only the user who put a file *into* the Shared folder can remove that original file. When any other user drags the file out of the folder, the Mac automatically creates a *copy* of the file. Not even the Administrator can remove a file that another user put in the Shared folder (log in as root, if you must remove a file; see pages 458–459).

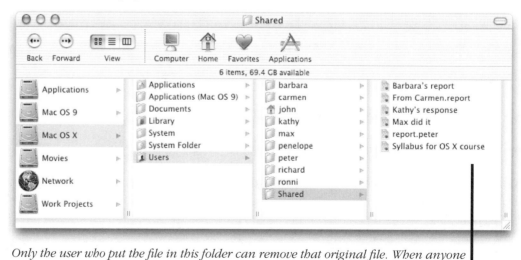

*Only the user who put the file in this folder can remove that original file. When anyone
else drags that file out of the Shared folder, the Mac automatically creates a copy.*

When any user drags a file out of the Shared folder, the Mac automatically makes a **copy;** the only user who can remove a file from the Shared folder is the **original owner.**

When a user makes this copy, she becomes the "owner" and picks up the "Read & Write" permissions of the owner, no matter what permissions the original owner had set for the group and everyone else. So if you don't want other users to be able to make changes to a document, set the "owner" permissions to "Read only." **New owners** will not be able to save changes, as shown below, but the **original owner** is still able to make and save changes, even though the permissions are "Read only."

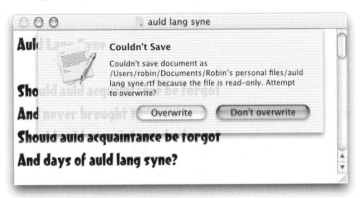

*If you are the **original owner** of this file, you will be allowed to overwrite the file so your changes are saved, even though the owner permissions are set for "Read only."*

*If you are **not** the original owner of this file, you will **not** be allowed to overwrite this file.*

The Shared folder is owned by the system so no one is allowed to make changes, not even the Administrator.

**Post a File
for Others to Copy**

If you put a file in your **Public** folder, everyone else on the Mac has access to it, just like in the Shared folder, but other users have to open your Home folder to get to it. Files in the Public folder are also accessible over a network, as explained in the following chapter, whereas files in the Shared folder are only available to users on the local Mac.

If you threw away your Public folder because you thought you'd never need it, follow the steps below to create a new one. **If you still have your Public folder, skip** to page 624.

**Do You Need to Make
a New Public Folder?**

I do hope you heeded the warnings early in the book not to throw away or rename any of the folders in your Home area, particularly the one named **Public.** If you did, it's really okay—you can create a new one, plus the Drop Box inside of it, and the new folder will work just like the original. It will even have the fancy little icon on it.

To make a new Public folder (if you previously threw yours away):

1. Open your Home window (click on the Home icon in the window Toolbar, or press Command Option H).

2. To make the new folder, press Command Shift N. A new, untitled folder will appear in your Home window.

3. Rename the folder **Public.** Click anywhere to set the name (or hit Return or Enter).

4. Now you need to create a Drop Box folder inside the Public folder. So double-click on the new Public folder to open its window.

5. To make the new folder, press Command Shift N. A new, untitled folder will appear in your Public window.

6. Rename the folder **Drop Box.** Be sure to use a capital D and B, and put a space between the words. Click anywhere to set the name (or hit Return or Enter).

7. Now you have to change the permissions for Drop Box so other users can put files into this folder, but not open it: Click once on the folder, then press Command I to Get Info. You'll get the Info window as shown on the opposite page, the illustration on the left.

Tip: You can recreate any of the folders you might have thrown away that you now realize you need, such as Pictures or Sites.

8. Click on the triangle next to "Ownership & Permissions." The Drop Box folder you just made probably has the permissions shown below, left, so the owner can "Read & Write," but others can "Read only." That's not what you want.

9. Press on the "Everyone" menu (not "Group" yet) and choose "Write only (Drop Box)."

10. Now press on the Group menu and choose "Write only (Drop Box)."

11. Close the Info box and you're all set.

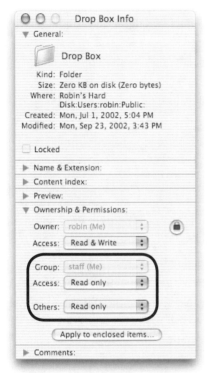

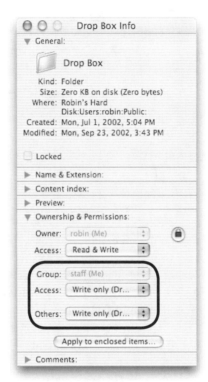

These are the permissions your Drop Box will have when you first make it.

With "Write only" permissions, your Public folder and Drop Box are back to their original states.

Using the Public Folder

As I mentioned on the previous page, you can put files in your **Public folder** to share with other users on the same Mac. File Sharing does not need to be turned on to do this (to share files in your Public folder over a network, Personal File Sharing does need to be turned on, as discussed in the following chapter).

Just drop files into your Public folder and all other users on the Mac can copy them to their Home folder.

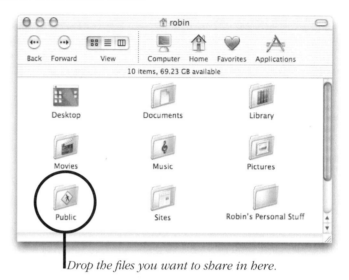

Drop the files you want to share in here.

To pick up a file in a Public folder, click once on that user's Home folder, then click on their Public folder. Just drag a file out—it will be automatically copied for you. Notice most of the other folders in every other user's Home have the "Do not enter" symbol, as shown on page 616.

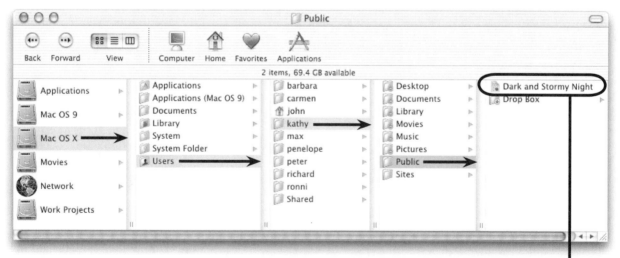

John is the user here, as you can see by the Home icon. He opened Kathy's Home folder to get to her Public folder, where she stored a file he needs called "Dark and Stormy Night."

Inside each Public folder is a **Drop Box.** This is a place where you can leave a file *for that one particular user whose Home it is.* No one but that one user can see the file—no one else can even look inside the folder.

To put a file in someone's Drop Box, open their Home folder, then open their Public folder, then drag your file into their Drop Box. You'll get the message shown below every time you drop in a file.

Using the Drop Box

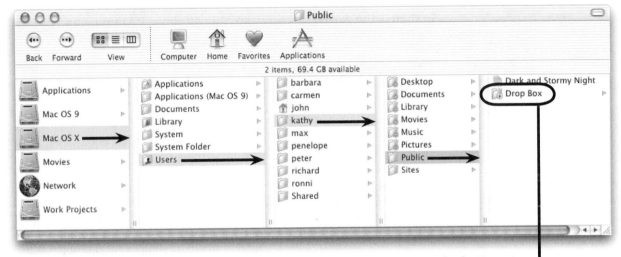

John is the user here, as you can see by the Home icon. He opened Kathy's Home folder to get to her Public folder, where he found her Drop Box, where he can drop in a file for her.

Drop Box

The Drop Box has an icon that indicates you can "write" to it, or put things inside of it. But that's all you can do—you can't open it.

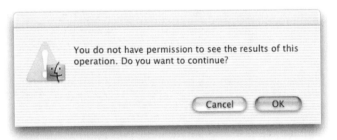

You'll get this message when you drop a file in someone's Drop Box because you will not be allowed to open the Drop Box folder to make sure the file transferred properly. You have to simply trust that it's there.

Change Permissions on Home Folders

You can **change the permissions** on any of your own Home folders, if you want others to have access to them. For instance, perhaps you used your digital camera and Image Capture to "offload" a whole bunch of family photos into your Pictures folder. Rather than copy the photos into your Public folder or the Shared folder, or drop them into individual family member folders, you can make your Pictures folder accessible and everyone else can go into the folder and view the photos.

To change the permissions, just follow the directions on pages 616–619.

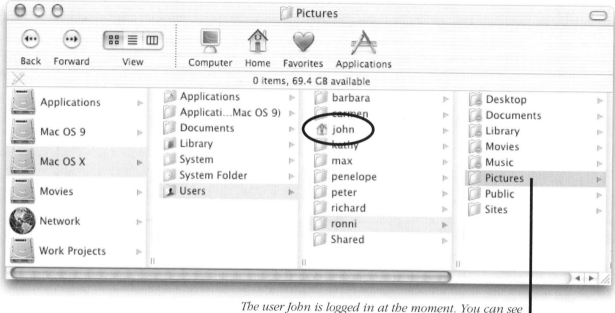

The user John is logged in at the moment. You can see that the user named Ronni has changed the permissions of her Pictures folder so all other users can access it.

Sharing Files between Several Macs

This chapter is only for you if you have more than one Mac in the same house or small office. If you do have more than one Mac, it is incredibly easy—in fact, it's so easy it's spooky—to **share files between Macs.** You can just drag a file onto the other computer's window, right there on your own Desktop. Or you can set it up so each person can get to the other person's entire hard disk. This works even if the other Macs are not using Mac OS X. If all the connected Macs use Jaguar, it's even easier to send files back and forth through Rendezvous. And if you have a Windows machine on your network, you can even share files with that computer as well!

Contents of this chapter

Simple Networking

The Macs you want to share files between must be **networked** together—you must have some sort of cable connecting them to each other or both to the same printer, or AirPort cards installed so they can connect to each other wirelessly. Networking a couple of Macs is a simple procedure.

There are entire books written on networking, and it *can* get very complex, so complex that people make a living being network specialists and in a large office there is usually a full-time *network administrator.* I am only going to explain the simplest method to get a couple of Macs talking to each other. We've got five Macs and a PC in this office, plus an iMac in the studio and a laptop in the library, plus three printers, all networked together, using a combination of DSL, Ethernet cables, and wireless AirPort. It is the coolest, most efficient way to get work done.

If you have a number of machines in your home office or small office, you will need something called a *switch* or *Ethernet hub* that can connect all of your machines together, including your printers. The switch/hub will have a number of Ethernet ports; you connect each Mac and printer to that box with *straight* (not crossover) Ethernet cables (I'll explain that in a minute).

If you have several computers in your office and a broadband connection, you probably have a *router* and all your Macs are connected into it—this means they're all set up for networking. Plug any network-capable printers into this router and you've got a fully networked small office. (In fact, with Apple's file sharing features, you can even network printers that are not connected to the hub and that weren't designed to be networkable; see page 350.)

If the router doesn't have enough ports for the Macs and printers in your office, you can buy a small hub or switch and connect the router to the hub/switch with a *crossover* Ethernet cable.

Peer-to-peer network

This simple network in a small office is called a **peer-to-peer network,** where every computer on the network is considered a "server," which is a computer that can "serve" files to others. This is different from a client-server situation in a large corporation, where lots of computers connect to one huge, main server and everyone gets files from that main server, rather than from each other's computers.

There are several possible ways you might want to connect. I'll explain them briefly here and you can skip directly to the pages you need.

How Do I Connect? Let Me Count the Ways

For all connections: *Read the First and Second Steps on the following page!*

Rendezvous: If both (or all) Macs are running Jaguar, you can use Rendezvous, which is part of iChat. With Rendezvous, you can send a single file or a folder full of files directly to another Mac. The other user must approve the incoming file.

**Mac running Jaguar
to
Mac running Jaguar**

You cannot see the files on another computer this way—it is strictly a method of sending requested files back and forth. And it's the fastest and easiest way to do so.

▾ Follow **Rendezvous:** pages 631–634.

Personal File Sharing: If both (or all) Macs are running any version of Mac OS X, you can connect directly to the other hard disks. If you connect as a **registered user who has Admin privileges,** you have access to their entire machine. You can't get into the folders belonging to other *users* on that machine, but you can get everywhere else.

**Mac running Jaguar
to
Mac running 10.1
or Jaguar**

You can leave files on that computer, or copy files from it to yours. The other person does not have to approve the process; they don't even have to be sitting at their Mac.

▾ Follow **Personal File Sharing as registered user (Admin):** Steps 1–3, pages 635–641.

If you connect as a **guest,** the only folders you have access to are the Public folders belonging to the users you connected to. All you can do is pick up any files they might have left in their Public folder, or leave files in their Drop Boxes (see Chapter 34 about those folders). If you connect as a **registered user with no Admin privileges,** you can access all of that user's Home folders.

▾ Follow **Personal File Sharing as guest:** Steps 1–3, pages 635–639 and 642.

Old Mac to new Mac: If you want to connect a Mac running OS 9 or earlier so you can get your old files onto your new computer, set up Personal File Sharing on both Macs. Then with your new Mac, connect to the old one.

**Mac running Jaguar or 10.1
to
an old Mac running OS 7, 8
or 9**

▾ Follow **Personal File Sharing as registered user:** Steps 1–2, pages 635–637.
Then follow **Share An Old Mac:** All of the steps, pages 645–649.

Jaguar to Windows: Yes, you can share files with a Windows machine.

**Mac running Jaguar
to
a PC running Windows**

▾ Follow **Windows File Sharing:** pages 650–655.

First Step: Ethernet Cables

You will probably have to buy **Ethernet cables.**

▼ If the cables are going to directly connect two computers (or any two Ethernet devices, like a Mac directly to a printer), you need **crossover cables.**

▼ If the cables are going from the computer into a hub, router, or switcher, you need **straight cables**—not crossover.

To tell if an Ethernet cable is crossover or not, hold both ends up, facing the same direction, with the locking clip facing up. Look at the colored wires coming through the end.

A straight cable has the colored wires in *exactly the same order.*

A crossover cable does *not* have the colored wires in the same order.

Second Step: Connect your Macs with Ethernet Cables

*At **www.DrBott.com** you can find hubs, switches, crossover Ethernet cables, straight Ethernet cables, network printing solutions, transceivers for older Macs that don't have RJ45 Ethernet ports, and much more.*

The first thing you must do before you can actually share files is **connect the computers together with cables.**

A. Connect two computers directly to each other using a **crossover Ethernet cable** for the fastest connection (for instance, G3 to G4 or iMac to G4). Just plug each end of the crossover cable into the Ethernet ports on each Mac. If the other Mac is too old to have an Ethernet port, you just need to get a transceiver adapter for the AAUI port; see page 674.

B. Connect any number of computers together with **straight Ethernet cables** that go from each computer into an Ethernet hub, router, or switch. If you have a high-speed connection, you already have a router that you can plug the Ethernet cables into.

C. Connect two computers directly to the same PostScript printer (either through Ethernet ports, if the printer has them, with crossover Ethernet cables; or through the regular serial port on older printers with something like a Farallon EtherMac iPrint adapter). Once both computers are connected to a printer, they are also connected to each other, whether the printer is turned on or not.

D. Connect two computers to a non-PostScript printer with Ethernet cables or a third-party solution. Once both computers are connected to a printer, they are also connected to each other, whether the printer is turned on or not. There are devices available that will connect anything to anything. For instance, Milan Technology has an adapter that will plug into the parallel port on your color inkjet (the parallel port is the long one) that you can then plug two Ethernet cables into. Other vendors have other great solutions. The best source for solutions from a variety of vendors is DrBott.com.

Rendezvous is part of the **iChat** software that comes with Jaguar. You can also send email, an Instant Message, or files to anyone on Rendezvous.

To use Rendezvous, you don't need to have a Mac.com account, nor an AIM account, as you must to use iChat. But both machines do need to have iChat installed (which automatically includes Rendezvous) and must be connected per the suggestions on pages 628 and 630.

To set up Rendezvous:

1. Open iChat: either single-click on its icon in the Dock, or double-click its icon in the Applications window.

2. The first time you open iChat, you get the dialog box shown below. Setting up iChat also sets up the information for Rendezvous.

   First and Last Names: This is how the other people on your network will identify you.

   Account Type: You don't need to choose an account type if you plan to use only Rendezvous. But if you are setting this up for iChat as well, choose "Mac.com" if you have a Mac.com account. Choose "AIM" as the account type if you have an AOL or an AIM screen name.

   Account Name and Password: Enter your screen name and password, if you have one of the accounts mentioned above. Otherwise, you can leave it blank if all you plan to do is Rendezvous. Click OK. Another message window will appear.

3. In the Rendezvous window, shown below, right, click "Yes."

Share Files with Rendezvous

iChat

Set up Rendezvous

See Chapter 33 for all the details about using iChat.

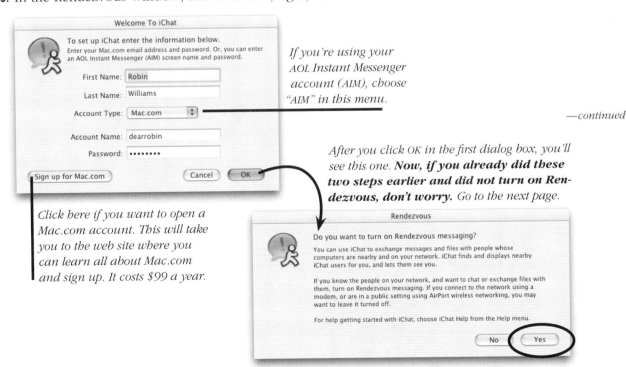

If you're using your AOL Instant Messenger account (AIM), choose "AIM" in this menu.

—*continued*

After you click OK in the first dialog box, you'll see this one. **Now, if you already did these two steps earlier and did not turn on Rendezvous, don't worry.** *Go to the next page.*

Click here if you want to open a Mac.com account. This will take you to the web site where you can learn all about Mac.com and sign up. It costs $99 a year.

It's not too late to set up Rendezvous

If you previously opened iChat and set it up but did not turn on Rendezvous, **or** if you want to change any of the settings (**or** turn off Rendezvous), use the iChat preferences:

1. While iChat is open, go to the iChat menu and choose "Preferences…."

2. In the "Accounts" pane, as shown below, check the box to "Enable local network messaging." Adjust any of the other settings per your liking.

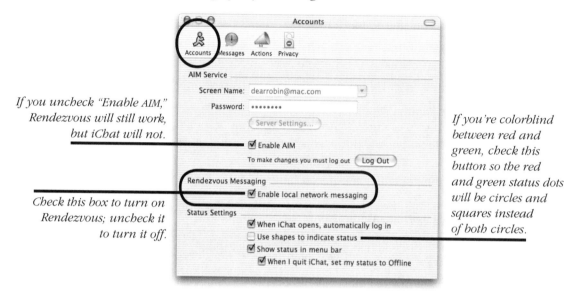

If you uncheck "Enable AIM," Rendezvous will still work, but iChat will not.

Check this box to turn on Rendezvous; uncheck it to turn it off.

If you're colorblind between red and green, check this button so the red and green status dots will be circles and squares instead of both circles.

Read the iChat information also!

Just about everything that applies to iChat (preferences, images, opening and closing, changing your availability message, what all the icons indicate, etc.) also applies to Rendezvous. So if you haven't already, read Chapter 33 about iChat to fill in any gaps you might have regarding Rendezvous.

To send a file to another computer on your local network:

1. Open iChat, which will activate Rendezvous.

2. If the Rendezvous window (shown below, left) doesn't appear, press Command 2, *or* go to the Window menu and choose "Rendezvous." Other users who also have Rendezvous set up and running will appear in the little window.

3. To send *one* file or a *folder* containing several files, drag it to the Rendezvous window and drop it on a name. You will be asked to confirm the transfer.

4. The other computer will get a message, shown below. When that user clicks "Save File," the file will be sent from one machine to another. Now that was pretty easy.

Send a file to another computer user

Scarlett cu2.jpg

Drag a file and drop it on the user's name.

The pictures in Rendezvous are coming from the Address Book; see Chapter 32.

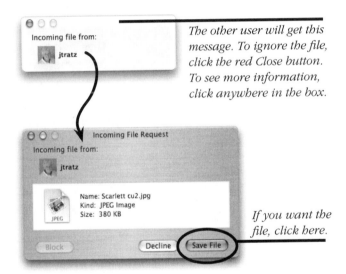

The other user will get this message. To ignore the file, click the red Close button. To see more information, click anywhere in the box.

If you want the file, click here.

—continued

Send a file through an Instant Message

Another way to send a file through Rendezvous:

1. Open iChat, which will activate Rendezvous.

2. If the Rendezvous window (shown below) doesn't appear, press Command 2, *or* go to the Window menu and choose "Rendezvous." Other users on your network who also have Rendezvous installed and running will appear in the little window.

3. Select the name of the user to whom you want to send a file, then click the "Instant Message" icon at the bottom, the one with the little bubble. This opens an Instant Message (IM) window, shown below-right, on both your computer and the other user's computer.

4. Start a dialog with the other person—send at least one message.

5. Now you can do one of two things:

   Either: Drag the file into the message box and send it (hit Return or Enter).

   Or: Click the paperclip icon to open the standard Open dialog box where you can find and select the file you want to send, then send it (hit Return or Enter).

6. The receiving user will see the file in the sender's message bubble. Click once on the file name and it will download to the Desktop (unless you changed your downloads default in the Internet system preferences' Web pane).

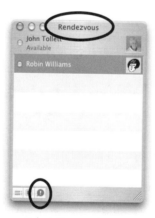

a. Select the user's name, then click this button to open an IM window. Here John is about to send me a file.

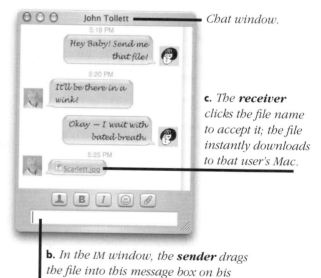

Chat window.

*c. The **receiver** clicks the file name to accept it; the file instantly downloads to that user's Mac.*

*b. In the IM window, the **sender** drags the file into this message box on his computer, then hits Return or Enter.*

Personal File Sharing

Okay, so you have your two Macs either directly connected to each other with a crossover Ethernet cable, or you have several Macs all connected into a router, hub, or switcher with straight Ethernet cables, as explained on pages 628 and 630. Now you need to turn on **Personal File Sharing.**

Turn on file sharing on every Mac that you want to share files between.

To turn on Personal File Sharing:

1a. Open the System Preferences: click on the icon in the Dock, or from the Apple menu, choose "System Preferences…."

1b. Single-click on the Sharing icon. You'll get the pane shown below.

1c. Make sure there is a checkmark for "Personal File Sharing."

Step 1: Set up Sharing preferences

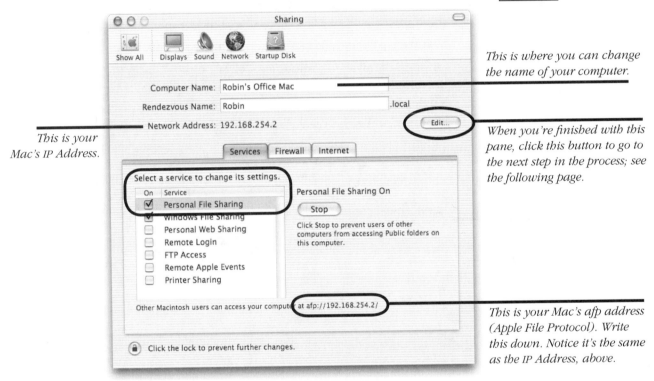

This is where you can change the name of your computer.

This is your Mac's IP Address.

When you're finished with this pane, click this button to go to the next step in the process; see the following page.

This is your Mac's afp address (Apple File Protocol). Write this down. Notice it's the same as the IP Address, above.

1d. If necessary, change the **Computer Name** to something that will tell you and others on the network which Mac this is. For instance, you might name it "G4 by the West Window" or "Cliff's Business Mac." You want a distinctive name that will tell you exactly which Mac this is when looking at a list; names like Mac1, Mac2, and Mac3 are not going to help much unless you paste big name tags on each Mac in your office.

1e. Write down the **afp address** on a piece of paper, and label it as the afp Address that shows up in the Sharing preferences pane for that particular computer. The afp (and the IP) Address might change now and then, so don't be surprised if that happens.

Step 2: Check your Network Pane

If you have a working DSL, cable, or other **broadband** connection, your Macs are all connected with Ethernet cables through the hub or router. This means your Network settings are probably right where you need them.

If you have a telephone **dial-up** connection, but your Macs are connected through Ethernet, you need to make a few adjustments in your Network preferences pane. It would be a good idea to make a new Location (see opposite page).

If you are connected through **AirPort,** walk through the Network preferences and make sure things are set up correctly for you. It would be a good idea to make a new Location (see opposite page).

Network preferences

To open the Network preferences pane:

2a. If you're continuing from Step 1, click the "Edit..." button in the Sharing preferences pane, circled on the previous page.

Or open the System Preferences: click on the icon in the Dock, or from the Apple menu, choose "System Preferences...." Single-click on the Network icon (there's probably a Network icon right in the toolbar). You'll get the pane shown below.

Choose "Built-in Ethernet" here, unless you want to connect to a Mac using AirPort, then choose "AirPort."

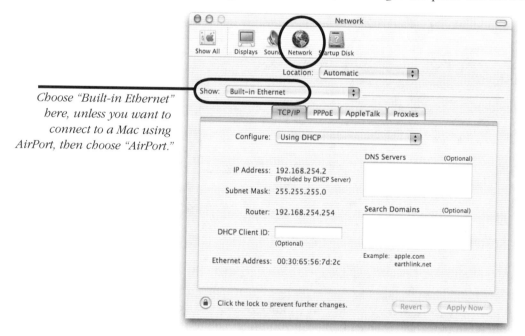

2b. From the Show menu, make sure "Built-in Ethernet" is chosen.

2c. Click the **AppleTalk** pane and check the box to "Make AppleTalk Active." (If all the Macs are connected with Ethernet, you really don't need AppleTalk anymore, but it won't hurt.)

2d. Click "Apply Now."

a. Before you make a **new Location, save the current one:**
From the Location pop-up menu, choose "New Location...."

Give it a name you will remember, such as "Santa Fe Dial-up."
Click the "Apply Now" button in the bottom-right corner.

b. Now you need to make a *new* Location for the file sharing setup.
To make a new Location, from the Location pop-up menu, choose
"New Location...."

Name the Location something you will recognize, such as "Office
Network" or "Connect to the Boss." Click OK. Now you will make
your settings for this Location.

c. If you have a **dial-up** connection, your Network preferences
probably has the "Show" option selected as "Internal Modem"
because that's how you connect to the Internet. You need to
change this to "Built-in Ethernet" so you can connect to the other
computers in your office.

If you want to connect through **AirPort,** choose "AirPort" in the
"Show" pop-up menu. The AirPort Base Station itself might be
connected to DSL or other broadband, or to a telephone connection, but if you want to connect to another Mac through an AirPort
connection, you need to select "AirPort" in the "Show" menu.

Make a new Location,
if necessary

This pop-up menu should display the name of your new Location.

Choose "Built-in Ethernet" here, unless you want to connect to a Mac using AirPort, then choose "AirPort."

d. Adjust the **settings** in the TCP/IP pane according to the information
in Chapter 30. (Most of the settings will be automatic and you can
just leave them as they are.)

e. Click the **AppleTalk** tab and turn on "Make AppleTalk Active."

f. When you have adjusted the settings for the new Location, click
the "Apply Now" button in the bottom-right corner.

So now when you need to use your dial-up to connect to the Internet,
choose your dial-up location and apply it; when you want to share files with
other Macs, choose your Ethernet location and apply it. See page 656.

Your AirPort location should work for both the Internet and file sharing; it
seems to work better than using the default "Automatic."

—go to Step 3

Step 3: Connect

You've set up all the computers running Mac OS X with the file sharing specifications in Steps 1 and 2, right? Plus they are all connected with Ethernet cables or AirPort.

(If your Macs are connected through a PostScript printer instead of Ethernet cables, make extra sure that AppleTalk is turned on; see Step 2.)

Mac OS X provides you with several ways to actually make the connection. Let's start with the Go menu, and then I'll tell you some shortcuts.

To connect to another Mac on your network:

3a. Click on any blank area of the Desktop to make the Finder active. Once the Finder is active, you should see the Go menu.

3b. From the Go menu, choose "Connect to Server…," or press Command K. You'll get the dialog box shown below, left.

If you see the same computer listed more than once, don't worry—at some point that computer had another IP address. That's why you want to know which one it has today.

*The * is your list of computers on the network that are running AppleTalk. "Local" is everyone on the network with Personal File Sharing turned on, even if they're not running AppleTalk.*

When you click a computer name, the columns slide over to give you details about the selected computer. Notice you now have a scroll bar if you want to go back to the list of server options.

3c. In the left side, choose "Local," and on the right side should appear the names of the other computers on your network that have file sharing turned on. Notice in the example above you see "Scarlett's Computer," which is still running Mac OS 9.0.

If your Macs are using AppleTalk, you'll see them also listed in the * servers option.

3d. Select the name of the computer you want to share files with. This moves the columns over to give you details about the selected Mac in the last column, as shown above.

Or you can type in the AFP address in the "Address" field. Type **afp://** and then the address (see page 635 for the address). Click the "Connect" button.

3e. You'll get the dialog box shown below, where you can choose to connect to the other Mac as a Guest or as a Registered User.

*See page 643–644 about adding the user name and password to your **keychain** so you can connect without having to even see this dialog box.*

Guest: You will only be allowed to see and copy files from the Public folder of the user on the other Mac. The only folder you can put files into is the Drop Box folder of the other user.

If you don't understand about Public folders and Drop Boxes, please see page 652 and 653.

Registered user: You must know the user name and password of the computer you are connecting to.

If you enter the **Administrator's user name** and password, you have access to the entire computer.

If you enter a **regular user's name and password,** you will have access to all of the Home folders of that user, but no other files on the computer or any partitions.

3f. When this dialog box appears, it shows up with your name in it, as shown below, left (actually, it shows up with the name of the current user of this computer, which might or might not be you). That's kind of confusing because it makes you think it wants *your* password. ***It doesn't—you need to enter the user name (either the long name or the short name) and password of the user whose files you want to connect to.***

Entering the name and password that you use on this computer you're sitting at won't get you anywhere at all.

*Enter the name and password of any user **on the other computer,** per the description of access in 3e, above.*

—continued

Connect as Registered User and Administrator

See page 642 about connecting as a guest or regular user.

3g. Let's say you connected to the other Mac as a **Registered User** and you entered the name and password of an **Administrator** on that Mac (as opposed to the name and password of a user who does not have Admin privileges). You will see the dialog box shown below. In this example, the other Mac has two partitions and one user/Administrator (jtratz). Double-click on any partition you want to mount on your Mac.

You can connect to more than one volume (disk) at once: Command-click on each one you want to connect to, then click OK.

3h. After you click the OK button in the step above, you will see a server icon on your Desktop and/or in your Computer folder, as shown below, and perhaps a "Volumes" window will open, displaying the server icon as well.

This "Volumes" window sometimes appears and sometimes doesn't. You won't be able to find the folder icon for this window once you close it—it's invisible. But if you want it back again, try this:

From the Go menu, choose "Go to Folder...."
In the little box that appears, type the name of your hard disk, a slash, and then Volumes, *as shown below. Click the "Go" button.*

The server icon (the icon for the other computer) will always be in your Computer window.

If you have your Finder preferences set to show connected servers on your Desktop, you'll find an icon there as well.

3i. Double-click the server icon wherever you find it, as explained in Step 3h, which will open a window that displays the contents of the other Macintosh!

Ta da! You're sharing files

It might *look* like it's one of your own windows, but it's really displaying the files on the other computer. *Anything you delete from this window will be immediately deleted from the other Mac.*

To make it easier to share files, *press Command N to open a new window. Now you can have this window from the other Mac open, plus a window from your own Mac, and you can drag files back and forth from one to the other. Any files you drag back and forth will be automatically copied from one place to the other—not moved.*

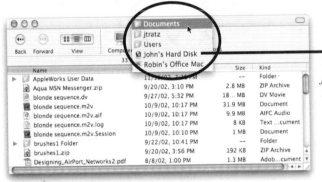

This tells me the Documents folder I'm looking at is actually the one on "John's Hard Disk."

Once you start opening files on the other computer, there is **no visual clue** *whose computer you are working on! Since all of the other user's Home folders are named exactly the same as yours, it's easy to get confused. Keep checking the path from the title bar: Command-click the title bar to get the menu you see above.*

Tip: If you like to check the path regularly, you might want to put the "Path" button right in your Toolbar. To do so, Shift-click on the Toolbar button to get the Customize pane, then drag the "Path" icon up to the Toolbar. Click "Done."

Path

*Connect as Guest
or Registered regular User
(not an Admin user)*

When you connect as a **guest,** you do not have access to the entire Mac—you will have access to any or all users on the other Mac, but all you'll be able to see are their Public folders and Drop Boxes, as shown below.

If you connect as a **regular user** (that is, you enter someone's name and password who is a user on that other computer but who does not have Admin privileges), you will have access to all of the folders that belong to that one user. You can also access the Public Folders and Drop Boxes of any other user on that computer.

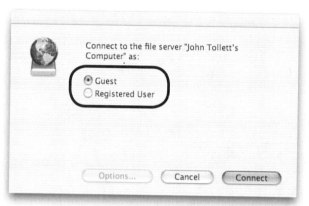

Connect as a guest, or as a registered user with the name and password of a regular user.

As a guest, you have access to any user's Public Folder or Drop Box on that Mac.

Double-click a user name, or Command-click on several users and then click OK.

If you later decide you want to access another user, just do Step 3 over again and choose another.

You will be able to copy files from a user's Public folder, as shown here. Or you can drop files into a user's Drop Box.

Do you **connect** to another Mac **regularly**? You can add the password for a Mac into your Keychain so you don't have to type the password each time you want to connect. Then add an alias of that server icon to your Favorites folder. Next time you want to connect to that computer, open your Favorites window, double-click the server icon, and you are instantly connected.

Connect with a Double-Click

To add the password to a keychain:

1. Go through the connection process as explained on the previous pages, until you come to the dialog box shown below.

Note: See pages 466–473 if you want to know more about Keychain.

2. Enter the correct user name and password, then click the Options..." button. You'll get the dialog box shown below. Check the box to "Add Password to Keychain." Click OK.

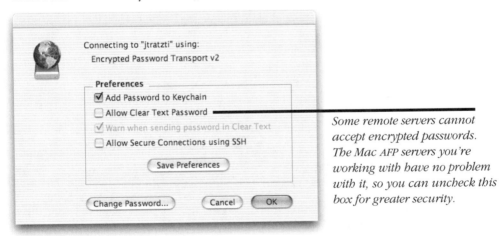

Some remote servers cannot accept encrypted passwords. The Mac AFP servers you're working with have no problem with it, so you can uncheck this box for greater security.

—continued

3. After you are connected, drag the server icon up to the Favorites icon in the Toolbar and drop it on the heart. This will make an alias in the Favorites folder, as shown below.

Here you see aliases to three different Macs.

If the other computer's IP address changes, the alias won't work anymore. Darn. You'll just have to connect the old-fashioned regular way, then make a new alias.

4. Now whenever you want to connect to that Mac, open the Favorites folder and double-click on the alias. The other Mac will be instantly mounted in your hard disk, and its window will open.

You can even do this with remote servers. The icon shown above, "Kate at Production," is the FTP site at Peachpit Press in Berkeley, California. I double-click that icon here in Santa Fe, New Mexico, and I am instantly connected with Kate's computer in Berkeley. Then I just drag my files into her folder and she's got 'em. Amazing.

Delete the Keychain Access password

Keychain Access

You can **delete the Keychain Access** password, if you like, to prevent easy access to the other Mac.

1. Click on the Applications icon in the Toolbar to open the Applications folder.

2. Double-click the Utilities folder.

3. Double-click the Keychain Access icon to get the window shown to the right.

4. Select the keychain for the connection you want to delete, then click the Remove button in the toolbar.
Click "Save Changes."

You must restart your Mac before this takes effect.

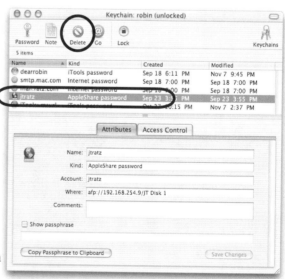

Connect the two Macs per one of the suggestions on page 630. Actually, you can share files with Macs running System 7.1, as well as up through Mac OS 9.2. Do the following four steps on the Mac running OS 9 (or earlier), then connect as usual from your Mac OS X machine. This is a great way to transfer files from your older Mac to your new one.

Share Mac OS 9 Files with Mac OS X

1. Set up File Sharing in Mac OS 9:

a. Go to the Apple menu, slide down to "Control Panels," and choose "File Sharing."

b. Follow each of the callouts below to set up File Sharing properly.

If you're connecting to a Mac running System 7 through 8.1, you'll find this in the Sharing Setup control panel.

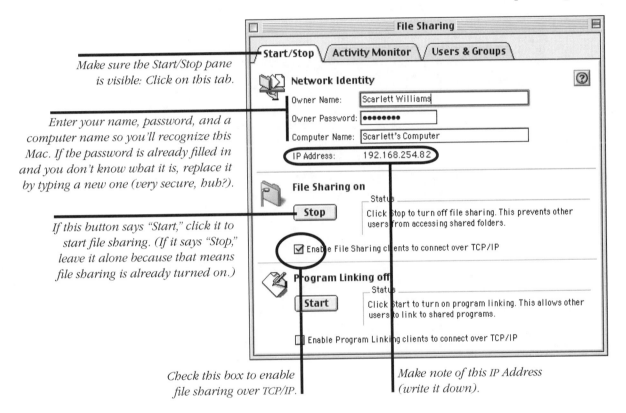

Make sure the Start/Stop pane is visible: Click on this tab.

Enter your name, password, and a computer name so you'll recognize this Mac. If the password is already filled in and you don't know what it is, replace it by typing a new one (very secure, huh?).

If this button says "Start," click it to start file sharing. (If it says "Stop," leave it alone because that means file sharing is already turned on.)

Check this box to enable file sharing over TCP/IP.

Make note of this IP Address (write it down).

—continued

2. Set up File Sharing User in Mac OS 9:

*If you're connecting to a
Mac older than OS 9, open the
Users & Groups control panel.*

a. If the File Sharing control panel is not already open, go to the Apple
menu, slide down to "Control Panels," and choose "File Sharing."

b. Click the "Users & Groups" tab.

Click here to close.

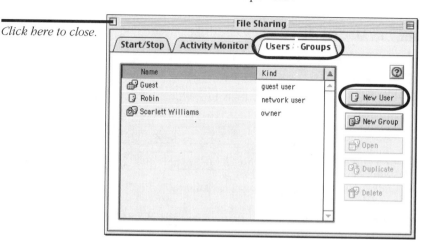

c. Click the button, "New User."

d. In the "Identity" pane, shown below, type in a name and password.
Write down this name and password on a piece of paper!

e. From the "Show" menu, choose "Sharing," and make sure the box
is checked to "Allow user to connect to this computer."

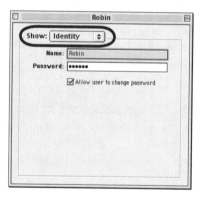 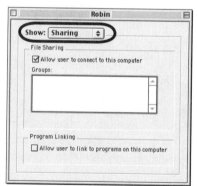

f. Click the close box to put this little dialog box away.

g. Click the close box to put the File Sharing control panel away.

3. Set up File Sharing Info in Mac OS 9:

a. Click once on the hard disk icon that you want to share files from.

b. Press Command I, or go to the File menu, choose "Get Info," then choose "Sharing."

In earlier systems, go to the File menu and choose "Sharing."

c. If you do not see "Sharing" in the "Show" pop-up menu in the Get Info box, as circled below, choose "Sharing" from that menu.

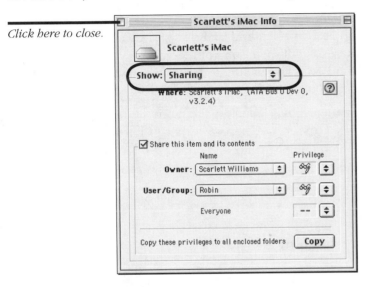

Click here to close.

d. Check the box to "Share this item and its contents."

e. In the "User/Group" pop-up menu, choose the name of the user you created in Step 2.

f. In the "Privilege" column, choose the "Read & Write" icon (the eyeglasses and pencil).

g. Close the Get Info box.

4. Set up AppleTalk Ethernet in Mac OS 9:

a. Go to the Apple menu, slide down to "Control Panels," and choose "AppleTalk."

b. In the "Connect via" pop-up menu, choose "Ethernet."

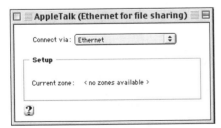

c. Close the AppleTalk control panel. If you are asked to save changes, click "Yes."

Connect and share files   Okay, now that the OS 9 Mac is ready, go to the OS X machine, connect to the other Mac, and share files.

To connect to the Mac OS 9 machine and share files:

1. In the OS X Mac Finder, go to the Go menu and choose "Connect to Server…." (If you don't see the Go menu, click on the Desktop and try again.)

2. In the "Connect to Server" dialog box, in the left pane, click either "*" or "Local." Depending on how your computers are networked, the other Mac will be in one of these lists. Since you turned on AppleTalk on both machines, the other computer is probably listed in both sections.

3. In the pane on the right side, the name of the OS 9 Mac will appear. Single-click the name, then click the "Connect" button, or double-click the computer name.

When you choose the computer name here, that name automatically appears in the "At" pop-up menu above, and its address appears in the "Address" field below.

When the Address field shows the name of a computer, it puts "%20" in place of every empty space. Don't let that worry you in this case.

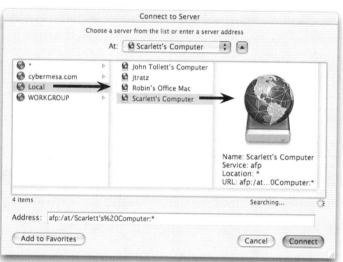

4. You'll get the dialog box shown below. Enter the name and password that you set up as a User on the OS 9 machine, in Step 2 on page 646. The click the "Connect" button.

5. You'll get the dialog box shown below. Select a hard disk, then click the OK button. If there is more than one partition on the other Mac and you previously set up sharing privileges in the Get Info box for the others, you'll see those listed here as well.

6. On your Desktop and/or in your Computer window, you'll see a network icon for the disk you selected above. Double-click that icon to open the hard disk on the other computer.

7. The window that opens displays the files on the Mac OS 9 computer. To make it easier to copy these files from this computer to your OS X machine, press Command N to open another window. Now you can drag files from one window to the other, between computers.

It's no easy task to keep track of which windows are on which machine! See the tip on page 641.

*Don't open any **applications** from the window of the other Mac because you will actually be working on the other machine at that point, which might affect the person using it.*

Share Files with a Windows Computer

Or do Steps 1–3 in the opposite direction: Make the new user in Windows (or use an existing user), and enter that person as a new account on your Mac.

Windows File Sharing lets you allow selected Windows users who are already on your *local* network to log in to your Macintosh and access your files, and you can send files to that Windows user as well. It's really amazing.

1. First, open the **Sharing** system preferences, as explained on page 635). You'll see the pane shown below.

   Check the box to select "Windows File Sharing."

   Write down the IP address that displays in the pane (circled below).

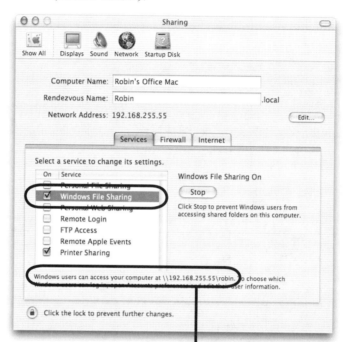

Write down this IP address. *This is what you will use to connect from the Windows computer to your Mac **except** you will change the user name at the end to the Windows user name. (Note that those are **back**slashes, not the forward slashes you use in a web address.)*

2. Then open the **Accounts** system preference (click the "Show All" button in the upper-left corner, then click the Accounts icon).

In the Accounts pane, click the "Users" tab. In the Users pane, create a new user for each Windows user that you want to allow access. Give the user a short name with all lowercase letters, no more than eight characters, no spaces. In this example, I created a new user called "robinpc." **Write down the short name and password.**

If you're making this for yourself, use a different name and short name because you cannot have two users with the same name.

Be sure to check the box "Allow user to log in from Windows."

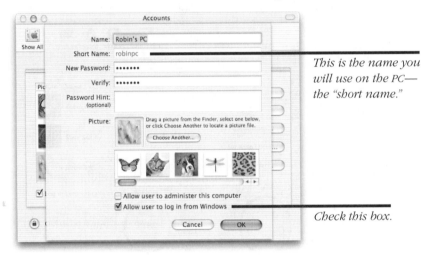

This is the name you will use on the PC— the "short name."

Check this box.

The main Administrator cannot share her account with a Windows user.

—continued

Now set up your PC to share

The "Control Panel" folder is inside the icon named "My Computer."

These directions use Windows 2000. If you're using a different version of Windows, the steps might be slightly different, but you should be able to follow along.

Click OK.

3. Now, **on the Windows machine,** make a new user (use the "Users and Passwords" Control Panel).

Check the box "Users must enter a user name and password..." and then the "Add" button will become available. Click "Add."

Enter the user's *short name* exactly as you created it on your Mac, in all lowercase letters.

Enter the password exactly as you created it, including any capital letters. Click "Next."

You will be asked to choose the level of use.

After you click the "Finish" button, Windows will set up a new user for the machine.

Go to the Start menu, log off of the current user, and log back on as the new user.

4. On the Windows machine, open the icon named "My Network Places."

In the window, shown below, double-click "Add Network

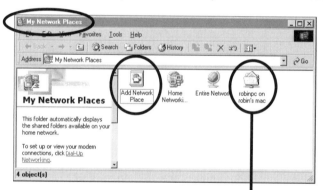

After you create the new Network Place, an icon appears in this window. To connect next time you log on, just double-click this icon.

5. Enter the IP address that you wrote down in Step 1, ***except*** substitute the name of the PC user, as shown in the example below.

*Notice this is the name of the new user I set up on the Mac, **not** the name that the Sharing window told me to type, as shown on page 650.*

6. Click "Next" and enter a name so you will recognize this network place. I recommend naming it the short name of the user so you won't get confused. Then click the "Finish" button.

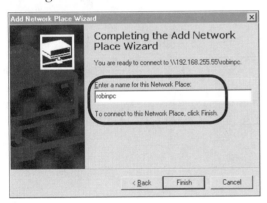

7. The Home window *of the user you created* on the Mac will appear on the Windows screen, as shown below. See the tips on the following page for sharing files.

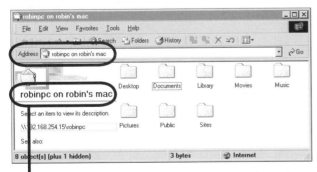

This tells me I'm looking at the Home window of the user "robinpc" on my Mac. wow.

**Share files
back and forth**

On the PC, the user can access any files in these folders *that the new user you created on the Mac has placed in them*. In this example, that is the user "robinpc" on the Mac. Note that this is not **your** Home folder (assuming you are the main user—it is the Home folder of the **new** user you made on your Mac in Step 2)! For security reasons, the PC cannot log in to the main Administrator's account.

To make files accessible to ANYONE using the Macintosh, put the Windows files in the ***Public folder.***

To make files accessible ONLY to that PC user on the Mac (the Mac user "robinpc," in this example), put the files in any other folder *except* Public.

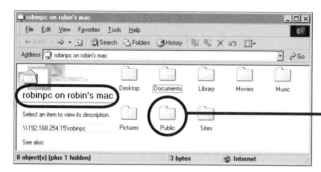

Any files the PC user puts in the Public folder will be available to any user on the Mac.

On the Mac, you will see the new user that you created on your Macintosh ("robinpc" in this example).

> **If you log in as that other user,** you can put files into any folder in your Home window and they will be accessible on the PC.

> **If you do NOT log in as that user,** you can put files in the **_Drop Box_** (inside the Public folder) and they will be accessible on the PC.

On the Mac, *any user can put files into this Drop Box and the PC user can get them.*

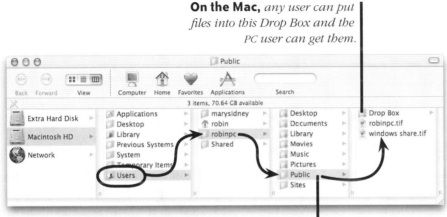

On the PC, *I put files in the Public folder and now any user can get them on the Mac.*

In this example, I am logged into my Mac as "robin" (you can tell because only the user "robin" has a Home icon instead of a generic folder icon), and I'm the main Administrator. Using the Column View in the window, I can easily open the "Users" folder and find the "robinpc" user's Home window, as shown above, and I can copy any files that person has put into the Public folder.

Disconnect

This is the contextual menu to eject a selected server.

Disconnect from any connected servers in the same ways you disconnect from any other hard disk.

▼ **Either** drag the server icon to the Trash basket.

▼ **Or** select the server icon. Go to the File menu and choose "Eject."

▼ **Or** select the server icon and press Command E for Eject.

▼ **Or** Control-click on a server icon to get the contextual menu; choose "Eject."

Other Tips

Here are a couple of **extra tips** to make networking easier.

▼ Put a "Connect" icon in your Toolbar; see pages 80–81 about customizing the Toolbar. Drag the Connect icon up to the Toolbar.

▼ Once you are connected, drag the server icon up to the Finder window Toolbar and drop it on the Favorites icon. Now that server is in the Favorites menu (which is in the Go menu), in your Open and Save As dialog boxes, and in the Favorites window. Just double-click it to connect. If you added the user name and password to your Keychain, as explained on page 643, you'll go straight to the server with just that double-click.

▼ Remember that Location you created on pages 637? Well, you can use the Location menu under the Apple menu to switch locations, as shown below.

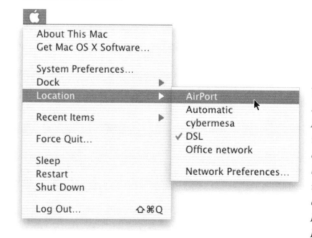

*Well, this is **supposed** to switch your locations, but I have found that it often neglects to switch the actual connection from, say, the built-in modem to the built-in Ethernet. So if you can't connect after changing Locations, choose "Network Preferences..." to check the "Show" menu setting.*

Sharing Files over the Internet

Built into your Mac are a number of ways to **share files with anyone in the world,** or with yourself when you are away from your own Mac. If you have a .Mac account, you can put up to 100 megabytes of stuff in your iDisk that other .Mac members can pick up or that you can access from a remote location. Or you can set up a web page with the HomePage feature in .Mac that lets anyone, even Windows users, access certain files in your iDisk. You can even turn on FTP access on your own Mac on your Desktop and people can download files from your Mac using a web browser, and they can download or upload files to you with an FTP program, such as Transmit or Fetch.

You can also turn on "Personal Web Sharing" on your Mac so your friends, family, and co-workers can view web pages that you store in your Sites folder. Oh, it's all so amazing.

All of the details about sharing files over the Internet using Mac.com features are explained in The Little Mac iApps Book, *by John Tollett and me.*

Contents of this chapter

Personal Web Sharing

One way you can share files with anyone in the world over the Internet is through the **Personal Web Sharing** feature on your Mac: In the Sites folder (which is in your Home window) you can place web pages, whole web sites, QuickTime movies, documents of any sort, and folders. From any computer, someone can use a web browser to access these special shared folders on your Mac. Depending on the quality and speed of your Internet connection, Web Sharing can function as a local area network or as an easy way to share files across the Internet or within a corporate intranet.

Personal Web Sharing does *not* provide you with the ability to remotely upload files to a shared folder. To upload files to your computer from somewhere else, use FTP access, as explained on pages 664–666, or your .Mac account and iDisk, as mentioned on pages xxi–xxii.

1) Get this information

There are **two pieces of information** a person needs to have before attempting to Web Share: the short user name and the computer's IP address, both from the computer you or someone else wants to connect to.

1. The **short user name** is the name chosen when the Mac was first set up, or when someone was established as a new user.

   To find the short name, go to System Preferences and click the Accounts icon. Select the name in the list, then click "Edit User…." You'll see the short name.

   You can log into any user's folder, not just the currently active user.

2. The **computer's IP address** is shown in the Sharing preferences: Go to System Preferences and click the Sharing icon. In the "Services" pane, as shown on the opposite page, you see the "Network Address," which is the IP address.

   Important note: If the computer uses a **broadband connection,** the IP address is usually the same for a long time.

   If the computer uses a **dial-up telephone modem connection,** this number will change everytime it connects to the Internet! This means if you want to do Web Sharing, you (or the other user) must *first* connect to the Internet, *then* look here and find out what the IP address is while it's connected, and tell the person you want to share with what that number is. That IP address *will only be good for that Personal Web Sharing session until you disconnect.*

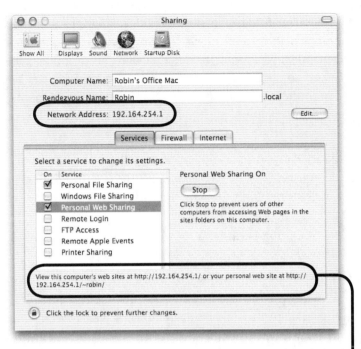

In Step 3 on page 661, you'll come back to this pane and check
"Personal Web Sharing." If you like, you can go ahead and do
it now. Then you'll see this line of information at the bottom of
the pane. Notice it's the same number as the "Network Address"
at the top of the pane.

Depending on how and to which service you connect, your
Network Address might look something like this:

snd-pa-010caburp0560.dialsprint.net.

That's perfectly fine. That's the "number" you'll use as your
IP address.

2) Put files in your Sites folder

There are **two separate folders** on your hard drive that are available for Web Sharing. One is available to all users, the **Sites folder;** every user can Web Share their own files. The other folder can only be modified (files added or deleted) by an Administrator of that particular computer, the **Documents** folder deep inside the main Library folder. You can put documents, movies, photos, or entire folders full of stuff that you want to share in either of these folders.

Sites

▼ **Sites folder:** This is the one every user will see in their own Home folder. Every user on the machine can put files into their own Sites folder for sharing with others. (If the original was thrown away, just make a new folder and name it "Sites.")

When Web Sharing is on, you (or anyone) can access files in the Sites folder with a web browser. You just type in:

http://network.address/~username/

Use the IP address of the Mac, the short user name, and be sure to include the ending slash (/) or it won't work.

> ***Important note:*** You might see a file called "index.html" and a folder called "images" in your Sites folder. If you do, take them out of there or no one will see your files (see page 663 for details of this).

▼ **WebServer Documents folder:** Only Administrators can modify the contents of this folder for Web Sharing.

To find this folder, open your Home folder, then open your Library folder, then open the WebServer folder, then open the Documents folder (see the illustration on the opposite page). This folder is full of files, but you can throw them all away (or copy them somewhere, if that makes you feel better), then replace them with your own web pages.

When Personal Web Sharing is on, you (or anyone) can access files in the WebServer Documents folder with a web browser. Someone would type into their browser:

http://network.address/

Your network address, of course, is the IP address of your Mac.

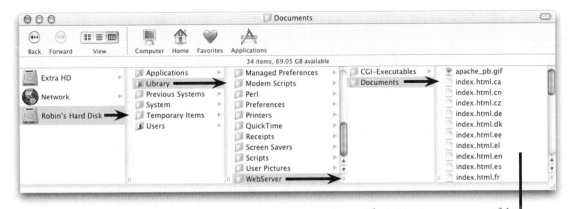

As an Administrator, you can safely delete everything in this folder and replace it with your own files.

These are all the same web page in different languages. To see what they look like, drag any one of these files and drop it in the middle of your browser window.

See page 663 for an example of the difference between putting regular files in this folder and putting a web page in here.

3) Turn on Web Sharing

Only an Administrator can turn Web Sharing on or off, so if you want regular users to be able to Web Share, you must turn it on before they log in.

To turn on Personal Web Sharing, open System Preferences and click "Sharing." In the "Services" pane (as shown on page 659), check the box for "Personal Web Sharing." Write down the "Network Address" that you see at the top of this pane, or the web addresses it provides at the bottom of the pane.

4) Access the Sites folder

To access the Sites folder from another computer:

1. Open your browser.

2. In the Address field (circled, below), type
   http://
   followed by the IP **address** of the computer you want to access, followed by **~username/**, as explained on the previous page and as shown below. *Be sure to type the last slash or it won't work.*

   It should look something like this:
   http://192.162.244.123/~joe/   *or*

   http://san-odp-031caburbp7167.dialsprint.net/~let/

   Hit Return or Enter. You should see a page like the one below.

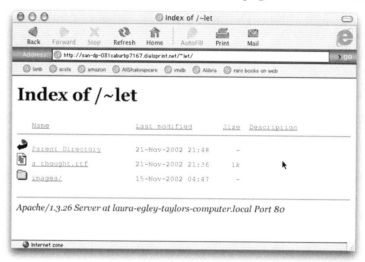

When you access another computer's folder through Web Sharing, a web page opens with a list view of the contents of the Sites folder (in this case), as shown above.

- ▼ **To download a file,** *don't* click on the file name link—drag the link to your Desktop and drop it there; this **transfers** the file to your computer.

- ▼ Click on a **folder link** to see a list of its contents, or drag the folder link to your Desktop to transfer the entire folder.

- ▼ If you click on a file name that is a link to a web page, you can view it in the browser just as you would any web site.

The **Sites folder** probably already has a web page from Apple in it, called "index.html," plus a folder called "images" that holds the graphics that are on Apple's web page. When those files are in the Sites folder, no one can access any other files you put in there; that page is just meant as a demo. So remove both of those files. It won't hurt anything.

Shown below are two other examples of files in the Sites folder.

- ▼ On the left you see **files** sitting inside the folder and what they will look like to someone accessing your folder through Web Sharing.

- ▼ On the right you see a **web page** with a graphic on it. If you know how to make web pages, you can put an entire site in this folder. The first page of your site must be named **index.html,** and it cannot be within another folder.

Put your own web site in the Sites folder

These are the original files that are probably in your Sites folder.

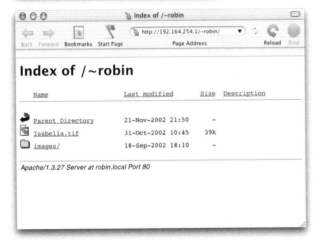

When you place individual files in the folder without an HTML page (which is a web page), this is what a person will see when accessing the folder. Drag any document link to the Desktop, or click a folder link to see what's in that folder.

When you put your own web page in the Sites folder, this is what a person will see when accessing the folder. You can add files to your web page so people can download them. Any images on your page can be dragged off to a person's Desktop.

Your Mac as an FTP Server

Transmit and Fetch are both shareware products, which means you can download them for free, and if you decide to keep and use one of them, pay its $25 fee online.

FTP (File Transfer Protocol) is a method of allowing access to a computer for either uploading or downloading files. Mac OS X includes FTP server software so you can do this from home or any small office.

Over the Internet, you can access files stored in a user's Home folder, no matter where in the world you are. To *download* files, a web browser is sufficient. To *upload* files to an FTP-enabled Mac, use an FTP "client," such as Transmit (**www.panic.com**) or Fetch (**www.FetchSoftworks.com**). Both of these utilities can also download files, as explained on the following pages.

Turn on FTP access

To enable FTP file sharing, you need to **turn on FTP access.** The person logging in to your Mac needs to know your current **IP address,** as well as the **user name** and **password** of the person who owns the files they want to access.

On the Mac that you want to make accessible, open System Preferences and choose "Sharing," as shown below. In the "Services" pane, check the box for "FTP Access."

Tip: You don't have to be across town or out of the country to take advantage of FTP sharing. If you have multiple Macs in your office that are not networked, you can use FTP sharing to transfer files between computers in the office. Make sure you trust anyone to whom you give FTP access—with the Administrator name and password they'll have access to your entire computer when "Allow FTP access" is turned on.

Note the "IP Address" at the bottom of the pane. That is the Internet Protocol address for this computer. The IP number is necessary to access a computer from the Internet.

- ▼ If you have a full-time **broadband** connection to the Internet, this number stays fairly constant. You can take the number with you to another computer or give it to someone else so files can be shared.

- ▼ If you have a **telephone dial-up** connection, this number will change every time you connect. So connect first, then make note of the IP address. The FTP session will only last until you disconnect.

With an **FTP client** such as Fetch or Transmit, not only can you download files from an FTP-enabled Mac, you can also upload files over the Internet from another computer.

To access an FTP-enabled Mac using Transmit:

1. Double-click the Transmit icon to open the application. You'll see the dialog box shown below.

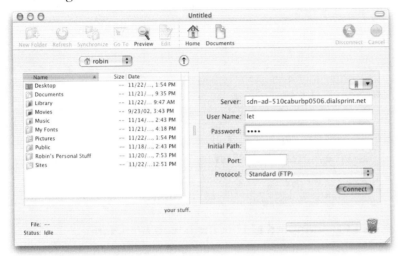

2. Enter the IP address into the "Server" field. *Do not type "http://."*

3. In the "User Name" field, type the user name for the account whose Home folder you want to access. (You do not need to type a ~.)

4. In the "Password" field, enter that User's account password.

5. Click "Connect."

Transmit opens a window that shows the folders and files on the other computer, as shown below.

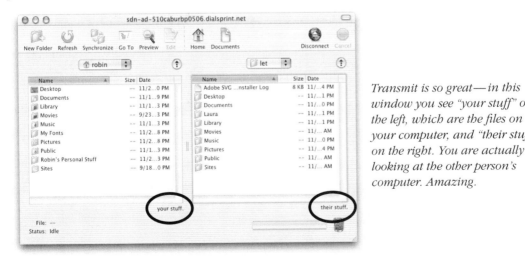

— continued

Use an FTP client for access

Transmit   Fetch

These are two of the available FTP clients. Both are great.

This is the IP address, user name, and password of the Mac that has FTP access turned on.

You can leave "Initial Path" and "Port" blank in this situation.

Fetch will ask for a "Host" name, which is the IP address, and the "User ID," which is the user name. And it will want the password also, of course.

Transmit is so great—in this window you see "your stuff" on the left, which are the files on your computer, and "their stuff" on the right. You are actually looking at the other person's computer. Amazing.

To open a folder on either computer, double-click its icon. If you navigate deep into the folder structure and want to return, click the pop-down menu at the top of the window to access the folder hierarchy.

To download a file (copy it from their computer to your computer), find the file you want in the right-side window, and drag it to a folder on the left side.

To upload a file or folder (send a copy of it from your computer to theirs), in the left-side window find the file you want to send, then drag that file to the right-side window.

Use a web browser for FTP access

With a current web browser, you can go to the FTP site and download files; you cannot upload files through the browser.

Read the information on page 664 and make sure you have those three pieces of data: the **current IP address,** the **user name,** and the **password** (not *your* user name and password, but the user name and password of the person whose Home folder you are going to access with FTP).

To access an FTP-enabled Mac using a web browser:

1. Open a web browser.

2. In the Address field, type **ftp://** and then the IP address, as shown below.

3. Hit the Return key or Enter key, or click the browser's Go button.

Only the most current web browsers will do this. If you use a browser and it doesn't work, try another browser.

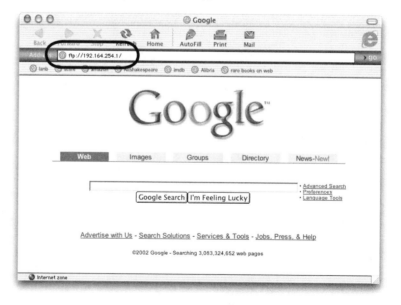

4. In the login dialog box that appears, as shown below, enter the User ID (short name) and password of the person whose Home folder you want to access. You can only access and share files in accounts for which you know the user name and password.

You don't need to enter anything in the "Account" field.

If you check "Remember Password," you won't have to enter it next time.

5. A web page containing the folders and files that belong to the targeted user opens in the browser, as shown below. Click on a folder (identified in the "Kind" column) to open another web page that lists the Folder contents.

To download a file, drag the link to your Desktop.

Or Control-click on a file to download it: From the contextual menu that appears, choose "Download Link to Disk" or something similar. In the "Save" dialog that opens, enter a file name and choose a location in which to save the file.

Security Issues   When you enable file sharing over the Internet with a broadband connection, you are opening your Mac up to **potential security risks.** To help
protect yourself, follow these simple guidelines.

▼ If you have multiple users, don't assign Administrator status
unnecessarily. In fact, if you want one extra step of protection,
create yourself a non-Admin user account and use it regularly,
even if you are the only user. Only log on as the Administrator
when you need to install software or change system-wide settings.

▼ Sharing files through your iDisk and Mac.com's HomePage (see
pages xxi–xxii) is quite safe since no one gets anywhere near your
Mac—the files are all on the Apple server.

▼ General file sharing as explained in Chapters 34 and 35 is relatively
safe. Just be sure to assign the privileges appropriately.

▼ Web sharing is fairly safe as well because there are no passwords
that can be taken, and you're only exposing one folder on your Mac.
Just make sure you don't put any files into the Sites folder or Web
Sharing Documents folder that you don't want to share. You can
assign few or no privileges (explained in Chapter 34) to the Sites
folders to even further limit access to them.

▼ Enabling FTP access is rather risky because passwords are not
encrypted as they go through the network. Make sure every user
has a safe and different password, and uncheck the "Allow FTP
access" box except when you need it.

▼ The Remote Login feature is the riskiest form of file sharing because
it allows users to connect to your Mac through a terminal emulator
(which years ago I dubbed the "terminator emulator"). I didn't even
explain how to do it in this chapter.

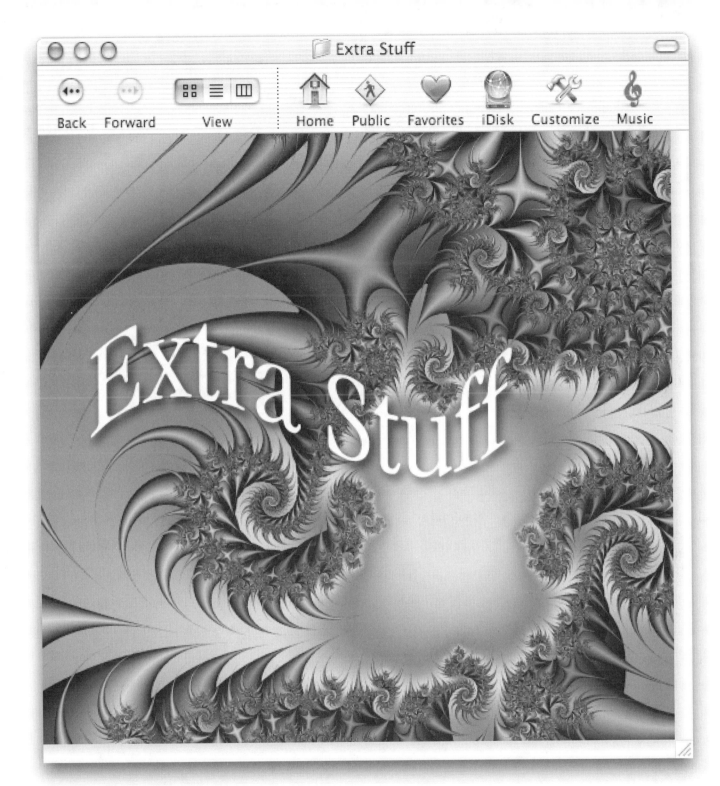

Ports & Peripherals

This chapter describes those places on the back or side of your computer where you plug things in **(ports)** and the things you plug into them **(peripherals).** You can spend years on your Mac without knowing the information in this chapter because one of the greatest things about the Mac is that if a cable fits into a port, it's the right match. It's not possible to plug something into the wrong place. So you don't really have to know anything about the back of your computer—it it fits, plug it in and move on. But when you get to the point where you want to know the difference between a FireWire port and a USB port and a serial port, then dive into this short chapter.

Contents of this chapter

What is a Peripheral?

A **peripheral** is any item (or "device") that is outside of the main computer box, but attached to it. Your monitor (except for iMacs) is actually a peripheral device, and so are your mouse, keyboard, and printer. Scanners, many CD writers, and external hard disks are peripherals. Devices that are internal (built in) on some machines might be external devices, or peripherals, on another. For instance, I have a little, lightweight PowerBook that has no built-in CD drive, but I bought an external CD drive that I can attach when I need it, so that CD drive is a peripheral. Many computers have built-in modems, others use modems as peripheral devices.

The main computer box is often called a CPU, although the CPU itself is actually a tiny chip in the middle of the main board (the motherboard) inside the box. So a CPU is not a peripheral. You might install a *card* (plastic board with circuitry on it) inside of your computer to expand its capabilities, such as a video card or a modem card. Some people consider that the devices on those cards are also peripherals because they are added on, even though they are in the computer box. (But isn't "internal peripheral" an oxymoron?)

What is a Port?

A **port** is a socket, a kind of receptacle, on the back or side of a computer or on the backs of peripheral devices. The port is where you connect the peripheral device. A port is very different from a regular socket like electrical sockets in the wall, in that information goes both ways through a port. A wall socket sends power in only one direction—to a device. A port sends information back and forth between the computer and the device.

There are lots of different kinds of ports, and peripherals are made to match a certain port type. For instance, you might have *USB* ports, to which you can only connect USB devices, such as *USB* printers. If you have *serial* ports, you'll connect *serial* printers.

The cables that connect peripherals to the CPU (or to another peripheral) have **connectors** on the ends. The connectors match the ports. On a Mac, if the connector matches the port, it works. You can't plug a connector into the wrong port. (Well, it's possible to shove a phone cable into the Ethernet port, as noted on page 674, but it really doesn't *fit*.)

On pages 674–677 are pictures of all these ports so you'll know exactly what you have (or don't have).

Connectors are the parts on the ends of the cables that actually make the connection to the other device. The connector is the part that tells you what kind of cable it is—an Ethernet cable has a very different connector from a serial cable, which is very different from a USB cable (as illustrated on the following pages).

Every connector is either **male or female;** take one look and you can guess why. The male or female shape is a very important identifying feature. When you start connecting lots of things together (like to project a presentation from the computer to a large wall screen), you will find yourself looking for either a male or female connector.

Another identifying feature of connectors are the **pins,** or slender metal prongs on the male versions (not all connectors have pins). The number of pins is particularly useful in describing what you need. For instance, I once needed a cable for a video card that I installed in my computer. I didn't know exactly what kind of cable I needed, so I counted the little pin holes and told the guy I needed a 15-pin connector and he thought I knew what I was talking about.

The **shape** is important. Some connectors are long and skinny, short and fat, rectangular or round, etc. Many connectors have identifying symbols that match the symbol on the port. On the next few pages are illustrations of the most common symbols that identify both the connectors and the ports.

On the back of your computer (not an iMac or laptop) you might see some larger, rectangular pieces that look like metal covers to openings. They are. Those are your **expansion slots;** the more slots you have, the more "expand-ability" your computer has.

You might buy an add-on like a video card for a second monitor. The card (also called a *board* or an *adapter*) is a flat, plastic piece with circuitry all over it and a port on one end. You open your computer box, and there are slots in the motherboard (the main board that runs the computer; of course it's a mother) where you stick this card in, usually perpendicular to the motherboard. You pop that rectangular metal piece out of the opening in the back of the Mac, and the port sticks out that end. Thus when you close the computer box, you have another port to which you can attach another peripheral.

You might get a game card, a modem card, a video card with extra VRAM (video RAM) just for your monitor, or other sorts of boards to expand the capability of your Mac.

Modem Ports

This is the port for an internal modem and the symbol that identifies it. (Don't get the modem port confused with the larger Ethernet port, as shown below.)

You probably have a telephone **modem port** for your *internal* modem, which looks exactly like an RJ11 phone jack in the wall of your house (because it is). Don't confuse the modem port with the Ethernet port; the Ethernet port, as shown below, is larger than the internal modem port.

You can plug any regular phone cable, like the kind you buy at the grocery store, into this port and the other end into a telephone or wall jack. This is one way to get connected to the Internet. When you use a phone cable and connect to this modem port, your connection is called a "dial up" connection—you are only connected to the Internet when your internal modem dials a phone number through this phone line.

An old Mac that doesn't have an *internal* modem will have a *serial* modem port instead, which is illustrated on page 677. This is to connect a modem that is contained in a separate, external box.

Ethernet Ports

This is what an RJ45 Ethernet port looks like, and the symbol that identifies it.

Ethernet (pronounced *eether-net*) is the most common *networking* system for local area networks (LANs), which means the computers that are connected together are close enough to be connected with cables (as opposed to a wide area network, a WAN). All newer Macs, including all iMacs, have Ethernet ports, which look like large phone jacks. You can use Ethernet even in your home or small office to connect several computers so you can send files back and forth (see Chapter 35).

Your printer might have an Ethernet port, in which case you can send data to the printer much faster than through the serial port. Even if it doesn't have an actual Ethernet port, you can get adapters for some printers so you can add the printer to your Ethernet network. In my office we use EtherMac iPrint Adapters from Farallon to network our good ol' workhorses—eight-year-old Apple LaserWriters. Also see page 350 about the incredibly easy way to network any printer to everyone else on the network, with the click of a button.

AAUI Ports

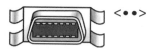

This is what an AAUI port looks like, and the symbol that identifies it.

Older Macs have **AAUI ports** (which stands for Apple Adapter Unit Interface) takes a variety of adapters for different networking systems, but the symbol for its port is the same as the symbol for an Ethernet port because Ethernet has become the most commonly used local area network. As explained in Chapter 35, you can get an Ethernet adapter for this port, called a transceiver, so you can connect this computer to one that has an actual Ethernet port.

The **USB ports** are on Macs built since late 1998. USB stands for Universal Serial Bus, which replaces both the Apple Desktop Bus and the serial ports, as described on page 677. With USB, input devices (like mice and keyboards) as well as scanners, printers, Zip drives, and other devices can all connect into the same ports.

You can't daisychain USB devices, like you can the SCSI devices mentioned on page 678, but you can buy a **hub** (shown to the right). The hub connects into one of the USB ports on the Mac, and several devices can plug into the hub. You can connect another hub to the first one, and so on, so you can supposedly connect up to 127 USB devices to one Macintosh. I don't know why you would, but you could.

Also check the base or the back of your monitor—you might find USB ports, which is a great convenience. The backsides of many stand-alone flat panel monitors have USB ports. And your keyboard has a USB port on both sides.

One of the greatest things about USB devices is that you can **hot swap** them; that is, you can connect and disconnect devices such as keyboards, mice, Zip drives, printers, or scanners without having to shut down the computer like you do with SCSI, serial, and even ADB devices. Just don't swap devices while they're doing something, like copying to a Zip or scanning a photo or printing.

FireWire is Apple's trademarked version of the standard called IEEE 1394. It's a high-performance serial bus (see the description of a bus in the ADB explanation on page 677) for connecting up to 63 devices through one port on your Mac. FireWire is only built into the newer Macs, like the 1999 blue-and-white G3s and up. Many iMacs and laptops have FireWire ports.

The big deal about FireWire is this: It's extremely fast; you can connect 63 devices in any which way you like, such as in a star or tree pattern, and up to 16 in a single chain; you can hot swap them in and out without having to turn off the computer; they connect with a simple snap-in cable; and there's no termination necessary (see the SCSI explanation for termination, if you care). FireWire replaces the serial connection.

You can connect a vast array of consumer electronics to FireWire, such as digital cameras, video tapes, and camcorders, as well as DVD (digital video disk) drives, plus hard disks, optical disks, and printers.

You might hear the FireWire ports called IEEE, but IEEE actually stands for the professional society, Institute of Electrical and Electronics Engineers, and the IEEE is a standard they developed. For instance, the Ethernet standard is IEEE 802.3.

USB Ports

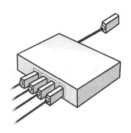

This drawing shows two USB ports and the symbol that identifies USB.

This is how a USB hub functions. The one connector goes into the computer's port, and the other connectors lead to extra devices.

FireWire Ports

This symbol identifies a FireWire port.

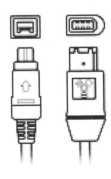

These are the two ends of a FireWire cable.

PCI Bus and Slots

PCI (Peripheral Component Interconnect) is yet another **bus** system. A bus is a system of hardware, software, and wiring that lets different parts of your computer communicate with each other. There are different kinds of buses, and PCI is focused on the expansion slots, which are described on page 673. PCI is now installed on most desktop computers, so if your computer was built in 1998 or later, it has PCI (except early iMacs). If your machine doesn't have PCI, it has what's called NuBus, Apple's prior technology.

When you read the specifications for a computer, it often brags about how many PCI slots it has. The more, the better if you plan to expand.

PC Slots and PC Cards

Most laptop computers, as well as other devices like digital cameras, have **PC slots** into which you slip **PC cards.** You might have heard these slots and cards referred to as PCMCIA, but that term is now limited to the association itself (the Personal Computer Memory Card International Association) and the cards and slots are simply called PC cards and slots.

PC cards are really little, as small as credit cards or half a stick of gum. There are a variety of PC cards for a variety of purposes. You can get cards for a cellular phone interface, Ethernet, global positioning system, hard drive, joystick, memory, modem, sound input and output, video capture, and much more. Cards that contain TV tuners, video teleconferencing, AM/FM radio tuners, and even CPUs (the CPU is the powerful chip that runs the entire computer) are available or in the works.

Unlike expansion slots, as explained on page 673, PC slots are accessible from the outside of the computer; like expansion slots, the purpose is to allow expanded capabilities. The slot, or socket, typically has a little flapping door covering the empty space where you slip in the card. Peek inside—you might actually have two sockets that you can use for two different cards.

None of the iMacs, iBooks, blue-and-white G3s, G4s, or newer machines have ADB ports or serial ports—Apple switched over to a new system, the Universal Serial Bus, which replaces both ADB and serial (below). Also, there are no SCSI connections on newer Macs. So unless you are using or working with an older Mac (like trying to connect an old Mac to your new one so you can copy files), **skip these two pages.**

Read this note before you take time to read this page

ADB stands for Apple Desktop Bus. A *bus* is a system of hardware, software, and wiring that lets all the different parts of your computer communicate with each other. There are different kinds of buses, and the ADB is specifically for *input devices*. An input device includes those items you input information into the computer with, such as a keyboard, mouse, trackball, joystick, or drawing tablet.

So most commonly, the ADB ports are where you connect your keyboard and mouse. Many Macs have only one ADB port on the back of the machine, plus one or two ADB ports on the keyboard, so you plug the keyboard into the port on the back of the computer box and then plug the mouse into the keyboard.

ADB Ports

This is what an ADB port looks like, and the symbol that identifies it.

A **serial port** is the little round one that looks similar to the ADB port, but it has more holes (to match the pins on the connector). There are two data wires in a serial cable, so the port can send and receive information at the same time.

There are usually two serial ports on the back of older Macs—one labeled with a little picture of a printer, and the other with a picture of a telephone. Although you can use either port for either a printer or an external modem cable, the printer port is actually slightly different in that it is the Mac's LocalTalk network port. This just means it's faster and more complex than the modem port, and if possible you should plug your serial printer cable into that one and the serial modem into the other one, although either one will work.

Until recently, almost all printers for the Mac were "serial printers," which means they connected to the serial port. As mentioned above, newer Macs don't have serial ports; they've been replaced with USB (see page 675).

Serial Ports
Printer and external modem ports

This is what a serial port looks like (above), and the symbols that identify the two on your Mac (below).

Also see page 674 regarding the **AAUI port,** which is the one you'll need to plug an Ethernet cable into so you can connect two Macs.

SCSI Ports

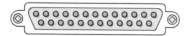

This is what one type of SCSI port looks like (above). There are actually several different shapes of SCSI ports, but they are all identified with the symbol below.

SCSI (pronounced *scuzzy,* not *sexy*) stands for Small Computer Systems Interface, which is a standard for connecting personal computers to peripheral devices and having them send information to each other.

There is only one SCSI port on older Macs, but there are two on the back of every SCSI device, which are things like scanners, extra hard disks, external CD drives, or CD writers. The ones on the device itself might look different, much larger, from the one on the back of your computer.

You can *daisychain* up to seven SCSI devices together; that is, you plug one SCSI device directly into the port on the computer, then hook the others to each other. To daisychain SCSI devices, you need a cable that has two connectors that match the two ports you are plugging into. For instance, a SCSI Zip drive uses the same connector as the Mac on both ends of its cable, but an older scanner might have two larger SCSI ports that are different from the SCSI port on the back of the Mac. So even if the ports on the two connecting devices are different, you can get cables with different connectors on each end.

Each device on the chain has to be pre-set to a different **SCSI address.** Look on any SCSI device and you'll see a tiny set of changeable numbers—that's the SCSI address. And SCSI devices have to be **terminated;** that is, the last device in the chain has to have a little stopper in the second port because the data goes in one port and out the other and gets confused if it finds an empty port. Some manufacturers use *internal termination,* which is great except it can limit the way devices are connected, and you have to *know* that device is internally terminated, which means you have to read the manual.

SCSI devices are infamous for being unpredictable—sometimes they don't work in one configuration of connections and termination, but they work if you just plug things in differently or if you turn them on in a different order. SCSI devices often refuse to *mount* (when a drive's icon appears on the Desktop, it is mounted) so often that there is a special little utility that most Mac users have called SCSIProbe to force them to mount. If you have SCSI devices, get SCSIProbe from the Internet at **www.download.com** or **www.shareware.com**.

Parallel Ports

Your Mac doesn't have a **parallel port,** but your printer might. It's a big, horsey-looking port that looks like it came from a PC, which it did; it looks much like the old SCSI port shown above. Parallel ports transfer data through eight wires, so all eight bits in a byte can go through the line at once (in parallel). Sounds like it should be fast, but most parallel ports are not capable of sending and receiving data at the same, which slows them down. The reason your printer might have a parallel port is because it can also plug into a PC. If the printer has a parallel port, it probably also has a serial port so it can print from an older Mac as well. Maximize your options.

Reformatting and Partitions

Hard disks are usually so huge these days that it is often a good idea to separate one large hard disk into several **partitions.** Each partition then acts like a separate hard disk, or volume—each partition has a separate icon, a separate window, and an individual name.

Using different partitions might also improve the speed of your Mac because it won't have to search the entire hard disk to find your data—it will just search the one partition that your work is stored on.

To create partitions, you have to **reformat** your hard disk. This will entirely destroy every piece of data on your disk, so make sure you back up everything you need before you reformat!

Contents of this chapter

Why Partition? If you have a large hard disk, you may want to think about **partitioning** it (separating it) into several smaller **volumes** (individual hard disks). This makes it easier for your computer to find what it needs, helps prevent files from becoming too fragmented, and can help your computer work faster. If you ever need to recover the data from a bad disk, it can sometimes be less expensive to recover an individual partition than to recover the entire hard disk. Or perhaps you need to install a different operating system such as Virtual PC so you can run Windows applications on your Mac—make a partition specifically for Windows stuff.

Dividing one disk into partitions can also help you keep things organized; you might have one small partition that is just for the operating system and its components, another partition for your applications, and another partition for your projects. Everything will still work together as if it was one big hard disk.

On the Mac I'm using at the moment, I separated the 20 gigabyte drive into three volumes: one for the Mac OS X operating system and applications, one for Mac OS 9 and applications that only work in Classic mode, and one for all my books and other projects.

If you plan to work with digital video and editing movies (which requires huge amounts of storage space), you'll need as much contiguous disk space as possible, and partitioning your hard disk is not recommended.

This is one hard disk partitioned into three separate volumes. Each volume looks and acts like a separate hard disk.

If you open up your Mac and look inside, you'll see a case like this icon inside your Mac—that's your hard disk. It fits in your hand. Amazing.

To partition your disk, you must **reformat** it. To *format* a disk means to prepare it for use; to *reformat* a disk means to wipe everything off the disk and prepare it for a fresh new use. There's no way to partition a disk without reformatting it first.

Once you have partitions, you can erase individual partitions without affecting the data on other volumes. For instance, while I was in the process of working with beta versions of Mac OS X and upgrading them constantly, it worked best to reformat just the one partition I had set aside for Mac OS X.

Sometimes you might need to reformat a disk because things get so screwy on your computer that, as a last resort, you totally reformat and start over from scratch. For instance, on a new iMac last year, all sorts of little things were going wrong—I couldn't receive faxes, eventually I couldn't even send faxes, my Zip drive wouldn't always work, sometimes I couldn't shut down, etc. So I backed up everything I had installed (as explained below) and reformatted and reinitialized the entire hard disk. Now everything works beautifully, as it should.

Very important: Reformatting your hard disk will absolutely positively without a doubt destroy every single thing on your entire hard disk and it will be impossible to recover any of it!!! If you have installed any new software or fonts at all or if you have created any new documents, before you reformat you must back them up (make copies of them) onto something like Zip or Jaz disks or onto CDs. If you don't feel comfortable doing that (see pages 170–177), have your power user friend help you. **Do not proceed without first backing up everything.**

Except: All of the software that came on your Mac will be restored at the end of this process, so don't worry about that. But even though the software applications themselves will be restored, any address lists you created in your email program, bookmarks in your browser, etc., will be gone.

You *don't* need to back up any software for which you have the original CD. You *do* need to back up software that you downloaded, especially if you didn't make a backup copy at the time you installed it. It's best, when downloading files, to always save the installer file, rather than the file that appears *after* you install it (as explained in Chapter 21).

If you're not perfectly clear on how to back up your necessary files, please have a friend over to help you, a friend who knows what she's doing!

If you've only had your computer a couple of days and haven't created anything of your own, go ahead and reformat and partition.

Why Reformat?

Tip: If reformatting doesn't fix squirrely problems like these, check your memory chips. Bad memory can make all sorts of weird things happen.

Back up everything you installed or created!!!

Reformat and Partition Your Hard Disk

Disk Utility

This is the Disk Utility that will format and partition disks for you. You can use it to erase a Zip disk or a partition (Disk Utility is in the Utilities folder).

Back up everything before you begin. I cannot be held responsible for any files you lose if you insist on not backing up everything you need! **Proceed at your own risk.**

You cannot reformat the disk that is running the computer, so you have to insert a system CD and let the system on the CD run the computer. What you are about to do is this: You're going to insert a system CD and start up from that CD, reformat the drive (destroying every iota of data on the entire hard disk), then reinstall everything like it was when it came from the factory. Follow these directions:

1. You have a CD called "Mac OS X" or "Mac OS X Install Disk 1." Put this CD in your Mac.

   You might also have one or more "Software Restore" disks for Mac OS X. Do *not* put the Restore disk in the Mac at this time—make sure you use the Install disk.

2. Wait for the CD to mount (its icon will appear on your Desktop and/or in your Computer window).

3. The "Welcome to Mac OS X" window should open automatically. If not, double-click the CD icon to open it.

4. Double-click the "Install Mac OS X" icon in the window to open the "Install Mac OS X" window, shown below.

Install Mac OS X

5. Click the "Restart" button. You'll be asked to enter the administrative password.

6. When you see the first installation window, ignore it and go up to the menu at the top of the screen. From the Installer menu, choose "Open Disk Utility...." The Disk Utility window opens, as shown on the opposite page.

7. Click the "Partition" tab.

8. In the upper-left corner you'll see names that represent two disks (or more if you have other drives connected), your big hard disk and the CD that started up your Mac. Click once on your hard disk, (or any disk you want to reformat) as shown on the opposite page.

9. In the Partition pane, under "Volume Scheme," there is a pop-up menu that says "Current." Click on this menu and choose the number of partitions you want to make. The "Volume Scheme"

panel below the menu will divide itself into equal parts according to the number of partitions you choose.

> If you decide later (like in a minute or two) that you want to make **more** partitions, click inside one of these partitions, then click the "Split" button.
>
> If you decide you want **fewer** partitions, click on a partition you want to delete, then click the "Delete" button.

10. Name each partition: Click in a partition box, then in the "Name:" edit box below "Volume Information," type a name.

    The "Format" choice is probably already selected as "Mac OS Extended." That's correct.

    Don't worry about the "Size" for now. Just click on each individual partition and name it.

11. Resize the partitions: Press on the dividing line between each partition and drag it up or down. You'll see the actual size reflected in the "Size" box. If you plan to do something like make a lot of movies, you probably want one extra-large partition.

These "names" indicate the hard disk and the CD. They actually indicate the disk sizes, not the names of the disks.

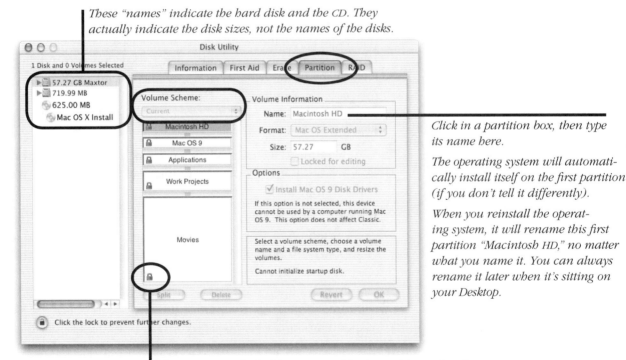

Click in a partition box, then type its name here.

The operating system will automatically install itself on the first partition (if you don't tell it differently).

When you reinstall the operating system, it will rename this first partition "Macintosh HD," no matter what you name it. You can always rename it later when it's sitting on your Desktop.

These icons are locked because in this picture I have already created the partitions (it's impossible to create a picture before I partition the disk because the picture gets destroyed along with all the other data on the disk).

*When **you** do this, the lock will be open. **Do not** click the lock to close it or you won't be able to copy files onto the disk!*

—continued

12. Okay, you've named and resized your partitions. This is your last chance to back out. ***If you really want to destroy every single piece of data on your Mac and start all over again with a perfectly clean slate,*** click "OK."

13. It doesn't take long. In a couple of seconds you can see the names of your new partitions in the panel on the left, as shown below.

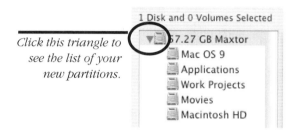

Click this triangle to see the list of your new partitions.

14. Now you're ready to quit the Disk Utility and re-install the operating system and software. There is no operating system on your Mac anymore because you just destroyed it, so you have to start up with a CD again.

> ***If the only install disk you have*** for Mac OS X is the one that's already in the machine, then quit Disk Utility (go to the Disk Utility menu and choose "Quit Disk Utility"). You will be taken back to the Installer window and the disk will go through the process of re-installing Mac OS X and all the software it had originally. You will be alerted when the installer wants you to insert Mac OS X Install Disc 2.
>
> You might need to re-install Mac OS 9 as well, depending on the CD you use. Many people like to install Mac OS 9 on a separate volume from OS X.
>
> ***If you have a number*** of Mac OS X "Software Restore" disks, you'll want to use those. But you have to swap CDs. So do this: Quit the Disk Utility, then quit the Installer. Choose "Restart" (you have no other choice). Instantly after clicking the "Restart" button, press the mouse button down *and hold it down*—this will force the CD tray to open or the CD to pop out of the slot (depending on the Mac you have). Take out the CD that's in the Mac and replace it with the "Software Restore" CD. It will go through the process of restoring all the software as if the Mac just came out of the factory.

15. Whew. When you restart after all is said and done, you'll see a separate hard disk icon for each volume you created. Good job.

If you prefer not to have the partition icons cluttering up your Desktop, since they all appear in your Computer window anyway, see page 131.

This is an example of a newly partitioned Mac. You can see the five different partitions that I named in the Disk Utility. Each one is an individual volume.

1. Can you reformat the hard disk that contains the operating system that is running the Mac?

   _____

2. What happens to all the data on a disk that you reformat?

   _____

3. What should you do very carefully before you divide your hard disk into partitions?

   _____

4. If you create four partitions, how many hard disk icons will appear on your Mac?

   _____

5. If you reformat your hard disk because it's acting a little weird and it still doesn't get better, what else should you check?

   _____

Answers on page 732.

Using the Classic Environment

Mac OS X is a fabulous operating system. But you still might have an app or two that hasn't been revised to run in OS X. So the Mac will open and run the OS 9 operating system in what is called the **Classic environment.** Applications that can't run in Mac OS X will automatically open in Mac OS 9. These applications are considered "Classic applications."

If you have Mac OS X on your machine but you start up your Mac with OS 9 most of the time, you'll need to know more about OS 9 than is in this chapter. If so, please read *The Little Mac Book, seventh edition,* from Peachpit Press.

Contents of this chapter

Opening Classic

The **Classic environment** does not open automatically when you start up in Mac OS X. If you double-click on a Classic application, it will open OS 9 for you, but I found there are fewer problems if I open Classic *first,* and *then* open the Classic application.

To open the Classic environment:

System Preferences icon

Classic icon

1. Open System Preferences: either click on the icon in the Dock, or go to the Apple menu and choose "Preferences...."

2. In System Preferences, click on the Classic icon, or choose "Classic" from the View menu.

3. In the Classic preferences pane, click the "Start" button. It takes a minute or two for Classic to get up and running.

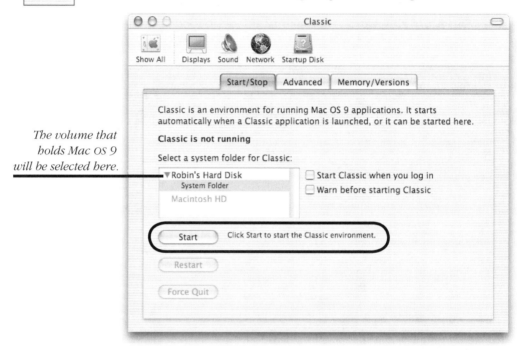

The volume that holds Mac OS 9 will be selected here.

After you start Classic, this preferences pane changes, as shown on page 710.

4. While Classic is starting, you'll see the window shown below, with the status bar telling you how much time is left, relatively.

If you want to see the whole "Desktop" and the extensions that are loading into Mac OS 9, click the disclosure triangle in the bottom-left corner of this small window.

Click here.

5. Click the triangle, as mentioned in Step 4, to display the OS 9 Desktop as it loads.

One thing you cannot do in Classic is get to the Mac OS 9 Desktop—this is the closest you will ever come. See page 706 for information about accessing any files you might have left on the Desktop last time you started up your Mac with OS 9.

First-time trouble?

If the first time you open Classic it says it **can't find a system,** try this:

1. Open System Preferences: either click on the icon in the Dock, or go to the Apple menu and choose "Preferences...."

2. In System Preferences, click the Startup Disk icon.

3. Select the Mac OS 9 System Folder or partition.

4. Click the "Show All" icon in the upper-left of the preferences pane.

5. Open the Classic preferences pane again and choose the OS 9 system as your startup volume.

6. Start Classic.

7. Go back to the Startup Disk (its icon is probably in the toolbar across the top of the pane) and reset your Mac OS X System Folder as the one to start up with.

Classic System Preferences

Once **Classic is up and running,** as explained on the previous two pages, you can make it automatically start up whenever you turn on your Mac, make it quit, restart, force quit, rebuild the Desktop, put it to sleep, and a few other things, as explained below.

Open the System Preferences (click that icon in the Dock), then click on the Classic icon to get the Classic preferences pane, as shown below.

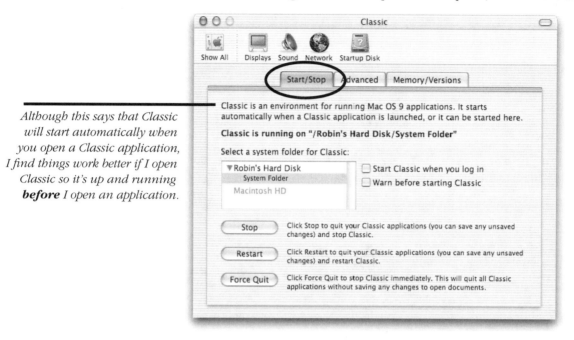

*Although this says that Classic will start automatically when you open a Classic application, I find things work better if I open Classic so it's up and running **before** I open an application.*

Start and Stop Classic

- If you use Classic applications everyday, **have Classic open automatically when you start up:** In the Classic pane above, check "Start Classic when you log in."

- ▼ **Stop Classic from running:** Click the "Stop" button. You will be asked to save any changes to documents, and all Classic applications will quit.

- ▼ **Restart Classic:** Click the "Restart" button. Sometimes this can fix things that are acting weirdly. You will be asked to save any changes to documents, and all Classic applications will quit.

- ▼ **Force quit Classic:** Click the "Force Quit" button in the Classic pane. Use this as a last resort when you can't stop or restart Classic and you're having problems with it (try rebuilding the Desktop first, as explained on the opposite page). All applications will quit instantly, and you'll lose any changes you made to documents that you hadn't already saved. Force-quitting Classic will not affect Mac OS X.

Or you can press Command Option Escape to get the "Force Quit Applications" window. Choose Classic, then click "Force Quit."

In the **Advanced** pane are several **Startup Options.** One of these deals with "extensions," small files that add functionality to the operating system and to individual applications (Mac OS X doesn't use extensions); see the information below and on the following pages regarding extensions.

▾ **Use preferences from home folder** is an option individual users can set so each one will have their own Mac OS 9 preferences while they're in Classic applications. See Chapter 20 about multiple users; after you set up a new user, come to this pane and click this box before that user ever opens Classic.

▾ **Put Classic to sleep** when you're not using it to save on processing power: Drag the slider bar to the number of minutes before Classic will sleep.

▾ **Rebuild Desktop:** If things act a little squirrely, like you double-click a file created with a Classic application and it doesn't open with that application, or if files don't have the correct icon in the Finder, try rebuilding the Desktop. The process does not affect your open applications or documents, and you do not have to restart to rebuild. Click the "Rebuild Desktop" button in the Advanced pane.

If you are an experienced Mac user and are accustomed to dealing with extensions, you'll be overjoyed to know you can turn them all off when starting Classic: choose **Turn Off Extensions** in the Advanced pane. This does not turn them off every time Classic starts up—it only works if you come to this Advanced pane and choose this option, and then click the "Start Classic" or "Restart Classic" button in this pane.

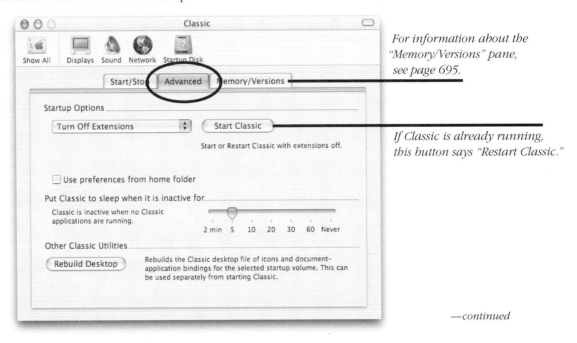

For information about the "Memory/Versions" pane, see page 695.

If Classic is already running, this button says "Restart Classic."

—continued

Or you can choose to **Open Extensions Manager** as Classic starts up so you can turn on or off extensions and control panels that you need or that you think might be causing trouble. Classic only opens certain extensions, so if you've installed a Classic application that needs extensions or control panels that Classic doesn't open, you can use this feature to turn them on. Otherwise that application might not work properly.

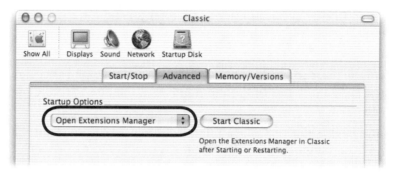

Start up Classic with certain keys held down

Another feature involves holding down certain keys when you start Mac OS 9. If you have a reason to hold down certain keys when you start OS 9, perhaps because a certain application requires it or for a particular trouble-shooting technique, ou can force Classic to act as if these keys are held down when you restart from the Advanced pane (not when you restart Classic in general or automatically on startup).

Click on the Advanced pane in the Classic preferences, and then choose **Use Key Combination.** You can press up to five keyboard characters in a row, one at a time, and they will appear in the edit box. You can't use the Delete key to get rid of these characters because the Mac thinks you want to add the Delete key to the combination; instead, press the "Clear Keys" button to remove the existing key combination and start over.

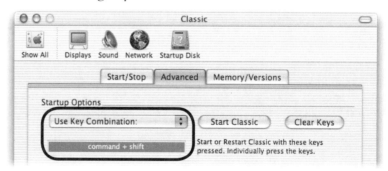

Quit Classic

Unfortunately, there is no visual clue that tells you whether Classic is open or has quit on you. I wish there was at least a little dot in the menu bar that would let me know that Classic is open because sometimes it up and quits altogether and I don't even know until I see that the triangles under my Classic applications in the Dock have suddenly disappeared. A great consolation when Classic crashes is that it doesn't affect Mac OS X—OS X just keeps running happily along.

Classic will quit automatically and safely when you Shut Down, Restart, or Log Out.

You can quit Classic yourself:

1. Open System Preferences: either click on the icon in the Dock, or go to the Apple menu and choose "Preferences…."

2. In System Preferences, click on the Classic icon, or choose "Classic" from the View menu.

3. In the Classic preferences pane, click the "Start/Stop" tab.

4. Click the "Stop" button.

Keyboard shortcut to quit

There is also a **keyboard shortcut** that will quit Classic. Be careful because if you use this shortcut, Classic and every application open in Classic will quit in less than one second and you will not be asked if you want to save any documents; *you won't get any warning, just zap—everything is gone.*

To use the keyboard shortcut, Classic must be active; that is, you need to have a Classic application open in front of you on the screen. Then press Command Option Shift Q.

Trouble at quitting time

If you have **trouble when quitting,** if Classic just won't quit or Mac OS X has trouble shutting down, you might have set up something in Mac OS 9 that is causing a problem. For instance, I've had a sound in my Shut Down Items folder in the System Folder for years in previous operating systems—when I shut down, I hear myself say, "Oooh, baby baby, goodbye." In OS X, this sound would try to play on Shut Down by opening iTunes, so iTunes would start up as I'm shutting down and that just couldn't be done.

So if you have trouble, check your Shut Down Items folder, check your control panels, and check anything else you might have set up in Mac OS 9 to happen on Shut Down.

Allocate Memory to Classic Applications

Mac OS X manages memory very well. In the Classic environment, Mac OS 9 is not so good at it. If a particular Classic application crashes regularly, it might be because it needs more RAM (random access memory) to accomplish what you're trying to do. If you don't have a lot of RAM (like 256 megabytes or less), don't try to open more than one or two applications in Classic. If you have plenty of RAM (or at least plenty for your most-used applications), you can **allocate more memory** to your Classic applications. (It's not possible, nor is it necessary, to allocate more memory to OS X applications.)

If you don't know what RAM is, or if you want to know how much you have in your Mac, see pages 220 or page 258.

To allocate more memory to a Classic application:

1. Make sure the application is not open—it must be quit. If it has an icon in the menu bar, there should be no triangle under it. If there is a triangle, press on the icon in the Dock and choose "Quit."

2. Find the original icon for the application in its folder. Not the folder icon—you must find the *application icon* itself.

    If an icon for this application is in the Dock, press on it and choose "Show in Finder." The application's folder will open and the application icon will be selected.

Check the "Kind" column to make sure you have selected the application icon.

3. Single-click on the application icon to select it.

4. Press Command I to get the Info window (*or* go to the File menu and choose "Get Info," *or* Command-click on the icon and choose "Get Info"). You'll get the Info window, as shown on the opposite page.

5. From the pop-up menu inside the Info window, choose "Memory." Only Classic applications have this option; if you don't see this option in the menu, either you did not select the actual application icon, or the application you selected is not a Classic application.

6. You see two boxes for memory allocation.

If you have enough built-in memory to handle it, raise the **Preferred Size** by at least 50 percent (if you don't have much memory, raise it by 25 percent).

Then raise the **Minimum Size** to match. This ensures the application will never open with less than what it needs.

Of course, you cannot allocate more memory than you have! And about 128 megabytes of your memory is needed to run Mac OS X and Classic. Adding more memory chips to your Mac is the cheapest and most effective way to add working power.

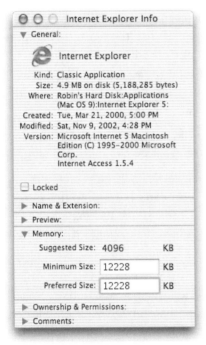

If a Classic app quits unexpectedly, allocating more memory to it will often fix the problem.

In the Classic system preferences, as described on page 691, you can see the memory allocations in the third tab, "Memory/Versions." To see only your applications (and not all the system processes running in the background), uncheck "Show background processes."

Installing and Opening Classic Applications

Here are a few tips and recommendations for **installing and opening Classic applications** in Mac OS X.

▼ The Administrator is the one who will have the fewest restrictions installing software. Make sure to log in as the Administrator (the name and password you used when you first turned on your Mac).

▼ If you partitioned your disk, it's best to install Classic applications (and store your documents) on a separate partition from the Mac OS X disk. This is primarily to avoid having access privilege problems (access privileges are discussed in Chapter 34). Information about partitioning your disk is in Chapter 38.

▼ The next best place for installing Classic applications is in the folder called "Applications (Mac OS 9)."

(If you partitioned your disk and installed Mac OS 9 on another partition, then this folder is on that other partition.)

▼ If you can't install a Classic application while running in Mac OS X, you'll have to restart your Mac in OS 9 (use the Startup Disk preferences in the System Preferences) and install directly into OS 9.

On some Macs, you can hold down the Option key when you restart to get the option to start up with either operating system, *if* the two operating systems are on two different partitions.

▼ If a Classic application installs an old version of QuickTime, make sure you reinstall the newest version. You can find it on the Mac OS 9 CD or download it from the Apple site.

▼ Time and technology move on—you can't hang onto the same software package you've owned for ten years and expect it to work with Classic. I'm afraid you'll have to upgrade if you've got really old stuff that won't work in Classic.

▼ As mentioned on page 692, Classic opens with a certain set of extensions, which might not include any special extensions that your application needs to run properly. Manage your extensions with the features mentioned on pages 691–692. If you don't know what extensions are or have any idea how to manage them, please call your local guru to come help you. Extension conflicts can be tricky and frustrating.

▼ Some applications are what's called "Carbon," which means they can open in both Mac OS 9 and OS X. Sometimes an application is capable of opening in OS X, but some of its features depend on extensions installed in Mac OS 9. In this case, you need to open the application in Classic (Mac OS 9) to get full functionality. **To force an application to open in Classic,** use the Info window.

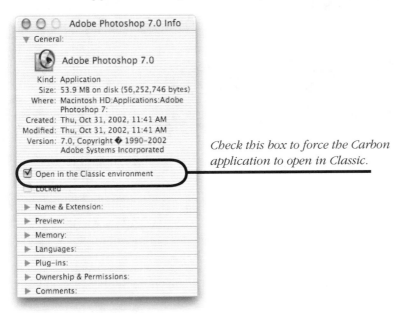

Check this box to force the Carbon application to open in Classic.

Please don't think this great app, Photoshop, needs to open in Classic—this is just an example of the Info window.

But if you have Photoshop plugin filters that only work in Mac OS 9, you can open the application in OS 9 so you have access to them.

Working in Classic If you've never worked in Mac OS 9, you'll find a number of minor things to be different from OS X. Let's start with the differences between the **windows,** since you will be using windows whenever you open a Classic application.

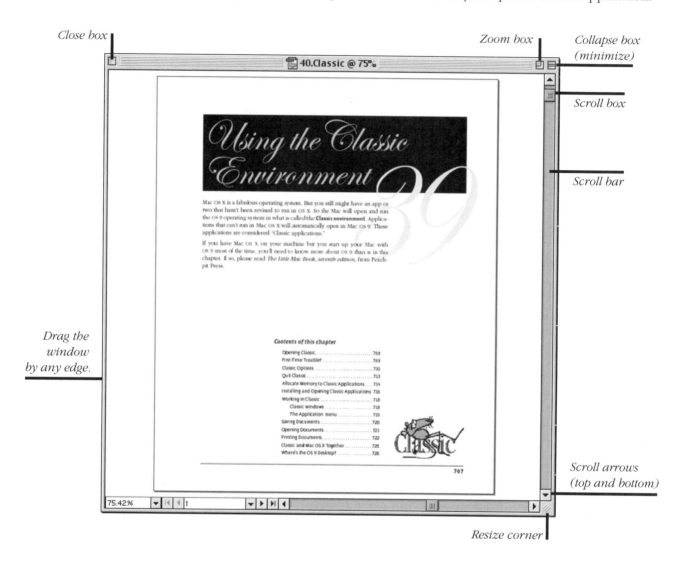

Close box

Zoom box

Collapse box (minimize)

Scroll box

Scroll bar

Drag the window by any edge.

Scroll arrows (top and bottom)

Resize corner

Classic windows **Moving the window:** In Classic, you can drag a window by any edge, as well as by the title bar. This is a feature I miss in OS X.

Red close button: The Classic *close box* to close a window is in the same position as the red close button in Mac OS X, but it's a boring gray box instead. It does the same thing.

Green zoom button: The Classic *zoom box* is in the right corner of the window. It does pretty much the same thing as the zoom button in OS X.

Yellow minimize button: You can't minimize a Classic window to the Dock. You can, however, click in the ***collapse box*** in the right corner (or double-click the title bar) to "roll up the windowshade," or "collapse" it, which leaves just the title bar on the screen.

If double-clicking the title bar does not roll up the window and you want it to, do this:

1. In the Classic environment, go to the Apple menu, down to Control Panels, and choose "Appearance."

2. Click the "Options" tab.

3. Click in the checkbox to "Double-click title bar to collapse windows."

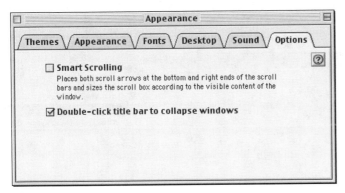

4. Notice in this control panel you can also turn on "Smart Scrolling," which puts both scroll arrows at the bottom of the scroll bar, which you probably have in Mac OS X. If you want this in OS 9, check the box.

5. Click in the close box to put away this control panel.

The Application menu

The **Hide Others** command is not under the Apple menu in OS 9. You'll find it in the **Application menu,** which is over in the far-right corner.

Also in this menu you'll see a list of all **open applications.** You can switch applications from here, which can be handy if you choose to hide your Dock.

The keyboard shortcut to **switch applications** works in Classic and Mac OS X seamlessly. Watch the Dock as you press Command Tab (hold down the Command key and tap the Tab key several times); you see that each time you hit the Tab key, the next *open* application in order is selected. When the icon of the application you want to be active is selected, let go of both the Tab and Command keys and the selected application will come forward.

Press Shift Command Tab to select applications in the reverse order.

In the Classic environment, this is the Application menu, over in the far-right of the menu bar.

Saving documents   The **Save As dialog box** is different in Mac OS 9. Similar, but different. You won't have the column view to navigate in, and you won't have your OS X Favorites (see Chapter 24 about Favorites). You can make Favorites, though, here in the Save As dialog box to make it easier to find your folder to save into; these Favorites won't appear in the OS X Favorites folder or Save As dialog box.

Favorites button. In Save As, you see your Favorite folders. In Open, you'll also see your Favorite documents.

Shortcuts button to access the files on your OS 9 Desktop, all volumes, servers, and even your iDisk.

Recents button shows the folders and volumes you have used recently.

*The **contents** listed in the window are the contents of the folder whose name appears here.*

Click on this menu to open it and choose another folder.

If you're accustomed to the column view, this menu is like going to the left in the columns.

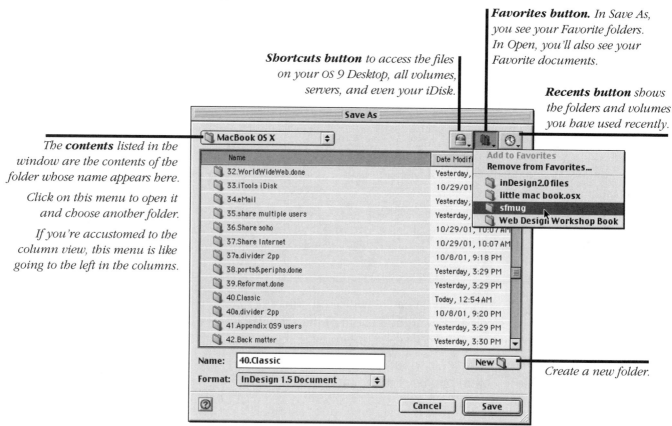

Create a new folder.

*Click on a **column heading** to organize the files by that heading.*

*Click on the **Sort Order triangle** (at the top of the scroll bar, as shown on the opposite page) to organize in the opposite direction.*

To add or remove a Favorite, select a folder, then use the Favorites button, as shown above.

The **Open dialog box** is just like the Save As dialog box shown on the opposite page, with the extra feature of showing a preview of many types of documents.

Opening documents

Favorites button. In Open, you'll see your Favorite documents as well as folders.

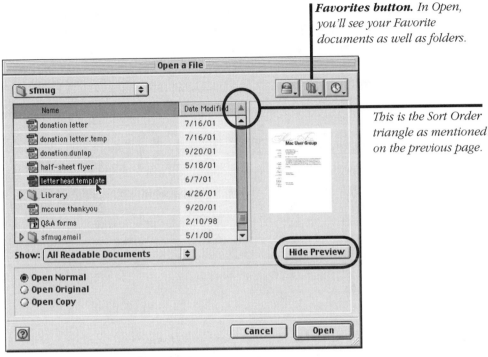

This is the Sort Order triangle as mentioned on the previous page.

*Click once on a file to see a **preview** of it, if one is available for that file type. If you don't see the preview area, click on the "Show Preview" button that will be where "Hide Preview" is in the example above.*

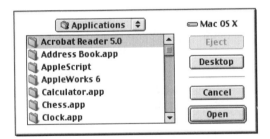

Some Classic applications will display this Open or Save As dialog box. It works the same as the other examples on these pages, but with fewer features for finding your folders and volumes.

Click on the menu at the top of the list to see the hierarchy of folders that the current folder is stored within.

Click the Desktop button to get to the Mac OS X Desktop, where you can open your hard disk and the other folders on it.

Printing documents

When you **print** in the Classic environment, you won't get the Print Center application. Instead, Mac OS 9 will use the Print Monitor, which you'll probably never actually see. The dialog box for printing will look different, but it's basically the same sort of thing: choose the pages you want to print, the quality, etc. Many applications will provide their own print dialog boxes that won't look anything like the one shown below, but they all have the same purpose and the same general features.

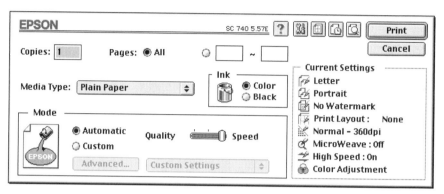

This is a typical sort of print dialog box for a small color printer.
For details, see the manual for your printer.

Before you print

Before you print for the first time in Classic, you will need to go to the Chooser, as explained on the following pages. If you have a color inkjet printer, you will probably need to install the software that came with it, if you haven't already, and you might need to restart in Mac OS 9 to install that software. If you have a PostScript printer, the LaserWriter 8 driver that is installed will work just fine.

Is your printer PostScript? Here's a good way to tell:

▼ If it prints black and white and cost around $1,000, it's probably PostScript.

▼ If it prints color and cost around $4,000, it's probably PostScript.

▼ If it prints color and cost from $50 to $800, it's definitely *not* PostScript.

Read more about PostScript and non-PostScript printers in Chapter 15.

To set up printing in Classic if you have a PostScript printer:

*Set up your
PostScript printer*

1. Turn on the printer and let it warm up.

2. Open a Classic application.

3. From the Apple menu, select "Chooser." You'll get the window shown below.

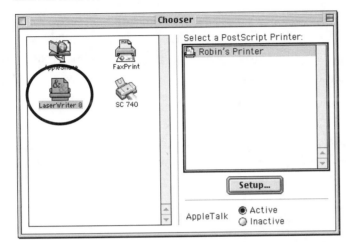

4. On the left side of the window, click once on the icon named "LaserWriter 8."

5. On the right side of the window, the name of your PostScript printer should appear. If it doesn't, these are the likely causes:

   ▾ The printer is not a PostScript printer.

   ▾ The printer is not turned on or is not quite warmed up enough.

   ▾ The cable attached to the printer is not plugged in snugly enough on both ends (you really shouldn't reattach it while the computer is on).

   ▾ The cable attached to the printer is a bad cable; try another one.

   ▾ If you're on a small network (a "peer-to-peer" network like you would most likely have at home or in a small office), the computer between you and the PostScript printer is turned off.

   ▾ If you've tried everything and the printer name still won't appear, rebuild the Desktop in Classic (see page 691) and start over.

6. When you get the name of your printer to appear on the right side, click once on it.

7. If the printer name does not have a little icon directly to the left of its name, like the one shown in the example, click the "Setup…" button. After the Mac runs the setup, the tiny icon will appear.

8. You're all set. Close the Chooser (click in its close box) and print your document.

Set up your non-PostScript printer

To set up printing in Classic if you have a non-PostScript printer:

1. If you *haven't* already installed your software, restart your computer in Mac OS 9 (see page 696 if you're not sure how to do that).

   If you *have* already installed your printer software, skip to step 4.

2. Use the CD that came with your printer and follow the instructions to install it.

3. Restart your Mac in OS X.

4. Turn on your printer and let it warm up (wait 'til all the noises stop).

5. Open a Classic application.

6. From the Apple menu, select "Chooser." You'll get the dialog box shown below.

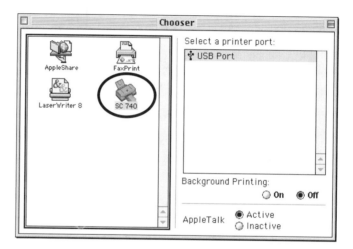

7. On the left side, click once on the type of printer you have. Above, I've selected an Epson 740. (I wish they'd name these printer drivers with names that match the printer, or at least the brand.) If you didn't install the software, you probably won't see the printer driver at all. Install the software as described in Steps 1 and 2.

8. On the right side, the name of your printer should appear. If it doesn't, these are the likely causes:

   ▼ The printer is not turned on or is not quite warmed up enough.

   ▼ The printer driver you selected on the left side is not the correct one; try another one.

   ▼ The cable attached to the printer is not plugged in snugly enough on both ends.

   ▼ If you've tried everything and the printer name still won't appear, rebuild the Desktop in Classic (see page 691) and start over.

   ▼ The cable attached to the printer is a bad cable; try another one.

When you open a **Classic** application, the Dock will keep you linked to **Mac OS X,** as you can see in the example below. Even if you choose to hide the Dock, when you move your mouse into that area the Dock will appear, even while you work in the Classic environment. It's great. You can jump back and forth all day long with the click of a button.

Classic and Mac OS X Together

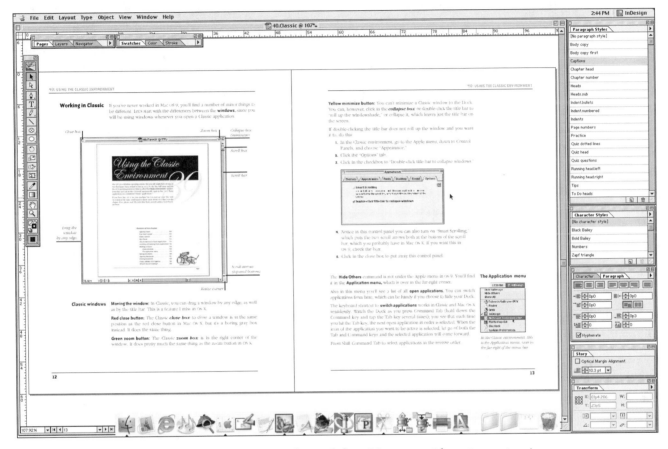

Here on my monitor you can see the Dock from Mac OS X, with my pages open in InDesign 1.5 in the Classic environment (although now I use version 2.0 in OS X). I hold down the Option key and click on the Finder icon in the Dock, and instantly I'm back in OS X and InDesign is hidden (it's hidden because I hold down the Option key when I clicked on the Finder icon).

Where's the OS 9 Desktop?

Maybe you used Mac OS 9 for a while and added Mac OS X to your Mac, or perhaps you switch back and forth between the operating systems. If so, you might feel nervous at first because you cannot get back to the **OS 9 Desktop** while running OS X. You can't get to the Desktop itself, but Mac OS X made a folder for you that contains all of the items you left on the other Desktop.

In fact, if you have more than one partition, OS X made a "Desktop Folder" for each partition. Just open the partition, and on the top level you'll see the folder.

Desktop (Mac OS 9)

If your hard disk is not separated into individual partitions, then Mac OS X made a folder for you on the OS X Desktop called "Desktop (Mac OS 9)." This folder is actually an alias, but it will open a window that will show you everything you had left on the Desktop.

You can also **open items** that you had left on the Desktop in any Classic Open dialog box, as shown on page 701. You can **save into** any folder you had on the Desktop through the Classic Save As dialog box, as shown on page 700. In both dialog boxes, use the Shortcuts button to choose the partition, then in the list you'll see the "Desktop Folder."

Where Did it Go?

For Experienced Mac OS 9 Users

If you have grown fondly familiar with previous Macintosh operating systems, it will be confusing at first to use Mac OS X because all your favorite tools and tricks have changed. Here is an overview of where you can find your old favorite features in brand new dress.

Contents in this chapter

Desktop and Finder Features

The **Desktop** and the **Finder** in Mac OS 9 look like the same thing. Actually, the Finder is the software that runs the Desktop, but when we would say, "Go to the Finder" or "Go to the Desktop," we meant the same place.

In Mac OS X, the Desktop and the Finder are more clearly separated. The Desktop is the background, and you can still place things on it and save to it. The Finder is a defined application with its own special windows. The menu across the top of the Desktop is the Finder menu, and all windows that display documents and application files are "Finder windows." Apple calls the Finder "the gateway to your computer and network."

Keep an eye on the menu bar and you will eventually become accustomed to recognizing when you are in the Finder and when you are working with some other feature of the system. See Chapter 9 for details.

This is the Application menu. At the moment, the Finder is the active application.

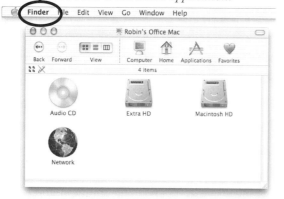

The name of this menu changes depending on which application is active.

*Although this might look like a Finder window, it's not. If the menu bar does not say "Finder" on the left side, then the window is an active application. Generally, you must **quit**, not just **close** the window, to put the application away.*

The Dock

You can't miss the Dock across the bottom of the screen. The Dock takes the place of Mac OS 9's application switcher, Apple menu, and Control Strip. Applications are to the left of the dividing line; all other files are stored on the right. The Trash basket cannot be moved, nor can you make an alias of it. You can move the Dock to either side: hold down the Control key, click on the dividing line, and choose a position from the menu. For a brief overview of the Dock, see Chapter 1; for all the details, see Chapter 8.

There are three different **window views** available for every Finder window. It can be confusing at first because although they look similar to what you are accustomed to, they act a little weird. You'll get used to it. For all the details and tips for working with these windows and views, see Chapter 6.

Window Views

Depending on which view you are in, you can click the **Back** and **Forward buttons** to go back or forward to previously viewed windows, just like web pages.

The **View button** gives you the same choices as the View menu: as Icon, List, or Column.

This is the **Icon View.** Double-click a folder to open that folder's contents in this same window (the contents of the new folder **replace** the current contents).

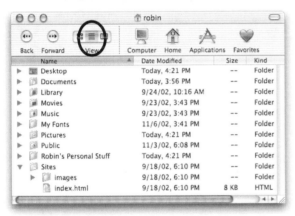

This is the **List View,** which acts very much like what you're used to.

This is the **Column View,** a brand new concept for the Mac. As you click each folder, its contents appear in a new column to the right. You can see that this window shows you (in the third column) what is in the Documents folder (selected in the second column) that belongs to the user named "robin" (selected in the first column).

Finder Windows   Windows for folders and disks are called **Finder windows.** See Chapter 6 for details about navigating through them without getting confused, and how to color the backgrounds of windows or add photographs as backgrounds, change the icon sizes, set global preferences and individual preferences, and even more (from the View menu, choose "Show View Options").

▼ Use the little colorful buttons in the top-left of the active window.

Red: Close the window. If it is an *application* window, this does not *quit* the application.

Yellow: Minimize the window, which sends an icon of the window to the Dock. Single-click that icon in the Dock to open the window again. Shift-click for slow motion (try it).

Green: Enlarge or reduce the size of the window.

Tip: When you open a window, you'll probably change the view and adjust the size, etc., to suit your purpose at the moment. If you click the **red** button and **close** the window, it **removes** all the customizing you did and when you reopen the window, you'll have to reset everything in the way you want it.

But if you click the **yellow** button and **minimize** the window, it **retains** all of your customizing, and when you reopen the window (click on its icon in the Dock), it will reappear exactly as you left it. Until another folder replaces the contents of the window.

▼ **Customize the Toolbar:** From the View menu, choose "Customize Toolbar…." Drag items from the panel into the Toolbar; drag them off the edge and drop them onto the Desktop to remove them. See Chapter 6.

▼ **If the Toolbar is showing** when you double-click a disk or folder icon, the contents of that folder **replace** the contents that were previously in that window space. That is, you don't get a brand-new window each time you open a folder. This can be nice as it reduces the clutter of lots of windows overlapping each other. Click the Back button to go back to the previously open window.

But sometimes you *want* a new, **separate** window. If so, either **hide the Toolbar** (click the Hide/Show Toolbar button in the upper-right of the window) *or* hold down the **Command key** when you double-click to open the folder or disk. You will get a new window in Icon view *and* the previous window will still be visible on your Desktop.

If you hold down the Option key instead of the Command key, you will get a new window *and* the previous window will disappear.

▼ **Same ol' tricks:** Hold down the Command key and click on the title of the window to see the hierarchy of the active window, as shown to the right.

Hold down the Command key to move an **un**active window without making it active.

Option–double-click a folder to open the window and make the previous window disappear.

Press Command Option W to close all open windows.

There has been a serious change in the way we **select multiple files** in some window views. Try these actions:

In a window that is in a **List** or **Column View,** click on an icon at the top of the list. Hold down the Shift key and click on an icon in the middle of the list. *Every file between the two clicks is selected.*

To select individual files that are not next to each other, hold down the Command key.

In a window that is in an **Icon View,** use the Command key *or* the Shift key to select more than one file.

A **file name** can have 256 characters, which is rarely useful. In Mac OS X, file name extensions are often very important! For instance, if you take the .rtf off of the name of a document you created in TextEdit, then TextEdit can't open it. If you name a folder with an extension of .dock, it's no longer a folder. See page 227 for details.

One window or several?

*Click this button to **hide or show the Toolbar.***

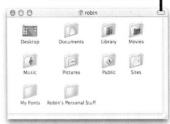

Selecting Files

Command-click the title.

Naming Files

Apple Menu

The **Apple menu** is not at all what it used to be. Below is a list of where you can find the comparable features in Mac OS X that you used to find in the Apple menu (some of the following items were eliminated from the Apple menu in Mac OS 9 as well).

To open the Applications folder directly, click once on this icon, found in the Finder window Toolbar.

Or use the Go menu, or press Command Option A.

About This Computer: This item is still the first item in the Apple menu, but it's called "About This Mac."

Apple System Profiler: It's still called "Apple System Profiler." Open the Applications folder, then open the Utilities folder. Or go to "About This Mac" and click the "More Info…" button.

AppleCD Audio Player: When you insert a music CD, iTunes automatically opens so you can play the CD. You can control this through the CDs and DVDs system preferences; see page 340.

Automated Tasks: Gone. But you can write and use scripts. See page 427 for a little bit of information, and check www.apple.com/applescript/macosx/script_menu for lots of information.

Calculator: This is now in the Applications folder, and it has been vastly improved. In fact, it's really great.

Chooser: Gone. When you are in an application and choose to print, you will automatically get the Print Center where you can set up and choose any printer on the network. To open the Print Center directly, go to the Applications folder, open the Utilities folder, and you'll find it in there. See Chapter 15.

Control Panels: Gone. Use System Preferences; see the following page.

Favorites: These are all stored in the Favorites window; click on the red heart in any Finder window. You can also access a submenu of Favorites from the Go menu, and you'll also find them in the Open and Save As dialog boxes. See Chapter 24.

Graphing Calculator: Gone.

Internet Access: The Control Panel is gone, but the Internet preferences pane is very similar. See the list of Internet features on page 719. See Chapters 30 and 31 for all the details.

Jigsaw Puzzle: Gone.

Key Caps: Open the Applications folder, then open the Utilities folder. It's still too small to be very useful, and it cannot display all of the available OpenType characters.

Network Browser: At the Desktop, click the Go menu, then choose "Connect to Server…." Or use Rendezvous, as explained in Chapter 35.

Note Pad: Gone. You can still use Stickies, though, and Stickies has more features than ever before.

Recent Applications, Recent Documents, Recent Servers: There are two different places to find your recently opened files.

- ▼ To open recent applications, utilities, and documents, use the Apple menu; choose "Recent Items."
- ▼ To open recent folders, favorites, and servers, use the Go menu. Servers will be listed under "Recent Folders."

You will also find Recent items in the Save As and Open dialog boxes. Use the General preferences to determine how many items appear in the Recent menu (open System Preferences, then click on General).

Scrapbook: Gone.

Sherlock: Sherlock no longer searches your hard disk, but only the Internet (press Command F at the Finder to search your hard disk). Click Sherlock's icon in the Dock. See Chapter 31 for details.

Stickies: Stickies are in the Applications folder, and they now have more features. You can add graphics, check spelling, search all notes, print all notes at once, and more. See pages 444–445.

Other:

- ▼ To store your most-used applications and other items for easy accessibility, use the Dock; see Chapter 8. (To add items to the Dock, just drag and drop the icons onto the Dock; drag them out of the Dock to remove them. This is okay because the Mac automatically creates aliases in the Dock for you.)
- ▼ For all the details about the new Apple Menu, see Chapter 9.

Control Panels

This is the System Preferences icon you'll find in the Dock.

Control panels are now called **System Preferences.** To access them, first open the System Preferences window, located in the Dock: click once on the icon in the Dock. Then click once on the various icons to get their individual preferences panes. See Chapter 22 for details. Below is a list of the most standard control panels in Mac OS 9 and where you can find comparable features.

AirPort: If you have an AirPort card installed, you'll see the AirPort icon in the menu bar, as circled below. If not, open the Applications folder, then open the Utilities folder, where you'll find the "AirPort Setup Assistant" and the "AirPort Admin Utility." See pages 452–453.

Appearance: There are no sound effects, and you can't choose a font for the system. You can't set up a theme for your Desktop, but individual users can customize their own Desktops (see the information about multiple users in Chapter 20).

    Desktop picture: In the System Preferences pane, click on "Desktop." See pages 127–128.

    Highlight colors: Use the General preferences pane. See page 136.

    Size of icons on the Desktop: Click on the Desktop. From the View menu, choose "Show View Options," then drag the "Icon Size" slider bar. See page 129 for details.

Apple Menu Options: Gone. To change the number of Recent Items, use the General preferences.

AppleTalk: Open the Network preferences pane. In the "Show" menu (the menu above the row of tabs, not the one in the menu bar), choose "Built-In Ethernet." Then click the "AppleTalk" tab.

Battery: If you have a laptop and you don't see the battery icon in the menu bar, go to the Energy Saver preferences, click the "Options" tab, and check the box to show the icon in the menu bar.

ColorSync: Use the ColorSync preferences pane. Also check out the ColorSync Utility, DigitalColor Meter, and Display Calibrator in the Utilities folder (which is in the Applications folder). See pages 461–462.

Control Strip: Use the Dock. See Chapter 8.

Date & Time: Use the Date & Time preferences pane. You can also use the Clock application in the Applications folder to make either an analog (with hands) or digital (with numbers) clock appear in the Dock or float around on your screen.

Energy Saver: Use the Energy Saver preferences pane. There is no automatic startup feature. Dang. But you can have your Mac automatically restart after a power failure.

Extensions Manager: There is no Extensions Manager for Mac OS X because there are no extensions. But you can access the Extensions Manager in Classic after starting or restarting OS 9: Open the Classic preferences pane. Click the "Advanced" tab. From the menu in the "Startup Options" section, choose "Open Extensions Manager." See Chapter 39.

File Exchange: Use the Get Info window (Command I) to choose an application for the selected document, or to choose an application for all documents of a particular file type, as shown to the right. See pages 142 and 428.

File Sharing: Use the Sharing preferences pane. You can set certain sharing privileges in the Get Info window: Select a file or group of files, then press Command I. Click the "Ownership & Permissions" triangle. See Chapters 34–36.

File Synchronization: Gone. If you have a .Mac account, you can download and use the application iSync.

General Controls: The General preferences pane is different from the General Controls control panel you are used to. Here you can change the overall color and highlight color, make several changes to the function of the scroll bars, choose the number of Recent items, and adjust the point size of font smoothing. See page 136.

Internet: For the "Web" and "Email" settings that used to be in this control panel, use the Internet preferences pane. See Chapter 30. For newsgroups, use Google.com on the web; see page 490.

Keychain Access: Use the Keychain Access utility: Open the Applications folder, then open the Utilities folder. See pages 466–473.

Launcher: Use the Dock. You can add applications, utilities, documents, photographs, folders, etc., to the Dock. See Chapter 8.

Location Manager: To *make* a new location, open the Network preferences pane and use the "Location" menu to choose "New Location…." To *use* any location, go to the Apple menu and use the "Location" submenu. See Chapter 31.

Memory: Gone. Mac OS X takes care of managing the memory for you and it does a much better job than OS 9. It is still possible to allocate memory for Classic applications, however, in the Get Info window (Command I), per usual. And you can see the memory allocations for Classic applications and processes in the Classic system preferences under the "Memory/Versions" tab; see Chapter 39.

Modem: Open the Network preferences pane. Make sure the "Show" menu (the menu above the row of tabs, not in the menu bar) has "Internal Modem" selected. Click the "Modem" tab and set your preferences. Also check the "PPP" tab and its "Options…" pane.

This is the Classic preferences icon.

The features of File Exchange are built into the Get Info window.

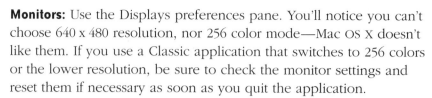

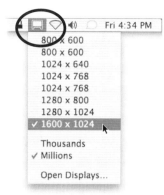

Internet Connect

*Use Internet Connect
in place of Remote Access.*

Monitors: Use the Displays preferences pane. You'll notice you can't choose 640 x 480 resolution, nor 256 color mode—Mac OS X doesn't like them. If you use a Classic application that switches to 256 colors or the lower resolution, be sure to check the monitor settings and reset them if necessary as soon as you quit the application.

You can put a Displays icon in the menu bar, as shown to the left, so you can change your monitor resolution easily. Open System Preferences, then single-click the Displays icon. Check the box, "Show displays in menu bar."

Mouse: Use the Mouse preferences pane.

Multiple Users: Use the Accounts preference pane to set up new users, and use the Login Items preferences pane to customize what each user can do. To severely limit a user's access, go to Accounts, make or select a user, then click the "Capabilities..." button. See Chapter 20.

Numbers: Use the International preferences pane.

QuickTime Settings: Use the QuickTime preferences pane.

Remote Access: To *set up* your dial-up connection, use the Network preferences pane. To *log on,* open the Applications folder and double-click "Internet Connect." Click the "Connect" button. See Chapter 31.

Remember when you are done to click the "Disconnect" button. If you happen to *close* the window and later want to connect again, first click the Internet Connect icon in the Dock to make it active, then go to the File menu and choose "New Connection" to get the window back.

If you use Internet Connect often, drag its icon right into the Dock.

Software Update: Use the Software Update preferences pane. Also see pages 138 and 306 about the command in the Apple menu to "Get Mac OS X Software...."

Sound: Use the Sound preferences pane. You cannot add your own alert sounds anymore. Dang.

Speech: Use the Speech preferences pane.

Startup Disk: Use the Startup Disk preferences pane. Also see Chapter 19 for keyboard shortcuts for restarting.

TCP/IP: Use the Network preferences pane.

Text: Use the International preferences pane.

Trackpad: Use the Mouse preferences pane.

Web Sharing: Use the Sharing preferences pane.

All of the **Internet functionality** you have grown accustomed to is still here, just in different places.

Internet Features

OmniWeb

This is the OmniWeb browser icon.

AirPort: If you have an AirPort card installed, you'll see the AirPort icon in the menu bar. If not, open the Applications folder, then open the Utilities folder. You'll find the "AirPort Setup Assistant" and the "AirPort Admin Utility." See pages 452–453.

Browsers: Microsoft Internet Explorer is the only browser included with Mac OS X, but you can of course install your own copy of Netscape or the America Online service. Try the OmniWeb browser—download it from **www.OmniGroup.com**.

Connect automatically: If you use a dial-up connection and want to make your Mac connect to the Internet automatically when you open an email program, a browser, Sherlock, etc., do this:

1. Open the Network preferences pane.
2. In the "Show" menu, choose "Internal Modem."
3. Click the PPP tab.
4. Click "PPP Options...."
5. Check the box to "Connect automatically when starting TCP/IP applications." Then click OK.

Internet: Use the Internet preferences pane to set web, email, and your iDisk settings, similar to the Internet control panel in OS 9.

Modem: Open the Network preferences pane. Make sure the "Show" menu (the menu above the row of tabs, not in the menu bar) has "Internal Modem" selected. Then click the "Modem" tab.

TCP/IP: Use the Network preferences pane.

Remote Access: To *set up* your dial-up connection, use the Network preferences pane. To *log on,* open the Applications folder and double-click "Internet Connect." Click the "Connect" button. See the notes about Internet Connect (under "Remote Access") on the opposite page. See Chapter 31 for details.

Web Sharing: Use the Sharing preferences pane. See Chapter 36.

▼ **Mac.com:** Check out the introduction on pages xxi–xxii for an overview of iTools, iDisk, and a special email account for you at Mac.com. See Chapter 32 for details on how to use the Mail program, and Chapter 36 about sharing files across the Internet. Use Image Capture to offload your digitial photos directly into your Pictures folder and create a slide show; see pages 433–437. And there are so many new applications free from Apple that I had to put them in another book, *The Little Mac iApps Book.*

Miscellaneous Features

This is a list of common features or actions you were familiar with in Mac OS 9 or previous versions and where they have gone to in OS X.

Application menu: The Application menu as we knew it in previous operating systems is gone, but the Dock takes its place. See Chapter 8.

▼ Use the Dock to switch between applications (fondly called "apps")—just click once on the icon for any open app.

▼ **Or** press Command Tab to switch between open apps; when you let go of both keys, the selected application (as shown in the Dock) will come forward. This even works when you are using an application in the Classic environment. Press Shift Command Tab to return to the previous application.

Hide or Show other applications: Just to the *right* of the Apple menu is the name of the currently active application. In that menu you'll find the commands to "Hide Others" and "Show All."

Empty Trash: Press and hold the mouse button on the Trash basket and you'll get a little pop-up menu to "Empty Trash." If you empty the trash this way, you won't get the warning message. If you use the "Empty Trash" command in the Finder menu or press Command Shift Delete to empty the trash, you *will* get a warning message. **To turn off the warning,** go to the Finder menu and choose "Preferences...."

Shut Down: From the Apple Menu, choose "Shut Down." On some keyboards, you can press Control Eject (the Eject key is the one in the top-right on newer keyboards; it has a triangle over a bar).

Restart: From the Apple Menu, choose "Restart."

Sleep: From the Apple Menu, choose "Sleep." To set the sleep conditions, use the Energy Saver preferences pane.

Force quit in OS X: There are several ways to force quit, and they won't even make your entire computer crash.

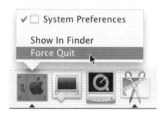

▼ Press Command Option Escape. From the little menu that appears, choose the application name and click "Force Quit."

▼ **Or** hold down the Option key, click the app icon in the Dock, then choose "Force Quit" from the pop-up menu that appears.

▼ **Or** if possible, go to the Apple Menu and choose "Force Quit...." From the little menu that appears, choose the app and click "Force Quit."

Force quit Classic: Use the technique above. Or open the System Preferences window, click the "Classic" icon, then the "Force Quit" button.

Rebuild the Desktop: You cannot rebuild the Desktop in OS X, but you can rebuild the OS 9 Desktop: In the Classic preferences pane, click the "Advanced" tab, then click the "Rebuild Desktop" button. The Mac will rebuild the Desktop immediately—you don't have to restart.

Aliases: Aliases work pretty much the same. Use the same keyboard shortcuts you are familiar with (except to make an alias in the same window is Command L, not Command M). You can still Command-Option-drag to create an alias in a new folder or on the Desktop, and find an original with Command R. See Chapter 23.

Favorites: These are all stored in the Favorites window; click on the red heart in any Finder window Toolbar to open the Favorites window, or press Command Option F. You can also access a submenu of Favorites from the Go menu, and you'll find them in the Save As and Open dialog boxes. See Chapter 23.

Startup Disk: There is a Startup Disk preferences pane where you can choose to start up your Mac with OS 9 or OS X. On some machines (G4s, iBooks, slot-loading iMacs, and PowerBooks with FireWire) you can hold down the Option key when you turn on the Mac and you'll get a choice of which operating system to boot with *if* you installed OS X and OS 9 on two separate partitions.

Startup Items: There is a "StartupItems" folder, but don't touch it. Use the Login Items preferences pane to choose which applications or documents will open on login. See Chapter 20.

Control Strip: Use the Dock. To access your most-used preference panes more easily, drag their icons to the Toolbar in the System Preferences window (you can't drag them to a Finder window, the Dock, or to the Desktop. Dang.)

Print the window: Take a screen shot with the tricks explained on page 476 or use the Grab utility, then print the screen shot.

Get Info windows: Select the icon, then from the File menu, choose "Get Info," *or* use the Command I shortcut. Depending on the file you select, there are more options now in the Info window—you can even see a preview of a graphic file or watch a movie! You can specify which applications open which sorts of documents, change the sharing privileges, and more. See pages 477–479.

Memory allocation and virtual memory: Mac OS X uses completely different memory management than previous operating systems. There is no Memory control panel; you cannot allocate memory to individual OS X applications; you cannot turn off virtual memory; you cannot set up a RAM disk. You can, however, still change the memory allocation of Classic (OS 9) applications as usual, using Show Info.

Spring-loaded folders: Press the Spacebar to spring open a folder. Customize the specs: from the Finder menu, choose "Preferences...."

Tabbed windows: Gone. But you can put folders in the Dock.

Labels: Gone.

mom.jpg

The name of an alias is no longer in italic. You see a tiny (very tiny) arrow in the bottom-left corner.

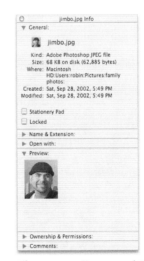

If you press Command Option I, the Get Info window is the Show Inspector window and will change its content depending on what you click on. Try it.

Utilities and Small Applications

A number of your favorite **utilities and small applications** have changed their name or location.

Calculator: The new and improved Calculator is in the Utilities folder, which is in the Applications folder. See page 428.

Disk Utility

Disk First Aid: Use the Disk Utility: Open the Applications folder, then open the Utilities folder, where you'll find the icon shown to the left. See page 455.

Drive Setup: Use the Disk Utility, as described above. See Chapter 38.

Erase Disk: Use the Disk Utility as described above.

Extensions Manager: There is no Extensions Manager for OS X. To access the Extensions Manager in Classic after starting or restarting OS 9, open the Classic preferences pane. Click the "Advanced" tab. From the menu in the "Startup Options" section, choose "Open Extensions Manager." See Chapter 40.

Key Caps: Open the Applications folder, then open the Utilities folder. You'll find it in the Utilities folder.

Scrapbook: The Scrapbook is gone. Stickies can now contain images, sounds, etc., and even has a spell checker.

Screen Saver: Use the Screen Effects preferences pane. Apple has provided a number of photographs and images for you to use, or you can use your own. See pages 330–336.

Screen shots: As usual, Command Shift 3 takes a screen shot of the entire screen. Command Shift 4 gives you a crosshair with which you can select a portion of the screen. See page 476 for other tricks.

Sherlock: Still there, but it now searches only the web. Click once on the Sherlock hat in the Dock, or double-click the Sherlock application in the Applications folder.

To search your hard disk, press Command F at the Finder.

SimpleText: SimpleText is gone; use TextEdit, found in the Applications folder. TextEdit has a spelling checker and many other more advanced features. Also, it is capable of using "Unicode," which lets you type with over 65,000 characters in a font instead of the 256 we have been limited to all these years. See pages 446–449.

Fonts

Name: Comic Sans MS
Kind: FFIL
Size: 124 KB
Created: 9/20/.02
Modified: 10/3/02
Version: 2.10

Not only can you use your existing TrueType and PostScript **fonts** in Mac OS X, you can also use some Microsoft Windows fonts, which means using cross-platform files can be less of a problem. You do not need Adobe Type Manager to display PostScript fonts clearly on the screen nor to rasterize fonts sent to your PostScript printer.

You cannot touch the fonts that are stored in the System Folder, but you can customize the fonts in the various Fonts folders which are located in the various Library folders. In the multi-user environment of Mac OS X, there is a *root* Fonts folder, plus individual users of that Macintosh have their own *user* Fonts folders. Applications can also open their own fonts. This means different users can have different font collections. See Chapter 26 for more information.

Apple also created a new font format called "data fork suitcase format"; fonts of this sort have a suffix of .dfont (and a file type of dfon). But most people don't need to worry about that.

If you know what QuickDraw is, Apple has replaced it with what is called Quartz.

▼ **To install new fonts:** Drag font files into the *appropriate* Fonts folder.

That is, to install the fonts so **only you** have access to them, click the Home button in a Finder window to see *your* user folder. Open *your* user folder icon, then open *your* Library folder icon, then you'll see *your* Fonts folder. Drag the fonts into this folder so *you* have access to them.

If you have administrative access to this computer and you want **every user** to have access to the new fonts, drag them into the *root* Fonts folder, as shown below: click the Computer icon in the Finder window Toolbar, then open the hard disk that has Mac OS X on it, then open the Library folder icon, then you'll see the Fonts folder that is accessible to all users. Drag the fonts into this folder so every user has access to them.

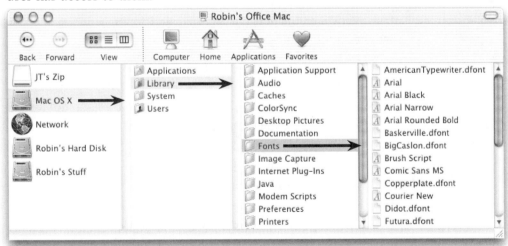

*Here you can see the path to the Fonts folder that stores fonts for all users (follow the selected items from left to right): Mac OS X hard disk, to the Library folder, to the Fonts folder. Because the Fonts folder is selected, you see the list of files in that folder. Drag files into the **selected Fonts folder icon,** or click once on an empty space in the last column and then drag items into the last column.*

Networking and File Sharing

Mac OS X is very involved with networking and file sharing. Below is a list of where you will find your old features. Also see Chapters 34–36.

Network Browser: Instead, at the Desktop, click on the Go menu. Then click "Connect to Server." Or use Rendezvous; see Chapter 35.

Chooser: Instead, to share from servers, see the tip above. Or set up any printer to share; see page 350.

File Sharing: Instead, use the Sharing preferences pane.

Web Sharing: Instead, use the Sharing preferences pane.

Disconnect from server: Select the server icon on the Desktop or in the Computer window, then from the File menu, choose "Eject," *or* drag the server icon to the Trash.

Printing

You don't need to go to the **Chooser** to select or change a printer. When you choose to print from any application, the **Print Center** will automatically appear and you can select any printer that is connected and turned on. If you need to go to the Print Center directly, you'll find it in the Utilities folder, which is in the Applications folder. See Chapter 15 about printing.

Desktop printers: Gone.

Print Window, Print Desktop: Gone. Make screen shots as explained on page 721 and print them.

Using Classic (Mac OS 9)

While running your Mac under OS X, you may need to open older applications in the "Classic" environment, Mac OS 9. You can just open any OS 9 application and the Mac will automatically open Classic, but you will have fewer problems if you open Classic first, then open your OS 9 application. See Chapter 39 for details.

Open Classic: Open the System Preferences window and click on the Classic icon. In the "Start/Stop" tab, click the button "Start."

Automatically open Classic on startup: Open the Classic preference, as explained above. Click the checkbox, "Start Classic when you login."

Force quit a Classic application: From the Apple menu, choose "Force Quit…." You'll get a dialog box with all of the open applications listed. Click once on the app you want to force quit, then click the "Force Quit" button.

Force quit Classic while in OS X: Open the System Preferences and click on the Classic icon. Click the button "Force Quit." Or use the technique above to force quit.

Restart Classic: Open the System Preferences and click the Classic icon. Click "Restart." You will be asked to save any unsaved documents.

There are a number of things you can do that will make the **transition** to working in Mac OS X a little easier.

Have Classic open on startup. If you have old applications that cannot run in OS X, have Classic open on startup so when you double-click an application, Classic is ready and waiting.

Fix your windows. It might make you crazy that every time you open a folder window, the previous folder's contents disappear, plus the view of the window is generally a surprise. You can do several things to make your windows behave as you are accustomed to (although you might want to just get used to the OS X method!)

To always open folders into their own, separate window:

Either click once in the Hide/Show Toolbar button in the upper-right of any Finder window. As long as the Toolbar is hidden, folders will always open in new windows. (Click the button again to revert to opening folders in the same window.)

This is the Hide/Show Toolbar button.

Or go to the Finder menu and choose "Preferences…." Check the box to "Always open folders in a new window."

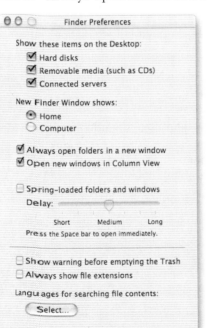

Setting your Finder Preferences to these settings will help you through the transition to Mac OS X by making your Mac behave more like you are used to.

Show the status bar. You might choose to view your windows without the Toolbar, but still want to see the status bar: Open any Finder window. Go to the View menu and choose "Show Status Bar."

Open new windows to Home. The default is set so that every time you ask for a new window, it automatically opens the Computer level window. If you keep your disk icons on the Desktop, then this Computer window is just a repeat of what you see on your Desktop. So change the default to open new Finder windows to your Home window, which is much more useful. In the Finder Preferences window, as shown above, click the radio button so "New Finder Window shows" Home.

Make a folder of aliases. If you store a lot of application icons in the Dock, the Dock gets very full and the icons become very tiny and difficult to select. Instead of putting every application's icon in the Dock, only store the ones you use the most. For the rest, put aliases of all your apps into one folder, then put that one folder into the Dock. Press on the folder icon to pop up a list where you can select the app, as shown below.

It takes a split second for the folder menu to pop up, unless you hold down the Control key as you click—then it pops up instantly. If you *click* on the folder icon in the Dock, its *window* appears on the Desktop.

This is the pop-up menu from a folder of aliases in the Dock.

Take advantage of Favorites. You might not have used Favorites much in Mac OS 9, but they are a lifesaver in OS X. Put aliases of the folders and documents you use most often into the Favorites window—just drag their original icons and drop them onto the Favorites icon in the Toolbar (if your Toolbar is still showing; if not, select the document or folder and press Command T). Now you don't have to go digging through disappearing windows to find the things you need the most. Just click the Favorites icon in the Toolbar or press Command Option F to open the Favorites window.

Favorites are also important when you use the **Open** or **Save As** dialog boxes. To prevent yourself from having to hunt down your folder to open or save into, make it a Favorite. Then in the Open or Save As dialog box, click to open the menu and your folders are right in that list—you won't have to navigate through the columns to find them.

Your Favorite folders will appear in the Open or Save As menu.

Put folders in the Toolbar. Sometimes you have to really wiggle around to move a file from one folder to another. If you have folders that you get into and store files into regularly, put them in the Toolbar (just drop the folder on the Toolbar and the Mac will put its alias there). Even if your folder is on a different partition, you can put it in the Toolbar. That way you can open it with one click.

These folders are stored on another partition so it's always a pain in the boompah to get files into and out of them. As an icon in the Toolbar, I can open them with a click, and I can drop files directly into them from anywhere in the Finder.

Keep your most-used folder or two in the Dock. It's crazy-making to have to search for the folder you need the most. Once your folder is in the Dock, click once on it to open it as a window, or press on it to open the folder to a pop-up menu.

Now, once you've done this, that window will stay in the View and arrangement you prefer and won't be taken over by any other folder window **unless** you click the Finder icon in the Dock to open a new window *while* your work folder is open. See, when you click the Finder icon, it activates your open work folder and all new folders will replace that work folder. So you need to get in the habit of using Command N to open a new window rather than clicking on the Finder icon to get a new window. I guarantee this won't make much sense until you have the problem. Once you have the problem, come back here, walk yourself through this process, and you'll see what a great tip it is.

*Single-click the folder icon in the Dock to open its **window** looking just like it did last time you opened it.*

*Press on the folder icon to get a pop-up **menu** of its contents.*

Control-press on the folder icon to make the pop-up menu appear instantly instead of pausing for a second.

Because all folders look the same in the Dock, I customized several folder icons so I can tell what's what. See page 117.

Do you miss the windowshade feature, where you could double-click a title bar and it rolled up the window, but stayed right there on the Desktop? If so, then download WindowShade X at **www.unsanity.com/haxies.php.** It's great. When you install it, its preferences will start a new row in the System Preferences main pane.

Accent Marks

Tilde	Press	Let go, then press
˜	Option n	Spacebar
ã	Option n	a
Ã	Option n	Shift a
ñ	Option n	n
Ñ	Option n	Shift n
õ	Option n	o
Õ	Option n	Shift o

Diaeresis	Press	Let go, then press
¨	Option u	Spacebar
ä	Option u	a
Ä	Option u	Shift a
ë	Option u	e
Ë	Option u	Shift e
ï	Option u	i
Ï	Option Shift f	
ö	Option u	o
Ö	Option u	Shift o
ü	Option u	u
Ü	Option u	Shift u
ÿ	Option u	y
`	Option Shift ` (` is next to 1, or next to Spacebar; the same key as the regular ˜key)	

Circumflex	Press	Let go, then press
^	Option i	Spacebar
â	Option i	a
Â	Option Shift m	
ê	Option i	e
Ê	Option i	Shift e
î	Option i	i
Î	Option Shift d	
ô	Option i	o
Ô	Option Shift j	
û	Option i	u
Û	Option i	Shift u

Acute	Press	Let go, then press
´	Option e	Spacebar
á	Option e	a
Á	Option e or Option Shift y	Shift a
é	Option e	e
É	Option e	Shift e
í	Option e	i
Í	Option e or Option Shift s	Shift i
ó	Option e	o
Ó	Option e or Option Shift h	Shift o
ú	Option e	u
Ú	Option e or Option Shift ;	Shift u

Grave	Press	Let go, then press
`	Option ` (` is next to 1, or next to Spacebar; the same key as the regular ˜key)	Spacebar
à	Option `	a
À	Option `	Shift a
è	Option `	e
È	Option `	Shift e
ì	Option `	i
Ì	Option `	Shift i
ò	Option `	o
Ò	Option ` or Option Shift l (letter el)	Shift o
ù	Option `	u
Ù	Option `	Shift u

Miscellaneous	Press:
å	Option a
Å	Option Shift a
ç	Option c
Ç	Option Shift c

Quiz Answers

3. The Mouse
1. Single-click.
2. Double-click.
3. Single-click.
4. Double-click.
5. Double-click.
6. Single-click.
7. Single-click.
8. Control-click.
9. Shift-click or Command-click
10. Command-click.

4. Keys and the Keyboard
1. Tab.
2. Return or Enter.
3. *Hide menu bar:* F9
   Open Bookmarks folder: F5
   Close all open windows: Option Command W
   Tile windows vertically: Shift Command L
   Go to first page: Shift Command PageUp
   Go to previous view: Command LeftArrow
4. Escape key: c
   Option key: l
   Control key: q
   Command key: f
   Tilde key: d
   Asterisk: t
   Shift key: m
   Forward slash: p
   Backslash: j
   Tab key: e
   Delete key: i
   PageUp key: a
   PageDown key: h
   LeftArrow key: u
   RightArrow key: s
   UpArrow key: b
   DownArrow key: o
   Home key: g
   End key: r
   Forward Delete: n
   Enter key: k
   Spacebar key: v

5. Menus
1. "Close."
2. Three (New, Macros, and Open Recent).
3. Seven (Open, Save As, Properties, Insert, Mail Merge, Page Setup, Print).
4. Two.
5. Seven.
6. Command W.
7. You'll get a dialog box with Print options.
8. Seven menus.
9. Five edit boxes.
10. Command Period.

6. Windows
1. See page 65.
2. Click in the yellow button, double-click the title bar, or press Command M.
3. By the size of the scrollers.
4. Hold down the Command key and drag the title bar.
5. The red button has a dot in it.
6. Single click.
7. List View with a Size column, then click the Size column heading.
8. Command–double-click on a folder, or hide the Toolbar and then open the folder.
9. Click on any column heading.
10. Hold down the Option key as you drag the thumb.
11. From the View menu, choose "Arrange by Name."
12. Press Command Option W.
13. Hold down the Command key and click on the name in the title bar.
14. Use the General preferences.
15. From the View menu, choose "Show Status Bar."

7. Icons
application:	TextEdit
hard disk:	Mac OS X
CD:	FontDisc
folder:	Ryan's Writings
document:	sonnets.idd
Zip disk:	Little Mac Book
unknown document:	PkgInfo
selected icon:	Favorites
locked icon:	Holiday Letter
Trash can:	wastebasket icon
DVD:	CASABLANCA
ready to rename:	All Things Hushed
stationery/template:	To Do List

8. Dock
1. Hold down the Control key, click on the dividing line of the Dock, choose "Position on screen," then choose Left, Right, or Bottom. Or go to the Dock preferences (see answer 9).
2. Drag the item out of the Dock and drop it on the Desktop.
3. Drag items anywhere else in the Dock (apps to the left, everything else to the right).
4. The Finder window and the Trash basket.
5. Web sites, folders, documents, applications, or any icon at all on your entire hard disk.
6. It opens the folder in a window.
7. It opens a menu from which you can select any item in the folder.
8. Press on the dividing line and drag it larger or smaller.
9. a) Control-click on the dividing line and choose "Dock Preferences…."
   b) Go to the Apple menu and choose "Dock…," then choose "Dock Preferences…."
   c) Open the System Preferences, then click on the Dock icon.
10. Go to the Dock preferences (see #9), and choose "Automatically hide and show the Dock," or hold down the Control key, click on the dividing line of the Dock, and choose "Turn Hiding On."

9. Desktop and Finder
1. Computer window.
2. Desktop folder in your Home.
3. From the Finder menu, open Preferences; check the "Home" box.
4. Yes.
5. Use "View Options" from the View menu ("Show View Options").
6. Use the Desktop preferences in the System Preferences pane.
7. Use "View Options" from the View menu ("Show View Options").
8. From the application menu, choose "Hide Others."
9. Option-click on the Desktop.
10. Shared folder in Users folder.

10. Folders

1. To organize and contain your files.
2. It appears in the active window.
3. Command N.
4. Select the folder, wait until you see the border (visual clue) around the name, then type.
5. Double-click on it.
6. Folder opens to a window and you see the files that are stored inside.
7. *To expand:* select folder(s), press Command RightArrow.
   To compress: select folder(s), press Command LeftArrow.
8. Press Command A to select all; press Command LeftArrow.
9. You don't have folders all over the screen, and you can select items from more than one folder simultaneously.
10. Put a folder in the Toolbar; put a folder in the Dock; make an alias of a folder on the Desktop; put a folder in the Favorites window; Command–doube-click to open the folder in a new window; Command Shift N to open another window.

11. Selecting and Copying Files

1. a
2. c
3. b
4. c
5. c
6. False; always check to make sure you're not copying unnecessary or duplicate files.
7. False; it's the Shift key or Command key.
8. True (assuming they are in the same window).
9. True of course.
10. False; Tab will select files alphabetically.

12. Opening Documents and Applications

1. Document.
2. The application will open and display this document.
3. Application.
4. The application will open.
5. Make sure the window is in List View, then click on the "Kind" column header.
6. New opens a brand-new, blank document. Open opens a document you or someone else has already created and named.
7. a. The two lists.
   b. "typos.rtf" or "sherlock tips."
   c. Documents
   d. "From" menu at top

13. Word Processing

1. Select first, then do it to it.
2. I-beam: ⌶
   Insertion point: |
   Pointer: ▸
3. I-beam.
4. Insertion point.
5. Either the character to its left, or the specifications you choose from the menu while the insertion point is flashing.

6. Usually Command B for Bold, Command I for Italic, Command U for Underline. Some applications also use a Shift key in combination (for instance, Command Shift B to change to Bold).
7. Press Command B (or whatever the command is), type the bold word(s), then press Command B again to toggle off the command.
8. 1) Select the paragraph (press-and-drag over it with the text tool, or try triple-clicking on it).
   2) Cut the paragraph (from the Edit menu, choose "Cut," or press Command X).
   3) Position the I-beam where you want to insert the paragraph, then click to set the insertion point at that spot.
   4) Paste (from the Edit menu, choose "Paste," or press Command V).
9. *Cut:*   Command X.
   Copy: Command C.
   Paste: Command V.
10. "Cut" removes the item and places it on the Clipboard. "Clear" removes the item and does *not* place it on the Clipboard—it's just gone.

14. Saving Documents

1. A.
2. B.
3. You would select the Pictures folder.
4. That column would move over to the left and the contents of the Hogmanay folder would appear in the right-hand column.
5. Tab key.
6. The "Where" menu.
7. Your Home folders would appear in the left-hand column.
8. Close the document or revert.
9. In RAM.
10. Save As from the File menu.

15. Printing Documents

1. See page 234.
2. See page 234.
3. In the Printer List, click once to select the printer that you want to be the default. From the Printers menu, choose "Make Default."
4. Use Page Setup. Some applications have this option in their own print dialog box.
5. In the Print dialog box, choose the "Layout" pane.
6. Click on the Print Center icon in the Dock, then choose "Show Queues."
7. If there is only one job running, there is no difference. If more than one job: "Hold" stops one job from printing. "Stop Queue" stops all jobs from printing.
8. In the Print dialog box, choose "Collate" in the "Copies & Pages" pane.
9. Drag the Print Center icon from the Utilities folder down to the Dock. Or, while a job is printing and the Print Center icon is already in the Dock, click once on the icon to get the pop-up menu and choose "Keep in Dock."
10. "Output Options."

16. Closing and Quitting

1. Close.
2. Quit.
3. Close.
4. Quit.
5. Close.
6. Quit.
7. Six applications are open.
8. Press on the Sherlock icon in the Dock and choose "Quit" from the pop-up menu.
9. Log Out or Shut Down (Restart will also work).
10. Apple menu, choose Force Quit; or Option-click an application icon in the Dock and choose Force Quit; or press Command Option Escape and choose Force Quit.

17. Using the Trash

1. It has something in it.
2. When you choose "Empty Trash" from the Finder menu.
3. Drag the file to the Trash; Select the file, from the File menu choose "Move to Trash"; Select item, press Command Delete; Hold down Control key and click on item, then select "Move to Trash."
4. It opens to a window, displaying its contents.
5. Click the Trash basket, then drag the item out of the window.
6. Press Command Z.
7. No.
8. Temporarily: Hold down the Option key when you choose "Empty Trash" from the Finder menu, or use the Trash pop-up menu in the Dock.
   Permanently: Uncheck the warning box in the Finder Preferences.
9. Unlock it.
10. Drag the file down toward the Dock and the Trash will pop up. Or use the keyboard shortcut Command Delete.

18. Ejecting Disks

1. Drag the disk to the Trash; Select the disk and choose "Eject" from the File menu (or press Command E); Hold down the Control key and click on the disk, then choose "Eject" from the contextual menu; Press F12; Press the Media Eject key.
2. Check the Dock to see if "TextEdit" or other word processing program is open; it might have opened the ReadMe file. Then quit that program.
3. The computer cannot "read" the disk; its icon does not show up on the Desktop.
4. Hold down the mouse or the Media Eject key on restart, or use the paperclip.

19. Restart, Shut Down, or Log Out

1. Shut Down.
2. Log Out.
3. Solid triangle.
4. All applications will automatically quit.
5. Command Option W.

20. Multiple Users and their Homes
1. Yes, any regular user can be given Administrative privileges.
2. No, only Admins can create more users.
3. The only way to change the short name is to delete the user and create another.
4. The original Admin is the first one in the list.
5. It has a space in it, and it can be found in the dictionary.
6. No. The user passwords are case sensitive.
7. Login preferences, the Login Window pane.
8. No, the files are reassigned to an Admin of your choice.
9. Simple Finder; click the "Capabilities" button.
10. Use the Login Items system preferences.

21. Downloading and Installing
1. Disk Copy.
2. .bin.
3. StuffIt Expander.
4. Unmount the disk image; toss the .sit and .img.
5. A .smi doesn't need Disk Copy.
6. For backup.
7. It needs to be mounted and unmounted.
8. Admin.
9. In the main Applications folder on the main hard disk.
10. In the user's Home folder (make a new folder for applications, if you like).

22. System Preferences
1. Mouse preferences; set to fastest speed.
2. Desktop.
3. File Sharing; set File Sharing to Start.
4. Keyboard preferences.
5. Displays; change the "Resolution."
6. Date & Time; set to correct time.
7. Users.
8. Internet.
9. Network.
10. Universal Access.

23. Aliases
1. A representation of the real file. An alias goes and gets the real file.
2. 2 to 3 K.
3. Select a file, then from the File menu choose "Make Alias." Or select a file, then press Command L. Or hold down the Control key, click on the file, choose "Make Alias." Or hold down Command and Option, drag the file to another window or to the Desktop.
4. Drop the file on the Favorites icon in the Toolbar.
5. Nothing.
6. Nothing; they stay, now useless, right where you left them.
7. Click once on the alias. From the File menu, choose "Show Original" (or press Command R).
8. On the Desktop.
9. The file is actually put into the **real** folder.
10. Nothing. The alias can still find it.

24. Favorites
1. No.
2. Documents, applications, disks, servers, web pages, folders, photographs, partitions.
3. No. It would be better to make a folder full of aliases and put that folder in the Dock.
4. Yes.
5. It *moves* the file into the Favorites window without making an alias.
6. An alias is made and placed in the Favorites folder.
7. Save the document, then drag the title bar icon to the Desktop.
8. Folders and disks.
9. Yes you can. It can come in handy if you save files directly onto it.
10. No, not every item in the Favorites window is necessarily an alias.

25. Search
1. No. The more characters you give the computer, however, the faster it can find your file.
2. No. It is not "case specific," meaning it does not check for caps and lowercase letters.
3. Yes. A space is a character to the computer.
4. Choose "Specific Places," then check the disk or folder name.
5. Choose "date created" "is after" 03/10/03. Click +. Choose "and" "is before" 03/20/03. Click +. Choose "name" "contains" budget.
6. Double-click the file name right there in the list of results.
7. Get Info.
8. Select the file in either pane, then press Command R.
9. Drag its icon right out of the top portion of the Results list and into the Trash.
10. Click on the header name (Name, Size, Kind, Date) of the view you want them sorted (organized) by.

26. Fonts
1. Serif faces.
2. In very large type only.
3. OS stands for oldstyle and indicates the font includes lovely oldstyle numerals and perhaps some other special characters.
4. In your Fonts folder, which is in your Library folder, which is in your Home folder.
5. In the Fonts folder in the Library folder on the main hard disk (not in the System's Library folder!).
6. A font where every character is designed to take up the same amount of space as every other character.
7. Proportional.
8. No because there is no designed style for either of those fonts.
9. Yes, Windows .ttf and .otf.
10. I hope so!

27. Applications on the Mac
1. Preview
2. AppleScript
3. Image Capture
4. Chess
5. Stickies
6. Mail
7. DVD Player
8. Acrobat Reader or Preview
9. TextEdit
10. iTunes

28. Utilities on Your Mac
1. Show Info.
2. Network Utility.
3. NetInfo Manager.
4. Key Caps
5. Disk Utility.
6. Apple System Profiler
7. Grab, as well as the keyboard shortcuts.
8. Keychain Access.
9. Show Info.
10. Disk Utility.

29. What is the Internet?
1. Email, newsgroups, mailing lists, World Wide Web.
2. 2.5Mbps.
3. Listserv.
4. A web site.
5. The "table of contents" page, often the first page you come to.
6. So you can see the web pages.
7. You can access the Internet by going through America Online.
8. No.
9. Log on to AOL, the double-click your browser icon.
10. The Macintosh!

31. Using the World Wide Web
1. b
2. d
3. a
4. c
5. a
6. d
7. a
8. b
9. c
10. d
11. c
12. b
13. d

38. Reformatting and Partitions
1. No.
2. It is erased off the disk, removed forever.
3. Back up.
4. Four.
5. Check your memory chips.

*This index is dedicated to one of my favorite people, **Phil Russell** of the Corvallis Mac User Group, who always appreciates a good index.*

with love,
Robin

B

R

Colophon

I wrote and produced this entire
book in Adobe InDesign 2.0. I used
Snapz Pro X and keyboard shortcuts
to make thousands of screen shots.
I cleaned up the screen shots in
Photoshop 7.

The fonts used are ITC Garamond
for the body copy, Bailey Bold
for the heads and subheads,
and ITC Edwardian Script for
the chapter heads.

I have a Microsoft-free environment.
Instead of Microsoft products, I use:
Netscape (www.Netscape.com) *or*
OmniWeb (www.OmniGroup.com);
Mariner Write word processor
  (www.MarinerSoftware.com);
Apple's Mail as an email client.